Lecture Notes in Artificial Intelligence   12061

Subseries of Lecture Notes in Computer Science

More information about this series at http://www.springer.com/series/1244

Mehdi Dastani · Huimin Dong ·
Leon van der Torre (Eds.)

Logic and Argumentation

Third International Conference, CLAR 2020
Hangzhou, China, April 6–9, 2020
Proceedings

 Springer

Editors
Mehdi Dastani 🆔
Utrecht University
Utrecht, The Netherlands

Huimin Dong 🆔
Zhejiang University
Hangzhou, China

Leon van der Torre 🆔
University of Luxembourg
Esch-sur-Alzette, Luxembourg

ISSN 0302-9743 ISSN 1611-3349 (electronic)
Lecture Notes in Artificial Intelligence
ISBN 978-3-030-44637-6 ISBN 978-3-030-44638-3 (eBook)
https://doi.org/10.1007/978-3-030-44638-3

LNCS Sublibrary: SL7 – Artificial Intelligence

This Springer imprint is published by the registered company Springer Nature Switzerland AG
The registered company address is: Gewerbestrasse 11, 6330 Cham, Switzerland

Preface

This book constitutes the refereed proceedings of the Third International Conference on Logic and Argumentation, CLAR 2020, held in Hangzhou, China, as part of the International Conferences on Logic and Artificial Intelligence at Zhejiang University (ZJULogAI). The conference was originally planned to be in April and that the conference is postponed to a later date in 2020 because of the COVID-19.

The CLAR series started as a regional workshop hosted by Zhejiang University in 2016 and has been held every two years ever since. It highlights recent advances in the two fields of logic and argumentation and aims at bringing together researchers from various disciplines such as logic, formal argumentation, artificial intelligence, philosophy, computer science, linguistics, and law.

The call for papers of CLAR 2020 attracted 31 high-quality submissions and the final program consisted of 14 regular papers and 7 short papers. Each paper was selected based on an average of three reviews. The Program Committee of CLAR 2020 consisted of 53 top researchers from 19 countries. The number of submissions to the CLAR series is growing, with 11 at CLAR 2016 and 16 at CLAR 2018. This year we decided to accept more papers, which were presented at the conference to promote communication between researchers in the areas relevant to CLAR from inside and outside of China.

The topics of accepted papers cover the focus of the CLAR series very well, including formal models of argumentation, logics for decision making and uncertain reasoning, formal models of evidence, confirmation, and justification, logics for group cognition and social network, reasoning about norms, formal representations of natural language and legal texts, as well as applications of argumentation on climate engineering.

As Program Committee chairs, we would like to thank all the members of the Program Committee for investing their valuable time in providing high-quality reviews, which are crucial for the quality and success of the conference. We are grateful for the continued financial support from the Department of Philosophy at Zhejiang University and the generous support of Springer in publishing proceedings. We would also like to acknowledge the use of EasyChair for organizing the reviewing process. Finally, we thank all those colleagues and students at Zhejiang University, for their efforts in making the conference happen.

February 2020

Mehdi Dastani
Huimin Dong
Leon van der Torre

Organization

Program Committee Chairs

Mehdi Dastani	Utrecht University, The Netherlands
Huimin Dong	Zhejiang University, China
Leon van der Torre	University of Luxembourg, Luxembourg

Program Committee

Thomas Ågotnes	University of Bergen, Norway
Pietro Baroni	University of Brescia, Italy
Stefano Bistarelli	Università di Perugia, Italy
Alexander Bochman	Holon Institute of Technology, Israel
Thomas Bolander	Technical University of Denmark, Denmark
Walter Carnielli	State University of Campinas, Brazil
Weiwei Chen	Sun Yat-sen University, China
Zoé Christoff	University of Bayreuth, Germany
Agata Ciabattoni	Vienna University of Technology, Austria
Valeria de Paiva	Samsung Research America, USA, and University of Birmingham, UK
Dragan Doder	Utrecht University, The Netherlands
Shanshan Du	Wuhan University, China
Massimiliano Giacomin	University of Brescia, Italy
Guido Governatori	CSIRO, Australia
Norbert Gratzl	Ludwig Maximilian University of Munich, Germany
Davide Grossi	University of Groningen, The Netherlands
Jiahong Guo	Beijing Normal University, China
Andreas Herzig	Université Paul Sabatier, IRIT-CNRS, France
Wesley Holliday	UC Berkeley, USA
Fengkui Ju	Beijing Normal University, China
Souhila Kaci	Université de Montpellier, France
Hannes Leitgeb	Ludwig Maximilian University of Munich, Germany
Hengfei Li	Shandong Jianzhu University, China
Beishui Liao	Zhejiang University, China
Fenrong Liu	Tsinghua University, China
Hu Liu	Sun Yat-sen University, China
Emiliano Lorini	Université Paul Sabatier, IRIT-CNRS, France
Réka Markovich	University of Luxembourg, Luxembourg
Alessandra Marra	University of Bayreuth, Germany
Thomas Meyer	University of Cape Town, South Africa
Sara Negri	University of Helsinki, Finland
Nir Oren	University of Aberdeen, UK

Eric Pacuit	University of Maryland, USA
Gabriella Pigozzi	Université Paris-Dauphine, France
Henry Prakken	Utrecht University and University of Groningen, The Netherlands
R. Ramanujam	Institute of Mathematical Sciences, Chennai, India
Olivier Roy	University of Bayreuth, Germany
Katsuhiko Sano	Hokkaido University, Japan
Chenwei Shi	Tsinghua University, China
Guillermo R. Simari	Universidad Nacional del Sur, Argentina
Sonja Smets	University of Amsterdam, The Netherlands
Christian Straßer	Ruhr-University Bochum, Germany
Johan van Benthem	University of Amsterdam, The Netherlands, and Stanford University, USA
Yì N. Wáng	Zhejiang University, China
Xuefeng Wen	Sun Yat-sen University, China
Stefan Woltran	Vienna University of Technology, Austria
Jiachao Wu	Shandong Normal University, China
Yun Xie	Sun Yat-sen University, China
Yuming Xu	Shandong University, China
Tomoyuki Yamada	Hokkaido University, Japan
Fan Yang	University of Helsinki, Finland
Teng Ying	Zhejiang University City College, China
Zhe Yu	Sun Yat-sen University, China

Additional Reviewers

Youan Su	Hokkaido University, Japan
Sunil Simon	Indian Institute of Technology Kanpur, India

Contents

Long Presentations

Group Belief

Thomas Ågotnes[1,2] and Yì N. Wáng[3(✉)]

[1] Southwest University, Chongqing, China
[2] University of Bergen, Bergen, Norway
thomas.agotnes@uib.no
[3] Zhejiang University, Hangzhou, China
ynw@xixilogic.org

Abstract. While logical formalizations of group notions of knowledge such as common and distributed knowledge have received considerable attention in the literature, most approaches being based on modal logic, group notions of *belief* have received much less attention. In this paper we systematically study standard notions of group knowledge and belief under different assumptions about which properties knowledge and belief have. In particular, we map out (lack of) preservation of knowledge/belief properties against different standard definitions of group knowledge/belief. It turns out that what is called group belief most often is not actually belief, i.e., does not have the properties of belief. In fact, even what is called group knowledge is sometimes not actually knowledge either. For example, under the common assumption that belief has the KD45 properties, distributed belief is not actually belief (it does not satisfy the D axiom). In the literature there is no detailed completeness proof for axiomatizations of KD45 with distributed belief that we are aware of, and there has been some confusion regarding soundness of such axiomatizations related to the mentioned lack of preservation. In this paper we also present a detailed completeness proof for a sound axiomatization of KD45 with distributed belief.

Keywords: Knowledge · Belief · Doxastic logic · Epistemic logic · Group belief · Distributed belief

1 Introduction

Different notions of group knowledge, such as common knowledge or distributed knowledge, have received considerable attention in the epistemic logic literature [5,8,20]. While most frameworks for epistemic logic are based on the modal logic S5 for modeling individual knowledge, frameworks for belief usually are based on weaker systems such as KD45 or K45. Group belief is routinely defined in the same way as group knowledge in such belief logics, but has received far less attention in the literature. In this paper we take a systematic look at standard notions of group knowledge and belief under different assumptions about which properties knowledge and belief have. A key question is whether or not properties of belief (e.g., KD45 or K45 properties) are *preserved* under the operations

© Springer Nature Switzerland AG 2020
M. Dastani et al. (Eds.): CLAR 2020, LNAI 12061, pp. 3–21, 2020.
https://doi.org/10.1007/978-3-030-44638-3_1

defining group knowledge from individual knowledge. We map out the answers to that question, for different assumptions about what the properties of knowledge and belief are against different definitions of group knowledge.

As an example, if we assume that individual belief has the KD45 properties it is not guaranteed that *distributed* belief has it – the intersection of two serial, transitive and Euclidean binary relations is not necessary serial, so distributed belief on KD45 lacks the *consistency* property (D axiom). Thus, if we assume that belief has the KD45 properties, then "distributed belief" *is not belief*. In fact, we argue that group belief *most often* is not belief; only under very weak or very strong assumptions about what belief is, are standard notions of group belief actually belief. Similarly, group *knowledge* is not always (S5) knowledge either.

Some of these observations are folklore in the epistemic/doxastic logic community. However, we are not aware of any existing systematic study. And there is evidence that more awareness of the properties of group belief is needed. As far as we are aware, no completeness proof for KD45 with distributed belief exists in print. Furthermore, there is a problem with the soundness of an axiomatization of doxastic logic with distributed belief on KD45 in the literature [8], exactly due to the lack of preservation of the consistency property for distributed belief on KD45. In this paper we provide a detailed completeness proof for a sound axiomatization of KD45 with distributed belief.

The rest of the paper is organized as follows. In the next section we introduce the background from the literature: modal logics of knowledge and belief, definitions of group knowledge and belief, and standard (combinations of) axioms corresponding to properties of knowledge and belief. In Sect. 3 we systematically look at (lack of) preservation of properties under different notions of group belief. A few preservation results have been established already in existing work on graph aggregation [6]. Key observations here are summed up in Fig. 1. In Sect. 4 we discuss axiomatizations of KD45 with distributed belief in the literature and present a detailed completeness result for a sound axiomatization. We discuss related and future work and conclude in Sect. 5.

2   Background

We briefly review the standard language and semantics of modal epistemic and doxastic logic. We refer to, e.g., [8] for more details.

Let PROP be a countable set of propositional variables, let AG be a finite set of agents, and let $\mathrm{GR} = \wp(\mathrm{AG}) \setminus \{\emptyset\}$ be the set of groups, i.e., the set of all nonempty sets of agents. We define the following variants of the epistemic language with individual belief operators B_a and with or without various combinations of group belief operators E_G, C_G and D_G.

Definition 1 (languages).

$$(\mathcal{BL}) \quad \varphi ::= p \mid \neg\varphi \mid (\varphi \wedge \varphi) \mid B_a\varphi$$
$$(\mathcal{BLC}) \quad \varphi ::= p \mid \neg\varphi \mid (\varphi \wedge \varphi) \mid B_a\varphi \mid E_G\varphi \mid C_G\varphi$$
$$(\mathcal{BLD}) \quad \varphi ::= p \mid \neg\varphi \mid (\varphi \wedge \varphi) \mid B_a\varphi \mid D_G\varphi$$
$$(\mathcal{BLCD}) \, \varphi ::= p \mid \neg\varphi \mid (\varphi \wedge \varphi) \mid B_a\varphi \mid E_G\varphi \mid C_G\varphi \mid D_G\varphi$$

where $p \in$ PROP, $a \in$ AG and $G \in$ GR. Boolean operators such as $\top$, $\rightarrow$, $\vee$ and so on are defined as usual.

While some works (e.g., [8]) use the notation K_a for both individual knowledge and the more general notion of individual belief, we chose to use B_a for both, treating knowledge as a special case of belief – belief as a generalization of knowledge. E_G is the operator for what is called *general belief*, or *everybody-believes* or *mutual belief*, C_G is *common belief*, and D_G is *distributed belief* (or knowledge).

A Kripke model M (over agents AG and propositional variables PROP) is a triple (S, R, V), where S is a nonempty set of states, $R : \text{AG} \rightarrow \wp(S \times S)$ assigns to every agent a a binary relation R_a on S, and $V : \text{PROP} \rightarrow S$ is a valuation which associates with every propositional variable a set of states where it is true. For any $s \in S$, the pair (M, s) is called a *pointed model*.

Definition 2 (satisfaction). *The truth in, or satisfaction by, a pointed model (M, s) with $M = (S, R, V)$ of a formula φ, denoted $(M, s) \models \varphi$, is defined inductively as follows.*

$$
\begin{aligned}
(M, s) &\models p & &\textit{iff} & &s \in V(p) \\
(M, s) &\models \neg\varphi & &\textit{iff} & &\text{not } (M, s) \models \varphi \\
(M, s) &\models (\varphi \wedge \psi) & &\textit{iff} & &(M, s) \models \varphi \text{ and } (M, s) \models \psi \\
(M, s) &\models B_a\varphi & &\textit{iff} & &\text{for all } t \in S, \text{ if } sR_at \text{ then } (M, t) \models \varphi \\
(M, s) &\models E_G\varphi & &\textit{iff} & &\text{for all } t \in S, \text{ if } sR_G^Et \text{ then } (M, t) \models \varphi \\
(M, s) &\models C_G\varphi & &\textit{iff} & &\text{for all } t \in S, \text{ if } sR_G^Ct \text{ then } (M, t) \models \varphi \\
(M, s) &\models D_G\varphi & &\textit{iff} & &\text{for all } t \in S, \text{ if } sR_G^Dt \text{ then } (M, t) \models \varphi
\end{aligned}
$$

where $R_G^E = \bigcup_{a \in G} R_a$, R_G^C is the transitive closure of R_G^E, and $R_G^D = \bigcap_{a \in G} R_a$. We say that φ is (globally) true in a model, if it is satisfied at all states of that model.

As discussed below, we restrict the class of models depending on which properties we assume that belief has, the strongest assumption being that the relations are *equivalence relations* in the case of *knowledge*.

The semantics for group belief given above are the standard definitions in the literature. In particular, the definition of the common knowledge/belief relation as the transitive closure of the union of the individual knowledge/belief relations is the one used in, e.g., the standard textbook [8][1] – not only for knowledge but also for weaker notions of belief. Some works, however (e.g., [4,5,19]), use a slightly different definition, namely the *reflexive* transitive closure – although almost always only in the context of S5 knowledge, in which case the two definitions are equivalent. In the following we will still consider the latter as a possible, alternative definition for common belief a few times. When referring to common belief we will henceforth mean the former definition, using transitive closure, if not otherwise stated. The latter definition, using the reflexive transitive closure, will be referred to as "the alternative definition" when needed.

Given a class $\mathscr{C}$ of models and a formula φ, we say φ is *valid* in $\mathscr{C}$ if and only if φ is globally true in all models of $\mathscr{C}$. We usually do not choose a class of models arbitrarily, but are rather interested in those based on a certain set of conditions over the binary relations in a model. Such conditions are often called *frame conditions*. In this paper we are going to focus on only some frame conditions, namely those that play the most prominent roles in the context of knowledge and belief. These conditions are

(l) *seriality*: $\forall s \in S \ \exists t \in S \ sR_a t,$
(r) *reflexivity*: $\forall s \in S \ sR_a s,$
(t) *transitivity*: $\forall s, t, u \in S \ ((sR_a t \ \& \ tR_a u) \Rightarrow sR_a u),$
(s) *symmetry*: $\forall s, t \in S \ (sR_a t \Rightarrow tR_a s),$ and
(e) *Euclidicity*: $\forall s, t, u \in S \ ((sR_a t \ \& \ sR_a u) \Rightarrow tR_a u).$

It is well known that these frame conditions are characterized by the axioms

D $B_a \varphi \rightarrow \neg B_a \neg \varphi,$
T $B_a \varphi \rightarrow \varphi,$
4 $B_a \varphi \rightarrow B_a B_a \varphi,$
B $\neg \varphi \rightarrow B_a \neg B_a \varphi,$ and
5 $\neg B_a \varphi \rightarrow B_a \neg B_a \varphi,$

respectively (see, e.g., [3]). There are 32 combinations of these 5 frame properties, potentially giving rise to 32 classes of models, but some of the combinations are equivalent.

In Table 1 we list the 32 different combinations over the 5 frame properties, and the corresponding logics over the language $\mathcal{BL}$ (i.e., the set of valid formulas on the corresponding model classes). There are 15 different logics up to logical equivalence. For logics based on the language $\mathcal{BLC}$, we add a superscript ^{C} to the name, as in K^C, D^C, T^C, $S4^C$, $S5^C$, $KD4^C$, $K45^C$, and so on. Similarly, for logics based on the language $\mathcal{BLD}$, we add a superscript ^{D}, e.g., $K45^D$, $KD45^D$, and so on. We can use this notation for logics over $\mathcal{BLCD}$ as well.

---

[1] The concrete definition of the semantics of common belief in [8], as well as in many other works (e.g. [7,9,12,13,15–17,22]), is that $(M, s) \models C_G \varphi$ iff $\forall k \geq 1 : (M, s) \models E_G^k \varphi$, where $E_G^1 \varphi$ stands for $E_G \varphi$ and $E_G^{k+1} \varphi$ for $E_G E_G^k \varphi$. As noted by [8, Lemma 2.2.1] that definition is equivalent to using the transitive closure (for arbitrary models, not only S5 models).

Table 1. Model classes and corresponding logics over the language $\mathcal{BL}$, with alternative names from the literature. Names of logics that are equivalent to one with fewer characterization axioms/frame conditions are in parentheses.

Frame cond.	Full name	Short name	Equivalent logic	Frame cond.	Full name	Short name	Equivalent logic
—	K	—	—	lrt	(KDT4)	—	S4
l	KD	D	—	lrs	(KDTB)	—	B
r	KT	T	—	lre	(KDT5)	—	S5
t	K4	—	—	lts	(KD4B)	—	S5
s	KB	—	—	lte	KD45	—	—
e	K5	—	—	lse	(KDB5)	—	S5
lr	(KDT)	—	T	rts	(KT4B)	—	S5
lt	KD4	—	—	rte	(KT45)	—	S5
ls	KDB	—	—	rse	(KTB5)	—	S5
le	KD5	—	—	tse	(K4B5)	—	K4B
rt	KT4	S4	—	lrts	(KDT4B)	—	S5
rs	KTB	B	—	lrte	(KDT45)	—	S5
re	KT5	S5	—	lrse	(KDTB5)	—	S5
ts	K4B	—	—	ltse	(KD4B5)	—	S5
te	K45	—	—	rtse	(KT4B5)	—	S5
se	KB5	—	K4B	lrtse	(KDT4B5)	—	S5

As is convention, because of the correspondence between frame conditions and characterization axioms, we often use the names of the corresponding logics to refer to the class of models. For example, the word "T models" simply stands for the class of models based on reflexive frames, and similarly "S5 models" means the class of models based on reflexive and Euclidean (and therefore also transitive and symmetric) frames. As already mentioned, we use "knowledge" as a special case of belief, i.e., when belief is assumed to have the S5 properties.

3   Group Belief in Different Logics

In this section we look at (the lack of) preservation of properties of belief when going from individual to group belief. Syntactically, this corresponds to whether group belief satisfies the same axioms as individual belief; semantically it corresponds to whether frame conditions are preserved under the group belief operations (union, intersection, etc.). As mentioned in the previous section we only consider combinations of the five frame conditions seriality, reflexivity, transitivity, symmetry and Euclidicity.

Definition 3 (preservation). *Given a model $M = (S, R, V)$ and a combination of frame conditions $\mathscr{F}$ (i.e., $\mathscr{F} \subseteq \{l, r, t, s, e\}$), we say that:*

1. $\mathscr{F}$ is preserved for general belief in M, *or general belief preserves $\mathscr{F}$ in M, if R_G^E satisfies $\mathscr{F}$ whenever R_a satisfies $\mathscr{F}$ for every $a \in G$, for any group G;*
2. $\mathscr{F}$ is preserved for common belief in M, *or common belief preserves $\mathscr{F}$ in M, if R_G^C satisfies $\mathscr{F}$ whenever R_a satisfies $\mathscr{F}$ for every $a \in G$, for any group G;*
3. $\mathscr{F}$ is preserved for distributed belief in M, *or distributed belief preserves $\mathscr{F}$ in M, if R_G^D satisfies $\mathscr{F}$ whenever R_a satisfies $\mathscr{F}$ for every $a \in G$, for any group G.*

A combination of frame conditions is preserved for a variant of group belief on a class of models iff it is preserved in every model in that class.

This notion of preservation is standard in modal logic [3]. It also corresponds to what is called *collective rationality* in [6] (see Sect. 5 for more details).

It is preservation on a class of models we are interested in. This says that the properties are *guaranteed* to hold on that model class, for example that Euclidicity is preserved for common belief on S5 models. Conversely, if a combination of properties is *not* preserved on a class of models it means that there is at least one model in that class where it is not preserved.

Lemma 1. *The following hold:*

1. *Seriality*
   (a) is preserved for general and common belief on the class of all models;
   (b) is preserved for distributed belief on the class of all reflexive models;
   (c) is not preserved for distributed belief on the class of $\mathscr{F} \cup \{l\}$ models, for any $\mathscr{F} \subseteq \{t, e\}$;
   (d) is not preserved for distributed belief on the class of $\{l, s\}$ models.
2. *Reflexivity is preserved for general, common and distributed belief on the class of all models.*
3. *Transitivity*
   (a) is not preserved for general belief on the class of all $\mathscr{F} \cup \{t\}$ models, for any $\mathscr{F} \subseteq \{l, r, s, e\}$;
   (b) is preserved for common and distributed belief on the class of all models.
4. *Symmetry is preserved for general, common and distributed belief on the class of all models.*
5. *Euclidicity*
   (a) is not preserved for general belief on the class of all $\mathscr{F} \cup \{e\}$ models, for any $\mathscr{F} \subseteq \{l, r, t, s\}$;
   (b) is preserved for common belief on the class of all symmetric models;
   (c) is not preserved for common belief on the class of all $\mathscr{F} \cup \{e\}$ models, for any $\mathscr{F} \subseteq \{l, t\}$;
   (d) is preserved for distributed belief on the class of all models.

Proof.

1. (a) Straightforward: the (transitive closure of) the union of serial relations is serial.
   (b) Follows from point 2 below.

(c) The following KD45 model is a counter-example for all the cases; the distributed belief relation is not serial:

$$\overset{ab}{\circlearrowleft} \bullet_t \xleftarrow{\ a\ } \bullet_s \xrightarrow{\ b\ } \bullet_u \overset{ab}{\circlearrowleft}$$

(d) The following KB model is a counter-example; the distributed belief relation is not serial:

$$\bullet_t \xleftrightarrow{\ a\ } \bullet_s \xleftrightarrow{\ b\ } \bullet_u$$

2. Follows from [6, Prop. 6][2].

3. (a) Consider the following S5 counterexample with two agents (which is also a counterexample for weaker logics):

$$\overset{ab}{\circlearrowleft}\bullet_s \xleftrightarrow{\ a\ } \overset{ab}{\circlearrowleft}\bullet_t \xleftrightarrow{\ b\ } \overset{ab}{\circlearrowleft}\bullet_u$$

This frame is transitive, however, $sR^E_{\{a,b\}}t$ and $tR^E_{\{a,b\}}u$ but not $sR^E_{\{a,b\}}u$.

(b) The common belief relation is transitive by definition. For distributed belief, assume that $sR^D_G t$ and $tR^D_G u$. That means that $sR_a t$ for every $a \in G$ and that $tR_a u$ for every $a \in G$; which again means that $sR_a u$ for every $a \in G$ by transitivity of the individual relations and thus that $sR^D_G u$.

4. The cases for general and distributed belief follow from [6, Prop. 8][3].

5. (a) Follows from the same counter-example as in the case of transitivity.

(b) Let the individual relations be symmetric and Euclidean, and let $sR^C_G t$ and $sR^C_G u$. Since there is a G-path from s to t and all relations are symmetric, there is a G-path from t to s and thus $tR^C_G s$. By transitivity of R^C_G, $tR^C_G u$.

(c) The KD45 counter-model in the case for seriality works as a counter-model in this case as well: we have that $sR^C_{\{a,b\}}t$ and $sR^C_{\{a,b\}}u$ but not $tR^C_{\{a,b\}}u$.

(d) Let the individual relations be Euclidean, and let $sR^D_G t$ and $sR^D_G u$. That means that $sR_a t$ and $sR_a u$ for any $a \in G$, and thus by Euclidicity of R_a that $tR_a u$ for any $a \in G$. But that means that $tR^D_G u$.

Note that Lemma 1 implies preservation of certain combinations of properties. For example, while Euclidicity is not preserved for common belief on the class of all models, the combination of Euclidicity and symmetry is.

From these preservation results we can deduce (the lack of) properties of group belief operators, under different assumptions about the properties of individual belief. In addition to *preservation*, sometimes group belief gets *new* properties; e.g., common belief is always transitive by definition. The results are shown in Table 2 and illustrated in Fig. 1.

---

[2] In the terminology of [6], general, common and distributed belief all correspond to *unanimous aggregation rules*.

[3] In the terminology of [6], general and distributed belief all correspond to *neutral aggregation rules*.

Table 2. Frame conditions and their preservation for group belief operators. The column EB (for general belief) lists the maximal combination of properties (among $\{l, r, t, s, e\}$) that R_G^E is guaranteed to satisfy for any G in any model with the frame conditions given in the same row. Similar conventions are used for the columns CB for common belief and DB for distributed belief. The column CBr is for the alternative definition of common belief using the reflexive transitive closure instead of just the transitive closure. **Bold** indicates that some frame condition(s) are not preserved.

Frame cond.	EB	CB	CBr	DB	Frame cond.	EB	CB	CBr	DB
K	K	K4	S4	K	S4	**T**	S4	S4	S4
D	D	KD4	S4	**K**	B	B	S5	S5	B
T	T	S4	S4	T	S5	**B**	S5	S5	S5
K4	**K**	K4	S4	K4	K4B	**KB**	K4B	S5	K4B
KB	KB	K4B	S5	KB	K45	**K**	**K4**	**S4**	K45
K5	**K**	**K4**	**S4**	K5	KD5	**KD**	**KD4**	**S4**	**K5**
KD4	**KD**	KD4	S4	**K4**	KDB	KDB	S5	S5	**KB**
KD45	**D**	**KD4**	**S4**	**K45**					

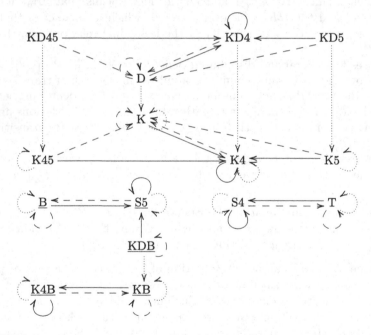

Fig. 1. Solid arrows represent common belief (transitive closure of the union), dashed arrows represent general belief (everybody-knows), and dotted arrows represent distributed belief. An arrow from one class to another means that group belief defined over individual belief having properties of the first class (i) has properties of the second class and (ii) does not have all the properties of any other of the classes we consider that strictly includes the second class. For example, distributed belief on KD45 is K45, and is not KD45 or KD4. For the alternative definition of common belief using the reflexive transitive closure, common belief is either S5 (underlined) or S4 (not underlined).

We leave a discussion of most of these results to Sect. 5, but let us point to one in particular here: that seriality is not preserved for distributed belief on KD45. This has caused some confusion; for example is an axiomatization of KD45 with distributed belief given in [8] not sound. In the next section we correct that result.

4   Axiomatization of KD45^D

An axiomatization of KD45 with distributed belief is given in [8]. A completeness result is claimed, however without a proof. Furthermore, the axiomatization is in fact not sound, due to the issue mentioned at the end of the previous section (Theorem 3.4.1 (e) is incorrect)[4]: the consistency (D) axiom for distributed belief is not valid (in the class of KD45 models). As far as we know, there is no detailed proof of completeness for axiomatizations of KD45 with distributed belief in print. In this section we look into the KD45 logic with distributed belief (i.e., KD45^D, which is based on the language $\mathcal{BLD}$), provide a (corrected) axiomatization for it, and present a detailed soundness and completeness proof.

The axiomatization for the logic KD45^D is given in Fig. 2. It consists of a typical **KD45** proof system (with axioms PC, K, D, 4, 5, and rules MP and N) for individual belief, and a **K45** proof system (with axioms PC, K$_D$, 4$_D$, 5$_D$, and rules MP and N$_D$[5]) for distributed belief with additional axioms DB1 and DB2 characterizing the effect of group inclusion on distributed belief. The soundness of **BLD** is not hard to verify by Lemma 1 (or Table 2 for a quick reference). What remains is to show the completeness of **BLD**.

PC	all instances of tautologies	MP	from φ infer $B_a\varphi$
K	$B_a(\varphi \to \psi) \to (B_a\varphi \to B_a\psi)$	D	$B_a\varphi \to \neg B_a\neg\varphi$
4	$B_a\varphi \to B_aB_a\varphi$	5	$\neg B_a \to B_a\neg B_a\varphi$
K$_D$	$D_G(\varphi \to \psi) \to (D_G\varphi \to D_G\psi)$	4$_D$	$D_G\varphi \to D_GD\varphi$
5$_D$	$\neg D_G \to D_G\neg D_G\varphi$	N	from φ infer $B_a\varphi$
DB1	$D_{\{a\}}\varphi \leftrightarrow B_a\varphi$	DB2	$D_G\varphi \to D_{G'}\varphi$ if $G \subseteq G'$

Fig. 2. Axiomatization **BLD**, with $\varphi, \psi \in \mathcal{BLD}$, $a \in$ AG and $G, G' \in$ GR.

In the presence of distributed belief operators, the typical canonical model definition for KD45^D does not give us a proper model, thus the method cannot be applied straightforwardly. We adapt the method of the completeness proof from [23] which can be traced back to [10,14,21]. The proof is presented in this way.

---

[4] We refer here to the 1995 hardcover edition of [8]. The result appears to have been corrected in a later (2003) paperback edition; still without a proof of completeness however.

[5] The necessitation rule N$_D$ for distributed belief, i.e., "from φ infer $D_G\varphi$", is provable via N, DB1 and DB2; hence omitted.

We start in Sect. 4.1 by showing that **BLD** is sound and complete with respect to the class of all *pseudo* KD45 models, in which distributed belief is treated as individual belief (i.e., in the operator D_G, the group G is treated as if it is an individual). Then, in Sect. 4.2, we define a translation between pseudo KD45 models and (genuine) KD45 models using the model construction methods of *unraveling* and *folding*. We show that the translation preserves truth of KD45^D in Sect. 4.3, which leads to the completeness of **BLD**.

4.1   Pseudo Soundness and Completeness

Definition 4 (KD45 pre-model). *A KD45 pre-model (pre-model for short) for* AG *over* PROP *is a tuple* $M = (S, R, V)$ *such that* S *is a domain and* V *is a valuation function defined as usual, while* $R : $ AG $\cup$ GR $\to \wp(S \times S)$ *assigns to every single agent a KD45 relation (i.e., a serial, transitive and Euclidean relation) on* S, *and to every group of agents a K45 relation (i.e., a transitive and Euclidean relation) on* S. *A* pointed pre-model *is a pair consisting of a pre-model and a state of it.*

A KD45 pre-model for AG over PROP can be seen as a model for AG $\cup$ GR over PROP, where every individual is assigned a KD45 relation, and every group is treated similarly to an individual, but assigned a K45 relation.

Satisfaction at a pointed pre-model is therefore analogous to that at a pointed model. More precisely, given any pre-model $M = (S, R, V)$ and $s \in S$,

$$
\begin{aligned}
(M, s) &\models p &&\text{iff}\quad s \in V(p) \\
(M, s) &\models \neg\varphi &&\text{iff}\quad \text{not } (M, s) \models \varphi \\
(M, s) &\models (\varphi \wedge \psi) &&\text{iff}\quad (M, s) \models \varphi \text{ and } (M, s) \models \psi \\
(M, s) &\models B_a\varphi &&\text{iff}\quad \text{for all } t \in S, \text{ if } sR_a t \text{ then } (M, t) \models \varphi \\
(M, s) &\models D_G\varphi &&\text{iff}\quad \text{for all } t \in S, \text{ if } sR_G t \text{ then } (M, t) \models \varphi.
\end{aligned}
$$

The only difference between the above and Definition 2 is in the interpretation of $D_G\varphi$, where for pre-models, we interpret using the preliminary R_G relation instead of $R_G^D = \bigcap_{a \in G} R_a$. In this sense, D_G operators behave similarly to a B_a operator. This is not, of course, sufficient – we want distributed and individual belief to have certain interaction properties. In particular we need to make the axiomatization **BLD** sound in the class of all semantic structures, but it is not the case at the moment, for the axioms DB1 and DB2 are not valid in the class of all pre-models. For this reason we define the notion of a *pseudo model*.

Definition 5 (KD45 pseudo model). *A KD45 pseudo model (pseudo model for short)* $M = (S, R, V)$ *is a pre-model such that*

- $R_a = R_{\{a\}}$ *for every agent* a, *and*
- $R_{G'} \subseteq R_G$ *for every* $G, G' \in$ GR *such that* $G \subseteq G'$.

It is not hard to see that **BLD** is sound with respect to the class of all pseudo models, for the KD45-ness of individual belief and K45-ness of distributed belief are required by definition of a pre-model, and DB1 and DB2 are fulfilled by the additional constraints for being a pseudo model.

We continue to show that **BLD** is also complete with respect to the class of all pseudo models. Later we shall show that any pseudo model is equivalent to a genuine model, so that the "pseudo" completeness result leads to a completeness result after all.

The *canonical pseudo model* M is a triple (S, R, V) such that:

- S is the set of all maximal **BLD** consistent sets of $\mathcal{BLD}$ formulas;[6]
- R is such that for all $\Phi, \Psi \in S$,
  - For all $a \in$ AG, $\Phi\ \mathsf{R}_a\ \Psi$ iff for all $\varphi \in \mathcal{BLD}$, if $B_a \varphi \in \Phi$ then $\varphi \in \Psi$, and
  - For all $G \in$ GR, $\Phi\ \mathsf{R}_G\ \Psi$ iff for all $\varphi \in \mathcal{BLD}$, if $D_G \varphi \in \Phi$ then $\varphi \in \Psi$;
- V is the valuation defined by $V(p) = \{\Phi \in S \mid p \in \Phi\}$ for all $p \in$ PROP.

It is not hard to verify that the canonical pseudo model is in indeed a pseudo model (in particular, one can check that R_a is a KD45 relation for any agent a, R_G is a K45 relation for any group G, and the additional properties of pseudo models also hold for R_G). The rest of the pseudo completeness proof goes just like a standard canonical model method (cf. [3]), and together with the pseudo soundness results argued above, we get the following.

Lemma 2 (pseudo soundness and pseudo completeness). *BLD is sound and strongly complete with respect to the class of all KD45 pseudo models.*

4.2   Translating a Pseudo Model to a Model

As mentioned above, pseudo soundness and completeness is not sufficient – pseudo models are not proper models. For a proper completeness result we need to show that any consistent set of formulas has a proper model. What remains to do is to show that when a set of formulas has a pseudo model, it must also have a genuine model. We do this by introducing a truth-preserving translation from a pseudo model to a genuine model. In this section we introduce definitions of such a translation, with its truth-perseverance shown in the next section.

To transform a pseudo model to a genuine model, we keep the same domain and valuation function, but redefine the uncertainty relation for every agent. We cannot just keep the uncertainty relation for each agent from the pseudo model and simply drop those for groups, for this will lead to a loss of uncertainty for groups which may finally make the resulting model not equivalent to the pseudo model. Technically speaking, in order to translate a pseudo model (S, R, V) to a genuine model (S, R', V), we need to define what R'_a is for every agent a. By doing so we have to somehow merge the information for groups containing a into it. For example, by the definition of a pseudo model, $R_{\{a,b,c\}}$ is a subset of $R_{\{a\}} \cap R_{\{b\}} \cap R_{\{c\}} \cap R_{\{a,b\}} \cap R_{\{b,c\}} \cap R_{\{a,c\}}$ but not necessary equal to the

---

[6] We refer to a modal logic textbook, say [3], for a definition of a *(maximal) consistent set of formulas*.

latter.[7] If we only keep the uncertainty relations for individuals, formulas such as $D_{\{a,b\}}\varphi$ may have a different truth value before and after the translation.

We shall follow the method of *unraveling and folding* used in [23] which can be traced back to the early papers [10,14,18]. Yet we cannot simply reuse all the definitions and lemmas there, as there are subtle differences due to the lack of reflexivity of the uncertainty relations. The following definitions and intermediate results are adaptions of similar constructs from the S5 case found in [23].

Definition 6 (treelike pre-models). *Given any pre-model $M = (S,R,V)$, a path of M from a state s_0 to a state s_n is a finite non-empty sequence of the following form:*

$$\langle s_0, R_{\tau_0}, \ldots, R_{\tau_{n-1}}, s_n \rangle$$

where each s_i $(0 \le i \le n)$ is a state in S, and each τ_j $(0 \le j < n)$ is either an agent or a group of agents such that $s_j R_{\tau_j} s_{j+1}$ holds in M. Repetitions of states or relations are allowed in a path.

The reduction of a path is obtained by recursively replacing all of its segments of the type $\langle x, R_\tau, y, R_\tau, z \rangle$ with $\langle x, R_\tau, z \rangle$. Note that the reduction of a path is unique, and is still a path, due to the transitivity of relations.

A reduced path is a path that is identical to its reduction. A pre-model M is called treelike, *if for any two states $s,t \in S$ there is at most one reduced path from s to t.*

Definition 7 (extensions and grafts). *Let $M = (S,R,V)$ be a pre-model, and τ an agent or a group of agents. Let s and t be two paths of M.*

- *s is called a τ-extension of t in M, if s extends t with $\langle R_\tau, u \rangle$ for some $u \in S$;*
- *s is called a τ-graft of t in M, if s and t are different τ-extensions of the same path.*

We illustrate the notions of a τ-extension and a τ-graft in Fig. 3.

Definition 8 (unraveling). *Given a pre-model $M = (S,R,V)$, its unraveled structure $M^u = (T,Q,\nu)$ is defined as follows:*

- *T is the set of all reduced paths of M;*
- *Given τ an agent or a group of agents, for any $s,t \in T$, $s Q_\tau t$ holds, iff*
  - *t is a τ-extension of s in M, or*
  - *s is a τ-graft of t in M;*
- *$\nu : \text{PROP} \to \wp(T)$ is such that for any $s \in S$ and any $s \in T$ which ends with s, $s \in \nu(p)$ iff $s \in V(p)$.*

---

[7] The two must be equal in a genuine model, but we cannot simply define $R_{\{a,b,c\}}$ to be the intersection of all of its subsets, for that already makes a pseudo model to be a genuine model. The whole method collapses then: we encounter the very problem that the canonical model is not a genuine model (mostly because the intersection of relations is not modally definable), which violates the starting point of the canonical model method. This was discussed in more detail already in [18].

Fig. 3. Illustrations of a τ-extension and a τ-graft. For the graph on the left, the path below is a τ-extension of the path on top, while for the graph on the right, the two paths are τ-grafts of each other.

Lemma 3. *The unraveling of a pseudo model is a treelike pre-model.*

Proof. Given a pseudo model $M = (S, R, V)$ and its unraveling $M^u = (T, Q, \nu)$, we must show all of the following properties:

1. for every $a \in \text{AG}$, Q_a is serial, transitive and Euclidean;
2. for every $G \in \text{GR}$, Q_G is transitive and Euclidean;
3. for all $s, t \in T$ there is at most one reduced path of M^u from s to t.

We show these properties below.

1. Given $a \in \text{AG}$ and $s, t, u \in T$ (i.e., s, t, u are reduced paths of M),
   – Seriality. Suppose $s = \langle s_0, R_b, x \rangle$ for some $b \in \text{AG}$ and $x \in S$, i.e., the path that extends s_0 with $\langle R_b, x \rangle$. By the seriality of R_a, there exists $y \in S$ such that xR_ay. Consider the path $x = \langle s, R_a, y \rangle$. By definition, x is an a-extension of s in M. A subtlety is that x is a reduced path of M only when $a \neq b$. If $a = b$, $s = \langle s_0, R_a, x, R_a, y \rangle$. Let $y = \langle s_0, R_a, y \rangle$, which is a reduction of x. Clearly y is an a-graph of s. By the definition of unraveling, $s \, Q_a \, y$. This shows that there is a state of T, i.e., x or y, that s links to via Q_a; hence the seriality of Q_a.
   – Transitivity. Suppose $s \, Q_a t$ and $t \, Q_a u$. We must show $s \, Q_a u$. By the definition of Q_a, the supposition gives us four possible combinations of whether t is an a-extension or a-graft of s, and whether u is an a-extension or a-graft of t. By the definitions, it is not hard to verify that u is either an a-extension or a-graft of s (again, a subtlety is to enforce that s, t and u are all reduced paths). Thus $s \, Q_a u$, as wanted.
   – Euclidicity. Suppose $s \, Q_a t$ and $s \, Q_a u$. Similarly to the above, we have four possibilities, and we can show that $t \, Q_a u$.
2. The proof goes in the same way as in the case of individual belief. That Q_G lacks seriality is due to the lack of seriality of R_G.
3. Suppose there are two reduced paths (called *meta-paths* here) of M^u from s to t. The length of each meta-state (which is a path of M) is non-decreasing along each meta-path. For a Q_τ that comes from a τ-extension, a different $Q_{\tau'}$ leads to a different meta-state, with $R_{\tau'}$ recorded in it. For a Q_τ that comes from a τ-graft, a different $Q_{\tau'}$ also leads to a different meta-state. An observation here is that there is no way to revisit a meta-state in a reduced meta-path. The only way to keep the size of a meta-state (which is a path

of M) not growing is via a τ-graph, but this cannot be made consecutively (otherwise not a reduced path). This guarantees the uniqueness of the reduced meta-path from s to t.

Definition 9 (folding). *Let $M = (S, R, V)$ be a treelike pre-model. M^f, the folding of M, is the tuple (S, Q, V) such that for all agents a, Q_a is the transitive and Euclidean closure of $R_a \cup \bigcup_{G \ni a} R_G$.*

Technically speaking, folding can be defined on any pre-model, but the name only makes sense for treelike pre-models, which is also revealed by Lemma 5.

Proposition 1. *Let (S, Q, V) be the folding of a treelike pre-model (S, R, V). For every agent a, Q_a is a KD45 (i.e., serial, transitive and Euclidean) relation.*

Proof. Seriality by that of R_a; transitivity and Euclidicity by definition.

Applying the processes of unraveling and folding, we can translate a pseudo model into a genuine model. In the next subsection, we show the procedure of unraveling and folding is truth preserving.

4.3   Truth Preservation of the Translation

We introduce with necessary adaptions the notions of *trans-equivalence* and *trans-bisimulation* from [23], which are generalizations of modal equivalence and bisimulation that are relations over the set of (pointed) models to relations between a set of (pointed) models and a set of (pointed) pre-models.

Definition 10 (trans-equivalence). *Let (M, s) be a pointed model and (M', s') a pointed pre-model. We say (M, s) and (M', s') are trans-equivalent, denoted $(M, s) \equiv^T (M', s')$, if $\{\varphi \mid (M, s) \models \varphi\} = \{\varphi \mid (M', s') \models \varphi\}$.*

Definition 11 (trans-bisimulation). *Let $M = (S, R, V)$ be a model and $M' = (S', R', V')$ a pre-model. A non-empty binary relation $Z \subseteq S \times S'$ is called a trans-bisimulation between M and M', if the following hold for all $s \in S$ and $s' \in S'$ such that sZs':*

- *(Atom) $s \in V(p)$ iff $s' \in V'(p)$, for all propositional variables p;*
- *(Zig) for all $G \in \mathrm{GR}$ and $t \in S$ such that $sR_G^D t$, there is a path of M' from s' to some t', such that tZt' and all the edges in the path are of the form R'_τ such that $G \subseteq \tau$;*
- *(Zag) for all $\tau \in \mathrm{AG} \cup \mathrm{GR}$ and $t' \in S'$ such that $s'R'_\tau t'$, there is a state $t \in S$ such that tZt' and $sR_\tau t$ when $\tau \in \mathrm{AG}$ and $sR_\tau^D t$ when $\tau \in \mathrm{GR}$.*

We write $Z : (M, s) \rightleftarrows^T (M', s')$ if Z is a bisimulation between M and M' such that sZs'. Moreover, $(M, s) \rightleftarrows^T (M', s')$ means that there is a $Z \subseteq S \times S'$ such that $Z : (M, s) \rightleftarrows^T (M', s')$.

We shall also make use of the notion of a standard bisimulation (see e.g., [3]). For a distinction, the existence of a standard bisimulation is denoted by $\rightleftarrows$, and we use $\rightleftarrows^T$ for trans-bisimulation.

Lemma 4 (conditional invariance of trans-bisimulation). *Given a pointed model (M, s) and a pointed pre-model (M', s'), if $(M, s) \rightleftarrows^{\mathrm{T}} (M', s')$ and there exists a pointed pseudo model (M'', s'') such that $(M', s') \rightleftarrows (M'', s'')$, then $(M, s) \equiv^{\mathrm{T}} (M', s')$.*

Proof. Suppose $Z : (M, s) \rightleftarrows^{\mathrm{T}} (M', s')$ and $Y : (M', s') \rightleftarrows (M'', s'')$. We show that for any formula ψ, $(M', s') \models \psi$ iff $(M, s) \models \psi$. The proof can be carried out by induction on formulas. The only interesting cases are for $B_a\varphi$ and $D_G\varphi$. Let $M = (S, R, V)$, $M' = (S', R', V')$ and $M'' = (S'', R'', V'')$.

The case for $B_a\varphi$. Sufficiency. Suppose $(M, s) \models B_a\varphi$, and we must show $(M', s') \models B_a\varphi$. For any state $t' \in S'$ such that $s'R'_at'$, it suffices to show $(M', t') \models \varphi$. By (Zag) there is a state $t \in S$ such that tZt' and sR_at. From $(M, s) \models B_a\varphi$ it follows $(M, t) \models \varphi$. We get $(M', t') \models \varphi$ by the induction hypothesis, as was to be shown.

For necessity, suppose $(M', s') \models B_a\varphi$, and we must show $(M, s) \models B_a\varphi$. Given any state t of M such that sR_at (equivalent to $sR^D_{\{a\}}t$ as M is a model), it suffices to show $(M, t) \models \varphi$. By (Zig) there is a path of M' from s' to some t' such that (i) tZt' and (ii) every edge in the path is of the form R'_τ with $\{a\} \subseteq \tau$. It follows from $(M', s') \rightleftarrows (M'', s'')$ that there is a path of M'' from s'' to some t'' such that (i) $t'Yt''$ and (ii) every relation in the path is of the form R_τ with $\{a\} \subseteq \tau$. $s''R''_at''$ holds since M'' is a pseudo model. Since we have $(M'', s'') \models B_a\varphi$ by the invariance of bisimulation, $(M'', t'') \models \varphi$ and so $(M', t') \models \varphi$. By the induction hypothesis we get $(M, t) \models \varphi$, as was to be shown.

The case for $D_G\varphi$ can be shown analogously to the case for $B_a\varphi$.

Lemma 5 (truthful translation).

1. *(Unraveling preserves bisimulation) Let M be a pseudo model and s a state of it. For any reduced path $\boldsymbol{s}$ of M that ends with s, $(M, s) \rightleftarrows (M^u, \boldsymbol{s})$.*
2. *(Folding preserves trans-bisimulation) Let M be a treelike pre-model and s a state of it. Then $(M^f, s) \rightleftarrows^{\mathrm{T}} (M, s)$.*

Proof. 1. It is not hard to verify that the conditions of (Atom), (Zig) and (Zag) for standard bisimulation are satisfied between a pointed model and its unraveling.

2. Let $M = (S, R, V)$ be a treelike pre-model and $M^f = (S, Q, V)$ its folding. It suffices to show that $Z = \{(s, s) \mid s \in S\}$ is such that $Z : (M^f, s) \rightleftarrows^{\mathrm{T}} (M, s)$. (Atom) holds trivially.

(Zig) Suppose there is a $t \in S$ such that sQ^D_Gt for some group G. It suffices to show that there is a path of M from s to t such that all the edges in the path are of the form R_τ such that $G \subseteq \tau$. Suppose $G = a_1, \ldots, a_n$, and then by definition we have $Q^D_G = Q_{a_1} \cap \cdots \cap Q_{a_n}$, therefore (s, t) is in the transitive and Euclidean closure of $R_{a_i} \cup \bigcup_{H \ni a_i} R_H$, for all a_i with $1 \leq i \leq n$. It follows that there are n reduced paths of M from s to t such that:

$$\langle s, R_{\tau_{1,1}}, \ldots, R_{\tau_{1,m_1}} t \rangle$$
$$\vdots$$
$$\langle s, R_{\tau_{n,1}}, \ldots, R_{\tau_{n,m_n}} t \rangle$$

where each $\tau_{i,j}$ is either a_i or some $H \ni a_i$. Since M is treelike, there can only be a unique reduced path from s to t. It follows that (i) $m_1 = m_2 = \cdots = m_n$ (i.e., all possible reduced paths are of the same length; let us denote it by m) and (ii) $\tau_{1,j} = \tau_{2,j} = \cdots = \tau_{n,j}$ (i.e., all relations remain the same at the same position of each possible reduced path; let us denote it by τ_j) for all possible j. But since $\tau_{i,j}$ at least contains a_i (or is a_i itself), it follows that $G \subseteq \tau_j$ for each j. Therefore, $G \subseteq \tau_1 \cap \cdots \cap \tau_m$, as was to be shown.

(Zag) Suppose there is $t \in S$ such that $sR_\tau t$ for some agent or group τ, and it suffices to show $sQ_\tau t$ (if τ is an agent) and $sQ_\tau^D t$ (if τ is a group). If τ is an agent a, we get $sQ_a t$ by the definition of Q_a. Otherwise τ is a group G with $sR_G t$, and it follows from the definition of folding that $sQ_x t$ for all $x \in G$, and thus $sQ_G^D t$.

Theorem 1. **BLD** *is a sound and strongly complete axiomatization of* $KD45^D$.

Proof. The soundness of **BLD** is easy to verify. As for the completeness, given a **BLD**-consistent set of $\mathcal{BLD}$ formulas, it can be extended to a maximal consistent set Φ of formulas using the standard Lindenbaum construction. By the pseudo completeness lemma (Lemma 2), there is a pseudo model (M, s) such that $(M, s) \models \Phi$. For any reduced path s of M, it follows from Lemma 5 that $(M^u, s) \rightleftarrows (M, s)$ and $((M^u)^f, s) \rightleftarrows^T (M^u, s)$, where M^u is the unraveling of M (which is a treelike pre-model by Lemma 3) and $(M^u)^f$ is the folding of M^u (which is a genuine model by definition). By Lemma 4 $((M^u)^f, s) \equiv^T (M^u, s)$, and $(M^u, s) \equiv (M, s)$ by the known result of the invariance of standard bisimulation. Therefore, $((M^u)^f, s) \models \Phi$.

5   Discussion

We have studied the properties of different types of group belief under different assumptions about the properties of belief (including knowledge). These are summed up in Fig. 1. We emphasize that we have used standard definitions that are used for both group knowledge and group belief in the literature, in particular in the standard textbook [8].

We can make the, perhaps surprising, observation that many group attitudes to knowledge and belief used in the literature are not well defined in the sense that they do not actually have the properties it is assumed that knowledge or belief has. For example, general knowledge (everybody-knows) *is actually not knowledge*, and common belief or distributed belief *are most often not belief*. In particular:

- Under the standard assumption that knowledge has the S5 properties, what is sometimes called *general knowledge* or *mutual knowledge* in the literature, i.e., what everybody knows, is not actually knowledge. It is (KT)B but not S5, in particular it lacks both the positive and negative introspection properties.
- Under the assumption that belief is consistent (the D axiom) but not veridical (the T axiom), distributed belief is not actually belief (in any of the standard model classes). For example, distributed belief on KD45 is K45 but not KD45. We note that "D but not T" is an extremely weak assumption about belief, in fact a standard property distinguishing belief from knowledge.
- Under the common assumption that belief has the KD45 or just the K45 properties, then common belief is not actually belief. It is KD4 or K4, respectively, and not KD45 or K45. In general, common belief typically lacks negative introspection. More precisely, common belief loses negative introspection on any of the model classes without the B axiom (symmetry). If we take the reflexive transitive closure of the union instead of the transitive closure, common belief is S4 on both KD45 and K45 model classes, again lacking the negative introspection property.
- General belief is not well defined as a notion of belief on weaker model classes than S5 either; it loses both positive and negative introspection on any class that has them.

None of the three (four, if we count the alternative definition for common belief) notions of group belief are actually belief on the most common model class for belief, namely KD45. The only cases for which all three notions of group belief are well defined in the sense that they have belief properties, are K, (K)T, KB and (KT)B.

Under the common assumption that belief does not have the veridicality property, the only cases where all three notions are well defined, in the sense that group belief actually has the properties of belief, are K and KB – i.e., under very weak assumptions about the properties of belief. Thus, group belief, as defined in the literature, strictly speaking typically is not actually belief, except under very weak assumptions about what belief is.

We hope these observations might help clarify the properties of group belief and knowledge. There has been some confusion and missing details in the literature regarding group knowledge/belief in general and distributed knowledge/belief in particular, for example about what the empty group knows [1] or what distributed knowledge actually means [2] – and about soundness and completeness of axiomatizations of KD45 with distributed belief. In this paper we provided a detailed completeness proof for a sound axiomatization of KD45 with distributed belief, by adapting a technique used for the S5 case in [23] to the KD45 case.

It should also be noted that while group belief often has fewer properties than individual belief (like common or distributed belief on KD45 as mentioned above), sometimes it has *more* properties. For example, common belief on KDB is S5 – it gains both positive and negative introspection. The alternative definition of common belief using the reflexive transitive closure is in a way "better behaved"; it is always either S4 or S5. However, its requirement that common belief must imply truth (reflexivity) does not square well with standard assumptions about belief (indeed, while this definition is often found for group knowledge, it is rarely found for group belief for weaker variants of belief than S5).

A conceptually closely related work is by Endriss and Grandi on *graph aggregation* [6]; the aggregation of one graph for each agent over the same set of vertices into a collective graph over the same set, in the spirit of aggregation problems in social choice theory. Endriss and Grandi argue that this abstraction captures many concrete natural problems, including preference aggregation, social networks, and indeed group knowledge including general, common and distributed knowledge (belief is not mentioned explicitly but the argument does not rely on any particular properties of knowledge). And indeed, what we have called preservation of belief properties for different types of group belief in this paper, is exactly the same that [6] calls *collective rationality* of the corresponding aggregation rules with respect to the properties. Despite the close connection to the framework, we were only able to make use of some minor results from [6], in the proof of Lemma 1, as [6] focuses mostly on Arrow-style *impossibility* results.

The motivation behind this paper has been to take a critical look at *standard* definitions of group knowledge and belief in the literature; i.e., the interpretation of general, common and distributed knowledge and belief using union, transitive closure of union, and intersection of individual accessibility relations, respectively. These definitions appear in standard textbooks and in a myriad of other works, and understanding them is therefore important. Of course, other, perhaps less well known, formalizations of group belief exist, although they have not been the topic of the current paper. Of particular mention here is [11], which takes a critical look at different definitions of group belief from a philosophical perspective, and proposes some new formalizations in modal logic. An interesting direction for future work would be to investigate preservation of belief properties under different assumptions of individual belief, for other non-standard notions of group belief. More broadly, by using the impossibility results from [6] mentioned above, it might be possible to say something about the *impossibility* of other group belief operators under certain assumptions about belief.

Acknowledgments. We thank the anonymous reviewers for useful comments. Yì N. Wáng acknowledges funding support by the National Social Science Foundation of China (Grant No. 16CZX048, 18ZDA290).

References

1. Ågotnes, T.: What no one knows. In: 10th Conference on Logic and the Foundations of Game and Decision Theory (LOFT 2012), Sevilla, June 2012
2. Ågotnes, T., Wáng, Y.N.: Resolving distributed knowledge. Artif. Intell. **252**, 1–21 (2017)
3. Blackburn, P., de Rijke, M., Venema, Y.: Modal Logic, Cambridge Tracts in Theoretical Computer Science, vol. 53. Cambridge University Press, Cambridge (2001)

4. van Ditmarsch, H., van der Hoek, W., Kooi, B.: Concurrent dynamic epistemic logic. In: Hendricks, V., Jørgensen, K., Pedersen, S. (eds.) Knowledge Contributors. Synthese Library Series, pp. 105–143. Kluwer Academic Publishers, Dordrecht (2003). https://doi.org/10.1007/978-94-007-1001-6_6
5. van Ditmarsch, H., van der Hoek, W., Kooi, B.: Dynamic Epistemic Logic. Synthese Library, vol. 337. Springer, Dordrecht (2007). https://doi.org/10.1007/978-1-4020-5839-4
6. Endriss, U., Grandi, U.: Graph aggregation. Artif. Intell. **245**, 86–114 (2017)
7. Fagin, R., Halpern, J.Y.: Reasoning about knowledge and probability. J. ACM **41**, 340–367 (1994)
8. Fagin, R., Halpern, J.Y., Moses, Y., Vardi, M.Y.: Reasoning about Knowledge. The MIT Press, Cambridge (1995). Hardcover edition
9. Fagin, R., Halpern, J.Y., Moses, Y., Vardi, M.Y.: Common knowledge revisited. Ann. Pure Appl. Logic **96**(1–3), 89–105 (1999)
10. Fagin, R., Halpern, J.Y., Vardi, M.Y.: What can machines know? On the properties of knowledge in distributed systems. J. ACM **39**(2), 328–376 (1992)
11. Gaudou, B., Herzig, A., Longin, D., Lorini, E.: On modal logics of group belief. In: Herzig, A., Lorini, E. (eds.) The Cognitive Foundations of Group Attitudes and Social Interaction. SPS, vol. 5, pp. 75–106. Springer, Cham (2015). https://doi.org/10.1007/978-3-319-21732-1_4
12. Halpern, J.Y.: Using reasoning about knowledge to analyze distributed systems. Ann. Rev. Comput. Sci. **2**, 37–68 (1987)
13. Halpern, J.Y., Moses, Y.: Knowledge and common knowledge in a distributed environment. J. ACM **37**(3), 549–587 (1990)
14. Halpern, J.Y., Moses, Y.: A guide to completeness and complexity for modal logics of knowledge and belief. Artif. Intell. **54**, 319–379 (1992)
15. Halpern, J.Y., Fagin, R.: Modelling knowledge and action in distributed systems. Distrib. Comput. **3**, 159–177 (1989)
16. Halpern, J.Y., Moses, Y., Waalrts, O.: A characterization of eventual byzantine agreement. In: Proceedings of the Ninth Annual ACM Symposium on Principles of Distributed Computing, PODC 1990, pp. 333–346. ACM, New York (1990)
17. Halpern, J.Y., Tuttle, M.R.: Knowledge, probability, and adversaries. J. ACM **40**, 917–960 (1993)
18. van der Hoek, W., Meyer, J.J.C.: Making some issues of implicit knowledge explicit. Int. J. Found. Comput. Sci. **3**(2), 193–224 (1992)
19. Jamroga, W., van der Hoek, W.: Agents that know how to play. Fundam. Inf. **63**(2–3), 185–219 (2004)
20. Meyer, J.J.C., van der Hoek, W.: Epistemic Logic for AI and Computer Science. Cambridge University Press, Cambridge (1995)
21. van der Hoek, W., Meyer, J.J.: Making some issues of implicit knowledge explicit. Int. J. Found. Comput. Sci. **3**(2), 193–224 (1992)
22. Walther, D.: Satisfiability of ATEL with common and distributed knowledge is ExpTime-complete. Technical report, University of Liverpool (2005)
23. Wáng, Y.N., Ågotnes, T.: Public announcement logic with distributed knowledge: expressivity, completeness and complexity. Synthese **190**(1 supplement), 135–162 (2013)

Broadening Label-Based Argumentation Semantics with May-Must Scales

Ryuta Arisaka[✉] and Takayuki Ito

Nagoya Institute of Technology, Nagoya, Japan
ryutaarisaka@gmail.com, ito.takayuki@nitech.ac.jp

Abstract. The semantics as to which set of arguments in a given argumentation graph may be acceptable (acceptability semantics) can be characterised in a few different ways. Among them, the labelling-based approach allows for a concise and flexible determination of acceptability statuses of arguments through assignment of a label indicating acceptance, rejection, or undecided to each argument. In this work, we contemplate a way of broadening it by accommodating may- and must- conditions for an argument to be accepted and rejected, as determined by the number(s) of rejected and accepted attacking arguments. We show that the broadened label-based semantics can be used to express more mild indeterminacy than inconsistency for acceptability judgement when, for example, it may be the case that an argument is accepted and when it may also be the case that it is rejected. We identify that finding which conditions a labelling satisfies for every argument can be an undecidable problem, which has an unfavourable implication to semantics. We propose to address this problem by enforcing a labelling to maximally respect the conditions, while keeping the rest that would necessarily cause non-termination labelled undecided.

1 Introduction

Dung formal argumentation [19] provides an abstract view of argumentation as a graph of: nodes representing arguments; and edges representing attacks from the source arguments to the target arguments. Dung argumentation allows us to determine which arguments are acceptable in a given argumentation.

While the determination in Dung's seminal paper is through conflict-freeness: *no members of a set attack a member of the same set*, and defence: *a set of arguments defend an argument just when any argument attacking the argument is attacked by at least one member of the set*, there are other known approaches. With labelling, a labelling function assigns a label indicating either of: acceptance, rejection, and undecided (see e.g. [14,29]) to each argument, offering a fairly concise and also flexible (see e.g. [13]) characterisation of arguments' acceptability, based, in case of [13,14], just on the labels of the arguments it is attacked by. Acceptance and rejection conditions may be defined uniformly for every argument [14,29], or per argument, as in Abstract Dialectical Frameworks (ADF) [13], where acceptance status of an argument is uniquely determined

© Springer Nature Switzerland AG 2020
M. Dastani et al. (Eds.): CLAR 2020, LNAI 12061, pp. 22–41, 2020.
https://doi.org/10.1007/978-3-030-44638-3_2

for each combination of the acceptance/rejection/undecided labels of associated arguments.

1.1 Labelling-Approach with May-Must Scales

In this work, we aim to further explore the potential of labelling-approach by broadening the labelling in [14] with what we term *may-must acceptance scale* and *may-must rejection scale*, to be assigned, like in ADF, to each argument. The may-must acceptance scale (respectively may-must rejection scale) of an argument is specifically a pair of natural numbers (n_1, n_2) with n_1 indicating the minimum number of its attackers that need to be rejected (respectively accepted) in order that the argument can be accepted (respectively rejected) and n_2 the minimum number of its attackers that need to be rejected (respectively accepted) in order that it must be accepted (respectively rejected). That is, n_1 is the *may* condition, while n_2 is the *must* condition, for acceptance (respectively rejection) of the argument.

Thus, not only can they, through the must conditions, express exact conditions for acceptance/rejection of an argument as with [13,14], they can additionally describe minimal requirements to be satisfied in order that the argument can be accepted/rejected. The may-must scales lead to the following distinction to acceptance and rejection of an argument.

(1). It may be accepted.   (2). It must be accepted.

(i). It may be rejected.   (ii). It must be rejected.

Since each argument has its own may-must scales both for acceptance and rejection, depending on the specific numerical values given to them, we may have several combinations in $\{(1)\ (2)\ \text{neither}\}-\{(i)\ (ii)\ \text{neither}\}$. Hence, the concept of *aggregation* becomes relevant for obtaining an actual acceptability status of an argument. While (2)−(neither) (i.e. it must be accepted and it is not to be rejected), (neither)−(ii) (i.e. it is not to be accepted and it must be rejected), (2)−(ii) (i.e. the argument is both accepted and rejected at the same time) and (neither)−(neither) (i.e. it is neither accepted nor rejected) deterministically indicate acceptance, rejection, undecided and undecided for the acceptability status of the argument, the other combinations are more interesting.

Let us consider for example (1)−(i). Unlike (neither)−(neither) or (2)−(ii), either of which leads to immediate logical inconsistency, (1)−(i) expresses milder indeterminacy, since we can assume the possibilities of the argument to be accepted and of the same argument to be rejected simultaneously without logical contradiction. In fact, there may be more than one suitable label from among acceptance, rejection and undecided as the acceptability status of an argument, which differs from [13,14]. Such non-deterministic labels of argument(s) can trigger disjunctive branches to the labels of those arguments attacked by them.

1.2   Motivation for May-Must scales

In real-life argumentation, an argument which is attacked by a justifiable argument but by no other arguments can be seen differently from an argument which is attacked by a justifiable argument and which is also attacked by a lot more defeated (rejected) arguments. For example, if that argument is a scientific theory, one interpretation of the two cases is that, in the first case, it meets an objection without it having stood any test of time, and, in the second case, even though it is not defended against one objection, it withstood all the other objections, a lot more of them in number. Such an interpretation gives us a reasonable ground to judge that an argument, if found out to withstand an objection, attains greater credibility, that is to say, that an attacker being rejected has a positive, or at least a non-negative, impact on its acceptance.

Coupled with the other more standard intuition that an attacker of an argument being accepted has a non-positive impact on the argument's acceptance, we see that

- the larger the number of rejected attackers is, the more likely it can become that the argument is accepted, and
- the larger the number of accepted attackers is, the more likely it can become that the argument is rejected,

until there comes a moment where both acceptance and rejection of the argument become so compelling, with sufficient numbers of rejected and accepted attackers, that its acceptance status can no longer be determined. As with any reasonable real-life phenomenon, the acceptance and rejection judgement can be somewhat blurry, too. Introduction of the may- conditions allows the softer boundaries of acceptance and rejection to be captured based on the number(s) of accepted and rejected attacking arguments.

Moreover, with studies of argumentation expanding into multi-agent systems, for argumentation-based negotiations (Cf. two surveys [18,37] for two-party negotiations and a recent work on multi-party current negotiations [3]), strategic dialogue games and persuasions [2,6,24–28,31,35,36,38–41], and others, it is preferable that an argumentation theory be able to accommodate a different nuance of arguments' acceptability *locally* per argument, and yet somehow in a *logically principled* manner. Future applications into the domain in mind, may-must scales are given to each argument, like local constraints in ADF, ensuring the locality. Like in argumentation with graded acceptability [23] (see below for comparisons), however, may-must conditions are rooted in 'endogenous' information of an argumentation graph, to borrow the expression in [23], namely the cardinality of attackers, which aids retention of a level of abstractness defining monotonic conditions, i.e. a may- or a must- condition is satisfied minimally with n accepted or rejected attacking arguments, but also with any $(n \leq)$ m accepted or rejected attacking arguments. As we will show, it for example offers an easy characterisation of: possibly accepting an argument when 80% of attacking arguments are rejected; accepting an argument when 90% of attacking arguments are rejected; possibly rejecting an argument when 40%

of attacking arguments (but at least 1) are accepted; and rejecting an argument when 50% of attacking arguments (but at least 1) are accepted.

1.3   Related Work

Resembling situations are rather well-motivated in the literature. Argumentation with graded acceptability [23] relaxes conflict-freeness and defence in Dung abstract argumentation. For conflict-freeness, it permits a certain number k_1 of attackers to be accepted simultaneously with the attacked (see also set-attacks [34] and attack-tolerant argumentations [1,5,20,21,33]). For defence, it allows the defence by a set of arguments for the attacked to occur when a certain number k_2 of its attackers are attacked by a certain number k_3 of members of the set. Our work follows the general idea of conditionalising acceptance statuses of arguments on the cardinality of accepted and rejected attacking arguments. Indeed, $k_1 + 1$ corresponds to the must- condition of the may-must rejection scale in this work. On the other hand, unlike in [23] where dependency of acceptability status of an argument on the attackers of its attackers is enforced due to k_2 and k_3, we are more conservative about the information necessary for determining acceptability status(es) of an argument. We have it obtainable purely from its immediate attackers. Also, may- conditions are not considered in [23]. In particular, while both may- and must- conditions of the may-must acceptance scale of an argument interact with those of its may-must rejection scale (see Sect. 1.1), the interaction between the non-positive and the non-negative effects on the acceptance of the argument is, as far as we can fathom, not primarily assumed in [23].

Ranking-based argumentations (Cf. a recent survey [11]) order arguments by the degree of acceptability. There are many conditions around the ordering, giving them various flavour. Ones that are somewhat relevant to our setting (see Sect. 1.2) are in a discussion in [15], where we find the following descriptions:

- the more defence branches an argument has, the more acceptable it becomes.
- the more attack branches an argument has, the less acceptable it becomes.

Here, a branch of an argument is a chain of attacking arguments having the argument as the last one attacked in the chain, and an attack branch (respectively a defence branch) is a branch with an odd (respectively even) number of attacks. With the principle of reinstatement (that an attacker of an attacker of an argument has a propagating positive effect on the acceptance of the argument) assumed, these two conditions are clearly reasonable. By contrast, our approach assigns may- and must- acceptance and rejection conditions to each argument; thus, the reinstatement cannot be taken for granted, which generally makes it inapplicable to propagate argumentation ranks (which can be numerical values [7,8,16,21,30]) through branches by a set of globally uniform propagation rules. The cardinality precedence: the greater the number of immediate attackers of an argument, the weaker the level of its acceptability is [11], which in itself does not take into account acceptability statuses of the immediate attackers, does not always hold good with our approach, either.

For a label-based argumentation, non-deterministic labelling in argumentation as far back as we can see is discussed in [29], where an argument may be labelled as either rejected ($\{-\}$) or 'both accepted and rejected' ($\{+, -\}$) when, for example, it has just one attacker labelled $\{+, -\}$. Nonetheless, the criteria of label assignments are global (an argument may be accepted ($\{+\}$) just when the label(s) of all its attackers contain $-$; and may be rejected just when there exists at least one argument whose label contains $+$), not covering the various nuances to follow from locally given criteria. On more technical a point, while letting only $\{+, -\}$ (both accepted and rejected) be 'undecided' is sufficient in [29], that is not enough in more general a case, as we are to show in this paper. Indeed, with some argumentation graph and some may-must acceptance and rejection scales, it can happen that whether, for example, an argument is accepted, or both accepted and rejected, is itself an undecidable question.

Abstract Dialectical Frameworks (ADF) [13] is another labelling approach which accommodates, with 3 values [13] (which has been recently extended to multi-values [12]), local acceptance, rejection and undecided conditions. The label of an argument is determined into only one of the 3 labels for a given combination of its attackers' labels. Since its label is determined for every combination of its attackers' labels, the ADF labelling is very specific (or concrete). By contrast, the may-must conditions are more abstract in that they only specify, like in [14,23], the numbers of attackers but not exactly which ones. Apart from that the abstract specification is in line with [14], the level of abstractness is more favourable for our setting, since the may- and must- acceptance (or rejection) conditions, once satisfied with n rejected (or n accepted) attacking arguments, should remain satisfied with m rejected (or m accepted) attacking arguments so long as $n \leq m$, which they can handle in more principled a way. Moreover, the acceptance status of an argument is evaluated both for acceptance and for rejection with the two scales. The independent criteria are fitting for many real-life decision-makings, since it is common that assessments as to why a proposal (a suspect) should/must be accepted (guilty) and as to why it (the suspect) should/must be rejected (acquitted) are separately made before, based on them, a final decision is delivered. The may- must- conditions based on the cardinality of accepted or rejected attacking arguments are, as far as we are aware, not considered in ADF including [10,12]. Some more technical comparisons are found in the conclusion of this paper.

Fuzziness as a varying attack strength [30] and as a varying degree of acceptability of an argument [10,12,16] have been discussed in the literature, both of which are closely related to ranking-based argumentation. The kind of fuzziness that we deal with in this paper, however, is not, again borrowing the expression in [23], about 'exogeneously given information about the relative strength of arguments' or the relative degree of acceptability, but about an endogenous property of an argumentation graph, the cardinality of attackers.

1.4   Summary of Contribution and the Structure of the Paper

We broaden the labelling in [14] with a may-must acceptance scale and a may-must rejection scale for each argument, as we stated in Sect. 1.1, which helps *localise* the nuance of acceptability of an argument based on the cardinality of (accepted and rejected) attacking arguments. That those conditions only specify the numbers of (accepted and rejected) attacking arguments and that their satisfaction conditions are *monotonic* (Cf. Section 1.2) help the approach retain a level of abstractness that facilitates a principled explanation as to why an argument is accepted, rejected, or undecided. The may-must scales accommodate *two-way evaluation* for acceptance as well as rejection, and *non-deterministic labelling*.

Technically, we identify that finding a labelling that satisfies local criteria for each argument is not always possible due to a circular reasoning. We address this problem by enforcing a labelling to maximally respect local acceptance criteria, while keeping the rest that would necessarily cause non-termination labelled undecided.

In the remaining, we will see: technical preliminaries, specifically of Dung abstract argumentation labelling [14] (in Sect. 2); and present our label-based argumentation with may-must scales and identify its connection to the above-mentioned labelling (in Sect. 3). We will then draw conclusions with some technical remarks around ADF.

2   Technical Preliminaries

Dung abstract argumentation [19] considers an argumentation as a graph where a node represents an argument and where an edge between arguments represents an attack from the source argument to the target argument. Technically, let $\mathcal{A}$ denote the class of abstract entities that we understand as arguments, then a (finite) abstract argumentation is a tuple (A, R) with $A \subseteq_{\text{fin}} \mathcal{A}$ and $R \subseteq A \times A$. $a_1 \in A$ is said to attack $a_2 \in A$ if and only if, or iff, $(a_1, a_2) \in R$ holds. We denote the class of all Dung abstract argumentations by $\mathcal{F}^{\mathsf{D}}$.

One of the main objectives of representing an argumentation formally as a graph is to infer from it which set(s) of arguments may be accepted. Acceptability of a set of arguments is determined by whether it satisfies certain criteria.

In this paper, we will uniformly use labelling [14] for characterisation of the acceptability semantics; readers are referred to Dung's original paper [19] for an equivalent semantic characterisation through conflict-freeness and defence[1].

Let $\mathcal{L}$ denote $\{\mathsf{in}, \mathsf{out}, \mathsf{undec}\}$, and let Λ denote the class of all partial functions $\mathcal{A} \to \mathcal{L}$. Let Λ^A for $A \subseteq \mathcal{A}$ denote a subclass of Λ that includes all and only those $\lambda \in \Lambda$ that is defined for all and only members of A. For the order among

---

[1] Similar semantic characterisation with the conflict-freeness and the defence is, as with some of the ranking-based approaches or with ADF, not actually practical in this work, since the nuance of an attack in Dung abstract argumentation is only one of many that are expressible in our proposal.

members of Λ, let $\preceq$ be a binary relation over Λ such that $\lambda_1 \preceq \lambda_2$ for $\lambda_1, \lambda_2 \in \Lambda$ iff all the following conditions hold. (1) There is some $A \subseteq_{\text{fin}} \mathcal{A}$ such that $\lambda_1, \lambda_2 \in \Lambda^A$. (2) For every $a \in A$, $\lambda_1(a) = \text{in}$ (and respectively $\lambda_1(a) = \text{out}$) materially implies $\lambda_2(a) = \text{in}$ (and respectively $\lambda_2(a) = \text{out}$). We may write $\lambda_1 \prec \lambda_2$ when $\lambda_1 \preceq \lambda_2$ but not $\lambda_2 \preceq \lambda_1$.

Then, $\lambda \in \Lambda$ is said to be: a complete labelling of $(A, R) \in \mathcal{F}^D$ iff all the following conditions hold for every $a \in A$ [14].

1. $\lambda \in \Lambda^A$.
2. $\lambda(a) = \text{in}$ iff there exists no $a_x \in A$ such that a_x attacks a and that $\lambda(a_x) \neq \text{out}$.
3. $\lambda(a) = \text{out}$ iff there exists some $a_x \in A$ such that a_x attacks a and that $\lambda(a_x) = \text{in}$.

First of all, $(\Lambda^A, \preceq)$ is clearly a meet-semilattice (see [17] for all these notions around a lattice). Denote the set of all complete labellings of (A, R) by $\Lambda^{com}_{(A,R)}$. It is well-known that $(\Lambda^{com}_{(A,R)}, \preceq)$ is also a meet-semilattice.

A complete labelling λ of (A, R) ($\in \mathcal{F}^D$) is said to be also a preferred labelling of (A, R) iff, for every complete labelling λ_x of (A, R), $\lambda \prec \lambda_x$ does not hold. A preferred labelling λ of (A, R) is also a stable labelling of (A, R) iff, for every $a \in A$, $\lambda(a) \neq \text{undec}$ holds. Also, $\lambda \in \Lambda$ is called a grounded labelling of (A, R) iff λ is the meet of $\Lambda^{com}_{(A,R)}$ in $(\Lambda^A, \preceq)^2$.

For any such labelling λ of (A, R), we say that $a \in A$ is: accepted iff $\lambda(a) = \text{in}$; rejected iff $\lambda(a) = \text{out}$; and undecided, otherwise.

We call the set of all complete/preferred/stable/grounded labellings of (A, R) complete/preferred/stable/grounded semantics of (A, R).

Let $a_1 \rightarrow a_2$ or $a_2 \leftarrow a_1$ be a graphical representation of $(a_1, a_2) \in R$. A small concrete example $a_1 \leftrightarrows a_2$ should suffice for illustrating the relation among the semantics. Let $\lambda_1, \lambda_2, \lambda_3 \in \Lambda^{\{a_1, a_2\}}$ be such that $\lambda_1(a_1) = \text{in}$, $\lambda_1(a_2) = \text{out}$ (as shown below, to the left), that $\lambda_2(a_1) = \text{out}$, $\lambda_2(a_2) = \text{in}$ (as shown below, at the centre), and that $\lambda_3(a_1) = \lambda_3(a_2) = \text{undec}$ (as shown below, to the right).

$$\begin{matrix} \text{in} & & \text{out} & & \text{out} & & \text{in} & & \text{undec} & & \text{undec} \\ a_1 & \longleftrightarrow & a_2 & & a_1 & \longleftrightarrow & a_2 & & a_1 & \longleftrightarrow & a_2 \end{matrix}$$

Then, complete, preferred, stable and grounded, semantics of this argumentation are exactly $\{\lambda_1, \lambda_2, \lambda_3\}$, $\{\lambda_1, \lambda_2\}$, $\{\lambda_1, \lambda_2\}$ and $\{\lambda_3\}$.

3 Label-Based Argumentation Semantics with May-Must Scales

We present abstract argumentation with may-must scales, and characterise its labelling-based semantics in this section. In the remaining, for any tuple T of

---

[2] We make it more general here in light of some more recent argumentation studies (including this work) in which a grounded labelling is not necessarily a complete labelling [4,9], although, in case of Dung argumentation, it is trivial that a grounded labelling is the meet of $\Lambda^{com}_{(A,R)}$ in $(\Lambda^{com}_{(A,R)}, \preceq)$.

n-components, we make the following a rule that $(T)^i$ for $1 \leq i \leq n$ refers to T's i-th component. Since the two may-must scales (one for acceptance and one for rejection) define a nuance of acceptability of an argument, we call the pair a nuance tuple:

Definition 1 (Nuance tuple). *We define a nuance tuple to be* $(\boldsymbol{X}_1, \boldsymbol{X}_2)$ *for some* $\boldsymbol{X}_1, \boldsymbol{X}_2 \in \mathbb{N} \times \mathbb{N}$*. We denote the class of all nuance tuples by* $\mathcal{Q}$*. For any* $Q \in \mathcal{Q}$*, we call* $(Q)^1$ *its may-must acceptance scale and* $(Q)^2$ *its may-must rejection scale.*

Definition 2 (Abstract argumentation with may-must scales). *We define a (finite) abstract argumentation with may-must scales to be a tuple* (A, R, f_Q) *with:* $A \subseteq_{fin} \mathcal{A}$*;* $R \subseteq A \times A$*; and* $f_Q : A \rightarrow \mathcal{Q}$*, such that* $((f_Q(a))^i)^1 \leq ((f_Q(a))^i)^2$ *for every* $a \in A$ *and every* $i \in \{1, 2\}$*.*
We denote the class of all (finite) abstract argumentations with may-must scales by $\mathcal{F}$*, and refer to its member by* F *with or without a subscript.*

The role of a nuance tuple within an $(A, R, f_Q) \in \mathcal{F}$ is as was described in Sect. 1. If $a \in A$ is such that $((f_Q(a))^1)^1 = 2$ (the first component of the first component of $f_Q(a)$, which is the first component of $(f_Q(a))$'s may-must acceptance scale, which is the may condition of $(f_Q(a))$'s may-must acceptance scale) and $((f_Q(a))^1)^2 = 3$ (similarly, the must condition of $(f_Q(a))$'s may-must acceptance scale), then a can never be accepted unless there are at least 2 arguments attacking a that are rejected. Once there are at least 3 arguments attacking a that are rejected, then a must be accepted.

Given the nature of attack, it is not very intuitive to permit the value of may-condition to be strictly larger than that of must- condition of a may-must scale: an accepted attacking argument has a non-favourable effect on the argument(s) it attacks; if, say, 2 arguments attacking a need to be accepted in order that a can be rejected, intuitively 1 accepted argument attacking a does not produce strong enough non-favourable effect on a to reject it; also into the other direction, if, say, 3 arguments attacking a need to be accepted in order that a must be rejected, intuitively 4 accepted arguments attacking a still enforce rejection of a. It is for this reason that we are formally precluding the possibility in Definition 2.

Definitions for satisfaction of may- and must- conditions of the may-must scales are as below. Here and in the remaining, for any $F \equiv (A, R, f_Q)$ $(\in \mathcal{F})$, any $a \in A$ and any $\lambda \in \Lambda^A$, we denote by $\mathsf{pred}^F(a)$ the set of all $a_x \in A$ with $(a_x, a) \in R$, by $\mathsf{pred}^F_{\lambda, \mathsf{in}}(a)$ the set of all $a_x \in \mathsf{pred}^F(a)$ with $\lambda(a_x) = \mathsf{in}$, and by $\mathsf{pred}^F_{\lambda, \mathsf{out}}(a)$ the set of all $a_x \in \mathsf{pred}^F(a)$ with $\lambda(a_x) = \mathsf{out}$.

Definition 3 (May- and must- satisfaction). *Let* $\mathsf{sat} : \mathcal{F} \times \mathcal{A} \times \mathcal{L} \times \Lambda \rightarrow \{\mathsf{true}, \mathsf{false}\}$ *be a predicate which is such that, with* $F \equiv (A, R, f_Q)$ $(\in \mathcal{F})$*,* $a \in A$*, and* $\lambda \in \Lambda^A$*:*

- $\mathsf{sat}(F, a, \mathsf{in}, \lambda)$ *holds iff* $((f_Q(a))^1)^1 \leq |\mathsf{pred}^F_{\lambda, \mathsf{out}}(a)|$ *holds.*
- $\mathsf{sat}(F, a, \mathsf{out}, \lambda)$ *holds iff* $((f_Q(a))^2)^1 \leq |\mathsf{pred}^F_{\lambda, \mathsf{in}}(a)|$ *holds.*

We specifically write $\mathsf{sat}_\star(F, a, \mathsf{in}, \lambda)$ *just when* $((f_Q(a))^1)^2 \leq |pred^F_{\lambda, out}(a)|$ *holds. Similarly, we specifically write* $\mathsf{sat}_\star(F, a, \mathsf{out}, \lambda)$ *just when* $((f_Q(a))^2)^2 \leq |pred^F_{\lambda, in}(a)|$ *holds.*

For any $F \equiv (A, R, f_Q)$ $(\in \mathcal{F})$, *any* $a \in A$, *and any* $\lambda \in \Lambda^A$, *we say that* a *satisfies may- acceptance condition (respectively may- rejection condition) under* λ *iff* $\mathsf{sat}(F, a, \mathsf{in}, \lambda)$ *(respectively* $\mathsf{sat}(F, a, \mathsf{out}, \lambda)$*) holds; we say that* a *satisfies must- acceptance condition (respectively must- rejection condition) under* λ *iff* $\mathsf{sat}_\star(F, a, \mathsf{in}, \lambda)$ *(respectively* $\mathsf{sat}_\star(F, a, \mathsf{out}, \lambda)$*) holds.*

We specifically say that a *satisfies* may_s*- acceptance condition (respectively* may_s*- rejection condition) under* λ *iff* a *satisfies may- but not must- acceptance condition (respectively may- but not must- rejection condition).*

We say that a *satisfies not-may- acceptance condition (respectively not-may- rejection condition) under* λ *iff* a *does not satisfy may- acceptance condition (respectively may- rejection condition).*

Now, as we described in Sect. 1, acceptance and rejection variations give rise to several combinations. Here, we cover all possible cases exhaustively and precisely for each $\lambda \in \Lambda^A$.

(1) **Must-must**: $a \in A$ satisfies must- acceptance and rejection conditions under λ.

(2) **Must-may$_s$**: $a \in A$ satisfies must- acceptance (respectively must- rejection) condition and may$_s$- rejection (respectively may$_s$- acceptance) condition under λ.

(3) **Must-notMay**: $a \in A$ satisfies must- acceptance (respectively must- rejection) condition, and not-may- rejection (respectively not-may- acceptance) condition under λ.

(4) **May$_s$-may$_s$**: $a \in A$ satisfies may$_s$- acceptance and rejection conditions under λ.

(5) **May$_s$-notMay**: $a \in A$ satisfies may$_s$- acceptance (respectively may$_s$- rejection) condition, and not-may- rejection (respectively not-may- acceptance) condition under λ.

(6) **notMay-notMay**: $a \in A$ satisfies not-may- acceptance and not-may- rejection conditions under λ.

Following Kleene-Priest three values logic' negation [32] (assume: truth corresponds to acceptance, and falsehood corresponds to rejection), we obtain that not-may- acceptance (respectively not-may- rejection) of a is equivalent to must- rejection (respectively must- acceptance) of a. Thus, with the possible-world perspective (see any modern text on classical modal logic, e.g. [22]), satisfaction of:

- must- acceptance (respectively must- rejection) of $a \in A$ implies a's acceptance (respectively rejection) in every accessible possible world.
- may$_s$- acceptance (respectively may$_s$- rejection) of a implies a's acceptance (respectively rejection) in a non-empty strict subset of all accessible possible worlds and a's rejection (respectively acceptance) in the other accessible possible worlds.

– not-may- acceptance (respectively not-may rejection) is equivalent to must-rejection (respectively must- acceptance).

As a consequence, we obtain:

For (1), since a can either be accepted or rejected but not both simultaneously, this case where both acceptance and rejection of a are implied in every accessible possible world is logically inconsistent. Thus, the acceptability status of a is undecided.

For (2), in some accessible possible worlds, a's acceptance and rejection are both implied, leading to inconsistency, while in the other accessible possible worlds, only a's acceptance (respectively rejection) is implied. Hence, it is clear that a is not judged rejected (respectively accepted) here; however, whether a is accepted (respectively rejected) is indeterminate.

For (3), it is the case that a must be accepted (respectively rejected) in every possible world (respectively accepted). Hence, a is judged accepted (respectively rejected).

For (4), it is possible that only a's acceptance is implied in some accessible possible worlds, only a's rejection is implied in some other accessible possible worlds, and both a's acceptance and rejection are implied in the remaining accessible possible worlds. In short, all of: a being accepted; its being rejected; and its acceptance status being undecided are generally a possibility.

For (5), it is analogous to (2). It is clear that a is not judged rejected (respectively accepted); however, whether a is accepted (respectively rejected) is indeterminate.

For (6), we have logical inconsistency, and the acceptability status of a is undecided.

Figure 1 to the right summarises the expected acceptance statuses of an argument for a given combination. In the table, [must-a] (, [may$_s$-a], and respectively [not-a]) indicates the case where the argument satisfies must- acceptance (, may$_s$- acceptance, and respectively not-may- acceptance); analogously, [must-r], [may$_s$-r], and [not-r] are for rejection. In Fig. 1, the any entry abbreviates that either of in, out and

$$\begin{array}{c@{\quad}ccc} & \text{[must-r]} & \text{[may}_s\text{-r]} & \text{[not-r]} \\ \text{[must-a]} & \begin{bmatrix} \text{undec} & \text{in?} & \text{in} \\ \text{[may}_s\text{-a]} & \text{out?} & \text{any} & \text{in?} \\ \text{[not-a]} & \text{out} & \text{out?} & \text{undec} \end{bmatrix} \end{array}$$

Fig. 1. Corresponding expected acceptance status(es) of an argument for each combination of may- must- acceptance and rejection conditions. any is any of in, out, undec, in? is any of in, undec, and out? is any of out, undec.

undec is possible; the in? entry either of in and undec; and the out? entry either of out and undec.

To connect the labels assigned to $\mathsf{pred}^F(a)$, $F \in \mathcal{F}$, with the label of a expected from them, we describe that λ designates a label l for a when and only when l is expected from the labels of $\mathsf{pred}^F(a)$ under λ, and that the label of a is designated under λ when and only when: (1) λ designates the label for a; and also (2) $\lambda(a)$ is the label. Formally:

Definition 4 (Label designation). *For any $F \equiv (A, R, f_Q)$ $(\in \mathcal{F})$, any $a \in A$, and any $\lambda \in \Lambda$, we say that λ designates $l \in \mathcal{L}$ for a iff all the following conditions hold.*

1. *λ is defined for every member of $\mathsf{pred}^F(a)$.*
2. *If $l = \mathsf{in}$, then a satisfies may- acceptance condition but not must- rejection condition.*
3. *If $l = \mathsf{out}$, then a satisfies may- rejection condition but not must- acceptance condition.*
4. *If $l = \mathsf{undec}$, then either of the following holds.*
   - *a satisfies must- acceptance and must- rejection conditions.*
   - *a satisfies at least either may_s- acceptance condition or may_s- rejection condition.*
   - *a satisfies not-may- acceptance and not-may- rejection conditions.*

Definition 5 (Designated label). *For any $F \equiv (A, R, f_Q)$ $(\in \mathcal{F})$, any $a \in A$, and any $\lambda \in \Lambda$, we say that a's label is designated under λ iff all the following conditions hold.*

> 1. *λ is defined for a.*   2. *λ designates $\lambda(a)$ for a.*

It can be easily surmised from Fig. 1 that a labelling may designate more than one label for an argument:

Proposition 1 (Non-deterministic label designation). *There exist $F \equiv (A, R, f_Q)(\in \mathcal{F})$, $a \in A$, $\lambda \in \Lambda$, and $l_1, l_2 \in \mathcal{L}$ such that λ designates l_1 and l_2, and that $l_1 \neq l_2$.*

The intuitive understanding of the significance of label designation is: if λ is such that every argument's label is designated under λ, then λ is a 'good' labelling in the sense of every argument respecting the correspondences in Fig. 1.

Example 1 (Labelling). To illustrate these definitions around labelling, let us consider the following simple acyclic argumentation graph with associated nuance tuples. We let $\underset{Q}{a}$ be a graphical representation of an argument a with $f_Q(a) = Q$.

$$
\begin{array}{ccccccccc}
a_1 & \longrightarrow & a_2 & \longrightarrow & a_3 & \longleftarrow & a_4 & \longleftarrow & a_5 \\
((0,0),(1,1)) & & ((0,1),(1,2)) & & ((1,1),(1,1)) & & ((1,1),(1,1)) & & ((0,0),(1,1))
\end{array}
$$

Denote this argumentation (with the indicated nuance tuples) by F. There are 3 labellings in $\Lambda^{\{a_1,\dots,a_5\}}$ under which the labels of every argument is designated, as shown below. Let us call the labelling with the first (, second, third) label assignment λ_1 (, λ_2, λ_3).

$$
\begin{array}{ccccccccc}
\mathsf{in} & & \mathsf{out} & & \mathsf{in} & & \mathsf{out} & & \mathsf{in} \\
a_1 & \longrightarrow & a_2 & \longrightarrow & a_3 & \longleftarrow & a_4 & \longleftarrow & a_5 \\
((0,0),(1,1)) & & ((0,1),(1,2)) & & ((1,1),(1,1)) & & ((1,1),(1,1)) & & ((0,0),(1,1))
\end{array}
$$

$$\begin{array}{ccccccccc}
\overset{\text{in}}{a_1} & \longrightarrow & \overset{\text{in}}{a_2} & \longrightarrow & \overset{\text{undec}}{a_3} & \longleftarrow & \overset{\text{out}}{a_4} & \longleftarrow & \overset{\text{in}}{a_5} \\
((0,0),(1,1)) & & ((0,1),(1,2)) & & ((1,1),(1,1)) & & ((1,1),(1,1)) & & ((0,0),(1,1))
\end{array}$$

$$\begin{array}{ccccccccc}
\overset{\text{in}}{a_1} & \longrightarrow & \overset{\text{undec}}{a_2} & \longrightarrow & \overset{\text{in}}{a_3} & \longleftarrow & \overset{\text{out}}{a_4} & \longleftarrow & \overset{\text{in}}{a_5} \\
((0,0),(1,1)) & & ((0,1),(1,2)) & & ((1,1),(1,1)) & & ((1,1),(1,1)) & & ((0,0),(1,1))
\end{array}$$

To see that there are no other labellings under which the labels of all the arguments are designated, note firstly that, of the 5 arguments, the labels of a_1, a_5 and a_4 are designated under some $\lambda \in \Lambda^{\{a_1,\ldots,a_5\}}$ iff $\lambda(a_1) = \lambda(a_5) =$ in and $\lambda(a_4) =$ out hold. To see that that is the case, let us firstly note that $\mathsf{pred}^F(a_1) = \mathsf{pred}^F(a_5) = \emptyset$. Thus, expected acceptance statuses of both a_1 and a_5 are known with no dependency on other arguments.[3] It follows trivially from the associated nuance tuples that both a_1 and a_5 satisfy must- acceptance and not-may- rejection condition. From Fig. 1, then, in is the only one expected acceptance status for these two arguments. Vacuously, if any $\lambda \in \Lambda^{\{a_1,\ldots,a_5\}}$ designates only in for a_1 and a_5, it must deterministically hold that $\lambda(a_1) = \lambda(a_5) =$ in, if the two arguments' labels are to be designated under λ. Now for a_4, assume in label for a_5, it satisfies must- rejection condition (because there is 1 accepted attacking argument) and not-may- acceptance condition (because there is 0 rejected attacking argument), which finds in Fig. 1 the corresponding expected acceptance status of out. This is deterministic provided in label for a_5 is deterministic, which happens to be the case in this example.

A more interesting case is of a_2. Assume in label for a_1, then it satisfies may_s- acceptance condition (because there is 0 rejected attacking argument) and may_s- rejection condition (because there is 1 accepted attacking argument), which finds any in Fig. 1 indicating that any of the 3 labels is a possibility.

Finally for a_3 for which neither may_s- acceptance condition nor may_s- rejection condition can be satisfied, every combination of acceptability statuses of a_2 and a_4 leads to at most one of the 3 labels for a_3. Consequently, λ_1, λ_2 and λ_3 are indeed the only 3 possible labellings of F such that every argument's label is designated under them.   ♣

Since the labelling for Dung abstract argumentation (see Sect. 2) is such that any labelling that satisfies the acceptance and rejection conditions of every argument in $(A, R) \in \mathcal{F}^D$ is a complete labelling of (A, R), we would also like to define a complete labelling of $\mathcal{F}$ to be such that every argument's label is designated under it.

It is, however, problematic to call such a labelling a complete labelling, because, then, there may not exist a complete labelling, as the following example shows.

---

[3] This does not mean that an expected acceptance status of an argument a_x with $\mathsf{pred}^F(a_x) = \emptyset$ is deterministic: if a_x satisfies may_s- acceptance or rejection condition, there are multiple possible expected acceptance statuses. We simply mean that no other arguments are required to know which may- must- conditions a_x would satisfy.

Example 2 (Non-termination of choosing a labelling that designates every argument). Consider a_1 $\underset{((0,0),(1,1))}{\overset{\frown}{\longleftarrow}}$ and assume $\lambda \in \Lambda^{\{a_1\}}$ with $\lambda(a_1) = \text{in}$. Then, λ designates undec for a_1. However, if $\lambda(a_1) = \text{undec}$, it follows that λ designates in for a_1. Assume $\lambda(a_1) = \text{out}$ instead, then λ designates in for a_1. ♣

Theorem 1. *There exists some $(A, R, f_Q) \in \mathcal{F}$ and some $a \in A$ such that, for every $\lambda \in \Lambda^A$, λ designates $l \neq \lambda(a)$ for a.*

3.1 Maximally Designating Labellings

As the result of Theorem 1, generally with $(A, R, f_Q) \in \mathcal{F}$ with an arbitrary f_Q, we can only hope to obtain maximally designating labellings under which some arguments, even though their labels may not be designated, may still be assigned undec. Now, since dependency of arguments' acceptability statuses is, as with [13,14], from source argument(s)' to their target argument's, we may without loss of generality consider any maximality per strongly connected component (see below), from ones that depend on a fewer number of other strongly connected components to those with a larger number of them to depend on.

We recall the definition of a strongly connected component and then define the order among them (Definition 6). In parallel, we will also need to rely on a function that updates a labelling by changing the label of an argument whose label is not designated under the labelling (Definition 7), so we can tell whether we can have a every-argument-designating labelling (Definition 8).

Definition 6 (SCC and SCC-depth). *For any $F \equiv (A, R, f_Q)$ ($\in \mathcal{F}$), we say that (A_1, R_1) with $A_1 \subseteq A$ and $R_1 \equiv (R \cap (A_1 \times A_1))$ is a strongly connected component iff, for every $a_x \in A$ and every $a_y \in A_1$, we have: $\{(a_x, a_y), (a_y, a_x)\} \subseteq R^*$ iff $a_x \in A_1$. Here, R^* is the reflexive and transitive closure of R.*

Let $\Delta : \mathcal{F} \times \mathcal{A} \to 2^A$ be such that, for any $F \equiv (A, R, f_Q)$ ($\in \mathcal{F}$) and any $a \in A$, $\Delta(F, a)$ is the set of all arguments in a strongly connected component that includes a. Let $\delta : \mathcal{F} \times \mathcal{A} \to \mathbb{N}$ be such that, for any $F \equiv (A, R, f_Q)$ ($\in \mathcal{F}$) and any $a \in A$, $\delta(F, a)$ is:

- *0 iff there is no $a_x \in \Delta(F, a)$ and $a_y \in (A \backslash \Delta(F, a))$ such that $(a_y, a_x) \in R$.*
- *$1 + \max_{a_z \in A'} \delta(F, a_z)$ with: $A' = \{a_w \in (A \backslash \Delta(F, a)) \mid \exists a_u \in \Delta(F, a). (a_w, a_u) \in R\}$.*

For any $F \equiv (A, R, f_Q)$ ($\in \mathcal{F}$) and any $a \in A$, we say that $\Delta(F, a)$ (and also a) have the SCC-depth of n iff $\delta(F, a) = n$.

Example 3 (SCC-depth). If we have $a_1 \overset{Q_1}{\longleftrightarrow} a_2 \overset{Q_2}{\longrightarrow} a_3 \overset{Q_3}{\longrightarrow} a_4$ we have (denoting this graph by F) $\Delta(F, a_1) = \Delta(F, a_2) = \{a_1, a_2\}$, $\Delta(F, a_3) = \Delta(F, a_4) = \{a_3, a_4\}$, $\Delta(F, a_1)$ $(= \Delta(F, a_2))$ has SCC-depth 0, and $\Delta(F, a_3)$ $(= \Delta(F, a_4))$ SCC-depth 1. ♣

Definition 7 (Labelling update sequence). *Let Θ denote the class of all functions $\Lambda \to \Lambda$ such that for any $F \equiv (A, R, f_Q)$ $(\in \mathcal{F})$, any $\lambda_1 \in \Lambda^A$, any $A_1 \subseteq A$ and any $\theta^{F,A_1} \in \Theta$, $\theta^{F,A_1}(\lambda_1)$ is:*

- *λ_1 if, for every $a \in A_1$, a's label is designated under λ_1.*
- *$\lambda_2 \in \Lambda^A$, otherwise, such that there is some $a \in A_1$ such that (1) a's label is not designated under λ_1, that (2) λ_1 designates $\lambda_2(a)$ for a, and that (3) $\lambda_1(a_x) = \lambda_2(a_x)$ for every $a_x \in (A\backslash\{a\})$.*

For any $F \equiv (A, R, f_Q)$ $(\in \mathcal{F})$, any $\lambda_1 \in \Lambda^A$, and any $A_1 \subseteq A$, we say that $(\lambda_1, \ldots, \lambda_n) \in (\Lambda^A)^n$ for $2 \leq n$ $(\in \mathbb{N})$ is an update sequence for A_1 iff, for every $1 \leq i \leq n-1$, there exists some $\theta_i^{F,A_1} \in \Theta$ such that $\theta_i^{F,A_1}(\lambda_i) = \lambda_{i+1}$.

Definition 8 (Convergence and contamination). *For any $F \equiv (A, R, f_Q)$ $(\in \mathcal{F})$ and any $A_1 \subseteq A$, we say that an update sequence $(\lambda_1, \ldots, \lambda_n)$ for A_1:*

- *updates $a_x \in A_1$ iff there exists some $m \leq n$ such that $\lambda_{m-1}(a_x) \neq \lambda_m(a_x)$;*
- *converges iff there exists some $m \leq n$ such that $\lambda_{m-1} = \lambda_m$; and*
- *contaminates $a_x \in A_1$ iff $(\lambda_1, \ldots, \lambda_n)$ updates a_x twice.*

Convergence is decidable with loop detection due to a member of $\mathcal{F}$ having a finite number of arguments.

With the notions we have introduced, we can obtain a maximally-designating labelling λ, maximal in the sense that any change of the label of an argument which is not designated under λ into a label which λ designates for it would find no converging update sequence, and would lead to contamination of the argument so long as updating is fair. The fair and unfair update sequences are at any rate an update sequence, thus it suffices to enumerate every possible one of them for including the fair one(s).

Definition 9 (Maximally-designating labelling). *For any $F \equiv (A, R, f_Q)$ $(\in \mathcal{F})$ and any $\lambda_1 \in \Lambda$, we say that λ_1 is a maximally-designating labelling of F up to $n \in \mathbb{N}$ iff both of the following conditions hold.*

1. *λ_1 is a maximally-designating labelling of F up to every $i \leq n-1$.*
2. *for every $a \in A$, with $\delta(F, a) = n$, either every $a_x \in \Delta(F, a)$'s label is designated under λ_1 or else all of the following conditions hold.*
   (a) *For every $a_x \in \Delta(F, a)$, if a_x's label is not designated under λ_1, then $\lambda_1(a_x) = \mathsf{undec}$.*
   (b) *There exists no pair of $n \in \mathbb{N}$ $(2 \leq n)$ and an update sequence $(\lambda_1, \ldots, \lambda_n)$ for $\Delta(F, a)$ such that $(\lambda_1, \ldots, \lambda_n)$ converges.*
   (c) *There exists a pair of $n \in \mathbb{N}$ $(2 \leq n)$ and an update sequence $(\lambda_1, \ldots, \lambda_n)$ for $\Delta(F, a)$ such that it contaminates every and only $a_x \in \Delta(F, a)$ whose label is not designated by λ_1.*

We simply say that λ is a maximally-designating labelling of F iff λ is a maximally-designating labelling of F up to every $n \in \mathbb{N}$.

Existence of a maximally-designating labelling is guaranteed for any $F \equiv (A, R, f_Q)$ $(\in \mathcal{F})$, since, again, A is finite. For the example in Example 2, we have one maximally designating labelling $\lambda \in \Lambda^{\{a_1\}}$ with $\lambda(a_1) = $ undec. We note that this definition correctly picks up the source of non-termination without a false positive from non-deterministic labels, due to the condition (b).

We define the condition under which $\lambda \in \Lambda$ is regarded a complete, preferred, stable or grounded labelling of a given $F \equiv (A, R, f_Q)$ $(\in \mathcal{F})$ by relying on maximally-designating labellings. Later, we show that specific may-must conditions to every argument reduces each type of a labelling of (A, R, f_Q) to the same type of labelling for the corresponding Dung abstract argumentation (A, R), thus confirming the adequacy of these definitions.

Definition 10 (Labelling). *For any $F \equiv (A, R, f_Q)$ $(\in \mathcal{F})$ and any $\lambda \in \Lambda$, we say that λ is:*

- *a complete labelling of F iff $\lambda \in \Lambda^A$ and also λ is a maximally-designating labelling of F. We denote the set of all complete labellings of F by Λ_F^{com}.*
- *a preferred labelling of F iff $\lambda \in \Lambda_F^{com}$ and, for every $\lambda' \in \Lambda_F^{com}$, it does not hold that $\lambda \prec \lambda'$.*
- *a stable labelling of F iff $\lambda \in \Lambda_F^{com}$ and also, for every $a \in A$, $\lambda(a) \neq$ undec holds.*
- *a grounded labelling of F iff λ is the meet of Λ_F^{com} in $(\Lambda^A, \preceq)$.*

Definition 11 (Acceptability semantics). *For any $F \equiv (A, R, f_Q)$ $(\in \mathcal{F})$, we say that $\Lambda' \subseteq \Lambda$ is the complete (, preferred, stable, grounded) semantics of F iff every complete (, preferred, stable, grounded) labelling of F is in Λ' but no other.*

Example 4 (Semantics). Consider the example in Example 1, with the 3 maximally-designating labellings λ_1 (the first) λ_2 (the second), and λ_3 (the last).

$$
\begin{array}{ccccc}
\text{in} & & \text{out} & & \text{in} & & \text{out} & & \text{in} \\
a_1 & \longrightarrow & a_2 & \longrightarrow & a_3 & \longleftarrow & a_4 & \longleftarrow & a_5 \\
((0,0),(1,1)) & & ((0,1),(1,2)) & & ((1,1),(1,1)) & & ((1,1),(1,1)) & & ((0,0),(1,1))
\end{array}
$$

$$
\begin{array}{ccccc}
\text{in} & & \text{in} & & \text{undec} & & \text{out} & & \text{in} \\
a_1 & \longrightarrow & a_2 & \longrightarrow & a_3 & \longleftarrow & a_4 & \longleftarrow & a_5 \\
((0,0),(1,1)) & & ((0,1),(1,2)) & & ((1,1),(1,1)) & & ((1,1),(1,1)) & & ((0,0),(1,1))
\end{array}
$$

$$
\begin{array}{ccccc}
\text{in} & & \text{undec} & & \text{in} & & \text{out} & & \text{in} \\
a_1 & \longrightarrow & a_2 & \longrightarrow & a_3 & \longleftarrow & a_4 & \longleftarrow & a_5 \\
((0,0),(1,1)) & & ((0,1),(1,2)) & & ((1,1),(1,1)) & & ((1,1),(1,1)) & & ((0,0),(1,1))
\end{array}
$$

λ_1, λ_2 and λ_3 are the only 3 possible complete labellings of F, i.e. $\{\lambda_1, \lambda_2, \lambda_3\}$ is its complete semantics.

The relation among λ_1, λ_2 and λ_3 is such that $\lambda_3 \prec \lambda_1$, $\lambda_3 \not\preceq \lambda_2$, $\lambda_2 \not\preceq \lambda_3$, $\lambda_1 \not\preceq \lambda_2$, and $\lambda_2 \not\preceq \lambda_1$ all hold. Hence, $\{\lambda_1, \lambda_2\}$ is the preferred semantics of F, a subset of the complete semantics. Moreover, $\{\lambda_1\}$ is the stable semantics of F. On the other hand, none of $\lambda_1, \lambda_2, \lambda_3$ are the least in $(\{\lambda_1, \lambda_2, \lambda_3\}, \preceq)$, and thus they cannot be a member of the grounded semantics; instead, it is $\{\lambda_4\}$ with: $\lambda_4(a_1) = \lambda_4(a_5) = $ in; $\lambda_4(a_2) = \lambda_4(a_3) = $ undec; and $\lambda_4(a_4) = $ out. Clearly, λ_4 is the meet of $\{\lambda_1, \lambda_2, \lambda_3\}$ in $(\Lambda^{\{a_1, \ldots, a_5\}}, \preceq)$.   ♣

The relation among the semantics below follows from Definition 10 immediately, and is almost as expected.

Theorem 2 (Subsumption).
All the following hold for any $F \in \mathcal{F}$.

1. *The complete, the preferred, and the grounded semantics of F exist.*
2. *The preferred semantics of F is a subset of the complete semantics of F.*
3. *If the stable semantics of F exists, then it consists of all and only members λ of the preferred semantics of F such that, for every $a \in A$, $\lambda(a) \neq$ undec holds.*

However, it is not necessary that the grounded semantics be a subset of the complete semantics.

There is an easy connection to Dung abstract argumentation labelling (see Sect. 2).

Theorem 3 (Correspondences to acceptability semantics in Dung argumentation). *For any $F \equiv (A, R, f_Q)$ ($\in \mathcal{F}$), if $(f_Q(a))^1 = (|\text{pred}^F(a)|, |\text{pred}^F(a)|)$ and $(f_Q(a))^2 = (1,1)$ for every $a \in A$, then: $\Lambda_x \subseteq \Lambda$ is the complete (, preferred, stable, and respectively grounded) semantics of F iff Λ_x is that of (A, R).*

This should highlight some advantage of the level of abstractness of may-must scales, in that it is very easy to determine nuance tuples globally (but also locally) with just 4 specific natural numbers or expressions that are evaluated into natural numbers. For example, we can specify the requirement for: possible acceptance of an argument a to be rejection of 80% of attacking arguments; acceptance of a to be rejection of 90% of attacking arguments; possible rejection of a to be acceptance of at least 1 but otherwise 40% of attacking arguments; and rejection of a to be acceptance of at least 1 but otherwise 50% of attacking arguments, all rounded up to the nearest natural numbers. We then have: $F \equiv (A, R, f_Q)$ ($\in \mathcal{F}$) with: $(f_Q(a))^1 = (\lceil 0.8 * |\text{pred}^F(a)| \rceil, \lceil 0.9 * |\text{pred}^F(a)| \rceil)$ and $(f_Q(a))^2 = (\max(1, \lceil 0.4 * |\text{pred}^F(a)| \rceil), \max(1, \lceil 0.5 * |\text{pred}^F(a)| \rceil))$ for every $a \in A$.

4   Conclusion with Technical Comparisons

We proposed a labelling-based argumentation with may-must scales, to broaden the labelling for Dung abstract argumentation, specifically [14]. Just as a complete labelling of $(A, R) \in \mathcal{F}^D$ is one that assigns to each argument $a \in A$ the label expected from the acceptance and the rejection conditions induced by the labels it assigns to $\text{pred}^F(a)$, so is 'almost' a complete labelling of $(A, R, f_Q) \in \mathcal{F}$. As we have identified, however, such a labelling may not actually exist. We proposed a way of addressing it. We also noted the connection to Dung abstract argumentation labelling.

Detailed technical comparisons to ADF with 3 values [13], for its closest connection to $\mathcal{F}$ among [12,13], should be of formal interest. For now, we mention a couple of notable technical decisions taken in ADF that generate some obvious differences; however, more precise technical relations will be studied.

As a quick reminder, we state a formal definition of ADF with notations kept consistent with those used in this work:

A (finite) ADF is a tuple (A, R^a, C) with: $A \subseteq_{\text{fin}} \mathcal{A}$; a binary relation R^a over A; and $C = \{C_a\}_{a \in A}$ where each C_a is a function: $\Lambda^{\text{pred}(A, R^a, C)}(a) \to \mathcal{L}$. Let us denote the class of all ADF tuples by $\mathcal{F}^{\text{ADF}}$.

For the semantics, let $\text{twoVal} : \mathcal{A} \times \Lambda \to 2^{\Lambda}$, which we alternatively state $\text{twoVal}^{\mathcal{A}} : \Lambda \to 2^{\Lambda}$, be such that, for any $A \subseteq_{\text{fin}} \mathcal{A}$ and any $\lambda \in \Lambda^A$, we have: $\text{twoVal}^A(\lambda) = \{\lambda_x \in \Lambda^A \mid \lambda \preceq \lambda_x$ and λ_x is maximal in $(\Lambda^A, \preceq)\}$.
Every member of $\text{twoVal}^A(\lambda)$ is such that $\lambda(a) \in \{\text{in}, \text{out}\}$ for every $a \in A$.

Also, let $\Gamma : \mathcal{F}^{\text{ADF}} \times \Lambda \to \Lambda$, which we alternatively state $\Gamma^{\mathcal{F}^{\text{ADF}}} : \Lambda \to \Lambda$, be such that, for any $(A, R^a, C) \in \mathcal{F}^{\text{ADF}}$ and any $\lambda \in \Lambda^A$, $\Gamma^{(A, R^a, C)}(\lambda)$ satisfies all the following.

1. $\Gamma^{(A, R^a, C)}(\lambda) \in \Lambda^A$.
2. For every $a \in A$, if $\Gamma^{(A, R^a, C)}(\lambda)(a) \neq \text{undec}$, then there exists no $\lambda_x \in \text{twoVal}^A(\lambda)$ such that $C_a(\lambda_x \downarrow_{\text{pred}(A, R^a, C)(a)}) \neq \Gamma^{(A, R^a, C)}(\lambda)(a)$. Here, $\lambda_x \downarrow_{\text{pred}(A, R^a, C)(a)}$ denotes a member of $\Lambda^{\text{pred}(A, R^a, C)}(a)$ which is such that, for any $a_x \in \text{pred}^{(A, R^a, C)}(a)$, $\lambda_x(a_x) = \lambda_x \downarrow_{\text{pred}(A, R^a, C)(a)}(a_x)$ holds.

In a nutshell [13], $\Gamma^{(A, R^a, C)}(\lambda)$ gets a consensus of every $\lambda_x \in \text{twoVal}^A(\lambda)$ on the label of each $a \in A$: if each one of them says in for a, then $\Gamma^{(A, R^a, C)}(\lambda)(a) = \text{in}$, if each one of them says out for a, then $\Gamma^{(A, R^a, C)}(\lambda)(a) = \text{out}$, and for the other cases $\Gamma^{(A, R^a, C)}(\lambda)(a) = \text{undec}$.

Then the grounded semantics of $(A, R^a, C) \in \mathcal{F}^{\text{ADF}}$ contains just the least fixpoint of $\Gamma^{(A, R^a, C)}$; the complete semantics of (A, R^a, C) contains all and only fixpoints of $\Gamma^{(A, R^a, C)}$; and the others are defined in a usual way from the complete semantics.

Some differences are therefore easy to identify. For instance, the grounded semantics of $F \in \mathcal{F}$ may not be a subset of its complete semantics (Cf. Theorem 2), while ADF enforces the property via Γ. In view of recent studies [4,9] where the subsumption does not hold, we believe our characterisation can be accommodating. Consider the example in Example 4 for where a difference occurs.

Also, for any $(A, R, f_Q) \in \mathcal{F}$, which we also refer to by F, if a semantics $\Lambda \subseteq \Lambda^A$ of F is such that, for two distinct $\lambda_1, \lambda_2 \in \Lambda$, there exists some $a \in A$ such that (1) $\lambda_1(a) \neq \lambda_2(a)$, and that (2) $\lambda_1(a_x) = \lambda_2(a_x)$ for every $a_x \in \text{pred}^F(a)$, then Λ does not belong to a semantics of (A, R, C) (or (A, R^a, C) with $R \equiv R^a$) above. This is rather clear, because, for any $a \in A$, C_a is a function with its range of $\{\text{in}, \text{out}, \text{undec}\}$. An example of such Λ has been covered; see again Example 4.

References

1. Arieli, O.: Conflict-tolerant semantics for argumentation frameworks. In: del Cerro, L.F., Herzig, A., Mengin, J. (eds.) JELIA 2012. LNCS (LNAI), vol. 7519, pp. 28–40. Springer, Heidelberg (2012). https://doi.org/10.1007/978-3-642-33353-8_3
2. Arisaka, R., Hagiwara, M., Ito, T.: Deception/honesty detection and (mis)trust building in manipulable multi-agent argumentation: an insight. In: Baldoni, M., Dastani, M., Liao, B., Sakurai, Y., Zalila Wenkstern, R. (eds.) PRIMA 2019. LNCS (LNAI), vol. 11873, pp. 443–451. Springer, Cham (2019). https://doi.org/10.1007/978-3-030-33792-6_28
3. Arisaka, R., Ito, T.: Numerical abstract persuasion argumentation for expressing concurrent multi-agent negotiations. ArXiv e-prints arXiv:2001.08335 (2020). To also appear in IJCAI best of Workshops 2019 Springer Volume
4. Arisaka, R., Santini, F., Bistarelli, S.: Block argumentation. In: Baldoni, M., Dastani, M., Liao, B., Sakurai, Y., Zalila Wenkstern, R. (eds.) PRIMA 2019. LNCS (LNAI), vol. 11873, pp. 618–626. Springer, Cham (2019). https://doi.org/10.1007/978-3-030-33792-6_48
5. Arisaka, R., Satoh, K.: Coalition formability semantics with conflict-eliminable sets of arguments. In: AAMAS, pp. 1469–1471 (2017)
6. Arisaka, R., Satoh, K.: Abstract argumentation/persuasion/dynamics. In: Miller, T., Oren, N., Sakurai, Y., Noda, I., Savarimuthu, B.T.R., Cao Son, T. (eds.) PRIMA 2018. LNCS (LNAI), vol. 11224, pp. 331–343. Springer, Cham (2018). https://doi.org/10.1007/978-3-030-03098-8_20
7. Baroni, P., Romano, M., Toni, F., Aurisicchio, M., Bertanza, G.: Automatic evaluation of design alternatives with quantitative argumentation. Argument Comput. 6(1), 24–49 (2015)
8. Besnard, P., Hunter, A.: A logic-based theory of deductive arguments. Artif. Intell. 128(1–2), 203–235 (2001)
9. Bistarelli, S., Santini, F.: A Hasse diagram for weighted sceptical semantics with a unique-status grounded semantics. In: Balduccini, M., Janhunen, T. (eds.) LPNMR 2017. LNCS (LNAI), vol. 10377, pp. 49–56. Springer, Cham (2017). https://doi.org/10.1007/978-3-319-61660-5_6
10. Bogaerts, B.: Weighted abstract dialectical frameworks through the lens of approximation fixpoint theory. In: AAAI, pp. 2686–2693 (2019)
11. Bonzon, E., Delobelle, J., Konieczny, S., Maudet, N.: A comparative study of ranking-based semantics for abstract argumentation. In: AAAI, pp. 914–920 (2016)
12. Brewka, G., Pührer, J., Strass, H., Wallner, J.P., Woltran, S.: Weighted abstract dialectical frameworks: extended and revised report. CoRR, abs/1806.07717 (2018)
13. Brewka, G., Strass, H., Ellmauthaler, S., Wallner, J., Woltran, S.: Abstract dialectical frameworks revisited. In: IJCAI (2013)
14. Caminada, M.: On the issue of reinstatement in argumentation. In: Fisher, M., van der Hoek, W., Konev, B., Lisitsa, A. (eds.) JELIA 2006. LNCS (LNAI), vol. 4160, pp. 111–123. Springer, Heidelberg (2006). https://doi.org/10.1007/11853886_11
15. Cayrol, C., Lagasquie-Schiex, M.C.: Graduality in argumentation. J. Artif. Intell. Res. 23, 245–297 (2005)
16. da Costa Pereira, C., Tettamanzi, A.G.B., Villata, S.: Changing one's mind: erase or rewind? Possibilistic belief revision with fuzzy argumentation based on trust. In: IJCAI, pp. 164–171 (2011)
17. Davey, B.A., Priestley, H.A.: Introduction to Lattices and Order. Cambridge University Press, New York (2002)

18. Dimopoulos, Y., Moraitis, P.: Advances in argumentation-based negotiation. In: Negotiation and Argumentation in Multi-agent systems: Fundamentals, Theories, Systems and Applications, pp. 82–125 (2014)
19. Dung, P.M.: On the acceptability of arguments and its fundamental role in non-monotonic reasoning, logic programming, and n-person games. Artif. Intell. **77**(2), 321–357 (1995)
20. Dunne, P.E., Hunter, A., McBurney, P., Parsons, S., Wooldridge, M.: Weighted argument systems: basic definitions, algorithms, and complexity results. Artif. Intell. **175**(2), 457–486 (2011)
21. Gabbay, D.M., Rodrigues, O.: An equational approach to the merging of argumentation networks. J. Logic Comput. **24**(6), 1253–1277 (2014)
22. Garson, J.: Modal logic. In: Zalta, E.N. (ed.) The Stanford Encyclopedia of Philosophy (2018)
23. Grossi, D., Modgil, S.: On the graded acceptability of arguments in abstract and instantiated argumentation. Artif. Intell. **275**, 138–173 (2019)
24. Grossi, D., van der Hoek, W.: Audience-based uncertainty in abstract argument games. In: IJCAI, pp. 143–149 (2013)
25. Hadjinikolis, C., Siantos, Y., Modgil, S., Black, E., McBurney, P.: Opponent modelling in persuasion dialogues. In: IJCAI, pp. 164–170 (2013)
26. Hadoux, E., Beynier, A., Maudet, N., Weng, P., Hunter, A.: Optimization of probabilistic argumentation with Markov decision models. In: IJCAI, pp. 2004–2010 (2015)
27. Hadoux, E., Hunter, A.: Strategic sequences of arguments for persuasion using decision trees. In: AAAI, pp. 1128–1134 (2017)
28. Hunter, A.: Towards a framework for computational persuasion with applications in behaviour change. Argument Comput. **9**(1), 15–40 (2018)
29. Jakobovits, H., Vermeir, D.: Robust semantics for argumentation frameworks. J. Logic Comput. **9**, 215–261 (1999)
30. Janssen, J., Cock, M.D., Vermeir, D.: Fuzzy argumentation frameworks. In: IPMU, pp. 513–520 (2008)
31. Kakas, A.C., Maudet, N., Maritis, P.: Modular representation of agent interaction rules through argumentation. Auton. Agent. Multi-Agent Syst. **11**(2), 189–206 (2005)
32. Kleene, S.C.: Introduction to Meta-mathematics. North-Holland Publishing Co., Amsterdam (1952)
33. Leite, J., Martins, J.: Social abstract argumentation. In: IJCAI, pp. 2287–2292 (2011)
34. Nielsen, S.H., Parsons, S.: A generalization of Dung's abstract framework for argumentation: arguing with sets of attacking arguments. In: Maudet, N., Parsons, S., Rahwan, I. (eds.) ArgMAS 2006. LNCS (LNAI), vol. 4766, pp. 54–73. Springer, Heidelberg (2007). https://doi.org/10.1007/978-3-540-75526-5_4
35. Parsons, S., Sklar, E.: How agents alter their beliefs after an argumentation-based dialogue. In: Parsons, S., Maudet, N., Moraitis, P., Rahwan, I. (eds.) ArgMAS 2005. LNCS (LNAI), vol. 4049, pp. 297–312. Springer, Heidelberg (2006). https://doi.org/10.1007/11794578_19
36. Rahwan, I., Larson, K.: Argumentation and game theory. In: Simari, G., Rahwan, I. (eds.) Argumentation in Artificial Intelligence, pp. 321–339. Springer, Boston (2009). https://doi.org/10.1007/978-0-387-98197-0_16
37. Rahwan, I., Ramchurn, S.D., Jennings, N.R., Mcburney, P., Parsons, S., Sonenberg, L.: Argumentation-based negotiation. Knowl. Eng. Rev. **18**(4), 343–375 (2003)

38. Rienstra, T., Thimm, M., Oren, N.: Opponent models with uncertainty for strategic argumentation. In: IJCAI, pp. 332–338 (2013)
39. Riveret, R., Prakken, H.: Heuristics in argumentation: a game theory investigation. In: COMMA, pp. 324–335 (2008)
40. Sakama, C.: Dishonest arguments in debate games. In: COMMA, pp. 177–184 (2012)
41. Thimm, M.: Strategic argumentation in multi-agent systems. KI - Künstliche Intelligenz **28**(3), 159–168 (2014). https://doi.org/10.1007/s13218-014-0307-2

Semirings of Evidence

Michael Baur and Thomas Studer$^{(\boxtimes)}$

Institute of Computer Science, University of Bern, Bern, Switzerland
michael.baur@students.unibe.ch, thomas.studer@inf.unibe.ch

Abstract. In traditional justification logic, evidence terms have the syntactic form of polynomials, but they are not equipped with the corresponding algebraic structure. We present a novel semantic approach to justification logic that models evidence by a semiring. Hence justification terms can be interpreted as polynomial functions on that semiring. This provides an adequate semantics for evidence terms and clarifies the role of variables in justification logic. Moreover, the algebraic structure makes it possible to compute with evidence. Depending on the chosen semiring this can be used to model trust, probabilities, cost, etc. Last but not least the semiring approach seems promising for obtaining a realization procedure for modal fixed point logics.

Keywords: Justification logic · Semiring · Completeness

1 Introduction

Justification logic replaces the $\square$-operator from modal logic with explicit evidence terms [5,11,30]. That is, instead of formulas $\square A$, justification logic features formulas $t : A$, where t encodes evidence for A. Depending on the context, the term t may represent a formal proof of A [5,29] or stand for an informal justification (like direct observation, public announcement, private communication, and so on) for an agent's knowledge or belief of A. With the introduction of possible world models, justification logic has become an important tool to discuss and analyze epistemic situations [6,7,14,15,36].

The terms of justification logic represent explicit evidence for an agent's belief or knowledge. Within justification logic, we can reason about this evidence. For instance, we can track different pieces of evidence pertaining to the same fact, which is essential for distinguishing between factive and non-factive justifications. This is applied nicely in Artemov's analysis of Russel's Prime Minister example [8]. Evidence terms can also represent the reasoning process of an agent. Therefore, agents represented by justification logic systems are not logically omniscient according to certain complexity based logical omniscience tests [12–14].

In traditional justification logic, terms are built using the binary operations $+$ (called sum) and $\cdot$ (called application) and maybe other additional operations. Thus terms have the syntactic form of polynomials and are, in the context of the Logic of Proofs, indeed called proof polynomials.

© Springer Nature Switzerland AG 2020
M. Dastani et al. (Eds.): CLAR 2020, LNAI 12061, pp. 42–57, 2020.
https://doi.org/10.1007/978-3-030-44638-3_3

This syntactic structure of polynomials is essentially used in the proof of realization, which provides a procedure that, given a theorem of a modal logic, constructs a theorem of the corresponding justification logic by replacing each occurrence of □ with an adequate justification term [5].

The main contribution of the present paper is to look at the syntactic structure of justification terms *algebraically*, that is, we interpret justifications by a semiring structure. The motivation for this is threefold:

1. It provides an appropriate semantics for variables in evidence terms. It was always the idea in justification logic that terms with variables justify derivations from assumptions. The variables represent the input values, i.e., (arbitrary) proofs of the assumptions [5]. But this was not properly reflected in the semantics where usually variables are treated like constants: to each term (no matter whether it contains variables or not) some set of formulas is assigned. In our semiring semantics, ground terms (i.e. terms not containing variables) are interpreted as elements of a semiring and terms with variables are interpreted as polynomial functions on the given semiring of justifications. Thus terms with variables are adequately represented and the role of variables is clarified.

2. The algebraic structure of terms makes it possible to compute with justifications. Depending on the choice of the semiring, we can use the term structure to model levels of trust (Viterbi semiring), costs of obtaining knowledge (tropical semiring), probabilistic evidence (powerset semiring), fuzzy justifications (Łukasiewicz semiring), and so on.

3. Considering ω-continuous semirings, i.e. semirings in which certain fixed points exist, may provide a solution to the problem of realizing modal fixed point logics like the logic of common knowledge. In these logics, some modal operators can be interpreted as fixed points of monotone operations. It seems likely that their realizations also should be fixed points of certain operations on semirings.

1.1 Related Work

Our approach is heavily inspired by the semiring approach for provenance in database systems [25]. There the idea is to label database tuples and to propagate expressions in order to annotate intermediate data and final outputs. One can then evaluate the provenance expressions in various semirings to obtain information about levels of trust, data prices, required clearance levels, confidence scores, probability distributions, update propagation, and many more [26].

This semiring framework has been adapted to many different query languages and data models. The core theoretical work of those approaches includes results on query containment, the construction of semirings, and fixed points [3,4,19–21,23,24].

There are only few systems available where justification terms are equipped with additional structure. Two prominent examples are based on λ-terms (in contrast to the combinatory terms of the Logic of Proofs). The reflective lambda calculus [2] includes reduction rules on proof terms. The intensional lambda calculus [10] has axioms for evidence equality and also features a reduction relation on the terms.

2   The Syntax of SE

We begin by defining the justification language as usual except that we limit the number of variables by some arbitrary but fixed number n. That is, we use a countable set of constants $\mathsf{JConst} = \{0, 1, c_1, c_2, ...\}$ that includes two distinguished elements 0 and 1. Further we have a finite set of variables $\mathsf{JVar} = \{x_1, ..., x_n\}$.

Definition 1 (Justification Term). *Justification terms are*

$$c \in \mathsf{JConst}, \quad x \in \mathsf{JVar}, \quad s \cdot t, \quad and \quad s + t,$$

where s and t are justification terms. The set of all justification terms is called Tm. *A justification term that does not contain variables is called* ground term. GTm *denotes the set of all ground terms.*

Often we write only *term* for *justification term*. Further, we need a countable set of atomic propositions $\mathsf{Prop} = \{P_1, P_2, ...\}$.

Definition 2 (Formulas). *Formulas are* $\bot$, P, $A \to B$ *and* $t : A$, *where t is a justification term, $P \in \mathsf{Prop}$ and A, B are formulas. The set of all formulas is called* Fml.

The remaining logical connectives $\neg$, $\wedge$, $\vee$, and $\leftrightarrow$ are abbreviations as usual, e.g., $\neg A$ stands for $A \to \bot$.

Now we can define a deductive system for the logic SE about the semirings of evidence. It consists of the following axioms:

CL	Every instance of a propositional tautology
j	$x : (A \to B) \to (y : A \to x \cdot y : B)$
j+	$x : A \wedge y : A \to (x + y) : A$
a+	$(x + y) + z : A \to x + (y + z) : A$
c+	$x + y : A \to y + x : A$
0+	$x + 0 : A \leftrightarrow x : A$
am	$(x \cdot y) \cdot z : A \leftrightarrow x \cdot (y \cdot z) : A$
a0	$x \cdot 0 : A \leftrightarrow 0 : A \quad$ and $\quad 0 \cdot x : A \leftrightarrow 0 : A$
a1	$x \cdot 1 : A \leftrightarrow x : A \quad$ and $\quad 1 \cdot x : A \leftrightarrow x : A$
dl	$x \cdot (y + z) : A \leftrightarrow x \cdot y + x \cdot z : A$
dr	$(y + z) \cdot x : A \leftrightarrow y \cdot x + z \cdot x : A$

The rules of SE are:

$$\mathbf{MP} \quad \frac{A \quad A \to B}{B}$$

and

$$\mathbf{jv} \quad \frac{A(x)}{A(t)}$$

where x is a variable, t is a term, and $A(t)$ denotes the result of substituting t for x in $A(x)$.

The axiom schemes **a+**, **c+**, **0+**, **am**, **a0**, **a1**, **dl** and **dr** are called semiring axioms. In the axiom scheme **j+**, we find an important difference to traditional justification logic where $\vee$ is used instead of $\wedge$, see also Sect. 4 later. The idea for **j+** is to read $s + t : A$ as *both s and t justify A*. This is useful, e.g., in the context of uncertain justifications where having two justifications is better than just having one. The rule **jv** shows the role of variables in SE, which differs from traditional justification logic. In our approach a formula $A(x)$ being valid means that $A(x)$ is valid *for all justifications x*.

Let us mention two immediate consequences of our axioms. First a version of axiom **0+** with $x + 0$ is replaced by $0 + x$ is provable. Second, the direction from right to left in axiom **a+** is also provable.

Lemma 1. *The following formulas are derivable in* SE:

$$0 + x : A \leftrightarrow x : A \qquad and \qquad x + (y + z) : A \leftrightarrow (x + y) + z : A.$$

A theory is just any set of formulas.

Definition 3 (Theory). *A theory T is a subset of* Fml. *We use $T \vdash_{SE} F$ to express that F is derivable from T in* SE.

Often we drop the subscript SE in $\vdash_{SE}$ when it is clear from the context. Moreover, we use $\vdash_{CL}$ for the derivability relation in classical propositional logic.

A theory can compensate for the absence of constant specifications. Usually, systems of justification logic are parametrized by a constant specification, i.e., a set containing pairs of constants and axioms. One then has a rule saying that a formula $c : A$ is derivable if (c, A) is an element of the constant specification. Here we do not adopt this approach but simply use a theory that includes $c : A$.

Theorem 1 (Conservativity). *The logic* SE *is a conservative extension of the classical propositional logic* CL, *i.e., for all formulas A of the language of* CL, *we have*

$$\vdash_{SE} A \quad iff \quad \vdash_{CL} A.$$

Proof. The claim from right to left is trivial as SE extends CL. For the direction from left to right, we consider a mapping $^\circ$ from Fml to formulas of CL that simply drops all occurrences of $t :$. In particular, for any CL-formula A, we have $A^\circ = A$. Now it is easy to prove by induction on the length of SE derivations that for all $A \in$ Fml,

$$\vdash_{SE} A \quad implies \quad \vdash_{CL} A^\circ.$$

Simply observe that for any axiom A of SE, A° is a propositional tautology, and that the rules of SE respect the $^\circ$-translation. □

Now consistency of SE follows immediately.

Corollary 1 (Consistency of SE). *The logic* SE *is consistent.*

Proof. Assume towards contradiction that $\vdash_{SE}\bot$. It follows $\vdash_{CL}\bot$ by conservativity of SE over CL, which is a contradiction. □

3 The Semantics of SE

Our semantics of SE is similar to traditional semantics for justification logic in the sense that $t : A$ is given meaning by simply making use of an evidence relation that assigns a set of formulas to each evidence term. The novelty of our approach is the requirement that the interpretation of the terms forms a semiring.

Definition 4 (Semiring). $K = (S, +, \cdot, 0, 1)$, *where* S *is the domain, is a semiring, if for all* $a, b, c \in S$:

1. $(a + b) + c = a + (b + c)$, $a + b = b + a$ *and* $a + 0 = 0 + a = a$
2. $(a \cdot b) \cdot c = a \cdot (b \cdot c)$ *and* $a \cdot 1 = 1 \cdot a = a$
3. $(a + b) \cdot c = a \cdot c + b \cdot c$ *and* $c \cdot (a + b) = c \cdot a + c \cdot b$
4. $a \cdot 0 = 0 \cdot a = 0$

Thus, unlike in a ring, there is no inverse to $+$. We also do not require $\cdot$ to be commutative.

Note that we use $+$ and $\cdot$ both as symbols in our language of justification logic and as operations in the semiring. It will always be clear from the context which of the two is meant.

For the following, assume we are given a semiring $K = (S, +, \cdot, 0, 1)$. We use a function $I : \mathsf{JConst} \to S$ to map the constants of the language of SE to the domain S of the semiring. We call this function I an *interpretation* if $I(0) = 0$ and $I(1) = 1$. We now extend I to a homomorphism such that $I : \mathsf{Tm} \to S[\mathsf{JVar}]$, where $S[\mathsf{JVar}]$ is the polynomial semiring in JVar over S by setting:

1. $I(x) := x$ for variables x
2. $I(s + t) := I(s) + I(t)$ for terms s, t
3. $I(s \cdot t) := I(s) \cdot I(t)$ for terms s, t

Let $K = (S, +, \cdot, 0, 1)$ be a semiring with domain S. We define $\mathsf{Fml_S}$ as the set of formulas where we use elements of S instead of justification terms.

1. $\bot \in \mathsf{Fml_S}$
2. $P \in \mathsf{Fml_S}$, where $P \in \mathsf{Prop}$
3. $A \to B \in \mathsf{Fml_S}$, where $A \in \mathsf{Fml_S}$ and $B \in \mathsf{Fml_S}$
4. $s : A \in \mathsf{Fml_S}$, where $A \in \mathsf{Fml_S}$ and $s \in S$

Definition 5 (Evidence relation). *Let* S *be the domain of a semiring. We call* $J \subseteq S \times \mathsf{Fml_S}$ *an evidence relation if for all* $s, t \in S$ *and all* $A, B \in \mathsf{Fml_S}$:

1. $J(s, A \rightarrow B)$ and $J(t, A)$ imply $J(s \cdot t, B)$
2. $J(s, A)$ and $J(t, A)$ imply $J(s + t, A)$

Definition 6 (Valuation). *A valuation v is a function from* JVar *to* S.

The polynomial $I(t)$ can be viewed as a function $t_I : S^n \rightarrow S$. Hence, given an interpretation $I :$ JConst $\rightarrow S$ and a valuation v, every $t \in$ Tm can be mapped to an element $t_I(v(x_1), ..., v(x_n))$ in S, which we denote by t_I^v. By abuse of notation, we only mention the variables that occur in the term t. For a variable x we have

$$v(x) = x_I(v(x)) = x_I^v.$$

Given the definition of the polynomial function t_I, we find, e.g.,

$$x_I^v \cdot y_I^v = x_I(v(x)) \cdot y_I(v(y)) = (x \cdot y)_I(v(x), v(y)) = (x \cdot y)_I^v. \qquad (1)$$

For $A \in$ Fml we define $A_I^v \in$ Fml$_\mathsf{S}$ inductively:

1. $\perp_I^v := \perp$
2. $P_I^v := P$, where $P \in$ Prop
3. $(A \rightarrow B)_I^v := A_I^v \rightarrow B_I^v$, where $A \in$ Fml and $B \in$ Fml
4. $(s : A)_I^v := s_I^v : A_I^v$, where $A \in$ Fml and $s \in$ Tm

Let $A(x_1, ..., x_n) \in$ Fml. Then A_I denotes the function $A_I : S^n \rightarrow$ Fml$_\mathsf{S}$ with $A_I(y_1, ..., y_n) = A_I^v$ where v is such that $v(x_i) = y_i$.

Definition 7 (Semiring model). *A semiring model is a tuple $M = (K, *, I, J)$ where*

1. $K = (S, +, \cdot, 0, 1)$ *is a semiring*
2. $*$ *is a truth assignment for atomic propositions, i.e.,* $* :$ Prop $\rightarrow \{\mathbb{F}, \mathbb{T}\}$
3. I *is an interpretation, i.e.,* $I :$ JConst $\rightarrow S$
4. J *is an evidence relation.*

First we define truth in a semiring model for a given valuation. Because variables represent arbitrary justifications, we require a formula to be true for all valuations in order to be true in a semiring model. This means a formula with variables is interpreted as universally quantified.

Definition 8 (Truth in a semiring model). *Let $M = (K, *, I, J)$ be a semiring model, v a valuation and A a formula. $M, v \Vdash A$ is defined as follows:*

- $M, v \nVdash \perp$
- $M, v \Vdash P$ *iff* $P^* = \mathbb{T}$
- $M, v \Vdash A \rightarrow B$ *iff* $M, v \nVdash A$ or $M, v \Vdash B$
- $M, v \Vdash s : A$ *iff* $J(s_I^v, A_I^v)$

Further we set $M \Vdash A$ iff $M, v \Vdash A$ for all valuations v.

For a semiring model M and a theory T, $M \Vdash T$ means $M \Vdash A$ for all $A \in T$.

Definition 9 (Truth in a theory). *A theory T entails a formula F, in symbols $T \Vdash F$, if for each semiring model M we have that $M \Vdash T$ implies $M \Vdash F$.*

By unfolding the definitions, we immediately get the following lemma, which is useful to establish soundness of SE.

Lemma 2. *Let $M = (K, *, I, J)$ be a semiring model and let v and w be valuations with $v(x_i) = (t_i)_I^w$ for variables x_i and terms t_i. Then*

$$M, v \Vdash A(x_1, ..., x_n) \quad iff \quad M, w \Vdash A(t_1, ..., t_n).$$

Proof. By induction on the structure of A.

- Case $A = \bot$. We have $M, v \nVdash \bot$ and $M, w \nVdash \bot$.
- Case $A = P$. We have $M, v \Vdash P \Leftrightarrow P^* = 1 \Leftrightarrow M, w \Vdash P$.
- Case $A = B \rightarrow C$. We have $M, v \Vdash (B \rightarrow C)(x_1, ..., x_n)$
  $\Leftrightarrow M, v \Vdash B(x_1, ..., x_n) \rightarrow C(x_1, ..., x_n)$
  $\Leftrightarrow M, v \nVdash B(x_1, ..., x_n)$ or $M, v \Vdash C(x_1, ..., x_n)$
  $\overset{\text{I.H.}}{\Leftrightarrow} M, w \nVdash B(t_1, ..., t_n)$ or $M, w \Vdash C(t_1, ..., t_n)$
  $\Leftrightarrow M, w \Vdash B(t_1, ..., t_n) \rightarrow C(t_1, ..., t_n) \Leftrightarrow M, w \Vdash (B \rightarrow C)(t_1, ..., t_n)$.
- Case $A = s : B$. We have $M, v \Vdash (s : B)(x_1, ..., x_n)$
  $\Leftrightarrow M, v \Vdash s(x_1, ..., x_n) : B(x_1, ..., x_n)$
  $\Leftrightarrow J(s(x_1, ..., x_n)_I^v, B(x_1, ..., x_n)_I^v)$
  $\Leftrightarrow J(s_I(v(x_1), ..., v(x_n)), B_I(v(x_1), ..., v(x_n)))$
  $\Leftrightarrow J(s_I((t_1)_I^w, ..., (t_n)_I^w), B_I((t_1)_I^w, ..., (t_n)_I^w))$
  $\Leftrightarrow J(s(t_1, ..., t_n)_I^w, B(t_1, ..., t_n)_I^w) \Leftrightarrow M, w \Vdash s(t_1, ..., t_n) : B(t_1, ..., t_n)$
  $\Leftrightarrow M, w \Vdash (s : B)(t_1, ..., t_n)$.   □

Theorem 2 (Soundness). *Let T be an arbitrary theory. Then:*

$$T \vdash F \quad implies \quad T \Vdash F.$$

Proof. As usual by induction on the length of the derivation of F. Let $M = (K, *, I, J)$ be a semiring model such that $M \Vdash T$. To establish our claim when F is an axiom or an element of T, we let v be an arbitrary valuation and show $M, v \Vdash F$ for the following cases:

1. $F \in T$. Trivial.
2. **CL.** Trivial.
3. **j.** Assume $M, v \Vdash x : (A \rightarrow B)$ and $M, v \Vdash y : A$. That is $J(x_I^v, (A \rightarrow B)_I^v)$ and $J(y_I^v, A_I^v)$ hold, which by Definition 5 implies $J(x_I^v \cdot y_I^v, B_I^v)$. Hence by (1) we get $J((x \cdot y)_I^v, B_I^v)$, which yields $M, v \Vdash x \cdot y : B$.
4. **j+.** Similar to the previous case.
5. **a+.** Assume $M, v \Vdash (x + y) + z : A$. That is $J(((x + y) + z)_I^v, A_I^v)$. Because of

$$((x + y) + z)_I^v = (v(x) + v(y)) + v(z) = v(x) + (v(y) + v(z)) = (x + (y + z))_I^v,$$

   we get $J((x + (y + z))_I^v, A_I^v)$, which yields $M, v \Vdash x + (y + z) : A$.
6. The remaining axioms are treated similarly to the previous case.

The case when F has been derived by **MP** follows by I.H. as usual. For the case when $F = A(t)$ has been derived from $A(x)$ by **jv**, we find by I.H. that $M \Vdash A(x)$, which is

$$M, v \Vdash A(x) \text{ for all valuations } v. \tag{2}$$

Given the term t and an arbitrary valuation w, we find that there exists a valuation v such that $t_I^w = v(x)$. By Lemma 2 we get

$$M, v \Vdash A(x) \quad \text{iff} \quad M, w \Vdash A(t).$$

Thus using (2), we obtain $M, w \Vdash A(t)$. Since w was arbitrary, we conclude $M \Vdash A(t)$.   □

For the completeness proof, we consider the free semiring over $\mathsf{JConst} \cup \mathsf{JVar}$. We have for $s, t \in \mathsf{Tm}$:

- $[t]$ is the equivalence class of t with respect to the semiring equalities, see Definition 4;
- $[s] + [t] := [s + t]$;
- $[s] \cdot [t] := [s \cdot t]$;
- $S_{\mathsf{Tm}} := \{[t] : t \in \mathsf{Tm}\}$;
- $K_{\mathsf{Tm}} := (S_{\mathsf{Tm}}, +, \cdot, [0], [1])$ is the free semiring over $\mathsf{JConst} \cup \mathsf{JVar}$.

The following lemma states that our truth definition respects the semiring equalities.

Lemma 3. *Let T be a theory and s, t be ground terms with $[s] = [t]$. For each formula A we have*

$$T \vdash_{\mathsf{SE}} s : A \quad \text{iff} \quad T \vdash_{\mathsf{SE}} t : A.$$

Lemma 4. *Assume that we are given an interpretation $I : \mathsf{JConst} \to S_{\mathsf{Tm}}$ with $I(c) = [c]$, a term $s(x_1, ..., x_n)$, and a valuation $v : \mathsf{JVar} \to S_{\mathsf{Tm}}$ with $v(x_i) = [t_i]$. Then we have*

$$s(x_1, ..., x_n)_I^v = [s(t_1, ..., t_n)].$$

Proof. Induction on the structure of s:

- $c_I^v = [c]$ by definition of I.
- $(x_i)_I^v = [t_i]$ by definition of v.
- $(s_1 + s_2)_I^v = (s_1)_I^v + (s_2)_I^v$. By I.H. we have

$$(s_1)_I^v = [s_1(t_1, ..., t_n)] \quad \text{and} \quad (s_2)_I^v = [s_2(t_1, ..., t_n)].$$

Thus $(s_1)_I^v + (s_2)_I^v = [s_1(t_1, ..., t_n)] + [s_2(t_1, ..., t_n)] = [(s_1 + s_2)(t_1, ..., t_n)]$.
- $(s_1 \cdot s_2)_I^v = (s_1)_I^v \cdot (s_2)_I^v$. By I.H. we have

$$(s_1)_I^v = [s_1(t_1, ..., t_n)] \quad \text{and} \quad (s_2)_I^v = [s_2(t_1, ..., t_n)].$$

Thus $(s_1)_I^v \cdot (s_2)_I^v = [s_1(t_1, ..., t_n)] \cdot [s_2(t_1, ..., t_n)] = [(s_1 \cdot s_2)(t_1, ..., t_n)]$ □

We extend the notion of equivalence to formulas by defining the function

$$[\cdot] : \mathsf{Fml} \to \mathsf{Fml}_{S_{\mathsf{Tm}}}$$

as follows:

- $[\bot] := \bot$
- $[P] := P$
- $[A \to B] := [A] \to [B]$
- $[t : A] := [t] : [A]$

Intuitively $[A]$ is the formula where each justification term is replaced by its equivalence class in the free semiring. Observe that if $I(c) = [c]$ and $v(x) = [x]$, then $[A] = A_I^v$. Now we extend Lemma 4 to formulas.

Lemma 5. *Assume that we are given the interpretation* $I : \mathsf{JConst} \to S_{\mathsf{Tm}}$ *with* $I(c) = [c]$, *a formula* $A(x_1, ..., x_n)$, *and a valuation* $v : \mathsf{JVar} \to S_{\mathsf{Tm}}$ *with* $v(x_i) = [t_i]$. *Then we have*

$$A(x_1, ..., x_n)_I^v = [A(t_1, ..., t_n)].$$

Proof. Induction on the structure of A:

- $\bot_I^v = \bot = [\bot]$
- $P_I^v = P = [P]$
- $(A \to B)(x_1, ..., x_n)_I^v = A(x_1, ..., x_n)_I^v \to B(x_1, ..., x_n)_I^v$
  $\overset{\text{I.H.}}{=} [A(t_1, ..., t_n)] \to [B(t_1, ..., t_n)] = [(A \to B)(t_1, ..., t_n)]$
- $(s : A)(x_1, ..., x_n)_I^v = s(x_1, ..., x_n)_I^v : A(x_1, ..., x_n)_I^v$
  $\overset{\text{I.H. and L. 4}}{=} [s(t_1, ..., t_n)] : [A(t_1, ..., t_n)] = [(s : A)(t_1, ..., t_n)]$ □

Let $\mathsf{Prop2}$ be an infinite set of atomic propositions with $\mathsf{Prop} \cap \mathsf{Prop2} = \emptyset$. Then there exists an bijective function $f : S_{\mathsf{Tm}} \times \mathsf{Fml}_{S_{\mathsf{Tm}}} \to \mathsf{Prop2}$. We assume f to be fixed for the rest of this section. Based on this function we define a translation $'$ that maps formulas of Fml to pure propositional formulas containing atomic propositions from $\mathsf{Prop} \cup \mathsf{Prop2}$.

1. $\bot' := \bot$
2. $P' := P$
3. $(A \to B)' := A' \to B'$
4. $(t : A)' := f([t], [A])$

Let T be a theory. We define first $N := \{A' \mid A \in T \text{ or } A \text{ is an axiom of } \mathsf{SE}\}$ and then the corresponding theory:

$$T' := \{A(t_1, ..., t_n)' \mid A(x_1, ..., x_n)' \in N, t_i \in \mathsf{Tm}\}.$$

Suppose $A(x_1, ..., x_n)' \in T'$. Then there exist a formula $B(x_1, ..., x_n)' \in N$ and justification terms $s_1, ..., s_n$ such that $B(s_1, ..., s_n)' = A(x_1, ..., x_n)'$. This implies

$B(s_1(t_1, ..., t_n), ..., s_n(t_1, ..., t_n))' = A(t_1, ..., t_n)'$. Now we have $A(t_1, ..., t_n)' \in T'$. Therefore the following implication is proved:

$$A(x)' \in T' \Rightarrow A(t)' \in T' \tag{3}$$

In fact this does not only hold for formulas in T' but also for all formulas derived from T' by classical propositional logic.

Lemma 6. *If* $T' \vdash_{CL} A(x)'$ *then* $T' \vdash_{CL} A(t)'$.

Proof. Induction on the derivation of $A(x)'$. Note that T' contains all the axioms of CL. So we can omit this case.

1. If $A(x)' \in T'$ then $A(t)' \in T'$ by the above observation and thus $T' \vdash_{CL} A(t)'$.
2. If $A(x)'$ is obtained by **MP** from B and $B \to A(x)'$ then B can be written as $C(x)'$ because f is surjective. The induction hypothesis $(T' \vdash_{CL} C(t)'$ and $T' \vdash_{CL} C(t)' \to A(t)')$ yields $T' \vdash_{CL} A(t)'$. □

Lemma 7. $T \vdash_{SE} A \Leftrightarrow T' \vdash_{CL} A'$

Proof. Left to right by induction on a derivation of A:

1. If $A \in T$ or A is an axiom then $A' \in T'$ and therefore $T' \vdash_{CL} A'$.
2. If A is obtained by **MP** from B and $B \to A$ then the induction hypothesis $(T' \vdash_{CL} B'$ and $T' \vdash_{CL} B' \to A')$ immediately yields $T' \vdash_{CL} A'$.
3. If $A(t)$ is obtained by **jv** from $A(x)$ then the induction hypothesis is $T' \vdash_{CL} A(x)'$. By the previous lemma we conclude $T' \vdash_{CL} A(t)'$.

Right to left by induction on a derivation of A':

1. If $A(x_1, ..., x_n)' \in T'$ then there exist a formula $B(x_1, ..., x_n)' \in N$ and justification terms $s_1, ..., s_n$ such that $B(s_1, ..., s_n)' = A(x_1, ..., x_n)'$. Trivially we have $T \vdash_{SE} B(x_1, ..., x_n)$ and get by **jv** that $T \vdash_{SE} B(s_1, ..., s_n)$. Since f is injective, the only difference between $A(x_1, ..., x_n)$ and $B(s_1, ..., s_n)$ is that some terms may be replaced by equivalent ones (modulo the semiring). Therefore, we get $T \vdash_{SE} A(x_1, ..., x_n)$ by using the semiring axioms of SE and propositional reasoning.
2. If A' is a propositional tautology then so is A because f is injective, but some terms in A may be replaced by equivalent ones. We get $T \vdash_{SE} A$ again by using the semiring axioms and propositional reasoning.
3. If A' is obtained by **MP** from $B \to A'$ and B then B can be written as C'. The induction hypothesis $(T \vdash_{SE} C \to A$ and $T \vdash_{SE} C)$ implies $T \vdash_{SE} A$.

□

Lemma 7 gives us the ability to switch from SE to CL and vice versa. Therefore, we can use completeness of CL to obtain completeness for SE.

Theorem 3 (Completeness). *Let* T *be an arbitrary theory. Then:*

$$T \Vdash F \quad implies \quad T \vdash F.$$

Proof. We will prove the contraposition, which means for $T \nvdash F$ we will construct a semiring model M and find a valuation v, such that $M \Vdash T$ and $M, v \nVdash F$. Assume $T \nvdash F$. By Lemma 7 we get $T' \nvdash_{\mathsf{CL}} F'$. The completeness of CL delivers $* : \mathsf{Prop} \cup \mathsf{Prop2} \rightarrow \{\mathbb{F}, \mathbb{T}\}$, such that for the CL-model M_* consisting of $*$ we have $M_* \Vdash T'$ and $M_* \nVdash F'$. Now we can define the semiring model M:

- $M := (K_{\mathsf{Tm}}, *|_{\mathsf{Prop}}, I, J)$
- $*|_{\mathsf{Prop}}$ is the restriction of $*$ to Prop
- $I : \mathsf{JConst} \rightarrow S_{\mathsf{Tm}}, I(c) := [c]$
- $J := \{([t], [A]) \mid M_* \Vdash f([t], [A])\}$

In order to prove that M is a semiring model, we need to show that J is an evidence relation.

1. From $M_* \Vdash T'$ we derive $M_* \Vdash (s : (A \rightarrow B) \rightarrow (t : A \rightarrow s \cdot t : B))' \; \forall s, t \in \mathsf{Tm}$ and $\forall A, B \in \mathsf{Fml}$ by using the definition of T' and (3). It follows

$$M_* \Vdash f([s], [A \rightarrow B]) \rightarrow (f([t], [A]) \rightarrow f([s \cdot t], [B])).$$

By the truth definition in CL we find

$$\text{if } f([s], [A \rightarrow B])^* = \mathbb{T} \text{ and } f([t], [A])^* = \mathbb{T} \text{ then } f([s \cdot t], [B])^* = \mathbb{T}.$$

From the definition of J in M we get

$$\text{if } J([s], [A] \rightarrow [B]) \text{ and } J([t], [A]) \text{ then } J([s] \cdot [t], [B]).$$

2. From $M_* \Vdash T'$ we derive $M_* \Vdash (s : A \wedge t : A \rightarrow s + t : A)' \; \forall s, t \in \mathsf{Tm}$ and $\forall A \in \mathsf{Fml}$ by using the definition of T' and (3). It follows

$$M_* \Vdash f([s], [A]) \wedge f([t], [A]) \rightarrow f([s + t], [A]) \; \forall s, t \in \mathsf{Tm} \text{ and } \forall A \in \mathsf{Fml}.$$

By the truth definition in CL we find

$$\text{if } f([s], [A])^* = \mathbb{T} \text{ and } f([t], [A])^* = \mathbb{T} \text{ then } f([s + t], [A])^* = \mathbb{T}.$$

From the definition of J in M we get

$$\text{if } J([s], [A]) \text{ and } J([t], [A]) \text{ then } J([s] + [t], [A]).$$

Knowing that M is a semiring model we prove

$$M_* \Vdash A(t_1, ..., t_n)' \Leftrightarrow M, w \Vdash A(x_1, ..., x_n) \qquad (4)$$

by induction on the structure of A, where $w(x_i) = [t_i]$:

- Case $A = \bot$. We have $M_* \nVdash \bot'$ and $M, w \nVdash \bot$.
- Case $A = P$. We have $M_* \Vdash P' \Leftrightarrow M_* \Vdash P \Leftrightarrow P^* = \mathbb{T} \Leftrightarrow M, w \Vdash P$.

- Case $A = B \to C$. We have $M_* \Vdash (B \to C)(t_1, ..., t_n)'$
  $\Leftrightarrow M_* \Vdash B(t_1, ..., t_n)' \to C(t_1, ..., t_n)'$
  $\Leftrightarrow M_* \nVdash B(t_1, ..., t_n)'$ or $M_* \Vdash C(t_1, ..., t_n)'$
  $\Leftrightarrow M, w \nVdash B(x_1, ..., x_n)$ or $M, w \Vdash C(x_1, ..., x_n)$ (by induction hypothesis)
  $\Leftrightarrow M, w \Vdash B(x_1, ..., x_n) \to C(x_1, ..., x_n)$
  $\Leftrightarrow M, w \Vdash (B \to C)(x_1, ..., x_n)$.
- Case $A = s : B$. We have $M_* \Vdash (s : B)(t_1, ..., t_n)'$
  $\Leftrightarrow M_* \Vdash (s(t_1, ..., t_n) : B(t_1, ..., t_n))'$
  $\Leftrightarrow M_* \Vdash f([s(t_1, ..., t_n)], [B(t_1, ..., t_n)])$ (by definition of $'$)
  $\Leftrightarrow J([s(t_1, ..., t_n)], [B(t_1, ..., t_n)])$ (by definition of J)
  $\Leftrightarrow J(s(x_1, ..., x_n)_I^w, [B(t_1, ..., t_n)])$ (by Lemma 4)
  $\Leftrightarrow J(s(x_1, ..., x_n)_I^w, B(x_1, ..., x_n)_I^w)$ (by Lemma 5)
  $\Leftrightarrow M, w \Vdash s(x_1, ..., x_n) : B(x_1, ..., x_n)$
  $\Leftrightarrow M, w \Vdash (s : B)(x_1, ..., x_n)$

Now we show $M \Vdash T$, i.e. $M, w \Vdash T$ for all valuations w. Hence let w be an arbitrary valuation (assume $w(x_i) = [t_i]$) and $A(x_1, ..., x_n) \in T$. It follows $A(x_1, ..., x_n)' \in T'$ and by (3) also $A(t_1, ..., t_n)' \in T'$. From $M_* \Vdash T'$ we get $M_* \Vdash A(t_1, ..., t_n)'$. (4) implies $M, w \Vdash A(x_1, ..., x_n)$. Since w was arbitrary we conclude $M \Vdash T$.

Now we consider the special case of (4) where $w = v$ with $v(x) = [x]$. We have

$$M_* \Vdash A(x_1, ..., x_n)' \Leftrightarrow M, v \Vdash A(x_1, ..., x_n)$$

Remembering $M_* \nVdash F'$, we derive $M, v \nVdash F$, which finishes the proof.   □

4 Realization

Realization is concerned with the relationship between justification logic and modal logic. In this section, we let ∘ be the mapping from Fml to formulas of the modal logic K that replaces all occurrences of $s :$ in a formula of SE with □. We immediately get the following lemma.

Lemma 8. *For any formula A we have*

$$\vdash_{\mathsf{SE}} A \quad implies \quad \vdash_{\mathsf{K}} A^\circ.$$

To investigate mappings from modal logic to SE, we need the notion of an axiomatically appropriate theory.

Definition 10. *A theory T is called axiomatically appropriate if*

1. *for each axiom A of SE, there is a constant c such that $c : A \in T$ and*
2. *for each $B \in T$, there is a constant c such that $c : B \in T$.*

Using axiomatically appropriate theories, we get an analogue of modal necessitation in SE.

Lemma 9 (Internalization). *Let T be an axiomatically appropriate theory. For any formula A, there exists a ground term t such that*

$$T \vdash A \quad implies \quad T \vdash t : A.$$

For the following definition we need the notion of positive and negative occurrences of $\square$ within a given formula A. First we assign a polarity to each subformula occurrence within A as follows.

1. The only occurrence of A within A is given positive polarity.
2. If a polarity is already assigned to an occurrence $B \to C$ within A, then the same polarity is assigned to C and the opposite polarity is assigned to B.
3. If a polarity is already assigned to an occurrence $\square B$ within A, then the same polarity is assigned to B.

The leading $\square$ in an occurrence of $\square B$ within A has the same polarity as the occurrence of $\square B$ within A.

Definition 11. *A realization r is a mapping from modal formulas to Fml such that for each modal formula F we have $(r(F))^\circ = F$. A realization is normal if all negative occurrences of $\square$ are mapped to distinct justification variables.*

For the rest of this section, we require axiomatically appropriate theories T also to be schematic, which is a technical requirement saying roughly that T respects substitutions, for a discussion of this property see [30]. Schematicness is needed for the following two claims.

We are confident that Kuznets' realization procedure [28] can be applied in the context of SE. Thus we have the following:

Conjecture 1. Let T be an axiomatically appropriate theory such that for some constant c,

$$c : (A \to (A \vee B)) \in T \quad \text{and} \quad c : (B \to (A \vee B)) \in T.$$

Then there exists a realization r such that for all modal formulas F,

$$\vdash_{\mathsf{K}} F \quad implies \quad T \vdash_{\mathsf{SE}} r(F).$$

However, the realization obtained by the previous theorem will not be normal. In traditional justification logic normal realizations can be achieved using the $+$ operation, which there (unlike in SE) is axiomatized by $s : A \vee t : A \to s+t : A$.

Since we work with general theories (instead of simple constant specifications) and with variables that are interpreted universally, we can mimick the traditional $+$ operation and perform the usual realization procedure given in [5,30].

Conjecture 2. Let T be an axiomatically appropriate theory such that for some constant c

$$x : A \to c \cdot x \cdot y : (A \vee B) \in T \quad \text{and} \quad y : B \to c \cdot x \cdot y : (A \vee B) \in T.$$

Then there exists a normal realization r such that for all modal formulas F,

$$\vdash_{\mathsf{K}} F \quad implies \quad T \vdash_{\mathsf{SE}} r(F).$$

5   Applications

The semiring interpretation of evidence has a wide range of applications. Many of them require a particular choice of the semiring. The following are of particular interest to us (see also [26]):

- $V = ([0,1], \max, \cdot, 0, 1)$ is called the Viterbi semiring. We can think of the elements of V as *confidence scores* and use them to model trust.
- $T = (\mathbb{R}_+^\infty, \min, +, \infty, 0)$ is called the tropical semiring. This is connected to *shortest path problems*. In the context of epistemic logic, we can employ this semiring to model the costs of obtaining knowledge. Among other things, this might provide a fresh perspective on the logical omniscience problem, related to the approaches in [12–14].
- $P = (\mathcal{P}(S), \cup, \cap, \emptyset, S)$ is called the powerset lattice (semiring). This is closely related to the recently introduced subset models for justification logic [31–33]. This semiring can be used to model probabilistic evidence and aggregation thereof, see, e.g., [9].
- $F = ([0,1], \max, \max(0, a + b - 1), 0, 1)$ is called the Łukasiewicz semiring. We can use it to model fuzzy evidences. Ghari [22] provides a first study of fuzzy justification logic that is based on this kind of operations for combining evidence.

Another stream of possible applications emerges from the fact that terms with variables represent actual functions. If the underlying semiring is ω-continuous, then the induced polynomial functions are ω-continuous and, therefore, monotone [27]. Hence, they have least and greatest fixed points. Thus it looks very promising to consider this kind of semirings to realize modal fixed point logics like common knowledge.

Common knowledge of a proposition A is a fixed point of $\lambda X.(EA \wedge EX)$. There are justification logics with common knowledge available [6,18] but their exact relationship to modal common knowledge is still open.

We believe that non-wellfounded and cyclic proof systems [1,16,17,35] are the right proof-theoretic approach to settle this question. In those systems, proofs can be regarded as fixed points and hence justifications realizing those cyclic proofs will be fixed points in a semiring. For this purpose, making use of formal power series, which might be thought of as infinite polynomials, look very promising. First results in this direction have been obtained by Shamkanov [34] who presents a realization procedure for Gödel-Löb logic based on cyclic proofs.

Acknowledgements. We thank the anonymous reviewers for many helpful comments. We are grateful to Daniyar Shamkanov for the discussion about cyclic proofs and realization. This research is supported by the Swiss National Science Foundation grant 200020_184625.

References

1. Afshari, B., Leigh, G.E.: Cut-free completeness for modal mu-calculus. In: 2017 32nd Annual ACM/IEEE Symposium on Logic in Computer Science (LICS), pp. 1–12 (2017)
2. Alt, J., Artemov, S.: Reflective λ-calculus. In: Kahle, R., Schroeder-Heister, P., Stärk, R. (eds.) PTCS 2001. LNCS, vol. 2183, pp. 22–37. Springer, Heidelberg (2001). https://doi.org/10.1007/3-540-45504-3_2
3. Amsterdamer, Y., Davidson, S.B., Deutch, D., Milo, T., Stoyanovich, J., Tannen, V.: Putting lipstick on pig: enabling database-style workflow provenance. Proc. VLDB Endow. 5(4), 346–357 (2011)
4. Amsterdamer, Y., Deutch, D., Tannen, V.: Provenance for aggregate queries. In: Proceedings of the Thirtieth ACM SIGMOD-SIGACT-SIGART Symposium on Principles of Database Systems, PODS 2011, pp. 153–164. ACM (2011)
5. Artemov, S.: Explicit provability and constructive semantics. Bull. Symbolic Logic 7(1), 1–36 (2001)
6. Artemov, S.: Justified common knowledge. Theoret. Comput. Sci. 357(1–3), 4–22 (2006)
7. Artemov, S.: The logic of justification. Rev. Symbolic Logic 1(4), 477–513 (2008)
8. Artemov, S.: Tracking evidence. In: Blass, A., Dershowitz, N., Reisig, W. (eds.) Fields of Logic and Computation. LNCS, vol. 6300, pp. 61–74. Springer, Heidelberg (2010). https://doi.org/10.1007/978-3-642-15025-8_3
9. Artemov, S.: On aggregating probabilistic evidence. In: Artemov, S., Nerode, A. (eds.) LFCS 2016. LNCS, vol. 9537, pp. 27–42. Springer, Cham (2016). https://doi.org/10.1007/978-3-319-27683-0_3
10. Artemov, S., Bonelli, E.: The intensional lambda calculus. In: Artemov, S.N., Nerode, A. (eds.) LFCS 2007. LNCS, vol. 4514, pp. 12–25. Springer, Heidelberg (2007). https://doi.org/10.1007/978-3-540-72734-7_2
11. Artemov, S., Fitting, M.: Justification Logic: Reasoning with Reasons. Cambridge University Press, Cambridge (2019)
12. Artemov, S., Kuznets, R.: Logical omniscience via proof complexity. In: Ésik, Z. (ed.) CSL 2006. LNCS, vol. 4207, pp. 135–149. Springer, Heidelberg (2006). https://doi.org/10.1007/11874683_9
13. Artemov, S., Kuznets, R.: Logical omniscience as a computational complexity problem. In: Heifetz, A. (ed.) Proceedings of the Twelfth Conference Theoretical Aspects of Rationality and Knowledge (TARK 2009), pp. 14–23, Stanford University, California, 6–8 July 2009. ACM (2009)
14. Artemov, S., Kuznets, R.: Logical omniscience as infeasibility. APAL 165(1), 6–25 (2014)
15. Baltag, A., Renne, B., Smets, S.: The logic of justified belief, explicit knowledge, and conclusive evidence. APAL 165(1), 49–81 (2014)
16. Baston, C., Capretta, V.: The coinductive formulation of common knowledge. In: Avigad, J., Mahboubi, A. (eds.) ITP 2018. LNCS, vol. 10895, pp. 126–141. Springer, Cham (2018). https://doi.org/10.1007/978-3-319-94821-8_8
17. Bucheli, S., Kuznets, R., Studer, T.: Two ways to common knowledge. In: Bolander, T., Braüner, T. (eds.) Proceedings of M4M-6. ENTCS, vol. 262, pp. 83–98. Elsevier (2010)
18. Bucheli, S., Kuznets, R., Studer, T.: Justifications for common knowledge. J. Appl. Non-Class. Log. 21(1), 35–60 (2011)

19. Deutch, D., Moskovitch, Y., Tannen, V.: Provenance-based analysis of data-centric processes. VLDB J. **24**(4), 583–607 (2015). https://doi.org/10.1007/s00778-015-0390-5

20. Foster, J.N., Green, T.J., Tannen, V.: Annotated XML: queries and provenance. In: Proceedings of the Twenty-seventh ACM SIGMOD-SIGACT-SIGART Symposium on Principles of Database Systems, PODS 2008, pp. 271–280. ACM (2008)

21. Geerts, F., Unger, T., Karvounarakis, G., Fundulaki, I., Christophides, V.: Algebraic structures for capturing the provenance of SPARQL queries. J. ACM **63**(1), 1–63 (2016)

22. Ghari, M.: Pavelka-style fuzzy justification logics. Logic J. IGPL **24**(5), 743–773 (2016)

23. Green, T.J.: Containment of conjunctive queries on annotated relations. In: Proceedings of the 12th International Conference on Database Theory, ICDT 2009, pp. 296–309. ACM (2009)

24. Green, T.J., Ives, Z.G., Tannen, V.: Reconcilable differences. Theory Comput. Syst. **49**(2), 460–488 (2011)

25. Green, T.J., Karvounarakis, G., Tannen, V.: Provenance semirings. In: Proceedings of the Twenty-Sixth ACM SIGMOD-SIGACT-SIGART Symposium on Principles of Database Systems, pp. 31–40. ACM (2007)

26. Green, T.J., Tannen, V.: The semiring framework for database provenance. In: Proceedings of the 36th ACM SIGMOD-SIGACT-SIGAI Symposium on Principles of Database Systems, pp. 93–99. ACM (2017)

27. Kuich, W.: Semirings and formal power series: their relevance to formal languages and automata. In: Rozenberg, G., Salomaa, A. (eds.) Handbook of Formal Languages, vol. 1, pp. 609–677. Springer, Heidelberg (1997). https://doi.org/10.1007/978-3-642-59136-5_9

28. Kuznets, R.: A note on the use of sum in the Logic of Proofs. In: Drossos, C., Peppas, P., Tsinakis, C. (eds.) Proceedings of the 7th Panhellenic Logic Symposium, 15–19 July 2009, pp. 99–103. Patras University Press, Patras University, Patras (2009)

29. Kuznets, R., Studer, T.: Weak arithmetical interpretations for the Logic of Proofs. Logic J. IGPL **24**(3), 424–440 (2016)

30. Kuznets, R., Studer, T.: Logics of Proofs and Justifications. College Publications, London (2019)

31. Lehmann, E., Studer, T.: Subset models for justification logic. In: Iemhoff, R., Moortgat, M., de Queiroz, R. (eds.) WoLLIC 2019. LNCS, vol. 11541, pp. 433–449. Springer, Heidelberg (2019). https://doi.org/10.1007/978-3-662-59533-6_26

32. Lehmann, E., Studer, T.: Belief expansion in subset models. In: Artemov, S., Nerode, A. (eds.) LFCS 2020. LNCS, vol. 11972, pp. 85–97. Springer, Cham (2020). https://doi.org/10.1007/978-3-030-36755-8_6

33. Lehmann, E., Studer, T.: Exploring subset models for justification logic (submitted)

34. Shamkanov, D.: A realization theorem for the Gödel-Löb provability logic. Sbornik Math. **207**(9), 1344–1360 (2016)

35. Studer, T.: On the proof theory of the modal mu-calculus. Studia Logica **89**(3), 343–363 (2008). https://doi.org/10.1007/s11225-008-9133-6

36. Studer, T.: Decidability for some justification logics with negative introspection. J. Symbolic Logic **78**(2), 388–402 (2013)

Logic Programming, Argumentation and Human Reasoning

Marcos Cramer$^{(\boxtimes)}$ and Emmanuelle-Anna Dietz Saldanha

International Center for Computational Logic, TU Dresden, Dresden, Germany
marcos.cramer@tu-dresden.de

Abstract. The weak completion semantics, a computational logic approach, has been shown to adequately model various episodes of human reasoning. Since the inception of abstract argumentation in the 1990s, connections between argumentation semantics and logic programming semantics have been studied, but existing work on this connection has not yet covered the weak completion semantics. In this paper we define a novel translation from logic programs to abstract argumentation frameworks and show that under this translation the weak completion semantics corresponds to the grounded semantics of abstract argumentation. Combining this translation with argumentation semantics other than grounded semantics gives rise to novel logic programming semantics. We discuss the potential relevance of these novel semantics to modeling human reasoning and give an outlook on possible future research on this topic.

1 Introduction

Let us consider a famous psychological study from the literature, *Byrne's suppression task* [3]. This experiment shows that people with no prior exposure to formal logic suppress previously drawn conclusions when additional information becomes available. Consider the following example: *If she has an essay to finish, then she will study late in the library* and *she has an essay to finish.* Most participants (96%) concluded: *she will study late in the library.* If participants, however, receive an additional conditional: *If the library stays open, then she will study late in the library* then only 38% of them conclude: *She will study late in the library.* This shows that, although the conclusion is still correct under classical logic, participants seem to suppress that conclusion when given the additional conditional. This example shows that humans are capable to draw *non-monotonic* inferences.

Byrne [3] studied multiple variants of this suppression task, and it turned out that her results could not be straightforwardly explained in classical logic. On the other hand, logic programs interpreted under the weak completion semantics have been shown to be good predictors of human responses on Byrne's suppression task [11,19,20,22]. The weak completion semantics has also been shown to be a cognitively plausible model of human reasoning in the context of various other reasoning tasks [6,10,18].

© Springer Nature Switzerland AG 2020
M. Dastani et al. (Eds.): CLAR 2020, LNAI 12061, pp. 58–79, 2020.
https://doi.org/10.1007/978-3-030-44638-3_4

A new paradigm that recently emerged in the area of the psychology of reasoning is the integration of knowledge via argumentation [28]. There is strong evidence from psychology that arguments are the means for human reasoning [27]. In this paper we study the connection between such human reasoning tasks, the weak completion semantics and abstract argumentation. *Abstract argumentation* is a field of research within AI based on the idea of Dung [13] that under some conditions, the acceptance of arguments depends only on a so-called *attack* relation among the arguments, and not on the internal structure of the arguments. Dung called the directed graph that represents the arguments as well as the attack relation between them an *argumentation framework* (*AF*). Whether an argument is deemed acceptable depends on the decision about other arguments. Therefore the basic concept in abstract argumentation is a *set* of arguments that can be accepted together, called an *extension*. Crucially, there may be several of such extensions, and these extensions may be incompatible. An (*extension-based*) *argumentation semantics* takes as input an AF and produces as output a set of extensions.

Since the inception of abstract argumentation in the 1990s, connections between argumentation semantics and logic programming semantics have been studied. Already the seminal paper by Dung [13] introduced two possible ways of translating logic programs into argumentation frameworks. Later work has established a rich set of correspondences between logic programming semantics and argumentation semantics [4]. However, existing work on these correspondences has not yet covered the weak completion semantics.

In this paper we define a novel translation from logic programs to abstract argumentation frameworks and show that under this translation the weak completion semantics corresponds to the grounded semantics of abstract argumentation. Combining this translation with argumentation semantics other than grounded semantics gives rise to novel logic programming semantics that closely resemble the weak completion semantics, but also lead to different results in some crucial cases. We discuss the potential relevance of these novel semantics to modeling human reasoning and give an outlook on possible future research on this topic.

The paper is structured as follows: In Sect. 2 we introduce the formal preliminaries from abstract argumentation and logic programming that are required in this paper. In Sect. 3 we show how the various instances of the suppression task can be modeled within the weak completion semantics. Section 4 introduces our novel translation from logic programming to argumentation and presents a correspondence theorem between the weak completion semantics of logic programs and the grounded semantics of argumentation frameworks under this translation; the proof of this correspondence theorem is in the appendix. Furthermore, this section explains how our translation function can be used to define novel logic programming semantics. In Sect. 5 we discuss some properties of these novel semantics from the perspective of their potential use as models of human reasoning, highlighting that more empirical research is required to establish which of these semantics can predict human reasoning best. Section 6 concludes the paper.

2   Formal Preliminaries

In this section we introduce notions from abstract argumentation and logic programming that are required in this paper.

2.1   Abstract Argumentation

We define the required notions from abstract argumentation as introduced by Dung [13] and as explained in its current state-of-the-art form by Baroni et al. [1].

We start by defining the fundamental notion of *argumentation frameworks* and the auxiliary notions of *att-paths* and odd *att-cycles*.

Definition 1. *An* argumentation framework (AF) $F = \langle Ar, att \rangle$ *is a finite directed graph in which the set Ar of vertices is considered to represent arguments and the set $att \subseteq Ar \times Ar$ of edges is considered to represent the attack relation between arguments, i.e. the relation between a counterargument and the argument that it counters.*

Definition 2. *An att-path is a sequence $\langle a_0, \dots, a_n \rangle$ of arguments where $(a_i, a_{i+1}) \in att$ for $0 \le i < n$ and where $a_j \ne a_k$ for $0 \le j < k \le n$ with either $j \ne 0$ or $k \ne n$. An odd att-cycle is an att-path $\langle a_0, \dots, a_n \rangle$ where $a_0 = a_n$ and n is odd.*

Given an argumentation framework, we want to choose sets of arguments for which it is rational and coherent to accept them together. A set of arguments that may be accepted together is called an *extension*. Multiple *argumentation semantics* have been defined in the literature, i.e. multiple different ways of defining extensions given an argumentation framework. Before we consider specific argumentation semantics, we first give a formal definition of the notion of *argumentation semantics*:

Definition 3. *An* argumentation semantics *is a function σ that maps any AF $F = \langle Ar, att \rangle$ to a set $\sigma(F)$ of subsets of Ar. The elements of $\sigma(F)$ are called σ-extensions of F.*

Note 4. We usually define an argumentation semantics σ by specifying criteria which a subset of Ar has to satisfy in order to be a σ-extension of F.

In this paper we consider the complete, stable, grounded, preferred, CF2 and SCF2 semantics. The first four are based on the notion of *admissibility* and are widely studied in the abstract argumentation literature. The latter two are not based on the notion of admissibility, but have recently been shown to be good predictors of human judgments about argument acceptability [7–9]. We now first define the four admissibility-based semantics:

Definition 5. *Let* $F = \langle Ar, att \rangle$ *be an AF, and let* $S \subseteq Ar$. *The set* S *is called* conflict-free *iff there are no arguments* $b, c \in S$ *such that* b *attacks* c *(i.e. such that* $(b, c) \in att$). *Argument* $a \in Ar$ *is* defended *by* S *iff for every* $b \in Ar$ *such that* b *attacks* a *there exists* $c \in S$ *such that* c *attacks* b. *We say that* S *is* admissible *iff* S *is conflict-free and every argument in* S *is defended by* S. *We say that* S attacks a *if there exists* $b \in S$ *such that* b *attacks* a.

- S *is a* complete extension *of* F *iff* S *is admissible and* S *contains all the arguments it defends.*
- S *is a* stable extension *of* F *iff* S *is admissible and* S *attacks all the arguments of* $Ar \setminus S$.
- S *is the* grounded extension *of* F *iff* S *is a minimal with respect to set inclusion complete extension of* F.
- S *is a* preferred extension *of* F *iff* S *is a maximal with respect to set inclusion complete extension of* F.

The CF2 semantics was first introduced by Baroni *et al.* [2]. The idea behind it is that we partition the AF into *strongly connected components* and recursively evaluate it component by component by choosing maximal conflict-free sets in each component and removing arguments attacked by chosen arguments. We formally define it following the notation of Dvořák and Gaggl [14]. For this we first need some auxiliary notions:

Definition 6. *Let* $F = \langle Ar, att \rangle$ *be an AF, and let* $a, b \in Ar$. *We define* $a \sim b$ *iff either* $a = b$ *or there is an att-path from* a *to* b *and there is an att-path from* b *to* a. *The equivalence classes under the equivalence relation* $\sim$ *are called* strongly connected components *(SCCs) of* F. *We denote the set of SCCs of* F *by* $SCCs(F)$. *Given* $S \subseteq Ar$, *we define* $D_F(S) := \{b \in Ar \mid there\ exists\ a \in S\ such\ that\ (a, b) \in att\ and\ a \not\sim b\}$.

Definition 7. *Let* $F = \langle Ar, att \rangle$ *be an AF, and let* $S \subseteq Ar$. *We write* $F|_S$ *for the restricted AF* $\langle S, att \cap (S \times S) \rangle$.

We now recursively define CF2 extensions as follows:

Definition 8. *Let* $F = \langle Ar, att \rangle$ *be an AF, and let* $S \subseteq Ar$. *Then* S *is a CF2 extension of* F *iff either*

- $|SCCs(F)| = 1$ *and* S *is a maximal conflict-free subset of* Ar, *or*
- $|SCCs(F)| > 1$ *and for each* $C \in SCCs(F)$, $S \cap C$ *is a CF2 extension of* $F|_{C \setminus D_F(S)}$.

The SCF2 semantics was recently introduced by Cramer and van der Torre [9] motivated both by desirable formal principles that it satisfies as well as by its capacity to predict human judgments about the acceptability of arguments. For defining the SCF2 semantics, we first need some auxiliary notions:

Definition 9. *Let* $F = \langle Ar, att \rangle$ *be an AF, and let* $A \subseteq Ar$. *We define* $A^- = \{a \in Ar \mid a\ attacks\ some\ b \in A\}$.

Definition 10. *Let $F = \langle Ar, att \rangle$ be an AF, and let $A \subseteq Ar$. We say that A is strongly complete outside odd cycles iff for every argument $a \in Ar$ such that no argument in $\{a\} \cup \{a\}^-$ is in an odd att-cycle and $A \cap \{a\}^- = \emptyset$, we have that $a \in A$.*

We now recursively define SCF2 extensions as follows:

Definition 11. *Let $F = \langle Ar, att \rangle$ be an AF, and let $S \subseteq Ar$. Then S is an SCF2 extension of F iff either*

- *Ar contains at least one argument a such that a attacks itself and S is an SCF2 extension of $F|_{\{a \in S | (a,a) \notin att\}}$.*
- *Ar contains no argument a such that a attacks itself, $|SCCs(F)| = 1$ and S is a maximal conflict-free subset of Ar that is strongly complete outside odd cycles, or*
- *Ar contains no argument a such that a attacks itself, $|SCCs(F)| > 1$ and for each $C \in SCCs(F)$, $S \cap C$ is an SCF2 extension of $F|_{C \backslash D_F(S)}$.*

2.2   Logic Programming

The terminology and notation here is based on [12,17,25]. We assume a propositional language, in which *atoms* can be combined to *formulas* using the unary connective $\neg$ (*not*) and the binary connectives $\wedge$ (*and*), $\vee$ (*or*), $\leftarrow$ (*if*) and $\leftrightarrow$ (*if and only if*). The set of atoms is assumed to contain $\top$ (*true*), $\bot$ (*false*) and U (*undefined*). A *literal* is a formula that is of the form A or $\neg A$ for an atom A.

Definition 12. *Let F be a formula of the form $L_1 \wedge \ldots \wedge L_n$ where L_i is a literal for $1 \leq i \leq n$. Then $\text{pos}(F) = \{L_i \mid 1 \leq i \leq n \text{ and } L_i \text{ is an atom}\}$ and $\text{neg}(F) = \{L_i \mid 1 \leq i \leq n \text{ and } L_i \text{ is of the form } \neg A\}$.*

Definition 13. *Clauses are expressions of the forms $A \leftarrow L_1 \wedge \ldots \ldots \wedge L_n$ (rules), $A \leftarrow \top$ (facts), and $A \leftarrow \bot$ (assumptions), where A is an atom other than $\top$, U and $\bot$, and L_i is a literal for $1 \leq i \leq n$. A is the head and $L_1 \wedge \ldots \ldots \wedge L_n$, as well as $\top$ and $\bot$, are the body of the corresponding clauses. A program $\mathcal{P}$ is a finite set of clauses. A normal program $\mathcal{P}$ is a program without assumptions. If $\mathcal{P}$ is a program, then $\mathcal{P}^*$ denotes the normal program $\{A \leftarrow body \mid A \leftarrow body \in \mathcal{P}$ and $body \neq \bot\}$.*

Definition 14. *Let $\mathcal{P}$ be a program. The set of all atoms occurring in $\mathcal{P}$ is denoted by $\text{atoms}(\mathcal{P})$. A is undefined in $\mathcal{P}$ iff A is not the head of any clause in $\mathcal{P}$. The set of all atoms that are undefined in $\mathcal{P}$ is $\text{undef}(\mathcal{P})$.*

Three-Valued Logics. The various logic programming approaches that we will discuss in the following differ with respect to the underlying logic that they have originally been introduced with. Therefore, Table 1 shows the truth tables of the three-valued logics in consideration, where $\top$, $\bot$ and U denote the three truth-values *true*, *false* and *unknown* respectively. In particular, models under the

Table 1. Truth tables for three-valued logics. The gray highlighted $\top$'s indicate that formulas which are true under $\leftarrow_L$ ($\leftrightarrow_L$) are true under $\leftarrow_S$ ($\leftrightarrow_S$), and vice versa.

F	$\neg F$
$\top$	$\bot$
$\bot$	$\top$
U	U

$\wedge$	$\top$	U	$\bot$
$\top$	$\top$	U	$\bot$
U	U	U	$\bot$
$\bot$	$\bot$	$\bot$	$\bot$

$\leftarrow_L$	$\top$	U	$\bot$
$\top$	$\top$	$\top$	$\top$
U	U	$\top$	$\top$
$\bot$	$\bot$	U	$\top$

$\leftrightarrow_L$	$\top$	U	$\bot$
$\top$	$\top$	U	$\bot$
U	U	$\top$	U
$\bot$	$\bot$	U	$\top$

$\vee$	$\top$	U	$\bot$
$\top$	$\top$	$\top$	$\top$
U	$\top$	U	U
$\bot$	$\top$	U	$\bot$

$\leftarrow_S$	$\top$	U	$\bot$
$\top$	$\top$	$\top$	$\top$
U	$\bot$	$\top$	$\top$
$\bot$	$\bot$	$\bot$	$\top$

$\leftrightarrow_S$	$\top$	U	$\bot$
$\top$	$\top$	$\bot$	$\bot$
U	$\bot$	$\top$	$\bot$
$\bot$	$\bot$	$\bot$	$\top$

weak completion semantics introduced have originally been defined according to the three-valued Łukasiewicz logic [26], for which the set of connectives is $\{\neg, \wedge, \vee, \leftarrow_L, \leftrightarrow_L\}$. On the other hand, models under the well-founded semantics have originally been defined according to the three-valued S_3 logic [31], for which the set of connectives is $\{\neg, \wedge, \vee, \leftarrow_S, \leftrightarrow_S\}$. As the highlighted $\top$'s in Table 1 show, the models with respect to these logics coincide for formulas without nested implications or equivalences, and thus also for the models which are going to be discussed in this paper. Therefore, in the following, we will not need to further specify the respective underlying three-valued logic.

Definition 15. *Let $\mathcal{P}$ be a program. A three-valued interpretation I of $\mathcal{P}$ is a mapping from atoms($\mathcal{P}$) to the set of truth values $\{\top, \bot, U\}$ such that $I(\top) = \top$, $I(\bot) = \bot$ and $I(U) = U$. We represent an interpretation as a pair $I = \langle I^\top, I^\bot \rangle$ of disjoint sets of atoms, where $I^\top$ is the set of all atoms other than $\top$ that are mapped to $\top$ by I, and $I^\bot$ is the set of all atoms other than $\bot$ that are mapped to $\bot$ by I, and where $I^\top \cap I^\bot = \emptyset$. Atoms that do not occur in $I^\top \cup I^\bot$ are mapped to U.*

Definition 16. *Let $I = \langle I^\top, I^\bot \rangle$ and $J = \langle J^\top, J^\bot \rangle$ be two interpretations. We define $I \preceq_k J$ iff $I^\top \subseteq J^\top$ and $I^\bot \subseteq J^\bot$, and we define $I \preceq_t J$ iff $I^\top \subseteq J^\top$ and $J^\bot \subseteq I^\bot$.*

Definition 17. *Let F be a formula. The truth value of F under I, denoted $I(F)$ is determined according to the truth tables in Table 1.*

Definition 18. *Let I be an interpretation. I is a model of a formula F, if $I(F) = \top$. I is a model of $\mathcal{P}$ if I is a model for every clause occurring in $\mathcal{P}$, i.e. $I(C) = \top$ for all $C \in \mathcal{P}$. A model I of $\mathcal{P}$ is a $\preceq_k$-minimal ($\preceq_t$-minimal) model of $\mathcal{P}$ iff for any other model J of $\mathcal{P}$ it holds that $I \preceq_k J$ ($I \preceq_t J$). I is a $\preceq_k$-least ($\preceq_t$-least) model of $\mathcal{P}$ iff it is the only $\preceq_k$-minimal ($\preceq_t$-minimal) model of $\mathcal{P}$.*

Weak Completion Semantics. The weak completion semantics (WCS) has originally been introduced by Hölldobler and Kencana Ramli [19–21]. The following program transformation is a variation of Clark's completion [5].

Definition 19. *Let $\mathcal{P}$ be a program. Consider the following transformation for $\mathcal{P}$: 1. Replace all clauses in $\mathcal{P}$ with the same head $A \leftarrow body_1, A \leftarrow body_2, \ldots, A \leftarrow body_n$ by the single expression $A \leftarrow body_1 \vee body_2, \vee \cdots \vee body_n$. 2. Replace all occurrences of $\leftarrow$ by $\leftrightarrow$. The resulting set of equivalences is the* weak completion *of $\mathcal{P}$ (wc $\mathcal{P}$).*

As Hölldobler and Kencana Ramli [20] have shown, the model intersection property holds for weakly completed programs, which guarantees the existence of a least model for every program. These models can be computed by the following immediate consequence operator proposed by Stenning and van Lambalgen [33].

Definition 20. *Let I be an interpretation and $\mathcal{P}$ a program. The* Stenning and van Lambalgen *operator is defined as follows: $\Phi_{\mathcal{P}}(I) = \langle J^{\top}, J^{\perp} \rangle$, where*

$J^{\top} = \{A \mid there\ exists\ A \leftarrow body \in \mathcal{P}\ such\ that\ I(body) = \top\}$,
$J^{\perp} = \{A \mid A \notin \mathsf{undef}(\mathcal{P})\ and\ for\ all\ A \leftarrow body \in \mathcal{P}\ we\ find\ that\ I(body) = \perp\}$.

The $\preceq_k$-least fixed point of $\Phi_{\mathcal{P}}$, lfp $\Phi_{\mathcal{P}}$, is identical to the $\preceq_k$-least model of the weak completion of $\mathcal{P}$ (lm wc $\mathcal{P}$). It can be reached by iteratively applying $\Phi_{\mathcal{P}}$ to $I = \langle \emptyset, \emptyset \rangle$ [19]. We call the $\preceq_k$-least fixed point of Φ the *WCS model of $\mathcal{P}$*.

Kripke-Kleene Semantics. Fitting [15] provided an immediate consequence operator, whose least fixed point for a given program $\mathcal{P}$ corresponds to the least model of Clark's completion of $\mathcal{P}$ [5].

Definition 21. *Let I be an interpretation and $\mathcal{P}$ a normal program. The* Fitting *operator is defined as follows: $\Psi_{\mathcal{P}}(I) = \langle J^{\top}, J^{\perp} \rangle$, where*

$$J^{\top} = \{A \mid there\ exists\ A \leftarrow body \in \mathcal{P}\ such\ that\ I(body) = \top\},$$
$$J^{\perp} = \{A \mid for\ all\ A \leftarrow body \in \mathcal{P}\ we\ find\ that\ I(body) = \perp\}.$$

The operator Φ in Definition 20 differs with respect to the Fitting operator Ψ, in the specification of $J^{\perp}$ where the first line "$A \notin \mathsf{undef}(\mathcal{P})$ and" is dropped in Ψ.

The $\preceq_k$-least fixed point of $\Psi_{\mathcal{P}}$ is called the *Kripke-Kleene model* or *KK model of $\mathcal{P}$* (in the literature it is sometimes called *Fitting's model*).

Stable Model Semantics. Stable models originate from Gelfond and Lifschitz [16], and have been extended to three-valued stable models by Przymusinski [29]. For defining the stable model of a program, we first define the notion of a reduct:

Definition 22. *Let I be an interpretation and $\mathcal{P}$ a normal program. The reduct of $\mathcal{P}$ with respect to I, denoted by $\mathcal{P}|_I$, is obtained from $\mathcal{P}$ by replacing in the bodies of all clauses $\mathcal{P}$ each negative literal $\neg A$ by $I(\neg A)$, that is, with the truth value constant corresponding to the value of $\neg A$ under I.*

Definition 23. *Let I be an interpretation and $\mathcal{P}$ a normal program. I is a three-valued stable model or 3-St model of $\mathcal{P}$ if and only if I is a $\preceq_t$-minimal model of $\mathcal{P}|_I$. I is a two-valued stable model or 2-St model of $\mathcal{P}$ if and only if I is a 3-St model of $\mathcal{P}$ that does not assign the truth value U to any atom.*

Well-Founded Semantics. The Well-founded Semantics has first been presented by Gelder, Ross and Schlipf [34]. Since Przymusinski [29] established that the well-founded model coincides with the knowledge-least three-valued stable model, we use this characterization as our definition of the well-founded model:

Definition 24. *Let I be an interpretation and $\mathcal{P}$ a normal program. I is the well-founded model or WF model of $\mathcal{P}$ if I is the $\preceq_k$-least three-valued stable model of $\mathcal{P}$.*

Translation and Correspondence. Two main differences between the Weak Completion Semantics and the other logic programming approaches introduced above, have been identified [12]: (i) The weak completion semantics, and the Kripke-Kleene semantics deal differently with undefined atoms in a program. (ii) Additionally to (i), under certain circumstances, the weak completion semantics and the well-founded semantics deal differently with atoms involved in positive cycles. The following correspondence between WCS models and WF models can be established:

Theorem 25 (adapted from Theorem 11 in [12]). *For any program $\mathcal{P}$, not containing positive cycles, and interpretation I, I is a WCS model of $\mathcal{P}$ iff I is the WF model of*

$$\mathcal{P}^* \cup \bigcup_{A \in \mathsf{undef}(\mathcal{P})} \{A \leftarrow \neg A', A' \leftarrow \neg A\},$$

where for each $A \in \mathsf{undef}(\mathcal{P})$, an auxiliary atom A' is introduced that does not occur in $\mathcal{P}$.

2.3   Correspondence of Argumentation and Logic Programming

In his seminal paper [13], Dung provided two translations from logic programming to argumentation framework: One which captures the semantics of negation as possibly infinite failure, and one which captures the semantics of negation as finite failure. While the first one has been the basis for most of the more recent work on the correspondence between argumentation and logic programming, e.g. [4], we will here present Dung's second translation, because it closely resembles the translation that we will introduce and motivate in this paper.

Before we define the translation, we first need two auxiliary notions:

Definition 26. *Given a set $\mathcal{K}$ of literals, we define $\bigwedge \mathcal{K}$ to be $L_1 \wedge \cdots \wedge L_n$ if $\mathcal{K} = \{L_1, \ldots, L_n\}$ ($n \geq 1$), and we define $\bigwedge \mathcal{K}$ to be $\top$ if $\mathcal{K} = \emptyset$.*

Definition 27. *Given a literal L, we define the* complement *$\bar{L}$ of L as follows:*

$$\bar{L} := \begin{cases} \neg L \text{ if } L \text{ is an atom;} \\ A \quad \text{if } L \text{ is } \neg A \text{ for some atom } A. \end{cases}$$

Definition 28. *The translation $AF_{naff}(\mathcal{P})$ of a program $\mathcal{P}$ is the argumentation framework (Ar, att), where*

$$Ar := \{(\mathcal{K}, A) \mid \mathcal{K} \text{ is a set of literals such that } A \leftarrow \bigwedge \mathcal{K} \in \mathcal{P}\}$$
$$\cup \{(\{\neg A\}, \neg A) \mid A \in \mathsf{atoms}(\mathcal{P})\}$$
$$att := \{((\mathcal{K}, L), (\mathcal{K}', L')) \mid (\mathcal{K}, L) \in Ar, (\mathcal{K}', L') \in Ar \text{ and } \bar{L} \in \mathcal{K}'\}$$

Note 29. The subscript *naff* in $AF_{naff}(\mathcal{P})$ means *negation as finite failure.*

Dung [13] proved the following theorem that establishes a correspondence between the Kripke-Kleene model of a program $\mathcal{P}$ and the grounded extension of $AF_{naff}(\mathcal{P})$:

Theorem 30 (Theorem 56 in [13]). *Let $\mathcal{P}$ be a logic program, let E be the grounded extension of $AF_{naff}(\mathcal{P})$. Then the Kripke-Kleene model of $\mathcal{P}$ is $\langle \{A \mid (\mathcal{K}, A) \in E\}, \{A \mid (\mathcal{K}, \neg A) \in E\}\rangle$.*

Note that this correspondence between the Kripke-Kleene semantics of logic programs and the grounded semantics of argumentation frameworks depends on the translation between the two formalisms. If another translation is chosen, the grounded semantics may correspond to a different logic programming semantics. For example, under Dung's translation for *negation as possibly infinite failure* [13] as well as under the translation given by Caminada et al. [4], the grounded semantics corresponds to the well-founded semantics. For the translation that we will introduce in Sect. 4, we will show that the grounded semantics corresponds to the weak completion semantics.

3   The Suppression Task

Recall the suppression task from the introduction. Byrne carried out a psychological experiment that can be split up into four different cases (or variations) for each of three different groups of participants [3]. In the following, we will only discuss the results of the three different groups for the first two cases. Consider the information received by Group I in case 1:

$$\text{If she has an essay to finish, then she will study late in the library.} \tag{1}$$
$$\text{She has an essay to finish.} \tag{2}$$

Table 2. Logic program representation for the first two cases of the suppression task, according to Stenning and van Lambalgen [33].

Case	Program		Fact/Assumption
e	$\mathcal{P}_I^e = \{l \leftarrow e \wedge \neg ab_1,$	$ab_1 \leftarrow \perp,$	$e \leftarrow \top\}$
	$\mathcal{P}_{II}^e = \{\ell \leftarrow e \wedge \neg ab_1, \ell \leftarrow t \wedge \neg ab_2, ab_1 \leftarrow \perp, ab_2 \leftarrow \perp,$		$e \leftarrow \top\}$
	$\mathcal{P}_{III}^e = \{\ell \leftarrow e \wedge \neg ab_1, \ell \leftarrow o \wedge \neg ab_3, ab_1 \leftarrow \neg o, ab_3 \leftarrow \neg e,$		$e \leftarrow \top\}$
$\bar{e}$	$\mathcal{P}_I^{\bar{e}} = \{\ell \leftarrow e \wedge \neg ab_1,$	$ab_1 \leftarrow \perp,$	$e \leftarrow \perp\}$
	$\mathcal{P}_{II}^{\bar{e}} = \{\ell \leftarrow e \wedge \neg ab_1, \ell \leftarrow t \wedge \neg ab_2, ab_1 \leftarrow \perp, ab_2 \leftarrow \perp,$		$e \leftarrow \perp\}$
	$\mathcal{P}_{III}^{\bar{e}} = \{\ell \leftarrow e \wedge \neg ab_1, \ell \leftarrow o \wedge \neg ab_3, ab_1 \leftarrow \neg o, ab_3 \leftarrow e,$		$e \leftarrow \perp\}$

The participants had the option to choose from *She will study late in the library*, *She will not study late in the library*, or *She may or may not study late in the library*. 96% of the participants concluded that *She will study late in the library*.

Additionally to (1) and (2), Group II received the following information

$$\text{If she has a textbook to read, then she will study late in the library.} \quad (3)$$

Again, 96% of this group concluded that *She will study late in the library*. Additionally to (1) and (2), Group III received the following information:

$$\text{If the library stays open, then she will study late in the library.} \quad (4)$$

In this group, only 38% concluded that *She will study late in the library*. This is the so-called *suppression effect* as previously drawn conclusions were suppressed. One explanation why the percentage dropped significantly, is that participants might have thought about the necessity that *the library (has to) stay open* in order to *study late in the library*.

In the second case, Group I now received, instead of (2), the following information together with (1):

$$\text{She does not have an essay to finish.} \quad (5)$$

In this case, 46% of the participants concluded that *She will not study late in the library*. Similarly, in Group III, who received as information (1), (4) and (5), 63% concluded that *She will not study late in the library*. Yet, when Group II received as information (1), (3) and (5), then only 4% concluded that *She will not study late in the library*. Now the suppression effect can be observed in Group II. One explanation why the percentage dropped significantly in this group is that the participants might have thought about an alternative possibility for her to *study late in the library*, namely because *She has a textbook to read*.

Stenning and van Lambalgen [33] suggested to model Byrne's suppression task by representing the given statements within the experiment as logic program

Table 3. Models under the respective semantics for the programs of Table 2. Highlighted atoms show the differences between the Weak Completion Semantics and the others.

Case	Program	KK/2-St/3-St/WF model of $\mathcal{P}^*$	WCS model of $\mathcal{P}$	Byrne
e	$\mathcal{P}_{\mathrm{I}}^{e}$	$\langle\{e,\ell\},\{ab_1\}\rangle$	$\langle\{e,\ell\},\{ab_1\}\rangle$	96% L
	$\mathcal{P}_{\mathrm{II}}^{e}$	$\langle\{e,\ell\},\{\boxed{t},ab_1,ab_2\}\rangle$	$\langle\{e,\ell\},\{ab_1,ab_2\}\rangle$	96% L
	$\mathcal{P}_{\mathrm{III}}^{e}$	$\langle\{e,\boxed{ab_1}\},\{\boxed{o},\ell,ab_3\}\rangle$	$\langle\{e\},\{ab_3\}\rangle$	38% L
$\bar{e}$	$\mathcal{P}_{\mathrm{I}}^{\bar{e}}$	$\langle\emptyset,\{e,\ell,ab_1\}\rangle$	$\langle\emptyset,\{e,\ell,ab_1\}\rangle$	46% $\overline{L}$
	$\mathcal{P}_{\mathrm{II}}^{\bar{e}}$	$\langle\emptyset,\{e,\boxed{t},\ell,ab_1,ab_2\}\rangle$	$\langle\emptyset,\{e,ab_1,ab_2\}\rangle$	4% $\overline{L}$
	$\mathcal{P}_{\mathrm{III}}^{\bar{e}}$	$\langle\{\boxed{ab_1},ab_3\},\{e,\boxed{o},\ell\}\rangle$	$\langle\{ab_3\},\{e,\ell\}\rangle$	63% $\overline{L}$

clauses including licenses for inferences. Consider again (1), which is encoded by the clause $\ell \leftarrow e \wedge \neg ab_1$, where ab_1 is an *abnormality predicate* assumed (by default) to be false: ℓ holds if e is true and nothing abnormal is known ($\neg ab_1$), i.e. everything abnormal is false. (3) and (4) can be encoded analogously as the clauses $\ell \leftarrow t \wedge \neg ab_2$ and $\ell \leftarrow o \wedge \neg ab_3$, respectively. The dependency when the two conditionals (1) and (4) appear together was suggested to be encoded by means of their abnormalities as follows [33]:

$$ab_1 \leftarrow \neg o, \qquad\qquad ab_3 \leftarrow \neg e,$$

meaning that *Something is abnormal* (ab_1), with respect to $\ell \leftarrow e \wedge \neg ab_1$, if *the library is not open* ($\neg o$), and *Something is abnormal* (ab_3) with respect to $\ell \leftarrow o \wedge \neg ab_3$, if *She does not have an essay to finish*. Depending on the case, i.e. whether (2) or (5) is given to the participants, either $e \leftarrow \top$ or $e \leftarrow \bot$, holds.

The six logic programs representing the first two cases of the suppression task as proposed by Stenning and van Lambalgen are shown in Table 2. The superscript and superscripts of the programs denote the group and the case.

Table 3 depicts the results of the different semantics with respect to the programs in Table 2. The third column shows the models under the weak completion semantics: For Group II, t is unknown, and for Group III, o is unknown. This is different for the other semantics (second column) where for Group II, t is false, and for Group III, o is false. Consequently, under the weak completion semantics, ℓ is unknown in the cases of $\mathcal{P}_{\mathrm{II}}^{e}$ and $\mathcal{P}_{\mathrm{III}}^{\bar{e}}$, which coincides with the two suppression effects reflected in Byrne's results (last column). As for the other semantics, they fail to model the suppression effect in both cases.

As summarized in [11], all cases of the suppression task seem to be adequately modeled under the weak completion semantics. Note that the other two cases of the suppression task not discussed here can be modeled by means of abduction [24].

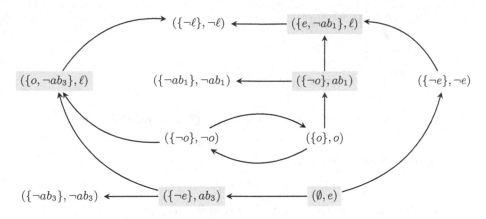

Fig. 1. The argumentation framework $AF_{wc}(\mathcal{P}^e_{\mathrm{III}})$ corresponding to $\mathcal{P}^e_{\mathrm{III}}$.

4   Translation, Correspondence and New LP Semantics

In this section we define a translation from logic programs to argumentation frameworks and show that under this translation, the weak completion semantics of logic programs corresponds to the grounded semantics of argumentation frameworks. Furthermore we use this translation function to define new logic programming semantics based on argumentation semantics.

Consider the following translation from a given program $\mathcal{P}$ to an AF:

Definition 31. *The translation $AF_{wc}(\mathcal{P})$ of a program $\mathcal{P}$ is the argumentation framework (Ar, att), where*

$$Ar := \{(\mathcal{K}, A) \mid \mathcal{K} \text{ is a set of literals such that } A \leftarrow \bigwedge \mathcal{K} \in \mathcal{P}\}$$
$$\cup \{((\{\neg A\}, \neg A) \mid A \in \mathsf{atoms}(\mathcal{P})\} \cup \{(\{A\}, A) \mid A \in \mathsf{undef}(\mathcal{P})\}$$
$$att := \{((\mathcal{K}, L), (\mathcal{K}', L')) \mid (\mathcal{K}, L) \in Ar, (\mathcal{K}', L') \in Ar \text{ and } \bar{L} \in \mathcal{K}'\}$$

Note 32. The subscript wc in $AF_{wc}(\mathcal{P})$ means *weak completion*, because this translation is closely linked to the weak completion of $\mathcal{P}$, as we will show below.

Example 33. Consider $\mathcal{P}^e_{\mathrm{III}}$, which we have already seen in Table 2 in Sect. 3 as the program that formalizes the first case for Group III in Byrne's suppression task: $\mathcal{P}^e_{\mathrm{III}} = \{\ell \leftarrow e \wedge \neg ab_1, \ \ell \leftarrow o \wedge \neg ab_3, \ ab_1 \leftarrow \neg o, \ ab_3 \leftarrow \neg e, \ e \leftarrow \top\}$.

The argumentation framework of $\mathcal{P}^e_{\mathrm{III}}$, $AF(\mathcal{P}^e_{\mathrm{III}})$, is depicted in Fig. 1. As usual, arrows indicate the attack relation between arguments. The five arguments highlighted in gray correspond to the five rules of $\mathcal{P}^e_{\mathrm{III}}$, five further arguments are of the form $(\{\neg A\}, \neg A)$ for atoms A of $\mathcal{P}^e_{\mathrm{III}}$, and $(\{o\}, o)$ is the only argument of the third type of arguments that correspond only to undefined atoms.

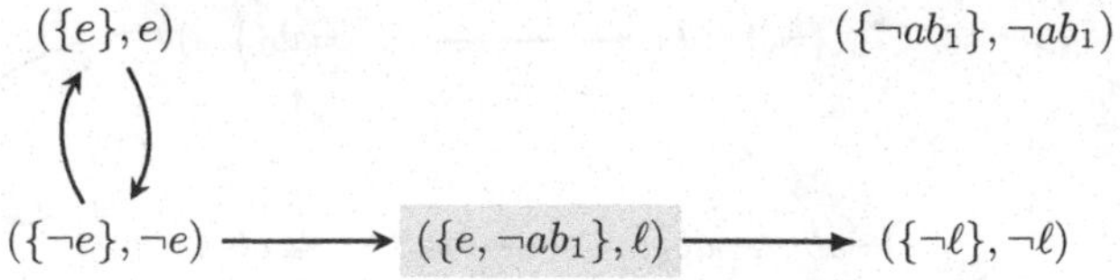

$$({\{e\}}, e) \qquad\qquad\qquad\qquad ({\{\neg ab_1\}}, \neg ab_1)$$

$$({\{\neg e\}}, \neg e) \longrightarrow ({\{e, \neg ab_1\}}, \ell) \longrightarrow ({\{\neg \ell\}}, \neg \ell)$$

Fig. 2. The argumentation framework $AF_{wc}(\mathcal{P}_0)$ corresponding to $\mathcal{P}_0$.

The grounded extension of $AF(\mathcal{P}_{\mathrm{III}}^e)$ is

$$E_0 := \{(\emptyset, e), ({\{\neg ab_3\}}, \neg ab_3)\}$$

The two stable, preferred, CF2 and SCF2 extensions of $AF(\mathcal{P}_{\mathrm{III}}^e)$ are E_1 and E_2:

$$E_1 := \{(\emptyset, e), ({\{\neg ab_3\}}, \neg ab_3), ({\{\neg o\}}, \neg o), ({\{\neg o\}}, ab_1), ({\{\neg \ell\}}, \neg \ell)\}$$
$$E_2 := \{(\emptyset, e), ({\{\neg ab_3\}}, \neg ab_3), ({\{o\}}, o), ({\{\neg ab_1\}}, \neg ab_1), ({\{e, \neg ab_1\}}, \ell), ({\{o, \neg ab_3\}}, \ell)\}$$

The complete extensions of $AF(\mathcal{P}_{\mathrm{III}}^e)$ are E_0, E_1 and E_2.   ▲

The following theorem, whose proof is in Appendix A, states that under the translation function AF_{wc}, the grounded semantics of argumentation frameworks corresponds to the weak completion semantics of logic programs.

Theorem 34. *Let $\mathcal{P}$ be a logic program, let E be the grounded extension of $AF_{wc}(\mathcal{P})$. Then the WCS model of $\mathcal{P}$ is $\langle \{A \mid (\mathcal{K}, A) \in E\}, \{A \mid (\mathcal{K}, \neg A) \in E\} \rangle$.*

Example 35. We continue Example 33. The grounded extension of $\mathcal{P}_{\mathrm{III}}^e$ is $E_0 = \{(\emptyset, e), ({\{\neg ab_3\}}, \neg ab_3)\}$, and the corresponding interpretation is

$$I = \langle \{A \mid (\mathcal{K}, A) \in E_0\}, \{A \mid (\mathcal{K}, \neg A) \in E_0\} \rangle \;=\; \langle \{e\}, \{ab_3\} \rangle,$$

which is indeed the WCS model of $AF(\mathcal{P}_{\mathrm{III}}^e)$.   ▲

We now look at how the translation function AF_{wc} can be used to map any argumentation semantics σ to a three-valued logic programming semantics σ-WCS:

Definition 36. *Let σ be an argumentation semantics and let $\mathcal{P}$ be a program. A three-valued interpretation I of $\mathcal{P}$ is called a σ-WCS model of $\mathcal{P}$ iff there exists a σ-extension E of $AF_{wc}(\mathcal{P})$ such that $I = \langle \{A \mid (\mathcal{K}, A) \in E\}, \{A \mid (\mathcal{K}, \neg A) \in E\} \rangle$.*

Definition 37. *A logic programming semantics $\mathcal{S}$ is an argumentation-WCS semantics iff there is an argumentation semantics σ such that $\mathcal{S}$ is identical to σ-WCS.*

By Theorem 34 we already know that grounded-WCS is the same as WCS, i.e. the weak completion semantics. Since any argumentation framework has a single grounded extension, any program has a single grounded-WCS model. For other semantics this is not the case. For example, an argumentation framework may have multiple preferred extensions, and hence a logic program may have multiple preferred-WCS models.

Example 38. Let us consider the program $\mathcal{P}_0 = \{\ell \leftarrow e \wedge \neg ab_1, ab_1 \leftarrow \bot\}$ that according to Stenning and van Lambalgen's license for inference approach corresponds to sentence (1) in Sect. 3. Figure 2 depicts $AF_{wc}(\mathcal{P}_0)$.[1] The grounded extension of $AF_{wc}(\mathcal{P}_0)$ is $E_0 := \{(\{\neg ab_1\}, \neg ab_1)\}$, so the (grounded-)WCS model of $\mathcal{P}_0$ is $I_0 := \langle \emptyset, \{ab_1\} \rangle$.

In the stable, preferred, CF2 and SCF2 semantics, there are two extensions, E_1 and E_2:

$$E_1 := \{(\{e\}, e), (\{e, \neg ab_1\}, \neg \ell), (\{\neg ab_1\}, \neg ab_1)\}$$
$$E_2 := \{(\{\neg e\}, \neg e), (\{\neg \ell\}, \neg \ell), (\{\neg ab_1\}, \neg ab_1)\}$$

These two extensions correspond to two $\mathcal{P}_0$-interpretations, I_1 and I_2, both of which are therefore stable-WCS models, preferred-WCS models, CF2-WCS models and SCF2-WCS models:

$$I_1 := \langle \{e, \ell\}, \{ab_1\} \rangle \quad \text{and} \quad I_2 := \langle \emptyset, \{e, \ell, ab_1\} \rangle.$$

The complete extensions of $AF_{wc}(\mathcal{P}_0)$ are E_0, E_1 and E_2, so the complete-WCS models of $\mathcal{P}_0$ are I_0, I_1 and I_2, which are also all the models of wc $\mathcal{P}_0$.   ▲

When we apply an LP semantics that allows for multiple models to the task of predicting what conclusions humans derive from given information, we need to specify how to combine the information that is present in the multiple models into a single prediction. There are two standard ways of combining the information from multiple interpretations into a single belief specification, namely *credulous belief* and *skeptical belief*. Credulously believing something means believing it as long as it is true in at least one of the given interpretations. Skeptically believing something means believing it only if it is true in all the given interpretations. Formally we define these notions as follows:

Definition 39. *Let $\mathcal{I}$ be a set of interpretations. The credulous belief set over $\mathcal{I}$, denoted $Cr(\mathcal{I})$, is the following set of literals:*

$$Cr(\mathcal{I}) := \{A \mid \text{ there is an } I \in \mathcal{I} \text{ such that } A \in I^\top\} \cup$$
$$\{\neg A \mid \text{ there is an } I \in \mathcal{I} \text{ such that } A \in I^\bot\}$$

The skeptical belief set over $\mathcal{I}$, denoted $Sk(\mathcal{I})$, is the following set of literals:

$$Sk(\mathcal{I}) := \{A \mid A \in \mathsf{atoms}(\mathcal{P}) \text{ and for every } I \in \mathcal{I}, A \in I^\top\} \cup$$
$$\{\neg A \mid A \in \mathsf{atoms}(\mathcal{P}) \text{ and every } I \in \mathcal{I}, A \in I^\bot\}$$

Example 40. We continue Example 38. Recall that I_1 and I_2 are the models of $\mathcal{P}_0$ in the stable-WCS, preferred-WCS, CF2-WCS and SCF2-WCS semantics. The credulous and skeptical belief sets over the set $\{I_1, I_2\}$ of interpretations are

$$Cr(\{I_1, I_2\}) = \{e, \neg e, \ell, \neg \ell, \neg ab_1\} \quad \text{and} \quad Sk(\{I_1, I_2\}) = \{\neg ab_1\}.$$

---

[1] Note that there is no argument that needs to represent $ab_1 \leftarrow \bot$ in $\mathcal{P}_0$.

So in this example, the credulous belief is inconsistent, whereas the skeptical belief is only the belief that the abnormality predicate ab_1 is false.   ▲

In general, the credulous belief over the complete-WCS, stable-WCS, preferred-WCS, CF2-WCS and SCF2-WCS models of a program $\mathcal{P}$ is inconsistent whenever $\mathcal{P}$ contains an undefined atom. For this reason, in the rest of the paper we will only consider skeptical belief sets over these semantics as potential predictors of human reasoning.

Reasoning skeptically from the set of complete-WCS models is the same as reasoning based on the (grounded-)WCS model. The reason for this is that the grounded extension is the $\subseteq$-least complete extension. As we will see in the next section, reasoning skeptically from the set of stable-WCS, preferred-WCS, CF2-WCS or SCF2-WCS models leads to predictions that in many cases coincide with the predictions of the weak completion semantics, while disagreeing with them in other cases.

5   Discussion on Cognitive Plausibility of New Semantics

In this section we combine theoretical observations and empirical data to compare the cognitive plausibility of the new logic programming semantics introduced in the previous section in contrast to the weak completion semantics. In particular, we provide support to the hypothesis that some of these novel semantics are better models of human reasoning than the weak completion semantics.

In the case of the six programs considered in Sect. 3, skeptical belief over stable-WCS, preferred-WCS, CF2-WCS or SCF2-WCS models corresponds to the (grounded-)WCS model. For a wide a range of programs, such as for the formalization of the second part of the suppression task, that has not be considered in this paper (see [11] for the formalization of these cases as logic programs) and other formalizations under the weak completion semantics (see [18]) this correspondence still seems to holds. Consequently, these semantics would yield the same results as the weak completion semantics, and thus they are also good candidates for being adequate cognitive theories.

5.1   Differences Among the Semantics

The next example shows that skeptical belief over stable-WCS, preferred-WCS, CF2-WCS and SCF2-WCS leads to different predictions than (grounded-)WCS:

Example 41. Consider the following two sentences:

> *If she has an essay to finish, she will study late in the library.*
> *If she does not have an essay to write, she will study late in the library.*

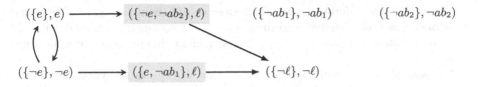

Fig. 3. The argumentation framework $AF_{wc}(\mathcal{P})$ corresponding to $\mathcal{P}_1$.

According to Stenning and van Lambalgen's license for inference approach, they are encoded as $\mathcal{P}_1 = \{\ell \leftarrow e \wedge \neg ab_1, ab_1 \leftarrow \bot, \ell \leftarrow \neg e \wedge \neg ab_2, ab_2 \leftarrow \bot\}$. Figure 3 depicts $AF_{wc}(\mathcal{P}_1)$.[2] The grounded extension of $AF_{wc}(\mathcal{P}_1)$ is

$$E_0 := \{(\{\neg ab_1\}, \neg ab_1), (\{\neg ab_2\}, \neg ab_2)\},$$

so the (grounded-)WCS model of $\mathcal{P}_1$ is $I_0 := \langle \emptyset, \{ab_1, ab_2\}\rangle$. In the stable, preferred, CF2 and SCF2 semantics, there are two extensions, E_1 and E_2:

$$E_1 := \{(\{e\}, e), (\{e, \neg ab_1\}, \ell), (\{\neg ab_1\}, \neg ab_1), (\{\neg ab_2\}, \neg ab_2)\}$$
$$E_2 := \{(\{\neg e\}, \neg e), (\{\neg e, \neg ab_2\}, \ell), (\{\neg ab_1\}, \neg ab_1), (\{\neg ab_2\}, \neg ab_2)\}$$

These two extensions correspond to the two following $\mathcal{P}_1$-interpretations,

$$I_1 := \langle \{e, \ell\}, \{ab_1, ab_2\}\rangle \quad \text{and} \quad I_2 := \langle \{\ell\}, \{e, ab_1, ab_2\}\rangle,$$

both of which are therefore stable-WCS models, preferred-WCS models, CF2-WCS models and SCF2-WCS models. The skeptical belief set over $\{I_1, I_2\}$ is

$$Sk(\{I_1, I_2\}) = \{\ell, \neg ab_1, \neg ab_2\}.$$

So while the (grounded-)WCS model tells us that neither ℓ nor $\neg \ell$ follow from $\mathcal{P}_2$, skeptical reasoning over stable WCS models, preferred-WCS models, CF2-WCS models or SCF2-WCS models tells us that ℓ does follow from $\mathcal{P}$. Note that the complete-WCS models of $\mathcal{P}_1$ are I_0, I_1 and I_2, which are also the models of wc $\mathcal{P}_1$.

Returning to the natural language sentences that we started with, this means that stable-WCS, preferred-WCS, CF2-WCS and SCF2-WC2 allow for the following inference, which (grounded-)WCS does not allow for:

If she has an essay to finish, she will study late in the library. (6)

If she doesn't have an essay to finish, she will study late in the library. (7)

Therefore she will study late in the library. (8)

▲

---

[2] Again, there are no arguments that need to represent $ab_1 \leftarrow \bot$ and $ab_1 \leftarrow \bot$ in $\mathcal{P}_1$.

Given that the inference from Sentence (6) and Sentence (7) to Sentence (8) is one where the different argumentation-WCS semantics considered in this paper make different prediction, we will now look at this inference in a bit more detail.

In classical logic as well as other logics that use the same syntax, e.g. intuitionistic logic or Łukasiewicz logic, the three sentences (6), (7) and (8) would usually be rendered as $e \rightarrow \ell$, as $\neg e \rightarrow \ell$ and as ℓ respectively. In classical logic, the set $\{e \rightarrow \ell, \neg e \rightarrow \ell\}$ entails the formula ℓ, i.e. the inference is deemed valid. One way of explaining the validity of this inference in classical logic is to note that in classical logic, $\{\varphi \vee \psi, \varphi \rightarrow \chi, \psi \rightarrow \chi\}$ entails χ for any formulas φ, ψ and χ, which is a variant of *disjunction elimination*. Furthermore in classical logic $(\varphi \vee \neg\varphi)$ is a tautology for any formula φ, which is called the *law of the excluded middle*. These two principles together ensure that $\{\varphi \rightarrow \chi, \neg\varphi \rightarrow \chi\}$ entails χ for any formulas φ and χ.

In intuitionistic logic and Łukasiewicz logic, $\{e \rightarrow \ell, \neg e \rightarrow \ell\}$ does not entail the formula ℓ, i.e. the inference from Sentence (6) and Sentence (7) to Sentence (8) is not deemed valid. Disjunction elimination still holds in these two logics, but the law of the excluded middle does not hold, so disjunction elimination cannot even be applied when all that is given is $e \rightarrow \ell$ and $\neg e \rightarrow \ell$.

To our knowledge, there have not yet been any empirical studies that test whether humans accept inferences of the form "If φ then χ. If $\neg\varphi$ then χ. Therefore χ." However, we consider it quite plausible that most humans do accept this inference, at least when φ is not instantiated with a vague proposition or with a proposition for which paradoxical information is provided. Indeed, most psychological theories of human reasoning predict that humans accept inferences of this form. Some such theories are based on classical logic, e.g. [32], and make this prediction due to its validity in classical logic or due to it being derivable with a short proof in some psychologically plausible calculus of classical logic like natural deduction, while other psychological theories of human reasoning like mental model theory [23] have been developed with the explicit goal of predicting some outcomes that classical-logic based approaches do not correctly predict, but still accept inferences like the one from (6) and (7) to (8).

Example 41 showed that inferences of the form "If φ then χ. If $\neg\varphi$ then χ. Therefore χ" are accepted by stable-WCS, preferred-WCS, CF2-WCS and SCF2-WCS as long as no additional information about φ and χ is provided. Do these semantics still allow χ to be concluded independently of what additional information is provided about φ and χ? In the case of stable-WCS the answer is yes, because each stable extension contains either the argument $(\neg\varphi, \neg\varphi)$ or an argument of the form $(\mathcal{K}, \varphi)$. In preferred, CF2 and SCF2 semantics, on the other hand, the addition of paradoxical information about φ, e.g. "If $\neg\varphi$ then φ", may lead to a situation where some or all extensions contain neither $(\neg\varphi, \neg\varphi)$ nor an argument of the form $(\mathcal{K}, \varphi)$. In this case, χ may become underivable according to preferred-WCS, CF2-WCS and SCF2-WCS. However this situation only appears when the information provided about φ is paradoxical in the sense of making two-valued reasoning about φ incoherent.

What our analysis of inferences of the form "If φ then χ. If $\neg\varphi$ then χ. Therefore χ" shows is that if future research confirms that such inferences are accepted by humans, this would be a problem for the weak completion semantics as originally defined, but it would not be the end for WCS-like theories of human reasoning, as WCS may be replaceable by closely related semantics such as stable-WCS, preferred-WCS, CF2-WCS and SCF2-WCS that accept such inferences (either unconditionally as in the case of stable-WCS, or in the absence of additional paradoxical information about φ, as in the case of preferred-WCS, CF2-WCS and SCF2-WCS).

5.2   Empirical Studies on Argumentation

Finally we would like to discuss what can be said about the relative cognitive plausibility of the various argumentation-WCS semantics for logic programming based on empirical studies about the cognitive plausibility of argumentation semantics. Three empirical studies [7,8,30] have been conducted to compare the cognitive plausibility of argumentation semantics, each with somewhat different methodology.

- The results of the study by Rahwan et al. [30] suggest that stable, preferred, CF2 and SCF2 predict human judgments about the acceptability of arguments better than grounded and complete semantics. Given that all the AFs used in this study have the same extensions under stable, preferred, CF2 and SCF2 semantics, these four semantics cannot be distinguished by the data of this study.
- The results of the first study by Cramer and Guillaume [7] confirm Rahwan et al.'s results that preferred, CF2 and SCF2 predict human judgments about arguments better than grounded and complete semantics, and additionally suggest that CF2 and SCF2 semantics predict human judgments better than preferred semantics. The study involves AFs that have no stable extensions; the way the predictions of semantics were specified in this study presupposes the existence of at least one extension in each semantics; therefore the stable semantics was discarded as a potential predictor on theoretical grounds.
- The results of the second study by Cramer and Guillaume [8] confirm their first study's results that CF2 and SCF2 are a better predictor of human judgments about arguments than preferred semantics. However, unlike the previous two studies, this study did not find a significant difference between CF2, SCF2, grounded and complete semantics as predictors of human judgments. This was the only study that involved an AF on which CF2 and SCF2 make different predictions, and on that AF the predictions of SCF2 were closer to human judgments than the predictions of CF2; however, this difference was not statistically significant, so further research is required to confirm this potential difference in the predictive capacity of SCF2 and CF2. Just like the previous study be the same authors, the stable semantics was discarded as a potential predictor on theoretical grounds.

While these studies give us valuable insight about the relative cognitive plausibility of argumentation semantics, one needs to be careful when transferring these results to the application of argumentation-WCS semantics to conditional reasoning that we have developed here. The studies cited above made the connection between natural language information and argumentation frameworks in ways that significantly differ from the connection that we used in this paper, i.e. the connection based on Stenning and van Lambalgen's license for inference approach and on the translation function AF_{wc}. In particular, two of the three existing studies completely excluded stable semantics, because it did not make meaningful predictions for the scenarios they considered, whereas stable-WCS does make meaningful predictions when modeling the suppression task. So further empirical work is required to make empirically well-founded claims about the relative cognitive plausibility of the various newly presented argumentation-WCS semantics here.

6   Conclusion

In this paper we have established a novel connection between logic programming and abstract argumentation by defining a translation function under which the grounded semantics of abstract argumentation corresponds to the weak completion semantics of logic programming, which has been shown to be a good model of human reasoning for various logical reasoning tasks. We make use of this connection to define various novel logic programming semantics that closely resemble the weak completion semantics, but that also exhibit some crucial differences. We have discussed the properties of these novel semantics from the point of view of their potential role as models of human reasoning, highlighting that more empirical research is required to establish which of these semantics can predict human reasoning best.

Acknowledgements. We would like to thank Christian Straßer for proposing a shorter proof of Theorem 34 (see appendix) that additionally has the advantage of establishing a useful correspondence between the weak completion semantics and the Kripke Kleene semantics.

A   Proof of Theorem 34

As mentioned in the Acknowledgements, the proof we present is based on a proof presented by Christian Straßer. It derives Theorem 34 from Theorem 30 with the help of Lemma 43, which establishes a correspondence between the weak completion semantics and the Kripke Kleene semantics.

Definition 42. *Given a program* $\mathcal{P}$, *define* $\mathcal{P}_{\mathsf{id}} := \mathcal{P} \cup \{A \leftarrow A \mid A \in \mathsf{undef}(\mathcal{P})\}$.

Lemma 43. *The WCS model of a program* $\mathcal{P}$ *is the KK-model of* $\mathcal{P}_{\mathsf{id}}$.

Proof. We prove this result by inductively proving that $\Phi^i_{\mathcal{P}}(\langle\emptyset,\emptyset\rangle) = \Psi^i_{\mathcal{P}_{\mathsf{id}}}(\langle\emptyset,\emptyset\rangle)$ for any $i \geq 1$ and any program $\mathcal{P}$ (where $\Phi^i_{\mathcal{P}}$ respectively $\Psi^i_{\mathcal{P}}$ denotes the ith iteration of the function based on a program $\mathcal{P}$). In the proof, we will sometimes make use of the following observation:

$(\star)$ If $A \notin \mathsf{undef}(A)$, $A \leftarrow body \in \mathcal{P}$ iff $A \leftarrow body \in \mathcal{P}_{\mathsf{id}}$.

Let $\langle J_i^\top, J_i^\perp \rangle = \Psi^i_{\mathcal{P}_{\mathsf{id}}}(\langle\emptyset,\emptyset\rangle)$ and $\langle K_i^\top, K_i^\perp \rangle = \Phi^i_{\mathcal{P}}(\langle\emptyset,\emptyset\rangle)$. We now show inductively that (i) $J_i^\top = K_i^\top$ and (ii) $J_i^\perp = K_i^\perp$.

We make use of a somewhat unusual variant of proof by induction in which both $i = 0$ and $i = 1$ are first established as separate base cases, and the induction step is from $i - 1$ and i to $i + 1$ for any $i > 0$.

First base case: $i = 0$. In this case, $J_i^\top = \emptyset = K_i^\top$ and $J_i^\perp = \emptyset = K_i^\perp$.

Second base case: $i = 1$. We discuss each point separately. Let $I = \langle\emptyset,\emptyset\rangle$.

Ad (i). Suppose $A \in J_1^\top$. Thus, there is a $A \leftarrow body \in \mathcal{P}_{\mathsf{id}}$ such that $I(body) = \top$. Since $I = \langle\emptyset,\emptyset\rangle$, $body$ is $\top$. In view of the definition of $\mathcal{P}_{\mathsf{id}}$, $A \leftarrow \top \in \mathcal{P} \cap \mathcal{P}_{\mathsf{id}}$ and so $A \in K_1^\top$. $K_1^\top \subseteq J_1^\top$ holds since $\mathcal{P} \subseteq \mathcal{P}_{\mathsf{id}}$.

Ad (ii). Suppose $A \in K_1^\perp$. Thus, $A \notin \mathsf{undef}(\mathcal{P})$ and for all $A \leftarrow body \in \mathcal{P}$, $I(body) = \perp$. By $(\star)$, for all $A \leftarrow body \in \mathcal{P}_{\mathsf{id}}$, $I(body) = \perp$ and hence $A \in J_1^\perp$.

Suppose now that $A \in J_1^\perp$. So, for all $A \leftarrow body \in \mathcal{P}_{\mathsf{id}}$, $I(body) = \perp$. Note that $A \notin \mathsf{undef}(\mathcal{P})$ since otherwise $I(A) = \perp$ which is impossible since $I = \langle\emptyset,\emptyset\rangle$. Since $\mathcal{P} \subseteq \mathcal{P}_{\mathsf{id}}$, $A \in K_1^\perp$.

Induction step: $i - 1, i \Rightarrow i + 1$ for any $i > 0$. Our inductive hypothesis is that $J_{i-1}^\top = K_{i-1}^\top$, $J_{i-1}^\perp = K_{i-1}^\perp$, $J_i^\top = K_i^\top$ and $J_i^\perp = K_i^\perp$. We again discuss (i) and (ii) separately. Let $I_i = \langle I_i^\top, I_i^\perp \rangle$ where $I_i^\top = J_i^\top = K_i^\top$ and $I_i^\perp = J_i^\perp = K_i^\perp$. Similarly for I_{i-1}.

Ad (i). Suppose $A \in K_{i+1}^\top$. Thus, there is a $A \leftarrow body \in \mathcal{P}$ for which $I_i(body) = \top$. Since $\mathcal{P} \subseteq \mathcal{P}_{\mathsf{id}}$, $A \leftarrow body \in \mathcal{P}_{\mathsf{id}}$. Thus, $A \in J_{i+1}^\top$.

For the other direction assume $A \in J_{i+1}^\top$. Thus, there is a $A \leftarrow body \in \mathcal{P}_{\mathsf{id}}$ for which $I_i(body) = \top$. Assume for a contradiction that $A \in \mathsf{undef}(\mathcal{P})$. Thus, $body = A$ and $A \in I_i^\top = K_i^\top$. Thus, there is a $A \leftarrow body' \in \mathcal{P}$ for which $I_{i-1}(body') = \top$. This contradicts $A \in \mathsf{undef}(\mathcal{P})$. So $A \notin \mathsf{undef}(\mathcal{P})$ and therefore $A \leftarrow body \in \mathcal{P}$. Thus, $A \in K_{i+1}^\top$.

Ad (ii). Suppose $A \in K_{i+1}^\perp$. Thus, $A \notin \mathsf{undef}(\mathcal{P})$ and for all $A \leftarrow body(\mathcal{P})$, $I_i(body) = \perp$. By $(\star)$, for all $A \leftarrow body \in \mathcal{P}_{\mathsf{id}}$, $I_i(body) = \perp$. Thus, $A \in J_{i+1}^\perp$.

Suppose now that $A \in J_{i+1}^\perp$. Thus, (†) for all $A \leftarrow body \in \mathcal{P}_{\mathsf{id}}$, $I_i(body) = \perp$. Assume for a contradiction that $A \in \mathsf{undef}(\mathcal{P})$. Then, since $A \leftarrow A \in \mathcal{P}_{\mathsf{id}}$, $I_i(A) = \perp$ and so $A \in I_i^\perp = K_i^\perp$. Since for all $B \in K_i^\perp (= \{C \mid C \notin \mathsf{undef}(\mathcal{P})$ and for all $C \leftarrow body \in \mathcal{P}, I_{i-1}(body) = \perp\})$, $B \notin \mathsf{undef}(\mathcal{P})$, this is a contradiction. So, $A \notin \mathsf{undef}(\mathcal{P})$ and by $(\star)$ and (†), for all $A \leftarrow body \in \mathcal{P}$, $I_i(body) = \perp$. Thus, $A \in K_{i+1}^\perp$. □

References

1. Baroni, P., Caminada, M., Giacomin, M.: Abstract argumentation frameworks and their semantics. In: Baroni, P., Gabbay, D., Giacomin, M., van der Torre, L. (eds.) Handbook of Formal Argumentation, pp. 159–236. College Publications, London (2018)
2. Baroni, P., Giacomin, M., Guida, G.: SCC-recursiveness: a general schema for argumentation semantics. Artif. Intell. **168**(1), 162–210 (2005)
3. Byrne, R.M.J.: Suppressing valid inferences with conditionals. Cognition **31**, 61–83 (1989)
4. Caminada, M., Sá, S., Alcântara, J., Dvořák, W.: On the equivalence between logic programming semantics and argumentation semantics. Int. J. Approx. Reason. **58**, 87–111 (2015)
5. Clark, K.L.: Negation as failure. In: Gallaire, H., Minker, J. (eds.) Logic and Data Bases, vol. 1, pp. 293–322. Plenum Press, New York (1978)
6. Costa, A., Dietz Saldanha, E.A., Hölldobler, S., Ragni, M.: A computational logic approach to human syllogistic reasoning. In: Gunzelmann, G., Howes, A., Tenbrink, T., Davelaar, E. (eds.) Proceedings of 39th Conference of Cognitive Science Society, pp. 883–888. Cognitive Science Society, Austin (2017)
7. Cramer, M., Guillaume, M.: Empirical cognitive study on abstract argumentation semantics. In: Computational Models of Argument - Proceedings of COMMA, pp. 413–424 (2018)
8. Cramer, M., Guillaume, M.: Empirical study on human evaluation of complex argumentation frameworks. In: Calimeri, F., Leone, N., Manna, M. (eds.) JELIA 2019. LNCS (LNAI), vol. 11468, pp. 102–115. Springer, Cham (2019). https://doi.org/10.1007/978-3-030-19570-0_7
9. Cramer, M., van der Torre, L.: SCF2 - an argumentation semantics for rational human judgments on argument acceptability. In: Proceedings of the 8th Workshop on Dynamics of Knowledge and Belief (DKB 2019) and the 7th Workshop KI & Kognition (KIK 2019), pp. 24–35 (2019)
10. Dietz, E.-A.: A computational logic approach to the belief bias in human syllogistic reasoning. In: Brézillon, P., Turner, R., Penco, C. (eds.) CONTEXT 2017. LNCS (LNAI), vol. 10257, pp. 691–707. Springer, Cham (2017). https://doi.org/10.1007/978-3-319-57837-8_55
11. Dietz, E.A., Hölldobler, S., Ragni, M.: A computational logic approach to the suppression task. In: Miyake, N., Peebles, D., Cooper, R.P. (eds.) Proceedings of the 34th Annual Conference of the Cognitive Science Society (COGSCI), pp. 1500–1505. Cognitive Science Society (2012)
12. Dietz, E.A., Hölldobler, S., Wernhard, C.: Modeling the suppression task under weak completion and well-founded semantics. J. Appl. Non Class. Log. (JANCL) **24**(1–2), 61–85 (2014)
13. Dung, P.M.: On the acceptability of arguments and its fundamental role in non-monotonic reasoning, logic programming and n-person games. Artif. Intell. **77**(2), 321–357 (1995)
14. Dvořák, W., Gaggl, S.A.: Stage semantics and the SCC-recursive schema for argumentation semantics. J. Log. Comput. **26**(4), 1149–1202 (2016)
15. Fitting, M.: A Kripke-Kleene semantics for logic programs. J. Log. Program. **2**(4), 295–312 (1985)

16. Gelfond, M., Lifschitz, V.: The stable model semantics for logic programming. In: Kowalski, R., Bowen, K.A. (eds.) Proceedings of the International Logic Programming Conference and Symposium, (ICLP/SLP), pp. 1070–1080. MIT Press, Cambridge (1988)
17. Hölldobler, S.: Logik und Logikprogrammierung 1: Grundlagen. Kolleg Synchron, Synchron (2009)
18. Hölldobler, S.: Weak completion semantics and its applications in human reasoning. In: Furbach, U., Schon, C. (eds.) Proceedings of the 1st Workshop on Bridging the Gap Between Human and Automated Reasoning (Bridging 2015), CEUR Workshop Proceedings, pp. 2–16 (2015). CEUR-WS.org
19. Hölldobler, S., Kencana Ramli, C.D.P.: Logic programs under three-valued Łukasiewicz semantics. In: Hill, P.M., Warren, D.S. (eds.) ICLP 2009. LNCS, vol. 5649, pp. 464–478. Springer, Heidelberg (2009). https://doi.org/10.1007/978-3-642-02846-5_37
20. Hölldobler, S., Kencana Ramli, C.D.P.: Logics and networks for human reasoning. In: Alippi, C., Polycarpou, M., Panayiotou, C., Ellinas, G. (eds.) ICANN 2009. LNCS, vol. 5769, pp. 85–94. Springer, Heidelberg (2009). https://doi.org/10.1007/978-3-642-04277-5_9
21. Hölldobler, S., Kencana Ramli, C.D.P.: Contraction properties of a semantic operator for human reasoning. In: Li, L., Yen, K.K. (eds.) Proceedings of the Fifth International Conference on Information, pp. 228–231 (2009)
22. Hölldobler, S., Philipp, T., Wernhard, C.: An abductive model for human reasoning. In: Logical Formalizations of Commonsense Reasoning. AAAI Spring Symposium Series Technical Reports, pp. 135–138. AAAI Press, Cambridge (2011)
23. Johnson-Laird, P., Khemlani, S.S.: Toward a unified theory of reasoning. Psychol. Learn. Motiv. **59**, 1–42 (2013)
24. Kakas, A.C., Kowalski, R.A., Toni, F.: Abductive logic programming. J. Log. Comput. **2**(6), 719–770 (1993)
25. Lloyd, J.W.: Foundations of Logic Programming. Springer, New York (1984). https://doi.org/10.1007/978-3-642-96826-6
26. Łukasiewicz, J.: O logice trójwartościowej. Ruch Filozoficzny **5**, 169–171 (1920). English translation: On three-valued logic. In: Łukasiewicz, J., Borkowski, L. (eds.) Selected Works, Amsterdam, North Holland, pp. 87–88 (1990)
27. Mercier, H., Sperber, D.: Why do humans reason? Arguments for an argumentative theory. Behav. Brain Sci. **34**(2), 57–74 (2011)
28. Oaksford, M., Chater, N.: New paradigms in the psychology of reasoning. Annu. Rev. Psychol. **71**(1), 305–330 (2020)
29. Przymusinski, T.C.: Well-founded semantics coincides with three-valued stable semantics. Fundamenta Informaticae **13**(4), 445–463 (1990)
30. Rahwan, I., Madakkatel, M.I., Bonnefon, J.F., Awan, R.N., Abdallah, S.: Behavioral experiments for assessing the abstract argumentation semantics of reinstatement. Cogn. Sci. **34**(8), 1483–1502 (2010)
31. Rescher, N.: Many-Valued Logic. McGraw-Hill, New York (1969)
32. Rips, L.J.: The Psychology of Proof: Deductive Reasoning in Human Thinking. MIT Press, Cambridge (1994)
33. Stenning, K., van Lambalgen, M.: Human Reasoning and Cognitive Science. A Bradford Book. MIT Press, Cambridge (2008)
34. Van Gelder, A., Ross, K.A., Schlipf, J.S.: The well-founded semantics for general logic programs. J. ACM **38**(3), 619–649 (1991)

Reasoning About Degrees of Confirmation

Šejla Dautović[1], Dragan Doder[2(✉)], and Zoran Ognjanović[1]

[1] Matematički Institut SANU, Belgrade, Serbia
shdautovic@mi.sanu.ac.rs
[2] Utrecht University, Utrecht, The Netherlands
d.doder@uu.nl

Abstract. We present a probabilistic logic for reasoning about degrees of confirmation. We provide a sound and strongly complete axiomatization for the logic. We show that the problem of deciding satisfiability is in PSPACE.

Keywords: Probabilistic logic · Measure of confirmation · Completeness theorem · Decidability

1 Introduction

In the last several decades, different tools are developed for representing and reasoning with uncertain knowledge, including probability as a dominant representation of uncertainty. One particular line of research concerns the formalization in terms of probabilistic logic. The modern development in this field started with Keisler's seminal work on probabilistic quantifiers [21]. After Nilsson [23] gave a procedure for probabilistic entailment which, given probabilities of premises, calculates bounds on the probabilities of the conclusion, researchers from the areas of logic, computer science and artificial intelligence started investigations about formal systems for probabilistic reasoning and provided several languages, axiomatizations and decision procedures for various probabilistic logics [3,10,12,13,15–19,24,25]. Those logics extend the classical (propositional or first order) calculus with expressions that speak about probability, while formulas remain true or false. They allow one to formalize statements of the form "the probability of α is at least a half." The corresponding probability operators behave like modal operators and the corresponding semantics consists of special types of Kripke models, with indistinguishability relations replaced with probability measures defined over the worlds.

This paper contributes to the field by proposing a logical formalization of the Bayesian measure of confirmation (or evidential support). Although contemporary Bayesian confirmation theorists investigated degrees of confirmation developing a variety of different probability-based measures, that field attracted little attention from the logical side, probably because of complexity of a potential formal language that would be adequate to capture those measures. In Carnap's book [2], one of the main tasks is "the explication of certain concepts

M. Dastani et al. (Eds.): CLAR 2020, LNAI 12061, pp. 80–95, 2020.
https://doi.org/10.1007/978-3-030-44638-3_5

which are connected with the scientific procedure of confirming or disconfirming hypotheses with the help of observations and which we therefore will briefly call *concepts of confirmation*". Carnap distinguished three different semantical concepts of confirmation: the classificatory concept ("a hypothesis A is confirmed by an evidence B"), the comparative concept ("A is confirmed by B at least as strongly as C is confirmed by D") and the quantitative concept of confirmation. The third one, one of the basic concept of inductive logic, is formalized by a numerical function c which maps pairs of sentences to the reals, where $c(A, B)$ is the *degree of confirmation* of the hypothesis A on the basis of the evidence B.

Bayesian epistemology proposes various candidate functions for measuring the degree of confirmation $c(A, B)$, defined in terms of subjective probability. They all agree in the following qualitative way: $c(A, B) > 0$ iff the posterior probability of A on the evidence B is greater than the prior probability of A (i.e., $\mu(A|B) > \mu(A)$), which correspond to the classificatory concept ("A is confirmed by B") [14]. Up to now, only the classificatory concept of confirmation is logically formalized, in our previous work [6].

In this paper, we formalize the quantitative concept of confirmation. We focus on the most standard[1] measure of degree of confirmation, called *difference* measure:

$$c(A, B) = \mu(A|B) - \mu(A).$$

Our formal language extends propositional logic with the unary probabilistic operators of the form $P_{\geq r}$ ($P_{\geq r}\alpha$ reads "the probability of α is at least r"), where r ranges over the set of rational numbers from the unit interval [24], and the binary operators $c_{\geq r}$ and $c_{\leq r}$, which we semantically interpret using the difference measure. The corresponding semantics consists of special types of Kripke models , with probability measures defined over the worlds.

Our main result is a sound and strongly complete (every consistent set of formulas is satisfiable) axiomatization for the logic. We prove completeness using a modification of Henkin's construction. Since the logic is not compact, in order to obtain strong variant of completeness, we use infinitary inference rules. From the technical point of view, we modify some of our earlier developed methods presented in [4,5,7–9,22,26,27,29]. We point out that our languages are countable and formulas are finite, while only proofs are allowed to be infinite. We also prove that our logic is decidable and we present complexity results.

Many measures on confirmation have been proposed over years. We point out that it was not our intention to take sides. We simply chose the difference measure because of its popularity. However, we discuss in Sect. 7 that our axiomatization technique can be easily modified to incorporate other measures of confirmation.

The contents of this paper are as follows. In Sect. 2 we recall the basic notions of probability. In Sect. 3 we present the syntax and semantics of our logic and defined the satisfaction relation. In Sect. 4 we propose an axiomatization for the logic, and we prove its soundness. In Sect. 5 we prove that the axiomatization is strongly complete with respect to the proposed semantics.

---

[1] According to Eells and Fitelson [11].

In Sect. 6 we present complexity results for the problem of deciding satisfiability. We conclude in Sect. 7.

2   Preliminaries

Let us introduce some basic probabilistic notions that will be use in this paper.

For a nonempty set $W \neq \emptyset$, we say that $H \subseteq 2^W$ is an *algebra of subsets* of W, if the following conditions hold:

1. $W \in H$,
2. if $A \in H$, then $W \setminus A \in H$, and
3. if $A, B \in H$, then $A \cup B \in H$.

For a given algebra H of subsets of W, a function $\mu : H \longrightarrow [0,1]$ is a *finitely additive probability measure*, if it satisfies the following properties:

1. $\mu(W) = 1$,
2. $\mu(A \cup B) = \mu(A) + \mu(B)$, whenever $A \cap B = \emptyset$.

For W, H and μ described above, the triple $\langle W, H, \mu \rangle$ is called a finitely additive *probability space*. The elements of H are called *measurable sets*.

For a probability measure μ, conditional probability is defined in the following way:

$$\mu(A|B) = \begin{cases} \frac{\mu(A \cap B)}{\mu(B)}, & \mu(B) > 0 \\ \text{undefined}, & \mu(B) = 0. \end{cases}$$

Note that, as a consequence of this definition, the difference measure $c(A, B) = \mu(A|B) - \mu(A)$ is also not defined when $\mu(B) = 0$.

3   The Logic LPP$_2^{\text{conf}}$: Syntax and Semantics

In this section we introduce the set of formulas of the logic LPP$_2^{\text{conf}}$, and the class of semantical structures in which those formulas evaluated.

3.1   Syntax

Let $\mathcal{P} = \{p, q, r, \dots\}$ be a denumerable set of propositional letters. For given rational numbers a and b such that $a < b$, let $[a, b]_Q$ denotes the set $[a, b] \cap Q$. The language of the logic LPP$_2^{\text{conf}}$ consists of

- the elements of set $\mathcal{P}$,
- classical propositional connectives $\neg$ and $\wedge$,
- the list of unary probability operators of the form $P_{\geq r}$, for every $r \in [0, 1]_Q$,
- the list of binary probability operators of the form $c_{\geq r}$, for every $r \in [-1, 1]_Q$, and
- the list of binary probability operators of the form $c_{\leq r}$, for every $r \in [-1, 1]_Q$.

Note that we use conjunction and negation as primitive connectives. The other propositional connectives, $\vee$, $\rightarrow$ and $\leftrightarrow$, are introduced as abbreviations, in the usual way.

The introduced language is used to define two types of formulas of $\text{LPP}_2^{\text{conf}}$. First, we have the set of classical propositional formulas over $\mathcal{P}$, denoted here by For_C. We will denote the propositional formulas by α, β and γ, possibly with subscripts. We denote the satisfiability relation of the classical propositional logic by $\models_C$. Now we define the second type of formulas.

Definition 1 (Probabilistic formula). *A basic probabilistic formula is any formula of the form:* $P_{\geq r}\alpha$ $c_{\geq r}(\alpha, \beta)$, $c_{\leq r}(\alpha, \beta)$, *where* $\alpha, \beta \in For_C$.

A probabilistic formula *is a Boolean combination of basic probabilistic formulas. We denote with For_P the set of all probabilistic formulas and denote arbitrary probabilistic formulas by ϕ and ψ, possibly with subscripts.*

Intuitively, $P_{\geq r}\alpha$ means that the probability that α is true is greater or equal to r, while $c_{\geq r}(\alpha, \beta)$ $(c_{\leq r}(\alpha, \beta))$ means that the formula β confirms the formula α with the degree at least r (at most r, respectively).

Example 1. The meaning of the formula

$$c_{\geq\frac{1}{2}}(\alpha, \beta) \rightarrow c_{\leq 0}(\neg\alpha, \beta)$$

is that if β confirms α to the degree $\frac{1}{2}$, then the degree that β confirms the negation of α is less or equal to zero.

The other types of probabilistic operators are usually defined as follows: $P_{<s}\alpha$ is $\neg P_{\geq s}\alpha$, $P_{\leq s}\alpha$ is $P_{\geq 1-s}\neg\alpha$, $P_{>s}\alpha$ is $\neg P_{\leq s}\alpha$, and $P_{=s}\alpha$ is $P_{\geq s}\alpha \wedge P_{\leq s}\alpha$. We use the following abbreviations to introduce other types of confirmation operators:

- $c_{=}(\alpha, \beta)$ is $c_{\geq}(\alpha, \beta) \wedge c_{\leq}(\alpha, \beta)$,
- $c_{>}(\alpha, \beta)$ is $c_{\geq}(\alpha, \beta) \wedge \neg c_{\leq}(\alpha, \beta)$ and
- $c_{<}(\alpha, \beta)$ is $c_{\leq}(\alpha, \beta) \wedge \neg c_{\geq}(\alpha, \beta)$.

Also, we denote both $\alpha \wedge \neg\alpha$ and $\phi \wedge \neg\phi$ by $\bot$ (and similarly for $\top$), letting the context determine the meaning.

One might think that $c_{<}(\alpha, \beta)$ might be defined simply as $\neg c_{\geq}(\alpha, \beta)$, in an analogous way as $P_{<s}$ is introduced. However, we will see that this does not hold under our satisfiability relation.

By a formula of $\text{LPP}_2^{\text{conf}}$ we mean either a classical of probabilistic formula.

Definition 2 (Formula of $\text{LPP}_2^{\text{conf}}$). *The set of formulas of $\text{LPP}_2^{\text{conf}}$ is*

$$For_{\text{LPP}_2^{\text{conf}}} = For_C \cup For_P.$$

We denote arbitrary formulas by ρ and σ (possibly with subscripts).

Thus, no mixing of pure propositional formulas and probability formulas is allowed.

Example 2. The expression

$$(\beta \rightarrow \alpha) \rightarrow c_{\geq 0}(\alpha, \beta)$$

is not a formula of the logic $\text{LPP}_2^{\text{conf}}$.

3.2   Semantics of LPP$_2^{\text{conf}}$

Now we define the structures in which we evaluate the formulas from $For_{\text{LPP}_2^{\text{conf}}}$.

Definition 3 (LPP$_2^{\text{conf}}$-**structure**). *An* LPP$_2^{\text{conf}}$-*structure is tuple* (W, H, μ, v)
where:

1. W *is a non- empty set of objects called* worlds.
2. $v : W \times \mathcal{P} \to \{true, false\}$ *assigns to each world* $w \in W$ *a two-valued evaluation* $v(w, \cdot)$ *of the propositional letters; it is then extended to all elements of* For_C *in the usual way.*
3. H *is an algebra of subsets of* W, *such that*

$$\{w \in W \mid v(w, \alpha) = true\} \in H,$$

   for every formula $\alpha \in For_{\text{LPP}_2^{\text{conf}}}$.
4. $\mu : H \longrightarrow [0, 1]$ *is a finitely additive measure.*

We denote with $\mathcal{M}(\text{LPP}_2^{\text{conf}})$ *the class of all* LPP$_2^{\text{conf}}$-*structures.*

Note that, according to Definition 3, the set of all worlds of an LPP$_2^{\text{conf}}$-structure M in which a classical propositional formula α has the values *true* is a measurable set. This requirement is crucial to ensure correctness of satisfiability relation. In order to relax the notation, we denote the mentioned set of worlds, $\{w \in W \mid v(w, \alpha) = true\}$, simply by $[\alpha]_M$. Thus, $[\alpha]_M \in H$ for every $M \in \mathcal{M}(\text{LPP}_2^{\text{conf}})$ and every $\alpha \in For_C$. Also, we write $[\alpha]$ instead of $[\alpha]_M$ when M is clear from the context.

Next we define the satisfiability of a formula in an LPP$_2^{\text{conf}}$-structure.

Definition 4 (Satisfiability). *Let* $M \in \mathcal{M}(\text{LPP}_2^{\text{conf}})$. *The* satisfiability relation $\models$ *is defined recursively as follows:*

1. $M \models \alpha$ *iff* $v(w, \alpha) = true$ *for every* $w \in W$,
2. $M \models P_{\geq r}\alpha$ *if* $\mu([\alpha]) \geq r$,
3. $M \models c_{\geq r}(\alpha, \beta)$ *if* $\mu([\beta]) > 0$ *and* $\mu([\alpha]|[\beta]) - \mu([\alpha]) \geq r$,
4. $M \models c_{\leq r}(\alpha, \beta)$ *if* $\mu([\beta]) > 0$ *and* $\mu([\alpha]|[\beta]) - \mu([\alpha]) \leq r$,
5. $M \models \neg\phi$ *iff* $M \not\models \phi$,
6. $M \models \phi \wedge \psi$ *iff* $M \models \phi$ *and* $M \models \psi$.

According to Definition 4, a classical formula α holds in an LPP$_2^{\text{conf}}$-structure M only if it holds in every world of M, and therefore represent certain information. In that case, the probability value of $[\alpha]_M$ has to be equal to 1, which will be ensured in the axiomatization by a variant of Necessitation rule.

Using Definition 4 and properties of reals, it is easy to obtain satisfiability for the other types of operators. For example,

$$M \models c_{<r}(\alpha, \beta) \text{ if } \mu([\beta]) > 0 \text{ and } \mu([\alpha]|[\beta]) - \mu([\alpha]) < r$$

holds. Now it is obvious that the operator $c_<$ is not equivalent to "negation of $c_\geq$," i.e., $M \not\models c_{\geq r}(\alpha, \beta)$ does not imply $M \models c_{<r}(\alpha, \beta)$, the reason is that $c([\alpha], [\beta])$ might simply be undefined in M (if $\mu([\beta]) = 0$).

At the end of this section, we define some basic semantical notions.

Definition 5 (Model). *For an $M \in \mathcal{M}(\mathrm{LPP}_2^{\mathrm{conf}})$ and a set of formulas T, we say that M is a* model *of T and write $M \models T$ iff $M \models \rho$ for every $\rho \in T$. T is* satisfiable, *if there is $M \in \mathcal{M}(\mathrm{LPP}_2^{\mathrm{conf}})$ such that $M \models T$.*

Now we define the notion of entailment relation between formulas.

Definition 6 (Entailment). *We say that a set of formulas T* entails *a formula ρ and write $T \models \rho$, if all models of T are models of ρ. Furthermore, ρ is* valid *if $\emptyset \models \rho$.*

4   Axiomatization of $\mathrm{LPP}_2^{\mathrm{conf}}$

In this section we present an axiomatization of our logic, which we denote $Ax(\mathrm{LPP}_2^{\mathrm{conf}})$. The axiom system $Ax(\mathrm{LPP}_2^{\mathrm{conf}})$ contains ten axiom schemes and five inference rules. In the following axiomatization, we assume that all the formulas respect Definition 1. For example, we consider only those instances of A9 and A10 for which $s(r + t) \leq 1$.

Axiom schemes:

(A1) All instances of classical propositional tautologies for both For_C and For_P.
(A2) $P_{\geq 0}\alpha$
(A3) $P_{\leqslant r}\alpha \rightarrow P_{<s}\alpha$ whenever $r < s$
(A4) $P_{<r}\alpha \rightarrow P_{\leqslant r}\alpha$
(A5) $(P_{\geqslant r}\alpha \wedge P_{\geqslant s}\beta \wedge P_{\geqslant 1}(\neg\alpha \vee \neg\beta)) \rightarrow P_{\geqslant r+s}(\alpha \vee \beta)$
(A6) $(P_{\leqslant r}\alpha \wedge P_{<s}\beta) \rightarrow P_{<r+s}(\alpha \vee \beta)$
(A7) $c_{\geq r}(\alpha, \beta) \rightarrow P_{>0}\beta$
(A8) $c_{\leq r}(\alpha, \beta) \rightarrow P_{>0}\beta$
(A9) $(P_{\geq t}\alpha \wedge P_{\geq s}\beta \wedge c_{\geq r}(\alpha, \beta)) \rightarrow P_{\geq s(r+t)}(\alpha \wedge \beta)$
(A10) $(P_{\leq t}\alpha \wedge P_{\leq s}\beta \wedge c_{\leq r}(\alpha, \beta)) \rightarrow P_{\leq s(r+t)}(\alpha \wedge \beta)$

Inference rules:

(R1) From $\{\rho, \rho \rightarrow \sigma\}$ infer σ
(R2) From α infer $P_{\geq 1}\alpha$.
(R3) From the set of premises $\{\phi \rightarrow P_{\geq r - \frac{1}{k}}\alpha \mid k \in \mathbb{N}, k \geq \frac{1}{r}\}$ infer $\phi \rightarrow P_{\geq r}\alpha$.
(R4) From the set of premises

$$\{\phi \rightarrow P_{>0}\beta\} \cup \{\phi \rightarrow ((P_{\geq t}\alpha \wedge P_{\geq s}\beta) \rightarrow P_{\geq s(r+t)}(\alpha \wedge \beta)) | t, s \in [0,1]_Q\}$$

infer $\phi \rightarrow c_{\geq r}(\alpha, \beta)$.

(R5) From the set of premises

$$\{\phi \to P_{>0}\beta\} \cup \{\phi \to ((P_{\leq t}\alpha \land P_{\leq s}\beta) \to P_{\leq s(r+t)}(\alpha \land \beta)) \mid t, s \in [0,1]_Q\}$$

infer $\phi \to c_{\leq r}(\alpha, \beta)$.

Let us briefly comment on the axiomatization $Ax(\text{LPP}_2^{\text{conf}})$. The axioms A1–A6 and the inference rules R1–R3 form the axiom system for the logic LPP_2 from [24]. The rule R3 is the so-called Archimedean rule. It ensures that the ranges of probability measures do not take non-standard values (in the sense of non-standard analysis). Intuitively, it claims that if probability is approximately close to r, then it must be r. The axioms A7 and A9, together with the rule R4 properly capture the third condition of Definition 4. Similarly, A8, A10 and R5 properly capture the fourth condition of Definition 4.

The rules R3-R5 are infinitary inference rules. The necessity of employing such rules comes form the non-compactness phenomena. Indeed, it is known that in real-valued probabilistic logic there exist inconsistent infinite sets of formulas, such that every finite subset is consistent. As pointed out in [20], one consequence of that fact is that any finitary axiomatization would not be strongly complete.

Let us now define some basic notions of proof theory.

Definition 7 (Proof, theorem). *Let* $T \subseteq For_{\text{LPP}_2^{\text{conf}}}$ *be a set of formulas. We write* $T \vdash_{Ax(\text{LPP}_2^{\text{conf}})} \rho$, *and we say that* ρ *is* deducible *from* T, *if there is an at most countable sequence of formulas* $\rho_0, \rho_1, ..., \rho_n$, *such that every* ρ_i *is an axiom or a formula from* T, *or it is derived from the preceding formulas by an inference rule. The sequence* $\rho_0, \rho_1, ..., \rho$ *is a* proof *of* ρ *from* T. *We write* $\vdash$ *instead of* $\vdash_{Ax_{\text{LPP}_2^{\text{conf}}}}$ *when it is clear from context.*

We say that ρ *is a* theorem *of* $Ax(\text{LPP}_2^{\text{conf}})$, *and write* $\vdash \rho$, *if* $\emptyset \vdash \rho$.

Note that the length of a proof might be any countable successor ordinal.

Definition 8 (Consistency). *A set of formulas* T *is* inconsistent *if there a formula* $\phi \in For_P$ *such that* $T \vdash \phi \land \neg\phi$, *otherwise it is* consistent.

T is maximally consistent set *(mcs) if it is consistent and every proper super-set of* T *is inconsistent.*

At the end of this section, we show that the axiom system $Ax(\text{LPP}_2^{\text{conf}})$ is sound.

Theorem 1 (Soundness). *The axiomatization* $Ax(\text{LPP}_2^{\text{conf}})$ *is sound with respect to the class of structures* $\mathcal{M}(\text{LPP}_2^{\text{conf}})$.

Proof. We need to show that every instance of an axiom scheme holds in every structure, and that the inference rules preserve the validity. Let us consider the axioms A7 and A9 and the rule R4. For A7, assume that $M \in \mathcal{M}(\text{LPP}_2^{\text{conf}})$ is a structure such that $M \models c_{\geq r}(\alpha, \beta)$, then $\mu([\beta]) > 0$, so $M \models P_{>0}\beta$. Now let us consider A9. Suppose that $M \models (P_{\geq t}\alpha \land P_{\geq s}\beta) \land c_{\geq r}(\alpha, \beta)$. Then $\mu([\alpha]) \geq t$,

$\mu([\beta]) \geq s$, $\mu([\beta]) \geq 0$ and $\mu([\alpha]|[\beta]) - \mu([\alpha]) \geq r$ i.e., $\mu([\alpha \wedge \beta]) \geq \mu([\beta])(r + \mu([\alpha]))$. This means that $\mu([\alpha \wedge \beta]) \geq s(r + t)$. Therefore, $M \models P_{\geq s(r+t)}(\alpha \wedge \beta)$.

Now let us consider R4. In order to show that it preserves validity, assume that $M \models \{\phi \rightarrow P_{>0}\beta\} \cup \{\phi \rightarrow ((P_{\geq t}\alpha \wedge P_{\geq s}\beta) \rightarrow P_{\geq s(r+t)}(\alpha \wedge \beta)) \mid t, s \in [0,1]_Q\}$. If $M \not\models \phi$, we have $M \models \phi \rightarrow c_{\geq r}(\alpha, \beta)$. Now suppose that $M \models \phi$. Then $M \models P_{>0}\beta$, i.e $\mu([\beta]) > 0$, and $M \models (P_{\geq t}\alpha \wedge P_{\geq s}\beta) \rightarrow P_{\geq s(r+t)}(\alpha \wedge \beta))$ for all $t, s \in [0,1]_Q$. If the numbers $t, s \in [0,1]_Q$ are such that $t \leq \mu([\alpha])$ and $s \leq \mu([\beta])$, then $M \models P_{\geq t}\alpha \wedge P_{\geq s}\beta$, so $M \models P_{\geq s(r+t)}(\alpha \wedge \beta)$, i.e., $\mu([\alpha \wedge \beta]) \geq s(r+t)$. Using the fact that rationals numbers are dense in reals, we conclude $\mu([\alpha \wedge \beta]) \geq \mu([\beta])(r + \mu([\alpha]))$ i.e., $\mu([\alpha]|[\beta]) - \mu([\alpha]) \geq r$, so with $\mu([\beta]) > 0$, $M \models c_{\geq r}(\alpha, \beta)$. Thus, $M \models \phi \rightarrow c_{\geq r}(\alpha, \beta)$. $\square$

5   Completeness of $Ax(\text{LPP}_2^{\text{conf}})$

In this section we show that the axiomatization $Ax(\text{LPP}_2^{\text{conf}})$ is strongly complete for the logic $\text{LPP}_2^{\text{conf}}$, i.e., we prove that every consistent set of formulas has a model. Completeness is proved in several steps, along the lines of Henkin construction. First, we prove that the deduction theorem holds for $Ax(\text{LPP}_2^{\text{conf}})$, using the implicative form of the infinitary rules. Then we use the deduction theorem to show that we can extend an arbitrary consistent set of formulas T to a maximal consistent set (Lindenbaum's theorem). The standard technique needs to be adapted in presence of infinitary inference rules. Third, we use the maximal consistent set to construct a canonical model. Finally, we show that the canonical model is indeed a model of T.

5.1   Lindenbaum's Theorem

We start by showing that the Deduction theorem holds.

Theorem 2 (Deduction theorem). *Let T be a set of formulas, and suppose that ρ and σ are two formulas such that either $\rho, \sigma \in For_C$ or $\rho, \sigma \in For_P$. Then*

$$T, \rho \vdash \sigma \text{ iff } T \vdash \rho \rightarrow \sigma.$$

Proof. The case when $\rho, \sigma \in For_C$ is a consequence of the fact that $Ax(\text{LPP}_2^{\text{conf}})$ extends classical propositional calculus. Let us consider the case when $\rho, \sigma \in For_P$. Here we will consider the nontrivial direction – from left to right, i.e., that $T, \phi \vdash \psi$ implies $T \vdash \phi \rightarrow \psi$. So, let us assume that $T, \phi \vdash \psi$. We proceed by the length of the inference. Here we only focus on the case when ψ is obtained by the rule R4, while the cases of applications of other infinitary rules can be handled in a similar way. Suppose that ψ is the formula $\phi_1 \rightarrow c_{\geq r}(\alpha, \beta)$, obtained from the set of premises $\{\phi_1 \rightarrow P_{>0}\beta\} \cup \{\phi_1 \rightarrow ((P_{\geq t}\alpha \wedge P_{\geq s}\beta) \rightarrow P_{\geq s(r+t)}(\alpha \wedge \beta)) \mid t, s \in [0,1]_Q\}$. By induction hypothesis

$T \vdash \phi \rightarrow (\phi_1 \rightarrow P_{>0}\beta)$, and
$T \vdash \phi \rightarrow (\phi_1 \rightarrow ((P_{\geq t}\alpha \wedge P_{\geq s}\beta) \rightarrow P_{\geq s(r+t)}(\alpha \wedge \beta)))$, for every $t, s \in [0,1]_Q$.

Then, by propositional reasoning we have

$T \vdash (\phi \wedge \phi_1) \rightarrow P_{>0}\beta$, and
$T \vdash (\phi \wedge \phi_1) \rightarrow ((P_{\geq t}\alpha \wedge P_{\geq s}\beta) \rightarrow P_{\geq s(r+t)}(\alpha \wedge \beta))$ for every $t, s \in [0,1]_Q$.

Applying R4 we obtain

$T \vdash (\phi \wedge \phi_1) \rightarrow c_{\geq r}(\alpha, \beta)$.

Using A1 and R1 we obtain

$T \vdash \phi \rightarrow (\phi_1 \rightarrow c_{\geq r}(\alpha, \beta))$
$T \vdash \phi \rightarrow \psi$. $\square$

Now we can prove the key step toward completeness.

Theorem 3 (Lindenbaum's Theorem). *Every consistent set of formulas can be extended to a maximal consistent set.*

Proof. Let T be an arbitrary consistent set of formulas. Assume that $\{\rho_i \mid i = 0, 1, 2, ...\}$ is an enumeration of all formulas from $For_{\text{LPP}_2^{\text{conf}}}$; it includes both non-probabilistic and probabilistic formulas. We construct T^* recursively, in the following way:

1. $T_0 = T$.
2. If the formula ρ_i is consistent with T_i, then $T_{i+1} = T_i \cup \{\rho_i\}$.
3. If the formula ρ_i is not consistent with T_i, then there are four cases:
   (a) If $\rho = \phi \rightarrow P_{\geq r}\alpha$, then

   $$T_{i+1} = T_i \cup \{\phi \rightarrow P_{<r-\frac{1}{k}}\alpha\},$$

   where k is a positive integer such that $r - \frac{1}{k} \geq 0$ and T_{i+1} is consistent.
   (b) If $\rho_i = \phi \rightarrow c_{\geq r}(\alpha, \beta)$, then $T_{i+1} = T_i \cup \{\psi_i\}$ where :

   $$\psi_i = \begin{cases} \phi \rightarrow P_{=0}\beta, & T_i \cup \{\phi \rightarrow P_{=0}\beta\} \nvdash \bot \\ \phi \rightarrow (P_{\geq t}\alpha \wedge P_{\geq s}\beta \wedge P_{<s(r+t)}(\alpha, \beta)), & T_i \cup \{\phi \rightarrow P_{=0}\beta\} \vdash \bot \end{cases}$$

   and t and s are two rational numbers from the unit interval such that T_{i+1} is consistent.
   (c) If $\rho_i = \phi \rightarrow c_{\leq r}(\alpha, \beta)$, then $T_{i+1} = T_i \cup \{\psi_i\}$ where:

   $$\psi_i = \begin{cases} \phi \rightarrow P_{=0}\beta, & T_i \cup \{\phi \rightarrow P_{=0}\beta\} \nvdash \bot \\ \phi \rightarrow (P_{\leq t}\alpha \wedge P_{\leq s}\beta \wedge P_{>s(r+t)}(\alpha, \beta)), & T_i \cup \{\phi \rightarrow P_{=0}\beta\} \vdash \bot \end{cases}$$

   and t and s are two rational numbers from the unit interval such that T_{i+1} is consistent.
   (d) Otherwise, $T_{i+1} = T_i$.
4. $T^* = \bigcup_{n=0}^{\infty} T_n$.

First, using Theorem 2 one can prove that the set T^* is correctly defined, i.e., there exist k, t and s from the steps 3(a)-3(b) of the construction. Here, we will consider the step 3(b), other two steps can be shown in a similar way.

Let us assume that $T \cup \{\phi \rightarrow c_{\geq r}(\alpha, \beta)\}$ is inconsistent. Then the set $T \cup \{c_{\geq r}(\alpha, \beta)\}$ is inconsistent as well. From Theorem 2 we obtain $T \vdash \neg c_{\geq r}(\alpha, \beta)$. Now suppose that the set $T \cup \{\phi \rightarrow P_{=0}\beta\}$ is inconsistent, and that the set $T \cup \{\phi \rightarrow (P_{\geq t}\alpha \wedge P_{\geq s}\beta \wedge P_{<s(r+t)}(\alpha, \beta))\}$ is inconsistent for every t and s. By Theorem 2, we obtain that $T \vdash P_{>0}\beta$ and $T \vdash \neg(P_{\geq t}\alpha \wedge P_{\geq s}\beta \wedge P_{<s(r+t)}(\alpha, \beta))$, for every t and s. Consequently,

$$T \vdash \top \rightarrow P_{>0}\beta$$

and

$$T \vdash \top \rightarrow ((P_{\geq t}\alpha \wedge P_{\geq s}\beta) \rightarrow P_{\geq s(r+t)}(\alpha, \beta)),$$

for all t and s, so from R4 we derive

$$T \vdash \top \rightarrow c_{\geq r}(\alpha, \beta).$$

Note that this contradicts with our assumption that $T \cup \{c_{\geq r}(\alpha, \beta)\}$ is an inconsistent set. Thus, there are rational numbers t and s such that the set

$$T \cup \{\phi \rightarrow (P_{\geq t}\alpha \wedge P_{\geq s}\beta \wedge P_{<s(r+t)}(\alpha, \beta))\}$$

is consistent.

Next we prove that T^* is a maximally consistent set. Note that every T_i is consistent by the construction. This still doesn't imply consistency of $T^* = \bigcup_{n=0}^{\infty} T_n$, because of the presence of the infinitary rules. In order to prove the consistency of T^*, we first show that it is deductively closed. If the formula ρ is an instance of some axiom, then $\rho \in T^*$ by construction of T^*. Next we prove that T^* is closed under the inference rules. Here we show that T^* is closed under the rule $R4$; the other cases are similar.

First we show that for every $\phi \in For_P$ either $\phi \in T^*$ or $\neg\phi \in T^*$ holds. Let i and j be the nonnegative integers such that $\rho_i = \phi$ and $\rho_j = \neg\phi$. From Theorem 2, it follows that either ϕ or $\neg\phi$ is consistent with $T_{max\{i,j\}}$. Then either $\phi \in T_{i+1}$ or $\neg\phi \in T_{j+1}$, so either $\phi \in T^*$ or $\neg\phi \in T^*$.

Let us show that T^* is closed under the inference rule R4. Assume that

$$\phi \rightarrow P_{>0}\beta, \phi \rightarrow ((P_{\geq t}\alpha \wedge P_{\geq s}\beta) \rightarrow P_{\geq s(r+t)}(\alpha, \beta)) \in T^*$$

for all $r, s \in [0, 1]_Q$. We need to show that $\phi \rightarrow c_{\geq r}(\alpha, \beta) \in T^*$. Assume that $\phi \rightarrow c_{\geq r}(\alpha, \beta) \notin T^*$. Then, by maximality of T^*, $\neg(\phi \rightarrow c_{\geq r}(\alpha, \beta)) \in T^*$. Thus, $\phi \in T^*$, so there is i such that $\phi \in T_i$. Let j be a nonnegative integer such that $\rho_j = \phi \rightarrow c_{\geq r}(\alpha, \beta)$. By the step 3(b) of the construction ot T^*, $\phi \rightarrow P_{=0}\beta \in T_{j+1}$, or there are $t', s' \in [0, 1]_Q$ such that $\phi \rightarrow (P_{\geq t'}\alpha \wedge P_{\geq s'}\beta \wedge P_{<s'(r+t')}(\alpha, \beta)) \in T_{j+1}$. Suppose that $\phi \rightarrow P_{=0}\beta \in T_{j+1}$, and let k be the nonnegative integer such that $\rho_k = \phi \rightarrow P_{>0}\beta$. Then

$$T_{\max\{i,k+1\}} \vdash P_{>0}\beta.$$

Note that we also have $T_{\max\{i,j+1\}} \vdash P_{=0}\beta$. Consequently, $T_{\max\{i,j+1,k+1\}} \vdash \perp$, a contradiction.

Now suppose that $\phi \rightarrow (P_{\geq t'}\alpha \wedge P_{\geq s'}\beta \wedge P_{<s'(r+t')}(\alpha, \beta)) \in T_{j+1}$, where $t', s' \in [0,1]_Q$. Let k' be the nonnegative integer such that $\rho_{k'} = \phi \rightarrow ((P_{\geq t'}\alpha \wedge P_{\geq s'}\beta) \rightarrow P_{\geq s'(r+t')}(\alpha, \beta))$. Then $T_{\max\{i,k'+1\}} \vdash (P_{\geq t'}\alpha \wedge P_{\geq s'}\beta) \rightarrow P_{\geq s'(r+t')}(\alpha, \beta)$. On the other hand,

$$T_{\max\{i,j+1\}} \vdash P_{\geq t'}\alpha \wedge P_{\geq s'}\beta \wedge P_{<s'(r+t')}(\alpha, \beta).$$

Thus, $T_{\max\{i,j+1,k'+1\}} \vdash \perp$, a contradiction. Consequently, the set T^* is deductively closed.

From deductive closedness of T^* we can prove that it is consistent. Indeed, if T^* is inconsistent, there is a formula $\phi \in For_P$ such that $T^* \vdash \phi \wedge \neg\phi$. But then there is a nonnegative integer i such that $\phi \wedge \neg\phi \in T_i$, a contradiction. □

5.2   Canonical Model

Now we are ready to prove our main result: the axiomatization $Ax(\mathrm{LPP}_2^{\mathrm{conf}})$ is strongly complete for the class of models $\mathcal{M}(\mathrm{LPP}_2^{\mathrm{conf}})$. For a given consistent set T, we actually build a structure which is a model of its maximal consistent superset T^*. Recall that the existence of such superset is provided by Theorem 3.

Definition 9 (Canonical model). *Let T^* be a mcs of formulas. The canonical model $M_{T^*} = (W, H, \mu, v)$ is defined as follows:*

- *$W = \{w \mid w$ is a classical propositional interpretation such that $w \models_C T^* \cap For_C\}$,*
- *$H = \{[\alpha] \mid \alpha \in For_C\}$, where $[\alpha] = \{w \in W \mid w \models_C \alpha\}$,*
- *$\mu : H \rightarrow [0,1]$ such that $\mu([\alpha]) = \sup\{r \in [0,1]_Q \mid T^* \vdash P_{\geq r}\alpha\}$,*
- *for every world w and every propositional letter $p \in \mathcal{P}, v(w,p) = true$ iff $w \models_C p$.*

It can be checked that this definition is correct, and that $M_{T^*} \in \mathcal{M}(\mathrm{LPP}_2^{\mathrm{conf}})$ for every mcs T^*. The proof is pretty much the same as the proof of the corresponding result for the logic LPP_2 [24], so we omit it here.

Now we formulate the completeness theorem for our logic.[2]

Theorem 4. (Strong completeness of $\mathrm{LPP}_2^{\mathrm{conf}}$). *A set of formulas T is consistent iff there is an $M \in \mathcal{M}(\mathrm{LPP}_2^{\mathrm{conf}})$, such that $M \models T$.*

Proof. Note that the direction form right to left follows from Theorem 1. For the other direction, suppose that T is a consistent set of formulas. By Theorem 3, there is a maximally consistent superset T^* of T, which we can use to construct the canonical model M_{T^*}. We need to show that M_{T^*} is a model of T^*. It is sufficient to show that $\rho \in T^*$ iff $M_{T^*} \models \rho$, for every formula $\rho \in For_{\mathrm{LPP}_2^{\mathrm{conf}}}$. In the case when ρ is a propositional formula, that follows from the construction of

---

[2] The usual formulation of strong completeness is $T \vdash \rho$ iff $T \models \rho$. It is well known that this formulation is equivalent to the formulation of Theorem 4.

M_{T^*} and the completeness theorem for propositional logic. In the case when ρ is a probabilistic formula ϕ, we use induction on the complexity of the formulas. The cases when ϕ is a conjunction or a negation are straightforward. The case when ϕ is $P_{\geq r}\alpha$ is essentially the same as in [24].

Let ϕ be of the form $c_{\geq r}(\alpha, \beta)$.

($\Rightarrow$) Assume that $c_{\geq r}(\alpha, \beta) \in T^*$. Let $\{t_n \mid n \in \mathbf{N}\}$ and $\{s_n \mid n \in \mathbf{N}\}$ be two strictly increasing sequences of numbers from $[0,1]_Q$, such that $lim_{n\to\infty}t_n = \mu([\alpha])$ and $lim_{n\to\infty}s_n = \mu([\beta])$. Let n be any number from $\mathbf{N}$. Then $T^* \vdash P_{\geq t_n}\alpha \wedge P_{\geq s_n}\beta$. Using the assumption $c_{\geq r}(\alpha, \beta) \in T^*$, the axioms A7 and A9 and propositional reasoning, we obtain $T^* \vdash P_{>0}\beta$ and $T^* \vdash P_{\geq s_n(r+t_n)}(\alpha \wedge \beta)$. Finally, by Definition 9 we have $\mu([\beta]) > 0$ and $\mu([\alpha \wedge \beta]) \geq lim_{n\to\infty}s_n(r+t_n) = \mu([\beta])(r + \mu([\alpha]))$, i.e.,

$$\mu([\beta]) > 0$$

and

$$\mu([\alpha]|[\beta]) - \mu([\alpha]) \geq r.$$

($\Leftarrow$) Now assume that $\mu([\beta]) > 0$ and $\mu([\alpha]|[\beta]) - \mu([\alpha]) \geq r$, i.e., $\mu([\alpha \wedge \beta]) \geq \mu([\beta])(r + \mu([\alpha]))$. We will show that

$$T^* \vdash P_{>0}\beta$$

and

$$T^* \vdash (P_{\geq t}\alpha \wedge P_{\geq s}\beta) \to P_{\geq s(r+t)}(\alpha \wedge \beta) \text{ for all } t, s \in [0,1]_Q.$$

Suppose that $T^* \not\vdash P_{>0}\beta$. By maximality $T^* \vdash P_{=0}\beta$, i.e., $\mu([\beta]) = 0$, a contradiction. So we have that $T^* \vdash P_{>0}\beta$.

If $t > \mu([\alpha])$ or $s > \mu([\beta])$, then $T^* \not\vdash P_{\geq t}\alpha \wedge P_{\geq s}\beta$. By maximality of T^*, $T^* \vdash \neg(P_{\geq t}\alpha \wedge P_{\geq s}\beta)$, and consequently $T^* \vdash (P_{\geq t}\alpha \wedge P_{\geq s}\beta) \to P_{\geq s(r+t)}(\alpha \wedge \beta)$. If $t \leq \mu([\alpha])$ and $s \leq \mu([\beta])$, then $s(r + t) \leq \mu([\alpha \wedge \beta])$ by assumption, so $T^* \vdash P_{\geq s(r+t)}(\alpha \wedge \beta)$ by Definition 9. Now the result follows from the fact that T^* is deductively close.

The case when ϕ us $c_{\leq r}(\alpha, \beta)$ can be proved in a similar way. $\square$

6   Decidability

In this section, we discuss decidability of LPP_2^{conf}. We distinguish two cases, since we have two types of formulas. We start with propositional formulas.

Theorem 5. *The problem of deciding whether a formula from For_C is satisfiable in an LPP_2^{conf} structure is NP-complete.*

Proof. This result follows straightforwardly from the same complexity result for propositional formulas under the classical semantics. Indeed, if α is propositionally unsatisfiable, then, according to our definition of satisfiability, α also does not hold in any model from $\mathcal{M}(LPP_2^{conf})$, since $v(w, \alpha) = false$ for every world w. For the other direction, note that if α is propositionally satisfiable, then it is satisfied in the model (W, H, μ, v), where $W = \{w\}$ (which uniquely determines $H = \{\emptyset, W\}$ and $\mu(\emptyset) = 0, \mu(W) = 1$), with $v(w, \cdot)$ being an evaluation function such that $v(w, \alpha) = true$. $\square$

Let us now turn to the probabilistic formulas.

Theorem 6. *There is a PSPACE procedure deciding whether a formula from For_P is satisfiable in an LPP_2^{conf} structure.*

Proof. Here we use the complexity result of Fagin, Halpern and Megiddo about polynomial weight formulas [13]. Those formulas are Boolean combinations of polynomial equations and inequalities, with integer coefficients and with variables of the form $w(\alpha)$, where $\alpha \in For_C$ and w stands for "weight" (probability). For example $(3w(p)w(p \lor q) + w(q \to p) \geq 2) \land 5w(q) \geq 1$ is a polynomial weight formula. Those formulas are evaluated in a Kripke structure with a probability measure over possible worlds, just like in our logic. A PSPACE decision procedure for satisfiability of polynomial weight formulas is proposed in [13]. In short, the authors reduce the problem to a problem in the quantifier-free theory of real closed fields and then apply Canny's decision procedure from [1]. Instead of repeating the same strategy for our logic, we rather translate the formulas of our language to polynomial weight formulas, and then apply the procedure from [13]. Our simple translation has two steps. First, we use the mapping f, defined recursively as follows

- $f(P_{\geq r}\alpha) = w(\alpha) \geq r$,
- $f(c_{\geq r}(\alpha, \beta)) = w(\beta) \geq 0 \land w(\alpha \land \beta) - w(\alpha)w(\beta) \geq rw(\beta)$,
- $f(c_{\leq r}(\alpha, \beta)) = w(\beta) \geq 0 \land w(\alpha \land \beta) - w(\alpha)w(\beta) \leq rw(\beta)$,
- $f(\varphi \land \psi) = f(\varphi) \land f(\psi)$,
- $f(\neg\varphi) = \neg f(\varphi)$.

Note that we need to further transform the obtained formulas, since polynomial weight formulas allow only integer coefficients. For that reason, we apply the function g, whose role is to clear the denominators. Instead of giving a formal definition, we illustrate how g works in practice. (We assume that the rational constants are given in form of fractions using coprime integers.) For example, if θ is the formula

$$w(p)w(p \to q) \geq \frac{2}{3} \lor w(q) \leq \frac{4}{5},$$

then $g(\theta)$ is

$$3w(p)w(p \to q) \geq 2 \lor 5w(q) \leq 4.$$

Obviously, a formula $\varphi \in For_P$ is satisfiable iff $g(f(\varphi))$ is a satisfiable polynomial weight formula. Thus, our result follows. □

7   Conclusion

In this paper we presented the probabilistic logic LPP_2^{conf} which allows reasoning about degrees of confirmation. The language contains both classical propositional formulas and probabilistic formulas, and it extends the language of LPP_2 [24] with the binary operators that model measure of confirmation. We proposed an axiomatization for the logic and prove strong completeness. Since the logic is not compact, the axiomatization contains infinitary rules of inference. We also proved that the problem of deciding whether a probabilistic formula of our logic is satisfiable is in PSPACE.

There are two avenues for further research. First, it would be interesting to see if a more expressive language could be built on top of this logic. For example, nesting of probability operators would allow expressions of the form $c_{\geq r}(\alpha, P_{\geq s}\beta)$, which model the situation in which probabilistic boundaries of one formula confirms (to some degree) another formula. Another interesting direction would be a first order extension, in which we could express the statements like $(\forall x)c_{\geq r}(\alpha(x), \beta(x))$.

Second, in this paper we modeled the difference measure. We chose this measure simply because it is most standard measure of confirmation. However, we can easily adapt the technique developed here to capture the other popular measures from the literature (see, for example, [28]). For example, Carnap's relevance measure

$$\mu(A \wedge B) - P(A)P(B)$$

can be axiomatized by replacing A7-A10 and R4 and R5 with the following axiom schemes and inference rules:

(A7') $(P_{\geq t}\alpha \wedge P_{\geq s}\beta \wedge c_{\geq r}(\alpha, \beta)) \rightarrow P_{\geq r+st}(\alpha \wedge \beta)$
(A8') $(P_{\leq t}\alpha \wedge P_{\leq s}\beta \wedge c_{\leq r}(\alpha, \beta)) \rightarrow P_{\leq r+st}(\alpha \wedge \beta)$
(R4') From the set of premises

$$\{\phi \rightarrow ((P_{\geq t}\alpha \wedge P_{\geq s}\beta) \rightarrow P_{\geq r+st}(\alpha \wedge \beta)) \mid t, s \in [0,1]_Q\}$$

   infer $\phi \rightarrow c_{\geq r}(\alpha, \beta)$.
(R5') From the set of premises

$$\{\phi \rightarrow ((P_{\leq t}\alpha \wedge P_{\leq s}\beta) \rightarrow P_{\leq r+st}(\alpha \wedge \beta)) \mid t, s \in [0,1]_Q\}$$

   infer $\phi \rightarrow c_{\leq r}(\alpha, \beta)$.

For axiomatizing Carnap's relevance measure we need only eight axiom schemes. Note that we can also apply the similar technique for axiomatizing log-ratio measure

$$c(\alpha, \beta) = \log\left[\frac{P(\alpha|\beta)}{P(\alpha)}\right],$$

but the decidability results are not clear. In that case, we cannot translate a formula to an existential sentence in the first-order language of fields, as we have done in Sect. 6, so we cannot apply the procedure from [13].

References

1. Canny, J.F.: Some algebraic and geometric computations in PSPACE. In: Proceedings of the 20th Annual ACM Symposium on Theory of Computing, Chicago, Illinois, USA, 2–4 May 1988, pp. 460–467 (1988)

2. Carnap, R.: Logical Foundations of Probability, 2nd edn. The University of Chicago Press, Chicago (1962). 1st edition (1950)
3. Delgrande, J.P., Renne, B., Sack, J.: The logic of qualitative probability. Artif. Intell. **275**, 457–486 (2019)
4. Doder, D., Marinković, B., Maksimović, P., Perović, A.: A logic with conditional probability operators. Publications de L'Institut Mathematique Ns. **87**(101), 85–96 (2010)
5. Doder, D., Ognjanović, Z.: A probabilistic logic for reasoning about uncertain temporal information. In: Proceedings of the Thirty-First Conference on Uncertainty in Artificial Intelligence, UAI 2015, pp. 248–257 (2015)
6. Doder, D., Ognjanović, Z.: Probabilistic logics with independence and confirmation. Studia Logica **105**(5), 943–969 (2017)
7. Doder, D.: A logic with big-stepped probabilities that can model nonmonotonic reasoning of system P. Publications de L'Institut Mathematique Ns. **90**(104), 13–22 (2011)
8. Doder, D., Marković, Z., Ognjanović, Z., Perović, A., Rašković, M.: A probabilistic temporal logic that can model reasoning about evidence. In: Link, S., Prade, H. (eds.) FoIKS 2010. LNCS, vol. 5956, pp. 9–24. Springer, Heidelberg (2010). https://doi.org/10.1007/978-3-642-11829-6_4
9. Doder, D., Ognjanovic, Z., Markovic, Z.: An axiomatization of a first-order branching time temporal logic. J. UCS **16**(11), 1439–1451 (2010)
10. Doder, D., Savić, N., Ognjanović, Z.: Multi-agent logics for reasoning about higher-order upper and lower probabilities. J. Logic Lang. Inf. **29**, 77–107 (2020). https://doi.org/10.1007/s10849-019-09301-7
11. Eells, E., Fitelson, B.: Measuring confirmation and evidence. J. Philos. **97**(12), 663–672 (2000)
12. Fagin, R., Halpern, J.Y.: Reasoning about knowledge and probability. J. ACM **41**(2), 340–367 (1994)
13. Fagin, R., Halpern, J.Y., Megiddo, N.: A logic for reasoning about probabilities. Inf. Comput. **87**, 78–128 (1990)
14. Fitelson, B.: The plurality of Bayesian measures of confirmation and the problem of measure sensitivity. Philos. Sci. **66**(3), 378 (1999)
15. Frisch, A., Haddawy, P.: Anytime deduction for probabilistic logic. Artif. Intell. **69**, 93–122 (1994)
16. Gaifman, H.: A theory of higher order probabilities. In: Halpern, J.Y. (ed.) Proceedings of the Theoretical Aspects of Reasoning about Knowledge, pp. 275–292. Morgan-Kaufmann, San Mateo (1986)
17. Guelev, D.: A propositional dynamic logic with qualitative probabilities. J. Philos. Logic **28**, 575–605 (1999)
18. Halpern, J.Y.: An analysis of first-order logics of probability. Artif. Intell. **46**, 311–350 (1990)
19. Heifetz, A., Mongin, P.: Probability logic for type spaces. Games Econ. Behav. **35**, 31–53 (2001)
20. van der Hoek, W.: Some considerations on the logic $P_F D$. J. Appl. Non-Class. Log. **7**(3), 287–307 (1997)
21. Keisler, H.J.: Probability quantifiers. In: Barwise, J., Feferman, S. (eds.) Model Theoretic Logic, pp. 509–556. Springer, Berlin (1985)
22. Marinkovic, B., Ognjanovic, Z., Doder, D., Perovic, A.: A propositional linear time logic with time flow isomorphic to ω^2. J. Appl. Logic **12**(2), 208–229 (2014)
23. Nilsson, N.: Probabilistic logic. Artif. Intell. **28**, 71–87 (1986)

24. Ognjanović, Z., Rašković, M.: Some first-order probability logics. Theoret. Comput. Sci. **247**(1–2), 191–212 (2000)
25. Ognjanović, Z., Rašković, M., Marković, Z.: Probability Logics. Probability-Based Formalization of Uncertain Reasoning. Springer, Cham (2016). https://doi.org/10. 1007/978-3-319-47012-2
26. Ognjanović, Z., Doder, D., Marković, Z.: A branching time logic with two types of probability operators. In: Benferhat, S., Grant, J. (eds.) SUM 2011. LNCS (LNAI), vol. 6929, pp. 219–232. Springer, Heidelberg (2011). https://doi.org/10.1007/978-3-642-23963-2_18
27. Savić, N., Doder, D., Ognjanović, Z.: Logics with lower and upper probability operators. Int. J. Approximate Reasoning **88**, 148–168 (2017)
28. Tentori, K., Crupi, V., Bonini, N., Osherson, D.: Comparison of confirmation measures. Cognition **103**(1), 107–119 (2007)
29. Tomović, S., Ognjanović, Z., Doder, D.: Probabilistic common knowledge among infinite number of agents. In: Destercke, S., Denoeux, T. (eds.) ECSQARU 2015. LNCS (LNAI), vol. 9161, pp. 496–505. Springer, Cham (2015). https://doi.org/10. 1007/978-3-319-20807-7_45

Ideal Related Algebras and Their Logics
Extended Abstract

Ivo Düntsch[1,2]($\boxtimes$) and Wojciech Dzik[3]

[1] College of Mathematics and Informatics, Fujian Normal University,
Fuzhou, Fujian, China
D.Ivo@fjnu.edu.cn

[2] Department of Computer Science, Brock University, St. Catharines, ON, Canada
duentsch@brocku.ca

[3] Institute of Mathematics, University of Silesia, Katowice, Poland
wojciech.dzik@us.edu.pl

Abstract. We present previously unknown algebraic semantics for Sobociński's logics **S4.4**, also known as **S4.3DumB₂**, and the autoepistemic logic **KD45**. The operators on the respective algebras are generalizations of the unary discriminator defined via suitable ideals. We also explore unification and admissible rules for these logics.

Keywords: Modal logics · Frame semantics · Algebraic semantics ·
Unification · Admissible rules · Boolean algebras with operators ·
Closure algebras

1 Introduction

Boolean algebras with operators were introduced by Jónsson and Tarski [13]: A *(modal) operator* $f : B \rightarrow B$ is a function on a Boolean algebra B that is normal, i.e. $f(0) = 0$, and additive, i.e. $f(x) + f(y) = f(x + y)$ for all $x, y \in B$. It turned out that the class of modal algebras, i.e. Boolean algebras augmented with a modal operator, provide the algebraic semantics for the logic **K**. A well studied class of modal algebras are the closure algebras: A modal operator f is called a *closure operator* [16], if it satisfies

Cl₁ $x \leq f(x)$,
Cl₁ $f(f(x)) = f(x)$

for all $x \in B$. The class of closure algebras provides the semantics for the logic **S4**.

Following the investigation of the semilattice of modal operators in [6], we consider modal operators on a Boolean algebra B which are in some sense connected to an ideal of B, and determine their associated logics. The simplest (and the strongest) such operator, the unary discriminator, is obtained from the trivial ideal:

$$f(x) = \begin{cases} 0, & \text{if } x = 0, \\ 1, & \text{otherwise.} \end{cases}$$

M. Dastani et al. (Eds.): CLAR 2020, LNAI 12061, pp. 96–103, 2020.
https://doi.org/10.1007/978-3-030-44638-3_6

We will vary this theme into two directions: Firstly, keeping f as the identity on an ideal and sending the rest to 1, secondly, setting $f(x) = 0$ if $x \in I$ and $f(x) = 1$ otherwise; such f acts like an indicator function. Both variations coincide with the discriminator, if $I = \{0\}$, and they differ for larger ideals.

Our motivation and starting point were algebraic, and we were quite surprised that the modal logics obtained from our algebras are well known in the logic community. Indeed, the class of ideal algebras provides algebraic semantics for the logic **S4.4** of Sobociński [20], which is also known as **S4HDumB$_2$** in the parlance of denoting logics by their properties. The class of ideal indicator algebras which we study subsequently turns out to provide an algebraic semantics for the autoepistemic logic **KD45**. The logics **S4.4** and **KD45** play important roles in the area of logic of knowledge and belief, as well as in non–monotonic reasoning. In this case, the necessitation modality $\Box$ is interpreted as "is known" or "is believed". Autoepistemic reasoning, that is, reasoning of a rational agent capable of reasoning about its own knowledge and belief, naturally appears in this context. Each of the logics **S4.4** and **KD45** are maximal in their range, that is, among all logics which are indistinguishable as epistemic logics, see Schwarz [18].

Non–monotonic reasoning appears very naturally in logics of knowledge and belief, which is indicated by the following example: Let p be an elementary sentence and assume that the knowledge base or the belief set is empty. Therefore, we may assume that $\neg\Box p$ (p is not known) is the autoepistemic consequence of $\emptyset$; this can be expressed by $\emptyset \vdash \neg\Box p$. Now suppose that the initial belief set contains p. Then $\{p\} \vdash \Box p$ and $\{p\} \not\vdash \neg\Box p$, which demonstrates non-monotonic reasoning: After extending the knowledge base with p the formula $\neg\Box p$ becomes rejected.

We assume familiarity with basic concepts of modal logics, their syntax and algebraic and frame semantics. For both we recommend the monograph by Blackburn et al. [1] and the essay by Bull and Segerberg [4]. Similarities and differences between both kinds of semantics are well described by Blok [2]. Our main source for universal algebra is the monograph by Burris and Sankappanavar [5]. We will write names of (logical axioms) in the `teletype` font, and the corresponding logics in **bold**.

Proofs and details of the constructions will be provided in the full version of the paper.

2 Ideal Related Algebras and Their Logics

An *ideal algebra* is a structure $\langle B, f \rangle$, where B is a nontrivial Boolean algebra, I an ideal of B, and $f : B \to B$ is defined by

$$f(x) := \begin{cases} x, & \text{if } x \in I, \\ 1, & \text{otherwise.} \end{cases} \tag{2.1}$$

A special ideal algebra is an algebra $\langle B, f^1 \rangle$, where f^1 is the unary discriminator, for which $I = \{0\}$. By some abuse of notation we call henceforth $\langle B, f \rangle$ an *ideal algebra* if and only if there is some ideal I such that f satisfies (2.1). We observe in passing that the set of closed elements of an ideal algebra is $I \cup \{1\}$. Indeed, this property can be used as a definition for ideal algebras, see e.g. [3].

In the sequel, $\mathfrak{B} := \langle B, f \rangle$ will be an ideal algebra with associated ideal I, unless otherwise indicated; sometimes we shall indicate this by writing I_f for the ideal associated with f. Clearly, f is a closure operator. The class of ideal algebras is denoted by IMA, and the variety generated by IMA is denoted by **Eq(IMA)**.

Ideal algebras are a universal positive class, but not a quasi–variety, i.e. the class cannot be axiomatized by quasi–identities, see [5, Theorem 2.25]:

Theorem 1. $\langle B, f \rangle$ *is an ideal algebra if and only if* $(\forall x)[f(x) = x \text{ or } f(x) = 1]$.

Structurally, IMA is very simple:

Theorem 2. IMA *is locally finite, and thus,* **Eq(IMA)** *is generated by its subdirectly irreducible finite members.*

Considering that each minimal congruence ideal is generated by an atom, we obtain

Theorem 3. *If* $\mathfrak{B}$ *is not simple, then* $\mathfrak{B}$ *is subdirectly irreducible if and only if* I_f *is generated by an atom.*

Thus, IMA is generated by the finite ideal algebras $\langle B, f \rangle$, where $I_f = \{0\}$ or I_f is generated by an atom. Each finite subdirectly irreducible ideal algebra with at least two atoms is uniquely determined by the number $m+1$ of atoms it has - the atom a generating I_f and m other atoms. With some abuse of notation, we shall write $B(1, m)$ for a generic ideal algebra of this type. Noting that $B(1, n)$ is a homomorphic image of $B(1, m)$, if $n \leq m$, we see that $\mathbf{Eq}(B(1, n)) \subseteq \mathbf{Eq}(B(1, m))$. By Jónsson's Lemma [14, Corollary 3.5] the inclusion is strict, and we obtain

$$\mathbf{Eq}(B(1,1)) \subsetneq \mathbf{Eq}(B(1,2)) \subsetneq \ldots \subsetneq \mathbf{Eq}(B(1,n)) \subsetneq \ldots \subsetneq \mathbf{Eq}(1,\omega) = \mathbf{Eq}(\mathsf{IMA}).$$

It came as something of a surprise for us, that **Eq(IMA)** provides the algebraic semantics of the logic **S4.4**, first presented by Sobociński [20]. This logic extends **S4** by the axiom

R1. $p \wedge \Diamond \Box p \implies \Box p$.

S4.4 is properly contained in **S5**, and it is an extension of **S4.3** [20, p 306]. A detailed discussion of the syntax of **S4.4** is presented in [21]. Subsequently, this logic was called **S4R** by Segerberg [19], and **SW5** by Schwarz [18], who called it the "true logic of knowledge". In his temporal interpretation, Zeman [21] calls **S4.4** the "logic of the end of the world".

Theorem 4. Eq(S4.4) = Eq(IMA).

For the $\subseteq$ part it is sufficient to show that each finite algebra in **Eq(S4.4)** is a product of ideal algebras.

A different direction to generalize the discriminator considering an ideal are the structures $\langle B, f \rangle$ where I is an ideal of B and f is an indicator function with respect to I, i.e.

$$f(x) := \begin{cases} 0, & \text{if } x \in I, \\ 1, & \text{otherwise.} \end{cases} \tag{2.2}$$

We call such an algebra an *indI–algebra*, and denote their class by indI.

Theorem 5. $\langle B, f \rangle$ *is an indI–algebra if and only if* $(\forall x)[f(x) = 0$ *or* $f(x) = 1]$.

If $\langle B, f \rangle$ is an indI–algebra with determining ideal I, we let $I_f := \{x \in B : f(x) = 0\}$. We denote the class of these algebra by indI. Similar to ideal algebras we obtain

Theorem 6. indI *is locally finite, and thus,* **Eq(indI)** *is generated by its finite members. Furthermore,* $\langle B, f \rangle$ *is subdirectly irreducible if and only if* I_f *is generated by an atom.*

It turns out that the modal logic belonging to indI is the well known autoepistemic logic determined by the axioms KD45, where D is the axiom $\Box p \implies \Diamond p$, and 5 is the Euclidean axiom $\Diamond \Box p \implies \Box p$.

Theorem 7. Eq(KD45) = Eq(indI).

We also obtain a new frame condition for this logic:

Theorem 8. *The logic* **KD45** *is determined by frames with the condition*

$$(\forall x, y, z)[xRy \Rightarrow zRy].$$

3 Unification and Admissible Rules in Logics of Ideal Related Algebras

In this section we consider rules of inference and consequence relations of logics related to the algebras we have discussed. By a rule $r : A_1, \ldots, A_n/B$ we mean a subset $r \subseteq Fm^n \times Fm$ which is closed under substitutions. Recall that a rule $r : A_1, \ldots, A_n/B$ is *admissible in* L if for every substitution ε, $\varepsilon A_1, \ldots, \varepsilon A_n \in L \Rightarrow \varepsilon B \in L$, and it is *derivable in* L if $A_1, \ldots, A_n \vdash_L B$. A system L (or a consequence operation $\vdash_L$) is called *structurally complete* (SC) if every admissible rule in L is also derivable in L.

A rule $r : A_1, \ldots, A_n/B$ is called *passive*, if for every substitution ε, $\{\varepsilon A_1, \ldots, \varepsilon A_n\} \nsubseteq L$. For example, the rule P_2

$$\Diamond A \wedge \Diamond \neg A/ \ B \qquad\qquad (3.1)$$

or, equivalently, $\Diamond A \wedge \Diamond \neg A/\bot$, is admissible but not derivable in many modal logics, e.g in **S5**. Therefore, we call L *almost structurally complete* (ASC), if every rule which is admissible and not passive is derivable in L. Slightly abusing the terminology, we say that a modal logic L is (A)SC if its consequence relation $\vdash_L$, based on Modus Ponens and Necessitation, is (A)SC. For instance **S5** and, indeed, every extension of **S4.3** is ASC but, in general, not SC [8].

A substitution ε of formulas is called a *unifier* for a formula A in the logic L if $\varepsilon A \in L$. A formula is *unifiable* in L, if $\varepsilon A \in L$ for some substitution ε. Therefore, a rule $r : A_1, \ldots, A_n/ \ B$ is passive if and only if $r : A_1 \wedge \cdots \wedge A_n$ is not unifiable. For $L \supseteq \mathbf{K4D}$ unifiability of a formula in L as well as being a passive rule in L does not depend on the logic L and is decidable.

A *projective unifier* for A in L is a unifier such that $A \vdash \varepsilon(B) \leftrightarrow B$ for each formula B (see [9,11]); we say that a logic L enjoys *projective unification* if each L-unifiable formula has a projective unifier in L, when $\vdash_L$ is based on Modus Ponens and Necessitation. Projective unifiers (formulas, substitutions) were defined and extensively used by S. Ghilardi see e.g. [10,11]. It is known [8] that if a logic enjoys projective unification, then it is (almost) structurally complete. In [8] it is shown that a logic L containing **S4** enjoys projective unification if and only if **S4.3** $\subseteq L$.

In [12, p. 30] the following axiom D1 is defined:

$$\Box(\Box p \rightarrow q) \vee \Box(\Box q \rightarrow p).$$

This axiom has no connection with the axiom $\mathbf{D} : \Box p \rightarrow \Diamond p$. It is known that **S4.3** = **S4D1**, but **K4.3** $\neq$ **K4D1**. In [15] it is proved that a transitive modal logic L has projective unification if and only if **K4D1** $\subseteq L$.

Even though **KD45** and **S4.4** are not structurally complete, we obtain

Theorem 9. *The logics* **S4.4** *and* **KD45** *as well as their extensions enjoy projective unification and are almost structurally complete.*

Theorem 9 solves the problem of admissibility of rules that are not passive. Next, we look at passive rules. In [17] it is shown that for every consistent normal modal logic extending **KD4** all passive rules can be derived from the rule P_2 which is shown in (3.1). Hence, together with Theorem 9, we obtain

Corollary 1. *1. Each admissible rule in* **S4.4** *(as well as in any of its extensions) is derivable or can be derived by means of the rule P_2.*
2. Each admissible rule in **KD45** *(as well as in any of its extensions) is derivable or can be derived by means of the rule P_2.*
3. Admissibility of rules in **S4.4** *and in* **KD45** *is decidable.*

For a variety of algebras **K**, $\mathscr{F}_{\mathbf{K}}(\lambda)$ denotes its λ-generated free algebra. The following description of ASC, adopted here to closure algebras, is known, see [7], Corollary 3.2.

Theorem 10. *Let* **K** *be a locally finite variety of closure algebras. Then* **K** *is ASC iff for every finite subdirectly irreducible algebra* $\mathfrak{A}$ *in* **K** *,* $\mathfrak{A} \times \mathscr{F}(0)$ *embeds into* $\mathscr{F}(\omega)$.

In particular, $\mathscr{F}_{\mathsf{IMA}}(\lambda)$ and $\mathscr{F}_{\mathsf{indl}}(\lambda)$ denote the λ-generated free algebra in IMA and in indI, respectively. Based on Theorem 10 we have the following:

Theorem 11. *1. For every finite subdirectly irreducible ideal algebra* $\mathfrak{A}$*,* $\mathfrak{A} \times$ $\mathscr{F}_{\mathsf{IMA}}(0)$ *embeds into the free algebra* $\mathscr{F}_{\mathsf{IMA}}(\omega)$.
2. For every finite subdirectly irreducible indI algebra $\mathfrak{A}$*,* $\mathfrak{A} \times \mathscr{F}_{\mathsf{indl}}(0)$ *embeds into the free algebra* $\mathscr{F}_{\mathsf{indl}}(\omega)$.

The results above can be expressed in terms of quasi-varieties determined by ideal related algebras. Recall that a class of algebras is called a *quasi–variety* if it is axiomatized by quasi–identities, that is, by algebraic expressions of the form $t_1 = t_1' \wedge \cdots \wedge t_n = t_n' \Rightarrow t' = t''$, where all t_i, t_i', t', t'' are terms. Equivalently, a class of algebras is a quasi-variety if it is closed under isomorphic copies, subalgebras, reduced products, and contains the trivial algebra. A quasi–identity $t_1 = t_1' \wedge \cdots \wedge t_n = t_n' \rightarrow t' = t''$ is called *admissible* in a quasi-variety $\mathscr{Q}$, if it holds in the countable free algebra in $\mathscr{Q}$. It is called *derivable*, if $t_1 = t_1' \wedge \cdots \wedge t_n = t_n' \models t' = t''$ in $\mathscr{Q}$.

Theorem 12. *1. The quasivariety generated by* IMA *is axiomatized by equations obtained from the axioms of* **S4.4** *and the single quasi-identity* $\Diamond x \wedge \Diamond \neg x = 1 \rightarrow y = 1$.
2. The quasivariety generated by indI *is axiomatized by equations obtained from the axioms of* **KD45** *and the single quasi-identity* $\Diamond x \wedge \Diamond \neg x = 1 \rightarrow y = 1$.

Let us note that $\Diamond x \wedge \Diamond \neg x = 1 \rightarrow 0 = 1$ is a translation of the passive rule P_2, see e.g. [9].

4   Summary and Outlook

We have presented two universal classes of modal algebras related to ideals, and have investigated their algebraic and logical properties. It turned out that the considered algebras provided previously unknown semantics for well known autoepistemic logics. We have also discussed unification and admissible rules of these logics.

In logics of knowledge and belief (in particular in autoepistemic logic) Kripke frames are used as a semantics. The logics determined by ideal-related algebras are Kripke-complete, that is, they are determined by classes of Kripke frames. It is well known that some modal logics are Kripke-incomplete, i.e. they cannot be determined by (a class of) Kripke frames; for these logics the algebraic approach is necessary. We are not aware of immediate applications of the algebraic semantics approach to logic of knowledge and belief, but expect that our algebraic approach gives a new perspective and offers new methodology for studies on non-monotonic reasoning.

In the full paper we shall give all proofs and discuss the canonical frames of our algebra classes. We shall also consider projective unification and admissible rules for these systems in more detail, as well as their complexity.

Acknowledgements. We are grateful to the anonymous referees whose observations helped to increase the quality of the paper and who spotted an erroneous claim in the submitted version. We would like to thank Ewa Orłowska for her valuable input to this project. I. Düntsch gratefully acknowledges support by the National Natural Science Foundation of China, Grant No.61976053.

References

1. Blackburn, P., Rijke, M.D., Venema, Y.: Modal Logic. Cambridge University Press, Cambridge (2001)
2. Blok, W.: The lattice of modal logics: an algebraic investigation. J. Symbolic Logic **45**, 221–238 (1980)
3. Blok, W., Dwinger, P.: Equational classes of closure algebras I. Ind. Math. **37**, 189–198 (1975)
4. Bull, R., Segerberg, K.: Basic modal logic. In: Gabbay, D., Guenthner, F. (eds.) Handbook of Philosophical Logic, vol. 3, 2nd edn, pp. 1–88. Springer, Heidelberg (2001). https://doi.org/10.1007/978-94-017-0454-0_1
5. Burris, S., Sankappanavar, H.P.: A Course in Universal Algebra. Springer, New York (2012). The Millenium Edition, 2012 Update. http://www.math.uwaterloo.ca/~snburris/htdocs/ualg.html
6. Düntsch, I., Dzik, W., Orłowska, E.: On the semilattice of modal operators and decompositions of the discriminator. In: Hajnal Andréka and István Németi on Unity of Science: From Computing to Relativity Theory Through Algebraic Logic. Outstanding Contributions to Logic. Springer (2020, to appear). https://arxiv.org/abs/1805.11891v1
7. Dzik, W., Stronkowski, M.: Almost structural completeness; an algebraic approach. Ann. Pure Appl. Logic **167**(7), 525–556 (2013)
8. Dzik, W., Wojtylak, P.: Projective unification in modal logic. Logic J. IGPL **20**, 121–153 (2012)
9. Dzik, W., Wojtylak, P.: Modal consequence relations extending **S4.3**. An application of projective unification. Notre Dame J. Formal Logic **57**(4), 523–549 (2016)
10. Ghilardi, S.: Unication through projectivity. J. Symbolic Comput. **7**, 733–752 (1997)
11. Ghilardi, S.: Best solving modal equations. Ann. Pure Appl. Logic **102**, 183–198 (2000)
12. Hughes, G.E., Cresswell, M.J.: A Companion to Modal Logic. Methuen, London (1984)
13. Jónsson, B., Tarski, A.: Boolean algebras with operators I. Am. J. Math. **73**, 891–939 (1951)
14. Jónsson, B.: Algebras whose congruence lattices are distributive. Math. Scand. **21**, 110–121 (1967)
15. Kost, S.: Projective unification in transitive modal logics. Logic J. IGPL **26**(5), 548–566 (2018). https://doi.org/10.1093/jigpal/jzy013
16. McKinsey, J.C.C., Tarski, A.: The algebra of topology. Ann. Math. (2nd Ser.) **45**(1), 141–191 (1944)

17. Rybakov, V., Terziler, M., Gencer, C.: Unification and passive inference rules for modal logics. J. Appl. Non-Class. Log. **10**, 368–377 (2000)
18. Schwarz, G.: In search of a "true" logic of knowledge: the nonmonotonic perspective. Artif. Intell. **79**, 39–63 (1995)
19. Segerberg, K.: An Essay in Classical Modal Logic. Filosofiska föreningen och Filosofiska institutionen vid Uppsala universitet (1971)
20. Sobociński, B.: Modal system S4.4. J. Form. Log. **5**(4), 305–312 (1964)
21. Zeman, J.Z.: A study of some systems in the neighbourhood of S4.4. J. Form. Log. **12**(3), 341–357 (1971)

Computer-Supported Analysis of Arguments in Climate Engineering

David Fuenmayor[1](✉) and Christoph Benzmüller[1,2]

[1] Freie Universität Berlin, Berlin, Germany
david.fuenmayor@fu-berlin.de
[2] University of Luxembourg, Esch-sur-Alzette, Luxembourg

Abstract. Climate Engineering (CE) is the intentional large-scale intervention in the Earth's climate system to counter climate change. CE is highly controversial, spurring global debates about whether and under which conditions it should be considered. We focus on the computer-supported analysis of a small subset of the arguments pro and contra CE interventions as presented in the work of Betz and Cacean (2012), namely those drawing on the "ethics of risk"; these arguments point out uncertainties in future deployment of CE technologies. The aim of this paper is to demonstrate and explain the application of higher-order interactive and automated theorem proving (utilizing shallow semantical embeddings) to the logical analysis of "real-life" argumentative discourse.

Keywords: Argumentation · Knowledge representation · Higher-order logic · Automated theorem proving · Isabelle · Climate Engineering

1 Introduction

Climate Engineering (CE), aka. Geo-engineering, is the intentional large-scale intervention in the Earth's climate system in order to counter climate change. Proposed CE technologies (e.g., solar radiation management, carbon dioxide removal) are highly controversial, spurring global debates about whether and under which conditions they should be considered. Criticisms to CE range from diverting attention and resources from much needed mitigation policies to potentially catastrophic side-effects; thus the cure may become worse than the disease. The analyzed arguments around the CE debate presented in this paper originate from Betz and Cacean's book [6], which is a slightly modified and updated translation of a study commissioned by the German Federal Ministry of Education and Research (BMBF) on "Ethical Aspects of Climate Engineering" finalized in spring 2011. Betz and Cacean's work aimed at providing a quite complete overview of the arguments around CE at the time. However, it is to expect that it has become partially outdated meanwhile. The illustrative analysis carried out in the present paper

Supported by VolkswagenStiftung, grant *Consistent, Rational Arguments in Politics (CRAP)*.

M. Dastani et al. (Eds.): CLAR 2020, LNAI 12061, pp. 104–115, 2020.
https://doi.org/10.1007/978-3-030-44638-3_7

focuses on a small subset of the CE argumentative landscape, namely on those arguments concerned with the "ethics of risk" ([6] p. 38ff.) which point out (potentially dangerous) uncertainties in future deployment of CE.

Our objective is to further illustrate and explore an approach previously presented at the CLAR-2018 conference [14], which concerns the application of (higher-order) interactive theorem proving to the logical analysis of individual arguments and argument networks. In that work we reconstructed several variants of Gödel's ontological argument[1] using the proof assistant *Isabelle*; initially as networks of abstract nodes, which were mechanically tested for validity and (in)consistency after adding or removing dialectical relations (attack or support); and later each node became "instantiated" by identifying it with a formula of a target (higher-order modal) logic and the experiments were repeated. Employing theorem provers and model finders, we showed that, e.g., consistency results for the abstracted arguments provide no guarantee at all at the instantiated level, i.e., after the semantics of the argument nodes is added. Drawing on this and other similar results, we argued that the analysis of non-trivial natural-language arguments at the abstract argumentation level is useful, but of limited explanatory power. Achieving such explanatory power requires the extension of techniques from abstract argumentation with means for deep semantical analysis using expressive logic formalisms (cf. approaches inspired by Montague semantics [15]) and, vice versa, methods for semantical analysis can become enriched by integrating them with contemporary argumentation frameworks.

In the current work we are formalizing and evaluating an extract from a quite contemporary and controversial discourse topic (in contrast to the previous, more philosophical arguments). This time we focus from the beginning on instantiated argument networks and on the use of automated tools to support the process of reconstructing both individual arguments and attack (resp. support) relations, by adding missing (implicit) premises. We aim at illustrating how the utilization of reasoning technology for very expressive (e.g. higher-order) logics has realistic prospects in the analysis of "real-life" argumentative discourse. In particular, our results suggest that this technology can be very useful to help in the reconstruction of argument networks using structured, deductive approaches (e.g. *ABA* [12] and *Deductive Argumentation* [4,5])[2] and also to identify implicit

---

[1] Ontological arguments (or proofs) are arguments for the existence of a Godlike being, common since centuries in philosophy and theology. More recently, they have attracted the attention of logicians, not only because of their interesting history, but also because of their quite sophisticated logical structures.

[2] Our reason for choosing a deductive approach over a defeasible one had originally a technical motivation: the base logic provided (off-the-shelf) in *Isabelle/HOL* is classical (monotonic). In fact, the *shallow* semantical embedding of non-classical object logics reuses the consequence relation (i.e. the proof methods) of the meta-logic. Embedding a non-monotonic logic in *Isabelle/HOL* can certainly be done (e.g. by *deep* embeddings or by explicit modeling of a non-monotonic consequence relation), but we are not currently pursuing such an approach, since this would be more complex from a user perspective and also take a toll on the performance of automated tools). In this respect we have chosen to treat arguments as deductions, thus locating all fallibility of an argument in its (sometimes implicit) premises.

and idle premises in arguments (cf. our previous work [13]). The case study presented in Sect. 3 has been carried out employing the *Isabelle/HOL* proof assistant [16] for classical higher-order logic (HOL).[3] Sources for this case study have been made available online (https://github.com/davfuenmayor/CE-Debate). We encourage the interested reader to try out (and improve on) this work.

2   Framework

In previous work on the logical analysis of argumentative discourse, we have presented an interpretive approach named computational hermeneutics, amenable to partial mechanization using three kinds of automated reasoning technology: (i) theorem provers, which tell us whether a (formalized) claim logically follows from a set of assumptions; (ii) model finders, which give us (counter-)examples for formulas in the context of a background set of assumptions; and (iii) so-called "hammers", which automatically invoke (i) as to find minimal sets of relevant premises sufficient to derive a claim, whose consistency can later be verified by (ii). We exemplified this approach by using some implementations of (i-iii) for higher-order logic provided by the *Isabelle/HOL* proof assistant. In computational hermeneutics, we work iteratively on an argument by choosing (tentatively at first) a logic for formalization and then working back and forth on the formalization of its premises and conclusion, while getting real-time feedback about the suitability of our choices (including the chosen logic) from a proof assistant. In particular, following the interpretive "principle of charity" [10], we aim at formalizations which render the argument as logically valid, while having a consistent and minimal set of assumptions. These actions are to be repeated until arriving at a state of *reflective equilibrium*: a state where our arguments and claims have the highest degree of coherence and acceptability according to syntactic and, particularly, inferential criteria of adequacy (see [13,14]).

Drawing upon the literature on structured argumentation graphs, in particular on Besnard and Hunter's work [5], we conceive an argument as a pair consisting of (i) a set of formulas (premises), from which (ii) another formula (conclusion) logically follows according to a previously chosen logic for formalization. Besnard and Hunter further introduce and interrelate different kinds of *attack* relations between arguments (defeaters, undercuts, and rebuttals; cf. [5]) which can be all subsumed, as we do, by considering an attack between (a set of) arguments A and B as the inconsistency of the set of formulas formed by the conclusion(s) of A together with the premises of B. Drawing upon the work of Cayrol and Lagasquie-Schiex on bipolar argumentation frameworks (BAF) [9], we also consider *support* relations between arguments. The original support notion of BAFs will also be extended to the case where two (or more) arguments *jointly* support another one (as happens with arguments A47 and A48 jointly supporting A22 in our case study). To put it more formally:

---

[3] HOL, also known as Church's type theory, is a logic of functions formulated on top of the simply typed lambda-calculus, which also provides a foundation for functional programming [2].

Definition 1. *A (deductive) argument is an ordered pair $\langle \varphi, \alpha \rangle$, where $\varphi \vdash_{(L)} \alpha$ for some chosen logic L (which may not be explicitly mentioned). φ is the support, or premises/assumptions of the argument, and α is the claim, or conclusion, of the argument. Other constraints we set on arguments are consistency: φ has to be logically consistent (according to the chosen logic L); and minimality: there is no $\psi \subset \varphi$ such that $\psi \vdash \alpha$. For an argument $A = \langle \varphi, \alpha \rangle$ the function Premises(A) returns φ and Conclusion(A) returns (a singleton set containing) α. Note that while every pair $\langle \varphi, \alpha \rangle$ can be seen as a candidate argument during the process of formal reconstruction, only those pairs which satisfy the given constraints are considered as arguments proper.*

Definition 2. *An argument A attacks (is a defeater of) B iff the set $Conclusion(A) \cup Premises(B)$ is inconsistent. Notice that this definition subsumes the more traditional one for classical logic, $Conclusion(A) \vdash \neg X$ for some $X \in Premises(B)$, while allowing for paraconsistent formalization logics where explosion (inconsistency) does not necessarily follow from pairs of contradictory formulas. This definition can be seamlessly extended to two (or more) arguments: A_1 and A_2 (jointly) attack B iff the set $Conclusion(A_1) \cup Conclusion(A_2) \cup Premises(B)$ is inconsistent.*

Definition 3. *An argument A supports B iff $Conclusion(A) \vdash X$ for some $X \in Premises(B)$. This definition can be seamlessly extended to two (or more) arguments: A_1 and A_2 (jointly) support B iff $Conclusion(A_1) \cup Conclusion(A_2) \vdash X$ for some $X \in Premises(B)$.*

We want to highlight the similarity in spirit between ours and Besnard and Hunter's [5] "descriptive approach" to reconstructing argument graphs (from natural language sources); where we have some abstract argument graph as the input, together with some informal text description of each argument. Thus, the task becomes to find the appropriate logical formulas for the premises and conclusion of each argument, compatible with the choice of the logic of formalization. As will become clear when analyzing our case study in Sect. 3, there is a need for finding appropriate "implicit" premises which render the individual arguments logically valid and additionally honor their intended dialectical role in the input abstract graph (i.e., attacking or supporting other arguments). This interpretive aspect, in particular, has been emphasized in our computational hermeneutics approach [13,14], as well as the possibility of modifying the input abstract argument graph as new insights, resulting from the formalization process, appear. In their exposition of structured argumentation (see, e.g., [5]) Besnard and Hunter duly highlight the fact that "richer" logic formalisms (i.e., more expressive than "rule-based" ones like, e.g., logic programming) are more appropriate for reconstructing "real-world arguments". Such representational and interpretive issues are tackled in our approach by the use of different (combinations of) non-classical and higher-order logics for formalization. For this we utilize the shallow semantical embeddings (SSE) approach to combining logics [3]. SSE exploits HOL as a meta-logic in order to embed the syntax and semantics of diverse object logics

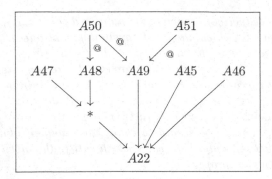

Fig. 1. Abstract argumentation network for the ethics of risk cluster in the CE debate (arrows labeled with @ indicate *attack*); the * indicates a *joint support*.

(e.g. modal, deontic, paraconsistent), thereby turning theorem proving systems for higher-order logics into universal reasoning engines [1].

3 Case Study

3.1 Individual (Component) Arguments

As has been observed by Betz and Cacean [6], incalculable side-effects and imponderables constitute one of the main reasons against CE technology deployment. Thus, arguments from the *ethics of risk* primarily support the thesis: "CE deployment is morally wrong" (named T9 in [6]) and make for an argument cluster with a non-trivial dialectical structure which we aim at reconstructing in this section. We focus on six arguments from the ethics of risk, which entail that the deployment of CE technologies (today as in the future) is not desirable because of being morally wrong (argument A22). Supporting arguments of A22 are: A45, A46, A47, A48, A49 (using the original notation in Betz and Cacean's work [6]). In particular, two of these arguments, namely A48 and A49, are further attacked by A50 and A51[4] (Fig. 1).

Ethics of Risk Argument (A22). The argument has as premise: "CE deployment is morally wrong" and as conclusion: "CE deployment is not desirable". Notice that both are formalized as (modally) valid propositions, i.e., true in

---

[4] We strive to remain as close as possible to the original argument network as introduced by Betz and Cacean [6] (with one exception concerning the dialectical relation among arguments A47, A48, A50 and A22, which will be commented upon later on). The reader will notice that some of the arguments could have been merged together. However, Betz and Cacean have deliberately decided not to do so. We conjecture that this is due to traceability concerns, given the fact that most arguments have been compiled from different bibliographic sources and authors. See [9] and [17] for a discussion on this issue.

all possible worlds or situations. We are thus presupposing a possible-worlds semantics for our logic of formalization while restricting ourselves, for the time being, to a propositional logic (to keep it simple). Also notice that we introduce two new, uninterpreted propositional constants ("CEisWrong" and "CEisNot-Desirable") and interrelate them by means of an implicit premise (A22-P2), but without further constraining their meaning at this stage of the modeling process. In general, term meanings (understood as their inferential roles) will gradually become determined as we add other companion arguments to the analysis.

Since this is the first argument to be represented in the proof assistant *Isabelle* in this work, we will pay special attention to the syntactic elements used for its formulation in the system. First notice that we use the keyword **consts** to introduce two non-interpreted constants; their type is $w{\Rightarrow}bool$, which corresponds to the type for characteristic functions of sets of worlds (of type w).

consts $CEisWrong{::}w{\Rightarrow}bool$ — type for world-contingent propositional constants
consts $CEisNotDesirable{::}w{\Rightarrow}bool$

Now we use *Isabelle*'s keyword **definition** to introduce interpreted constants (of Boolean type). The first two definitions introduce the premises of the argument, labeled *A22-P1* and *A22-P2*, and the last one introduces its conclusion, labeled *A22-C*.[5] We introduce an equivalence between two formulas (by employing the symbol $\equiv$) with the *definiendum* on its left-hand side and the *definiens* on its right-hand side. The expression $[\vdash P]$ for some proposition P stands for modal validity, i.e., truth in all worlds, formalized as: $\forall w.\ P(w)$ (not shown).

definition $A22\text{-}P1\ \equiv\ [\vdash CEisWrong]$
definition $A22\text{-}P2\ \equiv\ [\vdash CEisWrong \rightarrow CEisNotDesirable]$
definition $A22\text{-}C\ \equiv\ [\vdash CEisNotDesirable]$

Below we employ the model finder *Nitpick* [7] to find a model satisfying both premises and conclusion of the formalized argument. This shows consistency.

lemma assumes $A22\text{-}P1$ **and** $A22\text{-}P2$ **and** $A22\text{-}C$ **shows** *True*
    nitpick [*satisfy*] **oops** — Nitpick presents a simple model (not shown)

This first argument (A22) serves as a quite straightforward illustration of the role of implicit, unstated premises in enabling the reconstruction of a candidate argument as a valid argument (proper). Since, in our approach, we treat arguments as deductions, we will encode them as meta-logical theorems stating that a formula (conclusion) logically follows from a collection of other formulas (premises) in this form: $\varphi_1,\ \ldots\ \varphi_n \vdash \alpha$ (recall *Definition 1* in Sect. 2); which is encoded using *Isabelle* notation as **assumes** φ_1 **and** $\ldots$ φ_n **shows** α.[6] In this first example, we utilize the tableaux-based prover *blast* to verify that the conclusion follows from the premises.

---

[5] Notice that we will keep this same suffix convention throughout this work.
[6] Notice the similarity to sequents in Gentzen-type deductive systems. In fact, *Isabelle/HOL*'s meta-logic is based upon (higher-order) Gentzen-type natural deduction. It is also worth mentioning that our implementation in *Isabelle/HOL* handles arguments as (sequent-like) inferences independently from each other. This is dif-

theorem *A22-valid*: **assumes** *A22-P1* **and** *A22-P2* **shows** *A22-C*
   using *A22-C-def A22-P2-def A22-P1-def assms(1) assms(2)* **by** *blast*

Termination Problem (A45). CE measures do not possess viable exit options. If deployment is terminated abruptly, catastrophic climate change ensues.[7] Notice that we add as implicit premise (A45-P1) that there a real possibility of CE interventions being terminated abruptly.

   consts *CEisTerminated::w⇒bool* — world-contingent propositional constants
   consts *CEisCatastrophic::w⇒bool*
   definition *A45-P1* ≡ [⊢ ◊*CEisTerminated*] — additional (implicit) premise
   definition *A45-P2* ≡ [⊢ *CEisTerminated → CEisCatastrophic*]
   definition *A45-C* ≡ [⊢ ◊*CEisCatastrophic*]

Notice that we have introduced in the above formalization the ◊ modal operator to signify that a proposition is possibly true (e.g. at a future point in time).

   theorem *A45-valid*: **assumes** *A45-P1* **and** *A45-P2* **shows** *A45-C*
   using *A45-C-def A45-P1-def A45-P2-def assms(1) assms(2)* **by** *blast*

No Long-Term Risk Control (A46). Our social systems and institutions are possibly not capable of controlling risk technologies on long time scales and of ensuring that they are handled with proper technical care [6]. Notice that we can make best sense of this objection as (implicitly) presupposing a risk of CE-caused catastrophes (A46-P2).

   consts *RiskControlAbility::w⇒bool*
   definition *A46-P1* ≡ [⊢ ◊¬*RiskControlAbility*]
   definition *A46-P2* ≡ [⊢ ¬*RiskControlAbility → ◊CEisCatastrophic*] — implicit
   definition *A46-C* ≡ [⊢ ◊*CEisCatastrophic*]

As before, we can use automated tools to find further implicit premises, which may actually correspond to modifications to the logic of formalization. In fact, the argument A46 needs a (stronger) modal logic *K4* to succeed, so the corresponding additional premise is: *Ax4*: [⊢ ∀φ. □φ → □□φ] (which can be read intuitively as: "necessary propositions are so, necessarily" corresponding to transitivity of the accessibility relation, cf. possible-worlds semantics for modal logic).

   lemma assumes *A46-P1* **and** *A46-P2* **shows** *A46-C*
   nitpick oops — counterexample found (not shown – modal axiom 4 is required).
   theorem *A46-valid*: **assumes** *A46-P1* **and** *A46-P2* **and** *Ax4* **shows** *A46-C*
   using *A46-C-def A46-P1-def A46-P2-def assms(1) assms(2) assms(3)* **by** *blast*

---

ferent than having the premises for all arguments as axioms in a same theory resp. knowledge-base and drawing conclusions as theorems. In our approach, two arguments with mutually inconsistent premises will not cause any problems nor trivialize anything. In the same vein, conflicting arguments with the same explicit premises are also possible; the cause for the conflicting conclusions is to be found in additional (implicit) premises.

[7] Cf. Betz and Cacean's work [6] for sources for these and other proposed theses and arguments in the CE debate.

CE Interventions Are Irreversible (A47). As presented in [6], this argument consists of a simple sentence (its conclusion), which states that CE represents an irreversible intervention, i.e., that once the first interventions in world's climate have been set in motion, there is no way to "undo" them. In the following arguments we work with a predicate logic (including quantification), and thus introduce an additional type ("e") for actions (interventions).

> **typedecl** e — introduces a new type for actions
> **consts** $CEAction::e \Rightarrow w \Rightarrow bool$ — notice type for (world-dependent) predicates
> **consts** $Irreversible::e \Rightarrow w \Rightarrow bool$
> **definition** $A47\text{-}C \equiv [\vdash \forall I.\ CEAction(I) \rightarrow Irreversible(I)]$

No Ability to Retain Options After Irreversible Interventions (A48). Irreversible interventions (of any kind) narrow the options of future generations in an unacceptable way, i.e., it is wrong to carry them out [6].

> **consts** $WrongAction::e \Rightarrow w \Rightarrow bool$
> **definition** $A48\text{-}C \equiv [\vdash \forall I.\ Irreversible(I) \rightarrow WrongAction(I)]$

Unpredictable Side-Effects Are Wrong (A49). As long as side-effects of CE technologies cannot be reliably predicted, their deployment is morally wrong [6]. A49-P2 suggests that interventions with unpredictable side-effects are wrong.

> **consts** $USideEffects::e \Rightarrow w \Rightarrow bool$
> **definition** $A49\text{-}P1 \equiv [\vdash \forall I.\ CEAction(I) \rightarrow USideEffects(I)]$
> **definition** $A49\text{-}P2 \equiv [\vdash \forall I.\ USideEffects(I) \rightarrow WrongAction(I)]$ — implicit
> **definition** $A49\text{-}C \equiv [\vdash \forall I.\ CEAction(I) \rightarrow WrongAction(I)]$

> **theorem** $A49\text{-}valid$: **assumes** $A49\text{-}P1$ **and** $A49\text{-}P2$ **shows** $A49\text{-}C$
>   **using** $A49$-C-def $A49$-P1-def $A49$-P2-def assms(1) assms(2) **by** blast

Mitigation Is Also Irreversible (A50). Mitigation of climate change (i.e., the "preventive alternative" to CE), too, is, at least to some extent, an irreversible intervention with unforeseen side-effects [6].

> **consts** Mitigation::e — constant of same type as actions/interventions
> **definition** $A50\text{-}C \equiv [\vdash Irreversible(Mitigation) \wedge USideEffects(Mitigation)]$

All Interventions Have Unpredictable Side-Effects (A51). This defense of CE states that we do never completely foresee the consequences of our actions (anyways), and thus aims at somehow trivializing the concerns regarding unforeseen side-effects of CE.

> **definition** $A51\text{-}C \equiv [\vdash \forall I.\ USideEffects(I)]$

3.2 Reconstructing the Argument Graph

The claim that an argument (or a set of arguments) attacks resp. supports
another argument is, in our approach, conceived as an argument in itself, which
also needs to be reconstructed as logically valid by (possibly) adding implicit
premises. Below we introduce our generalized *attack* resp. *support* relations
between arguments along the lines of structured and bipolar argumentation (cf.
[5] and [9] respectively; and also recall *Definitions* 2 and 3 in Sect. 2).[8]

> **abbreviation** *attacks1* $\varphi \ \psi \quad \equiv (\varphi \wedge \psi) \longrightarrow False$ — for one attacker
> **abbreviation** *supports1* $\varphi \ \psi \quad \equiv \varphi \longrightarrow \psi$ — for one supporter
> **abbreviation** *attacks2* $\gamma \ \varphi \ \psi \ \equiv (\gamma \wedge \varphi \wedge \psi) \longrightarrow False$ — for two attackers
> **abbreviation** *supports2* $\gamma \ \varphi \ \psi \equiv (\gamma \wedge \varphi) \longrightarrow \psi$ — for two supporters

Does A45 Support A22? In this example, as in others, we have utilized
three kinds of automated tools integrated into *Isabelle*: the model finder *Nitpick* [7], which finds a counterexample to the claim that A45 supports A22
(without further implicit premises); the tableaux-based prover *blast*,[9] which can
indeed verify that by adding an implicit premise (if CE is possibly catastrophic
then its deployment is wrong) the support relation obtains; and the "ham-
mer" tool *Sledgehammer* [8], which automatically finds minimal sets of assumptions needed to prove a theorem. Let us recall the corresponding definitions:
$A45\text{-}C \equiv [\vdash \Diamond CEisCatastrophic]$ and $A22\text{-}P1 \equiv [\vdash CEisWrong]$.

> **lemma** *supports1 A45-C A22-P1* **nitpick oops** — countermodel found
> **theorem assumes** $[\vdash \Diamond\ CEisCatastrophic \rightarrow CEisWrong]$ — implicit
> **shows** *supports1 A45-C A22-P1* **using** *A22-P1-def A45-C-def assms(1)* **by** *blast*

Does A46 Support A22? The same implicit premise as before is needed
(recall the definition: $A46\text{-}C \equiv [\vdash \Diamond CEisCatastrophic]$).

> **lemma** *supports1 A46-C A22-P1* **nitpick oops** — countermodel found
> **theorem assumes** $[\vdash \Diamond CEisCatastrophic \rightarrow CEisWrong]$ — implicit
> **shows** *supports1 A46-C A22-P1* **using** *A22-P1-def A46-C-def assms(1)* **by** *blast*

Do A47 and A48 (together) Support A22? Here we have diverged from
the argument network as introduced in Betz and Cacean [6], where A48 is rendered as an argument supporting A47. We claim that our reconstruction is more
faithful to the given natural language description of the arguments and also better represents their intended dialectical relations. Also notice that an implicit
premise is needed to reconstruct this support relation as logically valid, namely
that if every CE action is wrong, then deployment of CE is wrong. (Let us recall
again the definitions: $A47\text{-}C \equiv [\vdash \forall I.\ CEAction(I) \rightarrow Irreversible(I)]$ and
$A48\text{-}C \equiv [\vdash \forall I.\ Irreversible(I) \rightarrow WrongAction(I)].$)

---

[8] Notice that we use *Isabelle*'s keyword **abbreviation** to introduce these definitions
as "syntactic sugar".
[9] This is a prover among several others integrated into *Isabelle* [16].

lemma *supports2 A47-C A48-C A22-P1* **nitpick oops** — countermodel found
theorem assumes $[\vdash \forall I.\ CEAction(I) \to WrongAction(I)] \longrightarrow [\vdash CEisWrong]$
   shows *supports2 A47-C A48-C A22-P1*
   using *A22-P1-def A47-C-def A48-C-def assms(1)* **by** *blast*

Does A49 Support A22? Note that the previous implicit premise is needed too (recall the definition: $A49\text{-}C \equiv [\vdash \forall I.\ CEAction(I) \to WrongAction(I)]$).

 lemma *supports1 A49-C A22-P1* **nitpick oops** — countermodel found
 theorem assumes $[\vdash \forall I.\ CEAction(I) \to WrongAction(I)] \longrightarrow [\vdash CEisWrong]$
   shows *supports1 A49-C A22-P1* **using** *A22-P1-def A49-C-def assms(1)* **by** *blast*

Does A50 Attack Both A48 and A49? Here, again, we diverge from Betz and Cacean's [6] original argument network. We think that, given the natural language description of the arguments, an attack relation between A50 and A48 is better motivated than between A50 and A47 (as originally presented). The indirect attack towards the main thesis (conclusion of A22) persists, since A47 and A48 jointly support A22 (see above). Also notice that we employ an additional, implicit premise to reconstruct the attack relation, namely that mitigation of climate change is not a wrong action. (Let us recall again the corresponding definitions: $A50\text{-}C \equiv [\vdash Irreversible(Mitigation) \land USideEffects(Mitigation)]$, $A48\text{-}C \equiv [\vdash \forall I.\ Irreversible(I) \to WrongAction(I)]$ and finally $A49\text{-}P2 \equiv [\vdash \forall I.\ USideEffects(I) \to WrongAction(I)]$.)

  lemma *attacks1 A50-C A48-C* **nitpick oops** — countermodel found
  lemma *attacks1 A50-C A49-P2* **nitpick oops** — countermodel found

  theorem assumes $[\vdash \neg WrongAction(Mitigation)]$ — implicit premise
    shows *attacks1 A50-C A48-C*
    using *A48-C-def A50-C-def assms(1)* **by** *blast*
  theorem assumes $[\vdash \neg WrongAction(Mitigation)]$ — implicit premise
    shows *attacks1 A50-C A49-P2*
    using *A49-P2-def A50-C-def assms(1)* **by** *blast*

Does A51 Attack A49? Notice that the previous additional premise is required again to reconstruct this attack relation as logically valid. (Recall the definitions: $A49\text{-}P2 \equiv [\vdash \forall I.\ USideEffects(I) \to WrongAction(I)]$ and $A51\text{-}C \equiv [\vdash \forall I. USideEffects(I)]$.)

  lemma *attacks1 A51-C A49-P2* **nitpick oops** — countermodel found
  theorem assumes $[\vdash \neg WrongAction(Mitigation)]$ — implicit premise
    shows *attacks1 A51-C A49-P2* **using** *A49-P2-def A51-C-def assms(1)* **by** *blast*

4   Challenges and Prospects

We are working on extending the current analysis to other argument clusters in the CE discourse, as presented in [6] (also drawing on more recent sources). An analysis at the abstract level, e.g. by using Dung's dialectic semantics [11], is also in sight (also extended with support relations, cf. BAF [9]). Preliminary experiments have shown that the expressivity of higher-order logic (HOL) indeed allows us to encode Dung's definitions for complete, grounded, preferred and stable semantics in *Isabelle/HOL* and to use automated tools for HOL to carry out computations. This can be very useful for prototyping tasks and as well for reasoning with arguments at the abstract and structural level in an integrated fashion. Further work is necessary to obtain a satisfactorily usable and scalable implementation. We are further working on utilizing shallow semantic embeddings (SSE) of non-classical logics (modal, intensional, deontic, paraconsistent, among several others) into HOL in order to continue fostering a logico-pluralist approach towards the reconstruction of structured argument graphs (e.g. by employing attack resp. support relations parameterized with different base logics). Concerning the prospects for a fully automated argument reconstruction process, it is worth mentioning that the initial step from natural language to formal representations lies outside our proposed framework. For example, in the presented case study we have "outsourced" the argumentation-mining task to the researchers who carried out the analysis (Betz and Cacean), while the semantic-parsing task was carried out "manually" by us. However, we are much impressed by recent progress in natural language processing (NLP) for these applications and follow with great interest the latest developments in the argumentation mining community. Another important challenge concerns the problem of coming up with candidates for additional (implicit) premises that render an inference valid, which is an instance of the old problem of abduction. The evaluation of candidate formulas is indeed supported by our tool-set, e.g. (counter)model finders can determine (in)consistency automatically, and theorem provers and "hammers" help us verify validity using minimal sets of assumptions (also useful to identify "question-begging" ones). The creative part of coming up with (plausible) candidates is, however, still a task for humans in our approach. Abductive reasoning techniques for the kind of expressive logics we work with (e.g. intensional, first- and higher-order) remain, to the best of our knowledge, very limited, so as to support full automation. We could reuse techniques and tools for some less expressive fragments of HOL (in cases where formalized arguments are bound to remain inside those fragments); but in general we strive for the finest granularity level in the semantic analysis (e.g. along the lines of Montague semantics [15]). With all its pros and cons, this is the distinguishing aspect of our approach.

Acknowledgements. We thank the anonymous reviewers for their valuable remarks and comments, which significantly helped to improve the final version of this paper.

References

1. Benzmüller, C.: Universal (meta-)logical reasoning: recent successes. Sci. Comput. Program. **172**, 48–62 (2019)
2. Benzmüller, C., Andrews, P.: Church's type theory. In: Zalta, E.N. (ed.) The Stanford Encyclopedia of Philosophy. Metaphysics Research Lab, Stanford University, summer 2019 edn. (2019)
3. Benzmüller, C., Paulson, L.C.: Quantified multimodal logics in simple type theory. Log. Univers. (Special Issue on Multimodal Logics) **7**(1), 7–20 (2013). https://doi.org/10.1007/s11787-012-0052-y
4. Besnard, P., Hunter, A.: Elements of Argumentation, vol. 47. MIT Press, Cambridge (2008)
5. Besnard, P., Hunter, A.: Constructing argument graphs with deductive arguments: a tutorial. Argum. Comput. **5**(1), 5–30 (2014)
6. Betz, G., Cacean, S.: Ethical Aspects of Climate Engineering. KIT Scientific Publishing, Karlsruhe (2012)
7. Blanchette, J.C., Nipkow, T.: Nitpick: a counterexample generator for higher-order logic based on a relational model finder. In: Kaufmann, M., Paulson, L.C. (eds.) ITP 2010. LNCS, vol. 6172, pp. 131–146. Springer, Heidelberg (2010). https://doi.org/10.1007/978-3-642-14052-5_11
8. Blanchette, J.C., Böhme, S., Paulson, L.C.: Extending Sledgehammer with SMT solvers. J. Autom. Reasoning **51**(1), 109–128 (2013). https://doi.org/10.1007/s10817-013-9278-5
9. Cayrol, C., Lagasquie-Schiex, M.C.: Bipolar abstract argumentation systems. In: Simari, G., Rahwan, I. (eds.) Argumentation in Artificial Intelligence, pp. 65–84. Springer, Boston (2009). https://doi.org/10.1007/978-0-387-98197-0_4
10. Davidson, D.: Inquiries into Truth and Interpretation: Philosophical Essays, vol. 2. Oxford University Press, Oxford (2001)
11. Dung, P.M.: On the acceptability of arguments and its fundamental role in nonmonotonic reasoning, logic programming and n-person games. Artif. Intell. **77**(2), 321–357 (1995)
12. Dung, P.M., Kowalski, R.A., Toni, F.: Assumption-based argumentation. In: Simari, G., Rahwan, I. (eds.) Argumentation in Artificial Intelligence, pp. 199–218. Springer, Boston (2009). https://doi.org/10.1007/978-0-387-98197-0_10
13. Fuenmayor, D., Benzmüller, C.: A computational-hermeneutic approach for conceptual explicitation. In: Nepomuceno-Fernández, Á., Magnani, L., Salguero-Lamillar, F.J., Barés-Gómez, C., Fontaine, M. (eds.) MBR 2018. SAPERE, vol. 49, pp. 441–469. Springer, Cham (2019). https://doi.org/10.1007/978-3-030-32722-4_25
14. Fuenmayor, D., Benzmüller, C.: Computational hermeneutics: an integrated approach for the logical analysis of natural-language arguments. In: Liao, B., Ågotnes, T., Wang, Y.N. (eds.) CLAR 2018. LASLL, pp. 187–207. Springer, Singapore (2019). https://doi.org/10.1007/978-981-13-7791-4_9
15. Janssen, T.M.V.: Montague semantics. In: Zalta, E.N. (ed.) The Stanford Encyclopedia of Philosophy. Metaphysics Research Lab, Stanford University, spring 2020 edn. (2020)
16. Nipkow, T., Wenzel, M., Paulson, L.C. (eds.): Isabelle/HOL. LNCS, vol. 2283. Springer, Heidelberg (2002). https://doi.org/10.1007/3-540-45949-9
17. Prakken, H.: Modelling support relations between arguments in debates. In: Chesñevar, C., Falappa, M., Ferme, E. (eds.) Argumentation-Based Proofs of Endearment. Essays in Honor of Guillermo R. Simari on the Occasion of his 70th Birthday, pp. 349–365. College Publications, London (2018)

A Logic of Knowledge and Belief
Based on Abstract Arguments

Xu Li and Yì N. Wáng(⊠)

Department of Philosophy, Zhejiang University, Hangzhou, China
ynw@xixilogic.org

Abstract. We introduce a logic of knowledge and belief in a framework in which belief has a standard KD45 characterization and knowledge undergoes the classical tripartite analysis that knowledge is justified true belief, which has a natural link to the studies of logics of evidence and justification. The characterization of knowledge is based on a flexible model that avoids unwanted properties concerned with the problem of logical omniscience. We axiomatize the logic, prove its soundness and completeness, and then extend the logic to a multi-agent setting. We also compare our framework with existing logics of knowledge and belief.

Keywords: Knowledge · Belief · Epistemic logic · Doxastic logic · Justified true belief

1 Introduction

Modern studies in epistemic logic and doxastic logic was initiated in [26,46] and later examined extensively in [20,33]. Most variants of epistemic and doxastic logics do not mix the two notions. Although there are traditions characterizing both knowledge and belief in one framework (say, [29,38]), this has received far less attention compared with the efforts made in either side.

For the literature on the logics of both knowledge and belief, and in particular of the relationship between them, there are various approaches that can largely be classified into two categories: those treating both knowledge and belief as primitive concepts, and those where knowledge or belief is a derived concept. We will look more into this in Sect. 5, but just to mention here approaches based on the famous tripartite definition of knowledge dating back to Plato, that knowledge is "justified true belief" (though Gettier [23] argues this is insufficient), which falls into the second category (see, e.g., [32] for an implementation in logic). Our work lies in this category as well.

We study knowledge and belief in the field of modal logic. We interpret belief using a primitive KD45 relation (a binary relation that is serial, transitive and Euclidean), and interpret knowledge as a true belief which has an appropriate

Funding support by the National Social Science Foundation of China (Grant No. 16CZX048, 18ZDA290).

M. Dastani et al. (Eds.): CLAR 2020, LNAI 12061, pp. 116–130, 2020.
https://doi.org/10.1007/978-3-030-44638-3_8

argument, in the sense that all of the basic facts in the argument are beliefs. This clearly relates to the work on logical approaches in the justification of knowledge [10,40], in particular, the fruitful direction of justification logic [3,4,21], which will be discussed in Sect. 5.

The application of justification logic in the discipline of epistemic logic [6,7] connects to the problem of logical omniscience. In normal modal systems, all logical validities are *necessarily* true, since the technical characterization in a normal epistemic logic makes it true that the modal box operator is closed under logical consequence. This becomes a problem when the modal box is used to express knowing and believing in epistemic and doxastic logics. Classical modal systems, such as those between S4 and S5 which are typically used to characterize knowledge and those like KD45 and K45 for belief, all have the problem of logical omniscience. This problem has been recognized already in [26, p. 31], and we refer to [36,37] for more details. One of the main solutions to this problem was to view knowledge or belief defined in this way to be *implicit* or *potential* (or more generally, some concept that is not knowledge or belief, but closely related), that one can only obtain in an ideal case, such as having an extreme power of reasoning. Only when the one is *aware* of the implicit knowledge or belief, it becomes *explicit*. This tradition has attracted a lot of attention since the seminal work on the logic of (un)awareness [19].

There have been solutions to the problem of logical omniscience without using the notion of awareness, since very early [16,27] to very new attempts [11,18]. For example, [45] introduces a logic of knowledge that does not have the problem by means of treating "knowing p" requiring the truth of p and the truth of its "epistemic counterparts". This has a close relationship to our model, and will be discussed in Sect. 5. Our framework avoids the problem of logical omniscience for knowledge, due to a similar style of construction.

The paper is presented in this way. We first introduce a logic of knowledge and belief called LKB in the next section. An axiomatization of LKB is introduced in Sect. 3, and we show its soundness and completeness there. In Sect. 4 we extend LKB to characterize multiple agents. We discussed related work in Sect. 5 and conclude in Sect. 6.

2   The Logic LKB

In this section we introduce a logic LKB for reasoning about knowledge and belief in a framework based on abstract justification. We first introduce the language of LKB, called $\mathcal{L}$ here. We assume a countably infinite set P of propositional variables.

Definition 1 (languages). *The language $\mathcal{L}$ for LKB is given by the following grammar rule:*

$$\varphi ::= p \mid \neg\varphi \mid (\varphi \wedge \varphi) \mid B\varphi \mid K\varphi,$$

where $p \in P$. Moreover, let $\mathcal{PL}$ be the language of propositional logic, i.e., the sublanguage of $\mathcal{L}$ without the operators B and K.

$B\varphi$ and $K\varphi$ are read as "the agent *believes* φ" and "the agent *knows* φ", respectively. For simplicity, here we focus on a single-agent system. We shall study a multi-agent extension in Sect. 4. Other propositional connectives are defined by usual abbreviations.

Now we introduce the formal models for LKB.

Definition 2 (models). *A model is a quadruple $M = (W, R, S, V)$ such that:*

- *W is a non-empty set of (possible) worlds (or states),*
- *$R \subseteq W \times W$ is a binary relation that is serial, transitive and Euclidean,*
- *$S : W \to \wp(\wp(\wp(W)))$ is an argumentation function, and*
- *$V : P \to \wp(W)$ is a valuation that assigns every propositional variable a set of possible worlds.*

As usual, M, together with a state w of it, forms a pointed model *(M, w).*

In the above definition, it is clear that (W, R, V) forms a standard Kripke model, more precisely, a *KD45 model*, as the relation R is serial, transitive and Euclidean. This follows the classical way of modeling belief [20,33]. What deserves extra explanation is the argumentation function S, which maps a state to a set of sets of sets of states. This has a flavor of neighborhood semantics [15]. Intuitively, a set of states will be used to stand for the states where a formula is true. A set of formulas is understood as a argument (or proof). Hence S will be used in an interpretation to link a state to a set of arguments, which will play an important role in the interpretation of knowledge.

Let us first introduce the formal semantics.

Definition 3 (satisfaction). *Given a model $M = (W, R, S, V)$ and a world $w \in W$, that a formula α is* satisfied *(or* true*) in the pointed model (M, w) (notation: $M, w \models \alpha$) is inductively defined as follows:*

$$M, w \models p \qquad \textit{iff } w \in V(p)$$
$$M, w \models \neg\varphi \qquad \textit{iff not } M, w \models \varphi$$
$$M, w \models (\varphi \wedge \psi) \quad \textit{iff } M, w \models \varphi \textit{ and } M, w \models \psi$$
$$M, w \models B\varphi \qquad \textit{iff for all } u \in W, \textit{ if } wRu \textit{ then } M, u \models \varphi$$
$$M, w \models K\varphi \qquad \textit{iff } M, w \models \varphi \textit{ and there exists } X \in S(w) \textit{ such that: } [\![\varphi]\!]_M \in X$$
$$\textit{and for all } \psi \in \mathcal{PL} \cup \{\varphi\}, \textit{ if } [\![\psi]\!]_M \in X \textit{ then } M, w \models B\psi$$

where $[\![\varphi]\!]_M = \{x \in W \mid M, x \models \varphi\}$ denotes the truth set of φ in M (similarly for the truth set of ψ). We omit the subscript M when it is clear from the context.

A formula φ is called valid, *denoted $\models \varphi$, if for all pointed models (M, w), $M, w \models \varphi$; otherwise it is called* invalid. *For any set Γ of formulas, we say φ is a* semantic consequence *of Γ, denoted $\Gamma \models \varphi$, if every pointed model (M, w) that satisfies all formulas of Γ also satisfies φ.*

The interpretation of $K\varphi$ follows the tripartite definition of knowledge, that knowledge is "justified true belief", as it can be easily observed from the interpretation that the truth of $K\varphi$ implies the truth of φ and $B\varphi$, and that there is an argument for φ.

More precisely, $K\varphi$ is true, if φ is true and there is an *appropriate* argument of it, in the sense that all propositional formulas following that argument, together with φ itself, must be believed to be true. In short, an argument comprises the truth sets of its consequences, and an appropriate argument is one such that the consequences are beliefs. A technical issue here is that we could not enforce the belief of all formulas in an argument, or otherwise the inductive definition contains a vicious circle. A typical solution is to consider only simpler formulas (say, according to modal depths), but to make it simple in this paper we consider only propositional formulas and the relevant formula φ. This does get an intuitive explanation: beliefs and disbeliefs are not so important for an argument compared to basic facts. We give an example below to make the above clearer.

Example 1. Consider an agent who *believes* that the number 47 is a prime and all her argument for this is that 47 is not divisible by 7. We may all agree that the agent does not *know* that 47 is a prime since the composite 8 is also not divisible by 7 and the agent's belief happens to be true.

Let p denote the proposition "47 is a prime" and q "8 is a prime", respectively. In the above setting, we see that the agent proposes an argument/reason for p, i.e., every number not divisible by 7 is a prime. In addition to p, the argument leads to other consequences including q. In the formal semantics the argument is represented by some $X \in S(w)$ which comprises the truth sets of its consequences (i.e., the truth sets of p and q).[1]

This scenario can be modeled in our framework by a model $M = (W, R, S, V)$ with $W = \{w\}$, $R = \{(w, w)\}$, $S(w) = \{\{\{w\}, \emptyset\}\}$, $V(p) = \{w\}$ and $V(q) = \emptyset$. Note that $S(w)$ here consists of a unique argument, i.e., $X = \{[\![p]\!], [\![q]\!]\} = \{\{w\}, \emptyset\}$. The *frame* (W, R) on which M is based is typically represented by the following diagram:

It is not hard to verify that $M, w \models Bp$ and $M, w \models p$. Now one can see that $M, w \not\models Kp$: the two consequences of the unique argument X, i.e., p and q, are not all beliefs, for $M, w \not\models Bq$.

Two immediate notes are:

1. We have chosen to model arguments in a semantic way, i.e., truth sets of consequences are used in the interpretation of arguments. We could have used a syntactical method to interpret an argument as a set of formulas (consequences of the argument). A benefit of the latter is to give us a weaker logic that lacks the rule of the replacements of equivalents. We on the other hand tend to admit this rule (see Proposition 1).
2. The interpretation of the knowledge operator includes an $\exists\forall$ type of identification of the appropriate arguments, which may lead to undecidability. A natural constraint can be enforced on the argumentation function S so

---

[1] There are of course other consequences following from this argument, e.g., 1 is a prime, 2 is a prime, etc. But for simplicity, we limit our focus in the formal model.

that there is only a finite number of possible arguments in each state. For simplicity we do not carry out the constraint in this paper.

We list some (in)validities of the logic regarding the characterization of knowledge, including those for characterizing that knowledge is true belief.

Proposition 1 (LKB knowledge). *The following properties hold for all formulas φ and ψ:*

1. *(verity)* $\models K\varphi \to \varphi$
2. *(being belief)* $\models K\varphi \to B\varphi$
3. *(replacement of equivalents) if* $\models \varphi \leftrightarrow \psi$ *then* $\models K\varphi \leftrightarrow K\psi$

The following hold for some formulas φ and ψ:

1. *(lack of distribution over implication)* $\not\models K(\varphi \to \psi) \to (K\varphi \to K\psi)$
2. *(lack of positive introspection)* $\not\models K\varphi \to KK\varphi$
3. *(lack of negative introspection)* $\not\models \neg K\varphi \to K\neg K\varphi$
4. *(lack of generalization) Even if* $\models \varphi$, *it is not necessarily* $\models K\varphi$
5. *Even if* $\models \varphi \to \psi$, *it is not necessarily* $\models K\varphi \to K\psi$.

Proof. The first two clauses can be seen easily from the definitions.

3. Assume $\models \varphi \leftrightarrow \psi$. Let $M = (W, R, S, V)$ be a model and $w \in W$. We need to show that $M, w \models K\varphi \leftrightarrow K\psi$, namely $M, w \models K\varphi$ if and only if $M, w \models K\psi$. Without loss of generality, suppose $M, w \models K\varphi$, and it suffices to show that $M, w \models K\psi$. By definition $M, w \models \varphi$ and there is an appropriate argument X for φ, in the sense that $X \in S(w)$ and $[\![\varphi]\!] \in X$ and $\forall \chi \in \mathcal{PL} \cup \{\varphi\} : [\![\chi]\!] \in X \Rightarrow M, w \models B\chi$. By the assumption we have $[\![\varphi]\!] = [\![\psi]\!]$. Moreover, $\models B\varphi \leftrightarrow B\psi$ (B is a standard KD45 modal operator). Therefore X is also appropriate for ψ. This shows $M, w \models K\psi$, and thus $M, w \models K\varphi \leftrightarrow K\psi$.

4. We give a countermodel. Consider the model $M_1 = (W_1, R_1, S_1, V_1)$ such that $W_1 = \{w, u, v\}$, $R_1 = \{(w, w), (u, u), (v, v)\}$, with (W_1, R_1) illustrated below:

and $V_1(p) = \{w\}$, $V_1(q) = \{w, v\}$, $S_1(w) = \{\{\{w, u, v\}\}, \{\{w\}\}\}$ and $S_1(u) = S_1(v) = \emptyset$.

We have $M_1, w \models K(p \to q)$, because (1) $M_1, w \models p \to q$ and (2) $\{\{w, u, v\}\}$ is an appropriate argument since $[\![p \to q]\!]_{M_1} = \{w, u, v\} \in \{\{w, u, v\}\}$ and $M_1, w \models B\psi$ for any $\psi \in \mathcal{PL} \cup \{(p \to q)\}$ (for $\{x \in W_1 \mid wRx\} \subseteq \{w, u, v\}$). Similarly, we have $M_1, w \models Kp$, but $M_1, w \not\models Kq$. So, $M_1, w \not\models K(p \to q) \to (Kp \to Kq)$.

5. consider a countermodel $M_2 = \{W_2, R_2, S_2, V_2\}$ with (W_2, R_2) illustrated below:

$S(w) = \{\{\{w, u\}\}\}$, $S(u) = \emptyset$, and $V(p) = \{w, u\}$. We have $M_2, w \models Kp$ and $M_2, u \not\models Kp$. Thus $M_2, w \not\models BKp$. Since $\models KKp \to BKp$, $M_2, w \not\models KKp$.

6. Consider a countermodel $M_3 = \{W_3, R_3, S_3, V_3\}$ with W_3, R_3 illustrated below:

$S(w) = \emptyset$ and $Vp = \emptyset$. We have $M_3, w \models \neg Kp$ but $M_3, w \not\models K\neg Kp$.
7. The model M_3 introduced in clause 6 is a suitable countermodel, since $\models \neg(p \wedge \neg p)$ and $M_3, w \not\models K\neg(p \wedge \neg p)$.
8. It is clear that $\models p \to (p \vee q)$. Using the model M_1 in clause 4, we can show that $M_1, w \models Kp$. We can also show that $M_1, w \not\models K(p \vee q)$. Therefore $\not\models Kp \to K(p \vee q)$.

Remark 1. The lack of generalization and distribution over implication for knowledge is what we would like to see, for these are direct causes of the problem of logical omniscience. The reader may instead want to have the principles of positive and negative introspection. Here we presented a logic without these principles mainly for the purpose of pursuing a simple and flexible framework. If one would like to enforce, for example, positive introspection, it can be done by adding the following constraint on the argumentation function S in a model: for all worlds w, for all $X \in S(w)$,

1. for all formulas φ, if $[\![\varphi]\!] \in X$ then $[\![K\varphi]\!] \in X$, and
2. for all worlds u such that wRu, if $X \in S(w)$, then $X \in S(u)$.

Remark 2. The semantics we introduced for LKB still has the problem of logical omniscience for the belief operator. We choose to do so mainly to keep the interpretation simple. Our framework extends easily if we adopt a weaker interpretation for the belief operator that does not involve the problem.

Moreover, the weak logic LKB does not enforce some relationships between knowledge and belief either. For example, positive and negative introspection ($B\varphi \to KB\varphi$, $\neg B\varphi \to K\neg B\varphi$, $K\varphi \to BK\varphi$ and $\neg K\varphi \to B\neg K\varphi$) are not valid.

3 Axiomatization

In this section we introduce a sound and complete axiomatization of the logic LKB, i.e., **LKB**, which is given in Fig. 1. The axioms PC, K, D, 4, 5 and the rules N and MP form an axiomatization of the standard KD45 logic of belief. There are a few more axioms and rules for the characterization of knowledge.

The soundness of **LKB** is not hard to verify. All the axioms are valid, and the rules preserve validity, some of which are shown in Proposition 1. As for the completeness, we prove by the canonical model method, and this will be our main task for the rest of this section.

We refer to a modal logic textbook (say, [12]) for the definitions of *proof*, *deduction* and a *(maximal) consistent* set of formulas in an axiomatization. A well-known Lindenbaum's Lemma claims that any consistent set of formulas is a subset of a maximal consistent set of formulas, which also holds for **LKB**.

Axioms:

PC All the instances of propositional tautologies
K $B(\varphi \to \psi) \to (B\varphi \to B\psi)$
D $B\varphi \to \neg B\neg\varphi$
4   $B\varphi \to BB\varphi$
5   $\neg B\varphi \to B\neg B\varphi$
KB $K\varphi \to B\varphi$
TK $K\varphi \to \varphi$

Rules:

N   from φ infer $B\varphi$
RE from $(\varphi \leftrightarrow \psi)$ infer $(K\varphi \leftrightarrow K\psi)$
MP from φ and $(\varphi \to \psi)$, infer ψ

Fig. 1. The axiomatization **LKB**

As a notational convention, the set of all maximal consistent sets of $\mathcal{L}$ formulas is denoted MCS. Moreover, we shall write $[\![\varphi]\!]^c$ for the set of all maximal consistent sets of formulas containing φ, i.e., $[\![\varphi]\!]^c = \{\Gamma \in MCS \mid \varphi \in \Gamma\}$.

We first introduce some properties of maximal consistent sets of formulas.

Lemma 1. *Let* $\Gamma \in MCS$. *The following hold:*

1. Γ *is closed under modus ponens, i.e., if* $\varphi, (\varphi \to \psi) \in \Gamma$, *then* $\psi \in \Gamma$;
2. *For all formulas* φ, *either* $\varphi \in \Gamma$ *or* $\neg\varphi \in \Gamma$, *but not both*;
3. $[\![\varphi]\!]^c = [\![\psi]\!]^c$ *if and only if* $\varphi \leftrightarrow \psi$ *is a* **LKB** *theorem.*

Proof. The first two clauses can be shown in the same way as in the literature. Now for the third:

From left to right. Suppose $\nvdash_{\mathbf{LKB}} \varphi \leftrightarrow \psi$, then $\{\varphi, \neg\psi\}$ or $\{\neg\varphi, \psi\}$ is consistent. Without loss of generality, we consider the first case, i.e., $\{\varphi, \neg\psi\}$ is consistent. Then there is $\Delta \in MCS$ such that $\{\varphi, \neg\psi\} \subseteq \Delta$. By the second clause of this lemma, $\psi \notin \Delta$, which implies that $[\![\varphi]\!]^c \neq [\![\psi]\!]^c$, as is to be shown.

From right to left. Suppose $[\![\varphi]\!]^c \neq [\![\psi]\!]^c$ and $\vdash_{\mathbf{LKB}} \varphi \leftrightarrow \psi$. Without loss of generality, consider the case when there exists $\Delta \in MCS$ such that $\varphi \in \Delta$ and $\psi \notin \Delta$. It follows that $\nvdash_{\mathbf{LKB}} \varphi \leftrightarrow \psi$, for otherwise there is a violation of the first and second clauses of this lemma.

Definition 4 (canonical model). *The* canonical model *for* **LKB** *is the structure* $M^c = (W^c, R^c, S^c, V^c)$ *where:*

- $W^c = MCS$, *i.e., the set of all maximal consistent sets of formulas;*
- R^c *is binary relation on* W^c *defined by:* $(w, u) \in R^c$ *iff for all formula* φ, *if* $B\varphi \in w$ *then* $\varphi \in u$;
- $S^c : W^c \to \wp(\wp(\wp(W^c)))$ *is such that* $S^c(w) = \{\{[\![\varphi]\!]^c\} \mid K\varphi \in w\}$;
- V^c *is the valuation defined by:* $V^c(p) = [\![p]\!]^c$ *for all* $p \in P$.

It is easy to see that $M^c = (W^c, R^c, V^c)$ forms the canonical model for the standard KD45 logic. Since **LKB** includes an axiomatization of KD45 as a subsystem, we can use the classical method to show that R^c is serial, transitive and Euclidean (cf., say, [12]). Moreover, S^c matches the type of an argumentation function. It is not hard to verify that the canonical model is a model of LKB.

Lemma 2 (truth). *For any formula $\varphi \in \mathcal{L}$ and any $w \in MCS$:*

$$\mathcal{M}^c, w \models \varphi \quad \textit{iff} \quad \varphi \in w$$

Proof. First of all, we can define the modal degree of any formula $\varphi \in \mathcal{L}$, notation $d(\varphi)$, as follows:

$$\begin{aligned}
d(p) &= 0 \\
d(\neg\varphi) &= d(\varphi) \\
d((\varphi \wedge \psi)) &= \max(d(\varphi), d(\psi)) \\
d(B\varphi) &= d(\varphi) + 1 \\
d(K\varphi) &= d(\varphi) + 1.
\end{aligned}$$

Our proof is carried out by nested induction on $d(\varphi)$ and within that on the structure of φ. The case $d(\varphi) = 0$ is trivial. Suppose for every φ such that $d(\varphi) \leq n$: $\mathcal{M}^c, w \models \varphi \Leftrightarrow \varphi \in w$. We are going to show that the same holds for all φ such that $d(\varphi) \leq n + 1$. The only interesting case is the inductive step for $K\varphi$:

From left to right. Suppose $K\varphi \notin w$. We claim that $\{[\![\varphi]\!]^c\} \notin S^c(w)$. Suppose not, there must be a ψ such that $K\psi \in w$ and $[\![\psi]\!]^c = [\![\varphi]\!]^c$. This implies that $\vdash_{\textbf{LKB}} \varphi \leftrightarrow \psi$ by Lemma 1(3). Therefore $\vdash_{\textbf{LKB}} K\varphi \leftrightarrow K\psi$ by rule the RE. But $K\varphi \notin w$, this contradicts the fact that w is closed under modus ponens. Thus $\{[\![\varphi]\!]^c\} \notin S^c(w)$. Since $d(\varphi) < d(K\varphi)$, by the induction hypothesis, $[\![\varphi]\!] = [\![\varphi]\!]^c$, therefore $\{[\![\varphi]\!]\} \notin S^c(w)$, and so $\mathcal{M}^c, w \not\models K\varphi$.

From right to left. We need to show that: (1) $\mathcal{M}^c, w \models \varphi$ and (2) there is X in $S^c(w)$ such that $[\![\varphi]\!] \in X$ and $\forall \psi \in \mathcal{PL} \cup \{\varphi\} : [\![\psi]\!] \in X \Rightarrow \mathcal{M}^c, w \models B\psi$. For (1), from $\vdash K\varphi \rightarrow \varphi$ it follows that $\varphi \in w$. Since $d(\varphi) < d(K\varphi)$, $\mathcal{M}^c, w \models \varphi$ by the induction hypothesis. For (2), since $K\varphi \in w$, $\{[\![\varphi]\!]^c\} \in S^c(w)$. We claim that $\{[\![\varphi]\!]^c\}$ is the suitable X. Firstly, by the induction hypothesis, $[\![\varphi]\!] = [\![\varphi]\!]^c$, so $[\![\varphi]\!] \in \{[\![\varphi]\!]^c\}$. Secondly, for each $\psi \in \mathcal{PL} \cup \{\varphi\}$, $[\![\psi]\!] = [\![\psi]\!]^c$ by the induction hypothesis. If $[\![\psi]\!] \in \{[\![\varphi]\!]^c\}$, it must be that $[\![\psi]\!]^c = [\![\psi]\!] = [\![\varphi]\!]^c$. By Lemma 1(3), it follows that $\vdash_{\textbf{LKB}} \varphi \leftrightarrow \psi$. Since $K\varphi \in w$ and $\vdash_{\textbf{LKB}} K\varphi \rightarrow B\varphi$, $B\varphi \in w$. Therefore $B\psi \in w$. So it suffices to show that $\mathcal{M}^c, w \models B\psi$, which is a standard result for a normal modal logic. Therefore, $\mathcal{M}^c, w \models K\varphi$.

With the above lemma, a standard argument leads us to the following theorem.

Theorem 1 (soundness and completeness). *For any formula φ and any set Γ of formulas, $\Gamma \vdash_{\textbf{LKB}} \varphi$ if and only if $\Gamma \models \varphi$.*

4   Extending to Multiple Agents

In this section we study the extension of LKB to allow multiple agents. Let A be a finite set of agents. It is natural to introduce the following multi-agent language:

Definition 5 (language $\mathcal{L}^m$). *The language $\mathcal{L}^m$ is given as follows:*

$$\varphi ::= p \mid \neg\varphi \mid (\varphi \wedge \varphi) \mid B_a\varphi \mid K_a\varphi,$$

where $p \in P$ is a propositional variable and $a \in A$.

To make a difference, we shall call the multi-agent extension of LKB the logic LKB^m. Definitions of the semantics can also be extended naturally from the single-agent case.

Definition 6 (LKB^m models). *An LKB^m model (or simply, a model, when there is no confusion in the context) is a tuple $M = (W, R, S, V)$ such that:*

- *W is a non-empty set of worlds;*
- *$R : A \rightarrow \wp(W \times W)$ assigns every agent a serial, transitive and Euclidean relation on W; for convenience, we write R_a for $R(a)$ for any $a \in A$;*
- *$S : W \rightarrow \wp(\wp(\wp(W)))$ is an* argumentation function; *and*
- *$V : P \rightarrow \wp(W)$ is a valuation that assigns every propositional variable a set of possible worlds.*

As usual, M, together with a state w of it, forms a pointed model *(M, w).*

Definition 7 (LKB^m satisfaction). *Given an LKB^m model $M = (W, R, S, V)$ and a world $w \in W$, that a formula α is* satisfied *in the pointed model (M, w) (notation: $M, w \models \alpha$) is defined as follows:*

$$
\begin{aligned}
&M, w \models p && \textit{iff } w \in V(p) \\
&M, w \models \neg\varphi && \textit{iff } \text{not } M, w \models \varphi \\
&M, w \models (\varphi \wedge \psi) && \textit{iff } M, w \models \varphi \text{ and } M, w \models \psi \\
&M, w \models B_a\varphi && \textit{iff } \text{for all } u \in W, \text{ if } wR_au \text{ then } M, u \models \varphi \\
&M, w \models K_a\varphi && \textit{iff } M, w \models \varphi \text{ and there exists } X \in S(w) \text{ such that: } [\![\varphi]\!] \in X \\
&&& \text{and for all } \psi \in \mathcal{PL} \cup \{\varphi\}, \text{ if } [\![\psi]\!] \in X \text{ then } M, w \models B_a\psi .
\end{aligned}
$$

Conventions are made as in Definition 3.

The extension goes smoothly by equipping the knowledge and belief operators, together with their semantic counterparts, for all the agents. In fact, we can carry out in the same way to reach an axiomatization for the multi-agent logic. The axiomatization **LKBm** given in Fig. 2 is a sound and complete axiomatization of the logic LKB^m.

Theorem 2 (LKBm soundness and completeness). *For any $\mathcal{L}^m$ formula φ and any set Γ of $\mathcal{L}^m$ formulas, $\Gamma \vdash_{\textbf{LKBm}} \varphi$ if and only if $\Gamma \models \varphi$.*

Axioms:

PC	All the instances of propositional tautologies
Km	$B_a(\varphi \to \psi) \to (B_a\varphi \to B_a\psi)$
Dm	$B_a\varphi \to \neg B_a\neg\varphi$
4m	$B_a\varphi \to B_aB_a\varphi$
5m	$\neg B_a\varphi \to B_a\neg B_a\varphi$
KBm	$K_a\varphi \to B_a\varphi$
TKm	$K_a\varphi \to \varphi$

Rules:

Nm	from φ infer $B_a\varphi$
REm	from $(\varphi \leftrightarrow \psi)$ infer $(K_a\varphi \leftrightarrow K_a\psi)$
MP	from φ and $(\varphi \to \psi)$, infer ψ

Fig. 2. The axiomatization **LKBm**

Proof. The theorem can be shown in very much the same way as for LKB.

Remark 3 (global vs. local argumentation functions). In the definition of a model for the multi-agent logic, we kept the argumentation function S the same as in a model for the single-agent logic. One may argue that we also have a reason to introduce an argumentation function for each agent:

$$S : A \to W \to \wp(\wp(\wp(W))).$$

Both options have an explanation.

For what we defined above, for an agent to achieve knowledge, an argument must be *global*, in the sense that it works as well for all other agents. What this represents is more like a mathematical proof which does not easily get refused by others. Yet a *local* argumentation function allows an agent to have its own argument for something, even though others may disagree. This is perhaps more like an argument in daily life.

Our framework allows the flexibility of making a distinction between global and local argumentation, which we expect a good impact on the approaches to reasoning about different levels of knowledge.

That said, we do not introduce a logic for knowledge based on local argumentation. One of the main difficulties is to understand what higher-order knowledge means in this case. For example, a formula $K_aK_b\varphi$ requires that agent a has an argument for $K_b\varphi$, which in turn requires that agent b has an argument for φ. But do we assume there is information adopt in common by both agents, say some simple tautologies? How can these be characterized? We leave such questions for future work.

5   Related Work

In this section we compare our work with existing literature. As already mentioned in the introduction, there have been a great amount of work in the area of logics of knowledge, belief and their relationships, which connects to the research on the concepts of proof, evidence and justification, and the logics of them.

Of special relevance is Williamson's work on knowledge and evidence [43,44]. In a later development [45], he introduces a logic of knowledge which is capable of solving the problem of logical omniscience, based on the idea that "knowing p requires safety from the falsity of p and of its epistemic counterparts." Formally, a model is a structure (W, R, V), where R consists of triples $\langle w, w^*, f \rangle$ in which w and w^* are worlds, and f is a function mapping a formula in w to a counterpart formula of it in w^* which may endure extra constraints. Knowledge is interpreted in a way that:

$$w \models K\varphi \text{ iff for all } \langle w, w^*, f \rangle \in R, w^* \models f(\varphi).$$

By an epistemic counterpart, he refers to a belief that is alike in various epistemically relevant respects, such as how they are formed, which circumstance they are formed in, etc. Our framework, though technically quite different, are conceptually close to this type of modeling.

Justification logics [3,4,21] are a family of modal logics with the modalities replaced with justification terms, inspired by the logic of proofs [1,2] where a justification of a formula is largely a deductive proof of it, or more precisely, a "proof polynomial" that encodes a proof. Fitting [21] adapted Artemov's framework using a semantic solution that can be traced back to [34]. An evidence function $\mathcal{E}$ is added to a standard Kripke model, making a quadruple $(W, R, \mathcal{E}, V)$. The function $\mathcal{E}$ assigns an evidence set of formulas to each proof polynomial t at each world w that consists of everything t justifies at w. The interpretation looks as follows:

$$M, w \models t : \varphi \quad \text{iff} \quad \varphi \in \mathcal{E}(w, t) \text{ and for all } u, \text{ if } wRu \text{ then } M, u \models \varphi.$$

Along the line of [21], Artemov and Nogina [6,7] introduced justification into the framework of epistemic logic. A model there is a quintuple $(W, R, R^e, \mathcal{E}, V)$ where (W, R, V) is a standard Kripke model with the binary relation R used for interpreting potential knowledge in the standard way. $\mathcal{E}$ is an evidence function as in [21], together with an extra relation R^e, the justification of a formula φ is interpreted as follows:

$$w \models t : \varphi \quad \text{iff} \quad \varphi \in \mathcal{E}(w, t) \text{ and for all } u, \text{ if } wR^eu \text{ then } M, u \models \varphi$$

This is used to model a type of explicit knowledge. We need to point out here that the concept of justification has been brought into the field of epistemic logic already in [10].

Although epistemic justifications are mainly used to characterize only the notion of knowledge, the differences in the interpretation of implicit and explicit knowledge has a technical similarity to that of belief and knowledge in this paper. This similarity is even more obvious when implicit/potential knowledge is regarded as belief.

Now we move on the literature on logics with both knowledge and belief, in particular the relationship between them. These can be classified into two categories:

(i) those taking both knowledge and belief as primitive and focus on the interaction properties between the two notions;

(ii) those in which knowledge or belief is not a primitive, but a derived notion
from the other or some notions different from the two.

In the first category, various axioms that hold for knowledge and/or belief
have been discussed already in [26]. The JTB definition of knowledge ("justified
true belief") has been implemented in epistemic logic in [32]. In [29], a combined
system of knowledge and belief was introduced based on Kripke semantics (the
notions of common knowledge and belief are also studied there). In their models,
two accessibility relations are used to represent epistemic uncertainty and doxastic uncertainty, respectively. The logic in [29] has some interesting validities
characterizing the relationship between knowledge and belief. For example, for
all agents a and formulas φ, the following are valid:

$$K_a\varphi \rightarrow B_a\varphi \text{ (and also } K_a\neg\varphi \rightarrow \neg B_a\varphi)$$
$$B_a\varphi \leftrightarrow K_a B_a\varphi \text{ and } \neg B_a\varphi \leftrightarrow K_a\neg B_a\varphi$$
$$K_a\varphi \leftrightarrow B_a K_a\varphi \text{ and } \neg K_a\varphi \leftrightarrow B_a\neg K_a\varphi$$

And $B_a\varphi \rightarrow B_a K_a\varphi$ is invalid there. Some of these principles, together with
others (such that $B\varphi \leftrightarrow \neg K\neg K\varphi$), were examined in [38] and followed by [28].
Also based on [38], recently [8,9] introduced a logic of knowledge and belief using
a topological style of semantics. Different logics were introduced for reasoning
about knowledge and belief in a combined way in [41,42]. More sophisticated
constructions are used there, which goes further away from the topic here. In
[30], formulas of the forms $K\varphi$, $C^\varphi\psi$ and $B^\varphi\psi$ are taken to be primitive, which
are interpreted as "the agent knows φ", "the agent is certain of ψ under the
evidence φ" and "the agent believes ψ under the evidence φ", respectively. Then
$B\varphi$ ("φ is believed") is defined as $B^\top\varphi$.

In the second category, besides the well-known JTB analysis of knowledge
using belief and many work in this strand (see, e.g., [31,39,44]), there are also
approaches defining belief out of knowledge. For example, [22] defines belief in
terms of knowledge and plausibility: an agent believes φ if he knows that φ is
more plausible than $\neg\varphi$. [13] defines belief in a similar fashion. It's worth noting
that, though from a very different motivation, their models have a flavor of
neighborhood semantics which is similar to ours (we use a neighborhood function
that selects the truth set of not mere a single formula). In [35], Moses and Shoham
suggest that belief be viewed as defeasible knowledge. In particular, they come
up with a definition of belief to be knowledge-relative-to-assumptions, and make
a connection to the notion of nonmonotonicity.

6   Conclusion

In this paper we introduced a logic of knowledge and belief in which we provided with an alternative implementation of the tripartite analysis of knowledge (knowledge = justified true belief). Our work has a conceptual link to

the research on justification logic, bringing a formal notion of justification into the definition of knowledge, yet different in that justification is used in forming knowledge out of true belief, instead of forming explicit knowledge out of implicit knowledge. Our model is a combination of standard KD45 model for belief with an argumentation function for knowledge that is of a flavor of the neighborhood semantics.

We introduced a sound and completeness axiomatization for our logic, and extended it to model multiple agents. In the multi-agent setting, we had two options, to model *global* or *local* arguments. We studied a logic of global arguments, and leave that of local ones for future work. As the reader may observe, our logic characterizes a weak notion of knowledge, without the problem of logical omniscience, but also lacking properties such as positive and negative introspection ($K\varphi \to KK\varphi$ and $\neg K\varphi \to K\neg K\varphi$) as well as the principle for the interaction between belief and knowledge (e.g. $B\varphi \to KB\varphi$). The model we propose is capable of modeling these principles by imposing further constraints (see Remark 1 for an example). We leave this also for future work.

One of the requirements of a formula to be knowledge is to have an *argument* for it. Occasionally we used other words, such as "proof", "justification", "evidence", etc., in place of "argument", though we do not in fact impose any structures of the argument – it is simply treated as a set of formulas. This is one of the reasons we call it "abstract argument" as in the title. Our work, however, does not have a direct link to the study of formal argumentation, in particular that of abstract argumentation framework [17]. We are interested in achieving a connection to that, perhaps by means of bringing an argumentation framework into the interpretation of knowledge, so that only the accepted ones are counted as arguments.

Also interesting to look into are the group notions of knowledge and belief. It is a natural task to study the extensions of our logic by incorporating common and distributed knowledge/belief. We are interested in comparing these with the logic of knowledge and belief presented in [29], and also extensions of justification logic with common knowledge [5,14] and distributed knowledge [24,25]. Other interesting tasks include modeling dynamics in our framework.

References

1. Artëmov, S., Straßen, T.: The basic logic of proofs. In: Börger, E., Jäger, G., Kleine Büning, H., Martini, S., Richter, M.M. (eds.) CSL 1992. LNCS, vol. 702, pp. 14–28. Springer, Heidelberg (1993). https://doi.org/10.1007/3-540-56992-8_3
2. Artemov, S.N.: Logic of proofs. Ann. Pure Appl. Logic **67**(1), 29–59 (1994)
3. Artemov, S.N.: Operational modal logic. Technical report, Mathematical Sciences Institute, Cornell University (1995)
4. Artemov, S.N.: Explicit provability and constructive semantics. Bull. Symbolic Logic **7**(1), 1–36 (2001)
5. Artemov, S.N.: Justified common knowledge. Theoret. Comput. Sci. **357**(1), 4–22 (2006)
6. Artemov, S.N., Nogina, E.: Introducing justification into epistemic logic. J. Logic Comput. **15**(6), 1059–1073 (2005)

7. Artemov, S.N., Nogina, E.: On epistemic logic with justification. In: Proceedings of the 10th Conference on Theoretical Aspects of Rationality and Knowledge, pp. 279–294. National University of Singapore (2005)

8. Baltag, A., Bezhanishvili, N., Özgün, A., Smets, S.: The topology of full and weak belief. In: Hansen, H.H., Murray, S.E., Sadrzadeh, M., Zeevat, H. (eds.) TbiLLC 2015. LNCS, vol. 10148, pp. 205–228. Springer, Heidelberg (2017). https://doi.org/10.1007/978-3-662-54332-0_12

9. Baltag, A., Bezhanishvili, N., Özgün, A., Smets, S.: A topological approach to full belief. J. Philos. Logic **48**(2), 205–244 (2019). https://doi.org/10.1007/s10992-018-9463-4

10. van Benthem, J.F.A.K.: Reflections on epistemic logic. Logique et Analyse **34**(133–134), 5–14 (1991)

11. Bjerring, J.C., Skipper, M.: A dynamic solution to the problem of logical omniscience. J. Philos. Logic **48**(3), 501–521 (2019). https://doi.org/10.1007/s10992-018-9473-2

12. Blackburn, P., de Rijke, M., Venema, Y.: Modal Logic, Cambridge Tracts in Theoretical Computer Science, vol. 53. Cambridge University Press, Cambridge (2001)

13. Bonanno, G.: Logics for belief as maximally plausible possibility. Studia Logica (2019). https://doi.org/10.1007/s11225-019-09887-w

14. Bucheli, S., Kuznets, R., Studer, T.: Justifications for common knowledge. J. Appl. Non-Class. Logics **21**(1), 35–60 (2011)

15. Chellas, B.F.: Modal Logic: An Introduction. Cambridge University Press, Cambridge (1980)

16. Chisholm, R.M.: The logic of knowing. J. Philos. **60**(25), 773–795 (1963)

17. Dung, P.M.: On the acceptability of arguments and its fundamental role in nonmonotonic reasoning, logic programming and n-person games. Artif. Intell. **77**(2), 321–357 (1995)

18. Dutant, J.: Epistemic logics for derived knowledge and belief (manuscript)

19. Fagin, R., Halpern, J.: Belief, awareness, and limited reasoning. Artif. Intell. **34**(1), 39–76 (1988)

20. Fagin, R., Halpern, J.Y., Moses, Y., Vardi, M.Y.: Reasoning About Knowledge. The MIT Press, Cambridge (1995)

21. Fitting, M.: The logic of proofs, semantically. Ann. Pure Appl. Logic **132**(1), 1–25 (2005)

22. Friedman, N., Halpern, J.Y.: Modeling belief in dynamic systems, Part I: foundations. Artif. Intell. **95**(2), 257–316 (1997)

23. Gettier, E.L.: Is justified true belief knowledge? Analysis **23**(6), 121–123 (1963)

24. Ghari, M.: Distributed knowledge with justifications. In: Lassiter, D., Slavkovik, M. (eds.) ESSLLI 2010-2011. LNCS, vol. 7415, pp. 91–108. Springer, Heidelberg (2012). https://doi.org/10.1007/978-3-642-31467-4_7

25. Ghari, M.: Distributed knowledge justification logics. Theory Comput. Syst. **55**(1), 1–40 (2014). https://doi.org/10.1007/s00224-013-9492-x

26. Hintikka, J.: Knowledge and Belief: An Introduction to the Logic of Two Notions. Cornell University Press, Ithaca (1962)

27. Hintikka, J.: Impossible possible worlds vindicated. J. Philos. Logic **4**(4), 475–484 (1975). https://doi.org/10.1007/BF00558761

28. Klein, D., Roy, O., Gratzl, N.: Knowledge, belief, normality, and introspection. Synthese **195**(10), 4343–4372 (2018). https://doi.org/10.1007/s11229-017-1353-8

29. Kraus, S., Lehmann, D.: Knowledge, belief and time. Theoret. Comput. Sci. **58**(1), 155–174 (1988)

30. Lamarre, P., Shoham, Y.: Knowledge, certainty, belief, and conditionalisation (abbreviated version). In: Principles of Knowledge Representation and Reasoning, pp. 415–424. Elsevier (1994)
31. Lehrer, K., Paxson, T.: Knowledge: undefeated justified true belief. J. Philos. **66**(8), 225–237 (1969)
32. Lenzen, W.: Recent Work in Epistemic Logic, Acta Philosophica Fennica, vol. 30. North-Holland, Amsterdam (1978)
33. Meyer, J.J.C., van der Hoek, W.: Epistemic Logic for AI and Computer Science, Cambridge Tracts in Theoretical Computer Science, vol. 41. Cambridge University Press, Cambridge (1995)
34. Mkrtychev, A.: Models for the logic of proofs. In: Adian, S., Nerode, A. (eds.) LFCS 1997. LNCS, vol. 1234, pp. 266–275. Springer, Heidelberg (1997). https://doi.org/10.1007/3-540-63045-7_27
35. Moses, Y., Shoham, Y.: Belief as defeasible knowledge. Artif. Intell. **64**(2), 299–321 (1993)
36. Stalnaker, R.: The problem of logical omniscience. I. Synthese **89**(3), 425–440 (1991)
37. Stalnaker, R.: The problem of logical omniscience, II. In: Context and Content: Essays on Intentionality in Speech and Thought, Chap. 14. Oxford University Press (1999)
38. Stalnaker, R.: On logics of knowledge and belief. Philos. Stud. **128**(1), 169–199 (2006)
39. Swain, M.: Epistemic defeasibility. Am. Philos. Q. **11**(1), 15–25 (1974)
40. Van Benthem, J., Fernández-Duque, D., Pacuit, E., et al.: Evidence logic: a new look at neighborhood structures. Adv. Modal Logic **9**, 97–118 (2012)
41. Voorbraak, F.: The logic of objective knowledge and rational belief. In: van Eijck, J. (ed.) JELIA 1990. LNCS, vol. 478, pp. 499–515. Springer, Heidelberg (1991). https://doi.org/10.1007/BFb0018462
42. Voorbraak, F.: As Far as I Know: Epistemic Logic and Uncertainty. Ph.D. thesis, Utrecht University, January 1993
43. Williamson, T.: Knowledge as evidence. Mind **106**, 717–742 (1997)
44. Williamson, T.: Knowledge and Its Limits. Oxford University Press, Oxford (2000)
45. Williamson, T.: Probability and danger. Amherst Lect. Philos. **4**, 1–35 (2009)
46. von Wright, G.H.: An Essay in Modal Logic. Studies in Logic and the Foundations of Mathematics. North-Holland Publishing Company, Amsterdam (1951)

A Meta-level Annotation Language
for Legal Texts

Tomer Libal$^{(\boxtimes)}$ (iD)

University of Luxembourg, Luxembourg City, Luxembourg
shaolintl@gmail.com

Abstract. There are many legal texts which can greatly benefit from
the support of automated reasoning. Such support depends on the existence of a logical formalization of the legal text. Among the methods
used for the creation of these knowledge bases, annotation tools attempt
to abstract over the logical language and support non-logicians in their
efforts to formalize documents. Nevertheless, legal documents use a rich
language which is not easy to annotate. In this paper, an existing annotation tool is being extended in order to support the formalization of a
complex example - the GDPR's article 13. The complexity of the article
prevents a direct annotation using logical and deontical operators. This is
overcome by the implementation of several macros. We demonstrate the
automated reasoning over the formalized article and argue that macros
can be used to formalize complex legal texts.

Keywords: Automated reasoning · Knowledge bases · Annotation
tools

1 Introduction

Computer systems are playing a substantial role in assisting people in a wide
range of tasks, including searching in large data and decision-making; and their
employment is progressively becoming vital in an increasing number of fields.
One of these fields is legal reasoning: New court cases and legislations are accu-
mulated every day and navigating through the vast amount of complex information is far from trivial. In addition, the understanding of those texts is reserved
only for experts in the legal domain despite the fact that they are usually of
interest to the general public.

A key component of legal reasoning is the transformation of legal texts into
a machine readable format. This transformation must capture the legal understanding of the text in order to allow computers to reason over it.

Supporting automated reasoning over legislation is an old idea, dating back
to LEGOL [23] and made popular by the formalisation of the British Nationality
Act [21]. These approaches and others (see for example [4,22]) were based on
the use of the Prolog programming language for the formalization of the legislation. Since then, many other systems have followed the same path and the
formalization of legal texts in Prolog is also done today [13].

© Springer Nature Switzerland AG 2020
M. Dastani et al. (Eds.): CLAR 2020, LNAI 12061, pp. 131–150, 2020.
https://doi.org/10.1007/978-3-030-44638-3_9

Prolog is very suitable for such formalizations but still depends on the works of programmers and logicians. In order to verify that the formalization is correct, methodologies were created which allow legal experts to be able to give back feedback to the programmers and logicians [1]. In addition to Prolog-based, legal knowledge bases were created which are based on other logical formalizations, such as IO logics [19] and modal logics [11].

In order to allow legal experts to create knowledge bases directly, user friendly interfaces can be created which aim at hiding the logical complexity. Annotation editors for legal texts [12, 16] allow users to add a legal interpretation to texts by the use of annotations. The editor then produces a logical formalization which can be used for automated reasoning.

Despite the advances described above, "good" logical formalizations are hard to achieve [3]. Among the most important properties of such formalizations, one can list faithfulness to the original text, efficient support for the required reasoning operations and being well engineered [20]. In order to be faithful to the original text, one must not only describe the legal terms and their logical relations in a faithful way but also meta-level concepts such exceptions, counterfactuals and deeming provisions. This normally increases the complexity of the formalization. Being well engineered, on the other hand, normally means being simple and easy to verify, validate, update and maintain.

The tension between the two can be demonstrated by looking at the third paragraph of article 13 of the GDPR[1]:

"Where the controller intends to further process the personal data for a purpose other than that for which the personal data were collected, the controller shall provide the data subject prior to that further processing with information on that other purpose and with any relevant further information as referred to in paragraph 2.".

This paragraph discusses cases not handled by previous paragraphs and ask to apply certain points in a new context. Attempting to faithfully represent this paragraph while keeping to the best engineering principals is not easy.

One approach for tackling such problems is to manually simplify the structure of the sentence such that logical annotations then become easier. In the example above, one can copy the relevant parts of the previous paragraphs and replace parts of their context with the one of paragraph 3.

From the engineering point of view, there are several problems with this approach. First, manual processing and copying is error-prone. By delegating work to the computer, we decrease the chance of error as long as the algorithm is correct. Second, it might be a tedious and time-consuming work which can be automated by a computer. Lastly, the manual work needs to be repeated when a change to the understanding or context of the legislation occurs.

In this paper, an extension to the NAI Suite's annotation editor [12] is discussed. The NAI Suite follows a certain methodology which aims at being faithful and well engineered at the same time. This methodology, closely related to the Isomorphism approach [2], uses two levels of annotations in order to create an

---

[1] https://eur-lex.europa.eu/eli/reg/2016/679/oj.

intermediary representation of the legal text which is faithful and well engineered, in the sense defined above. This intermediary representation is then translated automatically into logical representations which can then be used for efficient automated reasoning.

This methodology is still insufficient when facing the GDPR's paragraph from above. The two levels of annotations which are supported cover vocabulary and logical relations, but the paragraph requires complex modifications of a cross referenced paragraph as well.

The extension to the NAI Suite discussed in this paper supports an additional level of annotations. These meta-level annotations can handle complex legal structures, such as the one in the above example. In addition to this extension, a domain specific language (DSL) for describing meta-level annotations is presented and applied to these annotations. It is then being shown that with hardly any change to the original text, a formalization is created which can be used for automated reasoning. Some examples of automated query answering are demonstrated.

In the next section, an introduction to the NAI Suite, its theoretical foundations and its graphical user interface is given. The following section describes the extension of the tool, while Sect. 4 demonstrates how the new features can be applied to easily formalize and reason over article 13. A conclusion and future work discussion are given last.

2   The NAI Suite

The NAI suite integrates novel theorem proving technology into a usable graphical user interface (GUI) for the computer-assisted formalization of legal texts and applying automated normative reasoning procedures on these artifacts. In particular, NAI includes

1. a legislation editor that graphically supports the formalization of legal texts,
2. means of assessing the quality of entered formalizations, e.g., by automatically conducting consistency checks and assessing logical independence,
3. ready-to-use theorem prover technology for evaluating user-specified queries wrt. a given formalization, and
4. the possibility to share and collaborate, and to experiment with different formalizations and underlying logics.

NAI is realized using a web-based Software-as-a-service architecture, cf. Fig. 1. It comprises a GUI that is implemented as a Javascript browser application, and a NodeJS application on the back-end side which connects to theorem provers, data storage services and relevant middleware. Using this architectural layout, no further software is required from the user perspective for using NAI and its reasoning procedures, as all necessary software is made available on the back end and the computationally heavy tasks are executed on the remote servers only. The results of the different reasoning procedures are sent back to the GUI and displayed to the user. The major components of NAI are described in more detail in the following.

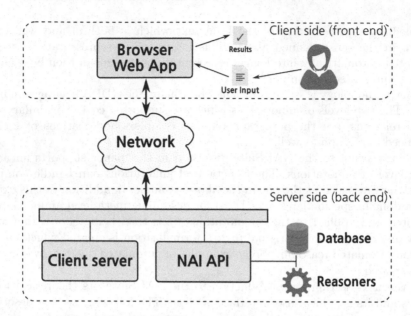

Fig. 1. Software-as-a-service architecture of the NAI reasoning framework. The front end software runs in the user's browser and connects to the remote site, and its different services, via a well-defined API through the network. Data flow is indicated by arrows.

2.1 The Underlining Logic

The logical formalism underlying the NAI framework is based on a universal fragment first-order variant of the deontic logic **DL*** [11], denoted **DL*₁**. Its syntax is given by

Definition 1 (Syntax of DL*₁). *Let V, P and F be disjoint sets of symbols for variables, predicate symbols (of some arity) and function symbols (of some arity), respectively. **DL*₁** formulas ϕ, ψ are given by:*

$$\phi, \psi ::= p(t_1, \ldots, t_n) \mid \neg\phi \mid \phi \wedge \psi \mid \phi \vee \psi \mid \phi \Rightarrow \psi$$
$$\mid \mathsf{Id}\,\phi \mid \mathsf{Ob}\,\phi \mid \mathsf{Pm}\,\phi \mid \mathsf{Fb}\,\phi$$
$$\mid \phi \Rightarrow_{\mathsf{Ob}} \psi \mid \phi \Rightarrow_{\mathsf{Pm}} \psi \mid \phi \Rightarrow_{\mathsf{Fb}} \psi$$

where $p \in P$ is a predicate symbol of arity $n \geq 0$ and the t_i, $1 \leq i \leq n$, are terms. Terms are freely generated by the function symbols from F and variables from V.

DL*₁ extends Standard Deontic Logic (SDL) with the normative concepts of ideal and contrary-to-duty obligations, and contains predicate symbols, the standard logical connectives, and the normative operators of obligation (Ob), permission (Pm), prohibition (Fb), their conditional counter-parts, and ideality (Id). Free variables are implicitly universally quantified at top-level.

This logic is expressive enough to capture many interesting normative structures. For details on its expressivity and its semantics, we refer to previous work [11].

2.2 The Reasoning Module

The NAI suite supports formalizing legal texts and applying various logical operations on them. These operations include consistency checks (non-derivability of falsum), logical independence analysis as well as the creation of user queries that can automatically be assessed for (non-)validity. After formalization, the formal representation of the legal text is stored in a general and expressive machine-readable format in NAI. This format aims at generalizing from concrete logical formalisms that are used for evaluating the logical properties of the legal document's formal representation.

There exist many different logical formalisms that have been discussed for capturing normative reasoning and extensions of it. Since the discussion of such formalisms is still ongoing, and the choice of the concrete logic underlying the reasoning process strongly influences the results of all procedures, NAI uses a two-step procedure to employ automated reasoning tools. NAI stores only the general format, as mentioned above, as result of the formalization process. Once a user then chooses a certain logic for conducting the logical analysis, NAI will automatically translate the general format into the specific logic resp. the concrete input format of the employed automated reasoning system. Currently, NAI supports only the DL^*_1 logic from Sect. 2.1; however, the architecture of NAI is designed in such a way that further formalisms can easily be supported.

The choice in favor of DL^*_1 is primarily motivated by the fact that it can be effectively automated using a shallow semantical embedding into normal (bi-)modal logic [11]. This enables the use of readily available reasoning systems for such logics; in contrast, there are few to none automated reasoning systems available for normative logics (with the exception of [9]). In NAI, we use the MleanCoP prover [15] for first-order multi-modal logics as it is currently one of the most effective systems and it returns proof certificates which can be independently assessed for correctness [14]. It is also possible to use various different tools for automated reasoning in parallel (where applicable). This is of increasing importance once multiple different logical formalisms are supported.

2.3 The Annotation Editor

The annotation editor of NAI is one of its central components. Using the editor, users can create formalizations of legal documents that can subsequently used for formal legal reasoning. The general functionality of the editor is described in the following.

One of the main ideas of the NAI editor is to hide the underlying logical details and technical reasoning input and outputs from the user. We consider this essential, as the primary target audience of the NAI suite are not necessarily logicians and it could greatly decrease the usability of the tool if a solid knowledge about formal logic was required. This is realized by letting the user annotate legal texts and queries graphically and by allowing the user to access the different reasoning functionalities by simply clicking buttons that are integrated into the GUI. Note that the user can still inspect the logical formulae that result from the annotation process and also input these formulae directly. However, this feature is considered advanced and not the primary approach put forward by NAI.

The formalization proceeds as follows: The user selects some text from the legal document and annotates it, either as a term or as a composite (complex) statement. In the first case, a name for that term is computed automatically, but it can also be chosen freely. Different terms are displayed as different colors in the text. In the latter case, the user needs to choose among the different possibilities (which roughly correspond to logical connectives) and the containing text can be annotated recursively. Composite statements are displayed as a box around the text. An example of an annotation result is displayed in Fig. 2.

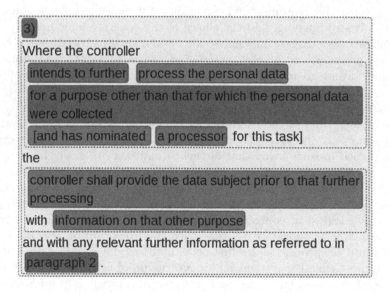

Fig. 2. GDPR article 13, paragprah 3: annotation

The editor also features direct access to the consistency check and logical independence check procedures (as buttons). When such a button is clicked, the current state of the formalization will be translated and sent to the back-end provers, which determine whether it is consistent resp. logically independent.

User queries are also created using such an editor. In addition to the steps sketched above, users may declare a text passage as *goal* using a dedicated annotation button, whose contents are again annotated as usual. If the query is executed, the back-end provers will try to prove (or refute) that the goal logically follows from the remaining annotations and the underlying legislation.

2.4   The Abstract Programming Interface (API)

All the reasoning features of NAI can also be accessed by third-party applications. The NAI suite exposes a RESTful (Representational state transfer) API which allows (external) applications to run consistency checks, checks for independence as well as queries and use the result for further processing. The exposure of NAI's REST API is particularly interesting for external legal applications that want to make use of the already formalized legal documents hosted by NAI. A simple example of such an application is a tax counseling web site which advises its visitors using legal reasoning over a formalization of the relevant tax law done in the NAI suite.

3   A Meta-level Annotation Language

An essential element in the compliance checking of privacy policies and data collection procedures, the GDPR's article 13[2] is concerned with their transparency. This article contains 4 paragraphs, where the first two contain each 6 subsections. The third paragraph extends and modify the second one while the last states a situation in which the three previous paragraphs do not hold.

Let us consider the first paragraph.

Paragraph 1 of GDPR's Article 13: Where personal data relating to a data subject are collected from the data subject, the controller shall, at the time when personal data are obtained, provide the data subject with all of the following information:

(a) the identity and the contact details of the controller and, where applicable, of the controller's representative;
(b) the contact details of the data protection officer, where applicable;
(c) the purposes of the processing for which the personal data are intended as well as the legal basis for the processing;
(d) where the processing is based on point (f) of Article 6(1), the legitimate interests pursued by the controller or by a third party;
(e) the recipients or categories of recipients of the personal data, if any;
(f) where applicable, the fact that the controller intends to transfer personal data to a third country or international organisation and the existence or absence of an adequacy decision by the Commission, or in the case of transfers referred to in Article 46 or 47, or the second subparagraph of Article 49(1), reference to the appropriate or suitable safeguards and the means by which to obtain a copy of them or where they have been made available.

The above paragraph is not easy to read but is even harder to annotate. There are several reasons.

---

[2] https://eur-lex.europa.eu/eli/reg/2016/679/oj.

– The structure of the paragraph is not trivial. It starts by declaring some conditions, then it states the obligation to communicate information. The exact information to communicate and other possible conditions are then specified in each item.
– Most conditions and the obligation are specified once only but the content of the obligation, i.e. the precise information which should be communicated to the data subject, is changing for each point.

In order to understand the paragraph, the reader is expected to reconstruct each of the 6 items with the relevant further conditions and the precise content of the obligation.

Clearly, new types of annotations must be added. For example, one can consider changing the precise information to communicate in each item as a replacement operation. Such operations are normally not a part of any logical language but of their meta-language. We need therefore a new kind of annotations for annotating meta-level concepts.

An even more complex structure appears in the third paragraph.

Paragraph 3 of GDPR's Article 13: Where the controller intends to further process the personal data for a purpose other than that for which the personal data were collected, the controller shall provide the data subject prior to that further processing with information on that other purpose and with any relevant further information as referred to in paragraph 2.

Here, in addition to all the issues which were just discussed, the annotation should also apply it to another, already existing, paragraph. The annotation should not only add further conditions to the referenced paragraph but modify it as well. For example, The sentence "the controller shall provide the data subject prior to that further processing with information on that other purpose and with any relevant further information as referred to in paragraph 2." requires the reader to adapt the obligations of paragraph 2 to the new processing.

Two possible solutions for annotating such complex legal structure come to mind. First, one can ask the user to simplify the structure manually. In the above case, the user will transform the complex sentence into many simple ones and will take care of replacing different values in the right places. This is the approach taken by current formalizations of the GDPR [19].

The solution suggested in this paper is to automatize this process by providing an additional layer of annotations for describing the complex structures of legal texts. These annotations will be called **macros**. Macros are tailored to specific situations and are capable of arbitrary modifications of the result. For example, in the case of paragraph 1, a macro could take the original sentence and break it down automatically into the several required sentences.

From the engineering point of view, the second approach is better. First, it saves the user from the need to copy and duplicate parts of the sentence. In addition, it generates automatically the relevant conditions of each item and thus is more rigorous. Lastly, by automatizing parts of the formalization process, future editions of this paragraph become easier - one just needs to change the relevant parts of the paper and the macro can be called again.

Clearly, a disadvantage of such an approach is the possible high number of required macros. For the purpose of having a precise and simple annotation of article 13, there is a need of 4 such macros. Nevertheless, as we will see next, these macros are general in nature and will possibly fit a wide range of legal sentences, which are usually of a restricted form. As a possible extension of the work discussed in this paper, there is also a plan to add to the NAI suite the ability to design new macros using a Domain Specific Language (DSL).

A possible such DSL is defined next. This DSL will be used in this paper to describe the macros which are required for the formalization of article 13.

Definition 2 (Annotation's syntax). *Annotations will be denoted using English capital letters $A, B, \ldots$ with possibly subscripts and superscripts. There are two types of annotations. Simple annotations, denoted by A^s are term annotations (also called vocabulary annotations), i.e. annotations applied to term and therefore do not contain any nested annotation. Complex annotations are of the form* ANNOT(*args*) *where* ANNOT *is the name of the logical connective which is used for the annotation and args is an ordered list of the top level annotations which are included in it. The connectives were described in Sect. 2.1.*

For example, a conjunction annotation over the term annotations $t(a, b)$ and $s(X, b)$ is denoted as $\mathrm{AND}(t(a, b), s(X, b))$.

Definition 3 (Parsing state). *Labels are defined as simple annotations which denote a name and are normally purely propositional. The parsing state is a pair* (*annots, map*) *where annots is an array of annotations which were extracted from the annotated texts and map is a mapping between labels and annotations. We denote the map which is obtained by setting the value y for the label x in map by $map(x, y)$. We denote the value which is associated with the label x in map by $map[x]$.*

Definition 4 (Macros). *A macro is a transformation from one parsing state into another and is denoted by* $(annots_1, map_1) \implies (annots_2, map_2)$. *Macros normally apply to only one annotation J_1 in the annots array. In these cases, we will simplify the notation and write* $(J_1, map_1) \implies (J_2, map_2)$. *In addition, when the map does not change, we will sometimes further simplify the notation and write $J_1 \implies J_2$.*

Lastly, we need to define occurrences of subterm annotations within annotations in order to be able to formally desscribe replacements.

Definition 5 (Subterm occurrences). *Given an arbitrary annotation A, we denote by $A[x]$ all occurrences of a subterm annotation x appearing in it. In the definition of a macro $(A[x], map_1) \implies (A[y], map_2)$, $A[y]$ on the right hand side is obtained from $A[x]$ by replacing all occurrences of x in A with y.*

For example, assuming that the conjunction in the previous example is denoted by A, the occurrences of the subterm b in it are denoted by $A[b]$.

We can denote the macro which replaces those occurrences of b with c using $A[b] \implies A[c]$.

We can now give a formal definition of the specific macros.

The Multi-obligation Macro. This macro takes two annotations, where the second annotation has the following restrictions. First, it must be a conjunction. Second, each conjunct except the first must be either a term, an "If/Then" or an "Always/If" annotation. Third, its first conjunct must be a term which contains the placeholder VAR. This placeholder can also appear anywhere in the first annotation.

Definition 6 (The multi-obligation macro). *The multi-obligation macro is defined by (M-OBS(C[VAR], AND(A[VAR], $B_1, .., B_n$)), map)*
$$\implies$$
(AND(IF-THEN-OB(AND($C[B_1^1], B_1^0$), $A[B_1^1]$)), ...,
IF-THEN-OB(AND($C[B_n^1], B_n^0$), $A[B_n^1]$))), map).
Where

- $n \geq 1$
- *For each $0 < i \leq n$, B_i is one of the following*
  - IF-THEN(B_i^0, B_i^1)
  - ALWAYS-IF(B_i^1, B_i^0)
  - *A simple annotation B_i^1. In this case B_i^0 is empty.*

Informally, when applied to two annotations, the macro does the following. For each conjunct beyond the first in the second annotation, the macro creates a new conditional obligation. The type of obligation and the form of conditions is defined according to the type of annotation:

- In case the annotation is simple, the set of conditions is the one defined in the first annotation and the obligation is the first conjunct, where the VAR placeholder is replaced by the simple annotation.
- In case the annotation is an "If/Then" or an "Always/If", we define the condition part of the annotation to be the first formula of the "If/Then" annotation and the second in "Always/If", while the conclusion part is defined to be the second formula and first, respectively. The set of conditions is a conjunction of the one defined in the first annotation and conditions of the complex annotation. The obligation is the first conjunct, where the VAR placeholder is replaced by the conclusion of the complex annotation.

Similarly to the above, any occurrence of the placeholder VAR in the conditions is replaced with the same term as in the obligation.

Paragraph 3 is relatively short syntactically but complex semantically. It expands on paragraph 2 and places further conditions and obligations. While paragraph 2 describes the obligations in case of the first data processing, paragraph 3 describes those in all subsequent ones. Clearly, additional macros are required. The first macro is used for cross-reference and allows the users of the editor to label annotated sentences with a certain name. Using this name, a second macro then takes the referenced annotated sentence, copies it and replaces relevant parts.

The Labeling Macro. This macro, which helps other macros to function by changing the state, expects two annotations. The first is a simple annotation denoting the label while the second can be any possible annotation. It enables the use of labels in other macros which are defined later. In our example, the simple annotation is just the term a13_p2 which is used to name the second paragraph, while the second annotation is the whole content of the second paragraph.

Definition 7 (The labeling macro). *The labeling macro is defined as follows*
$(LABEL(A^s, B), map) \Longrightarrow (B, map(A^s, B))$

The Copying Macro. This macro takes three arguments. An optional annotation containing further conditions, a conjunction of further obligations of the form stated in the Multi-obligation Macro and a label which is used in order to copy an annotated sentence. It uses the first conjunct of the second annotation to replace the obligation of the copied annotation and adds further obligations according to the other conjuncts. In our example, this macro copies the second paragraph, while adding further conditions referring to subsequent processing and the order between them. It then replaces the obligation to refer to the subsequent processing and adds a further obligation to communicate information about the purpose of the processing. It also states that the information should be communicated to the data subject before the processing takes place and not at the time of the collection, as is the case in paragraph 2.

Definition 8 (The copying macro). *The copying macro is defined as follows*
$(COPY(D_?[VAR], AND(E[VAR], F_1, ..F_m), G^s), map)$
$\Longrightarrow$
$(M\text{-}OBS(AND(D_?[VAR], C[VAR]), AND(E[VAR],$
$B_1, \ldots, B_n, F_1, \ldots, F_m)), map)$ *Where*

- $m \geq 0$
- $map[G^s] =$
  $M\text{-}OBS(C[VAR], AND(A[VAR], B_1, .., B_n))$ *with all the conditions as in Definition 6.*
- *For each* $0 \leq j \leq m$, F_i *is one of the following*
  - $IF\text{-}THEN(F_i^0, F_i^1)$
  - $ALWAYS\text{-}IF(F_i^1, F_i^0)$
  - *A simple annotation* F_i^1. *In this case* F_i^0 *is empty.*
- $D_?$ *refers to an optional arbitrary annotation.*

The last macro is based on the forth paragraph.

Paragraph 4 of GDPR's Article 13: Paragraphs 1, 2 and 3 shall not apply where and insofar as the data subject already has the information.

The last paragraph in the article has a standard legal form. Its purpose is to set exceptional circumstances in which other paragraphs do not hold. In our example, none of the obligations in the previous paragraphs should hold in case the data subject already has the required information.

In the previous subsection, we have seen a utility macro for labeling annotations. This macro is handy here as well as we will need to be able to refer to other annotations, in order to apply a macro for exceptional circumstances.

The Exception Macro. This macro gets a list of simple annotations, which denote labels of other annotations. It additionally gets an annotation which serves as the exceptional circumstances. When applied, this macro will add the negation of the exceptional circumstances to the conditions of all referred obligations in the state. In our example, it will make sure that all the obligations described in this article hold only in case the relevant information in the specific obligation is not already known to the data subject. Since many of these obligations are generated by one of the other macros, the exceptional circumstances can contain the VAR placeholder, similarly to the Multi-obligation and Copy macros. In our example, this placeholder is indeed used and is replaced, for every obligation, with the exact information which should be communicated and should not be already known.

Definition 9 (The exception macro). *The exception macro is defined as follows*
$$(EXCEP(A_1^s, \ldots, A_n^s, B), map) \implies (\emptyset, map(A_1^s, C_1)(\ldots)(A_n^s, C_n)) \ where$$

- $n \geq 1$
- *For each* $0 < i \leq n$
  - $map[A_i^s] = C_i'$
  - *In case* $C_i' = M\text{-}OBS(A, D)$, $C_i = M\text{-}OBS(AND(NOT(B), A), D)$
  - *Otherwise* $C_i = IF\text{-}THEN(NOT(B), C_i')$

A note about the above interpretation of legal exceptions. The macro defined in Definition 9 applies further conditions to previously defined sentences. The purpose of these further conditions is to specify situations in which these sentences are defeated. Most approaches to defeasible reasoning are based on non-monotonic logics [18]. Nevertheless, monotonic logics have been proposed as well [6]. Clearly, more discussion is required in order to justify the choice in Definition 9. While this discussion is beyond the scope of this paper, I would like to point out the main difference between the two approaches and suggest, in a very informal and imprecise way, a remedy, which is made possible by using the NAI Suite. Improving and implementing this remedy is planned as a future work.

In contrary to classical logics, non-monotonic logics allow a decrease in the amount of possible deductions given an increase in factual information. This advantage is no longer relevant if all possible knowledge is known in advance (please refer to Section 6 in [20] for more information). While knowing everything in advance is not feasible, knowing what is known in advance is. After all, the known information must be input into the NAI Suite and the total amount of relevant information is finite, since it must appear in the legislation, which is finite (or more precisely, can be finitely denoted). The NAI Suite can decide for each piece of information if it is known or not and adapt the reasoning process in order to take it into account.

It should be further noted that the macros abstract over the exact interpretation of exceptions. The precise treatment is handled by the underlining logic and theorem prover. It is true that in Definition 9 an explicit negation was used. The reason for that is that right now there is no other underlining logic. A better definition would use a new operator for denoting evidence which defeats obligations. The current underlining logic will interpret this operator as classical negation while a Prolog based solution would interpret it as a "negation as failure", etc.

4   Example: Automated Reasoning over GDPR Article 13

This section describes the formalization of article 13 of the GDPR using the NAI Suite and the extensions to the suite which were implemented in the previous section. The macros currently appear in the suite in the same drop list as the logical and normative connectives, just below a separator. In later versions of the tool, they will probably be allocated their own drop list.

The reader is invited to follow this section while simultaneously looking at the formalization in the tool itself. The formalization and queries which resulted from this work are integral artefacts of this paper and can be accessed via the NAI Suite web application[3]. This section will constantly make references to the tool.

4.1   Annotating Paragraph 1

The NAI Suite, as described in Sect. 2.3, requires us first to create a new legislation and then copy the original text into the editor pane. The first paragraph describes a situation in which a controller is obliged to communicate different information to the data subject, according to different conditions. Although not explicitly written, this paragraph also talks about processors and the processing of the data itself, as well as of its collection. In order to formalize the article, we must make these elements explicit in the text. We therefore add this information in brackets ('[','])') as can be seen in the already annotated text in the editor pane.

Given the explicit text of the paragraph, we are ready to annotate it. The first step of every formalization using the NAI Suite is to annotate all terms which are part of the vocabulary of the text. These terms correspond to the colorful annotations in the editor. There are many relations between the different legal terms. For example, the personal data of the data subject is being collected and

---

[3] Please login to https://nai.uni.lu using the email address: gdpr@nai.lu and password: nai. Please note that this account is write protected and cannot be changed. Note also that no registration is required in order to use the above account!.

processed and is subject to the supervision of a Data Privacy Officer (DPO). Such complex relations require an expressive language such as fist-order logic, which is used in the annotations of the article.

As an example of term annotations, one can consider the phrases "data subject" and "personal data", for which the following first-order terms were assigned (respectively): `data_subject(Subject)` and`personal_data(Data, Subject)`. When annotating terms, words starting with a lower-case letter are considered as constants while those starting with a capital letter are considered as variables which are quantified over the whole logical expression. The full list of the annotated legal terms can be found on the "Vocabulary" tab in the legislation editor.

Once all legal terms are annotated, we can proceed with annotating the relationsips between them. The structure of the paragraph is the following. A set of conditions for the whole paragraph is followed by an obligation to communicate information. The precise information to communicate then follows in each of the items, possibly with some further conditions.

The NAI suite supports such a sentence structure via the "Multi-obligation Macro". This macro accepts an annotation denoting the general conditions and a second annotation denoting the additional obligations and their specific conditions. When applied, the macro generates a conjunction of obligations, one for each of the annotated obligations and with the general conditions as well as the specific ones. We therefore annotate the whole paragraph 1 with this annotation.

We now proceed with annotating the conditions and obligations. First, we use the "And" connective to annotate all the general conditions, such as the existence of a processor and a controller, etc. We then proceed by using the "And" connective to annotate all the obligations. Each obligation can have one of three forms. A simple obligation contains just a term. The macro will convert this obligation into a conditional obligation where the conditions are all the general ones from the first conjunction. The more complex obligations are either "If/Then" and "Always/If".

The difference between these two connectives is syntactical only. While in "If/Then", the conditions are specified by the first annotation and the conclusion with the second, the order is reversed in "Always/If". By using one of these two annotations for the different obligations, the macro will know to add the additional, specific conditions to the conditions of each resulted obligation.

The application of the macro to the annotation of paragraph 1 generates multiple annotations. The DSL denotation of the generated annotation of the first item of paragraph 1 can be seen in Fig. 3

```
IF-THEN-OB(AND(processor(Processor),nominate(Controller,
Processor),personal_data_processed(Processor,Data,Time,
Justification,Purpose),personal_data(Data,Subject),
collected_at(Data,Time0),data_subject(Subject),
controller(Controller, Data)),communicate_at_time(Controller,
Subject,Time0,contact_details(Controller))))
```

Fig. 3. Generated annotation of item 1 in paragraph 1

The specific annotations can be seen by hovering with the mouse over the relevant parts of the text. The full formalization of this article can be seen on the "Formalization" tab. This formalization is a conjunction of the obligations specified in the article. Note that since some items contain more than just one obligation, the conjunction contains more than 6 conjuncts.

The annotation of paragraph 2 is similar.

4.2   Annotating Paragraph 3

Using the "Copy" macro, annotating this paragraph becomes relatively simple. The annotation takes 3 elements. The first contains optional additional conditions. Indeed, since we consider now further processing of the data, there are additional conditions such as the processor of the new processing, its purpose, etc. We also need, in the conditions, to stress that the new processing is different from the previous one. Finally, we group these further conditions in an "And" annotation.

The second element contains the further obligations. The first of which is the obligation template which contains the VAR placeholder. This element will replace the obligation template in the copied annotation which is referenced by the third element. The remaining items in this element are additional values which should be substituted for VAR in each of the generated obligations. These items add to those from the referenced annotation.

The annotated text can be seen in Fig. 2.

The resulting formalization, which can be seen at the bottom (the third element) of the "Formalization" tab, contains therefore more obligations that the referenced paragraph 2. In addition, all the obligations refer to the new purpose and state a new communication time, as stated in the new conditions.

Facilitating Correct Formalization. There is a further interesting issue which relates to this paragraph. Clearly, its annotation is far from trivial and is error prone. Still, by using macros and annotations, the chance of error occurring is reduced since there is a clear connection between the text itself and its annotation, as demanded by the Isomorphism approach to legal formalization [2]. This is not the case when the paragraph is translated into a logical formula manually. As an example, consider the DAPRECO formalization of the GDPR [19]. As mentioned in the introduction to this paper, this ambitious knowledge base contains a manual translation of almost all articles of the GDPR.

Nevertheless, if we focus on the translation of this paragraph[4], we can see several errors. First, the translation does not mention at all the fact that all of the required information mentioned in paragraph 2 is required here as well. Even more important though, there is no distinction between the two processing events of the data, except in the name of the variable used to denote them. There is a

---

[4] Please search for the text "statements51Formula" in https://raw.githubusercontent. com/dapreco/daprecokb/master/gdpr/rioKB_GDPR.xml, of a version no later than 11/2019.

relation between the times of the two occurrences but it is defined as "greater or equal". Clearly, this formalization will always apply to any processing, whether first or not, since one can substitute for the universally quantified variables the same processing and the same time.

Such an error is not easy to spot, when one translates regulations manually. On the other hand, when using annotations and macros, we could more easily spot this and use a correct annotation.

4.3 Annotating Paragraph 4

Annotating exceptions is now also relatively straightforward. We use the "Exception" macro to state all the annotations which should take an additional condition and the condition itself. The result can be seen in Fig. 4.

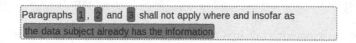

Fig. 4. Annotating the exception in paragraph 4

While in the intermediary annotations-based level we add a new annotation to faithfully capture the exception, in the underlining logical representation no new formula is added but existing formulae are modified to accommodate the exception. This is an example of an hierarchical formalization [20] which aims at being both faithful, well engineered and efficient.

4.4 Automated Reasoning over the GDPR

Section 2 has described several automated deduction based tools, such as consistency or independence checking. These tools can be used for checking the correctness of the formalization. Nevertheless, the main usage of automated deduction within the NAI Suite is for allowing the computer to answer questions and make legal deductions. Given a correctly formalized legislation, NAI can currently answer Yes/No questions. This is done by employing the state-of-the-art theorem prover MleanCoP [15], which in turn tries to build a formal proof that the question logically follows from the formalization and assumptions. Since first-order modal resolution is only semi-decidable [8], some negative answers cannot be given. The NAI Suite displays a warning in this case.

The main expected usage of this feature is by third-party tools, which will use the deduction engine of the NAI Suite over an already formalized legislation in order to answer arbitrary questions. For example, privacy policies can be checked automatically for compliance by constructing the relevant queries [17] and executing them in the NAI Suite.

Nevertheless, the NAI Suite also supports the possibility of writing queries directly in the tool. This feature is mainly used for testing and as a support tool for lawyers and jurists. Similarly, this feature can be used in order to demonstrate automatic reasoning over the article. The example consists of five questions relating to the precise time the controller is obliged to communicate different information to the data subject. These questions can be found and executed on the "Queries" menu of the tool. In the remaining of this section, they are described in detail.

Precise Time of Communicating Information in Case There is at Most One Processing of the Data. In order to be able to answer this question, three different scenarios are given. In each, we check if the controller is obliged to communicate specific information.

In all the example questions, the variable denoting the required information is instantiated with a specific one. In general, queries can also be executed over free variables and can represent a more general question.

The basic scenario which is described in all queries is the following. The birth date of the data subject Albert was collected on the 1/8/2017. The Controller Brian has nominated the Processor John to process the data for the purpose of improving the business. The processing took place on the 1/9/2017.

In the first question we assume that Albert does not yet know the Contact Details of the Data Protection Officer, who is named Charles. We ask if, in this case, Brian is obliged to communicate this information to Albert at the time of processing. When we execute the query, NAI tells us that this is not the case.

The way a theorem prover answers Yes/No questions is by trying to prove them. In case a proof is found, we have a mathematical argument that the answer is Yes. When a proof cannot be found, the theorem prover might answer that either the query is counter-satisfiable, or that the search for proof has timed out.

In the case the query is counter-satisfiable, we know that based on the information we have given, the prover has found cases where the opposite of what we have asked is true and that therefore, proving the validity of the argument is impossible. If we have given all relevant information, then this answer is effectively a No. On the other hand, if we have forgotten some important information, such as the fact that Brian is the Controller, then being counter-satisfiable means that in some cases, the answer is No, but in others, it might be Yes. For example, when we omit the information about the controller, it might be that it is not Brian who is obliged to communicate the data and therefore, we have found a counter example. This means that the quality of the answer is based on the quality of the question.

In the case the prover times out, we can only know that we have terminated its execution before an answer was found. Usually, the theorem prover answers in less than a second. While we can normally assume that a futile search for a proof usually means that there is none, we cannot count on this result.

For the first question, we have obtained the answer that a counter-example exists. By considering the "Vocabulary" tab, we can confirm that we have considered all relevant information and that therefore, this answer means no - Brian has no such obligation.

For the second question, the obligation was changed from communicating the information at the time of processing to communicating it at the time of the collection of data. The prover answers in this case Yes - Indeed, Brian is under such a legal obligation.

The last question checks if this obligation also holds when the information is not Charles contact details, but the purpose of processing. The prover still answers Yes.

Precise Time of Communicating Information in Case of a Second Processing of the Data. In the following two questions, we expand the case as follows. Besides nominating John to process the data, Brian has also nominated Chris to process it for the purpose of a collaboration with Facebook. Chris has processed the data on the 1/10/2017.

The first question in this group tries to determine, again in case Albert is not aware of this second purpose of processing his Data, if Brian is obliged to communicate this information at the time of the second processing. The prover answers No.

The last query states the same question, but places the time of communicating the information to before the time of the second processing. The prover affirms that this is indeed an obligation of Brian.

The examples above have shown how arbitrary Yes/No questions can be answered by the tool. In a similar fashion, questions can be asked by third-party tools via the exposed API (see Sect. 2.4), such as whether a certain privacy policy complies with the GDPR.

5   Conclusion and Future Work

The formalization of legal texts is a non-trivial and error-prone task. Annotations can help generating correct formalizations. Nevertheless, legal texts contain sentence structures which go beyond logical and deontic connectives. The solution which was described and demonstrated in this paper uses macros to describe meta-level properties and to annotate such structures.

The four macros which were introduced are relatively general and appear in other legal texts, as well as in other articles of the GDPR. The immediate followup of the current work is the formalization of articles 5 and 6, which have a similar structure. Other macros will be added when needed.

In addition, the macro DSL which was introduced in Sect. 3 can be extended into a macro editing functionality within the NAI Suite. Such a feature will allow users to create arbitrary macros and handle any kind of legal text efficiently.

Currently, the NAI suite supports an expressive deontic first-order language. This language is rich enough to describe many scenarios which appear in legal texts. Nevertheless, more work is required in order to capture all such scenarios. Among those features with the highest priority, we list support for exceptions, temporal sentences and arithmetic. In Sect. 4.3, one possible direction for addressing exceptions was given. Other possible solutions for these issues already exist in the form of tools such as non-monotonic reasoners [10], temporal provers [24] and SMT solvers [7].

On the level of usability, the tool currently does not give any information as to why a query is counter-satisfiable. The user needs to look on the vocabulary in order to determine possible reasons. Integrating a model finder, such as Nitpick [5], will help "debugging" formalizations and enriching the query language.

NAI's graphical user interface (GUI) aims at being intuitive and easy to use and tries to hide the underline complexities of the logics involved. A continuously updated list of new features can be found on the GUI's development website[5].

References

1. Bartolini, C., Lenzini, G., Santos, C.: An agile approach to validate a formal representation of the GDPR. In: Kojima, K., Sakamoto, M., Mineshima, K., Satoh, K. (eds.) JSAI-isAI 2018. LNCS (LNAI), vol. 11717, pp. 160–176. Springer, Cham (2019). https://doi.org/10.1007/978-3-030-31605-1_13
2. Bench-Capon, T.J., Coenen, F.P.: Isomorphism and legal knowledge based systems. Artif. Intell. Law 1(1), 65–86 (1992)
3. Bench-Capon, T.J., Robinson, G.O., Routen, T.W., Sergot, M.J.: Logic programming for large scale applications in law: a formalisation of supplementary benefit legislation. In: Proceedings of ICAIL, pp. 190–198 (1987)
4. Biagioli, C., Mariani, P., Tiscornia, D.: Esplex: a rule and conceptual model for representing statutes. In: Proceedings of ICAIL, pp. 240–251. ACM (1987)
5. Blanchette, J.C., Nipkow, T.: Nitpick: a counterexample generator for higher-order logic based on a relational model finder. In: Kaufmann, M., Paulson, L.C. (eds.) ITP 2010. LNCS, vol. 6172, pp. 131–146. Springer, Heidelberg (2010). https://doi.org/10.1007/978-3-642-14052-5_11
6. Boutilier, C.: Conditional logics of normality as modal systems. Proc. AAAI. 90, 594–599 (1990)
7. Bouton, T., Caminha B. de Oliveira, D., Déharbe, D., Fontaine, P.: veriT: an open, trustable and efficient SMT-solver. In: Schmidt, R.A. (ed.) CADE 2009. LNCS (LNAI), vol. 5663, pp. 151–156. Springer, Heidelberg (2009). https://doi.org/10.1007/978-3-642-02959-2_12
8. Fitting, M., Mendelsohn, R.L.: First-Order Modal Logic, vol. 277. Springer, Dordrecht (2012). https://doi.org/10.1007/978-94-011-5292-1
9. Governatori, G., Shek, S.: Regorous: a business process compliance checker. In: Proceedings of ICAIL, pp. 245–246. ACM (2013)
10. Kifer, M.: Nonmonotonic reasoning in FLORA-2. In: Baral, C., Greco, G., Leone, N., Terracina, G. (eds.) LPNMR 2005. LNCS (LNAI), vol. 3662, pp. 1–12. Springer, Heidelberg (2005). https://doi.org/10.1007/11546207_1
11. Libal, T., Pascucci, M.: Automated reasoning in normative detachment structures with ideal conditions. In: Proceedings of ICAIL, pp. 63–72. ACM (2019)
12. Libal, T., Steen, A.: NAI: the normative reasoner. In: Proceedings of ICAIL, pp. 262–263. ACM (2019)
13. de Montety, C., Antignac, T., Slim, C.: GDPR modelling for log-based compliance checking. In: Meng, W., Cofta, P., Jensen, C.D., Grandison, T. (eds.) IFIPTM 2019. IAICT, vol. 563, pp. 1–18. Springer, Cham (2019). https://doi.org/10.1007/978-3-030-33716-2_1

---

[5] https://github.com/normativeai/frontend/issues.

14. Otten, J.: Implementing connection calculi for first-order modal logics. In: Proceedings of IWIL, pp. 18–32 (2012)
15. Otten, J.: MleanCoP: a connection prover for first-order modal logic. In: Demri, S., Kapur, D., Weidenbach, C. (eds.) IJCAR 2014. LNCS (LNAI), vol. 8562, pp. 269–276. Springer, Cham (2014). https://doi.org/10.1007/978-3-319-08587-6_20
16. Palmirani, M., Cervone, L., Bujor, O., Chiappetta, M.: RAWE: an editor for rule markup of legal texts. In: Proceedings of RuleML (2013)
17. Palmirani, M., Governatori, G.: Modelling legal knowledge for GDPR compliance checking. In: Proceedings of JURIX, pp. 101–110 (2018)
18. Prakken, H., Sartor, G.: The three faces of defeasibility in the law. Ratio Juris **17**(1), 118–139 (2004)
19. Robaldo, L., Bartolini, C., Palmirani, M., Rossi, A., Martoni, M., Lenzini, G.: Formalizing gdpr provisions in reified I/O logic: the DAPRECO knowledge base. J. Logic Lang. Inf. 1–49 (2019). https://doi.org/10.1007/s10849-019-09309-z
20. Routen, T., Bench-Capon, T.: Hierarchical formalizations. Man-Mach. Stud. **35**(1), 69–93 (1991)
21. Sergot, M.J., Sadri, F., Kowalski, R.A., Kriwaczek, F., Hammond, P., Cory, H.T.: The British Nationality Act as a logic program. Commun. ACM **29**(5), 370–386 (1986)
22. Sherman, D.M.: Expert systems and ICAI in tax law: killing two birds with one AI stone. In: Proceedings of ICAIL, pp. 74–80. ACM (1989)
23. Stamper, R.: LEGOL: modelling legal rules by computer. In: Computer Science and Law, pp. 45–71 (1980)
24. Suda, M., Weidenbach, C.: A PLTL-prover based on labelled superposition with partial model guidance. In: Gramlich, B., Miller, D., Sattler, U. (eds.) IJCAR 2012. LNCS (LNAI), vol. 7364, pp. 537–543. Springer, Heidelberg (2012). https://doi.org/10.1007/978-3-642-31365-3_42

Towards an Executable Methodology for the Formalization of Legal Texts

Tomer Libal[1(✉)] and Alexander Steen[2]

[1] American University of Paris, Paris, France
shaolintl@gmail.com
[2] University of Luxembourg, Luxembourg City, Luxembourg

Abstract. A methodology for the formalization of legal texts is presented. This methodology is based on features of the NAI Suite, a recently developed formalization environment for legal texts. The ability of the tool to execute queries is used in order to drive a correct formalization until all queries are validated. The approach is studied on a fragment of the *Smoking Prohibition (Children in Motor Vehicles) (Scotland) Act 2016* of the Scottish Parliament.

Keywords: Legal reasoning · Deontic logic · Automated reasoning

1 Introduction

The generation and maintenance of knowledge bases as a formalized representation of domain specific information is a well-established approach for enabling the employment of automated procedures that process this information in a suitable way. In the context of Computational Law, knowledge bases may act as large repositories of interpretations of legal documents and therein contained norms, for the purpose of providing semantic access to them, e.g., for employment in legal drafting, compliance checking, and legal reasoning. While earlier research in Legal Informatics focused on structured document representations and information retrieval, e.g. [3], more recent work also addresses the logical structure of the legal documents' semantical content [14]. This structure is thereby captured by logical rules of some adequate logical formalism which describe the contained obligations, permissions, prohibitions, etc. and may then, in conjunction with a concrete state of affairs, be used to derive the legal consequences with respect to the given normative document using a deductive reasoning procedure.

In this paper, we follow the idea of using (semi-)automated reasoning technology for legal norms, but focus on the validation of legal knowledge bases themselves. Knowledge bases may be (partly) engineered by IT professionals since quite some expertise about its underlying technical details, e.g. knowledge about the computer-readable input format, is potentially necessary. How can we make sure that the representation of the legal norms actually captures the intended meaning? The knowledge engineering can of course include erroneous

M. Dastani et al. (Eds.): CLAR 2020, LNAI 12061, pp. 151–165, 2020.
https://doi.org/10.1007/978-3-030-44638-3_10

inputs because of limited domain knowledge available. Regardless of the domain expertise, general errors and inaccuracies may, of course, occur in any case. State-of-the-art methodologies for building legal ontologies [9] and for validating formal representations of legal texts [1] rely on communication between domain experts and IT experts for ensuring correctness. In the approach of Bartolini et al., the knowledge is modeled by IT experts and then translated algorithmically to a natural language representation. The latter representation is then given to domain experts who assess its correctness. Potential errors or problems are then reported back to the IT experts which try to accommodate the feedback. This whole process is repeated until certain quality criteria are met. Of course, communication between different domains is error-prone and laborious; the natural language translation result is still quite complex and might hinder the proper assessment of the data.

In contrast to this approach, we describe ongoing work towards a methodology that, intuitively speaking, treats the creation of legal knowledge bases as a domain-specific agile software engineering process. The methodology aims at enabling non-technical domain experts, here legal professionals, to control the knowledge engineering process by using a graphical and interactive interface that uses automated reasoning technology for providing real-time assessments of the given inputs. This design decision is in line with other systems that address the formalization of legal knowledge for non-technical audience, as done e.g. in "Oracle Policy Automation" (OPA) by Oracle Corporation.[1] The methodological approach in this paper is prototypically implemented in the new normative reasoning framework NAI [8]. NAI features a graphical annotation-based editor which abstracts from the underlying logical language of the knowledge base. It also incorporates easily accessible functionality for assessing the quality requirements of the presented methodology, including consistency, non-redundancy and functional correctness.

Additionally, the architecture of NAI is modular in the sense that it allows the use of different logics and reasoning engines that seem fit for the task at hand. It also provides an API, which can be used by other tools in order to reason over the formalized legislation. NAI is a web application and is readily available at https://nai.uni.lu. It is open-source and its source code is freely available at GitHub[2] under GPL-3.0 license.

The contributions of the paper are: A description of a new agile methodology inspired by behaviour-driven Development (BDD) for the creation and validation of legal knowledge bases. Furthermore, we show how the NAI tool can be used to implement this methodology by exemplarily formalizing a fragment of a concrete legal document and testing the resulting knowledge basis for correctness.

---

[1] See http://oracle.com/technetwork/apps-tech/policy-automation for further information.
[2] See https://github.com/normativeai.

2   Preliminaries

The logical formalism underlying the NAI framework is based on a universal fragment first-order variant of the deontic logic **DL*** [7], denoted **DL*$_1$**. Its syntax is given by

Definition 1 (Syntax of DL*$_1$). *Let V, P and F be disjoint sets of symbols for variables, predicate symbols (of some arity) and function symbols (of some arity), respectively. **DL*$_1$** formulas ϕ, ψ are given by:*

$$\phi, \psi ::= p(t_1, \ldots, t_n) \mid \neg\phi \mid \phi \wedge \psi \mid \phi \vee \psi \mid \phi \Rightarrow \psi$$
$$\mid \mathsf{Id}\,\phi \mid \mathsf{Ob}\,\phi \mid \mathsf{Pm}\,\phi \mid \mathsf{Fb}\,\phi \mid \phi \Rightarrow_{\mathsf{Ob}} \psi \mid \phi \Rightarrow_{\mathsf{Pm}} \psi \mid \phi \Rightarrow_{\mathsf{Fb}} \psi$$

where $p \in P$ is a predicate symbol of arity $n \geq 0$ and the t_i, $1 \leq i \leq n$, are terms. Terms are freely generated by the function symbols from F and variables from V.   ⌐

DL*$_1$ extends Standard Deontic Logic (SDL) with the normative concepts of ideal and contrary-to-duty obligations, and contains predicate symbols, the standard logical connectives, and the normative operators of obligation (Ob), permission (Pm), prohibition (Fb), their conditional counter-parts, and ideality (Id). Free variables are implicitly universally quantified at top-level.

This logic is expressive enough to capture many interesting normative structures. For details on its expressivity and its semantics, we refer to [7].

3   The NAI Suite

The NAI suite integrates novel theorem proving technology into a usable graphical user interface (GUI) for the computer-assisted formalization of legal texts and applying automated normative reasoning procedures on these artifacts. In particular, NAI includes

1. a legislation editor that graphically supports the formalization of legal texts,
2. means of assessing the quality of entered formalizations, e.g., by automatically conducting consistency checks and assessing logical independence,
3. ready-to-use theorem prover technology for evaluating user-specified queries wrt. a given formalization, and
4. the possibility to share and collaborate, and to experiment with different formalizations and underlying logics.

NAI is realized using a web-based Software-as-a-service architecture, cf. Fig. 1. It comprises a GUI that is implemented as a Javascript browser application, and a NodeJS application on the back-end side which connects to theorem provers, data storage services and relevant middleware. Using this architectural layout, no further software is required from the user perspective for using NAI and its reasoning procedures, as all necessary software is made available on the back end and the computationally heavy tasks are executed on the remote servers only. The results of the different reasoning procedures are sent back to the GUI and displayed to the user. The major components of NAI are described in more detail in the following.

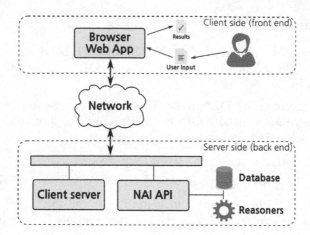

Fig. 1. Software-as-a-service architecture of the NAI reasoning framework. The front end software runs in the user's browser and connects to the remote site, and its different services, via a well-defined API through the network. Data flow is indicated by arrows.

3.1   The Reasoning Module

The NAI suite supports formalizing legal texts and applying various logical operations, such as consistency checks (non-derivability of falsum), logical independence analysis as well as the creation of user queries that can automatically be assessed for (non-)validity. After formalization, the formal representation of the legal text is stored in a general and expressive machine-readable format in NAI. This format aims at generalizing from concrete logical formalisms that are used for evaluating the logical properties of the legal document's formal representation.

There exist many different logical formalisms for capturing normative reasoning and extensions of it. Since the discussion of such formalisms is still ongoing, and the choice of the concrete logic underlying the reasoning process strongly influences the results of all procedures, NAI uses a two-step procedure to employ automated reasoning tools. NAI stores only the general format, as mentioned above, as the result of the formalization process. Once a user then chooses a certain logic for conducting the logical analysis, NAI will automatically translate the general format into the specific logic resp. the concrete input format of the employed automated reasoning system. Currently, NAI supports only the $\mathbf{DL^*}_1$ logic from Sect. 2; however, the architecture of NAI is designed in such a way that further formalisms can easily be supported. Some possible extensions, such as for the treatment of exceptions, are described in Sect. 5.

The choice in favor of $\mathbf{DL^*}_1$ is primarily motivated by the fact that it can be effectively automated using a shallow semantical embedding into normal (bi-)modal logic [7]. This enables the use of readily available reasoning systems for such logics; in contrast, there are few to none automated reasoning systems available for normative logics (with the exception of [5]). In NAI, we use the MleanCoP prover [11] for first-order multi-modal logics as it is currently one of the most effective systems and it returns proof certificates which can be independently assessed for correctness [10]. It is also possible to use various different tools for automated reasoning in parallel (where applicable). This is of increasing importance once multiple different logical formalisms are supported.

3.2 The Annotation Editor

The annotation editor of NAI is one of its central components. Using the editor, users can create formalizations of legal documents that can subsequently be used for formal legal reasoning. The general functionality of the editor is described in the following. A more detailed exemplary application on a concrete legal document is presented in Sect. 4.3.

One of the main ideas of the NAI editor is to hide the underlying logical details and technical reasoning input and outputs from the user. We consider this essential, as the primary target audience of the NAI suite are not necessarily logicians and it could greatly decrease the usability of the tool if a solid knowledge about formal logic was required. This is realized by letting the user annotate legal texts and queries graphically and by allowing the user to access the different reasoning functionalities by simply clicking buttons that are integrated into the GUI. Note that the user can still inspect the logical formulae that result from the annotation process and also input these formulae directly. However, this feature is considered advanced and not the primary approach put forward by NAI.

The formalization proceeds as follows: The user selects some text from the legal document and annotates it, either as a term or as a composite (complex) statement. In the first case, a name for that term is computed automatically, but it can also be chosen freely. Different terms are displayed as different colors in the text. In the latter case, the user needs to choose among the different possibilities (which roughly correspond to logical connectives) and the containing text can be annotated recursively. Composite statements are displayed as a box around the text. An example of an annotation result is displayed in Fig. 4a.

The editor also features direct access to the consistency check and logical independence check procedures (as buttons). When such a button is clicked, the current state of the formalization will be translated and sent to the back-end provers, which determine whether it is consistent resp. logically independent.

User queries are also created using such an editor. In addition to the steps sketched above, users may declare a text passage as *goal* using a dedicated annotation button, whose contents are again annotated as usual. If the query is executed, the back-end provers will try to prove (or refute) that the goal logically follows from the remaining annotations and the underlying legislation.

3.3 The Abstract Programming Interface (API)

All the reasoning features of NAI can also be accessed by third-party applications. The NAI suite exposes a RESTful (Representational state transfer) API which allows (external) applications to run consistency checks, checks for independence as well as queries and use the result for further processing. The exposure of NAI's REST API is particularly interesting for external legal applications that want to make use of the already formalized legal documents hosted by NAI. A simple example of such an application is a tax counseling web site which advises its visitors using legal reasoning over a formalization of the relevant tax law done in the NAI suite.

4   A Methodology for the Creation of Correct Formalizations

The formalization process essentially consists of translating an informal natural language text into a formal logical formula or code. As mentioned before, this step is essential for being able to apply automated reasoning techniques.

We can choose various formulae in the logic DL^*_1 which seem to describe a text at hand. Each of these formulae differs in the cases in which it holds, and in the consequences which can be derived from it.

A correct formalization means that the right formula is chosen. How can we pick up this formula? In [1], Bartolini et al. define a methodology for the validation of the formal representation of legal texts by a backward translation to a human-readable text. The text is then being validated by legal experts. Mockus and Palmirani [9] define a method for the iterative refinement of ontologies, which is inspired by a previous work by Peroni [13]. Peroni's work adapts approaches from the agile methodology in software engineering. The above approaches still depend on humans for validation. In this section we describe a new methodology which is based on Behaviour Driven Development (BDD)[3]. The "behaviours" defined by this methodology are validated by machines, similarly to those in software engineering.

4.1   Behaviour-Driven Development in Software Engineering

Behaviour-driven development (or BDD for short)[4] emerged from the process known as test-driven development (TDD). The concept behind BDD is to provide development and management teams with a shared process and shared tools, so that they can effectively collaborate while developing software. To this end, it combines the basic principles of TDD with object-oriented analysis and domain-driven design, to make the process of creating software as optimized and effective as possible.

In its core, BDD is simply the idea that software development should be governed by both technical proficiencies and business interests alike. However, besides the ideological concept, BDD does make use of specialized software in order to achieve the desired goals. The main tool of the method is a simple

---

[3] https://www.agilealliance.org/glossary/bdd/.

[4] The description is based on the definition in http://behaviour-driven.org/.

domain-specific language (DSL): Instead of complex lines of code, this language uses normal English words and logical constructs to express how the software should behave.

Using BDD in Software Engineering. BDD is a branch of the test-driven development method, which also uses domain-specific language to convert natural language phrases and statements into executable tests. We are talking about sentences that start with a conditional word (should, given, when, if, etc.) and define an outcome. For example:

- If I have two apples
- And my friend takes one
- Then I will have one apple

Basic Principles of BDD. BDD follows the basic principle that each unit of software must be individually tested. The process usually goes like this:

1. A test is designed for the specific software unit
2. The test is made to fail
3. The unit is then implemented into the test
4. The test is done again, verifying that the implementation of the unit makes it succeed

This basic outline allows the testing of both high and low-level software, as well as anything in between. When using the BDD methodology, the tests should be specified in terms of the desired behaviour of the unit in question. This behaviour is basically the requirements set by the business entity that commissioned the creation of the software.

Benefits of BDD. There are various benefits of using BDD in software engineering. In [12] they identify seven themes in which research has shown the advantages of BDD over other methods. Among the themes, three are especially relevant to legal formalization and are discussed below.

Cost. Some research suggests that BDD can help keep projects within budget. Findings are inconclusive about that. The same advantages can exist when formalizing legal texts.

Time. There is much evidence that BDD can reduces the development time. One of BDD's main goals is to keep implementation limited to passing the tests and therefore reduces implementation time. In addition, tests assure that changes to the code still conform to previous requirements. These benefits hold for legal formalization as well. There is much flexibility when formalizing legal text, from very specific and detailed formalization to a more abstract one. The level of detail depends on the intended use of the formalization. For example, if the intended queries we plan on executing over the text do not deal with specific laws regarding the age of the offender, there is no need to formalize those. Similarly, changes to formalizations are required from time to time, either because of changes in the law or the need to use a more detailed level. Tests ensure that those changes are compatible with previous requirements.

People. BDDs help bridge the gap between stack holders and programmers. The tests are normally written by stack holders and are automatically converted to code. This point is even more relevant to the legal domain. One of the main difficulties in legal formalization is the need to have both legal and technical/logical skills. The most popular approach to legal formalization depends on Prolog programming skills, for example. Using BDD in legal formalization will allow legal experts to write the tests while programmers and logicians will focus on the implementation of a formalization which satisfies them.

4.2   Towards Behaviour-Driven Development of Legal Formalization

BDD has been successfully used in software engineering and we believe that it can be adapted to legal text formalization as follows.

The lawyer writes down different scenarios which should be true (or false), given her interpretation of the legal text. The lawyer then annotates these scenarios in order to translate them into test formulae. In the last step, a person needs to annotate the legal text in a way such that all the test formulae will be validated. It should be noted that the person in the last step must not have a full legal understanding of the text and that in principle, this last step can even be executed by a machine, which tries different formalization possibilities until all test formulae are satisfied.

More formally and in alignment with the BDD process, we define the behaviour-driven development of a legal formalization as follows:

1. The legal expert writes down a set of legal cases and their intended resolution.
2. The cases naturally fail since they are not yet handled by the formalization. The failure is determined by the execution of the tests in a theorem prover.
3. Programmers or logicians then attempt to formalize the specific part of the legislation which covers those cases. If the number of possibilities is finite, this step can be automated in the future. Even if full automation is not possible, approaches like machine learning can make it more feasible.
4. The cases are executed again to verify that the formalization correctly captures the elements of the legislation which corresponds to the cases.

We need therefore to start with a comprehensive list of scenarios and their outcomes based on our legal interpretation. It should be noted that such scenarios are normally based on many articles or even on the whole text. In our example, we will derive them from one article only.

4.3   Case Study: Scottish Smoking Regulation

In this section we are going to demonstrate how the NAI suite can be used for implementing the above methodolgy on a legal text. The text we will use is the "Smoking Prohibition (Children in Motor Vehicles) (Scotland) Act 2016"[5]. This text is a good candidate for legal reasoning as it is short and relatively self contained. It has also featured in previous research [16].

This legislation contains 19 articles which go from describing the conditions of committing the offence to how a fine can be given and contested. In this example, we will focus on article 1 only. A more comprehensive formalization which includes sentences of the second part as well, is available online[6].

Article 1: Offence of smoking in a motor vehicle with children

1. It is an offence for an adult to smoke in a private motor vehicle when: (a) there is a child in the vehicle, and (b) the vehicle is in a public place.
2. Subsection (1) does not apply to a private motor vehicle that is designed or adapted for use as living accommodation and which, at the time the smoking occurs, is parked and is being used as living accommodation.
3. A person who commits an offence under subsection (1) is liable on summary conviction to a fine not exceeding level 3 on the standard scale.

In order to apply automated reasoning to this text, we first need to formalize our understanding of its meaning. In other words, we need to formalize a legal interpretation of the text.

There are various interpretations possible even for this, relatively simple, text. For the purpose of this example, we interpret the article as prohibiting adults to smoke in a private motor vehicle in case: (1) there is a child in the vehicle, (2) the vehicle is in public space and (3) the vehicle is not adapted or designed to be used, and at the same time is being used, as living accommodation.

Violating this prohibition, the adult is liable to a fine via a summary conviction.

Here we describe just a few of these scenarios. The reader is referred to the live example in the application for more cases.

The first step in the methodology is to create the vocabulary used in the formalization. As mentioned in Sect. 3.2, this is being done by using the *term* annotation on the text. The annotated terms can then be seen on the "Vocabulary" tab of the NAI suite. Figure 2 summarizes those for Article 1.

The test queries can now be created based on this vocabulary. The task of the lawyer is to consider different terms from the vocabulary and decide what is the expected outcome of them.

Scenario 1. An adult was smoking in a car which has a child in it and is not in public space. We expect the adult not to be liable to a fine.

Scenario 2. An adult was smoking in a car which has a child in it, is in public space and was not designed as living accommodation. We expect the adult to be liable to a fine.

---

[5] https://www.legislation.gov.uk/asp/2016/3/contents.
[6] Please visit https://nai.uni.lu and log in with the credentials: smoking@nai.lu / nai.

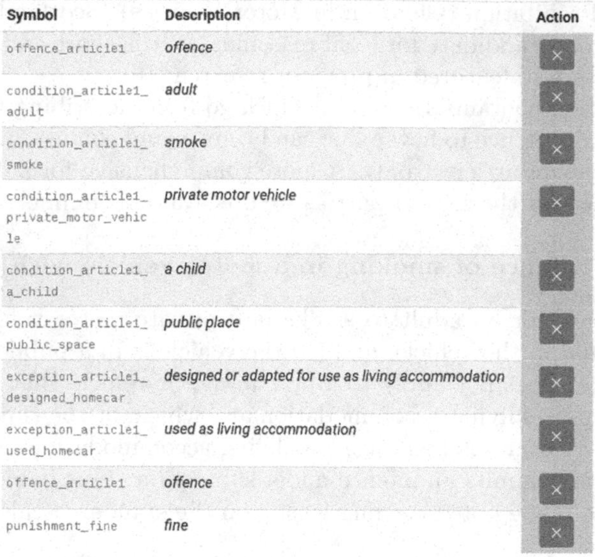

Symbol	Description	Action
offence_article1	*offence*	×
condition_article1_adult	*adult*	×
condition_article1_smoke	*smoke*	×
condition_article1_private_motor_vehicle	*private motor vehicle*	×
condition_article1_a_child	*a child*	×
condition_article1_public_space	*public place*	×
exception_article1_designed_homecar	*designed or adapted for use as living accommodation*	×
exception_article1_used_homecar	*used as living accommodation*	×
offence_article1	*offence*	×
punishment_fine	*fine*	×

Fig. 2. Vocabulary Smoking legislation article 1

The lawyer now uses the queries tab in the NAI suite in order to enter these two scenarios. In order to differentiate the test queries from case queries (queries written in order to solve a specific case), the test queries names are prefixed with "Test".

We can now annotate the two scenarios. We proceed first by annotating the conditions with the terms from the vocabulary. The user needs to select those from a drop down list. The expectation is then annotated as a goal. Within the goal, we annotate our expectation that the person is liable to a fine by using the *Permission* connective over the *punishment_fine* term. The two annotated scenarios, as well as their formalization, can be seen in Figs. 3a and b. When executing these queries, they naturally may fail. When annotating the legal text in the next phase, we must make sure that all the queries are now being validated.

We can now proceed with the last step - the annotation of Article 1. After some trial and error, we have ended up with the annotation in Fig. 4a. This annotation passes all of our test queries and we therefore conclude that it is a faithful formalization of our interpretation of Article 1. The $\mathbf{DL^*}_1$ formulae are shown in Fig. 4b.

It should be mentioned that on each step, we are advised to check the consistency of our annotations as well as those of the queries. The reasoning engine can find automatically inconsistencies in our annotations, which can lead to wrong results. In addition, it is recommended to check, on the "Formalization" tab, that each $\mathbf{DL^*}_1$ formula is independent. Dependent formulae are normally a sign of an incorrect formalization.

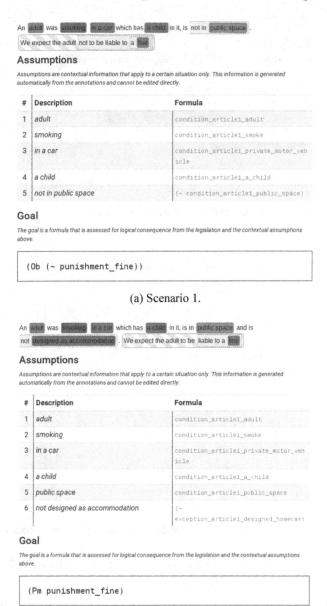

(a) Scenario 1.

(b) Scenario 2.

Fig. 3. Annotations and corresponding $\mathbf{DL^*_1}$ formulae of the different scenarios as presented by the NAI tool.

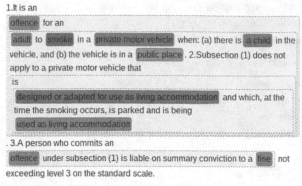

1.It is an

offence for an

adult to smoke in a private motor vehicle when: (a) there is a child in the vehicle, and (b) the vehicle is in a public place . 2.Subsection (1) does not apply to a private motor vehicle that

is

designed or adapted for use as living accommodation and which, at the time the smoking occurs, is parked and is being

used as living accommodation

. 3.A person who commits an

offence under subsection (1) is liable on summary conviction to a fine not exceeding level 3 on the standard scale.

(a) Annotations as entered into the editor.

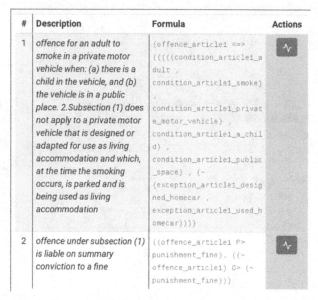

#	Description	Formula	Actions
1	*offence for an adult to smoke in a private motor vehicle when: (a) there is a child in the vehicle, and (b) the vehicle is in a public place. 2.Subsection (1) does not apply to a private motor vehicle that is designed or adapted for use as living accommodation and which, at the time the smoking occurs, is parked and is being used as living accommodation*	`(offence_article1 <=> (((((condition_article1_a dult , condition_article1_smoke) , condition_article1_privat e_motor_vehicle) , condition_article1_a_chil d) , condition_article1_public _space) , (~ (exception_article1_desig ned_homecar , exception_article1_used_h omecar))))`	
2	*offence under subsection (1) is liable on summary conviction to a fine*	`((offence_article1 P> punishment_fine), ((~ offence_article1) O> (~ punishment_fine)))`	

(b) Automatically created **DL**$*_1$ formulae corresponding to the annotations.

Fig. 4. Formalization of article 1 of the smoking legislation in NAI.

Case Queries. Given enough tests, we can increase our confidence that the formalization is faithful to our interpretation. we can now better trust it to resolve legal questions with regard to specific cases. Writing case queries is identical to the writing of test queries. As an example, consider the following case.

Case 1. A client got a fine while driving his home car while smoking. His teen daughter was sitting next to him. Is there a case to appeal this decision?

Here we want to check if there was an obligation in the law not to give our client the fine. In case it is true, an appeal should be successful. When we annotate the case above, we get that a conclusion cannot be drawn (the query is counter-satisfiable). The reason for that is because some of the conditions are not used. Since there might be two different values to these conditions which result in two different conclusions, the reasoner cannot determine if the query holds. In this case, we can find in the "Vocabulary" tab one further condition - the car should be in public space - and one further exception - the car should also be used as a home car, and not only be designed as one. We therefore ask the client to share more information about the case.

Case 2. The client adds further that he was indeed driving in public space. The home car though, was not used as a home car at the time. The client has removed the home facilities and is using the car for transportation of goods.

The addition of the new annotations gives us the answer that the policeman was indeed permitted to give the fine. The client could enjoy the exception of subsection (b), but he failed to use the car for accommodation. It seems better not to appeal the fine.

5   Conclusion and Future Work

In this paper we have described a new methodology for validating legal knowledge bases that is inspired by the behaviour-driven development approach from the field of software engineering. As a first step towards implementing this methodology, the NAI suite for normative reasoning is introduced and its application is demonstrated on an exemplary regulation.

The presented case study suggests that the NAI tool can be used by people without a strong IT background, as only few technical details are exposed to the user and most of the task is supported by a graphical user interface. In fact, one could argue that our approach also enables a broad range of users to contribute to the built-up of a reliable legal knowledge base; once the intended behaviour of the formalized norms are agreed upon (by legal experts), it is easy to automatically check compliance of the generated knowledge with the afore stated goal.

The tools presented in this paper are prototypes. Further work is required on both the tools and their supporting theories in order to make the formalization of legal texts easier and more intuitive. Among those improvements, the most notable ones relate to the supporting theory and to the usability of the user interface. We mention several such improvements here.

Currently, the NAI suite supports an expressive deontic first-order language. This language is rich enough to describe many scenarios which appear in legal texts. Nevertheless, more work is required in order to capture all such scenarios. Among those features with the highest priority, we list support for exceptions, temporal sentences and arithmetic. In this paper, we overcame the fact that subsection 1(b) is an exception to subsection 1(a) by explicitly mentioning the values of the conditions of the exception. This solution is not optimal since it requires the setting of values to these properties in all tests and cases. Possible support for these features already exists in the form of tools such as non-monotonic reasoners [6], temporal provers [15] and SMT solvers [4].

On the level of usability, the tool currently does not give any information as to why a query is counter-satisfiable. The user needs to look on the vocabulary in order to determine possible reasons. Integrating a model finder, such as Nitpick [2], will help "debugging" formalizations. Also, scalability of the proposed approach as to be investigated in larger case studies.

NAI's graphical user interface (GUI) aims at being intuitive and easy to use and tries to hide the underline complexities of the logics involved. A continuously updated list of new features can be found on the GUI's development website[7].

References

1. Bartolini, C., Lenzini, G., Santos, C.: An interdisciplinary methodology to validate formal representations of legal text applied to the GDPR. In: JURISIN (2018)
2. Blanchette, J.C., Nipkow, T.: Nitpick: a counterexample generator for higher-order logic based on a relational model finder. In: Kaufmann, M., Paulson, L.C. (eds.) ITP 2010. LNCS, vol. 6172, pp. 131–146. Springer, Heidelberg (2010). https://doi.org/10.1007/978-3-642-14052-5_11
3. Boella, G., Di Caro, L., Humphreys, L., Robaldo, L., Rossi, P., van der Torre, L.: Eunomos, a legal document and knowledge management system for the web to provide relevant, reliable and up-to-date information on the law. Artif. Intell. Law **24**(3), 245–283 (2016). https://doi.org/10.1007/s10506-016-9184-3
4. Bouton, T., de Oliveira, D.C.B., Déharbe, D., Fontaine, P.: veriT: an open, trustable and efficient SMT-solver. In: Schmidt, R.A. (ed.) CADE 2009. LNCS (LNAI), vol. 5663, pp. 151–156. Springer, Heidelberg (2009). https://doi.org/10.1007/978-3-642-02959-2_12
5. Governatori, G., Shek, S.: Regorous: a business process compliance checker. In: Proceedings of the 14th International Conference on Artificial Intelligence and Law, pp. 245–246. ACM (2013)
6. Kifer, M.: Nonmonotonic reasoning in FLORA-2. In: Baral, C., Greco, G., Leone, N., Terracina, G. (eds.) LPNMR 2005. LNCS (LNAI), vol. 3662, pp. 1–12. Springer, Heidelberg (2005). https://doi.org/10.1007/11546207_1
7. Libal, T., Pascucci, M.: Automated reasoning in normative detachment structures with ideal conditions. In: Proceedings of ICAIL, pp. 63–72 (2019). https://doi.org/10.1145/3322640.3326707
8. Libal, T., Steen, A.: NAI: the normative reasoner. In: Proceedings of ICAIL, pp. 262–263. ACM (2019)
9. Mockus, M., Palmirani, M.: Legal ontology for open government data mashups. In: 2017 Conference for E-Democracy and Open Government (CeDEM), pp. 113–124. IEEE (2017)
10. Otten, J.: Implementing connection calculi for first-order modal logics. In: IWIL@ LPAR, pp. 18–32 (2012)
11. Otten, J.: MleanCoP: a connection prover for first-order modal logic. In: 7th International Joint Conference, IJCAR, pp. 269–276 (2014). https://doi.org/10.1007/978-3-319-08587-6_20
12. Park, S., Maurer, F.: A literature review on story test driven development. In: Sillitti, A., Martin, A., Wang, X., Whitworth, E. (eds.) XP 2010. LNBIP, vol. 48, pp. 208–213. Springer, Heidelberg (2010). https://doi.org/10.1007/978-3-642-13054-0_20

---

[7] https://github.com/normativeai/frontend/issues.

13. Peroni, S.: A simplified agile methodology for ontology development. In: Dragoni, M., Poveda-Villalón, M., Jimenez-Ruiz, E. (eds.) OWLED/ORE 2016. LNCS, vol. 10161, pp. 55–69. Springer, Cham (2017). https://doi.org/10.1007/978-3-319-54627-8_5
14. Robaldo, L., Bartolini, C., Palmirani, M., Rossi, A., Martoni, M., Lenzini, G.: Formalizing GDPR provisions in reified I/O logic: the DAPRECO knowledge base. J. Logic Lang. Inf., 1–49 (2019). https://doi.org/10.1007/s10849-019-09309-z
15. Suda, M., Weidenbach, C.: A PLTL-prover based on labelled superposition with partial model guidance. In: Gramlich, B., Miller, D., Sattler, U. (eds.) IJCAR 2012. LNCS (LNAI), vol. 7364, pp. 537–543. Springer, Heidelberg (2012). https://doi.org/10.1007/978-3-642-31365-3_42
16. Wyner, A.Z., Gough, F., Lévy, F., Lynch, M., Nazarenko, A.: On annotation of the textual contents of Scottish legal instruments. In: JURIX, pp. 101–106 (2017)

Goal-Driven Structured Argumentation for Patient Management in a Multimorbidity Setting

Tiago Oliveira[1], Jérémie Dauphin[2(✉)], Ken Satoh[3], Shusaku Tsumoto[4], and Paulo Novais[5]

[1] MESM, Tokyo Medical and Dental University, Tokyo, Japan
tiago.oliveira.mesm@mri.tmd.ac.jp
[2] CSC, University of Luxembourg, Esch-sur-Alzette, Luxembourg
jeremie.dauphin@uni.lu
[3] National Institute of Informatics, Tokyo, Japan
ksatoh@nii.co.jp
[4] Shimane University, Izumo, Japan
tsumoto@med.shimane-u.ac.jp
[5] Algoritmi Centre, University of Minho, Braga, Portugal
pjon@di.uminho.pt

Abstract. We use computational argumentation to both analyse and generate solutions for reasoning in multimorbidity about consistent recommendations, according to different patient-centric goals. Reasoning in this setting carries a complexity related to the multiple variables involved. These variables reflect the co-existing health conditions that should be considered when defining a proper therapy. However, current Clinical Decision Support Systems (CDSSs) are not equipped to deal with such a situation. They do not go beyond the straightforward application of the rules that build their knowledge base and simple interpretation of Computer-Interpretable Guidelines (CIGs). We provide a computational argumentation system equipped with goal-seeking mechanisms to combine independently generated recommendations, with the ability to resolve conflicts and generate explanations for its results. We also discuss its advantages over and relation to Multiple-criteria Decision-making (MCDM) in this particular setting.

1 Introduction

Multimorbidity is the presence of two or more chronic medical conditions in an individual. It is a complex situation, particularly when the number of existing conditions is high and there are treatment conflicts [26]. These conflicts are typically: *drug-drug interactions*, when treatments have a negative combined effect on the patient; and *drug-disease interactions*, when a treatment for a condition negatively affects the evolution of another condition. Clinical Decision Support Systems (CDSSs) based on Computer-Intepretable Guidelines (CIGs) are not

© Springer Nature Switzerland AG 2020
M. Dastani et al. (Eds.): CLAR 2020, LNAI 12061, pp. 166–183, 2020.
https://doi.org/10.1007/978-3-030-44638-3_11

capable of combining different CIG executions to address multiple health conditions, as CIGs are designed to handle a single disease [10,21]. Furthermore, computational approaches that aim to tackle this problem [27,28] are limited in the dimensions of multimorbidity they consider, namely when it comes to: patient preferences, patient-specific prioritized goals, and decidable mechanisms for conflict resolution. These dimensions are considered to be fundamental in reasoning for patient management and, in what preferences and goals are concerned, should result from a discussion between patient and health care professional [16,25]. In recent years, several works call for the use of Multiple Criteria Decision-making (MCDM) methods to address conflicts in medical decision-making, produce decisions based on priorities over various criteria, and handle complexity in this setting [3,13]. However, a general MCDM method lacks the ability to explain and justify decisions and lay out their respective implications. These elements become opaque when scores are computed and presented.

We explore structured argumentation to formalize conflict resolution in multimorbidity and compute aggregated consistent sets of CIG recommendations that take into account the above-mentioned dimensions. The appeal of argumentation in comparison to other computational approaches is in reasoning with conflicting and incomplete information in a way that aims to emulate human reasoning, while allowing important conflicts to be highlighted and analyzed [2]. We augment the ASPIC+ [14] argumentation system for it provides sub-argument structure, important for explanations, and has been extensively studied and justified in regards to semantics for preferences over defeasible rules and mechanisms to perform defeasible reasoning. It also allows for contraposition, a useful feature when analyzing conflicts. We propose the ASPIC+G argumentation system for multimorbidity as a goal-driven argumentation system to select best solutions and map basic elements in multimorbidity reasoning to it. Following from this, we also provide a reasoning framework that takes into account drug-drug and drug-disease conflicts, patient preferences, and prioritized patient-specific goals. We demonstrate that the selected best solution can be used to derive in-depth explanations and provide mechanisms to produce justifications for conclusions. Finally, we show that the proposed argumentation system subsumes MCDM, with the added benefit of providing explanations for multimorbidity decisions.

2   Case Example

The case example to demonstrate the computational argumentation framework was adapted from a clinical case in [23], simplified for the sake of brevity and understanding. There are slight differences such as the addition of chronic kidney disease to showcase reasoning features.

Example 1. Patient A has a history of type 2 diabetes. Upon consultation and the completion of medical exams, it was possible to conclude that the patient, besides type 2 diabetes, has obesity, hypertension, and chronic kidney disease. The case is run in a CDSS with CIG agents that handle each health condition separately, yielding recommendations:

- **CIG Agent 1 (for obesity):** Define weight decrease (wd) as a therapy goal. To reduce weight, the patient should practice diet and exercise (de) [19].
- **CIG Agent 2 (for diabetes):** Define blood glucose decrease (gd) as a therapy goal. Sulfonylurea ($sulf$) or meglitinide (meg) can reduce blood glucose elevations, but they cause weight increase (wi). Metformin (met) can lower blood glucose, but its use in the presence of chronic kidney disease (ckd) should be avoided as it may accelerate chronic kidney disease ($ackd$). The patient should only take one of the drugs [20].
- **CIG Agent 3 (for kidney disease):** Define delay chronic kidney disease ($dckd$) as a therapy goal. The patient is advised to take angiotensin converting enzyme inhibitors ($acei$) as they delay the progression of chronic kidney disease to kidney failure [17].
- **CIG Agent 4 (for hypertension):** Define blood pressure decrease (bpd) as a therapy goal. Administer an angiotensin converting enzyme inhibitor ($acei$) or a calcium channel blocker (ccb) to decrease blood pressure. However, a calcium channel blocker compromises the effectiveness of glucose control drugs such as meglitinide or metformin [18].

Following the four CIG agents separately would produce *drug-disease interactions*. When considering CIG Agent 1 and CIG Agent 2, there is a conflict with the use of sulfonylurea and meglitinide from CIG Agent 2, as these drugs cause weight increase and this effect is contrary to the therapy goal outlined for obesity in CIG Agent 1, weight decrease. When adding the recommendations of CIG Agent 3 to the first two, other conflicts appear. The use of metformin for the treatment of diabetes is compromised by the recommendation to avoid the use of metformin in the presence of chronic kidney disease. Additionally, from CIG Agent 4, the recommendation to take a calcium channel blocker compromises the effectiveness of metformin and meglitinide. This is a *drug-drug interaction*. The mutually exclusive use of drugs for diabetes also constitutes drug-drug interactions.

In practice, the case is handled by establishing a priority over patient-specific goals and eliciting patient preferences [16]. Reproducing the source of the example [23], the health care professional acknowledges obesity is the most severe issue for the patient, thus weight decrease is the most preferred goal, followed by blood glucose decrease as the second goal, with blood pressure decrease at the same level. Delaying kidney disease is the least preferred goal. Additionally, the patient shows a clear preference for sulfonylurea or meglitinide, as the use of metformin has caused him severe adverse reactions in the past.

The knowledge enclosed in CIGs typically follows a task network model where each element is a task to carry out. A task recommending a treatment is normally called an *Action* and contains certain structured information about the treatments to be applied, respective outcomes and pre-conditions for application reflecting interactions [21]. This is the task we focus on and the basis for CIG Agent recommendations. Further ahead we use Example 1 to instantiate ASPIC+G. The process of preference elicitation and goal prioritization, including the functions that bring them about (e.g. severity of disease), are outside the scope of this work, so they will only be referred to as examples.

3   The ASPIC+G Argumentation System

The intuition behind ASPIC+G is that argumentation is often driven by goals which reflect the multiple objectives that may be achieved in a discussion. This fits reasoning in a multimorbidity setting particularly well due to the goal-oriented nature of the process.

3.1   Definition and Argument Construction

We define an ASPIC+G argumentation theory as follows.

Definition 1. *An argumentation theory in ASPIC+G is a tuple $\langle \mathcal{L}, \mathcal{R}, \mathrm{n}, \leqslant_{\mathcal{R}_d},$ $\mathcal{G}, \leqslant_{\mathcal{G}} \rangle$, where:*

- $\mathcal{L}$ *is a logical language closed under negation ($\neg$).*
- $\mathcal{R} = \mathcal{R}_s \cup \mathcal{R}_d$ *is a set of strict ($\mathcal{R}_s$) and defeasible ($\mathcal{R}_d$) rules of the form* $\phi_1, \ldots, \phi_n \to \phi$ *and* $\phi_1, \ldots, \phi_n \Rightarrow \phi$ *respectively, where* $n \geq 0$ *and* $\phi_i, \phi \in \mathcal{L}$;
- n *is a partial function s.t.* [1] $\mathrm{n} : \mathcal{R} \to \mathcal{L}$;
- $\leqslant_{\mathcal{R}_d}$ *is a partial pre-order over defeasible rules $\mathcal{R}_d$, denoting a preference relation, with a strict counterpart $<_{\mathcal{R}_d}$ given by $X <_{\mathcal{R}_d} Y$ iff $X \leqslant_{\mathcal{R}_d} Y$ and $Y \not\leqslant_{\mathcal{R}_d} X$;*
- $\mathcal{G} \subseteq \mathcal{L}$ *is a set of goals that the arguments will try to fulfil s.t. $\forall \, \theta \in \mathcal{G}$, there exists a rule $\phi_1, \ldots, \phi_n \to \phi$ in $\mathcal{R}_s$ or $\phi_1, \ldots, \phi_n \Rightarrow \phi$ in $\mathcal{R}_d$ s.t. $\phi = \theta$;*
- $\leqslant_{\mathcal{G}}$ *is a total pre-order on $\mathcal{G}$, denoting preferences over goals, with $<_{\mathcal{G}}$ given by $\phi <_{\mathcal{G}} \psi$ iff $\phi \leqslant_{\mathcal{G}} \psi$ and $\psi \not\leqslant_{\mathcal{G}} \phi$, and $\simeq_{\mathcal{G}}$ given by $\phi \simeq_{\mathcal{G}} \psi$ iff $\phi \leqslant_{\mathcal{G}} \psi$ and $\psi \leqslant_{\mathcal{G}} \phi$.*

In ASPIC+G, knowledge is represented either as strict rules or defeasible rules. Therefore, an undisputable fact is a strict rule with empty antecedents and a disputable fact is represented as a defeasible rule with empty antecedents. The relation $\leqslant_{\mathcal{G}}$ is a total pre-order which allows for equally preferred goals, as it is often the case that distinctions between goals cannot be specified. In order to understand the construction of arguments, we specify functions to convey argument features. Conc(A) denotes the conclusion of argument A. Sub(A) denotes the set of sub-arguments of A. DefRules(A) denotes the set of all defeasible rules used in A. Finally, TopRule(A) denotes the last inference rule used in the argument. We use the following definition for argument construction, adapted from [14].

Definition 2. *An argument A of an argumentation theory $\langle \mathcal{L}, \mathcal{R}, \mathrm{n}, \leqslant_{\mathcal{R}_d}, \mathcal{G}, \leqslant_{\mathcal{G}} \rangle$ has one of the following forms:*

---

[1] s.t.: such that.

- $A_1, \ldots, A_n \ \rightarrow \ \psi$ *if* $A_1, \ldots, A_n$ *are arguments s.t. there exists a strict rule* $\text{Conc}(A_1), \ldots, \text{Conc}(A_n) \rightarrow \psi$ *in* $\mathcal{R}_s$, *with* $\text{Conc}(A) = \psi$, $\text{Sub}(A) = \text{Sub}(A_1) \cup \ldots \cup \text{Sub}(A_n) \cup \{A\}$, $\text{DefRules}(A) = \text{DefRules}(A_1) \cup \ldots \cup \text{DefRules}(A_n)$, *and* $\text{TopRule}(A) = \text{Conc}(A_1), \ldots, \text{Conc}(A_n) \rightarrow \psi$;
- $A_1, \ldots, A_n \ \Rightarrow \ \psi$ *if* $A_1, \ldots, A_n$ *are arguments s.t. there exists a defeasible rule* $\text{Conc}(A_1), \ldots, \text{Conc}(A_n) \ \Rightarrow \ \psi$ *in* $\mathcal{R}_d$, *with* $\text{Conc}(A) = \psi$, $\text{Sub}(A) = \text{Sub}(A_1) \cup \ldots \cup \text{Sub}(A_n) \cup \{A\}$, $\text{DefRules}(A) = \text{DefRules}(A_1) \cup \ldots \cup \text{DefRules}(A_n) \cup \{\text{Conc}(A_1), \ldots, \text{Conc}(A_n) \Rightarrow \psi\}$, *and* $\text{TopRule}(A) = \text{Conc}(A_1), \ldots, \text{Conc}(A_n) \Rightarrow \psi$.

3.2   Attack, Defeat, and Goal Fulfilment

Attacks follow two of the three possible ways in ASPIC+ [14]. Arguments may be attacked on a conclusion of a defeasible inference (rebutting) or on a defeasible inference step itself (undercutting). Undermining attacks are represented as a special case of rebuttal. It is considered that an argument cannot be attacked on the conclusion of a strict inference. To define an undercutting attack, n is used to assign elements of $\mathcal{R}_d$ a well-formed formula in $\mathcal{L}$. $n(r) : r \in \mathcal{R}_d$ denotes that r is applicable and $\neg n(r)$ denotes that r is not applicable. An argument using r is undercut by any argument concluding $\neg n(r)$. The following definition of attack was adapted from [14].

Definition 3. *An argument* A *attacks an argument* B *iff* A *undercuts or rebuts* B, *where:* A *undercuts* B *(on* B′*) iff* $\text{Conc}(A) = \neg n(r)$ *for some* B′ $\in \text{Sub}(B)$ *s.t. the top rule* r *of* B′ *is defeasible;* A *rebuts* B *(on* B′*) iff* $\text{Conc}(A) = \neg \phi$ *for some* B′ $\in \text{Sub}(B)$ *of the form* $B''_1, \ldots, B''_n \Rightarrow \phi$.

The introduction of goals in argumentation demands the definition of a fulfilment relation.

Definition 4. *An argument* A *fulfils goal* $\theta \in \mathcal{G}$ *iff* $\text{Conc}(A) = \theta$. *If* A *fulfils a goal, we denote it with* $\text{Goal}(A)$. *For a set of arguments* S, *we write* $\text{Goal}(S)$ *for the set of goals fulfilled by the arguments in* S, *i.e.* $\text{Goal}(S) = \{\text{Goal}(A) \mid A \in S$ *s.t.* A *fulfils a goal* $\}$.

We use a preference order over arguments $\preceq$ determined by a weakest-link principle on $\leqslant_{\mathcal{R}_d}$, as described in [14]. To specify $\preceq$, we resort to an ordering of defeasible rule sets $\trianglelefteq_{\mathcal{R}_d}$, defined over an elitist criterion, i.e., the set with the overall weakest rule is the weakest. Therefore, given two sets of defeasible rules R and R': if $R = \emptyset$ then $R \ntrianglelefteq_{\mathcal{R}_d} R'$; if $R = \emptyset$ and $R' \neq \emptyset$ then $R' \trianglelefteq_{\mathcal{R}_d} R$; else, assuming a pre-order $\leqslant_{\mathcal{R}_d}$ over the elements in $R \cup R'$, if $\exists X \in R$ s.t. $\forall Y \in R'$, $X \leqslant_{\mathcal{R}_d} Y$, then $R \trianglelefteq_{\mathcal{R}_d} R'$.

Considering two arguments A and B, we say that $A \preceq B$ iff $\text{DefRules}(A) \trianglelefteq_{\mathcal{R}_d}$ $\text{DefRules}(B)$. We can define the strict counterpart $\prec$ directly under the weakest-link principle, in terms of $\trianglelefteq_{\mathcal{R}_d}$.

Attack and argument preference bring about a *defeat relation* $\mathcal{D}$. It is considered that: an argument A *successfully* rebuts an argument B if A rebuts B on B′

and A $\not\prec$ B'; an argument A *defeats* an argument B iff A undercuts or successfully rebuts B.

We now define an ASPIC+G framework as follows.

Definition 5. *An argumentation framework in ASPIC+G is a tuple* $(\mathcal{A}, \mathcal{D}, \mathcal{G}, \leqslant_\mathcal{G}, \mathcal{F})$, *where* $\mathcal{A}$ *is a set of arguments,* $\mathcal{D} \subseteq \mathcal{A} \times \mathcal{A}$ *is a binary relation of defeat,* $\mathcal{G}$ *is the set of goals,* $\leqslant_\mathcal{G}$ *is a preference order over goals, and* $\mathcal{F}$ *is a binary relation of fulfilment s.t.* $\mathcal{F} \subseteq \mathcal{A} \times \mathcal{G}$.

To select arguments, the framework uses the semantics presented in Dung's abstract argumentation framework [7], according to the following definition.

Definition 6. *Let* $(\mathcal{A}, \mathcal{D}, \mathcal{G}, \leqslant_\mathcal{G}, \mathcal{F})$ *be an ASPIC+G argumentation framework. For any* X $\in \mathcal{A}$, X *is acceptable with respect to some set* $S \subseteq \mathcal{A}$ *iff* $\forall$Y $\in$ A *s. t.* (Y, X) $\in \mathcal{D}$, $\exists$Z $\in S$ *s.t.* (Z, Y) $\in \mathcal{D}$. *Let* $S \subseteq \mathcal{A}$ *be a conflict free set, i.e., there are no* A, B *in* S *s.t.* (A, B) $\in \mathcal{D}$. *Then:* S *is an admissible extension iff* X $\in S$ *implies* X *is acceptable with respect to* S; *and* S *is a preferred extension iff it is a set inclusion maximal admissible extension.*

It is of interest within the context of multimorbidity to produce the *preferred*, and thus maximal sets of arguments, which are the most inclusive self-defended sets, containing all the sub-arguments that lead to a conclusion and the arguments that defend it.

3.3   Goal Set Ordering

The preferred extensions are viewed as consistent argumentation paths in the discussion and the possible solutions to solve a problem. However, it is necessary to compare the sets of goals that they fulfil in order to rank them. We now define a goal set ordering $\trianglelefteq_\mathcal{G}$ over sets of goals.

Definition 7. *Let* S *and* S' *be two finite sets of goals. We define the* goal set ordering, *denoted by the operator* $\trianglelefteq_\mathcal{G}$, *as:* $S' \trianglelefteq_\mathcal{G} S$ *iff* $S' = \emptyset$ *or* $\exists g \in (S \setminus S')$ *such that* $\forall g' \in (S' \setminus S)$, $g' \leqslant_\mathcal{G} g$.

A goal set ordering $S' \trianglelefteq_\mathcal{G} S$ denotes that S is at least as preferred as S', possibly more. The underlying principle is that the argumentation will always try to fulfil the goals by their order of importance. Due to the base relation $\leqslant_\mathcal{G}$ being a total pre-order, $\trianglelefteq_\mathcal{G}$ is also a total pre-order. We also allow for different goal extensions to be equally preferred by fulfilling goals of equal preference.

With the goal set ordering, it becomes possible to find the best goal-driven solutions, i.e., the *top preferred extensions*.

Definition 8. *Let* $F = (\mathcal{A}, \mathcal{D}, \mathcal{G}, \leqslant_\mathcal{G}, \mathcal{F})$ *be an ASPIC+G argumentation framework and* S *a preferred extension of* F. *We say that* S *is a* top preferred extension *of* F *iff for every preferred extension* S' *of* F, Goal(S') $\trianglelefteq_\mathcal{G}$ Goal(S).

ASPIC+G will be used to model Example 1 and demonstrate the outcomes of reasoning in multimorbidity using patient preferences and patient-specific goals.

4 Modelling Multimorbidity with ASPIC+G

We perform a mapping of basic components in CIG multimorbidity management to ASPIC+G and demonstrate its reasoning features. We also demonstrate how the given solutions can produce explanations.

4.1 Formalization and Reasoning

Let us consider $\mathbb{A}$ as a set containing all aggregated *Action* tasks recommended by all CIG agents, such as the ones in Example 1. We denote an action $A_{x,a} \in \mathbb{A}$, where x is the index and a the CIG agent recommending the action. For instance, $A_{1,2}$ is the first action recommended by CIG Agent 2. An action $A_{x,a}$ is a tuple $\langle t_{x,a}, O_{x,a}, P_{x,a} \rangle$, where:

- $t_{x,a}$ is a treatment;
- $O_{x,a} = \{(e_1, C_1, \lambda_1), \ldots, (e_n, C_n, \lambda_n) : n > 0\}$ stands for *outcomes* and is a set containing effects $(e_i, C_i, \lambda_i), i \in \{1, \ldots, n\}$ brought about by treatment $t_{x,a}$, where: e_i is a description of an effect; $C_i = \{c_1, \ldots, c_m : m \geq 0\}$ is a set with patient-specific conditions unifiable with the patient state $c_j, j \in \{1, \ldots, m\}$ that enable the occurrence of effect e_i over treatment $t_{x,a}$; λ_i is the impact of an effect e_i, if e_i is a positive effect, then $\lambda_i = \oplus$, otherwise, if it is a negative effect, $\lambda_i = \ominus$.
- $P_{x,a} = \{p_1, \ldots, p_n : n \geq 0\}$ denotes pre-conditions and contains constraints for the application of a treatment $t_{x,a}$.

From Example 1, we have the following actions in $\mathbb{A}$:

$A_{1,1} \langle de, \{(wd, \emptyset, \oplus)\}, \emptyset \rangle$;
$A_{1,2} \langle sulf, \{(gd, \emptyset, \oplus), (wi, \emptyset, \ominus)\}, \{\neg meg, \neg met\} \rangle$;
$A_{2,2} \langle meg, \{(gd, \emptyset, \oplus), (wi, \emptyset, \ominus)\}, \{\neg sulf, \neg met\} \rangle$;
$A_{3,2} \langle met, \{(gd, \emptyset, \oplus), (ackd, \{ckd\}, \ominus)\}, \{\neg sulf, \neg meg\} \rangle$;
$A_{1,3} \langle acei, \{(dckd, \emptyset, \oplus)\}, \emptyset \rangle$;
$A_{1,4} \langle acei, \{(bpd, \emptyset, \oplus), (\neg(meg \rightarrow gd), \emptyset, \ominus)\}, \{\neg ccb\} \rangle$;
$A_{2,4} \langle ccb, \{(bpd, \emptyset, \oplus), (\neg(meg \rightarrow gd), \emptyset, \ominus)\}, \{\neg acei\} \rangle$.

While there are CIG languages, such as PROForma [6], that encode the impact λ of an effect, this is not always the case. As such, we assume that this evaluation of effects is provided by either the CIG language or a joint assessment by health care professional and patient.

The next component of multimorbidity management is a set containing the contraries of effects $\mathbb{E} = \{C_1, \ldots, C_n : n \geq 0\}$ where each $C_i, i \in \{1, \ldots, n\}$, is a tuple (e_j, e_k) s.t. $\exists A_{x,a} = \langle t_{x,a}, O_{x,a}, P_{x,a} \rangle, A_{y,b} = \langle t_{y,b}, O_{y,b}, P_{y,b} \rangle \in \mathbb{A}$, s.t. $(e_j, C_j, \lambda_j) \in O_{x,a}$ and $(e_k, C_k, \lambda_k) \in O_{y,b}$. Example 1 provides effect contraries: $\mathbb{E} = \{(wd, wi), (dckd, ackd)\}$. The automatic retrieval of contraries from a CIG language may be performed by analysing the clinical effects with medical terminologies and identifying the medical concept (e.g., *weight*) and term denoting a transition (e.g, *increase, decrease*), with a posterior matching with its opposite. Given the freedom associated with the expression of these effects, contrary identification is not addressed herein.

The last component for reasoning in multimorbidity is the state of the patient $\mathbb{S} = \{s_1, \ldots, s_n : n \geq 0\}$, where each element is a condition manifested by the patient. In Example 1, we consider that $\mathbb{S} = \{ckd\}$, as this is the only element that interacts with the elements of other components.

With $\mathbb{A}$, $\mathbb{E}$ and $\mathbb{S}$ becomes possible to express applicability of treatments, treatment/effect relations, treatment conflicts, and effect conflicts in a logical language for ASPIC+G. The purpose is to aggregate the knowledge elements provided by CIG agents through argumentation and augment them with patient preferences over treatments and treatment goals.

Definition 9. *Let $\mathbb{A}$, $\mathbb{E}$ and $\mathbb{S}$, be the basic components for decision-making in multimorbidity. An argumentation theory in ASPIC+G for multimorbidity is a tuple $\langle \mathcal{L}, \mathcal{R}, \mathrm{n}, \leqslant_{\mathcal{R}_d}, \mathcal{G}, \leqslant_{\mathcal{G}} \rangle$, where* [2]:

- $\mathcal{R} = \mathcal{R}_d \cup \mathcal{R}_s$ are respectively defeasible and strict rules in which:
  - $\mathcal{R}_d = \mathcal{R}_1 \cup \mathcal{R}_2$ where $\mathcal{R}_1 = \{ \Rightarrow t_{x,a} \mid \exists A_{x,a} = \langle t_{x,a}, O_{x,a}, P_{x,a} \rangle \in$ $\mathbb{A}.\}$ and $\mathcal{R}_2 = \{ t_{x,a}, c_1, \ldots, c_n \Rightarrow e_z \mid \exists A_{x,a} = \langle t_{x,a}, O_{x,a}, P_{x,a} \rangle \in$ $\mathbb{A}, (e_z, \{c_1, \ldots, c_n\}, \oplus) \in O_{x,a}, n \geq 0\};$
  - $\mathcal{R}_s = \mathcal{R}_3 \cup \mathcal{R}_4 \cup \mathcal{R}_5 \cup \mathcal{R}_6$ where $\mathcal{R}_3 = \{ t_{x,a}, c_1, \ldots, c_n \to e_z \mid \exists A_{x,a} = \langle t_{x,a}, O_{x,a}, P_{x,a} \rangle \in \mathbb{A}, (e_z, \{c_1, \ldots, c_n\}, \ominus) \in O_{x,a}, n \geq 0\}$, $\mathcal{R}_4 = \{ t_{x,a} \to \neg t_{y,b} \mid \exists A_{x,a} = \langle t_{x,a}, O_{x,a}, P_{x,a} \rangle, A_{y,b} = \langle t_{y,b}, O_{y,b}, P_{y,b} \rangle \in \mathbb{A}, \neg t_{y,b} \in P_{x,a}\}$, $\mathcal{R}_5 = \{ e_j \to \neg e_k \mid (e_j, e_k) \in \mathbb{E}$ or $(e_k, e_j) \in \mathbb{E}$, and $\mathcal{R}_6 = \{ \to s \mid s \in \mathbb{S}\};$
- $\leqslant_{\mathcal{R}_d}$ is a partial pre-order over defeasible rules $\mathcal{R}_1$, denoting a preference relation over treatments;
- $\mathcal{G} = \{ e_1, \ldots, e_n \mid n \geq 0, \exists A_{x,a} = \langle t_{x,a}, O_{x,a}, P_{x,a} \rangle \in \mathbb{A}, (e_n, C_n, \oplus) \in O_{x,a}\}$ is a set of goals in terms of the positive effects of treatments;
- $\leqslant_{\mathcal{G}}$ is a total pre-order over treatment goals in $\mathcal{G}$.

Note that the treatments provided by CIG agents are handled as disputable facts and, thus, represented as defeasible rules with empty antecedents in $\mathcal{R}_1$. This stems from treatments being viewed as interventions that could be applied to the patient, but may not, given the context. Therefore, this element is defeasible. As for the treatment/effect relations, they are handled in two possible ways. In $\mathcal{R}_2$, this relation is depicted as a defeasible rule, when the effect of a treatment is positive. We consider that treatments only create a presumption in favour of their positive effect. However, when it comes to negative effects, we adopt a more conservative approach in $\mathcal{R}_3$, for negative effects are considered as something that compromises their corresponding positive effects, and, in a goal-driven search of solutions it is important to maximize the possibility of achieving the most preferred goals. For this reason, we represent a relationship between treatments and negative effects as strict rules. This also allows, by contraposition, to obtain the negation of treatments that compromise positive effects. $\mathcal{R}_4$

---

[2] We omit $\mathcal{L}$ and n, as they are implicit from the formalization.

represents drug-drug conflicts extracted from pre-conditions of actions, indicating that two treatments must not be combined. Similarly, $\mathcal{R}_5$ presents effects that are contrary to each other. This allows for the derivation of drug-disease conflicts. Finally, $\mathcal{R}_6$ is used to describe patient state, consisting of undisputable facts. Accordingly, we apply strict rules with no antecedents.

We now instantiate ASPIC+G for Example 1 by Definition 9. $\mathcal{L}$ consists of all atoms defined for Example 1 and their negations. n, $\mathcal{R}$, $\leqslant_{\mathcal{R}_d}$, $\mathcal{G}$, and $\leqslant_{\mathcal{G}}$ are as follows:

- $\mathcal{R}_d = \{\Rightarrow de, \Rightarrow sulf, \Rightarrow meg, \Rightarrow met, \Rightarrow acei, \Rightarrow ccb\} \cup \{de \Rightarrow wd, sulf \Rightarrow gd, r_1 : meg \Rightarrow gd, r_2 : met \Rightarrow gd, acei, ckd \Rightarrow dckd, acei \Rightarrow bpd, ccb \Rightarrow bpd\}$;
- $\mathcal{R}_s = \{sulf \rightarrow wi, meg \rightarrow wi, met, ckd \rightarrow ackd, ccb \rightarrow \neg r_1, ccb \rightarrow \neg r_2\} \cup \{sulf \rightarrow \neg meg, sulf \rightarrow \neg met, meg \rightarrow \neg met, acei \rightarrow \neg ccb\} \cup \{wd \rightarrow \neg wi, ackd \rightarrow \neg dckd\} \cup \{\rightarrow ckd\}$;
- $\mathcal{R} = \mathcal{R}_d \cup \mathcal{R}_s$;
- $\leqslant_{\mathcal{R}_d}: (\Rightarrow met) <_{\mathcal{R}_d} (\Rightarrow sulf), (\Rightarrow met) <_{\mathcal{R}_d} (\Rightarrow meg)$;
- $\mathcal{G} = \{wd, gd, dckd, bpd\}$;
- $\leqslant_{\mathcal{G}}: dckd <_{\mathcal{G}} gd \simeq_{\mathcal{G}} bpd <_{\mathcal{G}} wd$.

In $\mathcal{R}$, ASPIC+G allows for the representation of a situation in which a treatment negates defeasible rules r_1 and r_2, meaning that there is a medical circumstance in which these rules do not apply. In turn, these rules, due to their nature, are defeasible. The remaining defeasible rules reflect the possible treatments for diabetes, kidney disease, obesity, and hypertension. We need not be exhaustive in the listing of treatment conflicts in actions and treatment contraries, since the negation of the antecedent is obtained by contraposition. The relation $\leqslant_{\mathcal{R}_d}$ reflects the treatment preference of the patient for $sulf$ or meg over met. The goal set $\mathcal{G}$ contains the goals driving the treatment and their preference order is specified in $\leqslant_{\mathcal{G}}$. These goals are selected from positive effects in actions. wd is the most preferred goal since obesity is the most significant concern of the patient. bpd and gd are equally preferred. Lastly, $dckd$ is the least preferred.

By Definition 2, we build the arguments $\mathcal{A}$ for the argumentation framework along with representation of goals $\mathcal{G}$:

$\mathcal{A} = \{A_1 :\Rightarrow de, A_2 : A_1 \Rightarrow wd, A_2' : A_2 \rightarrow \neg wi, A_2'' : A_2' \rightarrow \neg sulf, A_2''' : A_2' \rightarrow \neg meg, B_1 :\Rightarrow sulf, B_2 : B_1 \Rightarrow gd, B_2' : B_1 \rightarrow \neg met, B_2'' : B_1 \rightarrow \neg meg, B_2''' : B_1 \rightarrow wi, B_2'''' : B_2''' \rightarrow \neg wd, C_1 :\Rightarrow meg, C_2 : C_1 \rightarrow gd, C_2' : C_1 \rightarrow \neg met, C_2'' : C_1 \rightarrow \neg sulf, C_2''' : C_1 \rightarrow wi, C_2'''' : C_2''' \rightarrow \neg wd, D_1 :\Rightarrow met, D_2 : D_1 \rightarrow gd, D_2' : D_1 \rightarrow \neg meg, D_2'' : D_1 \rightarrow \neg sulf, E_1 :\Rightarrow acei, E_1' :\rightarrow ckd, D_2''' : D_1, E_1' \rightarrow ackd, D_3 : D_2''' \rightarrow \neg dckd, E_2 : E_1, E_1' \Rightarrow dckd, E_3 : E_2 \rightarrow \neg ackd, E_4 : E_1', E_3 \rightarrow \neg met, E_5 : E_1 \Rightarrow bpd, E_6 : E_1 \Rightarrow \neg ccb, F_1 :\Rightarrow ccb, F_2 : F_1 \Rightarrow bpd, F_1' : F_1 \rightarrow \neg acei, F_1'' : F_1 \rightarrow \neg r_1, F_1''' : F_1 \rightarrow \neg r_2\}$;
$\mathcal{G} = \{G_1 : wd, G_2 : gd, G_3 : dckd, G_4 : bpd\}$.

By Definition 3, we are able to derive the attack relations among arguments. Additionally, by Definition 4, we establish the fulfilment relations between arguments and goals. Attacks, fulfilments, and sub-argument relations are represented in the graph of Fig. 1. The explanatory power of a graph, describing an ASPIC+G argumentation theory in the context of multimorbidity, lies in identifying how and where treatment conflicts arise in the clinical process leading up to a goal. The attacks in Fig. 1 are mostly rebuttals appearing from the drug-drug interactions caused by the group $sulf$, meg, and met and the group $acei$ and ccb and the contrary effects of treatments. From Fig. 1, it is also possible to identify that the argument for met (D_1) is also rebutted by an argument (E_4) resulting from the patient having chronic kidney disease and having to delay its progression. This attack is caused by a drug-disease interaction. The only undercutting attacks are made to argument C_2 by argument F_1'' and to argument D_2 by argument F_1'''. The arguments attack the applicability of rules r_1 (used in C_2) and r_2 (used in D_2) in the presence of ccb. This type of situation is useful for a physician to know in what circumstances a piece of knowledge is not valid. Going back to attacks brought about by the drug interactions, the attacks highlighted in blue do not result in defeat for $D_2'' \prec B_1$ and $D2' \prec C_1$. This happens due to the preferences of the patient expressed in $\leqslant_{\mathcal{R}_d}$ which, in turn, are responsible for $\mathrm{DefRules}(D_2'') \trianglelefteq_{\mathcal{R}_d} \mathrm{DefRules}(B_1)$ and $\mathrm{DefRules}(D_2') \trianglelefteq_{\mathcal{R}_d} \mathrm{DefRules}(C_1)$, i.e, the use of $sulf$ or meg is preferred to met and arguments that use the latter cannot defeat arguments that use one of the first two. The graph also determines which arguments fulfil the treatment goals established for the patient. By Definitions 6 and 7, we calculate the preferred extensions and respective goal sets:

- $S_1 = \{A_1, A_2, A_2', A_2''', E_1, E_1', E_2, E_3, E_4, E_5, E_6\}$, $\mathrm{Goal}(S_1) = \{G_1, G_3, G_4\}$;
- $S_2 = \{A_1, A_2, A_2', A_2''', D_1, D_2', D_2'', D2''', D_3, E_1', F_1, F_1', F_1'', F1''', F_2\}$, $\mathrm{Goal}(S_2) = \{G_1, G_4\}$;
- $S_3 = \{A_1, B_1, B_2, B_2', B_2'', B_2''', E_1, E_1', E_2, E_3, E_4, E_5, E_6\}$, $\mathrm{Goal}(S_3) = \{G_2, G_3, G_4\}$;
- $S_4 = \{A_1, B_1, B_2, B_2', B_2''', B_2'''', E_1', F_1, F_1', F_1'', F1''', F_2\}$, $\mathrm{Goal}(S_4) = \{G_2, G_4\}$;
- $S_5 = \{A_1, C_1, C_2, C_2', C_2'', C_2'''', E_1, E_1', E_2, E_2, E_3, E_4, E_5, E_6\}$, $\mathrm{Goal}(S_5) = \{G_2, G_3, G_4\}$;
- $S_6 = \{A_1, C_1, C_2', C_2''', C_2''''', E_1', F_1, F_1', F_1'', F_1''', F_2\}$, $\mathrm{Goal}(S_6) = \{G_4\}$.

There are six possible solutions for the argumentation theory in the form of preferred extensions: $S_1 - S_6$. Considering the already established goal ordering of $\leqslant_{\mathcal{G}}$, by Definition 7, we calculate the goal set ordering $\trianglelefteq_G$. Since extension S_1 fulfils wd, bpd and $dckd$, by Definition 8 it is the top preferred extension. This is the case due to the respective goal extension fulfilling the most preferred combination of goals and being the largest doing so. This means that in Example 1, patient A should practice diet and exercise and take angiotensin converting enzyme inhibitor to address obesity, hypertension and delay the progression of kidney disease. In this way, the ASPIC+G argumentation system ensures that the most important goals in the treatment process are achieved.

4.2 Explanation of Results

The explainable nature of argumentation, as analyzed in [8,29], also contributes to making it a useful tool in the domain. We do not intend to exhaustively show explanatory properties of ASPIC+G and leave this aspect for future work. Nonetheless, we present a feature that puts it in advantage in the later comparison with MCDM. We show how one can justify a given formula concluded by a top preferred extension using the notions of defense and sub-argument. In the upcoming formalization we will resort to a *defends* relation with the following definition.

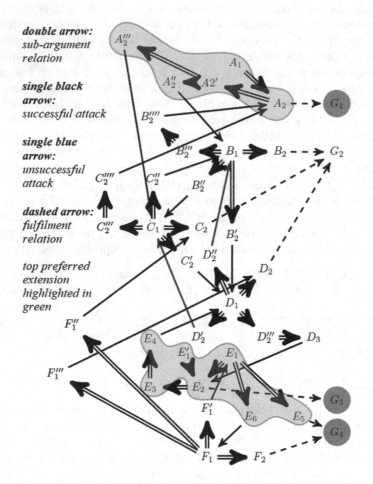

Fig. 1. Argumentation graph for Example 1.

Definition 10. *Let* $F = (\mathcal{A}, \mathcal{D}, \mathcal{G}, \leqslant_\mathcal{G}, \mathcal{F})$ *be an ASPIC+G argumentation framework. An argument* $\mathsf{C} \in \mathcal{A}$ *defends an argument* $\mathsf{A} \in \mathcal{A}$ *iff: there exists an argument* $\mathsf{B} \in \mathcal{A}$ *s.t.* B *attacks* A *and* C *attacks* B; *or there exists an argument* $\mathsf{B} \in \mathcal{A}$ *s.t.* B *defends* A *and* C *defends* B.

As mentioned, we regard an *explanation* for a conclusion as a justification and define it as follows.

Definition 11. *Let* $F = (\mathcal{A}, \mathcal{D}, \mathcal{G}, \leqslant_\mathcal{G}, \mathcal{F})$ *be an ASPIC+G argumentation framework generated from some argumentation theory and* S *a top preferred extension of* F. *The possible explanations of a conclusion* ϕ, *with* $\mathrm{Conc}(\mathsf{A}) = \phi$ *for some* $\mathsf{A} \in S$, *is the set* $\mathrm{Exp}(\phi, S) = \{\mathrm{Sub}(\mathsf{A}) \cup \{b \in \mathrm{Sub}(\mathsf{B}) \mid \mathsf{B}\ defends\ \mathsf{A}\} \mid \mathsf{A} \in S$ *s.t.* $\mathrm{Conc}(\mathsf{A}) = \phi\}$.

Thus, an explanation $\mathrm{Exp}(\phi, S)$ contains all the support (in the form of sub-arguments) and defense for a conclusion.

Example 2. Let $F = (\mathcal{A}, \mathcal{D}, \mathcal{G}, \leqslant_\mathcal{G}, \mathcal{F})$ be the ASPIC+G argumentation framework for Example 1 and S_1 its top preferred extension. The only explanation for top goal $(\mathsf{G}_1 : wd) = \mathrm{Conc}(\mathsf{A}_2)$ in $\mathrm{Exp}(wd, S_1)$ is the set $\{\mathsf{A}_1, \mathsf{A}_2, \mathsf{A}_2', \mathsf{A}_2'', \mathsf{A}_2'''\}$. Transforming this set into one containing its conclusions yields $\{de, wd, \neg wi, \neg sulf, \neg meg\}$.

In the explanation of Example 2, A_1 is a sub-argument of A_2 and therefore supports it. A_2' defends A_2 by being a sub-argument of both A_2'' and A_2''', which, in turn, defend A_2 by attacking B_1 and C_1 respectively. From the conclusions, de supports wd, and by concluding $\neg wi$, we are also concluding $\neg sulf$ and $\neg meg$, which are drugs that cause weight increase. Therefore, these arguments justify the fulfilment of weight decrease. With Definition 11 it becomes possible to explain why goals are fulfilled and why treatments are in the solution for patient management. Note that generating compound explanations for any combination of conclusions amounts to performing the union of their respective single explanations.

Some interesting properties of explanations include the *closure under the sub-argument relation* and *direct consistency*. The first ensures that for every argument in an explanation, all of its sub-arguments are also included in the explanation, and one can see that it is satisfied by the way the explanation sets are constructed. This property, together with the transitive nature of the notion of defense, ensures that every explanation also contains an explanation for every single one of its sub-conclusions, and hence provides maximal depth for the explanation. On the other hand, direct consistency guaranties that no two arguments in an explanation have opposite conclusions, and follows from the consistency of preferred extensions in ASPIC+ [14], since explanations are subsets of preferred extensions. Note that this last remark also implies that explanations are indirectly consistent, i.e. even after applying as many strict rules as desired to form new arguments from the ones present in an explanation, it is impossible to find two arguments with opposite conclusions. This ensures the well-behavior of the explanatory feature.

5   Relation with Multiple Criteria Decision

Our argumentation system can also be used to solve MCDM problems. There are numerous variations of MCDM methods [24], but there is no clear method proposed for health care, only a set of guidelines on how to conduct such an analysis, mainly criteria elicitation [13], which are not within the scope of this paper. Therefore, in this comparison we will focus on a general MCDM problem, defined as in [15].

Definition 12. *A multiple-criteria decision problem* $P = (D, C, agg)$ *consists of:*

1. *A sequence of decisions* $D = (d_1, ..., d_n)$;
2. *A sequence of criteria* $C = (c_1, ..., c_k)$, *where each* $c_i \in C$ *is a function* $c_i : D \to \mathbb{R}$;
3. *An aggregation function* $agg : \mathbb{R}^{|D| \times |C|} \to \mathbb{R}^{|D|}$.

We denote with V_P *the two-dimensional vector of the criteria values for each decision:*

$$V_P = \begin{bmatrix} c_1(d_1) & \cdots & c_k(d_1) \\ \vdots & \ddots & \\ c_1(d_n) & & c_k(d_n) \end{bmatrix}$$

In MCDM, a decision which is at least as good as every other one according to the aggregation function agg is called a *preferred decision*.

Definition 13. *Given a multiple-criteria decision problem* $P = (D, C, agg)$, *a decision* $d_i \in D$ *is preferred iff for all* $d_j \in D$ $agg(V_P)_j \leq agg(V_P)_i$.

We now provide a mapping to translate a problem into an argumentation theory in ASPIC+G, with a similar construction to the one done in [15].

Definition 14. *Let* $P = (D, C, agg)$ *be a multiple-criteria decision problem. We construct the argumentation theory* $P' = (\mathcal{A}, \mathcal{D}, \mathcal{G}, \leqslant_{\mathcal{G}}, \mathcal{F})$, *such that:*

1. $\mathcal{L}$ *is the smallest set closed under negation which contains all elements of* D *and* $\mathbb{R}$;
2. $\mathcal{R} = \mathcal{R}_1 \cup \mathcal{R}_2 \cup \mathcal{R}_3 \cup \mathcal{R}_4$, *where: a)* $\mathcal{R}_1 = \{\Rightarrow d_i \mid d_i \in D\}$; *b)* $\mathcal{R}_2 = \{d_i \to \neg d_j \mid d_i, d_j \in D\}$; *c)* $\mathcal{R}_3 = \{d_i \to v_{i,j} \mid d_i \in D, v_{i,j} \in V_P\}$; *d)* $\mathcal{R}_4 = \{v_{i,1}, ..., v_{i,k} \to agg(V_P)_i \mid v_{i,j} \in V_P, k = |C|\}$.
3. n *is the empty function;*
4. $\leq_{\mathcal{R}_d} = \emptyset$;
5. $\mathcal{G} = \{agg(V_P)_i \mid d_i \in D\}$;
6. $agg(V_P)_i \leq_{\mathcal{G}} agg(V_P)_j$ *iff* $agg(V_P)_i \leq agg(V_P)_j$.

In the resulting argumentation theory P', each decision d_i gives rise to a series of arguments which eventually lead to the fulfilment of the respective goal $agg(V_P)_i$. The preferred decisions are then retrieved in ASPIC+G in the form of *top preferred extensions* thanks to the ordering on the goals.

Theorem 1. *Let* $P = (D, C, agg)$ *be a multiple-criteria decision problem and* P' *its mapping into an argumentation theory in ASPIC+G as defined in Def. 14. Then, for all* $d \in D$, d *is a preferred decision in* P *iff there exists a top preferred extension in* P' *containing the argument* $\Rightarrow d$.

The proof of this theorem lies in the fact that all decisions are in conflict with each other thanks to the rules in $\mathcal{R}_2$. These being the only conflicts present in the framework, together with the lack of preferences over defeasible rules, ensures that every preferred extension represents exactly one decision and its consequences. By using the ranking over goals in ASPIC+G, which is derived from the ranking over the aggregations in P, we filter out the preferred extensions which do not represent preferred decisions, and hence obtain a bijection between preferred decisions in P and top preferred extensions in P'. [3] This shows that ASPIC+G can be built on top of MCDM, presenting the same data in a different kind of structure. While there has been some work on explainability in MCDM [12], our argumentative approach provides more transparency in the reasoning process and allows for explanations of preferred decisions (top preferred extensions), which is of extreme importance in medical reasoning for the sake of clarity and compliance with recommendations. Within a multimorbidity context, an MCDM method would produce a decision consisting of a set containing recommended treatments and respective aggregated score, which cannot easily be further decomposed and analyzed to demonstrate how that decision is brought about.

6 Related Work

Wilk et al. [27] propose a first order-logic framework in order to detect and mitigate adverse interactions (both drug-drug and drug-disease) between concurrently applied recommendations based on constraint logic programming. Reasoning requires that all stable solutions be encoded beforehand in the form of revision operators and computation mechanism is undecidable, as opposed to the computation of preferred extensions. Zamborlini et al. [28] use their transition-based medical recommendation model to represent interactions in association with recommendations from different CIGs. Interaction types are defined extensively. However, there is no reasoning mechanism to deal with conflicting recommendations. Spiotta et al. [22] propose a framework to analyze the temporal conformance of followed actions against a single CIG. Using answer set programming they provide explanations on conflicting situations, based on events in the state of a patient. There, the setting is different from the presented herein and the method does not aim to combine different CIGs.

Regarding argumentative approaches, Fox et al. [9] introduce argumentation to help physicians decide for or against treatments. There, patient preferences and patient-specific goals are not featured. Hunter and Williams [11] offer a formal approach to aggregating clinical evidence. Based on the available evidence, arguments are generated for claiming that one treatment is superior, or equivalent, to another. This approach does not concern multimorbidity nor the combination of different CIG recommendations. Brando et al. [5] developed an

---

[3] The complete proof is provided in the appendix.

argumentation-based decision support system which can be used to both represent medical decisions within a single guideline and dynamically choose the most suitable plans to achieve a unique goal. Goal prioritization is not featured.

Amgoud and Prade [1] propose an abstract argument-based framework for decision-making. They formulate a series of decision principles that are goal-driven. Yet, this argumentation framework would not fit decision-making in multimorbidity particularly well for it does not provide sub-argument structure, contrasting to our interest in showing a mapping from CIGs to rule patterns in argumentation. The notions of *pro* and *con* arguments are used to evaluate options, while our mechanism is solely based on explicit goal preferences and does not require the user to elicit all possible solutions beforehand. Muller and Hunter [15] formulate a structured argumentation framework for decision-making where goals are used to select decisions. In their work, there is a form of backward reasoning from goals to arguments and a direct comparison of their framework with MCDM. Given the importance of the latter in medical reasoning, we adapt their procedure to perform our own comparison. Note that the type of reasoning performed in our work goes in the opposite direction, from arguments to goals. We first check what are the possible preferred extensions, which, within the context, provide all possible treatment solutions without conflict and respective effects, and then verify which goals each solution fulfils in order to determine its ranking. This kind of reasoning and prioritization of goals are more adequate for assessing the recommendations proposed by CIG agents in a multimorbidity, as these recommendations are already the product of a reasoning process within the CIG agent. Black and Atkinson [4] present a dialogical argumentation framework for reasoning among different agents. Each agent, according to its perspective, has an input as to how a goal can be achieved. ASPIC+G does not possess this dialogical nature, nor it an objective in the current presentation. Furthermore, Black and Atkinson [4] do not specify an argument evaluation method, whereas our approach establishes detailed semantics for ordering preferred extensions based on respective goal sets.

7   Conclusions and Future Work

ASPIC+G models discussions driven by goals, where it is not only important to have explanatory arguments in favour or against a position, but also to know where paths lead to. As such, the presented argumentation system is a contribution in medical reasoning as it is fit for reasoning in multimorbidity. It combines the recommendations of agents, deriving drug-drug and drug-disease conflicts that arise from them, using patient preferences over treatments and preferred semantics so resolve the conflicts and produce solutions, then selecting the best solution based on patient-specific goal preferences. We also show that best solutions are capable of providing explanations in the form of sub-argument and defending argument sets, which are closed under the sub-argument relation, and both directly and indirectly consistent. ASPIC+G can be built on top of MCDM to produce preferred solutions, with the advantage of having a more transparent structure, an important feature in CDSSs. The present work does not specify preference elicitation or goal prioritization methods. We plan to address this and manage different types of preferences, mainly over defeasible rules, stemming from different sources. An example to be considered is the strength of evidence backing recommendations in relation to effects. We also plan to explore adding weights to the argumentation framework, in order to allow the representation of side effects of varying degrees of severeness and also therefore allowing for a slightly more detailed reasoning process.

8   Appendix

Proof of Theorem 1

Proof. We prove Theorem 1 in two steps:

- We first prove that if d_i is a preferred decision in P, then there exists a top preferred extension containing the argument $A :\Rightarrow d_i$.
  For all arguments A', there exists a j such that $(\Rightarrow d_j) \in Sub(A')$. If $j \neq i$, then the argument $A \rightarrow \neg d_j$ rebuts A' on $(\Rightarrow d_j)$. Since there are no preferences over the defeasible rules, this attack results in a defeat. Otherwise, $j = i$ and thus by construction, A' is not in conflict with A. Hence, the set containing A and all its super-arguments of the form $A \rightarrow \neg d_j$ make an admissible set, and therefore there exists a preferred extension E which contains them.
  Since d_i is a preferred decision in P, for all $d_j \in D$, $agg(V_P)_j \leq agg(V_P)_i$, and so $agg(V_P)_j \leq_G agg(V_P)_i$. By closure under strict rules, the argument A_{agg} with top rule $v_{i,j}, ... \rightarrow agg(V_P)_i$ is included in E. Hence, E is a top preferred extension which contains A.
- We now prove that if there exists a top preferred extension E containing the argument $A :\Rightarrow d_i$, then d_i is a preferred decision in P.
  By closure under strict rules, an argument A_{agg} with top rule $v_{i,j}, ... \rightarrow agg(V_P)_i$ is included in E. There is no $j \neq i$ for which there is an argument in E with conclusion $agg(V_P)_j$, as such an argument requires an argument of the form $\Rightarrow d_j$ as sub-argument, which would get rebutted by the argument $A \rightarrow \neg d_j$ which is in E by closure under strict rules. Take any other arbitrary preferred extension E'. By similar reasoning, E' may only contain one single argument with a conclusion of the form $agg(V_P)_j$ for some j. Since E is a top preferred extension, $GE_{E'} \trianglelefteq_{GE} GE_E$. E and E' are disjoint since they each only contain a single different argument of the form $agg(V_P)_x$, and hence $agg(V_P)_j \leq agg(V_P)_i$. Therefore, d_i is a preferred decision in P. $\qquad\square$

References

1. Amgoud, L., Prade, H.: Using arguments for making and explaining decisions. Artif. Intell. **173**(3–4), 413–436 (2009)

2. Atkinson, K., Bench-Capon, T., Modgil, S.: Argumentation for decision support. In: Bressan, S., Küng, J., Wagner, R. (eds.) DEXA 2006. LNCS, vol. 4080, pp. 822–831. Springer, Heidelberg (2006). https://doi.org/10.1007/11827405_80
3. Baltussen, R., Niessen, L.: Priority setting of health interventions: the need for multi-criteria decision analysis. Cost Eff. Resour. Alloc. **4**, 1–9 (2006)
4. Black, E., Atkinson, K.: Dialogues that account for different perspectives in collaborative argumentation. In: Proceedings of the 8th International Conference on Autonomous Agents and Multiagent Systems, vol. 2, pp. 867–874 (2009)
5. Brando, M., Glasspool, D., Boxwala, A.: Argumentation logic for the flexible enactment of goal-based medical guidelines. J. Biomed. Inform. **45**(5), 938–949 (2012)
6. Button, D.R., Fox, J.: The syntax and semantics of the PRO forma guideline modeling language. J. Am. Med. Inform. Assoc. **10**(5), 433–443 (2003)
7. Dung, P.M.: On the acceptability of arguments and its fundamental role in non-monotonic reasoning, logic programming and n-person games. Artif. Intell. **77**(2), 321–357 (1995)
8. Fan, X., Toni, F.: On computing explanations in argumentation. In: AAAI, pp. 1496–1502 (2015)
9. Fox, J., et al.: Towards a general model for argumentation services. In: AAAI Spring Symposium: Argumentation for Consumers of Healthcare, pp. 52–57 (2006)
10. Fraccaro, P., Casteleiro, M.A., Ainsworth, J., Buchan, I.: Adoption of clinical decision support in multimorbidity: a systematic review. JMIR Med. Inform. **3**(1), e4 (2015)
11. Hunter, A., Williams, M.: Aggregating evidence about the positive and negative effects of treatments. Artif. Intell. Med. **56**(3), 173–190 (2012)
12. Labreuche, C., Fossier, S.: Explaining multi-criteria decision aiding models with an extended shapley value. In: IJCAI, pp. 331–339 (2018)
13. Marsh, K., Ijzerman, M., Thokala, P., Baltussen, R., et al.: Multiple criteria decision analysis for health care decision making - emerging good practices: report 2 of the ISPOR MCDA emerging good practices task force. Value Health **19**(2), 125–137 (2016)
14. Modgil, S., Prakken, H.: The ASPIC+ framework for structured argumentation: a tutorial. Argument Comput. **5**(1), 31–62 (2014)
15. Muller, J., Hunter, A.: An argumentation-based approach for decision making. In: Proceedings of the 2012 IEEE 24th International Conference on Tools with Artificial Intelligence - Volume 01, ICTAI 2012, Washington, DC, USA, pp. 564–571. IEEE Computer Society (2012)
16. Muth, C., et al.: The Ariadne principles: how to handle multimorbidity in primary care consultations. BMC Med. **12**(1), 1–11 (2014)
17. NICE: Chronic kidney disease in adults : assessment and management. Technical report, January 2015
18. NICE: Hypertension in adults: diagnosis and management Y Your responsibility our responsibility. Technical report, August 2011
19. NICE: Obesity: identification, assessment and management management Y Your responsibility our responsibility. Technical report, November 2014
20. NICE: Type 2 diabetes in adults: management. NICE guideline (NG 28). Technical report, December 2015
21. Peleg, M.: Computer-interpretable clinical guidelines: a methodological review. J. Biomed. Inform. **46**(4), 744–763 (2013)
22. Spiotta, M., Terenziani, P., Dupré, D.T.: Temporal conformance analysis and explanation of clinical guidelines execution: an answer set programming approach. IEEE Trans. Knowl. Data Eng. **29**(11), 2567–2580 (2017)

23. Spollett, G.: Case study: a patient with uncontrolled type 2 diabetes and complex comorbidities whose diabetes care is managed by an advanced practice nurse. Diabetes Spectr. **16**(1), 32–36 (2003)
24. Triantaphyllou, E.: Multi-criteria Decision Making Methods: A Comparative Study. Applied Optimization, vol. 44, pp. 5–21. Springer, Boston (2000). https://doi.org/10.1007/978-1-4757-3157-6_2
25. Vermunt, N.P.C.A., Harmsen, M., Westert, G.P., Rikkert, M.G.M.O., Faber, M.J.: Collaborative goal setting with elderly patients with chronic disease or multimorbidity: a systematic review. BMC Geriatr. **17**(1), 167 (2017). https://doi.org/10.1186/s12877-017-0534-0
26. Wallace, E., Salisbury, C., Guthrie, B., Lewis, C., Fahey, T., Smith, S.M.: Managing patients with multimorbidity in primary care. BMJ **350**, h176 (2015)
27. Wilk, S., Michalowski, M., Michalowski, W., Rosu, D., Carrier, M., Kezadri-Hamiaz, M.: Comprehensive mitigation framework for concurrent application of multiple clinical practice guidelines. J. Biomed. Inform. **66**, 52–71 (2017)
28. Zamborlini, V., et al.: Analyzing interactions on combining multiple clinical guidelines. Artif. Intell. Med. **81**, 78–93 (2017)
29. Zeng, Z., Fan, X., Miao, C., Leung, C., Jih, C.J., Soon, O.Y.: Context-based and explainable decision making with argumentation. In: Proceedings AAMAS 2018, pp. 1114–1122 (2018)

Intuitionistic-Bayesian Semantics of First-Order Logic for Generics

Satoru Suzuki[✉]

Faculty of Arts and Sciences, Komazawa University,
1-23-1, Komazawa, Setagaya-ku, Tokyo 154-8525, Japan
bxs05253@nifty.com

Abstract. Generics are used frequently in various natural languages. Cohen's theory (1999) is one of the most promising theories of generics. Cohen proposes a probabilistic account of generics. Leslie (2007, 2008) points out the three shortcomings of Cohen's theory. Asher and Pelletier (2013) point out five more shortcomings of Cohen's theory. The aim of this paper is to propose a new version of logic for generics—First-Order Logic for Generics (FLG)—that can overcome all of the eight shortcomings. To accomplish this goal, we provide the language of FLG with an intuitionistic-Bayesian semantics.

Keywords: Bayesian semantics · Conceptual role · Conditionals · Generics · Intuitionistic Bayesianism · Natural language · Nonstandard probability theory · Philosophy of language · Probabilistic semantics · Stalnaker Thesis · Triviality result

1 Motivation: Cohen's Theory and Its Eight Shortcomings

The following sentences are examples of *generics*:

(1) Dogs bark.

(2) Mosquitoes carry the West Nile Virus.

Generics are used ubiquitously in various natural languages. Cohen's theory [2] is one of the most promising theories of generics. Cohen proposes a probabilistic account of generics. According to Leslie [8,9], we summarize Cohen's theory of generics as follows: Let $Alt(F)$ denote a contextually determined set of alternatives to a predicate F and $Alt(K)$ a contextually determined set of alternatives to a kind K. Cohen distinguishes between two different classes of generics: absolute and relative generics:

> *Absolute Generics*: 'Ks are F' is true iff the probability (*relative frequency*) that an arbitrary K that satisfies some predicate in $Alt(F)$ satisfies F is greater than 0.5.

© Springer Nature Switzerland AG 2020
M. Dastani et al. (Eds.): CLAR 2020, LNAI 12061, pp. 184–200, 2020.
https://doi.org/10.1007/978-3-030-44638-3_12

Relative Generics: '*K*s are *F*' is true iff the probability (relative frequency) that an arbitrary *K* that satisfies some predicate in *Alt*(*F*) satisfies *F* is greater than the probability (relative frequency) that an arbitrary member of *Alt*(*K*) that satisfies some predicate in *Alt*(*F*) satisfies *F*.

(1) is a true absolute generic because the probability that an arbitrary dog barks is greater than 0.5. (2) is a true relative generic because an arbitrary *mosquito* is far more likely to carry the virus than an arbitrary *insect*. Cohen adds the following condition to his theory:

Homogeneity: These truth conditions must hold for all salient partitions of a kind *K*.

For example, gender is a salient partition in animal kinds. Female and male chickens are almost as likely to be born. However, after a chick is found to be male, it is unfortunately customary to be killed and used as fertilizer and feedstock. As a result, over 80% of chickens become female. Despite this fact, (3) is a false generic:

(3) Chickens are female.

For Homogeneity is violated because the probability of an arbitrary male chicken being female is 0. Leslie [8,9] points out the following *three* shortcomings of Cohen's theory:

- **Shortcoming 1**: Cohen's theory wrongly makes (4) false for the same reason as (3).
  (4) Lions have manes.
- **Shortcoming 2**: The number of legs is considered to constitute a salient partition of the kind Dog. For example, Homogeneity is violated because the probability of an arbitrary dog that becomes three-legged by means of an unexpected accident being four-legged is 0. So (5) results in being false in Cohen's theory:
  (5) Dogs are four-legged.
- **Shortcoming 3**: Let us suppose that fleas also carry the virus. If the flea population grew so rapidly as to vastly outnumber all other insects, at some point it would cease to be the case that an arbitrary mosquito would be more likely than an arbitrary insect to carry the virus. At this point, (2) would fail to be a true relative generic on Cohen's theory. Intuitively, however, it would remain true.

On the other hand, Asher and Pelletier [1] point out the following five shortcomings of Cohen's theory:

- **Shortcoming 4**: Let us suppose that in a little more than 50, for example, 50.05% of the cases cats have (long) tails. Our intuitions say that in this case, the generic (6) is not true:
  (6) Cats have tails.
  But in Cohen's theory (6) is true.

- **Shortcoming 5**: In Cohen's theory, it is not at all clear how to adapt the *semantics* to capture uncertain inference.
- **Shortcoming 6**: The only way to have a chance of modeling *common-sense* reasoning patterns using probabilities is to use *nonstandard probabilities* in which probabilities can have *infinitesimal* values[1]. However, Cohen's theory has no structure for nonstandard probabilities. By means of the following example, we would like to illustrate what Asher and Pelletier seem to intend to say:

   Example 1 (Nonstandard Probabilities). *According to our* common sense, *the* two-dimensional geometric probability, *for example, of picking a point from the diagonal* $D_1(D_2)$ *of a rectangle, given that the point is on one of* D_1 *and* D_2, *will equal* $\frac{1}{2}$. *However, under* Kolmogorov probability theory, it equals $\frac{0}{0}$ *(undefined). On the other hand, under* nonstandard infinitesimal probability theory, *it equals* $\frac{1}{2}$.

- **Shortcoming 7**: The assignment of probabilities to formulae cannot be done in a *compositional* fashion due to the dependence of one formula on another: The probability assignment to $\mathbf{P}(\varphi \wedge \psi)$ cannot be defined in terms of $\mathbf{P}(\varphi)$ and $\mathbf{P}(\psi)$.
- **Shortcoming 8**: Cohen's theory cannot deal with *embedded generics* properly.

   The aim of this paper is to propose a new version of logic for generics—First-Order Logic for Generics (FLG)—that can overcome *all of the eight shortcomings of Cohen's theory* pointed out by Leslie [8,9] and Asher and Pelletier [1]. To accomplish this goal, we provide the language of FLG with an *intuitionistic-Bayesian semantics*.

   The structure of this paper is as follows. In Sect. 2, we touch upon conceptual roles, Bayesian semantics, the Ramsey Test, and the Stalnaker Thesis. In Sect. 3, we argue about Bayesian semantics and the triviality result. In Sect. 4, we show the four advantages of intuitionistic-Bayesian semantics. In Sect. 5, we define the language $\mathscr{L}_{\mathsf{FLG}}$ of FLG and provide FLG with an intuitionistic-Bayesian semantics. And furthermore, we give the logical forms of some generics and provide them with their truth conditions. In Sect. 6, we summarize the ways of overcoming the eight shortcomings by means of FLG. In Sect. 7, we finish with brief concluding remarks.

2   Bayesian Semantics, Ramsey Test, and Stalnaker Thesis

Harman says, in connection with truth-theoretic semantics and conceptual-role semantics, that

---

[1] For nonstandard probability theory, consult [14]. For the relation between epistemic modals and nonstandard probability theory, refer to [18].

··· meaning depends on role in conceptual scheme rather than on truth conditions. That is, meaning has to do with evidence, inference, and reasoning, including the impact sensory experience has on what one believes, the way in which inference and reasoning modify one's beliefs and plans, and the way beliefs and plans are reflected in action [4, p. 11].

Field argues against this view as follows:

My view rather is that truth-theoretic semantics and conceptual-role semantics must supplement each other: truth-theoretic semantics cannot account for certain differences in sense unaccompanied by differences in reference; and conceptual-role semantics ··· cannot properly answer questions ··· about relations between language and the world. But, taken together, I claim, truth-theoretic semantics and conceptual-role semantics provide an account of all the facts about meaning that there are [3, p. 380].

Field argues that there are two versions of truth-theoretic semantics. One is a *non-referential version* whose paradigm is as follows:

(7) 'Beethoven wohnte in Deutschland' is true iff Beethoven lived in Germany [3, p. 389].

The other version is a *referential version* whose paradigm is as follows:

(8) 'Beethoven lived in Germany' is true iff there are objects x and y and a relation R such that 'Beethoven' stands for x, 'Germany' stands for y, 'lived in' stands for R, and x bears R to y [3, p. 389].

The *referential meaning* of 'Beethoven lived in Germany' is given by (8) together with a specification of the referents of the three components of this sentence. To specify the referential meaning of a sentence is not fully to specify its meaning. *The meaning of a sentence is given by its referential meaning together with its conceptual role.* The following sentences have the same referential meaning (*Frege's Puzzle*).

(9)   Hesperus = Hesperus,
(10)   Hesperus = Phosphorus.

Field explains the difference in meaning between (9) and (10) by saying that these two sentences differ in conceptual role. Moreover, he explains the difference in conceptual role by saying that these two sentences differ in *subjective (Bayesian) conditional probability*. He argues that (9) and (10) have different conceptual role for an agent iff his or her subjective probability (*degree of belief*) of (9) under the condition Γ is different from his or her subjective probability of (10) under Γ, that is,

$$\mathbf{P}(\text{Hesperus} = \text{Hesperus}, \Gamma) \neq \mathbf{P}(\text{Hesperus} = \text{Phosphorus}, \Gamma),$$

when his or her belief state is represented by a conditional probability function $\mathbf{P}$ [3, pp. 389–390].

Remark 1 (Bayesian Probability). *Cohen interprets probability as relative frequency, whereas in this paper we consider Bayesian probability from a semantic point of view.*

Remark 2 (Binary Probability Function and Semantic Entailment). *In this paper we adopt as conditional probability functions not defined probability functions but primitive binary probability functions that take a formula and a set of formulae as arguments. For in this paper we intend to use these binary probability functions in order to define an after-mentioned semantic entailment in* FLG *of a set of formulae with a formula.*

As for evaluation of the acceptability of conditionals, Ramsey wrote as follows:

> If two people are arguing 'If φ, will ψ?' and are both in doubt as to φ, they are adding φ hypothetically to their stock of knowledge and arguing on that basis about ψ... [15, p. 155].

This is called the *Ramsey Test*. Stalnaker materialized this test in terms of subjective probability. Let **P** represent a belief state of one of these people, and let Γ denote his or her stock of knowledge. Then, for any φ, ψ, $\mathbf{P}(\varphi \to \psi, \Gamma) = \mathbf{P}(\psi, \{\varphi\} \cup \Gamma)$ is called the *Stalnaker Thesis* [17, p. 75].

3   Bayesian Semantics and Triviality Result

Suppose that the language $\mathscr{L}$ of first-order logic with equality is given. The set of all well-formed formulae of $\mathscr{L}$ is denoted by $\Phi_{\mathscr{L}}$. Suppose that both the *derivability* $\vdash_{\mathsf{IL}}$ *in intuitionistic first-order logic with equality* and the *derivability* $\vdash_{\mathsf{CL}}$ *in classical first order logic with equality* are defined. We define finite axiomatizability of superintuitionistic logics as follows:

Definition 1 (Finite Axiomatizability of Superintuitionistic Logics). *Let* IL $+ (\Psi_1(\varphi, \psi, \chi, \ldots) + \ldots + \Psi_n(\varphi, \psi, \chi, \ldots))$ *be the system of superintuitionistic first-order logic with equality that has* $\Psi_1(\varphi, \psi, \chi, \ldots), \ldots, \Psi_n(\varphi, \psi, \chi, \ldots)$ *as axioms besides the axioms of* IL. *If a system X of superintuitionistic first-order logic can be represented by $X =$* IL $+ (\Psi_1(\varphi, \psi, \chi, \ldots) + \ldots + \Psi_n(\varphi, \psi, \chi, \ldots))$, *for finite n, then X is said to be* finitely axiomatizable. *The derivability $\vdash_X$, for any finitely axiomatizable system X of superintuitionistic first-order logic with equality can be defined.*

First, let us consider a conditional probability function $\mathbf{P}_I : \Phi_{\mathscr{L}} \times \wp(\Phi_{\mathscr{L}}) \longrightarrow [0, 1]$ satisfying Conditions 1–11 below [13] for any $\varphi, \psi \in \Phi_{\mathscr{L}}$ and for any $\Gamma \subset \wp(\Phi_{\mathscr{L}})$:

Condition 1 $0 \leq \mathbf{P}_I(\varphi, \Gamma) \leq 1$,
Condition 2   If $\varphi \in \Gamma$, then $\mathbf{P}_I(\varphi, \Gamma) = 1$,
Condition 3 $\mathbf{P}_I(\varphi, \{\psi\} \cup \Gamma) \times \mathbf{P}_I(\psi, \Gamma) = \mathbf{P}_I(\psi, \{\varphi\} \cup \Gamma) \times \mathbf{P}_I(\varphi, \Gamma)$,
Condition 4 $\mathbf{P}_I(\varphi \to \psi, \Gamma) = \mathbf{P}_I(\psi, \{\varphi\} \cup \Gamma)$ (*Stalnaker Thesis*),
Condition 5 $\mathbf{P}_I(\varphi \wedge \psi, \Gamma) = \mathbf{P}_I(\varphi, \{\psi\} \cup \Gamma) \times \mathbf{P}_I(\psi, \Gamma)$,
Condition 6 $\mathbf{P}_I(\varphi, \{\psi, \chi\} \cup \Gamma) = \mathbf{P}_I(\varphi, \{\psi \wedge \chi\} \cup \Gamma)$,
Condition 7 $\mathbf{P}_I(\varphi, \{\psi \vee \chi\} \cup \Gamma) = \mathbf{P}_I(\varphi, \{\psi\} \cup \Gamma) \times \mathbf{P}_I(\varphi, \{\chi, \psi \to \varphi\} \cup \Gamma)$,
Condition 8 $\mathbf{P}_I(\varphi, \{\bot\} \cup \Gamma) = 1$,
Condition 9 $\mathbf{P}_I(\forall x F(x), \Gamma) = \lim_{n \to \infty} \mathbf{P}_I(F(t_1) \wedge F(t_2) \wedge \cdots \wedge F(t_n), \Gamma)$,
Condition 10 $\mathbf{P}_I(\varphi, \{\exists x F(x)\} \cup \Gamma)$
$= \lim_{n \to \infty} \mathbf{P}_I(\varphi, \{F(t_1) \vee F(t_2) \vee \cdots \vee F(t_n)\} \cup \Gamma)$,
Condition 11   For any $t, t', \mathbf{P}_I(t = t', \Gamma) = 1$ iff $\mathbf{P}_I(\varphi, \Gamma) = \mathbf{P}_I(\varphi', \Gamma)$,
where φ' is obtained from φ by replacing t
in zero or more (but not necessarily all) places by t'.

Second, let us consider a conditional probability function $\mathbf{P}_{S(\Psi_1 \wedge \dots \wedge \Psi_n)} : \Phi_{\mathscr{L}} \times \wp(\Phi_{\mathscr{L}}) \longrightarrow [0,1]$ satisfying Conditions 1–11 and Condition 12 below, for any $\varphi, \psi, \chi, \ldots \in \Phi_{\mathscr{L}}$ and for any $\Gamma \subset \wp(\Phi_{\mathscr{L}})$:

Condition 12 $\mathbf{P}_{S(\Psi_1 \wedge \dots \wedge \Psi_n)}(\Psi_1(\varphi, \psi, \chi, \ldots) \wedge \ldots \wedge \Psi_n(\varphi, \psi, \chi, \ldots), \Gamma) = 1$.

Third, let us consider a conditional probability function $\mathbf{P}_C : \Phi_{\mathscr{L}} \times \wp(\Phi_{\mathscr{L}}) \longrightarrow [0,1]$ satisfying Conditions 1–11 and Condition 13 below [13], for any $\varphi \in \Phi_{\mathscr{L}}$ and for any $\Gamma \subset \wp(\Phi_{\mathscr{L}})$:

Condition 13   If there is $\psi \in \Phi_{\mathscr{L}}$ such that $\mathbf{P}_C(\psi, \Gamma) \neq 1$,
then $\mathbf{P}_C(\varphi, \Gamma) + \mathbf{P}_C(\neg\varphi, \Gamma) = 1$.

Considering the strong soundness and completeness of intuitionistic first-order logic with respect to $\mathbf{P}_I{}^2$, we call $\mathbf{P}_I$ an *intuitionistic conditional probability function*. Considering the strong soundness and completeness of superintuitionistic first-order logics with respect to $\mathbf{P}_{S(\Phi_1 \wedge \dots \wedge \Phi_n)}$ for any finitely axiomatizable system X of superintuitionistic first-order logic[3], we call $\mathbf{P}_{S(\Phi_1 \wedge \dots \wedge \Phi_n)}$ a *superintuitionistic conditional probability function*. Considering the strong soundness and completeness with respect to $\mathbf{P}_C{}^4$, we call $\mathbf{P}_C$ a *classical conditional probability function*. On the basis of [13], we derive the following *triviality result*[5]:

Fact 1 (Triviality). *For any $\varphi, \psi \in \Phi_{\mathscr{L}}$ and any $\Gamma \subset \wp(\Phi_{\mathscr{L}})$, if $\mathbf{P}_C(\varphi, \Gamma) < 1$ and $\mathbf{P}_C(\psi, \Gamma) < 1$, then $\mathbf{P}_C(\varphi, \Gamma) = \mathbf{P}_C(\psi, \Gamma)$. Moreover, for any $\Gamma, \Delta \subset$*

---

[2] For the strong soundness and completeness of intuitionistic first-order logic with respect to $\mathbf{P}_I$, consult [12] and [13].
[3] For the strong soundness and completeness of superintuitionistic first-order logics with respect to $\mathbf{P}_{S(\Phi_1 \wedge \dots \wedge \Phi_n)}$, consult [13].
[4] For the strong soundness and completeness with respect to $\mathbf{P}_C$, consult [7] and [13].
[5] The arguments on triviality results originate in [10] and [11].

$\wp(\Phi_{\mathscr{L}})$, if both $\Gamma \setminus \Delta$ is finite and $\Delta \setminus \Gamma$ is finite, then, for any $\varphi \in \Phi_{\mathscr{L}}$, $\mathbf{P}_C(\varphi, \Gamma) = \mathbf{P}_C(\varphi, \Delta)$ unless $\mathbf{P}_C(\varphi, \Gamma) = 1$ or $\mathbf{P}_C(\varphi, \Delta) = 1$.

Field [3] explains the difference in meaning between two sentences by saying that they differ in *conceptual role*. Moreover, he explains the difference in conceptual role by saying that these two sentences differ in *subjective conditional probability*. However, Fact 1 shows that except for the trivial cases, the probability of one sentence under a condition is always the same as that of another sentence under it and the probability of a sentence under one condition is always the same as that of it under another condition. Therefore $\mathbf{P}_C$, which is constrained by *Stalnaker Thesis (Condition 4)*, cannot represent properly an agent's rational belief state. Condition 13 is necessary to prove *Fact 1*. Neither $\mathbf{P}_I$ nor $\mathbf{P}_{S(\Phi_1 \wedge \ldots \wedge \Phi_n)}$ satisfies Condition 13. Therefore neither invites the triviality result. Then in this sense both $\mathbf{P}_I$ in intuitionistic Bayesianism and $\mathbf{P}_{S(\Phi_1 \wedge \ldots \wedge \Phi_n)}$ in superintuitionistic Bayesianisms might represent an agent's rational belief states. Which can represent more properly an agent's rational belief states, $\mathbf{P}_I$ or $\mathbf{P}_{S(\Phi_1 \wedge \ldots \wedge \Phi_n)}$?

4   Four Advantages of Intuitionistic-Bayesian Semantics

There are an infinite number of superintuitionistic logics. However, in general, it is difficult to attach any significance to the axioms peculiar to them respectively. So it is difficult to attach any importance in conceptual roles to each superintuitionistic Bayesianism. Then we would like to consider the features of intuitionistic Bayesianism. We summarize Weatherson's *possible* (though not decisive) arguments [20] that intuitionistic Bayesianism has the three advantages over classical one as follows[6]:

1. According to *verificationism*, classical Bayesianism has no way of representing *complete uncertainty*: Because verificationism implies the failures of Laplace's principle of indifference, it cannot be said that uncertainty about φ is represented, as classical Bayesianism does, by assigning the probability $\frac{1}{2}$ to φ. Then classical Bayesianism must abandon either assigns the probability 1 to the law of the excluded middle or finite additivity. On the other hand, because intuitionistic Baysianism does not need to assign the probability 1 to the law of the excluded middle, it does not need to abandon finite additivity.
2. According to *antirealism about future*, no propositions about the future have positive probabilities. Also in this case, classical Bayesianism must abandon either assigns the probability 1 to the law of the excluded middle or finite additivity.
3. Intuitionistic Bayesianism can provide a justification for rejecting the positive arguments, e.g., *Dutch Book arguments*, for classical Bayesianism. All such Dutch Book arguments have assumed that the classical—rather than intuitionistic—reasoning is appropriate. But Weatherson argues that a Dutch Book argument is also possible even if the intuitionistic—rather than classical—reasoning is appropriate.

---

[6] Weatherson provides four arguments for intuitionistic Bayesianism. However, these four arguments can be reduced to the following three arguments.

In general, intuitionistic-Bayesian semantics on the basis of intuitionistic Bayesianism has these *three* advantages over classical-Bayesian semantics. The *fourth* advantage, which is most essential, is that, in providing a First-Order Logic for Generics (FLG) with its semantics, classical-Bayesian semantics can invites the *triviality result* (*Fact 1*), whereas intuitionistic-Bayesian semantics cannot invite it. For, as we explain in detail, in *Condition 15*, absolute generics will be probabilistically characterized by *indicative conditionals*, and furthermore, in *Condition 16*, relative generics will be also probabilistically characterized by indicative conditionals. So providing FLG with its classical-Bayesian semantics, via *Stalnaker Thesis* (*Condition 4*), can result in inviting the triviality result (*Fact 1*), whereas providing FLG with its intuitionistic-Bayesian semantics, via Stalnaker Thesis, cannot result in inviting the triviality result. These four are the reasons why we provide FLG with its intuitionistic-Bayesian semantics.

5   First-Order Logic for Generics (FLG)

5.1   Language of FLG

We define the language $\mathscr{L}_{\mathsf{FLG}}$ of FLG as follows:

Definition 2 (Language of FLG).

- Let $\mathscr{V}$ denote a set of individual variables, $\mathscr{C}$ a set of individual constants, and $\mathscr{P}$ a set of predicate symbols.
- The language $\mathscr{L}_{\mathsf{FLG}}$ of FLG is given by the following BNF grammar:

$$t ::= x \mid a,$$
$$\varphi ::= F_i(t) \mid \tilde{F}_m(t) \mid t = t' \mid \bot \mid \neg\varphi \mid \varphi \wedge \psi \mid \varphi \vee \psi \mid$$
$$\varphi \rightarrow \psi \mid \varphi \Rightarrow \psi \mid \varphi \Rrightarrow \psi \mid \forall x\varphi \mid \exists x\varphi,$$

where $x \in \mathscr{V}$, $a \in \mathscr{C}$, $F_{i \in \{1,2,\dots,m\}}, \tilde{F}_m \in \mathscr{P}$, and where there are neither nestings of $\Rightarrow$ nor those of $\Rrightarrow$.
- $\top$ and $\leftrightarrow$ are introduced by the standard definitions.
- $\tilde{F}_m$ is an $(F_1, F_2, \dots, F_m)$-membered superordinate predicate symbol of $F_{i \in \{1,2,\dots,m\}}$.

Example 2 (Superordinate Predicate Symbol). In the situation of (2) [Mosquitoes carry the West Nile Virus.], being an insect is a (being a mosquito, being a flea,...)-membered superordinate predicate.

- For any $F_{i \in \{1,2,\dots,m\}} \in \mathscr{P}$, there is an $(F_1, F_2, \dots, F_m)$-membered superordinate predicate symbol $\tilde{F}_m \in \mathscr{P}$ of $F_{i \in \{1,2,\dots,m\}}$.
- We interpret $\rightarrow$ as an indicative conditional connective, $\Rightarrow$ as an absolute generic conditional connective, and $\Rrightarrow$ as a relative generic conditional connective.

Remark 3 (Indicative Conditional Connective $\rightarrow$). In FLG, $\rightarrow$ is not a material conditional connective but an indicative conditional connective. The semantics of $\rightarrow$ is given by the Stalnaker Thesis (Condition 4).
- The set of all well-formed formulae of $\mathscr{L}_{\mathsf{FLG}}$ is denoted by $\Phi_{\mathscr{L}_{\mathsf{FLG}}}$.

5.2   Intuitionistic-Bayesian Semantics of FLG

Now we would like to introduce as a main semantic device of FLG a *temporal nonstandard conditional probability function* $\mathbf{P}_I^{(u)} : \Phi_{\mathscr{L}_{\mathsf{FLG}}} \times \wp(\Phi_{\mathscr{L}_{\mathsf{FLG}}}) \times \mathscr{U} \longrightarrow {}^*[0,1]$, where $^*[0,1]$ denotes the interval of *nonstandard reals in [0,1]* containing *infinitesimals*[7] in order to achieve the following two purposes:

1. In order to overcome Shortcoming 6 in Sect. 1,
2. In order to describe after-mentioned Conditions 15 (Diachronic Stability in Absolute Genericity) and 16 (Diachronic Stability in Relative Genericity).

Let $\mathscr{U}$ denote a set of *times*. Suppose that $\mathbf{P}_I^{(u)}$ satisfies not only Conditions 1–11 but also Conditions 14–16 below, for any $\varphi, \psi, \chi, \ldots \in \Phi_{\mathscr{L}_{\mathsf{FLG}}}$ and any $\Gamma \subset \wp(\Phi_{\mathscr{L}_{\mathsf{FLG}}})$; In any $(F_1, F_2, \ldots, F_m)$-membered superordinate predicate symbol $\tilde{F}_m$, $F_1, F_2, \ldots, F_m$ should be *jointly exhaustive* and *mutually exclusive*:

Condition 14 (($F_1, F_2, \ldots, F_m$)-Membered Superordinate Predicate Symbol $\tilde{F}_m$)
For any $u \in \mathscr{U}$ and for any $i, j \in \{1, 2, \ldots, m\}$,
$\mathbf{P}_I^{(u)}(\forall x((F_1(x) \vee F_2(x) \vee \cdots \vee F_m(x))$
$\leftrightarrow \tilde{F}_m(x)) \wedge \neg \exists x(F_i(x) \wedge F_j(x)), \Gamma) = 1.$

In Sect. 1 we summarized Cohen's distinction between absolute generics and relative generics. Cohen's theory has as an essential part Homogeneity that can bring the several shortcomings that were pointed out in Sect. 1. In place of Homogeneity, FLG has as semantically essential parts Diachronic Stability in Absolute Genericity and Diachronic Stability in Relative Genericity. The probabilistic relations that characterize absolute generics in Sect. 1 should be stable diachronically and formalized as follows:

Condition 15 (Diachronic Stability in Absolute Genericity)
$\mathbf{P}_I^{(u_1)}(\varphi \Rightarrow \psi, \Gamma) = 1$ for a particular $u_1 \in \mathscr{U}$
iff $\mathbf{P}_I^{(u)}(\varphi \rightarrow \psi, \Gamma) > \mathbf{P}_I^{(u)}(\varphi \rightarrow (\neg\psi \wedge \tilde{\psi}), \Gamma)$ for any $u \in \mathscr{U}$,
where $\tilde{\psi}$ is gained by substituting $\tilde{F}_m$ for each $F_{i \in \{1,2,\ldots,m\}}$ of ψ.

Remark 4 (Condition 15 and Triviality Result). *If we provide FLG with its classical-Bayesian semantics, then Condition 15 together with Stalnaker Thesis (Condition 4) can result in inviting the triviality result (Fact 1), whereas if we provide FLG with its intuitionistic-Bayesian semantics, Condition 15 together with Stalnaker Thesis cannot result in inviting the triviality result.*

Let us return to (3). Female and male chickens are almost as likely to be born. However, after a chick is found to be male, it is unfortunately customary to be killed and used as fertilizer and feedstock. As a result, over 80% of chickens become female. So according to Condition 15, (3) is a false absolute generic.

---

[7] For nonstandard probability theory, consult [14]. For the relation between epistemic modals and nonstandard probability theory, refer to [18].

Furthermore, the probabilistic relations that characterize relative generics in Sect. 1 also should be stable diachronically and formalized as follows:

> Condition 16 (Diachronic Stability in Relative Genericity)
> $\mathbf{P}_I^{(u_1)}(\varphi \Rightarrow \psi, \Gamma) = 1$ for a particular $u_1 \in \mathscr{U}$
> iff $\mathbf{P}_I^{(u)}(\varphi \rightarrow \psi, \Gamma) > \mathbf{P}_I^{(u)}(\tilde{\varphi} \rightarrow \psi, \Gamma)$ for any $u \in \mathscr{U}$,
> where $\tilde{\psi}$ is gained by substituting $\tilde{F}_m$ for each $F_{i \in \{1,2,\ldots,m\}}$ of ψ.

Remark 5 (Condition 16 and Triviality Result). *If we provide* FLG *with its classical-Bayesian semantics, then Condition 16 together with Stalnaker Thesis (Condition 4) can result in inviting the triviality result (Fact 1), whereas if we provide* FLG *with its intuitionistic-Bayesian semantics, Condition 16 together with Stalnaker Thesis cannot result in inviting the triviality result.*

According to Morgan and Mares [13], we define the semantic entailment $\Vdash_I^u$ relative to $u \in \mathscr{U}$ as follows:

Definition 3 ($\Vdash_I^u$). *Let Γ denote the finite set of well-formed formulae in $\mathscr{L}_{\mathsf{FLG}}$ and let φ denote a well-formed formula in $\mathscr{L}_{\mathsf{FLG}}$. Then*

$$\Gamma \Vdash_{\mathsf{FLG}}^{\mathbf{P}_I^{(u)}} \varphi$$
iff $\mathbf{P}_I^{(u)}(\varphi, \Gamma \cup \Delta) = 1$ for a particular $\mathbf{P}_I$-part of $\mathbf{P}_I^{(u)}$ and any $\Delta \subset \wp(\Phi_{\mathscr{L}_{\mathsf{FLG}}})$.

$$\Gamma \Vdash_{\mathsf{FLG}}^u \varphi$$
iff $\mathbf{P}_I^{(u)}(\varphi, \Gamma \cup \Delta) = 1$ for any $\mathbf{P}_I$-part of $\mathbf{P}_I^{(u)}$ and any $\Delta \subset \wp(\Phi_{\mathscr{L}_{\mathsf{FLG}}})$.

5.3 FLG-Logical Forms of Generics and Their Truth Conditions

Let us return to (1) [Dogs bark.]. Let $D(x)$ denote 'x is a dog', $V_1(x)$ 'x barks', $\tilde{V}_m$ ($V_1, V_2, \ldots, V_m$)-membered superordinate predicate symbol of $V_{i \in \{1,2,\ldots,m\}}$. Then the FLG-logical form of (1) is as follows:

$$(11) \quad \forall x (D(x) \Rightarrow V_1(x)).$$

On the basis of Condition 14 (($F_1, F_2, \ldots, F_m$)-Membered Superordinate Predicate Symbol $\tilde{F}_m$) and Condition 15 (Diachronic Stability in Absolute Genericity), we give the truth condition of the FLG-logical form of an absolute generic (1) by the Stalnaker Thesis without inviting the triviality result:

Proposition 1 (Truth Condition of (11)).

$$\Gamma \Vdash_{\mathsf{FLG}}^{\mathbf{P}_I^{(u_1)}} \forall x (D(x) \Rightarrow V_1(x))$$
for a particular $\mathbf{P}_I^{(u_1)}$ and a particular $\Gamma \subset \wp(\Phi_{\mathscr{L}_{\mathsf{FLG}}})$
iff for any $u \in \mathscr{U}$,
$$\lim_{n \to \infty} ((\mathbf{P}_I^{(u)}(V_1(t_1), \{D(t_1)\} \cup \Gamma) > \mathbf{P}_I^{(u)}(\neg V_1(t_1) \wedge \tilde{V}_m(t_1), \{D(t_1)\} \cup \Gamma))$$ *and*
$$(\mathbf{P}_I^{(u)}(V_1(t_2), \{D(t_2)\} \cup \Gamma) > \mathbf{P}_I^{(u)}(\neg V_1(t_2) \wedge \tilde{V}_m(t_2), \{D(t_2)\} \cup \Gamma))$$ *and $\cdots$ and*
$$(\mathbf{P}_I^{(u)}(V_1(t_n), \{D(t_n)\} \cup \Gamma) > \mathbf{P}_I^{(u)}(\neg V_1(t_n) \wedge \tilde{V}_m(t_n), \{D(t_n)\} \cup \Gamma))).$$

Proof.

$\Gamma \Vdash_{\mathsf{FLG}}^{\mathbf{P}_I^{(u_1)}} \forall x(D(x) \Rightarrow V_1(x))$

iff $\mathbf{P}_I^{(u_1)}(\forall x(D(x) \Rightarrow V_1(x), \Gamma) = 1$

iff $\lim\limits_{n\to\infty}(\mathbf{P}_I^{(u_1)}((D(t_1) \Rightarrow V_1(t_1))$

$\wedge(D(t_2) \Rightarrow V_1(t_2)) \wedge \cdots \wedge (D(t_n) \Rightarrow V_1(t_n)), \Gamma)) = 1$

iff $\lim\limits_{n\to\infty}((\mathbf{P}_I^{(u_1)}(D(t_1) \Rightarrow V_1(t_1), \Gamma) = 1)$ and $(\mathbf{P}_I^{(u_1)}(D(t_2) \Rightarrow V_1(t_2), \Gamma) = 1)$

and $\cdots$ and $(\mathbf{P}_I^{(u_1)}(D(t_n) \Rightarrow V_1(t_n), \Gamma) = 1))$

iff for any $u \in \mathscr{U}$,

$\lim\limits_{n\to\infty}((\mathbf{P}_I^{(u)}(D(t_1) \to V_1(t_1), \Gamma) > \mathbf{P}_I^{(u)}(D(t_1) \to (\neg V_1(t_1) \wedge \tilde{V}_m(t_1)), \Gamma))$ and

$(\mathbf{P}_I^{(u)}(D(t_2) \to V_1(t_2), \Gamma) > \mathbf{P}_I^{(u)}(D(t_2) \to (\neg V_1(t_2) \wedge \tilde{V}_m(t_2)), \Gamma))$ and $\cdots$ and

$(\mathbf{P}_I^{(u)}(D(t_n) \to V_1(t_n), \Gamma) > \mathbf{P}_I^{(u)}(D(t_n) \to (\neg V_1(t_n) \wedge \tilde{V}_m(t_n)), \Gamma)))$

iff for any $u \in \mathscr{U}$, for any $\mathbf{P}_I^{(u)}$,

$\lim\limits_{n\to\infty}((\mathbf{P}_I^{(u)}(V_1(t_1), \{D(t_1)\} \cup \Gamma) > \mathbf{P}_I^{(u)}(\neg V_1(t_1) \wedge \tilde{V}_m(t_1), \{D(t_1)\} \cup \Gamma))$ and

$(\mathbf{P}_I^{(u)}(V_1(t_2), \{D(t_2)\} \cup \Gamma) > \mathbf{P}_I^{(u)}(\neg V_1(t_2) \wedge \tilde{V}_m(t_2), \{D(t_2)\} \cup \Gamma))$ and $\cdots$ and

$(\mathbf{P}_I^{(u)}(V_1(t_n), \{D(t_n)\} \cup \Gamma) > \mathbf{P}_I^{(u)}(\neg V_1(t_n) \wedge \tilde{V}_m(t_n), \{D(t_n)\} \cup \Gamma)))$. ∎

Let us return to (2) [Mosquitoes carry the West Nile Virus.]. Let $I_1(x)$ denote 'x is a mosquito', $C(x, y)$ 'x carries y', w the West Nile Virus, $\tilde{I}_m$ ($I_1, I_2, \ldots, m$)-membered superordinate predicate symbol of $I_{i\in\{1,2,\ldots,m\}}$. Then the FLG-logical form of (2) is as follows:

$$(12) \quad \forall x(I_1(x) \Rightarrow C(x, w)).$$

On the basis of Condition 14 $((F_1, F_2, \ldots, F_m)$-Membered Superordinate Predicate Symbol $\tilde{F}_m)$ and Condition 16 (Diachronic Stability in Relative Genericity), we give the truth condition of the FLG-logical form of a relative generic (2) by the Stalnaker Thesis without inviting the triviality result:

Proposition 2 (Truth Condition of (12)).

$\Gamma \Vdash_{\mathsf{FLG}}^{\mathbf{P}_I^{(u_1)}} \forall x(I_1(x) \Rightarrow C(x, w))$

for a particular $\mathbf{P}_I^{(u_1)}$ *and a particular* $\Gamma \subset \wp(\Phi_{\mathscr{L}_{\mathsf{FLG}}})$

iff for any $u \in \mathscr{U}$,

$\lim\limits_{n\to\infty}((\mathbf{P}_I^{(u)}(C(t_1, w), \{I_1(t_1)\} \cup \Gamma) > \mathbf{P}_I^{(u)}(C(t_1, w), \{\tilde{I}_m(t_1)\} \cup \Gamma))$ *and*

$(\mathbf{P}_I^{(u)}(C(t_2, w), \{I_1(t_2)\} \cup \Gamma) > \mathbf{P}_I^{(u)}(C(t_2, w), \{\tilde{I}_m(t_2)\} \cup \Gamma))$ *and* $\cdots$ *and*

$(\mathbf{P}_I^{(u)}(C(t_n, w), \{I_1(t_n)\} \cup \Gamma) > \mathbf{P}_I^{(u)}(C(t_n, w), \{\tilde{I}_m(t_n)\} \cup \Gamma)))$.

Proof.

$\Gamma \Vdash_{\mathsf{FLG}}^{\mathbf{P}_I^{(u_1)}} \forall x (I_1(x) \Rightarrow C(x, w))$

iff $\quad \mathbf{P}_I^{(u_1)}(\forall x(I_1(x) \Rightarrow C(x, w), \Gamma) = 1$

iff $\quad \lim_{n \to \infty} (\mathbf{P}_I^{(u_1)}((I_1(t_1) \Rightarrow C(t_1, w)) \wedge (I_1(t_2) \Rightarrow C(t_2, w))$

$\wedge \cdots \wedge (I_1(t_n) \Rightarrow C(t_n, w)), \Gamma)) = 1$

iff $\quad \lim_{n \to \infty} ((\mathbf{P}_I^{(u_1)}(I_1(t_1) \Rightarrow C(t_1, w), \Gamma) = 1)$

and $(\mathbf{P}_I^{(u_1)}(I_1(t_2) \Rightarrow C(t_2, w), \Gamma) = 1)$

and $\cdots$ and $(\mathbf{P}_I^{(u_1)}(I_1(t_n) \Rightarrow C(t_n, w), \Gamma) = 1))$

iff $\quad$ for any $u \in \mathscr{U}$,

$\lim_{n \to \infty} ((\mathbf{P}_I^{(u)}(I_1(t_1) \to C(t_1, w), \Gamma) > \mathbf{P}_I^{(u)}(\tilde{I}_m(t_1) \to C(t_1, w), \Gamma))$ and

$(\mathbf{P}_I^{(u)}(I_1(t_2) \to C(t_2, w), \Gamma) > \mathbf{P}_I^{(u)}(\tilde{I}_m(t_2) \to C(t_2, w), \Gamma))$ and $\cdots$ and

$(\mathbf{P}_I^{(u)}(I_1(t_n) \to C(t_n, w), \Gamma) > \mathbf{P}_I^{(u)}(\tilde{I}_m(t_n) \to C(t_n, w), \Gamma)))$

iff $\quad$ for any $u \in \mathscr{U}$, for any $\mathbf{P}_I^{(u)}$,

$\lim_{n \to \infty} ((\mathbf{P}_I^{(u)}(C(t_1, w), \{I_1(t_1)\} \cup \Gamma) > \mathbf{P}_I^{(u)}(C(t_1, w), \{\tilde{I}_m(t_1)\} \cup \Gamma))$ and

$(\mathbf{P}_I^{(u)}(C(t_2, w), \{I_1(t_2)\} \cup \Gamma) > \mathbf{P}_I^{(u)}(C(t_2, w), \{\tilde{I}_m(t_2)\} \cup \Gamma))$ and $\cdots$ and

$(\mathbf{P}_I^{(u)}(C(t_n, w), \{I_1(t_n)\} \cup \Gamma) > \mathbf{P}_I^{(u)}(C(t_n, w), \{\tilde{I}_m(t_n)\} \cup \Gamma)))$. $\blacksquare$

Next we would like to consider embedded generics. (13) is an example of an embedded generic provided by Asher and Pelletier [1, p. 318] :

(13)   People who go to bed late don't get up early.

(13) is considered to express a high probabilistic relation between an object being a member of people and going to bed late and it not getting up early. Let $P(x)$ denote 'x is a member of people', $L(x)$ 'x goes to bed late', $G_1(x)$ 'x gets up early' and $\tilde{G}_m$ $(G_1, G_2, \ldots, G_m)$-membered superordinate predicate symbol of $G_{i \in \{1,2,\ldots,m\}}$. Then the FLG-logical form of (13) is as follows:

$$(14) \quad \forall x ((P(x) \wedge L(x)) \Rightarrow \neg G_1(x)).$$

On the basis of Condition 14 $((F_1, F_2, \ldots, F_m)$-Membered Superordinate Predicate Symbol $\tilde{F}_m)$ and Condition 15 (Diachronic Stability in Absolute Genericity), we give the truth condition of the FLG-logical form of an embedded generic (13) by the Stalnaker Thesis without inviting the triviality result:

Proposition 3 (Truth Condition of (14)).

$$\Gamma \Vdash_{\mathsf{FLG}}^{\mathbf{P}_I^{(u_1)}} \forall x((P(x) \wedge L(x)) \Rightarrow \neg G_1(x))$$

for a particular $\mathbf{P}_I^{(u_1)}$ *and a particular* $\Gamma \subset \wp(\Phi_{\mathscr{L}_{\mathsf{FLG}}})$

iff for any $u \in \mathscr{U}$,

$$\lim_{n \to \infty} ((\mathbf{P}_I^{(u)}(\neg G_1(t_1), \{P(t_1), L(t_1)\} \cup \Gamma)$$
$$> \mathbf{P}_I^{(u)}(\neg\neg G_1(t_1) \wedge \tilde{G}_m(t_1), \{P(t_1), L(t_1)\} \cup \Gamma)) \text{ and}$$
$$(\mathbf{P}_I^{(u)}(\neg G_1(t_2), \{P(t_2), L(t_2)\} \cup \Gamma)$$
$$> \mathbf{P}_I^{(u)}(\neg\neg G_1(t_2) \wedge \tilde{G}_m(t_2), \{P(t_2), L(t_2)\} \cup \Gamma)) \text{ and} \cdots \text{and}$$
$$(\mathbf{P}_I^{(u)}(\neg G_1(t_n), \{P(t_n), L(t_n)\} \cup \Gamma)$$
$$> \mathbf{P}_I^{(u)}(\neg\neg G_1(t_n) \wedge \tilde{G}_m(t_n), \{P(t_n), L(t_n)\} \cup \Gamma))).$$

Proof.

$$\Gamma \Vdash_{\mathsf{FLG}}^{\mathbf{P}_I^{(u_1)}} \forall x((P(x) \wedge L(x)) \Rightarrow \neg G_1(x))$$

iff $\mathbf{P}_I^{(u_1)}(\forall x((P(x) \wedge L(x)) \Rightarrow \neg G_1(x)), \Gamma) = 1$

iff $\lim\limits_{n \to \infty} (\mathbf{P}_I^{(u_1)}((((P(t_1) \wedge L(t_1)) \Rightarrow \neg G_1(t_1)) \wedge ((P(t_2) \wedge L(t_2)) \Rightarrow \neg G_1(t_2))$

$\wedge \cdots \wedge ((P(t_n) \wedge L(t_n)) \Rightarrow \neg G_1(t_n)), \Gamma)) = 1$

iff $\lim\limits_{n \to \infty} ((\mathbf{P}_I^{(u_1)}((P(t_1) \wedge L(t_1)) \Rightarrow \neg G_1(t_1), \Gamma) = 1)$

and $(\mathbf{P}_I^{(u_1)}((P(t_2) \wedge L(t_2)) \Rightarrow \neg G_1(t_2), \Gamma) = 1)$

and $\cdots$ and $(\mathbf{P}_I^{(u_1)}((P(t_n) \wedge L(t_n)) \Rightarrow \neg G_1(t_n), \Gamma) = 1))$

iff   for any $u \in \mathscr{U}$,

$\lim\limits_{n \to \infty} ((\mathbf{P}_I^{(u)}((P(t_1) \wedge L(t_1)) \to \neg G_1(t_1), \Gamma)$

$> \mathbf{P}_I^{(u)}((P(t_1) \wedge L(t_1)) \to (\neg\neg G_1(t_1) \wedge \tilde{G}_m(t_1)), \Gamma)) \text{ and}$

$(\mathbf{P}_I^{(u)}((P(t_2) \wedge L(t_2)) \to \neg G_1(t_2), \Gamma)$

$> \mathbf{P}_I^{(u)}((P(t_2) \wedge L(t_2)) \to (\neg\neg G_1(t_2) \wedge \tilde{G}_m(t_2)), \Gamma)) \text{ and} \cdots \text{and}$

$(\mathbf{P}_I^{(u)}((P(t_n) \wedge L(t_n)) \to \neg G_1(t_n), \Gamma)$

$> \mathbf{P}_I^{(u)}((P(t_n) \wedge L(t_n)) \to (\neg\neg G_1(t_n) \wedge \tilde{G}_m(t_n)), \Gamma)))$

iff   for any $u \in \mathscr{U}$,

$\lim\limits_{n \to \infty} ((\mathbf{P}_I^{(u)}(\neg G_1(t_1), \{P(t_1), L(t_1)\} \cup \Gamma)$

$> \mathbf{P}_I^{(u)}(\neg\neg G_1(t_1) \wedge \tilde{G}_m(t_1), \{P(t_1), L(t_1)\} \cup \Gamma)) \text{ and}$

$(\mathbf{P}_I^{(u)}(\neg G_1(t_2), \{P(t_2), L(t_2)\} \cup \Gamma)$

$> \mathbf{P}_I^{(u)}(\neg\neg G_1(t_2) \wedge \tilde{G}_m(t_2), \{P(t_2), L(t_2)\} \cup \Gamma)) \text{ and} \cdots \text{and}$

$(\mathbf{P}_I^{(u)}(\neg G_1(t_n), \{P(t_n), L(t_n)\} \cup \Gamma)$

$> \mathbf{P}_I^{(u)}(\neg\neg G_1(t_n) \wedge \tilde{G}_m(t_n), \{P(t_n), L(t_n)\} \cup \Gamma)))$.   ∎

(15) is another example of an embedded generic provided by Asher and Pelletier [1, p. 318] :

(15)   Dogs chase cats that chase mice.

(15) is considered to express a high probabilistic relation between the first being a dog and the second being a cat and the third being a mouse and the first chasing the second and the second chasing the third. Let $D(x)$ denote 'x is a dog', $C(x)$ 'x is a cat', $M(x)$ 'x is a mouse', $O_1(x,y)$ 'x chases y', and $\tilde{O}_k$ $(O_1, O_2, \ldots, O_k)$-membered superordinate predicate symbol of $O_{i \in \{1,2,\ldots,k\}}$. Then the FLG-logical form of (15) is as follows:

$$(16) \quad \forall x \forall y \forall z ((D(x) \wedge C(y) \wedge M(z)) \Rightarrow (O_1(x,y) \wedge O_1(y,z))).$$

On the basis of Condition 14 ($(F_1, F_2, \ldots, F_m)$-Membered Superordinate Predicate Symbol $\tilde{F}_m$) and Condition 15 (Diachronic Stability in Absolute Genericity), we give the truth condition of the FLG-logical form of another embedded generic (15) by the Stalnaker Thesis without inviting the triviality result:

Proposition 4 (Truth Condition of (16)).

$\Gamma \Vdash_{\mathsf{FLG}}^{\mathbf{P}_I^{(u_1)}} \forall x \forall y \forall z ((D(x) \wedge C(y) \wedge M(z)) \Rightarrow (O_1(x,y) \wedge O_1(y,z)))$
for a particular $\mathbf{P}_I^{(u_1)}$ *and a particular* $\Gamma \subset \wp(\Phi_{\mathscr{L}_{\mathsf{FLG}}})$
iff   for any $u \in \mathscr{U}$,
$\lim_{l \to \infty} \lim_{m \to \infty} \lim_{n \to \infty} ((\mathbf{P}_I^{(u)}(O_1(r_1,s_1) \wedge O_1(s_1,t_1), \{D(r_1), C(s_1), M(t_1)\} \cup \Gamma) >$
$\mathbf{P}_I^{(u)}(\neg(O_1(r_1,s_1) \wedge O_1(s_1,t_1)) \wedge (\tilde{O}_k(r_1,s_1) \wedge \tilde{O}_k(s_1,t_1)),$
$\{D(r_1), C(t_1), M(t_1)\} \cup \Gamma))$
and $\cdots$ *and* $(\mathbf{P}_I^{(u)}(O_1(r_1,s_1) \wedge O_1(s_1,t_n), \{D(r_1), C(s_1), M(t_n)\} \cup \Gamma) >$
$\mathbf{P}_I^{(u)}(\neg(O_1(r_1,s_1) \wedge O_1(s_1,t_n)) \wedge (\tilde{O}_k(r_1,s_1) \wedge \tilde{O}_k(s_1,t_n)),$
$\{D(r_1), C(t_1), M(t_n)\} \cup \Gamma))$
and $\cdots$ *and* $(\mathbf{P}_I^{(u)}(O_1(r_l,s_m) \wedge O_1(s_m,t_n), \{D(r_l), C(s_m), M(t_n)\} \cup \Gamma) >$
$\mathbf{P}_I^{(u)}(\neg(O_1(r_l,s_m) \wedge O_1(s_m,t_n)) \wedge (\tilde{O}_k(r_l,s_m) \wedge \tilde{O}_k(s_m,t_n)),$
$\{D(r_l), C(t_m), M(t_n)\} \cup \Gamma)))$.

Proof.

$\Gamma \Vdash_{\mathsf{FLG}}^{\mathbf{P}_I^{(u_1)}} \forall x \forall y \forall z ((D(x) \wedge C(y) \wedge M(z)) \Rightarrow (O_1(x,y) \wedge O_1(y,z)))$
iff $\mathbf{P}_I^{(u_1)}(\forall x \forall y \forall z ((D(x) \wedge C(y) \wedge M(z)) \Rightarrow (O_1(x,y) \wedge O_1(y,z))), \Gamma) = 1$
iff $\lim_{n \to \infty} (\mathbf{P}_I^{(u_1)}(\forall y \forall z ((D(r_1) \wedge C(y) \wedge M(z)) \Rightarrow (O_1(r_1,y) \wedge O_1(y,z)))$
$\wedge \forall y \forall z ((D(r_2) \wedge C(y) \wedge M(z)) \Rightarrow (O_1(r_2,y) \wedge O_1(y,z)))$
$\wedge \cdots \wedge \forall y \forall z ((D(r_n) \wedge C(y) \wedge M(z)) \Rightarrow (O_1(t_l,y) \wedge O_1(y,z))), \Gamma)) = 1$
iff $\lim_{l \to \infty} \lim_{m \to \infty} \lim_{n \to \infty} (\mathbf{P}_I^{(u_1)}(((D(r_1) \wedge C(s_1) \wedge M(t_1))$
$\Rightarrow (O_1(r_1,s_1) \wedge O_1(s_1,t_1))) \wedge \cdots \wedge$
$((D(r_1) \wedge C(s_1) \wedge M(t_n)) \Rightarrow (O_1(r_1,s_1) \wedge O_1(s_1,t_n))) \wedge \cdots \wedge$
$((D(r_1) \wedge C(s_m) \wedge M(t_1)) \Rightarrow (O_1(r_1,s_m) \wedge O_1(s_m,t_1))) \wedge \cdots \wedge$
$((D(r_1) \wedge C(s_m) \wedge M(t_n)) \Rightarrow (O_1(r_1,s_m) \wedge O_1(s_m,t_n))) \wedge \cdots \wedge$
$((D(r_l) \wedge C(s_1) \wedge M(t_1)) \Rightarrow (O_1(r_l,s_1) \wedge O_1(s_1,t_1))) \wedge \cdots \wedge$
$((D(r_l) \wedge C(s_1) \wedge M(t_n)) \Rightarrow (O_1(r_l,s_1) \wedge O_1(s_1,t_n))) \wedge \cdots \wedge$
$((D(r_l) \wedge C(s_m) \wedge M(t_1)) \Rightarrow (O_1(r_l,s_m) \wedge O_1(s_m,t_1))) \wedge \cdots \wedge$
$((D(r_l) \wedge C(s_m) \wedge M(t_n)) \Rightarrow (O_1(r_l,s_m) \wedge O_1(s_m,t_n))), \Gamma)) = 1$

iff $\lim\limits_{l\to\infty}\lim\limits_{m\to\infty}\lim\limits_{n\to\infty}((\mathbf{P}_I^{(u_1)}((D(r_1)\wedge C(s_1)\wedge M(t_1))$

$\Rightarrow (O_1(r_1,s_1)\wedge O_1(s_1,t_1)),\Gamma)=1)$

and $\cdots$ and $(\mathbf{P}_I^{(u_1)}((D(r_1)\wedge C(s_1)\wedge M(t_n))$

$\Rightarrow (O_1(r_1,s_1)\wedge O_1(s_1,t_n)),\Gamma)=1)$

and $\cdots$ and $(\mathbf{P}_I^{(u_1)}((D(r_l)\wedge C(s_m)\wedge M(t_n))$

$\Rightarrow (O_1(r_l,s_m)\wedge O_1(s_m,t_n)),\Gamma)=1))$

iff   for any $u\in\mathscr{U}$,

$\lim\limits_{l\to\infty}\lim\limits_{m\to\infty}\lim\limits_{n\to\infty}((\mathbf{P}_I^{(u)}((D(r_1)\wedge C(s_1)\wedge M(t_1))$

$\to (O_1(r_1,s_1)\wedge O_1(s_1,t_1)),\Gamma)$

$> \mathbf{P}_I^{(u)}((D(r_1)\wedge C(s_1)\wedge M(t_1))$

$\to (\neg(O_1(r_1,s_1)\wedge O_1(s_1,t_1))\wedge (\tilde{O}_k(r_1,s_1)\wedge \tilde{O}_k(s_1,t_1))),\Gamma))$

and $\cdots$ and $(\mathbf{P}_I^{(u)}((D(r_1)\wedge C(s_1)\wedge M(t_n))\to (O_1(r_1,s_1)\wedge O_1(s_1,t_n)),\Gamma)$

$> \mathbf{P}_I^{(u)}((D(r_1)\wedge C(s_1)\wedge M(t_n))$

$\to (\neg(O_1(r_1,s_1)\wedge O_1(s_1,t_n))\wedge (\tilde{O}_k(r_1,s_1)\wedge \tilde{O}_k(s_1,t_n))),\Gamma))$

and $\cdots$ and $(\mathbf{P}_I^{(u)}((D(r_l)\wedge C(s_m)\wedge M(t_n))\to (O_1(r_l,s_m)\wedge O_1(s_m,t_n)),\Gamma)$

$> \mathbf{P}_I^{(u)}((D(r_l)\wedge C(s_m)\wedge M(t_n))$

$\to (\neg(O_1(r_l,s_m)\wedge O_1(s_m,t_n))\wedge (\tilde{O}_k(r_l,s_m)\wedge \tilde{O}_k(r_l,s_m))),\Gamma)))$

iff   for any $u\in\mathscr{U}$,

$\lim\limits_{l\to\infty}\lim\limits_{m\to\infty}\lim\limits_{n\to\infty}((\mathbf{P}_I^{(u)}(O_1(r_1,s_1)\wedge O_1(s_1,t_1),\{D(r_1),C(s_1),M(t_1)\}\cup\Gamma)>$

$\mathbf{P}_I^{(u)}(\neg(O_1(r_1,s_1)\wedge O_1(s_1,t_1))\wedge (\tilde{O}_k(r_1,s_1)\wedge \tilde{O}_k(s_1,t_1)),$

$\{D(r_1),C(t_1),M(t_1)\}\cup\Gamma))$

and $\cdots$ and $(\mathbf{P}_I^{(u)}(O_1(r_1,s_1)\wedge O_1(s_1,t_n),\{D(r_1),C(s_1),M(t_n)\}\cup\Gamma)>$

$\mathbf{P}_I^{(u)}(\neg(O_1(r_1,s_1)\wedge O_1(s_1,t_n))\wedge (\tilde{O}_k(r_1,s_1)\wedge \tilde{O}_k(s_1,t_n)),$

$\{D(r_1),C(t_1),M(t_n)\}\cup\Gamma))$

and $\cdots$ and $(\mathbf{P}_I^{(u)}(O_1(r_l,s_m)\wedge O_1(s_m,t_n),\{D(r_l),C(s_m),M(t_n)\}\cup\Gamma)>$

$\mathbf{P}_I^{(u)}(\neg(O_1(r_l,s_m)\wedge O_1(s_m,t_n))\wedge (\tilde{O}_k(r_l,s_m)\wedge \tilde{O}_k(s_m,t_n)),$

$\{D(r_l),C(t_m),M(t_n)\}\cup\Gamma)))$.   ∎

6   Some Remarks on Overcoming of Shortcomings by Means of **FLG**

We summarize the ways of overcoming the eight shortcomings by means of FLG:

– **Shortcoming 1**: According to Leslie [8,9], Shortcoming 1 results from Homogeneity that is an essential part of Cohen's theory. We do not that this analysis
is correct. By means of FLG, we give the reason why it is not correct. In FLG,
let $M(x)$ denote 'x is male', $L(x)$ 'x is a lion', $S_1(x)$ 'x has manes', and $\tilde{S}_m$
$(S_1,S_2\ldots,S_m)$-membered superordinate predicate symbol of $S_{i\in\{1,2,\ldots,m\}}$.
Then whether the FLG-logical form of (4) is (17) or (18) is determined not
semantically in FLG *but pragmatically out of* FLG:

$$(17)\quad \forall x(L(x)\Rightarrow S_1(x)).$$

$$(18) \quad \forall x((M(x) \wedge L(x)) \Rightarrow S_1(x)).$$

It is determined pragmatically that FLG-logical form of (4) is (18). Then, according to Condition 15, (18) is a true absolute generic. If (18) is considered to be a logical form of (4) in Cohen's theory, then (18) is a true absolute generic, too.

- **Shortcoming 2**: We agree that Shortcoming 2 results from Homogeneity in Cohen's theory. On the other hand, the semantics of FLG does not requires Homogeneity. According to the *Diachronic Stability in Absolute Genericity (Condition 15)*, (5) is a *true* absolute generic in FLG.
- **Shortcoming 3**: We do not share with Leslie the intuition that (2) would remain true in the changed situation. We can explain our position in terms of the *Diachronic Stability in Relative Genericity (Condition 16)*. The truth of (2) in FLG requires Condition 16. But the changed situation would cause a violation of Condition 16.
- **Shortcoming 4**: The mere fact that 50.05% of cats have tails at a *particular time* is not sufficient to guarantee that (6) is true in FLG. For the truth of (6) in FLG requires the *Diachronic Stability in Absolute Genericity (Condition 15)* that is a much stronger condition than the fact above.
- **Shortcoming 5**: In FLG, it is clear how to adapt the semantics (i.e., *intuitionistic-Bayesian semantics*) to capture uncertain inference.
- **Shortcoming 6**: We have introduced *nonstandard probabilities* into the semantics of FLG.
- **Shortcoming 7**: As Szabó [19] argues, the most widely known objection to compositionality comes from Frege's Puzzle dealt in Sect. 2: Even if e and e' are synonyms, the truth values of sentences where they occur embedded within the clausal complement of a mental attitude verb may well differ. So we have a case of apparent violation of compositionality. Some (e.g., [5,16] and [6]) give up compositionality, but still provide *recursive* semantic clauses. In the semantics of FLG, we takes this line.
- **Shortcoming 8**: We have provided embedded generics (13) and (15) with their truth conditions in terms of FLG.

7 Concluding Remarks

In this paper we have proposed a new version of logic for generics—First-Order Logic for Generics (FLG)—that can overcome all of the eight shortcomings of Cohen's theory pointed out by Leslie [8,9] and Asher and Pelletier [1]. To accomplish this goal, we have provided the language of FLG with an intuitionistic-Bayesian semantics.

Acknowledgements. The author would like to thank three anonymous reviewers of CLAR 2020 for their very helpful comments.

References

1. Asher, N., Pelletier, F.J.: More truths about generic truth. In: Mari, A., et al. (eds.) Genericity, pp. 312–333. Oxford University Press, Oxford (2013)
2. Cohen, A.: Generics, frequency adverbs, and probability. Linguist. Philos. **22**, 221–253 (1999)
3. Field, H.H.: Logic, meaning, and conceptual role. J. Philos. **74**, 379–409 (1977)
4. Harman, G.: Meaning and semantics. In: Munitz, M.K., Unger, P.K. (eds.) Semantics and Philosophy, pp. 1–16. New York University Press, New York (1974)
5. Higginbotham, J.: Linguistic theory and Davidson's program. In: LePore, E. (ed.) Truth and Interpretation: Perspectives on the Philosophy of Donald Davidson, pp. 29–48. Blackwell, Oxford (1986)
6. Larson, R.K., Ludlow, P.: Interpreted logical forms. Synthese **95**, 305–355 (1993)
7. Leblanc, H.: Probabilistic semantics for first-order logic. Math. Logic Q. **25**, 497–509 (1979)
8. Leslie, S.J.: Generics and the structure of the mind. Philos. Perspect. **21**, 375–403 (2007)
9. Leslie, S.J.: Generics and the structure of the mind. Philos. Rev. **117**, 1–47 (2008)
10. Lewis, D.: Probabilities of conditionals and conditional probabilities. Philos. Rev. **85**, 297–315 (1976)
11. Lewis, D.: Probabilities of conditionals and conditional probabilities II. Philos. Rev. **95**, 581–589 (1986)
12. Mogan, C.G., Leblanc, H.: Probabilistic semantics for intuitionistic logic. Notre Dame J. Formal Logic **24**, 161–180 (1983)
13. Mogan, C.G., Mares, E.D.: Conditionals, probability, and non-triviality. J. Philos. Logic **24**, 455–467 (1995). https://doi.org/10.1007/BF01052599
14. Narens, L.: Theories of Probability. World Scientific, Singapore (2007)
15. Ramsey, F.P.: General propositions and causality. In: Mellor, D.H. (ed.) F. P. Ramsey: Philosophical Papers, pp. 145–163. Cambridge University Press, Cambridge (1990). Completed in 1929
16. Segal, G.: A preference for sense and reference. J. Philos. **86**, 73–89 (1989)
17. Stalnaker, R.C.: Probability and conditionals. Philos. Sci. **37**, 64–80 (1970)
18. Suzuki, S.: Epistemic modals, qualitative probability, and nonstandard probability. In: Aloni, M., et al. (eds.) Proceedings of the 19th Amsterdam Colloquium (AC 2013), pp. 211–218 (2013)
19. Szabó, Z.G.: Compositionality. Stanford Encyclopedia of Philosophy (2012)
20. Weatherson, B.: From classical to intuitionistic probability. Notre Dame J. Formal Logic **44**, 111–123 (2003)

Ambiguity Preference and Context Learning in Uncertain Signaling

Liping Tang[✉]

Institute of Logic and Cognition, Department of Philosophy,
Sun Yat-sen University, Guangzhou, China
tanglp3@mail.sysu.edu.cn

Abstract. Lexical ambiguity is present in many natural languages, but ambiguous words and phrases do not seem to be advantageous. Therefore, the presence of ambiguous words in natural language warrants explanation. We justify the existence of ambiguity from the perspective of the context dependence. The main contribution of the paper is that we constructed a context learning process such that the interlocutors can infer opponent's private belief from the conversation. A sufficient condition is proved to show if the learning can be successful. Furthermore, we investigate when the learning fails, how the interlocutors choose among degrees of ambiguous expressions through an adaptive learning.

Keywords: Ambiguity · Context learning · Uncertain signaling · Reinforcement learning

1 Introduction

Natural language involves various kinds of uncertainties such as vagueness, synonymy and ambiguity. Among those uncertainties, lexical ambiguity is one of the most common features in language. Lexical ambiguity lies in the fact that a word could have more than one interpretations. For example, the word "mole" in English can be used to refer to "a dark spot on the skin", to "a burrowing mammal", to "a spy". In terms of information transaction, ambiguity does not seem an optimal choice. It is because the use of ambiguous expressions may cause the failure of information transaction and misunderstandings. We have not run out of possible words, why not invent a new word for any one of the meanings for ambiguous words? Therefore, the existence of ambiguous words needs an explanation.

In linguistics and game theory, many people have discussed this problem, and in most works, it is argued that being precise is expensive and unnecessary. Language, therefore, optimizes the balance of the benefits of precision with the costs of lexicon size (see Piantadosi et al. 2012; O'Connor 2014a; Santana 2014). The core of this argument relies on the fact that the context of the conversation can fill in information gaps left by ambiguity. According to Grice's cooperative principle (see Grice 1968) the conversational inference is based on the notion

M. Dastani et al. (Eds.): CLAR 2020, LNAI 12061, pp. 201–218, 2020.
https://doi.org/10.1007/978-3-030-44638-3_13

of common ground. From Stalnaker (2002), common ground is defined as the mutually recognized shared information in a situation where an act of trying to communicate takes place. In a conversation, common ground is treated as the conversational context, which plays an essential role in the pragmatic understanding of the language.

Furthermore, the influence of the context on the use of language depends on how much mutual information the interlocutors share and what kind of vocabularies is available. As the context gets clear, the more ambiguous word may be sufficient for transferring the information. However, it has not been fully investigated that where the context comes from and how the context affects the interlocutors' choice of words with different degrees of ambiguity.

The goal of this paper is to justify the existence of ambiguity from the perspective of the context dependence. We construct a context learning process in a signaing game for building the common ground of the conversation along the interactions. After that, the interlocutors' preferences of ambiguous words can be tracked as the context varies.

More specifically, we consider two interlocutors, a sender (S) and a receiver (R), are conducting a conversation for transferring information. They both have some personal beliefs about the communicating information. As the communication goes on, the interlocutors gradually infer the other's private belief from the result of each interaction. After repeated interactions, players are able to form a common ground, which serves as the context for the conversation. In addition, during the learning process, interlocutors' choices of ambiguous words may change as their beliefs about the context vary.

The following graph summarises the discussion above.

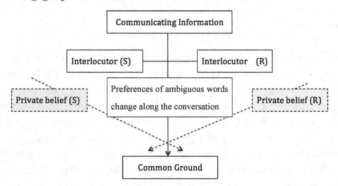

For implementing the idea above, we use Lewis's signaling game as our base model for the learning process (see Lewis 1969). Lewis's signaling game describes a very general communication scenario where a sender observes the situation (a state of the world) and then sends a signal to a receiver. The receiver takes an action based on the signal he receives. The payoff in the game depends on the state of the world and the action the receiver takes. The uncertainty of the signaling game comes from the receiver's ignorance of the true state. He can only obtain the information from the signals that the sender sends. The model has been widely used in exploring language communication (see O'Connor 2014b; Huttegger et al. 2010; Huttegger 2007; Zollman 2005; Jäger 2014).

Based on the Lewis's signaling game, we made two main changes to the model. The first change is to add players' private beliefs about the communicating information into the game. The second change is to expand the set of signals such that we can discuss ambiguous words with different degrees. With these two changes, we construct a context learning process through which the players are learning each other's beliefs during the repeated interactions. A sufficient condition is provided under which the learning is successful. After the players learned each other's private belief, they can form a mutual belief that serves as the common ground of the conversation. Furthermore, when the learning fails, though there is uncertainty about opponent's belief, we show that players still have a strong tendency to choose ambiguous expressions. We explore an uncertain signaling through the reinforcement learning mechanism.

The structure of the paper is the following. In Sect. 2, we first extend Lewis's signaling game such that each player has private belief about the communicating information. Then we discuss how players can learn opponent's private belief from the repeated communication. In Sect. 3, we establish a sufficient condition on the game under which the learning is successful. Under this condition, we discuss how the common ground of the conversation can be formed. In Sect. 4, we explore, when the learning fails, players' preferences of different ambiguous expressions through the reinforcement learning signaling. The paper ends with a comparison between our model and existing models on discussing uncertain signaling and pragmatic reasoning in conversation.

2 Signaling Game with Private Belief (SPB)

As the conversation goes, the interlocutors' beliefs about the communicating information change. For studying this dynamic process, we develop a new signaling game called signaling game with private belief (SPB). Based on Lewis's classical model, we assume that each player has private belief about the communicating information before the communication starts. Formally, we define players' private beliefs as partitions on the set of the states as follows.

Definition 1. *Given a set of finite states T, a private belief of player i indicated as B_i is defined as a partition on T. Each component of the belief partition is called an element of the partition that is indicated as $B_{ik}, k \in N$.*

When the game begins, nature reveals the information to the sender. At the same time, since the receiver has private information about the state, he is also aware of relative information about the true state[1]. The sender then sends a signal that carries information about the true state. By combining the signal information and his private information, the receiver takes an action that decides both players' benefits. Moreover, We argue that by observing the outcome of the game, the sender can possibly infer the receiver's private belief.

States and actions can have a broad interpretation. The most obvious way to understand them is that the state is some important fact about the outside

---
[1] Similar idea appeared in Santana (2014)'s work.

world and the action is some response to that fact. The state might be whether it is raining and the action might be to take an umbrella. But, the state might be something more internal, like the desire for the receiver to hold a certain belief. Similarly the action might be private, like coming to believe something.

Formally, SPB model is defined as follows.

Definition 2. *A signaling game with private belief (SPB) consists of the following parts:*

- *two players: player 1 and player 2;*
- *two roles: a sender and a receiver;*
- *a set of states $T : \{1, 2, \ldots, n\}$, each state is assumed to occur with the same probability.*
- *a set of possibly ambiguous signals S with conventional meanings;*
- *each player i has private belief B_i that is unknown to their opponents;*
- *a set of actions $\mathcal{A} : \{a_1, a_2, \ldots, a_n\}$;*
- *Sender's strategy is a function $f : T \to S$, the receiver's strategy is a function $g : S \times B_i \to \mathcal{P}(\mathcal{A}), i \in \{1, 2\}$, where $\mathcal{P}(\mathcal{A})$ is the power set on $\mathcal{A}$.*
- *A payoff function u for both players,*

$$u(t, A, B_{i \in \{1,2\}}) = \begin{cases} \frac{1}{|A|} & if a_t \in A, |A| \text{ represents the size of the set } A, \\ 0 & Otherwise. \end{cases}$$

where $t \in T$ and $A \in \mathcal{P}(\mathcal{A})$;

An example (Example 1) is provided below for illustrating the concepts of the game.

Example 1. The game consists of the following parts.

- Two players: player 1, player 2
- Two roles: a sender, a receiver
- A set of states $\{1, 2, 3, 4\}$ occuring with equal probability;
- A set of signals s_1, s_2 with commonly known conventional meanings (s_1 indicates the states $\{1, 2\}$, s_2 indicates the states $\{3, 4\}$).

$$1, 2 \| 3, 4$$
$$s_1 \| s_2$$

Since each signal can represent two different states, we say both signals are ambiguous. We use "$\|$" to indicate partitions on the meaning of signals and "$|$" to indicate the partitions of the private belief.

- Each player has a private belief about the states and does not know the opponent's belief. We assume that player 1's private belief is

$$1, 2 | 3, 4$$
$$B_{11} | B_{12}$$

which means that player 1 can distinguish $\{1,2\}$ from $\{3,4\}$ but not further. And player 2's private belief is

$$1|2,3,4$$

$$B_{21}|B_{22}$$

– A set of actions $\{a_1, a_2, a_3, a_4\}$

Firstly, we suppose that player 1 is the sender and player 2 is the receiver. Then, for each possible state, the game is played as follows.

Table 1. Play of the game in Example 1 (1)

State	Signal	Revealed information	Receiver's reasoning	Payoff
1	s_1	B_{21}	$B_{21} \cap s_1$	1
2	s_1	B_{22}	$B_{22} \cap s_1$	1
3	s_2	B_{22}	$B_{22} \cap s_2$	1/2
4	s_2	B_{22}	$B_{22} \cap s_2$	1/2

Table 1 shows for each state, what signal the sender sends, how the receiver reasons and what the outcome of the game is. For instance, the first row indicates that when state 1 occurs, the sender sends signal s_1. The receiver reads the information from the signal that is $\{1,2\}$, then combines it with his private belief B_{21} that is $\{1\}$, which yields the information $\{1\}$. Because $\{1\}$ is precise, the receiver is able to take the correct action which guarantees the best payoff for both players. In this example, the result holds trivially because the receiver's private belief already reveals the precise state information even without the information from the sender. Since the sender does not know the receiver's private belief, he sends the ambiguous signal anyway. But in row 3, the outcome information is $\{3,4\}$, which yields the finer information than the receiver's private belief. Hence, combining personal belief and signal information is essential in this case.

After communicating repeatedly, player 1 (sender) is able to infer player 2's (receiver) private belief by comparing the differences between the outcomes resulting from his inference and the actual outcome of the game. Player 1's inference about player 2's private belief with respect to Table 1 can be described as follows. For simplicity, we assume that both players know that players' belief partition contains two elements[2]. At each stage of the inference, from the sender's point of view, all the possible configurations of the receiver's private belief are listed.

At the initial stage, since only partitions with two elements are considered, the receiver' private belief has only three possibilities. They are

$$1|2,3,4 \quad 1,2|3,4 \quad 1,2,3|4$$

---

[2] This assumption is just for simplifying the illustration.

After state 1 occurs, the sender does some counterfactual reasoning. Specifically, the sender reasons that what the outcome of the game will be if he plays the game with the receiver who holds one of the three possible beliefs. It is easy to observe that only the first one yields payoff 1, which is consistent with the actual outcome in Table 1. Therefore, the other two possibilities are eliminated. Therefore, player 1 has learned that player 2's private belief is $1|2, 3, 4$.

The order of the occurrence of the states affect the learning process. If state 3 or state 4 occurs first, then the learning procedure may be different. The following analysis shows player 1's reasoning process when state 3 occurs first.

The initial stage is the same, there are three possibilities

$$1|2, 3, 4 \quad 1, 2|3, 4 \quad 1, 2, 3|4$$

After state 3 is communicated, the third possibility yields payoff 1 that is different from the actual payoff in Table 1. Therefore, the third posibility can be eliminated. Hence, two possibilities still remain.

$$1|2, 3, 4 \quad 1, 2|3, 4$$

After state 1 is communicated, applying the similar reasoning, player 1 infers player 2's private belief precisely as follows.

$$1|2, 3, 4$$

Therefore, in this simple toy game, in at most two steps, namely, after communicating state 3 or state 4 and state 1 or state 2, player 1 (sender) is able to infer player 2's (receiver) private belief correctly. In addition, if player 1 is lucky enough that state 1 or state 2 occurs earlier than state 3 or state 4, then player 1 is able to learn player 2's private belief quickly.

Similarly, player 2 is also able to infer player 1's private belief by playing the role of the sender. The following part shows the reasoning process where player 2 is the sender and player 1 is the receiver.

Table 2. Play of the game in Example 1 (2)

State	Signal	Revealed information	Receiver's reasoning	Payoff
1	s_1	B_{11}	$B_{11} \cap s_1$	1/2
2	s_1	B_{11}	$B_{11} \cap s_1$	1/2
3	s_2	B_{12}	$B_{12} \cap s_2$	1/2
4	s_2	B_{12}	$B_{12} \cap s_2$	1/2

Table 2 shows the outcomes of the game for different states. Player 2's inference about player 1's private belief with respect to Table 2 is simply described as follows.

At the initial stage, there are three possible beliefs.

$$1|2,3,4 \quad 1,2|3,4 \quad 1,2,3|4$$

After state 1, the first one can be eliminated.

$$1,2|3,4 \quad 1,2,3|4$$

After state 2, it keeps the same.

$$1,2|3,4 \quad 1,2,3|4$$

After state 3, only one belief remains. That is

$$1,2|3,4$$

In this process, state 1 (or state 2) and state 3 (or state 4) are important for player 2 to learn player 1's private belief.

Therefore, after a few rounds of signaling communication with role switching, both players can learn each other's private belief. After the opponents' beliefs are learned, both players can combine their beliefs. Then a common belief $1|2|3,4$ can be induced, which is obtained by taking the coarsest common refinement of the two belief partitions.

This common belief is important for further communication. It severs as the knowledge base for processing ambiguous expressions. For example, under this common belief, a two signal language s_1 and s_2 indicating the information $\{1,2,3\}$ and $\{4\}$ is sufficient to communicate precisely all the information in Example 1. Nevertheless, this kind of successful communication can not be achieved before the common belief is formed.

Moreover, if another set of signals $\{s_1, s_2, s_3,\}$ (with meanings $1,2||3||4$) is available as well, then the more ambiguous signal set $\{s_1, s_2\}$ (with meanings $1,2,3||4$) is preferred given that each signal is costly.

As a result, we have built a dynamic learning process between interlocutors through the repeated SPB model. After the learning is accomplished, even by using the ambiguous language, players might be able to communicate all the information precisely.

However, the learning may not be successful in the sense that some player's private belief can not be singled out from all possible belief partitions. Therefore, it is natural to ask under what conditions players' private belief is learnable. We answer this question in details in the next section.

3   When Is Private Belief Learnable?

In the previous section, we developed a learning procedure for players to learn each other's private belief in a conversation. However, there are situations in which the learning fails. The following is an example to demonstrate that players may sometimes fail to learn their opponent's private belief.

Example 2. Suppose there are six states $\{1, 2, 3, 4, 5, 6\}$ occurring with equal probability, the signal structure is the following.

$$12\|34\|56$$
$$s_1\|s_2\|s_3$$

Assume player 1's private belief and play 2's private belie are the followings:

$$1, 2, 3|4, 5, 6 \qquad 1, 2|3, 4, 5, 6$$
$$B_{11}|B_{12} \qquad B_{21}|B_{22}$$

Firstly, we assume that player 1 is the sender and player 2 is the receiver. Then from the sender's point of view, his inference is as follows.

Table 3. Play of the game in Example 2

State	Signal	Revealed information	Receiver's reasoning	Payoff
1	s_1	B_{21}	$B_{21} \cap s_1$	1/2
2	s_1	B_{21}	$B_{21} \cap s_1$	1/2
3	s_2	B_{22}	$B_{22} \cap s_2$	1/2
4	s_2	B_{22}	$B_{22} \cap s_2$	1/2
3	s_3	B_{22}	$B_{22} \cap s_3$	1/2
4	s_3	B_{22}	$B_{22} \cap s_3$	1/2

Following Table 3, we examine player 1's learning process for player 2's private belief. Similarly, we assume that player 1 knows that player 2's belief takes the form of a two-element partition on the set of the states. Therefore, player 1's learning process can be constructed as follows. Without lose of generality, we list player 1's learning process by communicating from state 1 to state 6.

At the initial stage, there are five possibilities.

$$1|2, 3, 4, 5, 6 \quad 1, 2|3, 4, 5, 6 \quad 1, 2, 3|4, 5, 6 \quad 1, 2, 3, 4, |5, 6 \quad 1, 2, 3, 4, 5|6$$

After state 1, the first possible belief can be eliminated.

$$1, 2|3, 4, 5, 6 \quad 1, 2, 3|4, 5, 6 \quad 1, 2, 3, 4, |5, 6 \quad 1, 2, 3, 4, 5|6$$

After state 2, it stays the same.

$$1, 2|3, 4, 5, 6 \quad 1, 2, 3|4, 5, 6 \quad 1, 2, 3, 4, |5, 6 \quad 1, 2, 3, 4, 5|6$$

After state 3, the second possible belief above can be eliminated.

$$1, 2|3, 4, 5, 6 \quad 1, 2, 3, 4, |5, 6 \quad 1, 2, 3, 4, 5|6$$

After state 4, it keeps the same.

$$1,2|3,4,5,6 \quad 1,2,3,4,|5,6 \quad 1,2,3,4,5|6$$

After state 5, one more possibility is eliminated.

$$1,2|3,4,5,6 \quad 1,2,3,4,|5,6$$

After state 6, two possibilities still remain.

$$1,2|3,4,5,6 \quad 1,2,3,4,|5,6$$

From this learning process, it is obvious that even though every state is communicated, player 1 still can not distinguish player 2's private belief from $1,2|3,4,5,6$ to $1,2,3,4,|5,6$. In other words, player 1 knows that player 2's private belief is one of these two, but there is no means for player 1 to figure out which one it is. Therefore, it is an example where players' private belief is not learnable. Thus, it arises a natural question that under what conditions players are able to learn each other's private belief. For answering this question, we examine more about the reason of the failure in Example 2.

We calculate the payoffs in the remaining two possible private belief under each state in Example 2.

Table 4. Payoff under each state

Private belief	State 1	State 2	State 3	State 4	State 5	State 6
$1,2|3,4,5,6$	1/2	1/2	1/2	1/2	1/2	1/2
$1,2,3,4,|5,6$	1/2	1/2	1/2	1/2	1/2	1/2

From Table 4, both possible beliefs yield the same payoffs under all the states. Recall that, in the learning process, the trigger for the sender to eliminate some private belief is the payoff differences. For example, in Example 2, from the initial stage to stage one, the private belief $1|2,3,4,5,6$ is eliminated from the possible set. It is because $1|2,3,4,5,6$ yields the payoff 1 for state 1, whereas all other possibilities yield $1/2$ for state 1. Since the true payoff is $1/2$, therefore, $1|2,3,4,5,6$ should be eliminated. The essential feature here is that the payoff differences resulting from different possible private beliefs provide the sender the opportunities to learn about the receiver's private belief. If all the possible private beliefs yield the same payoff, then the sender has no chance to learn anything.

Inspired by this phenomena, we established a sufficient condition under which the player's private belief is learnable. Before stating the condition, we first define formally what it means that two possible private belief are distinguishable.

Definition 3. *Given a SPB game with the set of states T, a set of actions $\mathcal{A}$ and a set of signals, we say that from the player i's point of view, two possible private beliefs B^1_{-i}, B^2_{-i} are distinguishable, if there exists a state j, such that $u(j, A_j | s_j \cap B^{1j}_{-i}) \neq u(j, A_j | s_j \cap B^{2j}_{-i})$, where $j \in T$, s_j is the corresponding signal, B^{1j}_{-i} and B^{2j}_{-i} are partition elements containing state j, and $A \in \mathcal{P}(\mathcal{A})$.*

Where B_{-i} indicates player i's opponent's possible private belief. $u(j, A_j | s_j \cap B^{1j}_{-i})$ is read as the payoff with respect to the receiver's action set A_j (indicating that $a_j \in A$) given signal s_j and the private information B^{1j}_{-i}.

The intuition behind this definition is just saying that if there exists a state under which two belief partitions yield different payoffs, then they are distinguishable. For example, in Example 2, the belief partitions $1|2, 3, 4, 5, 6$ and $1, 2|3, 4, 5, 6$ are distinguishable under state 1. Moreover, the structure of the game guarantees that under state 1, at least one of the two beliefs yields the wrong payoff and can be eliminated.

Now we can present the sufficient condition under which a private belief is learnable by using Definition 3.

Theorem 1. *Given the SPB game, if any two of receiver's possible private belief partitions from the sender's point of view are distinguishable, then the receiver's private belief is learnable.*

Proof: See Appendix.

Theorem 1 tells us under what conditions receiver's private belief is learnable. The sufficient condition meets our intuition that the payoff differences provide the sender an indication of distinguishing possible private beliefs from impossible ones. An example can illustrate the intuition behind the theorem.

Conversation A:

Ann: Hi, morning! Are you going to the bank?
Bob: Yes, I go there every day.

Conversation B

Ann: Hi, morning! Are you going to the bank?

Bob: Yes, I have an appointment with the financial manager.

In the two conversations above, because of the ambiguity of the word "bank", there maybe uncertainty in the conversation. In conversation A, Ann does not know which meaning of the bank that Bob is using. It is because from Bob's response, Ann can not distinguish the financial bank from the river bank. On the contrary, in conversation B, Ann can easily infer from Bob's response that Bob is using the word "bank" for the financial institute.

4   Uncertain Signaling and Ambiguity Preference

In the previous section, we provide a sufficient condition under which the players can learn opponents' private beliefs through the repeated signaling game. However, there are many situations such as Example 2 in which the learning fails. We want to ask if the players are uncertain about each other's belief, whether ambiguous signals can be chosen. In this section, we conduct simulation studies for exploring players' preferences of ambiguous expressions when the opponent's private belief is not fully learned.

The idea is to model a communicative scenario where given a set of signaling systems with different ambiguities, players are learning which signaling system is more optimal. A signaling system is a set of signals with conventional meanings with respect to the given set of the states. In the classical signaling game and our previous discussions, we consider a game with single signaling system only. In this section, we consider multiple signaling systems simultaneously.

In Lewis's signaling game, each equilibrium can be represented as a partition on a set of states, we call it a signaling system. For example, given a set of states $T : \{1, 2, 3, 4, 5, 6\}$, the separating equilibrium can be induced from the partition $\{1||2||3||4||5||6\}$, where we simply use $||$ to indicate the elements in the partition. One of the possible meaningful set of signals for the partition is that signal s_i carries the meaning of state i. Apparently, in the separating equilibrium, each signal precisely represents each state information.

One the other hand, the partial pooling equilibrium involves uncertainties for the meaning of the signals. For instance, the partition $\{1234||56\}$ can produce a partial pooling equilibrium, in which two signals are used and each signal carries the meanings of multiple states. Therefore, ambiguous signals can appear in the partial pooling equilibrium. We say that signaling system $\{1||2||3||4||5||6\}$ containing more signals is more precise than the signaling system $\{1234||56\}$. In general, for different partitions on the same set of states, the partition contains more signals is considered less ambiguity than the one with fewer signals. We assume that each signal in a partition have a cost c, then the partition with more signals is more precise but more expensive.

Assuming the existence of multiple signaling systems, we assign each signaling system a weight m by considering three factors. Firstly, the signaling system gains credences from two simultaneously occurring process: one is from the conversational information transaction, the other is from providing partial information about opponent's personal beliefs. In addition, we take into account of the cost of signals. Through keeping track of the weight of each signaling system in a reinforcement learning process, we show that ambiguous signaling systems have advantages in this uncertain signaling process.

The reinforcement learning has been widely applied in the studies of language evolution (see O'Connor 2014b; Skyrms 2010; Wagner 2009; Zollman 2005; Franke and van Rooij 2011). Reinforcement learning can be described by a simple urn model with two colored balls. Every time a ball is drawn from the urn randomly. Then, the same ball and another same colored ball are returned to the urn. As a result, the probability of the ball with the same color being drawn next time is increased. When reinforcement learning is applied in the signaling game, players' strategies can be imagined as drawing the colored balls from the urns of signals and acts.

We define the reinforcement learning for only sender's choice among the signaling systems. Since we assume the signaling systems are common knowledge, once the sender's strategy is fixed, the receiver's action is also fixed. Hence, it is sufficient to consider only the sender's strategy.

The updating rule is the following.

$$w_{P_i}(t+1) = w_{P_i}(t) + u_j + u_l - kc$$

where w_{P_i} is the weight for the signaling system P_i, u_j is the payoff for the result of communicating the state information j, u_l is the credence from learning the opponent's private beliefs while P_i is used. Formally, kc is the cost of the signaling system P_i in which k number of signals are contained. u_l is decided by counting how many possible belief partitions can be eliminated when P_i is used. $u_l = l$, if one possibility is eliminated. $u_l = 2l$, if two possibilities are eliminated. u_l is understood as how much impossibilities can be eliminated by using certain signals. The more impossible belief can be eliminated the more learning credences the signal can obtain. The learning here is an epistemic learning process which is also a process of reducing uncertainties.

By calculating the weight of each signaling system, we can define a response rule for the learning system to capture how frequently certain signals are used. The response rule for the reinforcement learning is defined as follows.

$$p_{P_i}(t) = \frac{w_{P_i}(t)}{\sum_j w_{P_j}(t)}$$

in which the probability of P_i being chosen is calculated by the proportion of the weight of P_i among the weight of all the possible partitions. The higher the probability of certain signaling system is, the more frequently this signaling system is used and hence more advantages this signaling system obtains in the evolutionary system.

We use Example 2 for the simulation study. The signaling systems under the consideration are

$$P_1 : 12||34||56 \quad P_2 : 1234||56 \quad P_3 : 123456$$

The costs of the signaling systems are $3c, 2c$ and c. The ambiguity increases from P_1 to P_3.

The reinforcement learning process is the following. Firstly, the occurring state and who plays the role of the sender are decided randomly with equal probability. Then, the sender chooses the signaling system by the response rule. The results of communication and learning are reflected on the weight w. We assume the original weights for all the signaling systems are the same.

If we assume the response probability $p_{P_i} = \frac{1}{3}, i = 1, 2, 3$ at time $t = 0$, we can calculate the expected weights according to the following equation.

$$E_{wP_i} = \frac{1}{2}\sum_j \frac{1}{6} * \frac{1}{3}(u_j + u_l) + \frac{1}{2}\sum_j \frac{1}{6} * \frac{1}{3}(u_j + u_l) - kc$$

Therefore,

$$E_{wP_1} = \frac{7}{12} + \frac{3}{2}l \approx 0.58 + 1.5l - 3c,$$

$$E_{wP_2} = \frac{4}{9} + 3l \approx 0.44 + 3l - 2c,$$

$$E_{wP_3} = \frac{1}{3} + \frac{7}{2}l \approx 0.33 + 3.5l - c$$

Apparently, for comparing E_{wP_i}, we have to specify the particular values of l and c. As the proportion of P_i changes along the learning process, it becomes impossible to calculate manually. Hence we conduct simulations to explore the dynamic of this learning process.

By changing the values of l and c, we got the simulation results by conducting each trial for 2000 generations.

Figure 1 presents one instance of simulation results for different values of l and c. The X axis shows the repeated times of communication. We repeated 2000 times for each trial. The Y axis shows the probability of each signaling system being chosen. It is obvious that in a short time of communication, the most precise signaling system P_1 still has some advantages. However, in the long run, the precise signaling system is dominated by the more ambiguous signaling systems P_2 and P_3.

For examining the stability of the result, we also conduct simulations for 200 trials for each case. During the 200 trails, we record the frequency of each signaling system being the best among the three with respect to the best average probability in each trial. For example, when $l = 0.2, c = 0.15$ (case (f)), in the 200 trials, 77% times, P_3 has the best average performance, P_2 takes 22.5% of the time while P_1 takes only 0.5% of the time. When $l = 0.1, c = 0.05$ (case (a)), among the 200 trials, P_3 has the best average performance 45% of the time, P_2 takes 41% of the time while P_1 takes 14% of the time. Overall, the most ambiguous signaling system has the best average performance among the given three signaling systems.

The explanation of the simulation results relies on two facts. Firstly, on balancing the information transaction and the costs of signals, the ambiguous signaling systems turn out to be more optimal. Secondly, the ambiguous signaling systems have advantages in the learning process in our models. When the communication is successful through using the ambiguous expression, which means the receiver's private belief plays an important role in the information transaction, as a result, the sender can infer the receiver's private belief through the outcome of this play. On the contrary, the precise signals do not have this merit.

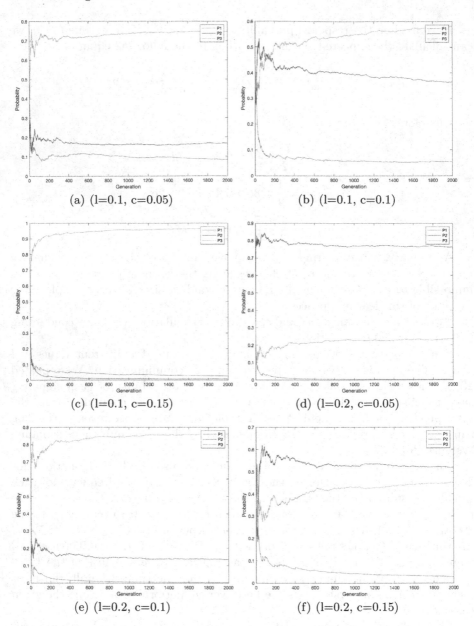

(a) (l=0.1, c=0.05)

(b) (l=0.1, c=0.1)

(c) (l=0.1, c=0.15)

(d) (l=0.2, c=0.05)

(e) (l=0.2, c=0.1)

(f) (l=0.2, c=0.15)

Fig. 1. The probability of each signaling system being chosen

To conclude, in this section, we use simulation studies to examine player's preference on ambiguous signals when the opponent's private belief is uncertain. Three factors are considered in the simulations: the benefits from information transactions, the partial information of opponents' belief through the learning and the cost of the signals. The simulation results show that more ambiguous signals are preferred in most of the situations.

5   Discussion and Conclusion

In the literature, there are many discussions about uncertain signaling and its communication features. We discuss the similarities and differences between our model and the established models in the literature. The models we concern are Santana's signaling model with belief context (see Santana 2014), the rational speech act model from Frank and Goodman (2012), the iterated response model by Franke and Jäger (2014) and the uncertain signaling model from Thomas (2017).

We proposed a dynamic learning procedure of private belief for communication, which differs from the models in which a common prior of beliefs is assumed. Santana's signaling model is a typical signaling game with a given context background. It studies the emergence of ambiguity in a cooperation signaling game. Based on Lewis's signaling game, a context is added to the model. Players combine both the signal information and the independent context information for making decisions. The paper argues that the evolution favors the ambiguous signaling. Our model has the similar motivation and structure as Santana's model. The major difference is that in Santana's model, the context is given as the common knowledge independent of the communication. One of the main contributions of our paper is building a learning process of the context belief during the communication. A dynamic perspective is taken in our model for both the context formation and the preference of ambiguities.

Our model is also different from the models built on the probabilistic (Bayesian) iterated learnings (see Frank and Goodman 2012; Goodman and Frank 2016; Franke and Jäger 2014). Rational language use is captured by a hierarchy over reasoning types in Franke and Jäger's hierarchy model. An iterated rationality reasoning is constructed on the strategy types in the model, which captures the back and forth pragmatics reasoning. Rational speech act game (in Frank and Goodman 2012) uses a Bayesian reasoning to predicate interlocutors' language use. Franke and Jäger's model and the Rational speech act model focus on the rationality and pragmatics in use of the language. The interlocutors' context belief is coded into the strategy types and the context information is not fully explored.

Thomas (2017)'s uncertain signaling model generates an adaptive dynamic to predicate ambiguous communication under which the players are lacking a common prior. Brochhagen's model focuses on the learning of the context belief, but only the adaptive dynamics is explored. It lacks a full analysis of whether and when a common context is possible to be established.

The investigation in this paper is built on the notion of information partition that is more basic than the concept of probability. The model follows Aumann (1976)'s tradition of "Agree to Disagree". The difference is that Aumann's theorem has a common prior assumption and is based on only one random variable. In our model, we works on multiple random variables (all possible private beliefs) and different priors. Another advantage of using information partition is that we can discuss the content of the information from the signals as well as from the context beliefs instead of just posterior probabilities. From the discussion in Geanakoplos and Polemarchakis (1982), the learning of posterior probability does not equal to learning the information itself. Hence, a model built on the notion of information partition has more potential for exploring belief updating and learning. Moreover, the discussion based on information partition can be easily extended to other related fields such as other extensive games and possible world semantics in Modal Logic.

To conclude, the paper tries to justify the existence of language ambiguity from the perspective of context dependence. When the context about the conversation is commonly known, the ambiguous expression is possible to communicate all the information. Furthermore, as the interlocutors' beliefs change during the repeated conversations, the interlocutors' preferences of degrees of ambiguity may change as well. The main contribution of the paper is that we construct a learning process for the players to update beliefs from the result of each conversation. We also establish a testing condition under which whether the learning process is successful. In addition, we discussed players's choice of ambiguous language when the opponent's private belief is not fully known. A reinforcement learning signaling game is developed for the uncertain signaling situations.

Acknowledgements. The author wishes to thank four anonymous reviewers for commenting on the previous manuscript of this paper. The research reported in this paper was supported by the Humanity and Social Science Youth Foundation of Ministry of Education of China (No. 17YJC72040004) and the National Humanity and Social Science Youth Foundation in China (No. 18CZX064).

Appendix

Theorem 1. *Given the SPB game, if any two of receiver's possible private belief partitions from the sender's point of view are distinguishable, then the receiver's private belief is learnable.*

Proof: This theorem can be proved from the players' reasoning process on inferring opponent's private belief by playing the SPB game repeatedly. The algorithm of this learning can be described as follows. For convenience, we eliminate the subscribe indicating the players in B in the proof.

Step 1 Since T is finite, we can list all the possible private belief partitions as a sequence $B : B^1, \ldots, B^m$;

Step 2 Calculate all the expected payoffs yielded by each $B^j, j \in \{1, 2, \ldots, m\}$ for each state $i, i \in \{1, 2, \ldots, n\}$;

Step 3 Pick the first two partitions in the sequence B, B^1 and B^2, since any belief partition are distinguishable, then there exists a state k such that $u(k, A_k|s_k \cap B^{1k}) \neq u(k, A_k|s_k \cap B^{2k})$. Therefore, once state k happens (the occurrence of state k can be guaranteed because players are playing this game repeatedly and every state is possible to occur.), by comparing the true payoff with the payoffs given by B^1 and B^2, There are two situations:

- One of the beliefs yields the true payoff, then the sender just return the correct partition back to the sequence B.
- Neither belief yields the true payoff, then both beliefs should be eliminated.

Step 4 Update the sequence B, then repeat from step 1.

Since for any two private belief partitions, they are distinguishable, and at least one of them is wrong. Hence, the list B can be eliminated to only one element in finite steps. The remaining belief partition is receiver's true private belief. Therefore, receiver's private belief is learnable. □

References

Aumann, R.J.: Agreeing to disagree. Ann. Stat. **4**, 1236–1239 (1976)

Frank, M.C., Goodman, N.D.: Predicting pragmatic reasoning in language games. Science **336**(6084), 998–998 (2012)

Franke, M., Gerhard, J.: Pragmatic back-and-forth reasoning. In: Reda, S.P. (ed.) Pragmatics, Semantics and the Case of Scalar Implicatures, pp. 170–200. Springer, London (2014). https://doi.org/10.1057/9781137333285_7

Geanakoplos, J.D., Polemarchakis, H.M.: We can't disagree forever. J. Econ. Theory **28**(1), 192–200 (1982)

Goodman, N.D., Frank, M.C.: Pragmatic language interpretation as probabilistic inference. Trends Cogn. Sci. **20**(11), 818–829 (2016)

Grice, H.P.: Utterer's meaning, sentence-meaning, and word-meaning. Found. Lang. **4**, 225–242 (1968)

Huttegger, S.M.: Evolution and explaining of meaning. Philos. Sci. **74**(1), 1–24 (2007)

Huttegger, S.M., Skyrms, B., Smead, R., Zollman, K.J.S.: Evolutionary dynamics of Lewis signaling games: signaling systems vs. partial pooling. Synthese **172**(1), 177–191 (2010)

Jäger, G.: Rationalizable signaling. Erkenntnis **79**(4), 673–706 (2013). https://doi.org/10.1007/s10670-013-9462-3

Zollman, K.J.S.: Talking to neighbors: the evolution of regional meaning. Philos. Sci. **72**(1), 69–85 (2005)

Lewis, D.: Convention. A Philosophical Study. Harvard University Press, Cambridge (1969)

Franke, M., Jäger, G., van Rooij, R.: Vagueness, signaling and bounded rationality. In: Onada, T., Bekki, D., McCready, E. (eds.) JSAI-isAI 2010. LNCS (LNAI), vol. 6797, pp. 45–59. Springer, Heidelberg (2011). https://doi.org/10.1007/978-3-642-25655-4_5

O'Connor, C.: Ambiguity is kinda good sometimes. Philos. Sci. **82**(1), 110–121 (2014a)

O'Connor, C.: The evolution of vagueness. Erkenntnis **79**(4), 707–727 (2013). https://doi.org/10.1007/s10670-013-9463-2

Piantadosi, S.T., Tily, H., Gibson, E.: The communicative function of ambiguity in language. Cognition **122**(3), 280–291 (2012)

Santana, C.: Ambiguity in cooperative signaling. Philos. Sci. **81**(3), 398–422 (2014)

Skyrms, B.: Signals: Evolution, Learning and Information. Oxford University Press, New York (2010)

Stalnaker, R.: Common ground. Linguist. Philos. **25**(5–6), 701–721 (2002)

Brochhagen, T.: Signalling under uncertainty: interpretative alignment without a common prior. Br. J. Philos. Sci., axx058. https://doi.org/10.1093/bjps/axx058

Wagner, E.: Communication and structured correlation. Erkenntnis **71**(3), 377–393 (2009). https://doi.org/10.1007/s10670-009-9157-y

A Decidable Multi-agent Logic for Reasoning About Actions, Instruments, and Norms

Kees van Berkel[1]($\boxtimes$), Tim Lyon[1], and Francesco Olivieri[2]

[1] Institut für Logic and Computation, TU Wien, Vienna, Austria
{kees,lyon}@logic.at
[2] Brisbane, Australia

Abstract. We formally introduce a novel, yet ubiquitous, category of norms: *norms of instrumentality*. Norms of this category describe which actions are obligatory, or prohibited, as instruments for certain purposes. We propose the *Logic of Agency and Norms* (LAN) that enables reasoning about actions, instrumentality, and normative principles in a multi-agent setting. Leveraging LAN, we formalize norms of instrumentality and compare them to two prevalent norm categories: *norms to be* and *norms to do*. Last, we pose principles relating the three categories and evaluate their validity vis-à-vis notions of deliberative acting. On a technical note, the logic will be shown decidable via the finite model property.

Keywords: Agency logic · Action constants · Action logic · Andersonian reduction · Decidability · Deontic logic · Norms of instrumentality

1 Introduction

The formal analysis of normative reasoning, roughly starting with the introduction of deontic logic in the 1950s [21], has been guided by the conviction that *action* and *agency* are pivotal components of normative reasoning [8,22]. In relation to this, an important development took place in the 1970s: the introduction of Propositional Dynamic Logic (PDL) [10]. Modal logics of PDL focus on the analysis of complex actions (or programs) and their relation to results. The framework was soon adapted to deontic reasoning [17] and it continues to receive attention to the present day [20]. The emphasis on action and agency in normative reasoning led to the distinction between two categories of norms: *norms to be* and *norms to do* [1,8]. Norms of the former category address *states of affairs*, without making reference to how such states of affairs are obtained by the agent. The latter category normatively prescribes *actions* to agents, yet, without specifying the possible outcomes that might be produced by the action.

However, there is a third category of norms merging both approaches, which, to the best of our knowledge, has not been formally investigated. These norms

© Springer Nature Switzerland AG 2020
M. Dastani et al. (Eds.): CLAR 2020, LNAI 12061, pp. 219–241, 2020.
https://doi.org/10.1007/978-3-030-44638-3_14

prescribe a specific normative relation between an action and a goal, with the action serving as an instrument to achieve the goal. We will refer to such norms as *norms of instrumentality*. Consider the following example:

> Although it is neither prohibited to use nonpublic information, nor is it prohibited to acquire financial profit on the stock market, it is in fact prohibited to use such information as an *instrument* to attain the latter.

The above principle is known as the law on 'insider trading' and belongs to this third category. Prohibitions of the form expressed above articulate which *actions* cannot be employed as *instruments* for achieving particular *goals*. Despite the ubiquity of normative constraints on instrumentality in legal, social, and ethical systems (e.g. protocols, rules of games, fairness constraints, etc.), an investigation of their philosophical ramifications in formal logic is absent. This work aims to provide the formal foundations for the analysis of norms of instrumentality.

In [1], a formal investigation of the first two norm categories is provided. The formalism employed there brings together Anderson's reduction of norms of the first class [2] and Meyer's reduction of norms of the second class [17] in a single system of modal logic called PDeL (i.e. deontic PDL). The first is a reduction of deontic operators to alethic formulae containing *violation constants* (e.g. a result A is obligatory when $\neg A$ strictly implies a violation). The second reduces deontic operators to formulae using action modalities and violation constants (e.g. an action Δ is obligatory when not performing Δ strictly implies a violation).

In [4], a third reduction is discussed, where action modalities of PDL are reduced to alethic formulae containing *action constants*. The resulting logic facilitates reasoning about agent-dependent actions within the object language and formally captures different notions of instrumentality (in a non-normative setting). Decidability of this logic was left as an open problem.

The current work brings together the three reductions found in [1] and [4], and introduces a *Logic of Agency and Norms* called LAN (Sect. 3). The resulting logic extends previous approaches by permitting us to reason with *agent-dependent* actions, as well as *agent-dependent* obligations and prohibitions, in multi-agent settings. The language of LAN will enable us to formally investigate the three norm categories; we will pose principles describing relations between the three categories and evaluate their validity vis-à-vis different notions of deliberative acting (Sect. 4). Last, we prove the decidability of LAN in Appendix A of the paper.

2   A Benchmark Example

In order to understand the distinct nature of the three kinds of norms, we provide an example protocol serving as a benchmark in developing our formal framework. In Sect. 5, we formalize and analyze the protocol using our developed logic.

A Hospital Health and Safety Protocol. The Health and Safety Committee of a public hospital in Vienna recently established a new set of guidelines to govern and redirect the behaviour of surgeons and nurses in the assistance and treatment of its patients. In particular, motivated by the increased awareness of the dangers of accidental self-inflicted wounds, caused by using sharp tools during surgery, the committee has proposed a new policy: that is, limiting the use of scalpels in surgery to surgeons and prohibiting assisting nurses the use of such instruments in the operation room. The protocol is summed up accordingly:

P1 A surgeon is obliged to use the prescribed scalpel to bring about a necessary incision during surgery.
P2 Assisting nurses are not allowed to use scalpels during surgery when the situation is not dire.[1]
P3 Nurses and surgeons alike have the obligations to (i) promote the health of their patients and (ii) preserve hygiene safety in the operation room.

First, we observe that the norm expressed by P1 is a norm belonging to the third, novel, category of *norms of instrumentality*; that is, it describes a norm that specifically relates an action as an instrument to a particular outcome. P2 is a prohibition subsumed under *norms to do*, and holds independent of the instrument's intended purpose. P3 is an obligation pertaining to *norms to be*, and holds independent of the instruments used to obtain (i) and (ii).

To stress the irreducibility of norms of instrumentality to norms to be and norms to do, consider the following: although a surgeon might be obliged to use a scalpel to ensure a required incision, it does not follow that she has the obligation to use scalpels independent of their intended purpose (some outcomes obtained by using scalpels could be prohibited), nor does it mean that she has the obligation to bring about the incision by any means necessary (some means could be prohibited). In fact, in case of P1, the surgeon has *only* the obligation to ensure the required incision by means of using the scalpel.[2]

To continue, the committee makes two *assumptions* in drafting the protocol:

T1 The protocol resolves all normative issues in surgical situations by offering rules of conduct that ultimately provide ways out of any possible conflict.
T2 The protocol assumes that the choices described, and suggested, to the agents can be consistently performed together.

The committee is aware that sub-ideal situations can occur (e.g. whenever an employee (in)voluntarily violates an initial rule). Given T1, the committee provides the following principle which activates whenever P3 cannot be satisfied:

---

[1] Notice that principle P2 incorporates a form of defeasible reasoning through explicit exception, for the present analysis of norms of instrumentality, the above will suffice.
[2] Notice that in the present example, we use a material tool to exemplify instruments. However, we stress that the notion of instrumentality is more general and refers to all actions serving goals; e.g. 'opening the window' is an instrument for 'changing the room's temperature' [22]. Following Von Wright [23], an action is a classified ϕ-instrument—where ϕ is the purpose—whenever the action serves the purpose of ϕ. Consequently, although in the above example reference is made to a 'scalpel' (i.e. a tool) the instrument under consideration—serving the purpose of 'the incision being made'—is in fact the action 'using the scalpel (for the purpose of incision)'. See [4] for a philosophical discussion on different notions of instrumentality.

E1 In case of failing to preserve hygiene standards during surgery (e.g., in the case of self-inflicted wounds) the employee in question is obliged to immediately leave the operation room and call the safety-emergency number.

The purpose of the above rule is to ensure that damage in sub-ideal scenarios is controlled. Principle E1 prescribes measures to be taken in case of failure to comply with other prescriptions. As can be seen, there is a close connection between principle E1 and what is called *contrary-to-duty* reasoning; that is, reasoning about secondary norms that arise from violating primary norms. We come back to this point during the formalization of the example in Sect. 5.

Last, the committee desires that the above protocol is captured in a logical system, enabling them (i) to analyse the consistency of the protocol and (ii) to reason with the protocol whenever critical circumstances occur. As can be observed, the logical language must contain agents, actions, results and violations, in order to facilitate the formal distinction between the three norm categories.

3   Deontic Logic of Actions, Agency and Norms

In what follows, we introduce the language, semantics and axiomatization of our Logic of Agency and Norms, henceforth, LAN (the logic will be a deontic extension of the machinery provided in [4]). As motivated in the introduction, we will employ a *reductionist approach* to norms via violation constants (following [17]) and to actions via action constants (following [4]). In order to reason with actions in a normative setting, we use a Boolean algebra of actions. The language of LAN will depend on this algebra of actions, which will enable us to talk about complex, compound actions as formulae in the object language.

Definition 1 (Algebra of Actions Act_{LAN}). *Let $Act = \{\delta_1, ..., \delta_n\}$ be a set of atomic action-types and let $\delta_i \in Act$. The language Act_{LAN} of complex action-types Δ is given via the following BNF grammar:*

$$\Delta ::= \delta_i \mid \Delta \cup \Delta \mid \overline{\Delta}$$

The operations $\cup$ and — represent *disjunction* and *complement* (resp.), allowing us to generate complex expressions such as 'closing-the-door *or* opening-the-window' and '*not* closing-the-window'. The *conjunction* operator & over actions is defined as $\Delta_1 \& \Delta_2 := \overline{\overline{\Delta_1} \cup \overline{\Delta_2}}$. Let $Agt = \{\alpha_1, \ldots, \alpha_n\}$ be a set of agent labels; we say Δ^{α_i} is an *agent-dependent action-type* iff $\Delta \in Act_{LAN}$ and $\alpha_i \in Agt$.

We let $Var = \{p_1, p_2, \ldots\}$ be a countable set of propositional variables, and for any $\alpha_i \in Agt$, we let $Wit^{\alpha_i} = \{\mathfrak{d}_1^{\alpha_i}, ..., \mathfrak{d}_n^{\alpha_i}\}$ be the set of propositional constants that witness the performance of atomic action-types δ_1, ..., δ_n by α_i (this is made formally precise in Definition 3). Let Wit be the union $\bigcup_{\alpha_i \in Agt} Wit^{\alpha_i}$ and note that $|Wit^{\alpha_i}| = |Act| = n$, for some $n \in \mathbb{N}$. Also, we take $\mathfrak{v}^{\alpha_i}$ to be a propositional constant witnessing a *norm violation* for agent α_i and let

$Vio = \{ \mathfrak{v}^{\alpha_i} \mid \alpha_i \in Agt \}$ be the set of all agential violation constants. Last, we let $Atoms = Var \cup Wit \cup Vio.^3$

Definition 2 (The Language $\mathcal{L}_{\mathsf{LAN}}$). $\mathcal{L}_{\mathsf{LAN}}$ *is given by the following BNF:*

$$\phi ::= p_i \mid \mathfrak{v}^{\alpha_j} \mid \mathfrak{d}_i^{\alpha_j} \mid \neg\phi \mid \phi \rightarrow \phi \mid \Box\phi \mid [\mathsf{N}]\phi$$

where $p_i \in Var$, $\alpha_j \in Agt$, $\mathfrak{v}^{\alpha_j} \in Vio$ *and* $\mathfrak{d}_i^{\alpha_j} \in Wit$.

In short, the operators $\wedge$, $\vee$ and $\equiv$ are defined in the usual way. Formulae of the form $\Box\phi$ and $[\mathsf{N}]\phi$ express, respectively, 'in all possible successor (future) states ϕ holds' and 'in the actual successor (future) state ϕ holds'. We take $\Diamond$ and $\langle\mathsf{N}\rangle$ as the duals of $\Box$ and $[\mathsf{N}]$, respectively. Last, we take $\mathfrak{d}_i^{\alpha_j}$ and $\mathfrak{v}^{\alpha_j}$ to stand for 'agent α_j has performed action δ_i' and 'agent α_j has violated a norm', respectively.

Following [4], we define a translation that maps agent-dependent action-types to formulae of $\mathcal{L}_{\mathsf{LAN}}$, enabling us to reason with actions inside the logic:

Definition 3 (Translation t between Act_{LAN} and $\mathcal{L}_{\mathsf{LAN}}$).

– *For any* $\delta_i \in Act$ *and* $\alpha_j \in Agt$, $t(\delta_i^{\alpha_j}) = \mathfrak{d}_i^{\alpha_j}$, *with* $\mathfrak{d}_i^{\alpha_j} \in \mathcal{L}_{\mathsf{LAN}}$.
– *For any* $\Delta \in Act_{\mathsf{LAN}}$ *and* $\alpha_i \in Agt$, $t(\overline{\Delta}^{\alpha_i}) = \neg t(\Delta^{\alpha_i})$.
– *For any* $\Delta, \Gamma \in Act_{\mathsf{LAN}}$ *and* $\alpha_i, \alpha_j \in Agt$, $t(\Delta^{\alpha_i} \cup \Gamma^{\alpha_j}) = t(\Delta^{\alpha_i}) \vee t(\Gamma^{\alpha_j})$.

Consequently, from the above we can derive $t(\Delta^{\alpha_i} \& \Gamma^{\alpha_i}) = t(\Delta^{\alpha_i}) \wedge t(\Gamma^{\alpha_i}).^4$

To demonstrate the potential of $\mathcal{L}_{\mathsf{LAN}}$, we present below the agency operators for *would, could* and *will*, as introduced in [4]. These operators will play a central role in determining an agent's compliance with the formalized example protocol in Sect. 5. We leave the introduction of normative operators to Sect. 4.

(1) For any $\Delta \in Act_{\mathsf{LAN}}$ and $\alpha_i \in Agt$, $[\Delta^{\alpha_i}]^{would}\phi := \Box(t(\Delta^{\alpha_i}) \rightarrow \phi)$
(2) For any $\Delta \in Act_{\mathsf{LAN}}$ and $\alpha_i \in Agt$, $[\Delta^{\alpha_i}]^{could}\phi := \Box(t(\Delta^{\alpha_i}) \rightarrow \phi) \wedge \Diamond t(\Delta^{\alpha_i})$
(3) For any $\Delta \in Act_{\mathsf{LAN}}$ and $\alpha_i \in Agt$, $[\Delta^{\alpha_i}]^{will}\phi := \Box(t(\Delta^{\alpha_i}) \rightarrow \phi) \wedge \langle\mathsf{N}\rangle t(\Delta^{\alpha_i})$

The above operators capture different relations between actions and results obtained at successor states. The first notion is interpreted as 'currently, by performing the action Δ, agent α_i *would* bring about ϕ' (i.e. Δ suffices for guaranteeing ϕ). This definition, however, does not ensure that the agent can in fact perform Δ. The second definition extends the first by adding a notion of ability to it, reading 'currently, by performing action Δ, agent α_i would bring about ϕ and agent α_i *could* currently perform Δ'. The third notion connects the actual course of events with the possible actions available to the agent, stating that 'currently, by performing Δ, agent α_i would bring about ϕ and agent α_i *will* actually execute Δ'. (Note that (3) implies (2), and (2) implies (1) within the logic LAN; see Definition 4).

---

[3] Following [1], to avoid paradoxes $\mathfrak{v}^{\alpha_i}$ is read as 'norm violation' instead of 'sanction'.
[4] We note in passing that one could define other action operators of PDL within the reduced logic LAN; for example 'composition' as $[\Delta^{\alpha_i}; \Gamma^{\alpha_i}]\phi := [\Delta^{\alpha_i}][\Gamma^{\alpha_i}]\phi$.

The logic LAN is specified through a Hilbert-axiomatization presented in Definition 4. The axioms $A1$, $A2$, $A4$ and $R1$ specify that both $\square$ and $[N]$ behave as normal modal operators. In addition, we make a few minimal assumptions for our logic: Axiom $A3$ ensures that every state has at most one actual successor. Axiom $A4$ guarantees that every actual future is also a possible future. Axiom $A5$ expresses that any list of available actions performable by different agents can be consistently performed together. Axiom $A5$ corresponds to clause T2 from the example of Sect. 2, and is an adaptation of the *independence of agents* principle (a pivotal condition for multi-agent STIT logics; see [3, Ch. 7]). Last, for our deontic setting we adopt a *weak contingency* axiom with respect to agent-dependent norm violations. This condition, captured by axiom A6, ensures that no agent α_i can end up in a state at which norm violations cannot be avoided; i.e. if there is a violation possible, there is also a successor state in which the violation is avoided. This axiom corresponds to requirement T1 made in Sect. 2. For a discussion of the contingency axiom A6 we refer to [2,18].

Definition 4 (Axiomatization of LAN).

A0 All propositional tautologies
A1 $\square(\phi \to \psi) \to (\square\phi \to \square\psi)$
A2 $[N](\phi \to \psi) \to ([N]\phi \to [N]\psi)$
A3 $\langle N \rangle \phi \to [N]\phi$
A4 $\square\phi \to [N]\phi$
A5 For distinct $\alpha_1, ..., \alpha_n \in Agt$ and not necessarily distinct $\Delta_1, ..., \Delta_n \in Act_{LAN}$,
   $(\Diamond t(\Delta_1^{\alpha_1}) \wedge ... \wedge \Diamond t(\Delta_n^{\alpha_n})) \to \Diamond(t(\Delta_1^{\alpha_1}) \wedge ... \wedge t(\Delta_n^{\alpha_n}))$
A6 For any $\alpha_j \in Agt$, $\Diamond \mathfrak{v}^{\alpha_j} \to \Diamond \neg \mathfrak{v}^{\alpha_j}$
R0 Modus Ponens: $\vdash_{LAN} \phi$ and $\vdash_{LAN} \phi \to \psi$ imply $\vdash_{LAN} \psi$
R1 Necessitation: $\vdash_{LAN} \phi$ implies $\vdash_{LAN} \square\phi$

A derivation of ϕ in LAN from a set Σ, written $\Sigma \vdash_{LAN} \phi$, is defined in the usual way (See [5, Def. 4.4]). When $\Sigma = \emptyset$, we say ϕ is a theorem, and write $\vdash_{LAN} \phi$.

The corresponding relational frames for LAN are those of [4], modified to a deontic setting using violation constants:

Definition 5 (Relational LAN Frames and Models). *An LAN-frame is a tuple $F = (W, \{W_{\mathfrak{d}_i^{\alpha_j}} : \mathfrak{d}_i^{\alpha_j} \in \mathcal{L}_{LAN}\}, \{W_{\mathfrak{v}^{\alpha_j}} : \mathfrak{v}^{\alpha_j} \in \mathcal{L}_{LAN}\}, R, R_N)$, such that:*

▶ *W is a non-empty set of worlds $w, v, u, ...$ such that:*
  (R1) *For each $\mathfrak{d}_i^{\alpha_j} \in Wit$, $W_{\mathfrak{d}_i^{\alpha_j}} \subseteq W$.*
  (R2) *For each $\mathfrak{v}^{\alpha_j} \in Vio$, $W_{\mathfrak{v}^{\alpha_j}} \subseteq W$.*
▶ *$R, R_N \subseteq W \times W$ are binary relations between worlds in W such that:*
  (R3) *For all $w, u, v \in W$, if $wR_N u$ and $wR_N v$, then $u = v$.*
  (R4) *For all $w, v \in W$, if $wR_N v$, then wRv.*
  (R5) *For all $w \in W$ and for all $1 \le i, j, \le n$, if there are (not necessarily distinct) action-types $\Delta_1, ..., \Delta_n$ such that for $1 \le i \le n$ there is a world $u_i \in W$, for which wRu_i and $u_i \in W_{t(\Delta_i^{\alpha_i})}$, then there is a world $v \in W$ such that wRv and $v \in W_{t(\Delta_1^{\alpha_1})} \cap ... \cap W_{t(\Delta_n^{\alpha_n})}$.[†]*

(R6) *For all $w \in W$ and all $\alpha_j \in Agt$, if there exists a $v \in W$ such that wRv and $v \in W_{\mathfrak{v}^{\alpha_j}}$, then there is a world $u \in W$ for which wRu and $u \in W - W_{\mathfrak{v}^{\alpha_j}}$.*

(†) *For an arbitrary Δ^{α_i}, s.t. $\Delta \in Act_{\mathsf{LAN}}$ and $\alpha_i \in Agt$, we define $W_{t(\Delta^{\alpha_i})}$ using the following recursive clauses: $W_{t(\delta_i^{\alpha_i})} = W_{\mathfrak{d}_i^{\alpha_i}}$, $W_{t(\overline{\Delta^{\alpha_i}})} = W - W_{t(\Delta^{\alpha_i})}$ and $W_{t(\Delta^{\alpha_i} \cup \Gamma^{\alpha_j})} = W_{t(\Delta^{\alpha_i})} \cup W_{t(\Gamma^{\alpha_j})}$.*

An LAN-*model is a tuple $M = (F, V)$ where F is an* LAN-*frame and V is a valuation function mapping propositional atoms to subsets of W, that is $V :$ $Atoms \mapsto \mathcal{P}(W)$, for which the following two restrictions hold:*

▶ $V(\mathfrak{d}_i^{\alpha_j}) = W_{\mathfrak{d}_i^{\alpha_j}}$, *for any* $\mathfrak{d}_i^{\alpha_j} \in \mathcal{L}_{\mathsf{LAN}}$.

▶ $V(\mathfrak{v}^{\alpha_j}) = W_{\mathfrak{v}^{\alpha_j}}$, *for any* $\mathfrak{v}^{\alpha_j} \in \mathcal{L}_{\mathsf{LAN}}$.

Let C_f^{LAN} be the class of LAN-*frames. (NB. One can easily show that $C_f^{\mathsf{LAN}} \neq \emptyset$.)*

The relation R represents transitions between successive states. Whereas transitions represented by R capture *possible* transitions from the current state, the relation R_N represents the *actual* transition from the current state. The only restrictions imposed are: there is at most one actual future **(R3)** and the actual future must be one of the possible futures **(R4)** (cf. A3 and A4 of Definition 4, resp.). The concept of 'actual future' is taken as state-dependent, which enables reasoning about states that would lie in the actual future of a counterfactual state (e.g., 'although it is Monday, if it would have been Thursday today, then it would actually be Friday tomorrow'; see [4]). Next, condition **(R5)** ensures that any combination of actions performed by distinct agents is consistent (cf. A5 of Definition 4). Condition **(R6)** enforces that, if there is a possible future in which a norm violation occurs for some agent, then there is also an alternative future available in which a norm violation is avoided for that agent (cf. A6 of Definition 4).

The semantics of $\mathcal{L}_{\mathsf{LAN}}$ is defined accordingly:

Definition 6 (Semantics for $\mathcal{L}_{\mathsf{LAN}}$). *Let M be an* LAN-*model and $w \in W$ of M. The* satisfaction *of a formula $\phi \in \mathcal{L}_{\mathsf{LAN}}$ in M at w is inductively defined as:*

(1) $M, w \vDash \chi$ *iff* $w \in V(\chi)$, *for any* $\chi \in Atoms$

(2) $M, w \vDash \neg\phi$ *iff* $M, w \nvDash \phi$

(3) $M, w \vDash \phi \rightarrow \psi$ *iff* $M, w \nvDash \phi$ *or* $M, w \vDash \psi$

(4) $M, w \vDash \Box\phi$ *iff*   *for all* $v \in W$ *s.t.* wRv *we have* $M, v \vDash \phi$

(5) $M, w \vDash [\mathsf{N}]\phi$ *iff*   *for all* $v \in W$ *s.t.* wR_Nv, *we have* $M, v \vDash \phi$

The semantic clauses for the dual operators $\Diamond$ and $\langle \mathsf{N} \rangle$, as well as global truth, validity and semantic entailment are defined as usual (see [5]).

(NB. propositional constants for actions and violations maintain their semantic interpretation in all models over a frame. See [4] for a discussion.)

The adequacy of LAN is directly obtained through a slight modification of the soundness and completeness proofs for the *logic of actions and expectations* presented in [4] (i.e. we substitute expectation constants for violation constants).

Theorem 1 (Adequacy [4]**).** *For all* $\phi \in \mathcal{L}_{\mathsf{LAN}}$, *we have that* ϕ *is an* LAN *theorem if and only if* ϕ *is valid with respect to the frame class* C_f^{LAN}.

Furthermore, the logic LAN is decidable and has the finite model property:

Theorem 2 (Finite Model Property). LAN *has the finite (tree) model property (FMP), i.e. every satisfiable formula is satisfiable on a finite, treelike model.*

Proof. The proof is presented in Appendix A at the end of this paper.

Corollary 1 (Decidability). *The satisfiability problem of* LAN *is decidable.*

As a closing comment, we observe that the decidability of LAN obtained here, implies decidability of the logic of *actions and expectations*, left as an open problem in [4] (this can be affirmed through a quick comparison of the axiomatizations).

4   Norms, Ability and Deliberation in LAN

The logic LAN allows us to reason about both actions and results. We can distinguish three different types of normative statements: normative statements about (1) results, (2) actions, and (3) actions in relation to results. We refer to the first two categories as *norms to be* and *norms to do*, respectively, and to the third category as *norms of instrumentality*. The last category articulates which actions must or must not be employed as instruments for obtaining particular goals (see [4,23] for a discussion of different notions of instrumentality). In this section, we demonstrate the expressive power of LAN through formalizing the aforementioned three categories, and use our formalization to investigate the dependencies between the different norm types. With this, we take a first step towards a formal analysis of norms of instrumentality. In the following section, we apply the attained notions to a formal analysis of our case study.

Before moving to our formal investigation, we need to establish some *desiderata* concerning the three norm-types and their interdependencies. First, we notice that according to [1], it is generally agreed upon that the categories of *norms to be* and *norms to do* cannot be completely reduced to one another. In Sect. 2 we discussed principle P1 of the protocol and argued that, in the case of obligations, *norms of instrumentality* are neither an instance of the former nor the latter category and, consequently, must be regarded as a category proper (the 'insider trading' example from Sect. 1 demonstrates the case for prohibitions). Still, we can identify several reasonable principles expressing certain interdependencies between the three categories:

D1 If a result is prohibited, then it will be prohibited regardless of the action used in obtaining it (i.e. prohibited given any action).
D2 If an action is prohibited, then its performance is prohibited irrespective of its outcome (i.e. prohibited given any outcome).

D3 If it is obligatory to perform a certain action to obtain a particular result (instrumentality), then it must be prohibited to not perform the action, as well as prohibited to not bring about the result.

In addition to the above, we will consider two pivotal principles from the realm of normative agency and investigate their effect on the three norm categories. The first is expressed as the *no vacuously satisfied norms* principle which states that all norms should be violable (see D4 below). This desideratum imposes a *deliberate* component on all norms (cf. Anderson's contingency principles [2,18] and Belnap and Horty's notion of deliberative agency [3,15]). As a second principle, we adopt a generalized variant of the 'ought implies can' principle—accredited to Immanuel Kant [16, A548/B576]—to which we will refer as the *norm implies can* principle. We will make a further distinction within the principle by considering two interpretations of the term 'can' (cf. [7] and [23] for different notions of ability). First, we take 'can' to denote 'possible' (D5 below). Second, we interpret 'can' as the stronger agentive notion of 'ability' (D6 below).

D4 Norms must be violable: If X is prohibited (obligatory), then (the negation of) X must be possible.
D5 Norms must be satisfiable: If X is obligatory (prohibited), then (the negation of) X must be possible.
D6 Norms must be agentively satisfiable: If X is obligatory (prohibited), then the agent must have the ability to guarantee (the negation of) X.
  (NB. Where X can be substituted for a result or an action.)

Clauses D5 and D6 express, respectively, the *weak* and *strong* norm implies can principle. We emphasize that for prohibitions (obligations), in order to fulfill (defy) its duty, an agent must ensure the *opposite* of what is forbidden (obligatory). In the following sections, we will see that the D1–D3 break down when we consider them together with the above deliberation constraints on norms D4–D6.

4.1 Norms to Be

In what follows, we will use the symbol F to refer to what is *forbidden* and we will use O to denote what is *obligatory*. Adapting Anderson's deontic reduction [2], we formally define the first category of *norms to be* (i.e. *forbidden to be* and *ought to be*, respectively) in accordance with principle D4 as follows:

F1. $\mathsf{F}[\top^{\alpha_i}]\phi := \Box(\phi \rightarrow \mathfrak{v}^{\alpha_i}) \wedge \Diamond\phi$
O1. $\mathsf{O}[\top^{\alpha_i}]\phi := \Box(\neg\phi \rightarrow \mathfrak{v}^{\alpha_i}) \wedge \Diamond\neg\phi$

We interpret $\mathsf{F}[\top^{\alpha_i}]\phi$ as 'ϕ is forbidden to become the case for agent α_i, iff (i) every possible transition to ϕ would mean a norm violation for agent α_i and (ii) ϕ is possible' and we read $\mathsf{O}[\top^{\alpha_i}]\phi$ as 'ϕ ought to become the case for agent α_i, iff (i) every possible transition to $\neg\phi$ would mean a norm violation for agent α_i and (ii) $\neg\phi$ is possible'. The first conjunct (i) of F1 and O1 corresponds to Anderson's reduction (referred to as the *reduction clause*), whereas the second conjunct (ii) captures that the norm can be violated (referred to as the *violation clause* of principle D4). We take $\top^{\alpha_i}$ to represent α_i's vacuously satisfied action: that is, $\top^{\alpha_i} := (\delta_1 \cup \overline{\delta_1})^{\alpha_i}$ (cf. the universal action [17]). We take $\bot^{\alpha_i} := (\delta_1 \& \overline{\delta_1})^{\alpha_i}$ to denote the impossible action, used in definitions F1$'$ and O1$'$ below.

We may extend the above formalizations to define *norms to be* in accordance with the more stringent principle D6. We write F$'$ and O$'$ to indicate what is forbidden and what is obligatory, respectively, within this paradigm:[5]

F1$'$. $\mathsf{F}'[\top^{\alpha_i}]\phi := \Box(\phi \to \mathfrak{v}^{\alpha_i}) \wedge \Diamond\phi \wedge \bigvee_{[\![\Delta^{\alpha_i}]\!] \in [\![Act^*_{\mathsf{LAN}}]\!]} \Box(t(\Delta^{\alpha_i}) \to \neg\phi)$

O1$'$. $\mathsf{O}'[\top^{\alpha_i}]\phi := \Box(\neg\phi \to \mathfrak{v}^{\alpha_i}) \wedge \Diamond\neg\phi \wedge \bigvee_{[\![\Delta^{\alpha_i}]\!] \in [\![Act^*_{\mathsf{LAN}}]\!]} \Box(t(\Delta^{\alpha_i}) \to \phi)$

The norms $\mathsf{F}'[\top^{\alpha_i}]\phi$ and $\mathsf{O}'[\top^{\alpha_i}]\phi$ are similar to $\mathsf{F}[\top^{\alpha_i}]\phi$ and $\mathsf{O}[\top^{\alpha_i}]\phi$ in that they contain a reduction clause and a violation clause. However, in addition they also contain a *norm implies ability* clause. This additional third clause expresses that (iii) 'there exists an action available to the agent that *would* serve as a suitable instrument for satisfying the norm' (cf. the 'would' operator, Sect. 3).

Principle D4 is explicitly satisfied by definition F1, O1, F1$'$, and O1$'$, whereas the latter two also explicitly satisfy D6. What is more, in LAN we derive that all four definitions satisfy D5 too. This result is obtained through the following reasoning: Suppose $\mathsf{F}[\top^{\alpha_i}]\phi$. By definition, $\Diamond\phi$ holds. Through basic LAN reasoning and the reduction clause, $\Diamond\mathfrak{v}^{\alpha_i}$ holds and, by applying axiom $A6$, we obtain $\Diamond\neg\mathfrak{v}^{\alpha_i}$. Last, from LAN reasoning and the reduction clause we can derive $\Diamond\neg\phi$. Similar arguments can be given for the remaining norms. Hence, we obtain the following LAN theorem:

$$\mathsf{F}[\top^{\alpha_i}]\phi \vee \mathsf{O}[\top^{\alpha_i}]\phi \vee \mathsf{F}'[\top^{\alpha_i}]\phi \vee \mathsf{O}'[\top^{\alpha_i}]\phi \to (\Diamond\phi \wedge \Diamond\neg\phi)$$

In other words, in LAN we derive that *norms to be* range over contingent state-of-affairs; i.e. the norms can be both satisfied and violated. We refer to this result as *the contingency property* of norms (cf. [2,18]).

4.2 Norms to Do

With respect to the second category of *norms to do*, we adopt Meyer's reduction [17] to the LAN setting and formally define our *forbidden to do* and *ought to do* operators, respectively, as follows:

---

[5] Notice, since Act_{LAN} represents a Boolean algebra of actions built over a finite number of actions types from Act, there are only finitely many equivalence classes $[\![\Delta^{\alpha_i}]\!] := \{\Gamma^{\alpha_i} \mid \vdash_{\mathsf{LAN}} t(\Gamma^{\alpha_i}) \equiv t(\Delta^{\alpha_i})\}$ of equivalent actions. We let $[\![Act^*_{\mathsf{LAN}}]\!]$ in F1$'$ and O1$'$ represent the set of all such equivalence classes *minus* the class $[\![\bot^{\alpha_i}]\!]$ of all impossible actions. Additionally, since obligatory or forbidden results are central to norms to be, as opposed to obligatory or forbidden actions, we impose the following restriction on F1, O1, F1$'$ and O1$'$: *the formula ϕ is free of action constants from Wit*. Without this restriction, norms to do could be seen as instances of norms to be—i.e. norms to bring about the witness of a performed action as a result—thus contradicting the observations made in [1] about the irreducibility of the two.

F2. $\mathsf{F}[\Delta^{\alpha_i}]\top := \Box(t(\Delta^{\alpha_i}) \to \mathfrak{v}^{\alpha_i}) \wedge \Diamond t(\Delta^{\alpha_i})$

O2. $\mathsf{O}[\Delta^{\alpha_i}]\top := \Box(\neg t(\Delta^{\alpha_i}) \to \mathfrak{v}^{\alpha_i}) \wedge \Diamond \neg t(\Delta^{\alpha_i})$

We read $\mathsf{F}[\Delta^{\alpha_i}]\top$ as 'the performance of Δ is forbidden for agent α_i, iff (i) every possible performance of Δ would mean a norm violation for agent α_i and (ii) Δ can be performed by α_i' and we interpret $\mathsf{O}[\Delta^{\alpha_i}]\top$ as 'Δ ought to be performed by agent α_i, iff (i) every possible performance of $\overline{\Delta}$ would mean a norm violation for agent α_i and (ii) $\overline{\Delta}$ can be performed by α_i'. We take $\top$ to represent the vacuously satisfied result; that is, we say that the norm applies independent of its result. The reduction clause (i) of F2 and O2 corresponds to Meyer's deontic reduction, whereas clause (ii) captures the norm's deliberative nature by requiring the possibility of norm violation.

The above, together with axiom A6, implies that also *norms to do* have the desired contingency characteristics; i.e. the following is an LAN theorem:

$$\mathsf{F}[\Delta^{\alpha_i}]\top \vee \mathsf{O}[\Delta^{\alpha_i}]\top \to (\Diamond t(\Delta^{\alpha_i}) \wedge \Diamond \neg t(\Delta^{\alpha_i}))$$

However, the distinction between D5 and D6 breaks down for norms to do: the implied contingency clause in these norms directly incorporates the notion of *ability*. This is due to our interpretation of actions, which corresponds to the use of actions in PDeL [1,17]; i.e. when an agent has an action at its disposal this means that it has the ability to guarantee its performance. Hence, in the current framework these two notions equate.

4.3 Norms of Instrumentality

So far, the first two categories have been formally defined on the basis of their converged interpretation in the literature (e.g., [1,8]) and extended with deliberative clauses. How should we formally capture the third, novel category of *norms of instrumentality*? The above analyses would suggest a definition comprising at least a reduction clause and a violation clause. However, with respect to norms of instrumentality this twofold reading does not suffice.

Let us first consider the obligations belonging to norms of instrumentality. First, recall that we take as *instruments* those actions that are suitable for serving a particular purpose. Hence, for an agent to be committed to such an obligation, we require that the prescribed action is in fact an *instrument* for bringing about the desired result; i.e. the action *would guarantee* the envisaged outcome. Observe that, given this reading, the strong *norm implies can* principle is immediately satisfied: i.e. the agent must be able to produce the desired result through the desired action. Hence, for the third category, we opt for a formalization that directly incorporates the agential notion of *would* (cf. Sect. 3). Second, we need to identify what it means for an agent to violate an obligation of the third category: If an agent α_i has the obligation to employ Δ (as an instrument) to obtain ϕ, then α_i violates this obligation whenever *either* α_i does not perform

Δ (independent of whether α_i produced ϕ) *or* α_i does not bring about ϕ (independent of whether α_i performed Δ). On the basis of the above two observations, we thus say that 'an agent α_i has the obligation to employ Δ as an instrument to obtain ϕ iff (i) performing $\overline{\Delta}$ or bringing about $\neg\phi$ would lead to a norm violation for agent α_i, (ii) such a norm violation is possible through $\neg\phi$ or $\overline{\Delta}$, and (iii) the performance of Δ by α_i would ensure ϕ (i.e. Δ is a ϕ-instrument for α_i).' We formally define this norm as follows:

O3. $\mathsf{O}[\Delta^{\alpha_i}]\phi := \Box(\neg(t(\Delta^{\alpha_i}) \wedge \phi) \rightarrow \mathfrak{v}^{\alpha_i}) \wedge \Diamond\neg(t(\Delta^{\alpha_i}) \wedge \phi) \wedge \Box(t(\Delta^{\alpha_i}) \rightarrow \phi)$

Notice that, in the three conjuncts of definition O3 we recognize: (i) the reduction clause, (ii) the violation clause, and (iii) the ability clause, respectively. Moreover, as with F1, O1, F1′, and O1′ we stipulate that ϕ must be free of action constants from Wit (in both O3 and F3).

Should we give a similar reading for prohibitions of this category? The answer is not straightforward. Let us reconsider the example from Sect. 1: 'it is prohibited to use non-public information as an instrument to attain financial profit on the stock market'. We say that an agent α_i violates this prohibition whenever α_i uses non-public information and consequently attains financial profit from it. However, should we additionally require that α_i is only subject to this prohibition whenever α_i has the strict ability to guarantee financial profit through using non-public information? The answer seems to be negative: we also desire to include cases in which α_i accidentally obtains financial profit on the stock market through using non-public information.[6] Nevertheless, in adopting the strong norm implies can principle we still require that the agent must have the *ability to avoid* violating the prohibition in question, thus satisfying its duty. Putting the above together, we say that 'agent α_i is prohibited to employ action Δ as an instrument for the purpose ϕ, iff (i) in every case in which Δ has been performed and ϕ has been successfully ensured, a norm violation has occurred, (ii) the norm can in fact be violated and, most importantly, (iii) either α_i has the ability to avoid performing Δ or there is an action to α_i's disposal that is a suitable instrument for avoiding ϕ.' Formally, this is expressed accordingly:

F3. $\mathsf{F}[\Delta^{\alpha_i}]\phi := \Box((t(\Delta^{\alpha_i}) \wedge \phi) \rightarrow \mathfrak{v}^{\alpha_i}) \wedge \Diamond(t(\Delta^{\alpha_i}) \wedge \phi) \wedge \theta$

$$\text{where } \theta := \Diamond\neg t(\Delta^{\alpha_i}) \vee \bigvee_{[\Gamma^{\alpha_i}] \in [Act^*_{\mathsf{LAN}}]} \Box(t(\Gamma^{\alpha_i}) \rightarrow \neg\phi)$$

The first two conjuncts of F3 correspond to the reduction and violation clause, respectively. The additional third conjunct explicitly stipulates the ability and instrumentality relations which enable the agent in question to fulfil its duty.

Let us discuss the interaction between the proposed definitions of norms of instrumentality and the list of desiderata presented at the beginning of this

---

[6] The assumption avoids risk by forbidding acts that possibly produce violations; e.g. 'it is forbidden to injure someone with a sharp tool, independent of the ability to guarantee the injury'. However, one could consider inclusion of instrumentality clauses for prohibitions when analyzing responsibility. We leave this for future work.

section. First, we observe that the second conjunct of F3, ensuring the prohibition's deliberative nature, invalidates principles D1 and D2. That is, an LAN-model can be constructed to show the following are satisfiable for some Δ^{α_i} and ϕ:

$$\mathsf{F}[\mathsf{T}^{\alpha_i}]\phi \wedge \neg\mathsf{F}[\Delta^{\alpha_i}]\phi, \quad \mathsf{F}'[\mathsf{T}^{\alpha_i}]\phi \wedge \neg\mathsf{F}[\Delta^{\alpha_i}]\phi, \quad \text{and } \mathsf{F}[\Delta^{\alpha_i}]\mathsf{T} \wedge \neg\mathsf{F}[\Delta^{\alpha_i}]\phi$$

The inconsistency of F3 with principles D1 and D2 can be understood as follows: a prohibition to bring about a result (action) should not imply that the result (action) must be avoided given any action (result), but only relative to those actions (results) possible. In other words, *impossible combinations* of actions and results are not forbidden because they are *inviolable*. Observe that D1 and D2 can be salvaged by abandoning principles D4, D5 and D6.

Second, as for the other two norm categories, definitions O3 and F3 imply the desired LAN theorem concerning the contingency of instrumentality norms:

$$\mathsf{O}[\Delta^{\alpha_i}]\phi \vee \mathsf{F}[\Delta^{\alpha_i}]\phi \rightarrow (\Diamond(t(\Delta^{\alpha_i}) \wedge \phi) \wedge \Diamond\neg(t(\Delta^{\alpha_i}) \wedge \phi))$$

Third, as stated by principle D3, when an agent α_i has the obligation to ensure ϕ, but only specifically through performing Δ, we would like to be able to derive that for α_i the state of affairs $\neg\phi$, as well as the performance of $\overline{\Delta}$, is prohibited. However, this principle only holds in our context when we forgo the weak *norm implies can* principle. In other words, by omitting the violation clause (ii) (and therefore the implied contingency property) of definitions F1, F1', F2, and O3, we obtain the following LAN theorems, satisfying principle D3:

$$\mathsf{O}[\Delta^{\alpha_i}]\phi \rightarrow (\mathsf{F}[\mathsf{T}^{\alpha_i}]\neg\phi \wedge \mathsf{F}[\overline{\Delta^{\alpha_i}}]\mathsf{T}) \quad \text{and } \mathsf{O}[\Delta^{\alpha_i}]\phi \rightarrow (\mathsf{F}'[\mathsf{T}^{\alpha_i}]\neg\phi \wedge \mathsf{F}[\overline{\Delta^{\alpha_i}}]\mathsf{T})$$

That in the present setting definition O3 is incompatible with principle D3, follows from the observation that impossible combinations of actions and states of affairs cannot be violated and, thus, will not classify as deliberative norms.

As a final remark, we believe that clause (iii) is pivotal for norms of instrumentality: That is, we do not want to commit agents to a cause whose outcome is merely accidental (i.e. uncontrollable). This would be too stringent. Instead, we desire that the envisaged outcome is a proper consequence of the agent's behaviour. In other words, when the agent has also the *ability* to fulfill its duty—i.e. guarantee that the action under consideration leads to the desired outcome—only then the agent can be demanded to ensure the outcome by performing the action. This claim is in line with principle D6, the strong, agentive reading of *norm implies can* where 'can' denotes 'ability' or 'choice' (cf. [3,7,15]). Given such a clause, our definitions avoid the overburdening of an agent by not committing the agent to a cause it cannot effectively fulfill. The following LAN theorems capture the strong *norm implies can* reading of O3 and F3:

$$\mathsf{F}[\Delta^{\alpha_i}]\phi \rightarrow [\Delta^{\alpha_i}]^{could}\phi \quad \text{and } \mathsf{O}[\Delta^{\alpha_i}]\phi \rightarrow [\Delta^{\alpha_i}]^{could}\phi$$

In conclusion, the final definitions—i.e. F1, F1', F2, F3, O1, O1', O2 and O3—are based on (i) Anderson's and Meyer's reduction, (ii) the *no vacuously*

Table 1. Formulae based on F1–F3, O1–O3, F1′ and O1′ considered with *only* the reduction clause (i) and considered with *all* clauses of the given definition. 'Yes' means the formula is a theorem for all Δ^{α_i} and ϕ; 'no' means otherwise. We let $\mathsf{F}^* \in \{\mathsf{F}, \mathsf{F}'\}$ and $\mathsf{O}^* \in \{\mathsf{O}, \mathsf{O}'\}$.

				Only clause (i)	Complete clauses
V1.	$\mathsf{F}^*[\mathsf{T}^{\alpha_i}]\phi \to \mathsf{F}[\Delta^{\alpha_i}]\phi$	and	$\mathsf{F}[\Delta^{\alpha_i}]\mathsf{T} \to \mathsf{F}[\Delta^{\alpha_i}]\phi$	yes	no
V2.	$\mathsf{O}[\Delta^{\alpha_i}]\phi \to \mathsf{O}^*[\mathsf{T}^{\alpha_i}]\phi$	and	$\mathsf{O}[\Delta^{\alpha_i}]\phi \to \mathsf{O}[\Delta^{\alpha_i}]\mathsf{T}$	yes	no, yes (resp.)
V3.	$\mathsf{O}^*[\mathsf{T}^{\alpha_i}]\phi \to \mathsf{F}[\Delta^{\alpha_i}]\neg\phi$	and	$\mathsf{O}[\Delta^{\alpha_i}]\mathsf{T} \to \mathsf{F}[\overline{\Delta^{\alpha_i}}]\phi$	yes	no
V4.	$\mathsf{F}^*[\mathsf{T}^{\alpha_i}]\phi \to \mathsf{O}[\Delta^{\alpha_i}]\neg\phi$	and	$\mathsf{F}[\Delta^{\alpha_i}]\mathsf{T} \to \mathsf{O}[\overline{\Delta^{\alpha_i}}]\phi$	no	no
V5.	$\mathsf{F}^*[\mathsf{T}^{\alpha_i}]\phi \equiv \mathsf{O}^*[\mathsf{T}^{\alpha_i}]\neg\phi$	and	$\mathsf{F}[\Delta^{\alpha_i}]\mathsf{T} \equiv \mathsf{O}[\overline{\Delta^{\alpha_i}}]\mathsf{T}$	yes	yes
V6.	$\mathsf{O}[\Delta^{\alpha_i}]\phi \to \mathsf{F}^*[\mathsf{T}^{\alpha_i}]\neg\phi \wedge \mathsf{F}[\overline{\Delta^{\alpha_i}}]\mathsf{T}$			yes	no
V7.	$\mathsf{O}[\Delta^{\alpha_i}]\phi \equiv \mathsf{O}[\Delta^{\alpha_i}]\mathsf{T} \wedge \mathsf{O}^*[\mathsf{T}^{\alpha_i}]\phi$			yes	no
V8.	$\mathsf{F}^*[\mathsf{T}^{\alpha_i}]\phi \wedge \mathsf{F}[\Delta^{\alpha_i}]\mathsf{T} \to \mathsf{F}[\Delta^{\alpha_i}]\phi$			yes	no

satisfied norms principle (of which the *weak norm implies can* principle was a logical consequence in LAN), and (iii) the *strong norm implies can* (i.e. ability) principle for norms of instrumentality. We saw that, by adopting principles enforcing minimal deliberative criteria on norms (i.e. D4 and D5), we canceled basic dependencies between the three categories (i.e. D1, D2 and D3). In Table 1 we gathered some LAN theorems that bear significance to the present analysis. For example, in losing the *norm implies can* principle altogether, we obtain interdependencies such as $V1-V3$ of Table 1 first column. That $\mathsf{O}[\Delta^{\alpha_i}]\phi$ implies $\mathsf{O}[\Delta^{\alpha_i}]\mathsf{T}$ with complete clauses ($V2$) is (in part) due to the ability clause, which ensures the violation clause necessary for the implied norm to do. The dependencies described by $V4$ and $V5$ are invariant to deliberation. Last, $V6-V8$ express some dependencies between combinations of norms. Still, further investigation of the proposed definitions and interdependencies is required. The present analysis establishes a first step towards such an investigation by exhibiting the expressive power of the logic LAN. Let us now formally address our case study.

5   The Benchmark Example Revisited

In what follows, we apply our formal machinery to the example of Sect. 2. We formalize the protocol in LAN by making use of definitions F1–F3 and O1–O3, and apply it to two concrete situations where an agent must invoke the protocol to make a decision. Our formalization will be used to demonstrate that the protocol is insufficient relative to its assumed aims (i.e. T1 and T2 of Sect. 2). We close by discussing the source of the aforementioned failure, arguing how the protocol and corresponding logic could be extended to repair such deficiencies.

For the formalization of the protocol, we take `sur` and `nur` to denote the agents 'surgeon' and 'nurse', respectively. The action language consists of the atoms `scalp`, `leave` and `call`, respectively describing 'using a scalpel', 'leaving the operation room' and 'calling the safety-emergency number'. Let incis, operation, dire, health, safety_nur and safety_sur be propositional atoms denoting 'the incision is made', 'the situation is an operation', 'the situation is dire', 'the patient's health is promoted', 'hygiene safety is promoted from the nurse's perspective' and 'hygiene safety is promoted from the surgeon's perspective', respectively. Consider the following possible formalization of the protocol:

P1. $(\text{operation} \wedge O[T^{sur}]\text{incis}) \rightarrow O[\text{scalp}^{sur}]\text{incis}$
P2. $(\text{operation} \wedge \neg\text{dire}) \rightarrow F[\text{scalp}^{nur}]T$
P3. $O[T^{nur}]\text{health} \wedge O[T^{nur}]\text{safety\_nur}$ and
$\quad O[T^{sur}]\text{health} \wedge O[T^{sur}]\text{safety\_sur}$
E1. $\neg\text{safety\_nur} \rightarrow (O[\text{leave}^{nur}]T \wedge O[\text{call}^{nur}]T)$ and
$\quad \neg\text{safety\_sur} \rightarrow (O[\text{leave}^{sur}]T \wedge O[\text{call}^{sur}]T)$

As an example of how to interpret the formulae above, we read P2 as: 'if there is an operation and the situation is not dire, then the nurse is prohibited to use the scalpel (irrespective of its outcome)'. We are currently interested in whether the protocol is consistent, and whether it can provide agents with sufficient tools to solve normative issues (in situations relevant to our example). Concerning the former, consistency will be shown via the construction of a model for P1–P3 and E1 (below). Regarding the latter, let us consider some possible situations.

Situation 1. In the operation room Anna, the head-surgeon, and a nurse named Bill are performing a tonsillectomy on a patient (i.e. the patient's tonsils are to be removed). Anna must make a final highly demanding dissection, involving both hands, when she realizes that another crucial incision had to be made using the harmonic scalpel (a scalpel that simultaneously cauterizes tissue). Since Anna is preoccupied and unable to do it, she appeals in this dire situation to Bill, asking whether he could make the other necessary incision with the harmonic scalpel, thus ensuring the patient's health. The situation is formalized accordingly:

(i) $\text{operation} \wedge \text{dire} \wedge [\overline{\text{scalp}}^{sur}]^{will}T$ (iii) $[\overline{\text{scalp}}^{nur}]^{would}\neg\text{health}$
(ii) $[\text{scalp}^{nur}]^{would}\text{incis}$ (iv) $\square(\text{incis} \rightarrow \text{health})$

Bill is aware of the new protocol: he knows he is not allowed to use scalpels in regular situations but remembers his duty to the patient's health too. What should Bill do? The protocol tells Bill that he has the obligation to promote the patient's health (i.e. $O[T^{nur}]\text{health}$, follows from P3). Since the surgical situation is dire (i) principle P2 does not apply. What is more, since using the scalpel to make the incision is Bill's only way to promote the patient's health— by (ii)–(iv)—Bill in fact has the obligation to make the incision with the scalpel; that is, the following is valid:

$$(i) \wedge (ii) \wedge (iii) \wedge (iv) \wedge P1 \wedge P2 \wedge P3 \wedge E1 \rightarrow O[\text{scalp}^{nur}]\text{incis}$$

Consequently, Bill is not prohibited from using the scalpel (i.e. $\neg F[\text{scalp}^{nur}]T$ follows from definition O3, LAN reasoning and V5).

Furthermore, to see whether Bill complies with the protocol when he *actually* brings about the incision with the scalpel—i.e. (v) $[\text{scalp}^{nur}]^{will}\text{incis}$—consider the corresponding LAN-model in Fig. 1. Namely, the model shows that Bill's behaviour (v), together with the formalized protocol P1–P3 and E1 and the present situation (i)–(iv), can be consistently represented together with Bill's actual norm compliance; i.e. (vi) $\langle N \rangle \neg \mathfrak{v}^{nur}$. For that reason, Bill's decision to make the incision using the scalpel preserves the state of compliance (nevertheless, as expected, it can still be the case that, due to some other action of Bill's, a violation is generated). (See [12] for a discussion of protocol consistency, compliance and model checking.) Conversely, if Bill actually decides to *not* use the scalpel, a norm violation will be inevitable; that is, the following is valid:

$$(i) \wedge (ii) \wedge (iii) \wedge (iv) \wedge P1 \wedge P2 \wedge P3 \wedge E1 \wedge \overline{[\text{scalp}^{nur}]}^{will} \top \rightarrow \overline{[\text{scalp}^{nur}]}^{will} \mathfrak{v}^{nur}$$

Last, we note that Fig. 1 also shows the consistency of the formalized protocol.

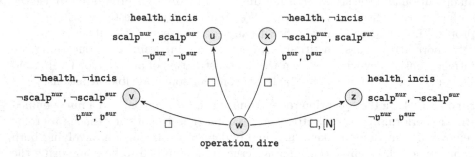

Fig. 1. An LAN-model satisfying P1–P3, E1 and (i)–(v); that is, showing the consistency of the protocol and Bill's actual behaviour with Bill being compliant in situation 1.

Situation 2. Let us continue the above example: right before Bill performs the procedure involving the scalpel, Bill accidentally hits his own arm with the harmonic scalpel and inflicts a painful wound. Bill and Anna know, since Bill has now violated his obligation (P3) to preserve the required hygiene safety, that he is obliged (E1) to immediately leave the operation room and call the safety-emergency number for assistance. However, Anna observes that the necessary incision still has to be made in order to secure the agent's health, so she concludes that Bill must stay and assist her immediately without further ado. The situation is formalized accordingly:

(vii) $\neg \texttt{safety\_nur}$ (viii) $[\texttt{leave}^{nur}]^{would} \neg \texttt{health}$

First, we observe that given E1 and (vii) , Bill has the obligation to leave (i.e. $O[\texttt{leave}^{nur}]\top$). However, through (viii), the act of leaving would imply that Bill violates his obligation to preserve the patient's health (i.e. $O[\top^{nur}]\texttt{health}$). In fact, the current situation and the formalized protocol are inconsistent; namely, (vii)–(viii), together with P1–P3 and E1, would render in LAN that Bill has an obligation to leave and to not leave (i.e. $\mathsf{O}[\mathtt{leave^{nur}} \& \overline{\mathtt{leave}}^{nur}]\top$). This inconsistency depends on the assumption T1 (cf. **(R6)** of Definition 5), which is the committee's assumption that there is a way out to every possible dilemma. In conclusion, the formalism tells us that the protocol is current inadequate.

The source of the conflict that arises in the second situation above relates to Chisholm's Paradox [9] and the issue of *contrary-to-duty* (CTD) reasoning. Principle E1, in fact, can be seen as a contrary-to-duty obligation and the present system suffers from the similar problem of detachment as the initial paradox does. In brief, a contrary-to-duty obligation is a specific obligation that comes into force whenever a primary obligation has been violated. What is more, their purpose is to (partially) *restore* compliance with the norm system (e.g. [11]). They are often referred to as secondary obligations, to denote the fact that they *depend upon* the possibility of violating *primary* obligations (cf. [9,19]). Such a violation is always possible when employing norms F1–F3, O1–O3, F1$'$, and O1$'$ with LAN due to the contingency requirements addressed in Sect. 4. An extension of our formalism to adequately account for such reasoning, is outside the scope of this paper, and so, we leave this to future work.

6 Conclusion

In this work, we provided the sound and complete logic LAN that brings together Anderson's reduction of *norms to be* and Meyer's reduction of *norms to do*. We introduced a new category of norms—*norms of instrumentality*—and analyzed its relationships with the former two classes vis-à-vis different notions of deliberative action. The technical contribution of this work consists in proving the finite model property and decidability of LAN. Since the non-normative logic presented in [4] is an instance of LAN, we also answered the open problem for that logic's decidability. These results show that LAN has the potential to be employed in automated reasoning with norms relating agency, actions and results.

In comparing the present logic with state of the art frameworks, we see three possible directions for future work. First, as mentioned in Sect. 5, a natural way to extend our framework would be to incorporate normative reasoning about subideal scenarios, involving a notion of contrary-to-duty norms that are primarily designed to bring the agent back into a state of compliance with the system. We aim to address this issue and analyze its relation to the three norm categories.

Second, our current analysis omitted consideration of permissions. The behaviour of permissions in relation to the three norm categories is not immediately clear. For example, although the notion of a weak permission appears equivalent to the dual of an unconditional obligation in the form of O1 or O2 , the concept of strong permission seems to require explicit formulations in permissive form (cf. [13]). Moreover, as argued in [13,14], the traditional way of representing permissions as duals of obligations is an over-simplification that cannot adequately model many real-life scenarios. We plan to extend our formalism to incorporate such permissions.

Last, since the logic LAN encompasses the Andersonian reductions analysed in [17], but uses a third reduction using action constants, we plan to devote future work to investigating the logic's relation to the deontic action logic PDeL.

Acknowledgments. Work funded by projects: FWF I2982, FWF W1255-N23, FWF Y544-N2, and WWTF MA16-028.

A   Finite Model Property and Decidability

In this appendix, we provide the main technical contribution of this paper: we show that LAN is decidable (Corollary 1), via proving the finite model property (FMP) for the logic (Theorem 2). Our strategy is, accordingly: first, we show that every satisfiable formula is satisfiable on a treelike model (Lemma 1). Second, we show that the depth of the treelike model can be bounded (Lemma 2). Last, we prove that the breadth of the model can be bounded (Lemma 3).

Lemma 1. *Every formula $\phi \in \mathcal{L}_{\mathsf{LAN}}$ satisfiable on a LAN-model, is satisfiable at the root of a treelike LAN-model.*

Proof. Let $M = (W, \{W_{\mathfrak{d}_j^{\alpha_i}} : \mathfrak{d}_j^{\alpha_i} \in \mathcal{L}_{\mathsf{LAN}}\}, \{W_{\mathfrak{v}^{\alpha_i}} : \mathfrak{v}^{\alpha_i} \in \mathcal{L}_{\mathsf{LAN}}\}, R, R_{\mathsf{N}}, V)$ be a LAN-model with $w \in W$ and assume $M, w \models \phi$ (i.e. ϕ is satisfiable). To show that ϕ is satisfiable at the root of a treelike model we evoke an unraveling procedure similar to the one in [5, Ch. 2.1]. We define the treelike model M^t as follows:

$$M^t = (W^t, \{W^t_{\mathfrak{d}_j^{\alpha_i}} : \mathfrak{d}_j^{\alpha_i} \in \mathcal{L}_{\mathsf{LAN}}\}, \{W^t_{\mathfrak{v}^{\alpha_i}} : \mathfrak{v}^{\alpha_i} \in \mathcal{L}_{\mathsf{LAN}}\}, R^t, R^t_{\mathsf{N}}, V^t), \text{ where}$$

- $W^t \subseteq \bigcup_{n \in \mathbb{N}} W^n$ is the set of all finite sequences $(w, w_1, ..., w_n)$ s.t. wRw_1, $w_1 R w_2, ..., w_{n-1} R w_n$;
- For each $\alpha_i \in Agt$ and each $\mathfrak{d}_j^{\alpha_i} \in Wit^{\alpha_i}$, $W^t_{\mathfrak{d}_j^{\alpha_i}} \subseteq W^t$ is the set of all finite sequences $(w, w_1, ..., w_n)$ s.t. $w_n \in W_{\mathfrak{d}_j^{\alpha_i}}$;
- For each $\alpha_i \in Agt$, $W^t_{\mathfrak{v}^{\alpha_i}} \subseteq W^t$ is the set of all finite sequences $(w, w_1, ..., w_n)$ s.t. $w_n \in W_{\mathfrak{v}^{\alpha_i}}$;
- For all $\boldsymbol{w}, \boldsymbol{u} \in W^t$, $\boldsymbol{w} R^t \boldsymbol{u}$ iff $\boldsymbol{w} = (w, w_1, ..., w_n)$, $\boldsymbol{u} = (w, w_1..., w_n, w_{n+1})$, and $w_n R w_{n+1}$;
- For all $\boldsymbol{w}, \boldsymbol{u} \in W^t$, $\boldsymbol{w} R^t_{\mathsf{N}} \boldsymbol{u}$ iff $\boldsymbol{w} = (w, w_1, ..., w_n)$, $\boldsymbol{u} = (w, w_1..., w_n, w_{n+1})$, and $w_n R_{\mathsf{N}} w_{n+1}$;
- For all $\boldsymbol{w} \in W^t$, $\boldsymbol{w} = (w, w_1, ..., w_n) \in V^t(p)$ iff $w_n \in V(p)$.

The model M^t is clearly treelike. Further, Prop. 2.14 and 2.15 of [5] imply:

(1) For any formula $\psi \in \mathcal{L}_{\mathsf{LAN}}$, each $u \in W$, and each $\boldsymbol{u} \in W^t$ of the form

$(w, w_1, ..., u)$, we have that $M, u \models \psi$ iff $M^t, \boldsymbol{u} \models \psi$.

This result, together with the assumption $M, w \models \phi$, implies $M^t, (w) \models \phi$, where (w) is the root of the treelike model M^t. To complete the proof, we must argue that M^t is a LAN-model, i.e., it satisfies conditions (R3)–(R6) of Definition 5:

(R3) Let $\boldsymbol{w}, \boldsymbol{u}, \boldsymbol{v} \in W^t$ and suppose $\boldsymbol{w} R_N^t \boldsymbol{u}$ and $\boldsymbol{w} R_N^t \boldsymbol{v}$. By definition of R_N^t we get (i) $\boldsymbol{w}$ is a sequence of the form $(w, w_1, ..., w_n)$, (ii) $\boldsymbol{u}$ is a sequence $(w, w_1, ..., w_n, w_{n+1})$, (iii) $\boldsymbol{v}$ is a sequence $(w, w_1, ..., w_n, w'_{n+1})$, (iv) $w_n R_N w_{n+1}$, and (v) $w_n R_N w'_{n+1}$. Since the original model M satisfies (R3), it follows from (iv) and (v) that $w_{n+1} = w'_{n+1}$, which, together with (ii) and (iii), implies $\boldsymbol{u} = \boldsymbol{v}$.

(R4) Let $\boldsymbol{w}, \boldsymbol{u} \in W^t$ and assume $\boldsymbol{w} R_N^t \boldsymbol{u}$. By definition of R_N^t we get (i) $\boldsymbol{w}$ is a sequence of the form $(w, w_1, ..., w_n)$, (ii) $\boldsymbol{u}$ is a sequence $(w, w_1, ..., w_n, w_{n+1})$, and (iii) $w_n R_N w_{n+1}$. Since the original model M satisfies (R4), it follows from (iii) that $w_n R w_{n+1}$, which, together with (i) and (ii), implies $\boldsymbol{w} R^t \boldsymbol{u}$.

(R5) Let $\boldsymbol{w} \in W^t$ and $Agt = \{\alpha_1, ..., \alpha_n\}$. Suppose there are (not necessarily distinct) action-types $\Delta_1, ..., \Delta_n \in Act_{\mathsf{LAN}}$ s.t. for $1 \leq i \leq n$ there exist $\boldsymbol{u}_i \in W^t$ s.t. $\boldsymbol{w} R^t \boldsymbol{u}_i$ and $\boldsymbol{u}_i \in W_{t(\Delta_i^{\alpha_i})}^t$. It follows that $\boldsymbol{w}$ is of the form $(w, w_1, ..., w_n)$ and each $\boldsymbol{u}_i$ is of the form $(w, w_1, ..., w_n, u_i)$ with $w_n R u_i$. The model M satisfies condition (R5), and hence there exists a world $v \in W$ s.t. $w_n R v$ and $v \in W_{t(\Delta_1^{\alpha_1})} \cap \cdots \cap W_{t(\Delta_n^{\alpha_n})}$. By definition of M^t, we have $\boldsymbol{v} = (w, w_1, ..., w_n, v) \in W^t$, implying that $\boldsymbol{w} R^t \boldsymbol{v}$ and $\boldsymbol{v} \in W_{t(\Delta_1^{\alpha_1})}^t \cap \cdots \cap W_{t(\Delta_n^{\alpha_n})}^t$.

(R6) Let $\boldsymbol{w} \in W^t$ and $\alpha_i \in Agt$. Assume there is a $\boldsymbol{v} \in W^t$ s.t. $\boldsymbol{w} R^t \boldsymbol{v}$ and $\boldsymbol{v} \in W_{\boldsymbol{v}^{\alpha_i}}^t$. This implies $\boldsymbol{w} = (w, w_1, ..., w_n)$ and $\boldsymbol{v} = (w, w_1, ..., w_n, v)$ with $w_n R v$. Since M satisfies (R6), there is a u s.t. $w_n R u$ and $u \in W - W_{v^{\alpha_i}}$. By definition of M^t, there is a $\boldsymbol{u} = (w, w_1, ..., w_n, u) \in W^t$ s.t. $\boldsymbol{w} R^t \boldsymbol{u}$ and $\boldsymbol{u} \in W^t - W_{\boldsymbol{v}^{\alpha_i}}^t$.

For the second transformation we define the following auxiliary concepts:

Definition 7 (Degree $deg(\cdot)$). *The* modal degree *is recursively defined as:*

- $deg(p) = deg(\mathfrak{d}_j^{\alpha_i}) = deg(\mathfrak{v}^{\alpha_i}) = 0;$
- $deg(\neg \phi) = \deg(\phi);$
- $deg(\phi \rightarrow \psi) = max\{\deg(\phi), deg(\psi)\};$
- $deg(\Diamond\phi) = deg(\Box\phi) = deg(\langle N \rangle \phi) = deg([N]\phi) = \deg(\phi) + 1.$

Definition 8 (Height $height(\cdot)$ and Depth). *Let M be a treelike model. We define the* height *of a node w in M recursively as follows:*

- $height(w) = 0$, *if w is the root of M;*
- $height(w) = height(u) + 1$, *if uRw in M.*

The depth *of M is the* maximum height *among all the worlds in M.*

Lemma 2. *Every formula ϕ satisfiable at the root of a treelike LAN-model, is satisfiable at the root of a treelike LAN-model with finite depth (specifically, with a depth equal to $deg(\phi)$).*

Proof. Let $M = (W, \{W_{\eth_j^{\alpha_i}} : \eth_j^{\alpha_i} \in \mathcal{L}_{\mathsf{LAN}}\}, \{W_{\mathfrak{v}^{\alpha_i}} : \mathfrak{v}^{\alpha_i} \in \mathcal{L}_{\mathsf{LAN}}\}, R, R_{\mathsf{N}}, V)$ be a treelike LAN-model with root $w \in W$ and assume $M, w \models \phi$. We first construct a treelike model M^d of finite depth by restricting the depth of M^d to $deg(\phi)$ and argue that ϕ is satisfiable at the root w of M^d. We define M^d as follows:

$$M^d = (W^d, \{W_{\eth_j^{\alpha_i}}^d : \eth_j^{\alpha_i} \in \mathcal{L}_{\mathsf{LAN}}\}, \{W_{\mathfrak{v}^{\alpha_i}}^d : \mathfrak{v}^{\alpha_i} \in \mathcal{L}_{\mathsf{LAN}}\}, R^d, R_{\mathsf{N}}^d, V^d), \text{ where}$$

– For all $w \in W$, $w \in W^d$ iff $height(w) \leq deg(\phi)$;
– For all $\eth_j^{\alpha_i} \in \mathcal{L}_{\mathsf{LAN}}$, $W_{\eth_j^{\alpha_i}}^d = W_{\eth_j^{\alpha_i}} \cap W^d$;
– For all $\mathfrak{v}^{\alpha_i} \in \mathcal{L}_{\mathsf{LAN}}$, $W_{\mathfrak{v}^{\alpha_i}}^d = W_{\mathfrak{v}^{\alpha_i}} \cap W^d$;
– $R^d = R \cap (W^d \times W^d)$;
– $R_{\mathsf{N}}^d = R_{\mathsf{N}} \cap (W^d \times W^d)$;
– For all $p \in Var$, $V^d(p) = V(p) \cap W^d$.

The model M^d is treelike with finite depth. Further, Lem. 2.33 in [5] gives us:

(2) For any formula $\psi \in \mathcal{L}_{\mathsf{LAN}}$ s.t. $deg(\psi) \leq deg(\phi)$ and any world $u \in W^d$ s.t.

$$height(u) \leq deg(\phi) - \deg(\psi), M, u \models \psi \text{ iff } M^d, u \models \psi.$$

From (2) we conclude that $M^d, w \models \phi$. Last, we show that M^d is a LAN-model:

(R3) Let $w, u, v \in W^d$ and assume $wR_{\mathsf{N}}^d u$ and $wR_{\mathsf{N}}^d v$. By definition of M^d, we know that $w, u, v \in W$ and that $wR_{\mathsf{N}} u$ and $wR_{\mathsf{N}} v$. Since the original model M satisfies property (R3), we have that $u = v$.

(R4) Let $w, u \in W^d$ and assume $wR_{\mathsf{N}}^d u$. By definition of M^d, we get $w, u \in W$ and $wR_{\mathsf{N}} u$. Since M satisfies property (R4), it follows that wRu. By the fact that $w, u \in W^d$ and the definition of M^d, we obtain $wR^d u$.

(R5) Let $w \in W^d$ and $Agt = \{\alpha_1, ..., \alpha_n\}$. Suppose there are (not necessarily distinct) complex action-types $\Delta_1, ..., \Delta_n \in Act_{\mathsf{LAN}}$ s.t. for $1 \leq i \leq n$ there exist $u_i \in W^d$ s.t. $wR^d u_i$ and $u_i \in W_{t(\Delta_i^{\alpha_i})}^d$. By definition of M^d, it follows that wRu_i holds for each $i \in \{1, ..., n\}$ with $height(u_i) \leq deg(\phi)$. Since M satisfies (R5), we know there exists a $v \in W$ s.t. wRv and $v \in W_{t(\Delta_1^{\alpha_1})} \cap \cdots \cap W_{t(\Delta_n^{\alpha_n})}$. We know $v \in W^d$ since $height(v) = height(u_i) \leq deg(\phi)$, which implies $wR^d v$ and $v \in W_{t(\Delta_1^{\alpha_1})}^d \cap \cdots \cap W_{t(\Delta_n^{\alpha_n})}^d$ by definition of M^d.

(R6) Let $w \in W^d$ and $\alpha_i \in Agt$. Assume there exists a $v \in W^d$ s.t. $wR^d v$ and $v \in W_{\mathfrak{v}^{\alpha_i}}^d$. By definition of M^d, we know that wRv holds with $height(v) \leq deg(\phi)$. Since M satisfies (R6), we know there exists a $u \in W$ s.t. wRu and $u \in W - W_{\mathfrak{v}^{\alpha_i}}$. Since $height(u) = height(v) \leq deg(\phi)$, it follows that $u \in W^d$, $wR^d u$, and $u \in W^d - W_{\mathfrak{v}^{\alpha_i}}^d$.

Lemma 3. *Every formula ϕ satisfiable at the root of a treelike LAN-model with finite depth equal to $deg(\phi)$, is satisfiable at the root of a treelike LAN-model with finite depth and finite branching (i.e., ϕ is satisfiable on a finite model).*

Proof. Let $M = (W, \{W_{\partial_j^{\alpha_i}} : \partial_j^{\alpha_i} \in \mathcal{L}_{\mathsf{LAN}}\}, \{W_{\upsilon^{\alpha_i}} : \upsilon^{\alpha_i} \in \mathcal{L}_{\mathsf{LAN}}\}, R, R_{\mathsf{N}}, V)$ be a treelike LAN-model with depth equal to $deg(\phi)$ with root $w \in W$ and assume $M, w \models \phi$. Let $Var(\phi)$ be the set of propositional variables occurring in ϕ. We define the set *Atoms* as $Var(\phi) \cup Wit \cup \{\upsilon^{\alpha_i} : \alpha_i \in Agt\}$. By Prop. 2.29 in [5], we know there are only a finite number of modal formulae (up to logical equivalence) built from the finite set *Atoms* with degree less than or equal to $deg(\phi)$. We use Θ to denote this collection of (equivalence classes of) formulae.

Using Θ, we first provide a *selection* procedure, similar to Thm. 2.34 of [5], to construct a finite model M^f and show that the root of this model satisfies ϕ. Last, we show that M^f is indeed a LAN-model. We construct M^f as follows:

$$M^f = (W^f, \{W^f_{\partial_j^{\alpha_i}} : \partial_j^{\alpha_i} \in \mathcal{L}_{\mathsf{LAN}}\}, \{W^f_{\upsilon^{\alpha_i}} : \upsilon^{\alpha_i} \in \mathcal{L}_{\mathsf{LAN}}\}, R^f, R^f_{\mathsf{N}}, V^f), \text{ where}$$

- W^f is the set obtained from the selection procedure (below);
- For all $\partial_j^{\alpha_i} \in \mathcal{L}_{\mathsf{LAN}}$, $W^f_{\partial_j^{\alpha_i}} = W_{\partial_j^{\alpha_i}} \cap W^f$;
- For all $\upsilon^{\alpha_i} \in \mathcal{L}_{\mathsf{LAN}}$, $W^f_{\upsilon^{\alpha_i}} = W_{\upsilon^{\alpha_i}} \cap W^f$;
- $R^f = R \cap (W^f \times W^f)$;
- $R^f_{\mathsf{N}} = R_{\mathsf{N}} \cap (W^f \times W^f)$;
- For all $p \in Var$, $V^f(p) = V(p) \cap W^f$.

Selection Procedure. We build our domain W^f by selecting a sequence of states $S_0, S_1, ..., S_{deg(\phi)}$ up to a height of $deg(\phi)$, where $S_0 = \{w\}$. Each subscript i of S_i represents that the states contained in the associated set are at a height of i in the original model M. Suppose that the sets $S_0, S_1, ..., S_i$ have already been chosen; we now explain how to select the set S_{i+1} with $i + 1 \le deg(\phi)$. For each formula $\psi \in \Theta$ equivalent to a formula of the form $\Diamond\chi$ or $\langle\mathsf{N}\rangle\chi$ with $deg(\psi) \le deg(\phi) - i$ s.t. $M, u \models \psi$ for some $u \in S_i \subseteq W$, we choose a $v \in W$ s.t. uRv (or, $uR_{\mathsf{N}}v$, depending on the modality in ψ) and $M, v \models \chi$. We define the domain $W^f = S_0 \cup S_1 \cup ... \cup S_{deg(\phi)}$.

The next statement is a consequence of this selection procedure [5, pp. 76–77]:

(3) For any formula $\psi \in \Theta$ s.t. $deg(\psi) \le deg(\phi)$ and any world $u \in W^f$ s.t.

$$height(u) \le deg(\phi) - \deg(\psi), M, u \models \psi \text{ iff } M^f, u \models \psi.$$

From (3), together with $M, w \models \phi$, $\phi \in \Theta$, $deg(\phi) \le deg(\phi)$, $w \in W^f$, and $height(w) \le deg(\phi)$, we infer $M^f, w \models \phi$. We show that M^f is an LAN-model:

(R3) Let $w, u, v \in W^f$ and assume $wR^f_{\mathsf{N}}u$ and $wR^f_{\mathsf{N}}v$. By definition of M^f, $wR_{\mathsf{N}}u$ and $wR_{\mathsf{N}}v$ hold. Since the model M satisfies (R3), we obtain $u = v$.

(R4) Let $w, u \in W^f$ and assume $wR^f_{\mathsf{N}}u$. By definition of M^f, $wR_{\mathsf{N}}u$ must hold. Since the original model M satisfies (R4), we have wRu, and because R^f is the set R restricted to W^f, which contains w and u, we infer $wR^f u$.

(R5) Let $w \in W^f$ and let $Agt = \{\alpha_1, ..., \alpha_n\}$. Suppose there are (not necessarily distinct) complex action-types $\Delta_1, ..., \Delta_n \in Act_{\mathsf{LAN}}$ s.t. for all $1 \le i \le n$ there exists a $u_i \in W^f$ s.t. $wR^f u_i$ and $u_i \in W^f_{t(\Delta_i^{\alpha_i})}$. By definition of M^f, this implies wRu_i, $u_i \in W_{t(\Delta_i^{\alpha_i})}$, and $height(u_i) \leq deg(\phi)$ for each $i \in \{1, ..., n\}$. Since M satisfies (R5), we know that there exists a v such that wRv and $v \in W_{t(\Delta_1^{\alpha_1})} \cap \cdots \cap W_{t(\Delta_n^{\alpha_n})}$, i.e., $M, w \models \Diamond(\bigwedge_{1 \leq i \leq n} t(\Delta_i^{\alpha_i}))$. Observe that because $height(w) + 1 = height(u_i) \leq deg(\phi)$ that $1 \leq deg(\phi)$, implying that $\Diamond(\bigwedge_{1 \leq i \leq n} t(\Delta_i^{\alpha_i})) \in \Theta$, because $deg(\bigwedge_{1 \leq i \leq n} t(\Delta_i^{\alpha_i})) = 0$. Consequently, by the selection procedure a $v' \in W$ such that $w\bar{R}v'$ and $M, v' \models \bigwedge_{1 \leq i \leq n} t(\Delta_i^{\alpha_i})$ must have been selected and placed in $S_{height(v')}$. Hence, there exists a $v' \in W^f$ s.t. $wR^f v'$ and $v' \in W^f_{t(\Delta_1^{\alpha_1})} \cap \cdots \cap W^f_{t(\Delta_n^{\alpha_n})}$.

(R6) Let $w \in W^f$, $\alpha_i \in Agt$, and assume there is a $v \in W^f$ s.t. $wR^f v$ and $v \in W^f_{\mathfrak{v}^{\alpha_i}}$. By definition of M^f we infer wRv and $v \in W_{\mathfrak{v}^{\alpha_i}}$ with $height(v) \leq deg(\phi)$; hence, there exists a $u \in W$ s.t. wRu and $u \in W - W_{\mathfrak{v}^{\alpha_i}}$ with $height(u) \leq deg(\phi)$. It follows that $M, w \models \Diamond \neg \mathfrak{v}^{\alpha_i}$. Since $height(w) = height(v) + 1 \leq deg(\phi)$, we know that $1 \leq deg(\phi)$, and so, $\Diamond \neg \mathfrak{v}^{\alpha_i} \in \Theta$. By the selection procedure, a $u' \in W$ s.t. wRu' and $u' \in W - W_{\mathfrak{v}^{\alpha_i}}$ must have been chosen and placed in $S_{height(u)}$; hence, $u' \in W^f$, $wR^f u'$, and $u' \in W^f - W^f_{\mathfrak{v}^{\alpha_i}}$.

Theorem 2. LAN *has the finite (tree) model property, i.e., every satsifiable formula is satisfiable on a finite, treelike model.*

Proof. Follows from Lemmas 1, 2, and 3.

Corollary 1. *The satisfiability problem of* LAN *is decidable.*

Proof. By [5, Thm. 6.15], we know that if a normal modal logic is finitely axiomatizable and has the FMP, then it is decidable, which is the case for LAN.

References

1. d'Altan, P., Meyer, J.J., Wieringa, R.J.: An integrated framework for ought-to-be and ought-to-do constraints. Artif. Intell. Law **4**(2), 77–111 (1996)
2. Anderson, A.R., Moore, O.K.: The formal analysis of normative concepts. Am. Sociol. Rev. **22**(1), 9–17 (1957)
3. Belnap, N., Perloff, M., Xu, M.: Facing the Future. Agents and Choices in our Indeterminist World. Oxford University Press, Oxford (2001)
4. van Berkel, K., Pascucci, M.: Notions of instrumentality in agency logic. In: Miller, T., Oren, N., Sakurai, Y., Noda, I., Savarimuthu, B.T.R., Cao Son, T. (eds.) PRIMA 2018. LNCS (LNAI), vol. 11224, pp. 403–419. Springer, Cham (2018). https://doi.org/10.1007/978-3-030-03098-8_25
5. Blackburn, P., de Rijke, M., Venema, Y.: Modal Logic. Cambridge University Press, Cambridge (2001)
6. Broersen, J.: Deontic epistemic stit logic distinguishing modes of mens rea. J. Appl. Logic **9**(2), 137–152 (2011)
7. Brown, M.A.: On the logic of ability. J. Philos. Logic **17**(1), 1–26 (1988)
8. Castañeda, H.N.: On the semantics of the ought-to-do. In: Davidson, D., Harman, G. (eds.) Semantics of Natural Language. Synthese Library, vol. 40, pp. 675–694. Springer, Dordrecht (1972). https://doi.org/10.1007/978-94-010-2557-7_21

9. Chisholm, R.: Contrary-to-duty imperatives and deontic logic. Analysis **24**, 33–36 (1963)
10. Fischer, M., Ladner, R.: Propositional dynamic logic of regular programs. J. Comput. Syst. Sci. **18**(2), 194–211 (1979)
11. Governatori, G.: Practical normative reasoning with defeasible deontic logic. In: d'Amato, C., Theobald, M. (eds.) Reasoning Web 2018. LNCS, vol. 11078, pp. 1–25. Springer, Cham (2018). https://doi.org/10.1007/978-3-030-00338-8_1
12. Governatori, G., Hashmi, M.: No time for compliance. In: 19th International Enterprise Distributed Object Computing Conference, pp. 9–18. IEEE (2015)
13. Governatori, G., Olivieri, F., Rotolo, A., Scannapieco, S.: Computing strong and weak permissions in defeasible logic. J. Philos. Logic **42**(6), 799–829 (2013). https://doi.org/10.1007/s10992-013-9295-1
14. Hansson, S.O.: The varieties of permission. In: Gabbay, D., Horty, J., Parent, X., van der Meyden, R., van der Torre, L. (eds.) Handbook of Deontic Logic and Normative Systems, pp. 195–240. College Publications, London (2013)
15. Horty, J.: Agency and Deontic Logic. Oxford University Press, Oxford (2001)
16. Kant, I.: Critique of Pure Reason. Cambridge University Press, Cambridge (2000)
17. Meyer, J.J.C.: A different approach to deontic logic: deontic logic viewed as a variant of dynamic logic. Notre Dame J. Formal Logic **29**(1), 109–136 (1988)
18. Pascucci, M.: Anderson's restriction of deontic modalities to contingent propositions. Theoria **83**(4), 440–470 (2017)
19. Prakken, H., Sergot, M.: Dyadic deontic logic and contrary-to-duty obligations. In: Nute, D. (ed.) Defeasible Deontic Logic, pp. 223–262. Springer, Dordrecht (1997). https://doi.org/10.1007/978-94-015-8851-5_10
20. Prisacariu, C., Schneider, G.: A dynamic deontic logic for complex contracts. J. Logic Algebraic Program. **81**(4), 458–490 (2012)
21. von Wright, G.H.: Deontic logic. Mind **60**(237), 1–15 (1951)
22. von Wright, G.H.: An Essay in Deontic Logic and the General Theory of Action. North Holland Publishing Company, Amsterdam (1968)
23. von Wright, G.H.: The Varieties of Goodness. Routledge & Kegan Paul, London and Henley (1972). fourth impression

Short Presentations

Preservation of Admissibility with Rationality and Feasibility Constraints

Weiwei Chen[✉]

Institute of Logic and Cognition and Department of Philosophy,
Sun Yat-sen University, Guangzhou 510275, China
chenww26@mail2.sysu.edu.cn

Abstract. The paper considers the problem of in what circumstances an aggregation rule guarantees an admissible output extension that represents a good compromise between several input extensions of abstract argumentation framework, each provided by a different individual. To achieve this, we introduce the concept of concrete admissibility for abstract argumentations by strengthening Dung's admissibility. We also define a model for extension aggregation that clearly separates the constraint supposed to be satisfied by individuals and the constraint that must be met by the collective decision. Using this model, we show that the majority rule guarantees admissible sets on newly defined admissible sets.

1 Introduction

Admissibility is an importance semantic property of argumentation frameworks. It lies in the heart of all semantics discussed in [8], and is shared by many more recent proposals [2]. Under Dung's argumentation framework [8], a set of arguments satisfies admissibility if it defends all its members in the sense that for any argument A in the set, either A is un-attacked, or if attacked by some argument B, then there is an argument in the set that attacks B, and it does not contain internal attacks.

When a group of agents are confronted with the same abstract argumentation framework, and each of them chooses an extension, we may wish to aggregate such extensions into a collective one, which represents the consensus of the group. Similar question has been received attention in the last decades or so (see, e.g., [1,4–6,17]). In this paper, we address the question of in what circumstances, an aggregation rule will guarantee admissible outputs during aggregation of extensions of abstract argumentation framework. In existing work, mention that Chen and Endriss [6] have shown that no aggregation rule preserves Dung's admissibility in general. Under their settings, all agents report extensions

Supported by the MOE Project of Key Research Institute of Humanities and Social Sciences in Universities, No. 18JJD720005, the China Postdoctoral Science Foundation Grant, No. 2019M663352, and the Philosophy and Social Science Youth Projects of Guangdong Province, No. GD19CZX03.

M. Dastani et al. (Eds.): CLAR 2020, LNAI 12061, pp. 245–258, 2020.
https://doi.org/10.1007/978-3-030-44638-3_15

that are admissible, and they aggregate such extensions by making use of a set of conceptually and computationally simple aggregation rules, quota rules, which have been studied in depth in judgment aggregation [7].

The graded semantics is a new theory of justification of arguments developed by Grossi and Modgil [13], in which the degree of acceptance of arguments can be weakened or strengthened. In the graded semantics, the number of attackers and defenders are given a fine-grained assignment when deciding whether a specific argument is acceptable. The notion of admissibility is extended to mn-admissibility. Such notion has the potential to require that if a set of arguments Δ is admissible, then any attacker of $A \in \Delta$ is attacked by more than one argument in Δ. While preserving Dung's admissibility is difficult, there is still no good news for the preservation of graded admissibility. Using the model proposed by Chen and Endriss [6], our results show that no quota rule can guarantee admisible outcomes on graded admissble sets. Thus, preserving graded admissibility is difficult as well.

In this paper, we introduce the concept of concrete admissibility and a new model for extension aggregation. When we consider whether an argument A is acceptable with respect to a set of arguments Δ, graded admissibility only considers the number of A's defenders in Δ, while in concrete admissibility, Δ included all defenders of A, i.e., for any attacker B of argument A, Δ includes all attacker of B.

For the model, we point out that in nearly all existing work on extension aggregation, there is only one single type of constraint (see, e.g., [6,17]). Such constraint is explicitly represented or left implicit. Following the model proposed by Endriss [10] for judgment aggregation [9,14], we introduce a model for extension aggregation that allows the constraints assumed to be satisfied by the individual agents can be different from the constraints met by the collective decision returned by the aggregation rule. Using this model, we show that the majority rule guarantees admissible outcomes on concretely admissible sets.

The paper is organized as follows. In Sect. 2, we review some of Dung's basic concepts of the theory of abstract argumentation. Section 3 recalls the preservation results of Dung's semantics introduced by Chen and Endriss [6]. In Sect. 4 we show that preserving new graded semantics yields similar impossibility results. In Sect. 5, we introduce concrete admissibility and a new model with integrity and feasibility constraints, and illustrates a positive result with majority rule. We conclude in Sect. 6 outlining some future research directions.

2   Abstract Argumentation

2.1   Abstract Argumentation Framework

In this section, we recall some of the basic concepts of the theory of abstract argumentation first introduced by [8]. An *argumentation framework* is a pair $AF = \langle Arg, \rightharpoonup \rangle$, in which Arg is a finite set of arguments and $\rightharpoonup$ is a binary relation on Arg. We say that A *attacks* B, if $A \rightharpoonup B$ holds for two arguments $A, B \in Arg$. For $\Delta \subseteq Arg$ and $B \in Arg$, we write $\Delta \rightharpoonup B$ (namely Δ attacks B) in case $A \rightharpoonup B$ for at least one argument $A \in \Delta$. For $\Delta \subseteq Arg$ and $C \in Arg$ we say that Δ *defends* C in case Δ attacks all arguments $B \in Arg$ with $B \rightharpoonup C$. We write 2^{Arg} for the powerset of Arg.

Given an argumentation framework $AF = \langle Arg, \rightharpoonup \rangle$, the question arises which subset Δ of the set of arguments Arg one should accept. Any such set $\Delta \subseteq Arg$ is called an *extension* of AF. Different criteria have been put forward for choosing an extension. While Dung has defined several semantic, notably complete, grounded, preferred, and stable semantics [8], it is worth mentioning that conflict-freeness, being self-defending, and admissibility are fundamental properties supposed to be satisfied by extensions of semantics.

Definition 1. *Let $AF = \langle Arg, \rightharpoonup \rangle$ be an argumentation framework and let $\Delta \subseteq Arg$ be a set of arguments. We adopt the following terminology:*

- *Δ is called conflict-free if there are no arguments $A, B \in \Delta$ such that $A \rightharpoonup B$.*
- *Δ is called self-defending if $\Delta \subseteq \{C \mid \Delta \text{ defends } C\}$.*
- *Δ is called admissible if it is both conflict-free and self-defending.*

Thus, a set of arguments is admissible if it is conflict-free and being self-defending. In the original paper, Dung defines some other semantics, including complete, grounded, preferred, and stable semantics [8]. All of them are admissibility-based in the sense that every extension of such semantics is admissible.

2.2 Abstract Argumentation Semantics and Propositional Logic

Following the work by Besnard and Doutre [3] and Chen and Endriss [6], we represent the properties of extensions in a purely syntactic manner, using a logical language. So fix an argumentation framework $AF = \langle Arg, \rightharpoonup \rangle$, think of Arg as a set of propositional variables, and let $\mathcal{L}_{AF}$ be the corresponding propositional language. Now extensions $\Delta \subseteq Arg$ correspond to models of formulas in $\mathcal{L}_{AF}$:

- $\Delta \models A$ for $A \in Arg$ if and only if $A \in \Delta$
- $\Delta \models \neg \varphi$ if and only if $\Delta \models \varphi$ is not the case
- $\Delta \models \varphi \wedge \psi$ if and only if both $\Delta \models \varphi$ and $\Delta \models \psi$

Given a formula φ, we use $\mathrm{Mod}(\varphi) = \{\Delta \subseteq Arg \mid \Delta \models \varphi\}$ to denote the set of all models of φ. Every formula φ identifies a property of extensions of AF, namely $\sigma = \mathrm{Mod}(\varphi)$. When using a formula φ to describe such a property of extensions, we usually refer to φ as an *integrity constraint*. The following simple result characterise the properties of being conflict-free and self-defending in terms of integrity constraints expressed in $\mathcal{L}_{AF}$.

Proposition 1. *Let $AF = \langle Arg, \rightharpoonup \rangle$ be an argumentation framework and let $\Delta \subseteq Arg$ be an extension. Then Δ is conflict-free if and only if:*

$$\Delta \models \mathrm{IC}_{CF} \quad \text{where} \quad \mathrm{IC}_{CF} = \bigwedge_{\substack{A, B \in Arg \\ A \rightharpoonup B}} (\neg A \vee \neg B)$$

That is, Proposition 1 states that $\mathrm{Mod}(\mathrm{IC}_{CF}) = \{\Delta \subseteq Arg \mid \Delta \text{ is conflict-free}\}$.

Proposition 2. *Let $AF = \langle Arg, \rightarrowtail \rangle$ be an argumentation framework and let $\Delta \subseteq Arg$ be an extension. Then Δ is self-defending if and only if:*

$$\Delta \models \mathrm{IC}_{SD} \quad where \quad \mathrm{IC}_{SD} = \bigwedge_{C \in Arg} [C \rightarrow \bigwedge_{\substack{B \in Arg \\ B \rightarrowtail C}} \bigvee_{\substack{A \in Arg \\ A \rightarrowtail B}} A]$$

We can now use the integrity constraints defined above to construct integrity constraints for the property of admissibility:

– Δ is admissible if and only if $\Delta \models \mathrm{IC}_{AD}$ where $\mathrm{IC}_{AD} = \mathrm{IC}_{CF} \wedge \mathrm{IC}_{SD}$.

Example 1. Consider the argumentation framework $AF = \langle \{A, B, C, D\}, \{A \rightarrowtail C, B \rightarrowtail C, C \rightarrowtail D\} \rangle$, as illustrated in Fig. 1. Then $\mathrm{IC}_{SD} = (\neg D \vee A \vee B) \wedge (\neg C)$, $\mathrm{IC}_{AD} = (\neg D \vee A \vee B) \wedge (\neg C) \wedge (\neg A \vee \neg C) \wedge (\neg B \vee \neg C) \wedge (\neg C \vee \neg D)$.

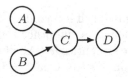

Fig. 1. An AF with four arguments

3 Preservation of the Dung's Admissibility

3.1 Extension Aggregation

In this section, we recall a model for extension aggregation defined by Chen and Endriss [6]. Such model allows a single type of constraint. Fix an argumentation framework $AF = \langle Arg, \rightarrowtail \rangle$. Let $U = \{1, \ldots, u\}$ be a finite set of *agents*. Suppose each agent $i \in U$ supplies us with an extension $\Delta_i \subseteq Arg$, reflecting her individual views of what constitutes an acceptable set of arguments in the context of AF. Thus, we are supplied with a *profile* $\boldsymbol{\Delta} = (\Delta_1, \ldots, \Delta_u)$, a vector of extensions, one for each agent. An *aggregation rule* is a function $F : (2^{Arg})^u \rightarrow 2^{Arg}$, mapping any given profile of extensions to a single extension.

Definition 2. *A quota rule F_q with quota q is the aggregation rule mapping any given profile of extensions to the extension including exactly those arguments accepted by at least q agents.*

The quota rules have low computational complexity in the sense that it is straightforward to compute outputs [11]. The nomination rule is the quota rule with quota $q = 1$. The majority rule is another example of quota rules for which its quota $q = \lceil \frac{u+1}{2} \rceil$.

3.2   Preservation of Dung's Admissibility

Chen and Endriss [6] have considered the problem of aggregation of alternative extensions by making use of quota rules. They exploit known encodings of argumentation semantics in propositional logic. They study the preservation of semantic properties of extensions, including conflict-freeness, self-defending, reinstating, admissibility, and I-Maximal properties. Our focus is admissibility.

Proposition 3 *(Chen and Endriss, 2018). Every quota rule F_q for u agents with a quota $q > \frac{u}{2}$ preserves admissibility for all argumentation frameworks AF with* $\mathrm{MaxDef}(AF) \leqslant 1$.

Note that $\mathrm{MaxDef}(AF)$ is the maximum number of attackers of an argument that itself is the source of an attack.

Theorem 1 *(Chen and Endriss, 2018). No quota rule preserves admissibility for all argumentation frameworks.*

Thus, no quota rule can guarantee the preservation of admissibility in general.

4   Preservation of Graded Admissibility

4.1   Graded Semantics

In this part, we present the graded semantics introduced by Grossi and Modgil [13]. The graded semantics can be seen as a generalisation of Dung's semantics. Extensions of the graded semantics are weakened or strengthened depending on level of self-defending and conflict-freeness they meet.

An argument A is defended by a set of arguments Δ whenever A is attacked by some argument B, there at least one argument in Δ that attacks B. Grossi and Modgil generalize the notion of defense to obtain the notion of *graded defense* [13].

Definition 3. *The defense function is defined as follows. For any $\Delta \subseteq Arg$:*

$$d(\Delta) = \{X \in Arg \mid \forall Y \in Arg : \text{IF } Y \rightharpoonup X \text{ THEN } \Delta \rightharpoonup Y\} \qquad (1)$$

Definition 4. *Let $AF = \langle Arg, \rightharpoonup \rangle$ be an argumentation framework, and m and n be two positive integers $(m, n > 0)$. The graded defense function for Δ is defined as follows. For any $\Delta \subseteq Arg$:*

$$d_n^m(\Delta) = \{X \in Arg \text{ s.t. } |\{Y \in \overline{X} \text{ s.t. } |\overline{Y} \cap \Delta| < n\}| < m\} \qquad (2)$$

where $\bar{X}$ denotes $\{Y \in Arg \mid Y \rightharpoonup X\}$.

So, $d_n^m(\Delta)$ denotes the set of arguments that have at most $m - 1$ attackers that are not counter-attacked by at least n arguments in Δ.

Example 2. Let us consider the argumentation framework depicted below.

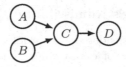

Let $\Delta = \{A, D\}$, it is easy to verify that $D \in d_1^1(\Delta)$ but $D \notin d_2^1(\Delta)$.

Definition 5. *A set of arguments Δ is said to be acceptable at grade mn(or, mn-acceptable) whenever all of its arguments are such that at most $m - 1$ of their attackers are not counter-attacked by at least n arguments in Δ.*

Definition 6. *A set of arguments Δ is said to be mn-self-defending whenever all of its arguments are such that at most $m - 1$ of their attackers are not counter-attacked by at least n arguments in Δ.*

Definition 7. *A set of arguments Δ is said to be at grade mn-admissible whenever Δ is mn-acceptable and being conflict-free.*

In fact, when $m = n = 1$, we recover the standard definition of being self-defending, admissibility. It is worth mentioning that Grossi and Modgil define graded admissibility as mn-acceptability plus l-conflict-freeness (a set of arguments Δ is said to be l-conflict-free whenever no arguments $A \in \Delta$ such that A is attacked by at least l arguments in Δ [13]). But for the sake of simplicity, we define graded admissibility as mn-acceptability plus Dung's notion of conflict-freeness.

4.2   Preservation Result for Graded Admissibility

In this section, we start with encoding the property of being graded self-defending in propositional logic and show a preservation result for such property. We then present a result for the property of graded admissibility. The following simple result characterises the property of being graded self-defending in terms of the integrity constraint expressed in $\mathcal{L}_{AF}$.

Proposition 4. *Let $AF = \langle Arg, \rightarrow \rangle$ be an argumentation framework and let $\Delta \subseteq Arg$ be an extension. Then Δ is mn-self-defending if and only if:*

$$\Delta \models \mathrm{IC}_{mnSD} \quad where \quad \mathrm{IC}_{mnSD} = \bigwedge_{C \in Arg} [C \rightarrow$$

$$\bigvee_{\{B_1,\dots,B_{(|\bar{C}|-m+1)}\} \in \binom{|\bar{C}|}{|\bar{C}|-m+1}} (\bigwedge_{i=1}^{|\bar{C}|-m+1} (\bigvee_{\{A_1,\dots,A_n\} \in \binom{|B_i|}{n}} (\bigwedge_{j=1}^{n} A_j)))] \quad (3)$$

To get the preservation results for being graded self-defending, we need a result regarding binary aggregation with integrity constraints [12], a variant of judgment aggregation.

Lemma 1 *(Grandi and Endriss, 2013). Let $AF = \langle Arg, \rightarrow \rangle$ be an argumentation framework and let φ be a clause in $\mathcal{L}_{AF}$ with k_1 positive literals and k_2 negative literals. Then a quota rule F_q for u agents preserves the property $\mathrm{Mod}(\varphi)$ if and only if:*

$$q \cdot (k_2 - k_1) > u \cdot (k_2 - 1) - k_1 \tag{4}$$

Note that a clause is a disjunction of literals, all integrity constraints can be translated into conjunctions of clauses. The following result shows that if we know the preservation result for some clauses, then we know results for the conjunction of such clauses.

Lemma 2 *(Grandi and Endriss, 2013). Let $AF = \langle Arg, \rightarrow \rangle$ be an argumentation framework, let φ_1 and φ_2 be integrity constraints in $\mathcal{L}_{AF}$, and let F be an aggregation rule that preserves both $\mathrm{Mod}(\varphi_1)$ and $\mathrm{Mod}(\varphi_2)$. Then F also preserves $\mathrm{Mod}(\varphi_1 \wedge \varphi_2)$.*

Thus, given a quota rule F_q and some clauses $\varphi_1, \ldots \varphi_l$, if F_q satisfies all clause φ_i, then it preserves $\mathrm{Mod}(\varphi_1 \wedge \cdots \wedge \varphi_l)$.

Example 3. Given an integrity constraint $\varphi = (\neg A \vee \neg B) \wedge C$. By Lemma 1, a quota rule preserves $\neg A \vee \neg B$ only if $q \cdot (2 - 0) > u \cdot (2 - 1) - 0$, i.e., only if $q > \frac{u}{2}$. A quota rule preserves C only if $q \cdot (0 - 1) > u \cdot (0 - 1) - 1$, which is always the case, thus, C is preserved by every quota rule. Thus, by Lemma 2, a quota rule preserves φ only if $q > \frac{u}{2}$.

Recall that the nomination rule is the quota rule for which its quota is 1.

Proposition 5. *The nomination rule preserves the property of being a mn-self-defending set.*

Proof. Recall that IC_{mnSD} is a conjunction of formulas of the form

$$C \rightarrow \bigvee_{\{B_1,\ldots,B_{(|\bar{C}|-m+1)}\}\in\binom{|\bar{C}|}{|\bar{C}|-m+1}} (\bigwedge_{i=1}^{|\bar{C}|-m+1} (\bigvee_{\{A_1,\ldots,A_n\}\in\binom{|B_i|}{n}} (\bigwedge_{j=1}^{n} A_j)))$$

which can be rewritten as

$$C \rightarrow \bigwedge_{B_1,\ldots,B_m\in\binom{|\bar{C}|}{m}} [\bigvee_{i=1}^{c_1}(A_{\pi_i(1)} \wedge \cdots \wedge A_{\pi_i(n)})_1] \vee \cdots \vee [\bigvee_{i=1}^{c_m}(A_{\pi_i(1)} \wedge \cdots \wedge A_{\pi_i(n)})_m], \tag{5}$$

where $c_i = \binom{|\bar{B}_i|}{n}$ for $i = 1, \cdots, m$, respectively. We take one such clause

$$C \rightarrow [\bigvee_{i=1}^{c_1}(A_{\pi_i(1)} \wedge \cdots \wedge A_{\pi_i(n)})] \vee \cdots \vee [\bigvee_{i=1}^{c_m}(A_{\pi_i(1)} \wedge \cdots \wedge A_{\pi_i(n)})], \tag{6}$$

which can be rewritten as

$$C \to \bigwedge_{j=1}^{n} [\bigvee_{i=1}^{m} (A_{\pi_i(j)} \vee \cdots \vee A_{\pi_{(|\bar{B}_j|-n)}(j)})]. \tag{7}$$

We take one such clause

$$C \to [\bigvee_{i=1}^{m} (A_{\pi_i(j)} \vee \cdots \vee A_{\pi_{(|\bar{B}_j|-n)}(j)})]. \tag{8}$$

Its number of positive literals is $(|\bar{B}_j| - n) \cdot m$, its number of negative literals is 1. Thus, according to Lemma 1, a uniform quota rule with quota q preserves it if and only if $q < \frac{(|\bar{B}_j|-n)\cdot m}{(|\bar{B}_j|-n)\cdot m-1}$. As IC_{mnSD} is a conjunction of such clauses, therefore we need to satisfy this inequality for all relevant m, n and B_j. This requirement is most demanding for largest values of n, and smallest of m and B_j. However, we point out that if $q = 1$, then $q < \frac{(|\bar{B}_j|-n)\cdot m}{(|\bar{B}_j|-n)\cdot m-1}$ is always the case. Thus, we have the proposition.

Theorem 2. *No quota rule preserves mn-admissibility for all argumentation frameworks.*

Proof. Recall that standard definition of admissibility is a special case of *mn*-admissibility for which $m = n = 1$. By Theorem 1, we get that no quota rule preserves 11-admissibility. Thus, we have the theorem.

Thus, we obtain a similar result for *mn*-admissibility.

5   Preservation Results for Concrete Admissbility

5.1   Concrete Admissibility

The graded semantics provides a theory of degree of justification of arguments. Under the graded semantics, the assignment of status of arguments are defined by the numbers of attackers and defenders. Theses graded semantics provide ways of strengthening or weakening the standard Dung semantics. While grade semantics appeals to the numbers of attackers and defenders to define acceptability of arguments, it is worth mentioning that, in some scenarios, given two arguments for which the numbers of attackers and defenders of such pair of arguments are different, but they share similar features. Consider the following example.

Example 4. Let us consider two sets of arguments $\Delta_1 = \{C, A\}$ in AF_1, $\Delta_2 = \{C, A, D, E\}$ in AF_2, as illustrated in Fig. 2. The numbers of defenders of C in AF_1 and AF_2 are different: C has one defender in AF_1, and C has three defenders in AF_2. But both of them are concretely defended in the sense that

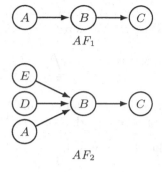

Fig. 2. Two argumentation frameworks

for every argument A, if C is defended by A, then A is included in Δ. Argument C has one defender in AF_1, namely A, and A is included in Δ_1; Argument C have three defenders in AF_2, namely A, D, E, and they are included in Δ_2. The similarity of C between AF_1 and AF_2 is not captured by Modgil and Grossi's graded semantics.

In above example, arguments share the same degree of justification of acceptability of arguments, can have different numbers of defenders.

Take an argument $A \in Arg$ and a set of arguments $\Delta \subseteq Arg$, under Dung's admissibility, we say that Δ defends A if for every attack $B \in Arg$ of argument A, Δ accepts at least one attacker of B, we say that Δ is admissible if Δ defends all its members and being conflict-free. We introduce the concept of *concrete admissibility*. We say that Δ *concretely defends* A if for every attacker B of arguments A, Δ accepts *all* attackers of B, i.e, Δ includes all defenders of A, we say that Δ satisfies concrete admissibility if Δ concretely defends all its members and Δ is conflict-free. Note that the requirement of concrete acceptability of arguments is a strong requirement.

We use the notion of concrete defense to define concrete admissibility.

Definition 8. *Take an argument $A \in Arg$ and a set of arguments $\Delta \subseteq Arg$. We say that Δ concretely defends A if Δ for every attacker B of arguments A, Δ accepts* all *attackers of B.*

For example, in Fig. 2, $\{A\}$ concretely defends C in AF_1, $\{A, D, E\}$ concretely defends C in AF_2.

Definition 9. *Take an argument $A \in Arg$ and a set of arguments $\Delta \subseteq Arg$. We say that Δ is* concretely admissible *if Δ concretely defends all of its members, and Δ is conflict-free.*

Recall that we use φ to refer a property of extensions, or an integrity constraint. The following simple result characterises the properties of being concrete defending in terms of the integrity constraint expressed in $\mathcal{L}_{AF}$.

Proposition 6. *Let $AF = \langle Arg, \rightharpoonup \rangle$ be an argumentation framework and let $\Delta \subseteq Arg$ be an extension. Then Δ is concrete defending if and only if:*

$$\Delta \models \mathrm{IC}_{CD} \quad \text{where} \quad \mathrm{IC}_{CD} = \bigwedge_{C \in Arg} \bigwedge_{\substack{B \in Arg \\ B \rightharpoonup C}} \bigwedge_{\substack{A \in Arg \\ A \rightharpoonup B}} [C \rightarrow A]$$

We can now use the integrity constraint defined above to construct the integrity constraint for the property of concrete admissibility:

- Δ is concretely admissible if and only if $\Delta \models \mathrm{IC}_{CA}$ where $\mathrm{IC}_{CA} = \mathrm{IC}_{CF} \wedge \mathrm{IC}_{CD}$.

Example 5. Consider the argumentation framework $AF = \langle \{A, B, C, D\}, \{A \rightharpoonup C, B \rightharpoonup C, C \rightharpoonup D\} \rangle$. Then $\mathrm{IC}_{SD} = (\neg D \vee A \vee B) \wedge (\neg C)$, $\mathrm{IC}_{CD} = (\neg D \vee A) \wedge (\neg D \vee B) \wedge (\neg C)$. In this example, $\{A, D\}$ and $\{B, D\}$ are admissible, but they are not concretely admissible. $\{A, B, D\}, \{A\}, \{B\}, \{A, B\}, \emptyset$ are all admissible and concretely admissible sets.

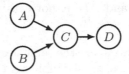

5.2   Concrete Admissibility and Prime Implicates

In the section, we generalize the notion of *prime implicate* to our context, a clause $\pi \in \mathcal{L}_{AF}$ is a prime implicate of a formula $\Gamma \in \mathcal{L}_{AF}$ if (i) $\Gamma \models \pi$ and (ii) for every clause $\pi' \in \mathcal{L}_{AF}$ with $\Gamma \models \pi'$ if $\pi' \models \pi$ then $\pi = \pi'$ [16]. In other words, the prime implicates are the logically strongest clauses entailed by Γ.

Recall that a clause is a disjunction of literals. A clause is simple if it has at most two literals, a clause is nonsimple if it cannot be simplified to a clause with less than three literals. A formula is simple if it logically equivalent to a conjunction of clauses with at most two literals (it is also called Krom formula). We first present three results concerning prime implicates.

Fact 3. *A formula Γ is simple if and only if all its prime implicates are simple.*

Lemma 3 *(Marquis, 2000). If $\Gamma \models \Gamma'$ is the case, then for every prime implicate π' of Γ' there exists a prime implicate π of Γ such that $\pi \models \pi'$.*

Definition 10 *(Endriss, 2018). A pair of formulas (Γ, Γ') is simple, if for every nonsimple prime implicate π' of Γ' there exists a simple prime implicate π of Γ such that $\pi \models \pi'$.*

Using the results above, we are now ready to present some results concerning the relation between self-defending and concrete defending, and the relation between Dung's admissibility and concrete admissibility.

Lemma 4. $\mathrm{IC}_{CD} \models \mathrm{IC}_{SD}$.

Proof. Recall that IC_{SD} is a conjunction of a collection of formulas of the form $C \rightarrow \bigwedge_{\substack{B \in Arg \\ B \rightarrow C}} \bigvee_{\substack{A \in Arg \\ A \rightarrow B}} A$. We take the one indexed by $C \in Arg$ and rewrite as $\bigwedge_{\substack{B \in Arg \\ B \rightarrow C}} (\neg C \vee \bigvee_{\substack{A \in Arg \\ A \rightarrow B}} A)$. This formula is a conjunction of a collection of clauses of the form $(\neg C \vee \bigvee_{\substack{A \in Arg \\ A \rightarrow B}} A)$. We take the one indexed by $B \in Arg$ with $B \rightarrow C$ and rewrite as $(\neg C \vee A_1 \vee A_2 \vee \ldots \vee A_n)$, in which $A_1, A_2, \ldots A_n$ defend C by attacking B. We denote it by φ'. Obviously φ' is a clause of IC_{SD}. We are going to show that there is at least one clause φ of IC_{CD} such that $\varphi \models \varphi'$.

Recall that IC_{CD} is a conjunction of a collection of formulas of the form $\bigwedge_{\substack{B \in Arg \\ B \rightarrow C}} \bigwedge_{\substack{A \in Arg \\ A \rightarrow B}} [C \rightarrow A]$. Let us consider one such formulas $\bigwedge_{\substack{B \in Arg \\ B \rightarrow C}} \bigwedge_{\substack{A \in Arg \\ A \rightarrow B}} [C \rightarrow A]$ which indexed by $C \in Arg$. This formula is a conjunction of a collection of formulas indexed by an argument $B \in Arg$ with $B \rightarrow C$. Let us consider one formula $\bigwedge_{\substack{A \in Arg \\ A \rightarrow B}} [C \rightarrow A]$ which indexed by $B \in Arg$ with $B \rightarrow C$. This formula can be rewritten as $(\neg C \vee A_1) \wedge (\neg C \vee A_2) \wedge \ldots \wedge (\neg C \vee A_n)$ in which $A_1, A_2, \ldots A_n$ defend C by attacking B as well. We denote it by $\varphi_1 \wedge \varphi_2 \wedge \ldots \wedge \varphi_n$. Since $A_1, A_2, \ldots A_n$ defending C by attacking B, we know that $(\neg C \vee A_i) \models (\neg C \vee A_1 \vee A_2 \vee \ldots \vee A_n)$ for $i \in \{1, 2, \ldots, n\}$. Thus, $\varphi_i \models \varphi'$ for $i \in \{1, 2, \ldots, n\}$.

Using the same construction, we can show that for every clause φ' of IC_{SD}, there is at least one clause φ of IC_{CD} such that $\varphi \models \varphi'$. Thus, $\mathrm{IC}_{CD} \models \mathrm{IC}_{SD}$.

Proposition 7. $(\mathrm{IC}_{CD}, \mathrm{IC}_{SD})$ *is simple.*

Proof. From Lemma 4, we know that $\mathrm{IC}_{CD} \models \mathrm{IC}_{SD}$. With Lemma 3, we know that for every prime implicate π' of IC_{SD} there exists a prime implicate π of IC_{CD} such that $\pi \models \pi'$. Obviously IC_{CD} is a conjunction of clauses with at most two literals. Thus, it is simple. By Fact 3, we have that every prime implicate of IC_{CD} is simple.

Putting together the above facts we are able to conclude that for every (simple and nonsimple) prime implicate π' of IC_{SD} there exists a simple prime implicate π of IC_{CD} such that $\pi \models \pi'$, and we are done.

Lemma 5. $\mathrm{IC}_{CA} \models \mathrm{IC}_{AD}$.

Proof. Recall that $\mathrm{IC}_{CA} = \mathrm{IC}_{CD} \wedge \mathrm{IC}_{CF}$, $\mathrm{IC}_{AD} = \mathrm{IC}_{SD} \wedge \mathrm{IC}_{CF}$. By Lemma 4, we get that $\mathrm{IC}_{CD} \models \mathrm{IC}_{SD}$. Thus, we have $\mathrm{IC}_{CA} \models \mathrm{IC}_{AD}$.

Proposition 8. $(\mathrm{IC}_{CA}, \mathrm{IC}_{AD})$ *is simple.*

Proof. Putting Lemma 5 and Lemma 3 together we get that for every prime implicate π' of IC_{AD} there exists a prime implicate π of IC_{CA} such that $\pi \models \pi'$. Since IC_{CF} is a conjunction of clauses with at most two literals, we know that IC_{CA} is a conjunction of clauses with at most two literals as well, i.e., IC_{CA} is simple. Thus, with Fact 3 we get that every (simple and nonsimple) prime implicate π' of IC_{AD} there exists a simple prime implicate π of IC_{CA} such that $\pi \models \pi'$. We are done.

5.3   A Model with Rationality and Feasibility Constraints

In nearly all existing work on judgment aggregation [12,15] as well as some work on extension aggregation [6], only a single type of constraint, namely the *integrity constraint* is considered. Integrity constraints decide what is permissible for both the input and the output. As we have shown in Sects. 3 and 4, Dung's admissibility and graded admissibility fail to be preserved under the model that allows for integrity constraints only. In this section, we propose a new model that allows for a distinction between rationality constraints and feasibility constraints. Let us illustrate the model with an example, adapted from [10]:

Example 6. A university council with 5 members needs to decide on the funding for three projects: (φ_1): refurbishing the university stadium, (φ_2): organising an international conference, (φ_3): building a new student dormitory. The budget is limited and it is not feasible to fund all three projects. However, the councilors are not required to keep this constraint in mind when casting their votes on the projects. Instead, they assumed to please at least one of the issues, i.e., it would be irrational for a councilor not to recommend any of the projects for funding. Suppose their votes are as follows:

Thus, every council's vote meets the rationality constraint. However, the outcome of the majority rule violates the feasibility constraint (Table 1).

Table 1. Scenario used in Example 6

	φ_1	φ_2	φ_3
Councillor 1	1	1	0
Councillor 2	0	0	1
Councillor 3	1	0	1
Councillor 4	1	1	0
Councillor 5	1	1	1

We reuse terminologies introduced in Sect. 3: let $AF = \langle Arg, \rightharpoonup \rangle$ be an argumentation framework, let U be a finite set of agents. Suppose that every agent provides an extension Δ_i, which gives rise to a profile of extensions $\Delta = \{\Delta_1, \ldots, \Delta_u\}$. A profile is Γ-rational if $\Delta_i \models \Gamma$ for all $i \in U$. Thus, we use Γ to define the permissible profiles of extensions, which is called a *rationality constraint*. An outcome is Γ'-feasible if the outcome satisfies such constraint. We call Γ' a *feasibility constraint*, which defines the acceptable outcomes.

Definition 11. *An aggregation rule $F : (2^{Arg})^u \rightarrow 2^{Arg}$ is said to guarantee Γ'-feasible on Γ-rational profiles if for every profile $\Delta \in \text{Mod}(\Gamma)^u$ it is the case that $F(\Delta) \in \text{Mod}(\Gamma')$.*

Thus, we say F guarantees Γ'-feasible outcomes on Γ-rational profiles if for any profile Δ for which $\Delta_i \models \Gamma$ for all $i \in U$ is the case, we have $\Delta \models \Gamma'$.

5.4   Preservation Results for Concrete Admissibility

In this section, we are ready to present a positive result for obtaining an admissible set on concretely admissible sets with rationality and feasibility constraints. Before going any further, we show a result from Endriss [10], which is needed to prove our main results.

Theorem 4 *(Endriss, 2018).   The majority rule guarantees Γ'-feasible outcomes on Γ-rational profiles if and only if $\Gamma \models \Gamma'$ and (Γ, Γ') is simple.*

Theorem 5. *The majority rule guarantees IC_{SD}-feasible outcomes on IC_{CD}-rational profiles.*

Proof. This theorem is a consequence of Lemma 4, Proposition 7, and Theorem 4.

In [6], we have shown that no uniform quota rule preserves admissibility for all argumentation frameworks. In contrast to this, we have a relatively positive result when the profiles we are considering are strengthened to concrete admissibility.

Theorem 6. *The majority rule guarantees admissible outcomes on concretely admissible profiles.*

Proof. This theorem is a consequence of Lemma 5, Proposition 8, and Theorem 4.

6   Conclusion

In this paper, we have explored the possibility of obtaining an admissible set of arguments during the aggregation of extensions of an abstract argumentation framework. We have introduced the concrete admissibility, which allows for strong assignments of status to arguments. To achieve this, we have proposed a model that allows for a clear distinction between integrity and feasibility constraints, which is supposed to be satisfied by individual decisions and collective decisions, respectively. We have shown the majority rule, a fair rule that is appealing on normative grounds, guarantees admissible sets on concrete admissible sets. In this paper, only admissibility is considered. Even though admissibility is a fundamental property of extension of argumentation framework, other properties are of particular interest as well. Thus, it is interesting to formulate variants for other semantics based on concrete admissibility, such as completeness, preferredness, stability, and consider the preservation of such semantic properties by making use of our new model. It would be natural to investigate whether it is possible to obtain positive results for such semantic properties using our new model.

References

1. Awad, E., Booth, R., Tohmé, F., Rahwan, I.: Judgement aggregation in multi-agent argumentation. J. Logic Comput. **27**(1), 227–259 (2017)
2. Baroni, P., Caminada, M., Giacomin, M.: An introduction to argumentation semantics. Knowl. Eng. Rev. **26**(4), 365–410 (2011)
3. Besnard, P., Doutre, S.: Checking the acceptability of a set of arguments. In: Proceedings of the 10th International Workshop on Non-Monotonic Reasoning (NMR) (2004)
4. Booth, R., Awad, E., Rahwan, I.: Interval methods for judgment aggregation in argumentation. In: Proceedings of the 14th International Conference on Principles of Knowledge Representation and Reasoning (KR) (2014)
5. Caminada, M., Pigozzi, G.: On judgment aggregation in abstract argumentation. J. Auton. Agents Multiagent Syst. **22**(1), 64–102 (2011)
6. Chen, W., Endriss, U.: Aggregating alternative extensions of abstract argumentation frameworks: preservation results for quota rules. In: Proceedings of the 7th International Conference on Computational Models of Argument (COMMA). IOS Press (2018)
7. Dietrich, F., List, C.: Judgment aggregation by quota rules: majority voting generalized. J. Theor. Politics **19**(4), 391–424 (2007)
8. Dung, P.M.: On the acceptability of arguments and its fundamental role in non-monotonic reasoning, logic programming and n-person games. Artif. Intell. **77**(2), 321–358 (1995)
9. Endriss, U.: Judgment aggregation. In: Brandt, F., Conitzer, V., Endriss, U., Lang, J., Procaccia, A.D. (eds.) Handbook of Computational Social Choice, pp. 399–426. Cambridge University Press, Cambridge (2016). Chap. 17
10. Endriss, U.: Judgment aggregation with rationality and feasibility constraints. In: Proceedings of the 17th International Conference on Autonomous Agents and Multiagent Systems (AAMAS 2018), July 2018
11. Endriss, U., Grandi, U., Porello, D.: Complexity of judgment aggregation. J. Artif. Intell. Res. (JAIR) **45**, 481–514 (2012)
12. Grandi, U., Endriss, U.: Lifting integrity constraints in binary aggregation. Artif. Intell. **199–200**, 45–66 (2013)
13. Grossi, D., Modgil, S.: On the graded acceptability of arguments in abstract and instantiated argumentation. Artif. Intell. **275**, 138–173 (2019)
14. Grossi, D., Pigozzi, G.: Judgment Aggregation: A Primer. Synthesis Lectures on Artificial Intelligence and Machine Learning. Morgan & Claypool Publishers, San Rafael (2014)
15. List, C., Pettit, P.: Aggregating sets of judgments: an impossibility result. Econ. Philos. **18**(1), 89–110 (2002)
16. Marquis, P.: Consequence finding algorithms. In: Kohlas, J., Moral, S. (eds.) Handbook of Defeasible Reasoning and Uncertainty Management Systems, vol. 5, pp. 41–145. Springer, Dordrecht (2000). https://doi.org/10.1007/978-94-017-1737-3_3
17. Rahwan, I., Tohmé, F.A.: Collective argument evaluation as judgement aggregation. In: Proceedings of the 9th International Conference on Autonomous Agents and Multiagent Systems (AAMAS), IFAAMAS (2010)

Uncertainty in Argumentation Schemes: Negative Consequences and Basic Slippery Slope

Davide Liga[1,2](✉) and Monica Palmirani[1]

[1] Alma Mater Studiourm - University of Bologna, Bologna, Italy
{davide.liga2,monica.palmirani}@unibo.it
[2] University of Luxembourg, Esch-sur-Alzette, Luxembourg
davide.liga@ext.uni.lu

Abstract. This study is an approach to encompass uncertainty in the well-known Argumentation Scheme from Negative Consequences and in the more recent "Basic Slippery Slope Argument" proposed by Douglas Walton. This work envisages two new kinds of uncertainty that should be taken into account, one related to time and one related to the material relation between premises and conclusion. Furthermore, it is argued that some modifications to the structure of these Argumentation Schemes or to their Critical Questions could facilitate the process of Knowledge Extraction and modeling from these two argumentative patterns. For example, the study suggests to change the premises of the Basic Slippery Slope related to the Control and the Loss of Control.

Keywords: Argumentation Schemes · Uncertainty · Argumentation

1 Introduction

In this first introductory Section, after a brief introduction to the theory of Argumentation Schemes and their associated Critical Questions, some conceptual issues related to the Basic Slippery Slope and Negative Consequences arguments are reported, such as the problem of designing a unique and definitive scheme that can represent all the types of Slippery Slope arguments, and the relation between the two schemes. We then introduce the problem and the importance of modelling Natural Language uncertainty in Argumentation Schemes. Moreover, we target some theoretical limitations and non-uniformity and suggest some potential way to tackle them. In Sect. 2, we briefly introduce the Argumentation Scheme from Negative Consequences, its structure and Critical Questions. In Sect. 3, a modelling for encompassing the uncertainty of this scheme is proposed following the approach of Baroni et al. [1] and suggesting the presence of a kind

This work was partially supported by the European Union's Horizon 2020 research and innovation programme under the MSCA grant agreement No 690974 'MIREL: MIning and REasoning with Legal texts'.

M. Dastani et al. (Eds.): CLAR 2020, LNAI 12061, pp. 259–278, 2020.
https://doi.org/10.1007/978-3-030-44638-3_16

of uncertainty defined as "Equal-Opposite Material Relation Uncertainty" and another one related to time. We also propose a different formalization of the Critical Questions that could enhance the uniformity of the scheme. In Sect. 4, we describe the Basic Slippery Slope Argument, its structure and its Critical Questions. Then, in the Sect. 5, we apply a formalization for encompassing the uncertainty of the scheme suggesting, also in this case, the presence of the two above-mentioned kinds of uncertainty. We also argue that a different formalization of the scheme could be advisable for both theoretical and practical reasons. The Sect. 6 concludes the paper.

1.1 Argumentation Schemes and Critical Questions

Before proceeding with our analysis, we briefly describe the concept of Argumentation Scheme and Critical Question following the theories of Walton et al. [10]. According to these theories, Argumentation Schemes describe stereotypical patterns of reasoning and can be seen as structures of inferential connections composed by premises supporting a conclusion.

Following this model, the two Argumentation Schemes analyzed in the present work, namely the Negative Consequence and the Basic Slippery Slope, will be represented as a set of *linked* premises [10] (for a the distinction between linked and convergent argument see Freeman [3]). The connection of these premises is thus described with a conjunction of the various semantic relations (see Fig. 1). For a more precise description of the concept of material (or semantic) relation, please refer to Macagno et al. [6].

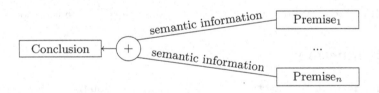

Fig. 1. Structure of an Argumentation Scheme

Although all the premises of an Argumentation Scheme provide semantic information (causal, definitional, and so on), some schemes contain *major* and *minor* premises, which seems to suggest the existence of a internal hierarchical order, with some premises having a stronger role in the inferential connection between premises and conclusion. In any case, all the Argumentation Schemes have a warranting function which enables the main inference to be drawn from the set of premises to the conclusion [6]. The warrant can be found in explicit or implicit premises [10] and it usually contains the main semantic relation. In this paper, we will follow the idea that the semantic connection between premises and conclusion, and the warranting function of the schemes, can be thought as an aggregate result of the actions of all the premises.

An Argumentation Scheme can be attacked in three ways [6], namely by arguing that:

- the premises are not true;
- the conclusion does not follow from the premises;
- the conclusion is false.

In other words, an attack can target premises, conclusions and the inferential connections. Moreover, the notion of attacking an Argumentation Scheme can be seen also from the point of view of its Critical Questions, since each Argumentation Scheme has a set of Critical Questions associated to it which aims at criticizing the scheme itself.

As explained by Walton et al. [10], the nature of Critical Questions may be somehow controversial, since they can sometimes target implicit premises, while other times they can be used as the starting point for an attack to a specific point of the scheme, requiring a further burden of proof. A clarification has been offered by Verheij [8], according to which critical questions have four roles:

- Questioning whether a premise holds;
- Pointing to exceptional situations in which the scheme defaults;
- Framing conditions for the correct use of a scheme;
- Indicating other arguments that might be used to attack the scheme.

1.2 The Basic Slippery Slope and the Negative Consequences Arguments

A common misunderstanding is that of confusing the Slippery Slope Argument and the Argument from Negative Consequences. We follow the idea that the first one is a subspecies of the second one, having its own characteristics [9]. These two argumentative patterns are conceptually similar, since their aim is similar: showing that an action may (will) result in a negative outcome. However, as will be described in Sect. 4, the Basic Slippery Slope argument proposed by Walton has a peculiar set of premises and if one these premises is missing, then we are not dealing with a Basic Slippery Slope, but with a different instance or subspecies of a Negative Consequences argument (notice that sometimes premises can be implicit, and if they are implicit they should not be considered missing) [9].

Importantly, this study must mention the existence of an extended debate about the uniqueness of the Slippery Slope Argument. The fact that the very existence of the Slippery Slope as a unique and definitive Argumentation Scheme is a topic of debate shows the non-triviality of analyzing the characteristics of this argumentative pattern. In this regard, Walton [11] identified four types of Slippery Slope Argument: one depending on causality, one depending on precedents, one depending on vagueness, and one that is a mixture of the previous ones. However, this study failed in finding common elements among those four types of Slippery Slope Argument. In fact, the problem of the Slippery Slope arguments is that they have a structure that can be difficult to understand and that can make it difficult to define a single, basic scheme embracing all the possible types and sub-types of Slippery Slope. For this reason, some scholars have argued that there is not such a unique and definitive structure that can include all these argumentative patterns [5]. A proposal of a "Basic Slippery Slope Argument" that could include all the typologies of Slippery Slope arguments has been proposed in Walton [9].

Following the formalization proposed in Baroni et al. [1], the present study proposes a modeling of the uncertainty of both the Basic Slippery Slope scheme and the Negative Consequences scheme.

1.3 The Problem of Uncertainty and Why It Is Useful

Baroni et al. [1] suggested the presence of at least three kinds of uncertainty that can be found in natural language:

- Uncertainty related to the presence and credibility of a source (e.g. expression referring to sources such as "According to professor Mario Rossi, ...") $[U_1]$;
- Uncertainty about the commitment (related to how the agents involved into an argument express their commitment, generally through the use of linguistic indicators) $[U_2]$;
- Uncertainty within the use of language (mostly related to the vagueness or ambiguity of some linguistic modifiers) $[U_3]$.

These three uncertainties are presented as a starting point for further extensions. The study suggests to investigate further to assess which kinds of uncertainty can be related to specific Argumentation Schemes.

Importantly, sometimes the source is not explicitly mentioned in the Argumentation Scheme, however we assume that any Argumentation Scheme has a source. If we consider Argumentation Schemes as patterns of reasoning that agents use to express and support their arguments, we assume that there is at least one basic source for any Argumentation Scheme: the arguer itself.

Baroni et al. [1] aimed at proposing a formalization for encompassing these kinds of natural language uncertainty directly within Argumentation Schemes. In this regard, they offer two examples: the Argumentation Scheme from Cause to Effect and the Argumentation Scheme from Position to Know, showing how to encompass Natural Language uncertainty into these two Argumentation Schemes. Finding a way to encompass uncertainty into Argumentation Schemes can be useful to evaluate argument strength and acceptability, because they can be "ranked" depending on their uncertainties, following the idea of the *preference-dependent* attack in Baroni et al. [2]. Interestingly, this way of encompassing uncertainty from Natural Language means that we can extract, from Natural Language, elements that can then be used within semi-formal and formal argumentation layers of evaluation. In other words, this methodology could be considered part of a broader approach in which linguistic indicators coming from Natural Language and Natural Arguments can provide elements of formal evaluation into Abstract Argumentation. This goes into the direction of building a common ground where Abstract Argumentation and Structured Argumentation can cooperate smoothly.

The ability to encompass uncertainty into Argumentation Schemes it is not only an elegant way to tighten the connection between Abstract Argumentation, NLP and Structured Argumentation; it can be useful also for practical purposes and applications: for example, in the legal domain, where modelling Legal Knowledge from Argumentation Schemes can be used to assess weakness and strength of legal argumentation [7]. Furthermore, this approach can be useful for several other applications of Formal Argumentation [4].

1.4 Theoretical Limitations and the Problem of Non-uniformity

In order to encompass uncertainty, this study suggests that some Argumentation Schemes should be reformulated. In some cases, in fact, the Argumentation Schemes formalized by Walton et al. [10] are not uniform. Particularly, these non-uniformities can be found in:

- How linguistic elements of uncertainty are used within the definition of Argumentation Schemes;
- How Critical Questions encompass uncertainty.

This is a long-term research goal which partially depends on the theoretical background. For example, it is not clear how the semantic links and the inferential warrants of Argumentation Schemes are inherited by their sub-types. Moreover, it is not always clear why some Critical Questions are targeting specific aspects of their scheme while the Critical Questions of other Argumentative Schemes seems focused on other aspects.

For example, similarly to Baroni et al. [1], we wonder why the Argumentation Scheme from Position to Know has two Critical Questions attacking the semantic information channeled by the two premises, while the Argumentation Scheme from Cause to Effect does not. As can be seen in Table 1, a further Critical

Table 1. An example of non-uniformity in the design of Critical Questions (CQs).

Argumentation Scheme "Position to Know"		
Component	Sentence	Targeted by:
Premise 1	α is in position to know in domain S containing preposition A	**CQ1** Is α in position to know?
Premise 2	α asserts that A (in domain S) is true (false)	**CQ3** Did α assert that A is true?
Argumentation Scheme "Cause to Effect"		
Component	Sentence	Targeted by:
Premise 1	If A occurs, then B occurs	**CQ1** How strong is the causal generalization?
Premise 2	In this case, A occurs	**MISSING**

Question could be added (as suggested by Baroni et al. [1]) targeting Premise 2 of the Cause to Effect argument. This could be something like "Does A actually occur?"

Moreover, why some Critical Questions explicitly target the main semantic relation of the inferential connection between premises and conclusion, while other schemes (even those sharing the same kind of main semantic relation) do not? For example, as will be described later, the Negative Consequence argument has a Critical Question targeting its causal relation, while the Slippery Slope argument (which is a sub-type of Negative Consequence argument) does not.

In this sense, it could be useful to harmonize the design of the Critical Questions or, at least, to clarify their scope (e.g., whether it is targeting an inferential connection, an explicit premise, an implicit premise, the semantic information of one premise, an aggregated semantic information, the whole inferential structure, and so on).

2   The Argumentation Scheme from Negative Consequences

The Argumentation Scheme from Negative Consequences is an argumentative pattern which points out the negative consequences of an action. For example, it is used by arguers who try to discourage people from bringing about specific actions, by claiming that those actions would have "bad consequences". Although there is also a positive counterpart (the Positive Consequences scheme), this work will focus only on the negative one, for reasons of space.

2.1   Structure of the Argumentation Scheme from Negative Consequences

The structure of this Argumentation Scheme is relatively straightforward:

Premise 1: If the agent α brings about (doesn't bring about) A, then B will occur.
Premise 2: B is a bad outcome (from the point of view of α's goals).
Conclusion: α should not bring about A.

As can be seen from the previous description, the scheme has a combination of two semantic connections: the causal relation of Premise 1 (in the form *if A then B*) and a definitional relation coming from Premise 2 (in the form *B is good/bad*) which aims at classifying the result of the previous causal relation.

Therefore, the inferential connection between premises and conclusion can be described as the aggregation of these two semantic connections (See Fig. 2). As already stated before, an Argumentation Scheme can be attacked in three ways: rebutting the conclusion of the Scheme, undermining a premise of the Scheme, undercutting the inferences between premises and conclusions. Regarding the ways of attacking an Argumentation Scheme from Negative Consequences, Walton et al. [10] propose three main Critical Questions:

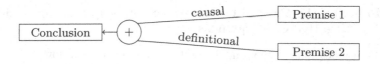

Fig. 2. Structure of the Negative Consequences Argumentation Scheme

Critical Question 1
How strong is the likelihood that the cited consequences will (may, must) occur?
Critical Question 2
What evidence supports the claim that the cited consequences will (may, must) occur, and is it sufficient to support the strength of the claim adequately?
Critical Question 3
Are there other opposite consequences (bad as opposed to good, for example) that should be taken into account?

3 Encompassing the Uncertainty of the Argumentation Scheme from Negative Consequences

The uncertainty of the Argumentation Scheme from Negative Consequence could be encompassed in the following way:

Premise 1:
{If the agent α brings about (doesn't bring about) A, then B will occur}$[U_1, U_t]$.
Explanation:
The assumption that if α brings (doesn't bring) about A, then B will occur may have a source. For this reason, there is an uncertainty U_1. Furthermore, we introduce a specific type of uncertainty that we call U_t, related to the use of the modal "will". A justification for adding this kind of uncertainty is that there are specific linguistic elements in Natural Language that are connected to the idea of time and can discriminate among different kinds of Negative Consequence arguments: for example, words such as "future" or verbal forms indicating an hypothetical results (e.g. "would") can be crucial to differentiate a Slippery Slope argument from a bare Negative Consequence argument [9].

Premise 2:
{B is a bad outcome (from the point of view of α's goals)}$[U_1]$.
Explanation:
The assumption that B is a bad outcome (from the point of view of α's goals) may have a source. For this reason, there is an uncertainty U_1.

Conclusion: {α should not bring about A}.[DU]
Explanation:
This is the Derived Uncertainty (DU).

3.1 Modelling the Critical Questions of the Argumentation Scheme from Negative Consequences

The Critical Questions of the scheme could be modelled as follows:

Critical Question 1
{How strong is the likelihood that the cited consequences will (may, must) occur?}$[U_3, U_t]$
Explanation:
The word "strong" implies a linguistic uncertainty (U_3). Also in this case, we suggest the presence of an uncertainty U_t, related to the use of the modals "will", "may" or "must".

Critical Question 2
{What evidence supports the claim that the cited consequences will (may, must) occur?}$[U_1, U_t]$ {and is it sufficient to support the strength of the claim adequately?}$[U_3]$
Explanation:
This Critical Question explicitly questions the source (evidences) that can support the argument. This can be considered an uncertainty about the source U_1, while we consider the verbal uncertainty related to the use of the modals "will", "may" or "must" as U_t. The second part refers again to the "strength" of the claim, so it is U_3.

Critical Question 3
{Are there other opposite consequences (bad as opposed to good, for example) that should be taken into account?}$[U_{eomr}]$
Explanation:
Here we formulate the presence of an uncertainty that we call "Equal-Opposite Material Relation". Baroni et al. [1] detected an analogous uncertainty within the Argumentation Scheme from Cause to Effect. In that case, Baroni et al. wondered what kind of uncertainty it was. We are attempting to give an answer to this question here. We argue that: when the main semantic (or "material") relation of an Argumentation Scheme (e.g. a causal relation [3]) produces effects that have an equal nature (i.e. they derive from the same material relation, e.g. a causal relation) but go towards an opposite direction w.r.t. the inferential connection of the Argumentation Scheme (i.e. these effects undercut the inference between premises and conclusion), we have an "Equal-Opposite Material Relation" (EOMR). Whenever an Argumentation Scheme is questioned in this way, there is an "Equal-Opposite Material Relation" (EOMR).

While we argue that the existence of a EOMR can be plausibly considered true, we underline that its theoretical usefulness in the analysis of Argumentation Schemes is not in the scope of this work and should be further investigated.

Following the ideas of Verheij [8], it seems that the role of the first Critical Question is to question whether Premise 1 holds. More precisely, it questions how strong is the probability that the causal information channeled by Premise 1 (i.e. the causal connection between the action A and the result B) occurs. While the role of the first Critical Question is clear, the second Critical Question seems somehow redundant and is split in two parts. In fact, while the first Critical Question is about *how strong is the likelihood* of the causal relation between A and B, the second one is about *what evidence supports* the same causal relation. Although, this appears as a partially redundant attack on the first premise, the role of the second Critical Question seems slightly different if we consider that it requires a burden of proof. This is made explicit in the second part of the question: "is [the evidence] sufficient to support the strength of the claim that *if A then B?*". Finally, the role of the third Critical Question, is to point to exceptional situations in which the scheme defaults. This means that this Critical Question is somehow related to the causal semantic information channelled by Premise 1.

Another aspect that should be mentioned is related to the definition of additional Critical Questions designed to reject each premise of the Scheme. This is a suggestion proposed by Baroni et al. [1], which aims at both uniforming the formulation of the Critical Questions and facilitating the modelling of their uncertainty. The Critical Questions 1 and 2 partially do it with regard to Premise 1, but they don't question the basic assumption that the agent is really bringing about (or not bringing about) the action A. In other words, the basic semantic information is not challenged. Furthermore, Premise 2 is not questioned at all. This means that we could add two new Critical Questions directly targeting the semantic information provided by the two premises:

Critical Question 4
{Is the agent α bringing about A?}$[U_1]$
Explanation:
This is undermining Premise 1; namely, it is as an uncertainty about the source's assumption that the agent α is bringing about A (U_1).

Critical Question 5
{Is B really a bad outcome from the point of view of α's goals?}$[U_1]$
Explanation:
This is undermining Premise 2; namely, it is an uncertainty about the source's assumption that B is a bad outcome from the point of view of α's goals (U_1).

4   The Basic Slippery Slope Argument

The Basic Slippery Slope Argument can be considered a general Argumentation Scheme designed to include all the types of Slippery Slope arguments that can be found in Natural Argumentation. As suggested by Walton [9], it can be considered a particular sub-type of the Argumentation Scheme from Negative Consequence, but with a more complex structure that span over a temporal sequence of events. This temporal sequence can be explicitly mentioned or it can be "compressed" by using special words that implicitly involve time spans (e.g. the word "future"). We will come back to this temporal aspect in the Sect. 4.1, which describe a proposal to encompass natural language uncertainties within the Basic Slippery Slope Argumentation Scheme.

Before describing the scheme, it is important to underline the difference with the Argumentation Scheme from Negative Consequences and the Slippery Slope arguments. The main conceptual difference between these two Schemes is that the Slippery Slope arguments have a sequence of actions that go in and out an undetermined "gray zone". In other words, the negative outcome must pass through a sequence of steps which has an undetermined nature.

4.1   The Structure of Basic Slippery Slope Argument

The general structure of the Basic Slippery Slope Argument described by Walton [9] is the following:

> **Initial Premise:** An agent α is considering carrying out an action A_0.
> **Sequential Premise:** Carrying out A_0 would lead to A_1, which would in turn lead to carrying out A_2, and so forth, through a sequence $A_2, \ldots, A_x, \ldots A_y, \ldots, A_n$.
> **Indeterminacy Premise:** There is a sequence $A_0, A_1, A_2, \ldots, A_x, \ldots A_y, \ldots, A_n$ that contains a sub-sequence $A_x, \ldots A_y$ called "the gray zone" where x and y are indeterminate points.
> **Control Premise:** α has control over whether to stop carrying out the actions in the sequence until α reaches some indeterminate point in the gray zone $A_x, \ldots A_y$.
> **Loss of Control Premise:** Once α reaches the indeterminate point in the gray zone $A_x, \ldots A_y$, α will lose control and will be compelled to keep carrying out actions until he/she reaches A_n.
> **Catastrophic Outcome Premise:** A_n is a catastrophic outcome that should be avoided if possible.
> **Conclusion:** A_0 should not be brought about.

Being a sub-type of the Negative Consequences argument, it can be noticed that the Sequential Premise is an evolution of Premise 1 of the Negative Consequences argument, while the Catastrophic Outcome Premise is an evolution of Premise 2 of the Negative Consequences argument. At the same time, it seems that the main semantic relation of the super-type, which is a causal relation (channeled by Premise 1) is preserved not only in the Sequential Premise, but also in the Loss of Control Premise (See Fig. 3). All the other premises, instead, seem to convey a definitional/classificatory value. In any case, also in the case of the Basic Slippery Slope, the final inferential strength connecting premises and conclusion can be described as the aggregation of the semantic information conveyed by the six linked premises.

Walton also suggested the possible presence of some contextual factors, called "drivers". A driver is described as a "catalyst that helps to propel the argument

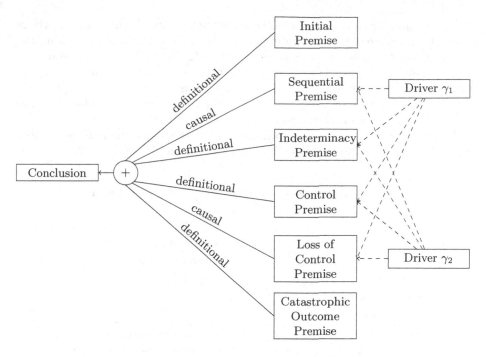

Fig. 3. Structure of the Basic Slippery Slope, dashed connections are optional links.

along the sequence in the argument, making it progressively harder for the agent to resist continuing" [9].

Walton chose not to clarify the nature of drivers in depth, maybe because a driver is an element that can be closely related to the peculiarities of the context where the argument takes place. Since the formulation of the Basic Slippery Slope Argument aims at designing a general model suitable for all the types of Slippery Slope argument, being too specific about the nature of drivers is probably not advisable. However, we may consider them as some sort of factors that can influence the main agent α either directly (influencing the actions of the agent α) or indirectly (perhaps, operating on the contextual environment).

Plausibly enough, we could even consider them as some sort of pseudo-agents, in some more specific instances of the Basic Slippery Slope argument. In this sense, the choice of the word "compelled" in the *Loss of Control Premise* is flexible enough to open the door for the possibility that the control (which is progressively lost by the agent α) flows towards some other drivers. In some more specific instances of Slippery Slope argument, a driver acquiring control over the sequence of actions could be, in our view, equivalent to consider that driver not anymore as a mere contextual factor, but as a proper agent involved into the sequence of the events of the slippery slope. For this reason, we may consider drivers as pseudo-agent or potential agents.

In any case, for the more general Basic Slippery Slope Argument, the drivers should be considered just as contextual factors that contribute in making the sequence flow towards the catastrophic result A_n. In such general instance of Slippery Slope argument, Walton suggest to model them as additional (optional) premises that can support some of the main premises of the scheme [9]. Intuitively, drivers are more likely to be connected with premises related to the sequence, and premises related to the control (see Fig. 3).

Following the Argumentation Scheme above, we can summarize the components of the Basic Slippery Slope Argument according to the Table 2.

Table 2. Components of the Basic Slippery Slope Argument.

Component	Comment
Agent α	Targeted agent
The critic β	Source agent
The drivers $\gamma_x \subseteq \Gamma$	Optional
A starting action A_0	
A catastrophic result A_n	
A sequence $A_0, A_1,$ $A_2, \ldots, A_x, \ldots A_y, \ldots, A_n$ (containing an indeterminate sub-sequence $A_x, \ldots A_y$)	The indeterminate sub-sequence is the "gray zone"

According to Walton, the main way of attacking a Slippery Slope is by asking if there is a bright line of separation in the so-called "gray zone". In other words, it is an attack to the Indeterminacy Premise and, indirectly, also to the premises related to the control and its loss. For this reason, the Basic Slippery Slope Argument has the following main Critical Question:

Main Critical Question
Is there a bright line in the gray zone?

In fact, if a bright line can be found into the allegedly "indeterminate gray zone", it means that the Slippery Slope does not exist at all.

5 Encompassing the Uncertainty of the Basic Slippery Slope Argument

Considering the Argumentation Scheme above and the formalization of Baroni et al. [1], we attempt to model the uncertainty behind each premise of the Basic Slippery Slope Argument. Also, we propose to reformulate some of the premises to eliminate some non-uniformities and because it seemed more appropriate for the modelling of uncertainty.

Initial Premise: {An agent α is considering carrying out an action A_0}$[U_1, U_2]$.
Explanation:
The observation "α is considering carrying out an action" has a source (the critic), for this reason there is an uncertainty connected to the source (U_1), which is to say, to the critic β.
The word "considering" could be seen as an uncertainty about the commitment (U_2) of the agent α.

Sequential Premise: {Carrying out A_0 would lead to A_1, which would in turn lead to carrying out A_2, and so forth, through a sequence $A_2, \ldots, A_x, \ldots A_y, \ldots, A_n$}$[U_1, U_t]$
Explanation:
The assumption "A_0 would lead to A_1 (...)" has a source, the critic β. For this reason, there is a source uncertainty U_1.
Similarly to the Negative Consequence argument, we introduce a specific type of uncertainty that we call U_t, related to the temporality of the sequence. A justification for adding this kind of uncertainty is that there are linguistic elements in Natural Language that are connected to the idea of time and can discriminate among different kinds of Slippery Slope Argument: words such as "future" or verbal forms indicating an hypothetical results (e.g. "would") can be crucial to detect, for example, the so-called "Compressed" Slippery Slope Argument [9]. Since temporality is an element that discriminates not just between Slippery Slope and non-Slippery Slope Arguments but also between different kinds of Slippery Slope arguments (e.g. the "Compressed" one), we argue that it is also important to model temporal expressions as a type uncertainty.

Indeterminacy Premise: {There is a sequence $A_0, A_1, A_2, \ldots, A_x, \ldots$ $A_y, \ldots, A_n$ that contains a sub-sequence $A_x, \ldots A_y$ called "the gray zone" where x and y are indeterminate points}$[U_1, U_3]$.
Explanation:
The assumption that there is a "gray zone" where x and y are not recognizable has a source (the critic β). So, also in this case there is an instance of uncertainty related to the source (U_1).
The expression "indeterminate" can be considered as a linguistic uncertainty (U_3).

Control Premise:* {α has control over whether to stop carrying out the actions in the sequence until α reaches some indeterminate point in the gray zone $A_x, \ldots A_y$}$[U_1, U_3]$.
Explanation:
The assumption that α will has control only until a certain point has a source (the critic β) and for this reason, there is an uncertainty U_1.
The expression "indeterminate" can be considered as a linguistic uncertainty (U_3).

Loss of Control Premise:* {Once α reaches the indeterminate point in the gray zone $A_x, \ldots A_y$, α will lose control}$[U_1, U_3]$ {and will be compelled to keep carrying out actions until he/she reaches A_n}$[U_1, U_3]$.
Explanation:
The assumption that α will lose control has a source (the critic β) and for this reason, there is an uncertainty U_1.
Moreover, the expression "indeterminate" can be considered as a linguistic uncertainty (U_3).
Interestingly, this premise can be considered as a group of two premises: the first one seems concerned with the concept that α will lose the control and can be considered partially overlapped with the previous premise, while the second one seems concerned with the direction of this loss (i.e. the direction of the loss is the catastrophic result A_n) and also with the existence of some not explicit compelling factors.
Always in the second part, we should consider the word "compelled" as linguistic uncertainty (U_3). A justification for this, is the fact that behind this word there is a potential crucial element in the definition of the drivers: why is the agent α compelled? What factors contribute to this condition? This definition, in fact, could be determinant in the definition of some more specific instance of Slippery Slope argument. So, we argue that also the general Basic Slippery Slope argument should encompass this element.

Catastrophic Outcome Premise: {A_n is a catastrophic outcome that should be avoided if possible}$[U_1]$.
Explanation:
The assumption that A_n is catastrophic has a source (the critic β) and for this reason, there is an uncertainty U_1.

Conclusion: {A_0 should not be brought about}[DU].
Explanation:
This is the Derived Uncertainty (DU).

As already suggested above, the Sequential Premise might be considered a derivation from the super-type's Premise 1, while the Catastrophic Outcome can be considered a derivation from the super-type's Premise 2. Interestingly, the premises of the sub-type (i.e., the premises of the Basic Slippery Slope argument) seems to reflect the same kinds of uncertainty of the super-type's premises (i.e., the premises of the Negative Consequence argument). In fact, U_1 and U_t seems to be inherited by the Sequential Premise from Premise 1, while U_1 is inherited by the Catastrophic Premise from Premise 2.

A similar phenomenon can be observed with the Critical Questions conveying the main semantic relation (which is a causal relation in the case of the two schemes analyzed in this work). In fact, the uncertainties U_1 and U_t seem to be inherited by the Critical Question 3 of the Basic Slippery Slope (i.e. the Critical Question related to the main causal relation) from the first two Critical Questions of the Negative Consequence Argument (i.e. the two Critical Questions focused on Premise 1, which we considered as partially redundant).

5.1   The Problem of the Non-uniformity

It is important to underline that there is a potential non-uniformity between the Control Premise and the Loss of Control Premise (for this reason, they have been marked with an asterisk).[1] It seems that the former wants to describe the fact of having control, while the latter is focused on the loss of control. However, the first one already says that the control exists *just until a specific point*, which implicitly means that the control is lost after reaching that point. In other words, the Control Premise is already about *losing* control (not just about *having* control).

On the other hand, while the Loss of Control Premise (which should be focused on the loss of the control) starts by mentioning the loss explicitly, it seems also focused on the description of another aspect: in fact, the second part of this premise (starting with "and will be compelled ...") seems more focused on the direction of the loss, rather than on the loss itself.

The partial overlapping between the Control Premise and the Loss of Control Premise (regarding the loss of control) along with the fact that the Loss Premise also mention a different concept (the direction of the Loss towards the catastrophic event A_n), could be a non-uniformity issue that can potentially affect the attempt to model knowledge starting from the this Argumentation Scheme.

For this reason, we argue that it is advisable to solve this non-uniformity. In this direction, we suggest a possible solution to reformulate the two premise avoid repetitions and ambiguities of the premises' scope. The solution could be that of having a premise for the loss of the control ("Loss of Control Premise") and another for the direction of the loss ("Slope Premise" or "Direction of the Loss Premise"). There is probably no need to create a premise which is just dedicated to the fact that the agent α have control until the point A_x.

Moreover, a "Direction of the Loss Premise" formulated in this way would give more importance and conceptual room to the potentialities behind the word "compelled" which is the only linguistic element referring to the potential existence of drivers.

Briefly, our suggestion can be described as follows:

Loss of Control Premise: $\{\alpha$ has control over whether to stop carrying out the actions in the sequence until α reaches some indeterminate point in the gray zone A_x, where the control is lost ... $A_y\}[U_1, U_3]$.
Explanation:
The assumption that α will have control only until a certain point has a source (the critic β) and for this reason, there is an uncertainty U_1.
The expression "indeterminate" can be considered as a linguistic uncertainty (U_3).

Direction of the Loss Premise: $\{\alpha$ is compelled to keep carrying out actions until he/she reaches $A_n\}[U_1, U_3]$.

---

[1] Also Baroni et al. [1] noticed a similar issue and suggested a different formulation for the Argumentation Schemes analyzed in their work and for the related Critical Questions.

Explanation:
The assumption that α is compelled to keep carrying out actions has a source (the critic β) and for this reason, there is an uncertainty U_1.
We should consider the word "compelled" as linguistic uncertainty (U_3), as already specified before.

As partially argued before, the fact of mentioning that the agent α has the control, before losing it, seems not necessary both from a logical point of view (losing it already imply having had it) and from the point of view of the practical implementation of the scheme in a real example: to instantiate a Basic Slippery Slope scheme there is no need to mention the fact of *having control* in a dedicated premise; on the contrary, to reach the theoretical purposes of the scheme, it should be sufficient to mention that the agent α lost it. This changes are not a mere linguistic change. We think that they can be useful for a better modelling of the knowledge and uncertainty within the Basic Slippery Slope Argumentation Scheme.

5.2 Modelling the Critical Questions of the Basic Slippery Slope Argumentation Scheme

As described by Baroni et al. [1], the Critical Questions can be used in the formulation of the uncertainty in the premises. For this reason, we can model the main Critical Questions of the Basic Slippery Slope Argument as follow:

Critical Question 1
{Is there a bright line in the gray zone?}$[U_1]$
Explanation:
This Critical Question can directly undermine the source's assumption that there is a Slippery Slope. For this reason there is an uncertainty U_1.

In the above-mentioned Critical Question, the "bright line" should be considered as a distinctive point in the sequence from A_0 to A_n where *agent α understands that it is time to stop*. It should be mentioned, however, that answering to this question is not simple, because the answer can depend on at least two points of view: the ability of α and the condition of the context (drivers included). In this sense, mentioning a "bright line" in the Critical Question is a good metaphorical resort, which however risks to hide the direction where the answers should be searched for. In fact, if the point of view is only on the "ability of α" to stop before the slope, the origin of the uncertainty would be intrinsically related with the agent. However, watching at the context (e.g. at the drivers involved into the sequence from A_0 to A_n), we may find that the origin of the uncertainty can be related to how drivers influence the slope. This distinction is not merely aesthetical. For example, if we wanted to investigate the presence of uncertainty related to the "bright line" in the gray zone directly within Natural Language sentences, we should consider not only those sentences in which the ability of the agent is mentioned, but also the sentences referred to contextual elements or drivers. This can be even more important in more specific instances of Slippery Slope arguments, where drivers could play a more defined role.

Also in this case, for uniformity, some Critical Questions may be explicitly formulated to attack the existence of each premise. This would produce other six Critical Questions:

Critical Question 2
{Is α considering carrying out A_0?}$[U_1, U_2]$
Explanation:
Questioning that A_n is considering carrying out A_0 would undermine the source's assumption that we are in a context of Slippery Slope (U_1).
While the verb "considering" can be seen as a U_2 (uncertainty about the commitment of the agent α).

Critical Question 3
{Is A_0 leading towards A_n?}$[U_1, U_t]$
Explanation:
Questioning that A_0 leading towards A_n would undermine the source assumption that we are in a context of Slippery Slope (U_1).
Moreover, since the sequence that would "lead" from A_0 to A_n is located into an indeterminate span of time, there could be an uncertainty connected to time also in this case (U_t).

Critical Question 4
{Does the sequence $A_0 \ldots A_n$ contain the indeterminate sub-sequence?} $[U_1, U_3]$
Explanation:
Questioning that the sequence from A_0 to A_n contain the indeterminate sub-sequence would undermine the source assumption that we are in a context of Slippery Slope (U_1).

Critical Question 5
{What elements indicate that α may lose the control?}$[U_1, U_3, U_t]$ {Are these elements strong enough to support the claim?}$[U_3]$
Explanation:
This Critical Question targets the potential presence of elements indicating that α could lose the control, undermining the existence of the Argumentation Scheme itself (U_1). While the word "strong" can be considered a linguistic uncertainty (U_3) and the word "may" can be referred to an uncertainty related to time (U_t).

Critical Question 6
{What elements indicate that α may be compelled to go towards A_n?}$[U_1, U_3, U_t]$ {Are these elements strong enough to support the claim?}$[U_3]$

Explanation:
This Critical Question targets the potential presence of elements indicating that α could be compelled to go towards A_n, undermining the existence of the Argumentation Scheme itself (U_1). While the word "strong" can be considered a linguistic uncertainty (U_3) and the word "may" can be referred to an uncertainty related to time (U_t).

Critical Question 7
{What elements indicate that A_n may be a catastrophe?}$[U_1, U_3, U_t]$ {Are these elements strong enough to support the claim?}$[U_3]$
Explanation:
This Critical Question targets the potential presence of elements indicating that A_n is a catastrophe, undermining the existence of the Argumentation Scheme itself (U_1). While the word "strong" can be considered a linguistic uncertainty (U_3) and the word "may" can be referred to an uncertainty related to time (U_t).

It should be noted that the Critical Questions 5, 6 and 7 are the most exposed to the problem of the time, basic characteristic element of the Slippery Slope Arguments. In fact, these questions could be not answerable, since their answers could be just arbitrary predictions on future events. For these reasons, they are formulated in terms of "What elements indicate that X may be true". Finally, it could be useful to underline that attacking the existence itself of the Argumentation Scheme is considered as an attack to the source of the argument (U_1).

At this point, it seems natural to envisage the existence of a Critical Question indicating the existence of a U_{eomr}, similarly to the Critial Question 3 of the super-type. In this sense, there would be another Critical Question questioning the existence of other factors (e.g. other consequences or even drivers) which despite being related to the same causal relation could go towards the opposite direction w.r.t the inference from premises to the conclusion.

Critical Question 8
{Are there other consequences or factors to be considered, which may be triggered through the sequential process from A_0 onward?}$[U_{eomr}, U_t]$
Explanation:
In this case, the main semantic relation (i.e. a causal relation) may produce effects or factors having an equal nature (i.e. they derive from the same causal material relation) but an opposite direction w.r.t. the inferential connection of the Argumentation Scheme, undercutting the inference between premises and conclusion (U_{eomr}). However, since these effects are in the future, there is an uncertainty related to time (U_t), channelled by the word "may".

6   Conclusions

In this paper, we encompassed the uncertainty of both the famous Argumentation Scheme from Negative Consequence and the novel Basic Slippery Slope Argument following the methodology proposed in Baroni et al. [1].

Noticeably, we described the presence of two potentially new kinds of uncertainty: one related to time (defined as U_t), and one related to the main semantic relation in the inferential connection between premises and conclusion, which we defined as "Equal-Opposite Material Relation" uncertainty (U_{eomr}).

Regarding the Argumentation Scheme from Negative Consequences, we suggested a partial reformulation of current model adding two more Critical Questions which target the semantic information channeled by the two premises of the scheme.

Regarding the Basic Slippery Slope Argument, we also suggested a reformulation of two premises in order to solve some non-uniformity that could affect the attempts to model knowledge from this Argumentation Scheme. Namely, we intervened in the two premises related to the loss of control to avoid redundancies. Moreover, similarly to the Negative Consequence argument, we suggested to add a new Critical Question for each premise, targeting the relative semantic information. Finally, we added another Critical Question which is related to the U_{eomr} uncertainty and is meant to target the potential existence of factors which may undercut the inferential connection between premises and conclusion despite being originated by the same main semantic relation of the scheme's inferential connection (i.e. the same causal relation).

In future research we will follow the suggestion of Baroni et al. [1] to use the modelled Argumentation Schemes with uncertainty together with Natural Language uncertainties in order to reach the "semi-formal argumentation with uncertainty". In this sense, some classifiers could be trained using NLP techniques in order to automatically evaluate the presence of uncertainty directly within Natural Language sentences.

This is a long-term research path which is strictly dependent on the formalization choices and on the theoretical background. In this regard, further studies on the philosophical side of the Argumentation Scheme theory can be crucial for a successful implementation of the present approach. For example, a more in-depth clarification about how the semantic links and the inferential warrants of an Argumentation Scheme are inherited by its sub-types could be useful for modeling uncertainty in a more appropriate way. Moreover, a further standardisation of the types (and sub-types) of Argumentation Schemes and Critical Questions is strongly advisable. We think that there is the need to reinforce the theoretical background designing Critical Questions in a more uniform way, making clear, and possibly unambiguous, what is the target of a Critical Question; for example, whether it is targeting an inferential connection, a (possibly implicit) premise, a semantic information, the whole inferential structure, and so on.

Acknowledgements. Davide Liga acknowledges Beishui Liao and Yì N. Wáng for their valuable guidance and support at Zhejiang University, and professor Leendert Van der Torre for his valuable suggestions and advice. We also acknowledge the anonymous reviewers for their important suggestions and observations.

References

1. Baroni, P., Giacomin, M., Liao, B., van der Torre, L.: Encompassing uncertainty in argumentation schemes. Front. Connect. Argum. Theory Nat. Lang. Process. 2014 (2014)
2. Bex, F., Modgil, S., Prakken, H., Reed, C.: On logical specifications of the argument interchange format. J. Log. Comput. **23**(5), 951–989 (2013)
3. Freeman, J.B.: Dialectics and the Macrostructure of Arguments: A Theory of Argument Structure, vol. 10. Walter de Gruyter, Berlin (2011)
4. Gabbay, D.M., Giacomin, M., Liao, B., van der Torre, L.: Present and future of formal argumentation. Dagstuhl Reports (2016)
5. Lode, E.: Slippery slope arguments and legal reasoning. Calif. Law Rev. **87**, 1469 (1999)
6. Macagno, F., Walton, D., Reed, C.: Argumentation schemes. History, classifications, and computational applications. J. Log. Appl. **4**(8), 2493–2556 (2017)
7. Palmirani, M.: A tool to highlight weaknesses and strengthen cases: CISpaces.org. In: Legal Knowledge and Information Systems: JURIX 2018: The Thirty-first Annual Conference, vol. 313, p. 186. IOS Press (2018)
8. Verheij, B.: Dialectical argumentation with argumentation schemes: an approach to legal logic. Artif. Intell. Law **11**(2), 167–195 (2003). https://doi.org/10.1023/B:ARTI.0000046008.49443.36
9. Walton, D.: The basic slippery slope argument. Informal Log. **35**(3), 273–311 (2015)
10. Walton, D., Reed, C., Macagno, F.: Argumentation Schemes. Cambridge University Press, Cambridge (2008)
11. Walton, D.N., Kuhse, H.: Slippery Slope Arguments. Clarendon Press, Oxford (1992)

Reasoning as Speech Acts

Chinghui Su, Liwu Rong$^{(\boxtimes)}$, and Fei Liang$^{(\boxtimes)}$

School of Philosophy and Social Development, Shandong University,
Shanda Nan Road 27, Jinan 250100, China
`pcs0929@gmail.com`, `hooeyrong@163.com`, `f.liang@sdu.edu.cn`

Abstract. By considering reasoning as speech acts, the paper gives a new perspective to evaluate good reasoning, that is, not only involving the consequence relation between premises and conclusions, but also involving the goal of doing reasoning by an agent. Moreover, in this paper, we propose a framework for characterizing the reasoning for persuasion from the logical perspective.

Keywords: Speech act · Reasoning · Persuasion · Action logic

1 Motivation

Consider the following conversation:

Edmund: Knowledge is not justified true belief. (1)

Alfred: Why? (Or why should I believe it?) (2)

Edmund: Well, here are two possible cases indicating that it is possible to have justified true belief without knowledge... (3)

Although the conversation proceeds back and forth and could last for a long time, it is clear to see that Edmund is trying to persuade Alfred to accept that "knowledge is not justified true belief" by a series of arguments. In fact, Edmund is demonstrating a speech act (assertion), involving reasoning from (3) to (1). It is commonly agreed that we can evaluate reasoning through concerning whether the conclusion logically follows from its premises via different standards, e.g. deductive reasoning, inductive reasoning, abductive reasoning, etc. What matters here is to evaluate the reasoning by the content of it only. In the above example, Edmund's argument is good if it is the case that: (1) is a logical consequence of (3)[1]. However, it seems to us that this evaluation is not enough since it ignores the aim of the argument, that is, to persuade Alfred to accept that

---

[1] Though the example is usually taken as deductive reasoning, the concept of logical consequence might also be concerned with inductive or abductive reasoning. That is, a good argument might not be truth preserving, while it is probability preserving (or has explanatory power).

All authors are supported by "Shandong University International Scientific Cooperation Seed Fund" (11090089395416). The third author is also supported by "Young Scholars Program of Shandong University" (11090089964225).

© Springer Nature Switzerland AG 2020

M. Dastani et al. (Eds.): CLAR 2020, LNAI 12061, pp. 279–286, 2020.
https://doi.org/10.1007/978-3-030-44638-3_17

"knowledge is not justified true belief". According to [3], "reasoning is characteristically addressed to problems", and then it should be seen as a mental activity with goals and purposes. That is, whether a certain argument expressed by a speech act is good depends on if it achieves its goal. In the example, Alfred believes that knowledge is justified true belief in the beginning, and Edmund is trying to persuade Alfred to give up this belief. If Alfred were to change his mind, then Edmund's speech act (what he said) is successful (in the sense of achieving his goal). Therefore, reasoning expressed by speech acts is $good^2$, if it satisfies two conditions: what an agent says constitutes good reasoning (informally) from $A_1, \ldots, A_n$ to B just in case (i) what the agent says exemplifies reasoning which satisfies certain standards (for example, validity) and that (ii) the audience (the agents spoke to) should accept B after the agents' speaking. (i) indicates that the content of the speech act instantiates a valid logical form, for example; and (ii) indicates that the goal of the speech act is achieved (for example, the audience's belief changed). In this paper, (ii) is our main concern.

To show that (i) and (ii) are different, though related to each other in most cases, let's see a real case that teaching students how to identify an invalid argument. While saying an invalid argument, at the same time the teacher shows reasoning exemplifying an invalid logical form. Does she succeed in teaching students how to identify an invalid argument? If yes, her speech act is successful and should be rendered *good*; otherwise, *not good*. On the other hand, while saying φ therefore φ, will people thereby turn to accept φ if they accept φ, given that they disbelieve φ at the beginning? Therefore, (i) and (ii) are different, though satisfying (i) may simultaneously satisfy (ii) in most cases. Since many people have focused on (i), we plan to take (ii) as our focus here. That is, we focus on reasoning hiding in speech acts.

2   General Idea

To give an adequate account of reasoning, some phenomena should be explained: (a) not all actual reasoning is good; (b) actual reasoning may be incomplete; and (c) not all valid arguments are good reasoning. To explain (a), Grice [3] proposes taking the derivability, as thought by the reasoner, to be derivable by canonical principles. To explain (b), Grice proposes that we shall consider ourselves facing different reasoning dealing with actual reasoning. To explain (c), Grice proposes that we shall treat reasoning as an activity with goals and purposes. In this paper, we propose that reasoning can be demonstrated by speech acts (in Austin's sense [1]), which is goal-oriented (e.g. persuading). In this sense, x reasons (informally) from A to B, in case (1) x thinks A and intends that, in thinking B, (2) he should be thinking something which would be the conclusion of a formally valid argument the premises of which are a supplementation of A. Although condition (2) is too strict to be satisfied by most of actual reasonings

---

2 According to [2], "good" is an incomplete predicate, for its precise meaning will be shown once being completed. In the present paper, whether "good" is ambiguous or incomplete is not our concern here.

since it implies that any mental activity which can be called reasoning should follow a formally valid argument, it still gives us a different perspective to think about reasoning practically, that is, reasoning as an action. To evaluate reasoning is to see if an agent achieve his/her goal after doing it (whether certain reasoning results in persuading audiences in question successfully). The idea is that, to explain the reason why a valid argument may (or may not) persuade people, we have to consider reasoning as speech acts and neglect the content of the reasoning, though usually the content is related to the goal (e.g. persuasion) of reasoning. There are three characters are involved in a *speech act*: what is said (locutionary act), speaker's intention (illocutionary act), and a result caused by what is said (perlocutionary act). Take a typical example, wedding ceremony. While saying "now I pronounce you husband and wife" (what is said), the priest has an intention to notarize the couple in front of him (speaker's intention). In general, the upshot will be two unrelated people becoming a couple, indicating that they are bounded in certain relationship. However, a possible upshot is that the priest's intention fails to be realized; for example, the wife runs away, after finding out her husband cheating on her all the time (e.g. flirting with other females). The thing is, perlocutionary act is what resulted from what is said, and we are not sure whether speaker's intention will be satisfied. When we consider reasoning demonstrated by speech acts, we can talk about what its end is and how to achieve its end. In this paper, we simply consider persuasion (to the audience) as the end of reasoning. Describing reasoning as an action towards persuasion, enables us to deal with each individual reasoning as a step of the process of persuasion. However, there are other ways to persuade except reasoning, we only focus on being persuaded to accept something by reasoning in this paper.

Describing reasoning as an action towards persuasion, enables us to deal with each individual reasoning as a step of the process of persuasion. However, there are other ways to persuade except doing a reasoning, we only focus on "being persuaded to accept φ after doing a reasoning" in this paper. In what follows, we give a formal framework to characterize "what is an agent being persuaded" (a logic for persuation). The basic idea is that we consider reasonings as actions with some structures, and the result of reasoning ("being persuaded to accept 'φ'") as information update: from the state of not accepting φ to the state of accepting φ. That is, the audience will accept φ, if the speaker persuades him/her successfully by a reasoning.

3   The Logic for Persuation

In [5], Herzig and Longin proposed a new logic for intention with cooperative principle and with assertive speech acts. They characterized the assertive type of speech acts by the form of $<i, j, A>$, where i is the author, j is the addressee, and A is a formula representing the propositional content of the act. In their example, $<u, s, Blue(sky)>$ represents a assertive speech act achieved by agent u's utterance towards agent s: "The sky is blue". Furthermore, each action associates with two modal operators *After* and *Before*, for example, Bel_i *Before*

$<j, i, p>$ Bel_j p means that the agent i believes that before informing that p, j believed that p. By introducing belief and intention operators, [5] could describe an agent's mental attitude before and after an assertive speech act. However, we also consider a speech act as a perlocutionary act, i.e. a result caused by what is said. What happened to the addressee when the author makes an assertion? A possible result may be belief adoption, as [5] suggested, "an agent adopts j's belief if he believes that j is competent at that belief." In our opinion, the process of belief adoption involves many different considerations, such as, the author's competence at p, the truthfulness and credibility of his report, and so on. All of these considerations can be concluded by Grice's cooperative principle, and the addressee make a belief adoption by his own reasoning and judgment. In this paper, we propose to give a description for reasoning as speech acts, and put more emphasis on the result caused by it rather than its content. By $P_i(\alpha_j, \varphi)$, we mean that "i is persuaded to accept φ after j did reasoning α. A simple idea is that the audience doesn't accept φ until the speaker has the reasoning α, regardless of the exact content of this reasoning. Unlike [5] intending to discover the relation between mental attitudes and describing the rules of belief adoption and intention generation, our work is to deal with each primitive and atomic reasoning as a step of the process of persuasion. In what follows, we give a formal frame work to characterize "an agent being persuaded by reasoning" (a logic for persuasion). The basic idea is that we consider reasonings as actions with some structures, and the result of reasoning ("being persuaded to accept something") as information update: from "the state of not accepting sth." to "the state of accepting sth.". That is, the audience will accept sth. after the speaker persuading him/her successfully by reasoning.

Let $\mathbf{A} = \{a, b, c, d, \ldots\}$ be a denumerable set of atomic reasoning actions, and $\mathbf{Ag} = \{i, j\}$ be a set of two agents (for simplicity, we only consider two agents' case). The set of arbitrary reasoning actions $\mathcal{R}$ are defined recursively as follows:

$$\alpha_i :: = a_i \mid (\alpha_i \oplus \alpha_i) \mid (\alpha_i; \alpha_i)$$

where $i \in \mathbf{Ag}$. In what follows, we use α, β, γ etc. to denote reasoning. Notice that, in this language, $\alpha_i; \beta_i$ means sequential reasoning, that is, agent i does reasoning α first and then does reasoning β. $\alpha_i \oplus \beta_i$ means "agent i chooses either reasoning α or reasoning β" intuitively. For example, to prove "φ", you have no idea whether the proof α or proof β could get it, you may try one of them arbitrarily.

Let $\mathbf{Atop} = \{p, q, r, \ldots\}$ be a denumerable set of atomic propositions. The set of formulas $\mathcal{F}$ are defined recursively as follows:

$$\varphi :: = p \mid \neg\varphi \mid [\alpha_i]\varphi \mid P_i(\alpha_j, \varphi) \mid (\varphi \vee \varphi) \mid (\varphi \wedge \varphi) \mid (\varphi \rightarrow \varphi)$$

where $i \in \mathbf{Ag}$. In what follows, we use φ, ψ, χ etc. to denote formulas. Intuitively, $[\alpha]\varphi$ means "φ holds after agent i doing reasoning α", and $P_i(\alpha_j, \varphi)$ means: "after agent j doing reasoning α, agent i has been persuaded to accept φ". Notice that it is possible that $j = i$, then it means an agent has been persuaded him(her)-self after doing reasoning α.

Definition 3.1 (Model and Frame).   *A model is a structure* $\mathfrak{M} = (W, N, R_{\alpha_i}, \mathbf{Ag}, V)$, *where:*

(1) W *is a non-empty set of states;*
(2) $N : W \times \mathbf{Ag} \rightarrow \mathcal{PP}(W)$ *s.t.*
   (a) *for any* $w \in W$, $i \in \mathbf{Ag}$ *and* $X, Y \subseteq W$, *if* $X \in N(w, i)$ *and* $X \subseteq Y$, *then* $Y \in N(w, i)$;
   (b) *for any* $w \in W$, $i \in \mathbf{Ag}$ *and* $X \subseteq W$, *if* $X \in N(w, i)$, *then* $\overline{X} \notin N(w, i)$, *where* $\overline{X} = W/X$;
   (c) *for any* $w \in W$, $i \in \mathbf{Ag}$ *and* $X, Y \subseteq W$, *if* $X \in N(w, i)$ *and* $Y \in N(w, i)$, *then* $X \cap Y \in N(w, i)$;
(3) R_{α_i} *is defined inductively as follows:*
   (a) $R_{a_i} \subseteq W \times W$, *and satisfies: for any* $w \in W$, *there exits* $v \in W$, *s.t.* $(w, v) \in R_{a_i}$.
   (b) $R_{\alpha_i \oplus \beta_i} = \{(w, u) \mid (w, u) \in R_{\alpha_i} \ or \ (w, u) \in R_{\beta_i}\}$;
   (c) $R_{\alpha_i ; \beta_i} = \{(w, u) \mid there \ exists \ v \in W, \ s.t. \ (w, v) \in R_{\alpha_i} \ and \ (v, u) \in R_{\beta_i}\}$;
(4) $V : \mathbf{Atop} \rightarrow \mathcal{P}(W)$.

A frame is a structure $\mathfrak{F} = (W, N, R_{\alpha_i}, \mathbf{Ag})$ *satisfying (1)-(3) above.*

In what follows, we use F to denote the class of all frames and M to denote the class of all models.

From (3a), It is not difficult to see that for any $w \in W$, there exits $v \in W$, s.t. $(w, v) \in R_{\alpha_i}$ for any α_i. Intuitively, $N(w, i)$ means "the set of all information agent i accepted in the state w". In this sense, the empty set (which corresponds to contradictory propositions) cannot be in any agent's information set in any state. Conversely, the whole set (which corresponds to tautologies) as the default information is in all agent's information sets in all states. Notice that our condition is a bit strict in the sense that it is not allowed that the inconsistent information exits in ant agent's information set in any state.

Definition 3.2 (Truth set). *Let* $\mathfrak{M}$ *be a model. For any* $\varphi \in \mathcal{F}$, *the* truth set $V(\varphi)$ *with respect to* $\mathfrak{M}$ *is defined recursively as follows: for any* $w, v \in W$,

(1) $V(\neg\varphi) = \overline{V(\varphi)}$;
(2) $V(\varphi \vee \psi) = V(\varphi) \cup V(\psi)$;
(3) $V(\varphi \wedge \psi) = V(\varphi) \cap V(\psi)$;
(4) $V(\varphi \rightarrow \psi) = \overline{V(\varphi)} \cup V(\psi)$;
(5) $V([\alpha_i]\varphi) = \{w \mid R_{\alpha_i}(w) \subseteq V(\varphi)\}$;
(6) $V(P_i(\alpha_j, \varphi)) = \{w \mid if \ v \in R_{\alpha_j}(w), \ then \ V(\varphi) \in N(v, i) \ for \ any \ v \in W\}$.

where $R_{\alpha_i}(w) = \{v \mid (w, v) \in R_{\alpha_i}\}$.

Definition 3.3 (Validity). *Let* $\mathfrak{F}$ *be a frame and* $\mathfrak{M}$ *be a model. A formula* φ *is* valid in $\mathfrak{M}$ *(note as:* $\mathfrak{M} \models \varphi$*) if* $V(\varphi) = W$; *a formula* φ *is valid in* $\mathfrak{F}$ *(note as:* $\mathfrak{F} \models \varphi$*) if* $V(\varphi) = W$ *for any* V. *A formula* φ *is valid in the class* M *of all models (note as:* M $\models \varphi$*) if it is valid in any model* $\mathfrak{M} \in$ M. *A formula* φ *is valid in the class* F *of all frames (note as:* F $\models \varphi$*) if it is valid in any frame* $\mathfrak{F} \in$ F. *A rule* $\varphi_1, \ldots \varphi_n / \psi$ *is valid in* $\mathfrak{M}$, *if* $\mathfrak{M} \models \varphi_1, \ldots, \mathfrak{M} \models \varphi_n$, *then* $\mathfrak{M} \models \psi$. *The validity of a rule in* $\mathfrak{F}$ *(or* M, *or* F*) is defined analogously as above.*

The axiomatization of the logic for persuasion **HP** is defined as follows:

Axioms:
  (a) all tautologies in propositional logic;
  (b) $[\alpha_i](\varphi \to \beta) \to ([\alpha_i]\varphi \to [\alpha_i]\beta)$;
  (c) $[\alpha_i](\varphi \wedge \psi) \leftrightarrow [\alpha_i]\varphi \wedge [\alpha_i]\psi$;
  (d) $[\alpha_i]\varphi \to \neg[\alpha_i]\neg\varphi$;
  (e) $[\alpha_i; \beta_i]\varphi \leftrightarrow [\alpha_i][\beta_i]\varphi$;
  (f) $[\alpha_j \oplus \beta_j]\varphi \leftrightarrow [\alpha_j]\varphi \wedge [\beta_j]\varphi$;
  (g) $P_i(\alpha_j, \varphi \to \psi) \to (P_i(\alpha_j, \varphi) \to P_i(\alpha_j, \psi))$;
  (h) $P_i(\alpha_j, \varphi) \wedge P_i(\alpha_j, \psi) \to P_i(\alpha_j, \varphi \wedge \psi)$;
  (i) $P_i(\alpha_j, \varphi) \to \neg P_i(\alpha_j, \neg\varphi)$;
  (j) $P_i(\alpha_j; \beta_j, \varphi) \leftrightarrow [\alpha_j]P_i(\beta_j, \varphi)$;
  (k) $P_i(\alpha_j \oplus \beta_j, \varphi) \leftrightarrow P_i(\alpha_j, \varphi) \wedge P_i(\beta_j, \varphi)$;

Rules:

$$\frac{\varphi \qquad \varphi \to \psi}{\psi} \ (MP) \qquad \frac{\varphi}{[\alpha_i]\varphi} \ ([\alpha]) \qquad \frac{\varphi}{P_i(\alpha_j, \varphi)} \ (P)$$

Corollary 3.4. *The following formulas hold in* **HP**:

(1) $P_i(\alpha_j, \varphi \wedge \psi) \to P_i(\alpha_j, \varphi) \wedge P_i(\alpha_j, \psi)$;
(2) $P_i(\alpha_j, \varphi) \vee P_i(\alpha_j, \psi) \to P_i(\alpha_j, \varphi \vee \psi)$;
(3) $\neg P_i(\alpha_j, \varphi \wedge \neg\varphi)$.

Proof. (1)

1.	$\varphi \wedge \psi \to \varphi$	Axioms (a)
2.	$P_i(\alpha_j, \varphi \wedge \psi \to \varphi)$	1, (P)
3.	$P_i(\alpha_j, \varphi \wedge \psi \to \varphi) \to (P_i(\alpha_j, \varphi \wedge \psi) \to P_i(\alpha_j, \varphi))$	Axiom (g)
4.	$P_i(\alpha_j, \varphi \wedge \psi) \to P_i(\alpha_j, \varphi)$	2,3, (MP)
5.	$P_i(\alpha_j, \varphi \wedge \psi) \to P_i(\alpha_j, \psi)$	1-4
6.	$P_i(\alpha_j, \varphi \wedge \psi) \to P_i(\alpha_j, \varphi) \wedge P_i(\alpha_j, \psi)$	4, 5, Axioms (a)

(2)

1.	$\varphi \to \varphi \vee \psi$	Axioms (a)
2.	$P_i(\alpha_j, \varphi \to \varphi \vee \psi)$	1, (P)
3.	$P_i(\alpha_j, \varphi \to \varphi \vee \psi) \to (P_i(\alpha_j, \varphi) \to P_i(\alpha_j, \varphi \vee \psi))$	Axiom (g)
4.	$P_i(\alpha_j, \varphi) \to P_i(\alpha_j, \varphi \vee \psi)$	2,3, (MP)
5.	$P_i(\alpha_j, \psi) \to P_i(\alpha_j, \varphi \vee \psi)$	1-4
6.	$P_i(\alpha_j, \varphi \vee \psi) \to P_i(\alpha_j, \varphi) \vee P_i(\alpha_j, \psi)$	4, 5, Axioms (a)

(3)

1.	$\neg(\varphi \wedge \neg\varphi)$	Axioms (a)
2.	$P_i(\alpha_j, \neg(\varphi \wedge \neg\varphi))$	1, (P)
3.	$P_i(\alpha_j, \neg(\varphi \wedge \neg\varphi)) \to \neg P_i(\alpha_j, \neg\neg(\varphi \wedge \neg\varphi))$	Axiom (i)
4.	$\neg P_i(\alpha_j, \neg\neg(\varphi \wedge \neg\varphi))$	2,3, (MP)
5.	$(\varphi \wedge \neg\varphi) \to \neg\neg(\varphi \wedge \neg\varphi)$	Axioms (a)
6.	$P_i(\alpha_j, (\varphi \wedge \neg\varphi) \to \neg\neg(\varphi \wedge \neg\varphi))$	5, (P)
8.	$P_i(\alpha_j, \varphi \wedge \neg\varphi) \to P_i(\alpha_j, \neg\neg(\varphi \wedge \neg\varphi))$	6, Axioms (g), (MP)
9.	$\neg P_i(\alpha_j, \neg\neg(\varphi \wedge \neg\varphi)) \to \neg P_i(\alpha_j, \varphi \wedge \neg\varphi)$	6, Axiom(a)
10.	$\neg P_i(\alpha_j, \varphi \wedge \neg\varphi)$	4,9, (MP)

$\square$

Theorem 3.5 (Soundness). **HP** *is sound with respect to* F.

Proof. As to axioms, the proofs for (a)–(f) are standard and can be found in [4, Chapter 5.6]. We only prove (g)–(k).

(g) In order to show $F \models P_i(\alpha_j, \varphi \to \psi) \to (P_i(\alpha_j, \varphi) \to P_i(\alpha_j, \psi))$, by Definition 3.3, it suffices to show that $\mathfrak{F} \models P_i(\alpha_j, \varphi \to \psi) \to (P_i(\alpha_j, \varphi) \to P_i(\alpha_j, \psi))$ for any $\mathfrak{F} \in F$, that is, it is enough to show that $V(P_i(\alpha_j, \varphi \to \psi) \to (P_i(\alpha_j, \varphi) \to P_i(\alpha_j, \psi))) = W$ for any $\mathfrak{F} \in F$ and for any V. Assume that it is not the case, that is, there exits a $w \in W$ s.t. $w \notin V(P_i(\alpha_j, \varphi \to \psi) \to (P_i(\alpha_j, \varphi) \to P_i(\alpha_j, \psi)))$. By Definition 3.2(4), $w \in V(P_i(\alpha_j, \varphi \to \psi))$ and $w \in V(P_i(\alpha_j, \varphi))$ but $w \notin V(P_i(\alpha_j, \psi))$. Hence, $w \in V(P_i(\alpha_j, \varphi \to \psi)) \cap V(P_i(\alpha_j, \varphi))$. Definition 3.2(6) implies that: for any $v \in W$, if $v \in R_{\alpha_j}(w)$, then $V(\varphi \to \psi) \in N(v, i)$ and $V(\varphi) \in N(v, i)$, by Definition 3.1(2c), which implies: for any $v \in W$, if $v \in R_{\alpha_j}(w)$, then $V(\varphi \to \psi) \cap V(\varphi) \in N(v, i)$ (*). By Definition 3.2(4), $V(\varphi \to \psi) \cap V(\varphi) \subseteq V(\psi)$. Combining with Definition 3.1(2a), (*) implies: for any $v \in W$, if $v \in R_{\alpha_j}(w)$, then $V(\psi) \in N(v, i)$, that is, $w \in V(P_i(\alpha_j, \psi))$ which contradicts with the assumption.

(h) It suffices to show that $V(P_i(\alpha_j, \varphi) \land P_i(\alpha_j, \psi) \to P_i(\alpha_j, \varphi \land \psi)) = W$ for any $\mathfrak{F} \in F$ and for any V, by Definition 3.2(4), it is enough to show that $V(P_i(\alpha_j, \varphi) \land P_i(\alpha_j, \psi)) \subseteq V(P_i(\alpha_j, \varphi \land \psi))$ for any $\mathfrak{F} \in F$ and for any V. It follows from 3.2(6) and 3.1(2c), and the proof is omitted.

(i) It suffices to show that $V(P_i(\alpha_j, \varphi) \to \neg P_i(\alpha_j, \neg\varphi)) = W$ for any $\mathfrak{F} \in F$ and for any V. By Definition 3.2(4), it is enough to show that $V(P_i(\alpha_j, \varphi)) \subseteq V(\neg P_i(\alpha_j, \neg\varphi))$ for any $\mathfrak{F} \in F$ and for any V. Let $w \in V(P_i(\alpha_j, \varphi))$, that is, for any $v \in W$, if $v \in R_{\alpha_j}(w)$, then $V(\varphi) \in N(v, i)$ by Definition 3.2(6). Definition 3.2(1) and 3.1(2b) implies that: for any $v \in W$, if $v \in R_{\alpha_j}(w)$, then $V(\neg\varphi) \notin N(v, i)$(*). Since $R_{\alpha_j}(w)$ is not empty by Definition 3.1(3a), (*) implies $w \in V(\neg P_i(\alpha_j, \neg\varphi))$ by Definition 3.2(1).

The proof for (j) is analogous with the proof for (e), and the proof for (k) is analogous with the proof for (f), hence proofs are omitted.

As to the rules, the proofs for the first two are standard and can be found in [4, Chapter 5.6]. We only prove the third one. By Definition 3.3, let $V(\varphi) = W$ for any $\mathfrak{F} \in F$ and for any V, it suffices to show that $V(P_i(\alpha_j, \varphi)) = W$ for any $\mathfrak{F} \in F$ and for any V. By Definition 3.2(6), it is enough to show that: for any $\mathfrak{F} \in F$ and for any V, "if $v \in R_{\alpha_j}(w)$, then $V(\varphi) \in N(v, i)$ for any $v \in W$" (*) holds. Since $W \in N(v, i)$ by Definition 3.1(2), (*) always holds. $\square$

Consider the following situation: two philosophers arguing whether we can justify our modal beliefs, such like "it is possible that Trump lost in the 2016 Presidential Election". One thinks so but the other not. As a philosopher, both are good at reasoning, and intend to convince another through reasoning. One may argue that we can justify our modal beliefs by conceivability: conceivability implies metaphysical possibility, by the argument which is proposed by David Chalmers, then the other philosopher accept it. In this case, we can use the formal language introduced above to characterize this process as follows: $P_1(\alpha_c, \varphi)$, $P_2(\alpha_1, \varphi)$, where φ stands for "conceivability is the key to justifying our modal beliefs", α_c stands for David Chalmers' arguments for φ. α_1 stands for Phi_1 showing the David Chalmers' arguments for φ. Philosopher 1 comes to accept φ after reading David Chalmers' arguments for φ. The first formula means: "after reading David Chalmers' argument, Phi_1 has been persuaded to accept φ", and the second formula means: "after Phi_1 showing the David Chalmers' argument to Phi_2, Phi_2 has been persuaded to accept φ".

4 Future Work

In the above section, we give a logic for persuasion to characterize the an agent being persuaded by reasoning. We showed the soundness of this logic, the completeness of this logic will be our next work. This logic has also some connections with argumentation theory and justification logic. Comparing these logics is also an interesting work for the future. Since our framework is quite rough (but general), in order to deal with some real arguments happened in our daily life, we should make the frame more fine. For example, if the audience undergoes certain information update, that is, from the state of not accepting φ to the state of accepting φ, the agent's intention is satisfied and the reasoning (the speech act) results in information update. However, sometimes persuasion is a matter of degree, for the achievement may come in degree. To explain this further, let's consider cycling. Many people are able to ride a bike, but it does not follow that each can demonstrate this very ability to the same degree. For example, an 20-miles cycle ride may be easy for some, but difficult for others. Similarly, after doing reasoning, the audience may raise the degree of credence to certain belief. Therefore, a fine-grained representation of belief-revision is called for, e.g. the degree of achieving the goal (persuasion).

References

1. Austin, J.: How to Do Things with Words. Oxford University Press, Oxford (1962)
2. Finlay, S.: Confusion of Tongues. Oxford University Press, Oxford (2014)
3. Grice, P.: Aspects of Reason. Oxford University Press, Oxford (2001)
4. Harel, D., Kozen, D., Tiuryn, J.: Dynamic Logic. MIT Press, Cambridge (2000)
5. Herzig, A., Longin, D.: A logic of intention with cooperation principles and with assertive speech acts as communication primitives. In: Proceedings of AAMAS, pp. 920–927 (2002)

Dynamics of Fuzzy Argumentation Frameworks

Zongshun Wang and Jiachao Wu$^{(\boxtimes)}$

School of Mathematics and Statistics, Shandong Normal University, Jinan 250300,
Shandong, China
wangzongshun1996@163.com, wujiachao1981@163.com

Abstract. Dung's theory of abstract argumentation plays an incremental role in artificial intelligence. The research about the dynamics theory of argumentation efficiently identifies the justified arguments when arguments or attacks change. However, the dynamics theory is absent in fuzzy argumentation framework (FAF). We want to calculate the semantics of the updated FAF by partially reusing the semantics of the previous FAF. In this paper, we explore the dynamics theory in FAFs. First, we introduce all the changes of FAF, including not only the changes of arguments and attacks but also the increases or decreases of their fuzzy degrees. Thus, the changes in FAFs are more complicated than standard AF. Then by extending Liao's division-based approach, we provide an efficient algorithm for computing some basic semantics. This algorithm conserves part of the semantics in the previous FAF. Thus, we can efficiently compute the belief degree to which arguments are justified.

Keywords: Dynamics of argumentation · Division-based approach · Fuzzy argumentation frameworks · Argumentation semantics

1 Introduction

Dung's theory [7] of argumentation frameworks (AFs) plays an increasingly important role in artificial intelligence and nonmonotonic reasoning. A Dung's AF is essentially a directed graph. The nodes represent the arguments and the arrows represent the attack relation between the arguments. Dung's theory is to seek reasonable subsets of the arguments under some criterions.

In order to handle the uncertain, incompleteness, and inconsistency of information, standard AFs are extended by quantifying arguments or attacks. More specifically, in these quantitative AFs, numerical values are combined with arguments/attacks, such as probabilistic AFs [9,12], fuzzy AFs (FAFs) [5,10,15], weighted AFs [8] and so on. FAFs characterize AFs by fuzzy arguments or fuzzy attack relation. In [10,15], the main task of FAFs is to find the subsets over

This work is supported by the National Natural Science Foundation of China (11601288), the Natural Science Foundation of Shandong (ZR2016AQ21) and the Excellent Young Scholars Research Fund of Shandong Normal University.

M. Dastani et al. (Eds.): CLAR 2020, LNAI 12061, pp. 287–307, 2020.
https://doi.org/10.1007/978-3-030-44638-3_18

justified fuzzy arguments. The extension semantics to FAFs have been proposed in [10,15]. Changes in arguments and attack relationships are intrinsic to various argumentation systems [2,4,11]. According to some research, arguments and their attack relation develop with the changes in basic knowledge or information or observations [3,6,14]. In [4], Cayrol et al. address the problem of the change of adding an argument in Dung's AF. They focus on the *change* of the argumentation systems and its extension. In [13], Liao et al. proposed a *division-based approach* for dynamics of AFs. The division-based approach provides an efficient algorithm for the dynamics of argumentation systems.

In quantitative AFs, the arguments and attack relation are also changed with the changes of basic knowledge, information, and observations. However, the research about the dynamics of quantitative AFs is absent. In this paper, we take the Gödel FAFs (GFAFs) as an example to explore the dynamics of quantitative AFs. However, the changes in the dynamics of FAFs are more complicated than standard AF. This is because FAF is changed not only by adding (or removing) arguments or attack relation but also by increasing (or decreasing) the belief degree of arguments or attack relation.

The main task of this paper is to provide an efficient algorithm for basic semantics in the updated FAF. We first establish the directionality principle in FAFs. Then we extend the division-based approach, each updated FAF is divided into three parts: unaffected FAF, affected FAF, conditioned FAF. We then compute the extension semantics of the updated FAF by computing the semantics of unaffected FAF and affected FAF under the conditioned FAF. In this way, we can calculate the complete, preferred and grounded semantics which partially reuses the extensions computed in the previous FAF.

This paper is structured as follows: In Sect. 2, we specify the motivation of the dynamics of FAF. In Sect. 3, we review some basic definitions of FAF and fuzzy set theory. In Sect. 4, we explore the various changes in the dynamics of FAFs. In Sect. 5, we extend the division-based method into the dynamics of FAFs. The paper ends with conclusions and remarks about future work.

2   Motivation

As we showed in the Introduction, changes in arguments and attack relationships are intrinsic to various argumentation systems. And compared with standard AFs, the dynamics of FAFs are more complicated. We first specify the intuition of the dynamics of FAFs. To understand the dynamics of FAFs, we consider the following example:

A patient goes to the hospital because of chest tightness. If we only make an empirical judgment about the patient, there are two diseases that may cause chest tightness: coronary heart disease and bronchitis. So we obtain two arguments:

A: The patient's chest tightness is caused by coronary heart disease;
B: The patient's chest tightness is caused by bronchitis.

Assuming that the patient's chest tightness is not caused by these two diseases at the same time. Thus these two arguments are contradictory. We can establish an FAF and the initial belief degree of that the patient's chest tightness is caused by coronary heart disease is 0.4 and the initial belief degree of that the patient's chest tightness is caused by bronchitis is 0.6. If we do a preliminary examination of the patient, the result of the examination shows that the patient has bronchitis and has no history of coronary heart disease. Consequently, the degree of A may naturally decrease and the degree of B may naturally increase, one may change the system by decreasing the degree of A into 0.1 and increasing the degree of B into 0.9. Therefore, in FAF, the change of initial degree of arguments or attack relation also changes the system. In addition, if we take a further examination of this patient, we have that patient suffers from cardiac failure. We then change the systems by adding the fuzzy argument 'the patient's chest tightness may be caused by cardiac failure'.

The dynamics of FAFs in this paper are shown as following:

1. adding arguments that interact with the previous FAF.
2. deleting arguments from the previous FAF.
3. adding attack relation which does not appear in the previous FAF.
4. deleting attack relation from the previous FAF.
5. increasing the initial belief degree of arguments.
6. decreasing the initial belief degree of arguments.
7. increasing the initial belief degree of attack relation.
8. decreasing the initial belief degree of attack relation.

Next, when a fuzzy argumentation system is changed by these above cases, we obtain an updated FAFs. Then, the main task is to find the belief degree to which arguments are justified. Thus, to cope with the semantics of updated FAFs, we extend Liao's division-based approach. By extending Liao's theory, we can compute the complete, preferred and grounded semantics which partially reuses the extensions computed in the previous FAF.

3   Preliminaries

Our work is based on Gödel fuzzy argumentation frameworks [15]. Let's first review the notions of fuzzy set and GFAFs.

3.1   Fuzzy Set Theory

We only show some notions of fuzzy set theory [16] that appear in this paper.

Let X be a nonempty set. A fuzzy set (X, S) is determined by its membership function $S\colon X \to [0,1]$, such that for each $x \in X$ the value $S(x)$ is interpreted as the grade of membership of x within X. Given some constant set X, we may denote a fuzzy set (X, S) as S for convenience. A crisp set S' is a classical set, namely for any $x \in X$, $S'(x) = 0$ or $S'(x) = 1$.

A fuzzy set S is contained in another fuzzy set S', if $\forall x \in X$, $S(x) \leq S'(x)$, which is denoted by $S \subseteq S'$.

A fuzzy set S is called a fuzzy point if its support is a single point $x \in X$, and is denoted by $(x, S(x))$. We denote all the support of S as $Supp(S)$, where $Supp(S) = \{x \mid S(x) \neq 0\}$.

A fuzzy point $(x, S(x))$ is contained in a fuzzy set S if it is a subset of S.

The t-norm is a binary operator on $[0, 1]$. In this paper, we focus on Gödel t-norm. Gödel t-norm $T : [0, 1] \times [0, 1] \to [0, 1]$ such that $\forall x, y \in [0, 1]$, $T(x, y) = min\{x, y\}$. For simplify, in this paper, we denote $*$ as Gödel t-norm, namely for any $x, y \in [0, 1]$, $x * y = T(x, y) = min\{x, y\}$.

3.2   Gödel Fuzzy Argumentation Frameworks

In this paper, an FAF consists of fuzzy arguments and fuzzy attack relation between the arguments, and Gödel FAF specializes it using Gödel t-norm.

Definition 1. *A fuzzy argumentation framework is a tuple $\langle \mathcal{A}, \rho \rangle$ where $\mathcal{A}$: $Args \to (0, 1]$ and $\rho : Args \times Args \to (0, 1]$ are total functions. We refer to $\mathcal{A}$ as a fuzzy set of arguments, and ρ as a fuzzy set of attacks, while Args is a crisp set of arguments.*

From [15], we call the elements in $\mathcal{A}$ as fuzzy arguments and the elements in ρ as fuzzy attack. We refer to an FAF using the Gödel t-norm as a GFAF. It is notable that Gödel t-norm is just a composition operator to combine fuzzy arguments and fuzzy attack relation. The FAFs explored in this paper all are GFAFs, and for simplify, we briefly denote GFAF as FAF.

An important distinction between the FAFs and AFs is that the attack relation may have no influence on the choice of acceptable arguments in FAF. We borrow the notions of sufficient attack and tolerable attack from [15].

Definition 2. *Given two arguments (A, a) and (B, b) as well as a fuzzy attack relation $((A, B), \rho_{AB})$, if $a * \rho_{AB} + b \leq 1$, then the attack is tolerable, otherwise it is sufficient.*

A sufficient attack *weakens* the attacked argument. If (A, a) sufficiently attacks (B, b), then (B, b) is weakened to (B, b') by (A, a), where $b' = 1 - a * \rho_{AB}$. We provide the definition of *weakening defend*.

Definition 3. *Given an $FAF = \langle \mathcal{A}, \rho \rangle$, a fuzzy set $S \subseteq \mathcal{A}$ weakening defends a fuzzy argument (C, c) in $\mathcal{A}$ if for any $(B, b) \in \mathcal{A}$ there is some $(A, a) \in S$ such that (A, a) weakens (B, b) to (B, b') and (B, b') tolerably attacks (C, c).*

We provide an alternate definition of *weakening defend*.

Definition 4. *Given an $FAF = (\mathcal{A}, \rho)$, a fuzzy set $S \in \mathcal{A}$ weakening defends a fuzzy argument $(A, a) \in \mathcal{A}$ if for any (B, b) sufficiently attacks (A, a) there exists $(C, c) \in S$ such that $c * \rho_{CB} = a$. Namely there exists (C, c) weakens (B, b) to $(B, 1 - a)$ and the attack relation from $(B, 1 - a)$ to (A, a) is clearly tolerable.*

It is notable that if the attack relation from A to B is always tolerable, namely $\mathcal{A}(A) * \rho_{AB} + \mathcal{A}(B) \leq 1$, then the attack relation has no influence in this system. Thus, for simplify, *we don't show this attack relation in this paper.*

We list the extensions semantics in GFAFs as follows.

Definition 5. *Given a GFAF* $= \langle \mathcal{A}, \rho \rangle$ *and* $S \subseteq \mathcal{A}$.
S is a conflict-free set if all attacks between the arguments in S are tolerable.
A conflict-free set S is an admissible extension if S weakening defends each element in S.
A conflict-free set S is a complete extension if it contains all the fuzzy arguments in $\mathcal{A}$ that S weakening defends.
An admissible extension is a preferred extension if it is maximal.
A complete extension is a grounded extension if it is minimal.
A conflict-free set is stable if it sufficiently attacks every element in $\mathcal{A}$ not in E.

In GFAFs, the grounded extension is unique and it is the least complete extension. The stable extensions coincide with the preferred extensions.

4   Dynamics of Fuzzy Argumentation Frameworks

In this section, we give the definition of *change* in FAFs. The notion of *change* is cited from [4], we introduce all the changes in FAFs. In [4,13], $\mathcal{I}$ denoted the *interactions* between arguments under the context of change. $\mathcal{I}$ represents the changed attack relation. For simplicity, we provide the notion of $\mathcal{I}$ in FAFs.

- $\mathcal{I}_{Ar_1:Ar_2}$ is the set of interactions related to Ar_2 and of the form $((A, B), \rho_{AB})$, $((B, A), \rho_{BA})$, or $((B, B'), \rho_{BB'})$, in which $A \in Ar_1$ and $B, B' \in Ar_2$.
- $\mathcal{I}_{Ar}$ is a set of interactions between the arguments in Ar, and of the form $((A, A'), \rho_{AA'})$, in which $A, A' \in Ar$.
- $\mathcal{I}_{(Ar_1, Ar_2)}$ is the set of interactions from the arguments in Ar_1 to the arguments in Ar_2, and of the form $((A, B), \rho_{AB})$, in which $A \in Ar_1$ and $B \in Ar_2$.

Analogously, we define a form of a set of fuzzy attack relation within FAF:

- ρ_{Ar} is a set of attack relation between the arguments in Ar, and of the form $((A, A'), \rho_{AA'})$, in which $A, A' \in Ar$.
- $\rho_{(Ar_1, Ar_2)}$ is the set of attack relation from the arguments in Ar_1 to the arguments in Ar_2, and of the form $((A, B), \rho_{AB})$, in which $A \in Ar_1$ and $B \in Ar_2$.

Definition 6. *Given an FAF* $= \langle \mathcal{A}, \rho \rangle$ *and* $Supp(\mathcal{A}) = Ar_1$.

1. *adding a set of fuzzy attack relation* $\mathcal{I}_{Ar_1}$ *(for any* $(A, B) \in Supp(\mathcal{I}_{Ar_1})$, $\mathcal{I}_{Ar_1}(A, B) > \rho(A, B) = 0)$ *is a change which is defined by:*

$$\langle \mathcal{A}, \rho \rangle \oplus \mathcal{I}_{Ar_1} = \langle \mathcal{A}, \rho \cup \mathcal{I}_{Ar_1} \rangle.$$

2. *removing a set of fuzzy attack relation $\mathcal{I}_{Ar_1} \subseteq \rho$ (for any $(A, B) \in Supp(\mathcal{I}_{Ar_1})$, $\mathcal{I}_{Ar_1}(A, B) = \rho(A, B)$) from FAF is a change which is defined by:*

$$\langle \mathcal{A}, \rho \rangle \ominus \mathcal{I}_{Ar_1} = \langle \mathcal{A}, \rho - \mathcal{I}_{Ar_1} \rangle.$$

3. *adding a set of fuzzy arguments $\mathcal{B}$ ($Supp(\mathcal{B}) = Ar_2$ and $Ar_1 \cap Ar_2 = \emptyset$) which interacts with FAF is a change which is defined by:*

$$\langle \mathcal{A}, \rho \rangle \oplus \langle \mathcal{B}, \mathcal{I}_{Ar_1:Ar_2} \rangle = \langle \mathcal{A} \cup \mathcal{B}, \rho \cup \mathcal{I}_{Ar_1:Ar_2} \rangle.$$

4. *removing arguments $\mathcal{B} \subseteq \mathcal{A}$ ($Supp(\mathcal{B}) = Ar_2$ and $\forall A \in Ar_2$, $\mathcal{B}(A) = \mathcal{A}(A)$) from FAF is a change which is defined by:*

$$\langle \mathcal{A}, \rho \rangle \ominus \langle \mathcal{B}, \mathcal{I}_{Ar_1:Ar_2} \rangle = \langle \mathcal{A} - \mathcal{B}, \rho - \mathcal{I}_{Ar_1:Ar_2} \rangle.$$

5. *increasing the initial belief degree of arguments, for simplify, we only increase the initial degree of an argument. We increase the initial degree of A into a, namely we use (A, a) replaces $(A, \mathcal{A}(A))$ and $a > \mathcal{A}(A)$, it is a change which is defined by:*

$$\langle \mathcal{A}, \rho \rangle \oplus (A, a) = \langle \mathcal{A} \cup (A, a), \rho \rangle.$$

6. *decreasing the initial belief degree of arguments, for simplify, we only decrease the initial degree of an argument, we first decrease the initial degree of A into 0, and the we increase the degree of A into a, namely, we use (A, a) replaces $(A, \mathcal{A}(A))$ and $a < \mathcal{A}(A)$, it is a change which is defined by:*

$$\langle \mathcal{A}, \rho \rangle \ominus (A, a) = \langle (\mathcal{A} - (A, \mathcal{A}(A))) \cup (A, a), \rho \rangle.$$

7. *increasing the initial belief degree of attack relation, for simplify, we increase the initial degree of an attack relation. We increase the initial degree of (A, B) into $\rho'(A, B)$, namely we use $((A, B), \rho'(A, B))$ replaces $((A, B), \rho(A, B))$ and $\rho'(A, B) > \rho(A, B)$, it is a change which is defined by:*

$$\langle \mathcal{A}, \rho \rangle \oplus ((A, B), \rho'(A, B)) = \langle \mathcal{A}, \rho \cup ((A, B), \rho'(A, B)) \rangle.$$

8. *decreasing the initial belief degree of attack relation, for simplify, we only decrease the initial degree of an argument, we first decrease the initial degree of (A, B) into 0, and then we increase the degree of (A, B) into $\rho'(A, B)$, namely, we use $((A, B), \rho'(A, B))$ replaces $((A, B), \rho(A, B))$ and $\rho'(A, B) < \rho(A, B)$, it is a change which is defined by:*

$$\langle \mathcal{A}, \rho \rangle \ominus ((A, B), \rho'(A, B)) = \langle \mathcal{A}, (\rho - ((A, B), \rho(A, B))) \cup ((A, B), \rho'(A, B)) \rangle.$$

Although we only increase the initial degree of an argument in (5)–(8), the case of multiple arguments can be done by iteratively applying the formalism of (5)–(8).

Next, we will define the dynamics of FAFs. Obviously, all the *changes* in Definition 6 are dynamics of FAFs. Additionally, the arbitrary combinations of 1–8 are also the dynamics of FAF. We introduce the dynamics of FAF when combined with an addition of FAF.

Definition 7. *Let* $FAF = \langle \mathcal{A}, \rho \rangle$, *where* $\mathcal{A} : Ar_1 \rightarrow (0, 1]$ *and* $\rho : Ar_1 \times Ar_1 \rightarrow (0, 1]$ *are total functions. An addition of FAF is represented as a tuple* $(\mathcal{B}, \mathcal{I}_{Ar_1} \cup \mathcal{I}_{Ar_1 : Ar_2})$, *in which* $\mathcal{B}$ *is a set of fuzzy arguments to be added and* $Ar_2 = Supp(\mathcal{B})$, $\mathcal{I}_{Ar_1} \cup \mathcal{I}_{Ar_1 : Ar_2}$ *is a set of fuzzy attacks to be added.*

In the above definition, we have some explanations about the addition of FAF. As far as the addition of fuzzy arguments $\mathcal{B}$ is considered, for each fuzzy argument $(A, a) \in \mathcal{B}$, there are two cases:

- $A \notin Ar_1$, then it coincides with the case 3 in Definition 6;
- $A \in Ar_1$, but $\mathcal{B}(A) > \mathcal{A}(A)$, then it coincides with the case 5 in Definition 6.

For each attack relation $(A, B) \in Supp(\mathcal{I}_{Ar_1}) \cup Supp(\mathcal{I}_{Ar_1 : Ar_2})$, there are also two cases:

- $(A, B) \in Supp(\mathcal{I}_{Ar_1 : Ar_2}) \backslash Supp(\mathcal{I}_{Ar_1})$, then it coincides with the case 1 in Definition 6;
- $(A, B) \in Supp(\mathcal{I}_{Ar_1})$, but $\rho(A, B) < \mathcal{I}_{Ar_1}(A, B)$, then it coincides with the case 7 in Definition 6.

From the above definition, an updated FAF with respect to an addition FAF is defined as follows:

Definition 8. *Let* $FAF = \langle \mathcal{A}, \rho \rangle$, *where* $\mathcal{A} : Ar_1 \rightarrow (0, 1]$ *and* $\rho : Ar_1 \times Ar_1 \rightarrow (0, 1]$ *are total functions. Let* $(\mathcal{B}, \mathcal{I}_{Ar_1} \cup \mathcal{I}_{Ar_1 : Ar_2})$ *be an addition. The updated FAF w.r.t.* $(\mathcal{B}, \mathcal{I}_{Ar_1} \cup \mathcal{I}_{Ar_1 : Ar_2})$ *is represented as follows:*

$$\langle \mathcal{A}^{\oplus}, \rho^{\oplus} \rangle = \langle \mathcal{A}, \rho \rangle \oplus (\mathcal{B}, \mathcal{I}_{Ar_1} \cup \mathcal{I}_{Ar_1 : Ar_2}) =_{def} \langle \mathcal{A} \cup \mathcal{B}, \rho \cup \mathcal{I}_{Ar_1} \cup \mathcal{I}_{Ar_1 : Ar_2} \rangle$$

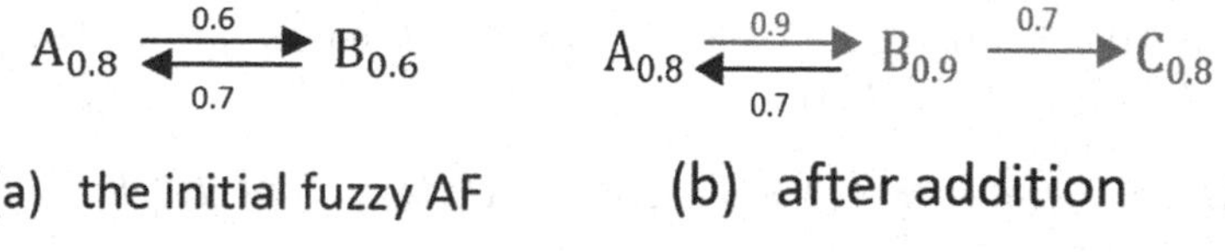

(a) the initial fuzzy AF   (b) after addition

Fig. 1. An example of updated FAF w.r.t. an addition of FAF (Example 1)

We provide an example to illustrate the above definition.

Example 1. *Let* $FAF = \langle \{(A, 0.8), (B, 0.6)\}, \{((A, B), 0.6), ((B, A), 0.7)\} \rangle$. *Suppose* $(\mathcal{B}, \mathcal{I}_{Ar_1} \cup \mathcal{I}_{Ar_1 : Ar_2})$ *be an addition, in which* $\mathcal{B} = \{(B, 0.9), (C, 0.8)\}$ *and* $\mathcal{I}_{Ar_1} \cup \mathcal{I}_{Ar_1 : Ar_2} = \{(A, B), 0.9), ((B, C), 0.7)\}$. *In Fig. 1, the arrows and nodes in red represent changed arguments and attack relation. Then we obtain an updated FAF* $\langle \mathcal{A} \cup \mathcal{B}, \rho \cup \mathcal{I}_{Ar_1} \cup \mathcal{I}_{Ar_1 : Ar_2} \rangle = \langle \{(A, 0.8), (B, 0.9), (C, 0.8)\}, \{((A, B), 0.9),$ $((B, A), 0.7), ((B, C), 0.7)\} \rangle$.

5 The Argumentation Semantics of Dynamic Fuzzy Argumentation Frameworks

In this section, we will extend the division-based approach in [13] to the dynamics of FAFs. In this paper, we only consider the efficient algorithms for calculating the complete, grounded and preferred semantics.

5.1 The Directionality Principle in FAFs

The division-based approach in [13] is based on the directionality principle, and thus we first extend the directionality principle into FAFs.

The notion of directionality principle is first provided in [1]. Intuitively, under Dung's AF, the justification status of an argument A is only depended on the status of the defeaters of the argument A (which in turn are affected by their defeaters and so on), while the arguments which only receive an attack from A (and in turn those which are attacked by them and so on) should not have any effect on the status of A. Then Baroni et al. extended the directionality principle by considering the unattacked set which doesn't receive attacks from outside. Here, we extend the directionality principle to FAFs. In FAFs, the belief degree of each argument is only depended on the belief degrees of attackers (which in turn are affected by their defeaters and so on).

Definition 9. *Given an $FAF = (\mathcal{A}, \rho)$, a fuzzy set $\mathcal{U} \in \mathcal{A}$ is unattacked if and only if there exists no $A \notin Supp(\mathcal{U})$, $B \in Supp(\mathcal{U})$ such that $(A, B) \in Supp(\rho)$. The set of unattacked sets of FAF is denoted as $US(FAF)$.*

We also provide the notion of restricted FAF. Let $FAF = \langle \mathcal{A}, \rho \rangle$. The restriction of FAF to $S \subseteq \mathcal{A}$ is $FAF \downarrow_S = \langle S, \rho_s \rangle$. The directionality criterion can then be defined, the semantics extensions of an unattacked set are not affected by the remaining parts of the FAF.

Definition 10. *A semantics S satisfies the directionality principle if and only if for any FAF, $\forall \mathcal{U} \in US(FAF)$:*

$$\mathcal{AE}_S(FAF, \mathcal{U}) = \mathcal{E}_S(FAF \downarrow_{\mathcal{U}}) \text{ where } \mathcal{AE}_S(FAF, \mathcal{U}) = \{E \cap \mathcal{U} \mid E \in \mathcal{E}_S(FAF)\}$$

Similar to Dung's AF, the complete, grounded and preferred semantics satisfy the directionality principle in FAF. This is because $\forall E \in \mathcal{AE}_{\mathcal{CO}}(FAF, U)$, there exists no fuzzy argument in E is sufficiently attacked by the fuzzy argument outside the unattacked set.

5.2 The Basic Theory of the Division-Based Approach in FAF

According to the definition of directionality principle, under a certain argumentation semantics $\mathcal{S} \in \{\mathcal{CO}, \mathcal{PR}, \mathcal{GR}\}$, the justified belief degree of argument is only affected by its attacker. Thus, as for a certain semantics that is based on the directionality principle, if an argument is not affected by the newly added argument and attack relation, then its justified degree will not change. Therefore, analogous to Liao's division-based theory in standard AF, in the updated FAF, we should identify the unaffected part and the affected part w.r.t. the changed arguments and attack relation. As far as the unaffected part of the updated FAF is concerned, its semantics can be conserved to calculate the semantics of the updated FAF. Thus, the complexity of computing the semantics of the dynamics of FAF might be decreased. Next, we should consider how to calculate the semantics of the affected part. We will Liao's approach by extending the notion of the conditioned part of the updated FAF to handle the problem. Finally, we combined these two parts of semantics and prove the soundness and completeness of the combined semantics. To cope with these problems, we extend the Liao's theory to FAF in the following section.

5.3   Conditioned Fuzzy Argumentation Frameworks

In order to handle the semantics of the updated FAFs, we extend the division-based approach to FAFs. Firstly, we restate the definition of conditioned FAF.

Definition 11. *Given a fuzzy argumentation framework* $FAF_1 = \langle \mathcal{A}_1, \rho_1 \rangle$, *a conditioned fuzzy argumentation framework w.r.t.* FAF_1 *is a tuple*

$$\mathrm{CFAF} = (\langle \mathcal{A}_2, \rho_2 \rangle, (C(\mathcal{A}_1), \rho_{(C(Ar_1), Ar_2)}))$$

in which

- $Ar_1 = Supp(\mathcal{A}_1)$, $Ar_2 = Supp(\mathcal{A}_2)$ *and* $C(Ar_1) = Supp(C(\mathcal{A}_1))$;
- $\langle \mathcal{A}_2, \rho_2 \rangle$ *is an FAF that is conditioned by* $C(\mathcal{A}_1)$, *in which* $\mathcal{A}_1 \cap \mathcal{A}_2 = \emptyset$;
- $C(\mathcal{A}_1) \subseteq \mathcal{A}_1$ *is a nonempty set of fuzzy arguments (called conditioning arguments) that attacks the fuzzy arguments in* $\mathcal{A}_2$, *i.e.,* $\forall A \in C(Ar_1)$, $\exists B \in Ar_2$, *s.t.* $(A, B) \in Supp(\rho_{(C(Ar_1), Ar_2)})$.

Since $\langle \mathcal{A}_1, \rho_1 \rangle$ is an FAF that independent of $\langle \mathcal{A}_2, \rho_2 \rangle$, we can obtain the reasonable set of FAF_1, i.e., the semantics extensions of FAF_1 is directly obtained by the corresponding criterion. Given a specific extension $E \in \mathcal{E}_\mathcal{S}(FAF_1)$, $C(\mathcal{A}_1)[E]$ is also called a condition of $\langle \mathcal{A}_2, \rho_2 \rangle$ under the reasonable extension E of FAF_1. $CFAF[E] = (\langle \mathcal{A}_2, \rho_2 \rangle, (C(\mathcal{A}_1)[E], \rho_{(C(Ar_1), Ar_2)}))$ is called an assigned CFAF. The semantics of an assigned $CFAF$ are related to the semantics of conditioning arguments, which are defined as follows:

Definition 12. *Let* $CFAF[E_1] = (\langle \mathcal{A}_2, \rho_2 \rangle, (C(\mathcal{A}_1)[E_1], \rho_{(C(Ar_1), Ar_2)}))$ *be an assigned CFAF w.r.t.* $FAF_1 = \langle \mathcal{A}_1, \rho_1 \rangle$, *in which* $E_1 \in \mathcal{E}_\mathcal{S}(FAF_1)$, $\mathcal{S} \in \{\mathcal{CO}, \mathcal{PR}, \mathcal{GR}\}$.

- *A set* $E \in \mathcal{A}_2$ *of fuzzy arguments is conflict-free if and only if there exists no* (A, a), $(B, b) \in E$ *s.t.* (A, a) *sufficiently attacks* (B, b) *w.r.t.* ρ_2.

- A fuzzy argument $(A, a) \in \mathcal{A}_2$ is weakening defended by a set $E \in \mathcal{A}_2$ of fuzzy arguments under the condition $C(\mathcal{A}_1)[E_1]$ if and only if the following two conditions hold:
  - $\forall (B, b) \in \mathcal{A}_2$, if (B, b) sufficiently attacks (A, a), then $\exists (C, c) \in E$ s.t. $c * \rho_{CB} = a$, or $\exists (D, d) \in C(\mathcal{A}_1)$, s.t. (D, d) is weakening defended by E_1 and $d * \rho_{DB} = a$;
  - $\forall (B, b) \in C(\mathcal{A}_1)$, if (B, b) sufficiently attacks (A, a), then $\exists (C, c) \in E_1$ s.t. $c * \rho_{CB} = a$.
- A conflict-free set E is admissible if and only if each argument in E is weakening defended by E under the condition $C(\mathcal{A}_1)[E_1]$.

Definition 13. Let $\mathrm{CFAF}[E_1] = (\langle \mathcal{A}_2, \rho_2 \rangle, (C(\mathcal{A}_1)[E_1], \rho_{(C(Ar_1), Ar_2)}))$ be an assigned CFAF w.r.t. $FAF_1 = \langle \mathcal{A}_1, \rho_1 \rangle$, in which $E_1 \in \mathcal{E}_S(FAF_1)$, $S \in \{CO, PR, GR\}$. Let $E \subseteq \mathcal{A}_2$ be an admissible set of fuzzy arguments.

- E is a preferred extension if and only if E is a maximal (w.r.t. set-inclusion) admissible set of fuzzy arguments.
- E is a complete extension if and only if each argument that is weakening defended by E under the condition $C(\mathcal{A}_1)[E_1]$ is in E.
- E is a grounded extension if and only if E is the minimal (w.r.t. set-inclusion) complete extension.
- E is ideal if and only if E is admissible and it is contained in every preferred set of fuzzy arguments. The ideal extension is the maximal (w.r.t. set-inclusion) ideal set.

5.4   The Division of Updated Fuzzy Argumentation Framework

The division of an FAF is based on the directionality principle of argumentation semantics. Notably, in this paper, if the attack relation has no influence in the FAF, i.e., the attack relation is always tolerable, then *we will not show this attack relation*. This can help us simplify the FAF. Given an $FAF = \langle \mathcal{A}, \rho \rangle$, for each pair arguments $A, B \in Ar$, if the attack relation from A to B is valid, i.e., A has influence on B, then we denote B is affected by A. Otherwise, B is independent of A. Based on this idea, the notion of reachability, as well as the notions of affected and unaffected between two arguments can be defined as follows:

Definition 14. Let $FAF = \langle \mathcal{A}, \rho \rangle$, where $Supp(\mathcal{A}) = Ar$. The reachability of two arguments $A, B \in Ar$ w.r.t ρ is recursively defined as follows:

- If there exists $(A, B) \in Supp(\rho)$, then B is reachable from A;
- If C is reachable from A, and B is reachable from C, then B is reachable from A.

Definition 15. Let $A, B \in Ar$, and ρ_{Ar} be a set of fuzzy attacks within Ar. We say that under the semantics that satisfies the directionality principle, B is affected by A, iff B is reachable from A w.r.t. ρ_{Ar}. Otherwise, B is unaffected by A w.r.t ρ_{Ar}. In addition, B is affected by $\mathcal{I}$, iff B is reachable from an argument w.r.t. $\mathcal{I}$.

Example 2. *Given an FAF with arguments A, B and C:*
$FAF = (\{(A, 0.6), (B, 0.7), (C, 0.8)\}, \{((A, B), 0.8), ((B, C), 0.6)\})$.
Here, from that $(A, 0.6)$ sufficiently attacks $(B, 0.7)$ and $(B, 0.7)$ sufficiently attacks $(C, 0.8)$, we have that B is reachable from A and C is reachable from B. Hence, C is reachable from A. From Definition 15, C is affected by A and B.

From the above definition, when an addition of FAF $\langle \mathcal{B}, \mathcal{I}_{Ar_1} \cup \mathcal{I}_{Ar_1:Ar_2} \rangle$ is added to an FAF $\langle \mathcal{A}, \rho \rangle$, we can identify the subset of $\mathcal{A}$ which is affected by $\mathcal{B}$ or $\mathcal{I}_{Ar_1} \cup \mathcal{I}_{Ar_1:Ar_2}$. The initial FAF will be divided into three parts:

- a component of $\mathcal{A}$ that is affected by $(\mathcal{B}, \mathcal{I}_{Ar_1} \cup \mathcal{I}_{Ar_1:Ar_2})$;
- a component of $\mathcal{A}$ that is unaffected by $(\mathcal{B}, \mathcal{I}_{Ar_1} \cup \mathcal{I}_{Ar_1:Ar_2})$;
- a subset of the unaffected component that conditions the affected components.

Therefore, we are ready to define the notion of the division of an updated FAF. Formally, we can provide the division of an updated FAF w.r.t. an addition $(\mathcal{B}, \mathcal{I}_{Ar_1} \cup \mathcal{I}_{Ar_1:Ar_2})$.

Definition 16. *Let $FAF = \langle \mathcal{A}, \rho \rangle$, and $Supp(\mathcal{A}) = Ar_1$. Suppose $(\mathcal{B}, \mathcal{I}_{Ar_1:Ar_2} \cup \mathcal{I}_{Ar_1})$ be an addition to the FAF. The updated FAF $\langle \mathcal{A}^\oplus, \rho^\oplus \rangle$ is divided into three parts: $\langle \mathcal{A}_a^\oplus, \rho_a^\oplus \rangle$, $\langle \mathcal{A}_u^\oplus, \rho_u^\oplus \rangle$, $(\mathcal{A}_c^\oplus, \rho_c^\oplus)$ where a, u and c stand for, respectively, affected, unaffected and conditioning.*
$\mathcal{A}_a^\oplus = \{(A, \mathcal{A}^\oplus(A)) \mid A \in Supp(\mathcal{B})$ *or A is affected by* $\mathcal{I}_{Ar_1} \cup \mathcal{I}_{Ar_1:Ar_2}$ *or A is affected by an argument* $C \in Supp(\mathcal{A}_a^\oplus)$ *w.r.t.* $\rho^\oplus\}$
$\mathcal{A}_u^\oplus = \mathcal{A}^\oplus - \mathcal{A}_a^\oplus$
$\mathcal{A}_c^\oplus = \{(A, \mathcal{A}^\oplus(A)) \in \mathcal{A}_u^\oplus \mid \exists B \in Supp(\mathcal{A}_a) \ s.t. \ (A, B) \in Supp(\rho^\oplus) \ w.r.t. \ \rho^\oplus\}$
$\rho_a^\oplus = \rho^\oplus \cap \rho_{Supp(\mathcal{A}_a^\oplus)}$
$\rho_u^\oplus = \rho^\oplus \cap \rho_{Supp(\mathcal{A}_u^\oplus)}$
$\rho_c^\oplus = \rho^\oplus \cap \rho_{(Supp(\mathcal{A}_c^\oplus), Supp(\mathcal{A}_a^\oplus))}$

From this definition, for a given updated FAF $\langle \mathcal{A}^\oplus, \rho^\oplus \rangle$, $\mathcal{A}_u^\oplus$ coincides with the arguments that are unaffected by $(\mathcal{B}, \mathcal{I}_{Ar_1} \cup \mathcal{I}_{Ar_1:Ar_2})$, $\mathcal{A}_a^\oplus$ coincides with the arguments that are affected by $(\mathcal{B}, \mathcal{I}_{Ar_1} \cup \mathcal{I}_{Ar_1:Ar_2})$ as well as the fuzzy arguments in $\mathcal{B}$, $\mathcal{A}_c^\oplus$ coincides with the fuzzy arguments in $\mathcal{A}_u^\oplus$ that condition $\mathcal{A}_a^\oplus$.

After we have the division of the updated FAF, the next step is to construct two sub-frameworks of the updated FAF $\langle \mathcal{A}^\oplus, \rho^\oplus \rangle$: the unaffected FAF and the affected FAF under the condition. The unaffected FAF is $\langle \mathcal{A}_u^\oplus, \rho_u^\oplus \rangle$. And the conditioned FAF w.r.t. $\langle \mathcal{A}_u^\oplus, \rho_u^\oplus \rangle$ is constructed according to $\langle \mathcal{A}_a^\oplus, \rho_a^\oplus \rangle$ and $(\mathcal{A}_c^\oplus, \rho_c^\oplus)$ as follows:
$$CFAF = (\langle \mathcal{A}_a^\oplus, \rho_a^\oplus \rangle, (\mathcal{A}_c^\oplus, \rho_c^\oplus))$$

From the Definition 16, we have $\mathcal{A}_c^\oplus \cap \mathcal{A}_a^\oplus = \emptyset$, $\mathcal{A}_c^\oplus \subseteq \mathcal{A}_u^\oplus$ and $\rho_c^\oplus \subseteq \rho_{(\mathcal{A}_c^\oplus, \mathcal{A}_a^\oplus)}$. Namely, it satisfies the definition of condition.

Example 3. *Let $FAF = \langle \mathcal{A}, \rho \rangle$, in which $\mathcal{A} = \{(A, 0.8), (B, 0.7), (C, 0.7), (D, 0.6), (E, 0.8), (F, 0.6), (G, 0.7)\}$ and $\rho = \{((A, B), 0.8), ((A, C), 0.7), ((C, D), 0.6), ((C, F), 0.6), ((B, D), 0.9), ((D, E), 0.9), ((E, D), 0.7), ((F, G), 0.7)\}$.*

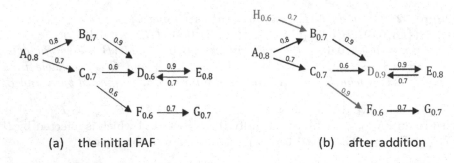

(a)   the initial FAF   (b)   after addition

Fig. 2. An example of the division of a fuzzy argumentation framework (Example 3)

Let $(\mathcal{B}, \mathcal{I}_{Ar_1:Ar_2} \cup \mathcal{I}_{Ar_1})$ be an addition FAF, in which $\mathcal{B} = \{(D, 0.9), (H, 0.6)\}$, $Ar_1 = Supp(\mathcal{A})$, $Ar_2 = Supp(\mathcal{B})$, and $\mathcal{I}_{Ar_1:Ar_2} \cup \mathcal{I}_{Ar_1} = \{((C, F), 0.9), ((H, B), 0.7)\}$. The updated FAF is $\langle \mathcal{A} \cup \mathcal{B}, \rho \cup \mathcal{I}_{Ar_1} \cup \mathcal{I}_{Ar_1:Ar_2} \rangle$, in this example, the division of the updated FAF is showed as follows:

- *$\langle \mathcal{A}_a^\oplus, \rho_a^\oplus \rangle = \langle \{(B, 0.7), (D, 0.9), (E, 0.8), (F, 0.6), (G, 0.7), (H, 0.6)\}, \{((B, D), 0.9), ((D, E), 0.9), ((E, D), 0.7), ((F, G), 0.7), ((H, B), 0.7)\} \rangle$;*
- *$\langle \mathcal{A}_u^\oplus, \rho_u^\oplus \rangle = \langle \{(A, 0.8), (C, 0.7)\}, \{((A, C).0.7)\} \rangle$;*
- *$(\mathcal{A}_c^\oplus, \rho_c^\oplus) = (\{(A, 0.8), (C, 0.7)\}, \{((A, B), 0.8), ((C, D), 0.6), ((C, F), 0.9)\}$.*

CFAF $= (\langle \mathcal{A}_a^\oplus, \rho_a^\oplus \rangle, (\mathcal{A}_c^\oplus, \rho_c^\oplus))$. *In this example, it is obvious that $\langle \mathcal{A}^\oplus, \rho^\oplus \rangle$ is equal to the combination of $\langle \mathcal{A}_u^\oplus, \rho_u^\oplus \rangle$ and CFAF.*

5.5   Computing the Semantics of an Updated Argumentation Framework Based on the Division

Under semantics $\mathcal{S} \in \{\mathcal{CO}, \mathcal{PR}, \mathcal{GR}\}$, based on the extensions of the two kinds of sub-frameworks, we will compute the extensions of $\langle \mathcal{A}^\oplus, \rho^\oplus \rangle$ by combining $\mathcal{E}_\mathcal{S}(\langle \mathcal{A}_u^\oplus, \rho_u^\oplus \rangle)$ and $\mathcal{E}_\mathcal{S}(CFAF[E])$, in which $E \in \mathcal{E}_\mathcal{S}(\langle \mathcal{A}_u^\oplus, \rho_u^\oplus \rangle)$.

Definition 17. *Let $\langle \mathcal{A}_u^\oplus, \rho_u^\oplus \rangle$ be the unaffected sub-framework of $FAF = \langle \mathcal{A}, \rho \rangle$ w.r.t an addition $(\mathcal{B}, \mathcal{I}_{Ar_1} \cup \mathcal{I}_{Ar_1:Ar_2})$, $\mathcal{E}_\mathcal{S}\langle \mathcal{A}_u^\oplus, \rho_u^\oplus \rangle$ be the set of extensions of $\langle \mathcal{A}_u^\oplus, \rho_u^\oplus \rangle$, and $CFAF[E_1] = (\langle \mathcal{A}_a^\oplus, \rho_a^\oplus \rangle, (\mathcal{A}_c^\oplus[E_1], \rho_c^\oplus))$ be an assigned conditioned sub-framework w.r.t. $E_1 \in \mathcal{E}_\mathcal{S}\langle \mathcal{A}_u^\oplus, \rho_u^\oplus \rangle$. The result of combining $\mathcal{E}_\mathcal{S}\langle \mathcal{A}_u^\oplus, \rho_u^\oplus \rangle$ and $\mathcal{E}_\mathcal{S}(CFAF[E_1])$, $\forall E_1 \in \mathcal{E}_\mathcal{S}\langle \mathcal{A}_u^\oplus, \rho_u^\oplus \rangle$, to form the set of combined extensions of $(\langle \mathcal{A}^\oplus, \rho^\oplus \rangle)$, denoted as $CombExt_\mathcal{S}(\langle \mathcal{A}^\oplus, \rho^\oplus \rangle)$, is defined as follows:*

$$CombExt_\mathcal{S}(\langle \mathcal{A}^\oplus, \rho^\oplus \rangle) = \{E_1 \cup E_2 \mid E_1 \in \mathcal{E}_\mathcal{S}(\langle \mathcal{A}_u^\oplus, \rho_u^\oplus \rangle) \wedge E_2 \in \mathcal{E}_\mathcal{S}(CFAF[E_1])\}$$

Next, we will prove that under each semantic $\mathcal{S} \in \{\mathcal{CO}, \mathcal{PR}, \mathcal{GR}\}$, the extension of an updated FAF $\langle \mathcal{A}^\oplus, \rho^\oplus \rangle$ coincides with the $CombExt_\mathcal{S}(\langle \mathcal{A}^\oplus, \rho^\oplus \rangle)$. Before the important theorem, we first figure out the relationship between a complete extension of an updated FAF and a complete extension of an assigned conditioned sub-framework of it. We have the following lemma:

Lemma 1. *For all $E \in \mathcal{E}_{CO}(\langle \mathcal{A}^{\oplus}, \rho^{\oplus} \rangle)$, it holds that $E \cap \mathcal{A}_a^{\oplus} \in \mathcal{E}_{CO}(\mathrm{CFAF}[E_1])$, in which $E_1 = E \cap \mathcal{A}_u^{\oplus}$.*

Proof. Since complete semantics satisfies the directionality criterion, and $\mathcal{A}_u^{\oplus}$ is an unattacked set, according to Definition 12, it holds that $E_1 = E \cap \mathcal{A}_u^{\oplus} \in \mathcal{E}_{CO}(\langle \mathcal{A}_u^{\oplus}, \rho_u^{\oplus} \rangle)$. According to the definition of assigned *CFAF*, it can be concluded that $E \cap \mathcal{A}_a^{\oplus} \subseteq \mathcal{A}_a^{\oplus}$ and $E \cap \mathcal{A}_a^{\oplus}$ is conflict-free. In order to prove that $E \cap \mathcal{A}_a^{\oplus}$ is a complete extension of *CFAF*$[E_1]$, we only need to verify the following two points:

- Every fuzzy argument in $E \cap \mathcal{A}_a^{\oplus}$ is weakening defended by $E \cap \mathcal{A}_a^{\oplus}$ under the condition $C(\mathcal{A}_u^{\oplus})[E_1]$, which is proved as follows:

  Since every fuzzy argument in $E \cap \mathcal{A}_a^{\oplus} \in E$ is weakening defended by E, it holds that $\forall (A, a) \in E \cap \mathcal{A}_a^{\oplus} \subseteq \mathcal{A}_a^{\oplus}$, if (B, b) sufficiently attacks (A, a), then there exists (C, c) in E s.t. $c * \rho_{CB} = a$. From the definition of $\mathcal{A}_a^{\oplus}$, (A, a) is only attacked by the fuzzy argument in $\mathcal{A}_a^{\oplus}$ and $\mathcal{A}_c^{\oplus}$. So, we have the following two cases:
  - (i) If $(B, b) \in \mathcal{A}_a^{\oplus}$, then (B, b) is attacked by $\mathcal{A}_a^{\oplus}$ or $\mathcal{A}_a^{\oplus}$. It holds that $\exists (C, c)$ in $E \cap \mathcal{A}_c^{\oplus}$ s.t. $c * \rho_{CB} = a$ or in $E \cap \mathcal{A}_a^{\oplus}$ s.t. $c * \rho_{CB} = a$ (satisfying the first condition of weakening defense of fuzzy arguments in an assigned *CFAF*, in Definition 12).
  - (ii) If $(B, b) \in \mathcal{A}_c^{\oplus}$, since the fuzzy argument in $\mathcal{A}_c^{\oplus}$ is only attacked by the fuzzy argument in $\mathcal{A}_u^{\oplus}$, we have that $\exists (C, c) \in E \cap \mathcal{A}_u^{\oplus} = E_1$ s.t. $c * \rho_{CB} = a$ (satisfying the second condition of weakening defense of fuzzy arguments in an assigned *CFAF*, in Definition 12).
- Every fuzzy argument which is weakening defended by $E \cap \mathcal{A}_a^{\oplus}$ under the condition $C(\mathcal{A}_u^{\oplus})[E_1]$ is in $E \cap \mathcal{A}_a^{\oplus}$, which is proved as follows:

  Since (A, a) in $\mathcal{A}_a^{\oplus}$ is attacked by $\mathcal{A}_c^{\oplus}$ or $\mathcal{A}_a^{\oplus}$, when (A, a) is weakening defended by $E \cap \mathcal{A}_a^{\oplus}$ under the condition $C(\mathcal{A}_u^{\oplus})[E_1]$, we have the following two cases:
  - (i) If (B, b) in $\mathcal{A}_a^{\oplus}$ sufficiently attacks (A, a), then according to the first condition of weakening defense of fuzzy arguments in Definition 12, there exists $(C, c) \in E \cap \mathcal{A}_a^{\oplus} \subseteq E$ s.t. $c * \rho_{CB} = a$ or $(D, d) \in E_1 \cap \mathcal{A}_c^{\oplus} \subseteq E$ s.t. $d * \rho_{DB} = a$.
  - (ii) If (B, b) in $\mathcal{A}_c^{\oplus}$ sufficiently attacks (A, a), then according to the second condition of weakening defense of fuzzy arguments in Definition 12, there exists $(C, c) \in E_1 \subseteq E$ s.t. $c * \rho_{CB} = a$.

  Consequently, for any (B, b) sufficiently attacks (A, a), there exists (C, c) in E s.t. $c * \rho_{CB} = a$. Therefore, (A, a) is weakening defended by E. According to the definition of complete extension, every fuzzy argument in $\mathcal{A}_a^{\oplus} \subseteq \mathcal{A}^{\oplus}$ that is weakening defended by E is in E, it holds that $(A, a) \in E$. Since $(A, a) \notin E_1$, it holds that $(A, a) \in E \cap \mathcal{A}_a^{\oplus}$.

Thus for all $E \in \mathcal{E}_{CO}(\langle \mathcal{A}^{\oplus}, \rho^{\oplus} \rangle)$, it holds that $E \cap \mathcal{A}_a^{\oplus} \in \mathcal{E}_{CO}(CFAF[E_1])$, in which $E_1 = E \cap \mathcal{A}_u^{\oplus}$. □

Based on the Lemma 1, we first show that the combined extensions are semantics extensions of the updated FAF. The result is formulated in the following theorem.

Theorem 1. *Under each argumentation semantics* $S \in \{CO, PR, GR\}$, $\forall E \in CombExt_S(\langle A^\oplus, \rho^\oplus \rangle)$, *it holds that* $E \in \mathcal{E}_S(\langle A^\oplus, \rho^\oplus \rangle)$, *in which* $E = E_1 \cup E_2$, *an extension by combining* $E_1 \in \mathcal{E}_S(\langle A_u^\oplus, \rho_u^\oplus \rangle)$ *and* $E_2 \in \mathcal{E}_S(CFAF[E_1])$.

Proof. Under complete semantics, let $E = E_1 \cup E_2$, where $E_1 \in \mathcal{E}_{CO}(\langle A_u^\oplus, \rho_u^\oplus \rangle)$ and $E_2 \in \mathcal{E}_{CO}(CFAF[E_1])$. In order to prove that E is a complete extension of $\langle A^\oplus, \rho^\oplus \rangle$, we need proof that: (1) E is conflict-free; (2) every fuzzy argument in E is weakening defended by E; (3) every fuzzy argument which is weakening defended by E is in E.

(1) First of all, E_1 and E_2 include no conflict which is entailed by the hypothesis $E_1 \in \mathcal{E}_{CO}(\langle A_u^\oplus, \rho_u^\oplus \rangle)$ and $E_2 \in \mathcal{E}_{CO}(CFAF[E_1])$. In addition, $\forall (A,a) \in E_1 \subseteq A_a^\oplus$, $\forall (B,b) \in E_2 \subseteq A_u^\oplus$, it holds that (B,b) does not sufficiently attack (A,a), for the reason that $A_u^\oplus$ is unaffected, and it also holds that (A,a) does not sufficiently attack (B,b). Otherwise, (B,b) is sufficiently attacked by a conditioning fuzzy argument that is accepted w.r.t. E_1. According to the second condition of acceptability of arguments in an assigned $CFAF$, (B,b) is not acceptable w.r.t. E_2 under the condition $C(A_u^\oplus)[E_1]$, i.e., $(B,b) \notin E_2$, contradicting $(B,b) \in E_2$. Thus E is conflict-free.

(2) We need prove that for any $(A,a) \in E$, if (B,b) sufficiently attacks (A,a), then there exists $(C,c) \in E$ s.t. $c * \rho_{CB} = a$, namely there exist elements in E weakening defends (A,a).

For any $(A,a) \in E$, there are two possible cases: $(A,a) \in E_1$ or $(A,a) \in E_2$.

(i) If $(A,a) \in E_1$, then $(A,a) \in A_u^\oplus$. Thus (A,a) is only attacked by the fuzzy arguments in A_u. Form the hypothesis $E_1 \in \mathcal{E}_{CO}(\langle A_u^\oplus, \rho_u^\oplus \rangle)$, (A,a) is weakening defended by E_1 in $\langle A_u^\oplus, \rho_u^\oplus \rangle$. Therefore E weakening defends (A,a).

(ii) If $(A,a) \in E_2$, then $(A,a) \in A_a^\oplus$ and (A,a) is weakening defended by E_2 under the condition $C(A_u^\oplus)[E_1]$ in $CFAF[E_1]$. If (B,b) sufficiently attacks (A,a), then $(B,b) \in A_a^\oplus$ or $(B,b) \in C[A_u^\oplus]$. Since (A,a) is weakening defended by E_2 under the condition $C(A_u^\oplus)[E_1]$ in $CFAF[E_1]$, it holds that:

(a) if $(B,b) \in C(A_u^\oplus)$, then from Definition 12, $\exists (C,c) \in E_1$ s.t. $c * \rho_{CB} = a$. Namely there exist elements in E weakening defends (A,a).

(b) if $(B,b) \in A_a^\oplus$, then from Definition 12, $\exists (C,c) \in E$ s.t. $c * \rho_{CB} = a$, or $\exists (D,d) \in C(A_1)$, s.t. (D,d) is weakening defended by E_1 and $d * \rho_{DB} = a$. Since E_1 is a complete extension, $(D,d) \in E_1$. Thus there exist elements in E weakening defends (A,a).

From (i) and (ii), it can be concluded that E weakening defends all the fuzzy arguments in E.

(3) We assume that $\exists (A,a) \in A^\oplus$ s.t. (A,a) is weakening defended by E, but $(A,a) \notin E$.

(i) If $(A, a) \in \mathcal{A}_u^\oplus$, then (A, a) is only attacked by the fuzzy arguments in $\mathcal{A}_u^\oplus$. Since (A, a) is weakening defended by E, we have that for any $(B, b) \in \mathcal{A}_u$ sufficiently attacks (A, a), there exists $(C, c) \in E$ s.t. $c * \rho_{CB} = a$. From that the fuzzy arguments in $\mathcal{A}_u^\oplus$ are only attacked by the fuzzy arguments in $\mathcal{A}_u^\oplus$, we have that $(C, c) \in \mathcal{A}_u^\oplus \cap E = E_1$. Thus (A, a) is weakening defended by E_1. According to that E_1 is a complete extension of $\langle \mathcal{A}_u^\oplus, \rho_u^\oplus \rangle$, it can be concluded that $(A, a) \in E_1$. But $(A, a) \notin E$. Thus it holds that $(A, a) \notin E_1$. Contradiction!

(ii) If $(A, a) \in \mathcal{A}_a^\oplus$, then (A, a) is only attacked by the fuzzy arguments in $\mathcal{A}_a^\oplus$ or $C(\mathcal{A}_u^\oplus)$. Since (A, a) is weakening defended by E, it holds that:

(a) If (A, a) is sufficiently attacked by a fuzzy argument (B, b) in $\mathcal{A}_a^\oplus$, then there exists $(C, c) \in E$ s.t. $c * \rho_{CB} = a$. It is obvious that $(C, c) \in E_1$ or E_2. Thus, if (B, b) sufficiently attacks (A, a), then $\exists (C, c) \in E_2$ s.t. $c * \rho_{CB} = a$, or $\exists (D, d) \in C(\mathcal{A}_u^\oplus)$, s.t. (D, d) is weakening defended by E_1 and $d * \rho_{DB} = a$ (satisfying the first condition of weakening defense of fuzzy arguments in Definition 12).

(b) If (A, a) is sufficiently attacked by a fuzzy argument (B, b) in $C(\mathcal{A}_u^\oplus)$, then there exists $(C, c) \in \mathcal{A}_u \cap E = E_1$ s.t. $c * \rho_{CB} = a$. Thus for any $(B, b) \in C(\mathcal{A}_u^\oplus)$, if (B, b) sufficiently attacks (A, a), then $\exists (C, c) \in E_1$ s.t. $c * \rho_{CB} = a$ (satisfying the second condition of weakening defense of fuzzy arguments in Definition 12).

Consequently, (A, a) is weakening defended by E_2 under the condition $C(\mathcal{A}_u^\oplus)[E_1]$. Since $(A, a) \notin E$, it holds that $(A, a) \notin E_2$. Contradicting that E_2 is a complete extension of $CFAF[E_1]$.

According to (i) and (ii), we have that for any (A, a) which is weakening defended by E is contained in E. Therefore, every fuzzy argument which is weakening defended by E is in E.

- Under the preferred semantics, $E = E_1 \cup E_2$ where $E_1 \in \mathcal{E}_{\mathcal{PR}}(\langle \mathcal{A}_u^\oplus, \rho_u^\oplus \rangle)$ and $E_2 \in \mathcal{E}_{\mathcal{PR}}(CFAF[E_1])$: since a preferred extension is also a complete extension, we only need to prove that E is a maximal complete extension (with respect to set inclusion) of $\langle \mathcal{A}^\oplus, \rho^\oplus \rangle$. Assume that E is not a maximal complete extension. Then there exists a preferred extension S of $\langle \mathcal{A}^\oplus, \rho^\oplus \rangle$ which strictly contains E. We suppose $S_1 = S \cap \mathcal{A}_u^\oplus$ and $S_2 = S \cap \mathcal{A}_a^\oplus$. Then from that $\mathcal{A}_a^\oplus \cap \mathcal{A}_u^\oplus = \emptyset$, we have that $S_1 \cap S_2 = \emptyset$. According to the directionality principle and the preferred semantics satisfy the directionality principle, from that $\mathcal{A}_u^\oplus$ is an unattacked set of $\langle \mathcal{A}^\oplus, \rho^\oplus \rangle$, we have that S_1 is a preferred extension of $\langle \mathcal{A}_u^\oplus, \rho_u^\oplus \rangle$. Thus if $E_1 \subsetneq S_1$, then contradicting that $E_1 \in \mathcal{E}_{\mathcal{PR}}(\langle \mathcal{A}_u^\oplus, \rho_u^\oplus \rangle)$. Therefore, $E_1 = S_1$, it follows that $E_2 \subsetneq S_2$. Since a preferred extension is also a complete extension, according to Lemma 1, it holds that S_2 is a complete extension of $CFAF[E_1]$. Contradicting that E_2 is a preferred extension of $CFAF[E_1]$. Consequently, we conclude that E is a maximal complete extension (i.e., preferred extension). Hence $E \in \mathcal{E}_{\mathcal{PR}}(\langle \mathcal{A}^\oplus, \rho^\oplus \rangle)$.

– Under grounded semantics, $E = E_1 \cup E_2$ where $E_1 \in \mathcal{E}_{\mathcal{GR}}(\langle \mathcal{A}_u^{\oplus}, \rho_u^{\oplus} \rangle)$ and $E_2 \in \mathcal{E}_{\mathcal{GR}}(CFAF[E_1])$: since the grounded extension is also a complete extension, we only need to prove that E is a minimal complete extension (with respect to set inclusion) of $\langle \mathcal{A}^{\oplus}, \rho^{\oplus} \rangle$. Assume that E is not a minimal complete extension. Then there exists a grounded extension S of $\langle \mathcal{A}^{\oplus}, \rho^{\oplus} \rangle$ which is strictly contained by E. We suppose $S_1 = S \cap \mathcal{A}_u^{\oplus}$ and $S_2 = S \cap \mathcal{A}_a^{\oplus}$. Then from that $\mathcal{A}_a^{\oplus} \cap \mathcal{A}_u^{\oplus} = \emptyset$, we have that $S_1 \cap S_2 = \emptyset$. According to the directionality principle and the grounded semantics satisfy the directionality principle, from that $\mathcal{A}_u^{\oplus}$ is an unattacked set of $\langle \mathcal{A}^{\oplus}, \rho^{\oplus} \rangle$, we have that S_1 is a grounded extension of $\langle \mathcal{A}_u^{\oplus}, \rho_u^{\oplus} \rangle$. Thus if $S_1 \subsetneq E_1$, then contradicting that $E_1 \in \mathcal{E}_{\mathcal{GR}}(\langle \mathcal{A}_u^{\oplus}, \rho_u^{\oplus} \rangle)$. Therefore, $E_1 = S_1$, it follows that $S_2 \subsetneq E_2$. Since a grounded extension is also a complete extension, according to Lemma 1, it holds that S_2 is a complete extension of $CFAF[E_1]$. Contradicting that E_2 is a grounded extension of $CFAF[E_1]$. As a result, we may conclude that E is a minimal complete extension (i.e., grounded extension). Hence $E \in \mathcal{E}_{\mathcal{GR}}(\langle \mathcal{A}^{\oplus}, \rho^{\oplus} \rangle)$.   □

According to Lemma 1, and Theorem 1, we immediately obtain Lemma 2.

Lemma 2. *Under each semantics $\mathcal{S} \in \{\mathcal{PR}, \mathcal{GR}\}$, $\forall E \in \mathcal{E}_{\mathcal{S}}(\langle \mathcal{A}^{\oplus}, \rho^{\oplus} \rangle)$, it holds that $E \cap \mathcal{A}_a^{\oplus} \in \mathcal{E}_{\mathcal{S}}(CFAF[E_1])$, in which $E_1 = E \cap \mathcal{A}_u^{\oplus}$.*

Proof. From Lemma 1, under complete semantics, $E \cap \mathcal{A}_a^{\oplus} \in \mathcal{E}_{\mathcal{CO}}(CFAF[E_1])$.

As far as preferred semantics are concerned, we need to prove that $E \cap \mathcal{A}_a^{\oplus}$ is a maximal complete extension. If $\exists E_2 \in \mathcal{E}_{\mathcal{PR}}(CFAF[E_1])$ and $E \cap \mathcal{A}_a^{\oplus} \subsetneq E_2$, then it follows that $E = (E \cap \mathcal{A}_u^{\oplus}) \cup (E \cap \mathcal{A}_a^{\oplus}) \subsetneq E_1 \cup E_2$. According to the directionality principle and $E_1 = E \cap \mathcal{A}_u^{\oplus}$, we have that E_1 is a preferred extension of $\langle \mathcal{A}_u^{\oplus}, \rho_u^{\oplus} \rangle$. From Theorem 1, we have that $E_1 \cup E_2$ is a preferred extension of $\langle \mathcal{A}^{\oplus}, \rho^{\oplus} \rangle$. This contradicts to the fact that E is a preferred extension of $\langle \mathcal{A}^{\oplus}, \rho^{\oplus} \rangle$. Hence, $E \cap \mathcal{A}_a^{\oplus} \in \mathcal{E}_{\mathcal{PR}}(CFAF[E_1])$.

As far as grounded semantics are concerned, we need to prove that $E \cap \mathcal{A}_a^{\oplus}$ is a minimal complete extension. If $\exists E_2 \in \mathcal{E}_{\mathcal{GR}}(CFAF[E_1])$ and $E_2 \subsetneq E \cap \mathcal{A}_a^{\oplus}$, then it follows that $E_1 \cup E_2 \subsetneq (E \cap \mathcal{A}_u^{\oplus}) \cup (E \cap \mathcal{A}_a^{\oplus}) = E$. According to the directionality principle and $E_1 = E \cap \mathcal{A}_u^{\oplus}$, we have that E_1 is a grounded extension of $\langle \mathcal{A}_u^{\oplus}, \rho_u^{\oplus} \rangle$. From Theorem 1, we have $E_1 \cup E_2$ is a grounded extension of $\langle \mathcal{A}^{\oplus}, \rho^{\oplus} \rangle$. This contradicts to the fact that E is a grounded extension of $\langle \mathcal{A}^{\oplus}, \rho^{\oplus} \rangle$. Hence, $E \cap \mathcal{A}_a^{\oplus} \in \mathcal{E}_{\mathcal{GR}}(CFAF[E_1])$.   □

Based on Lemmas 1 and 2, we show that the semantics extensions are the combined extension of the updated FAF. The result is formulated in the following theorem.

Theorem 2. *Under each semantics $\mathcal{S} \in \{\mathcal{CO}, \mathcal{PR}, \mathcal{GR}\}$, $\forall E \in \mathcal{E}_{\mathcal{S}}(\langle \mathcal{A}^{\oplus}, \rho^{\oplus} \rangle)$, it holds that $E \in CombExt_{\mathcal{S}}(\langle \mathcal{A}^{\oplus}, \rho^{\oplus} \rangle)$.*

Proof. Under each semantics $\mathcal{S} \in \{\mathcal{CO}, \mathcal{PR}, \mathcal{GR}\}$, $\forall E \in \mathcal{E}_{\mathcal{S}}(\langle \mathcal{A}^{\oplus}, \rho^{\oplus} \rangle)$ let $E_1 = \mathcal{A}_u^{\oplus} \cap E$, and $E_2 = \mathcal{A}_a^{\oplus} \cap E$. It holds that $E = E_1 \cup E_2$. According to Definition 10, Lemmas 1 and 2, it holds that $E_1 \in \mathcal{E}_{\mathcal{S}}(\langle \mathcal{A}_u^{\oplus}, \rho_u^{\oplus} \rangle)$ and $E_2 \in \mathcal{E}_{\mathcal{S}}(CFAF[E_1])$. According to Definition 17, it holds that $E \in CombExt_{\mathcal{S}}(\langle \mathcal{A}^{\oplus}, \rho^{\oplus} \rangle)$.   □

We give an example to illustrate the process of computing the extensions of an updated FAF by the division method.

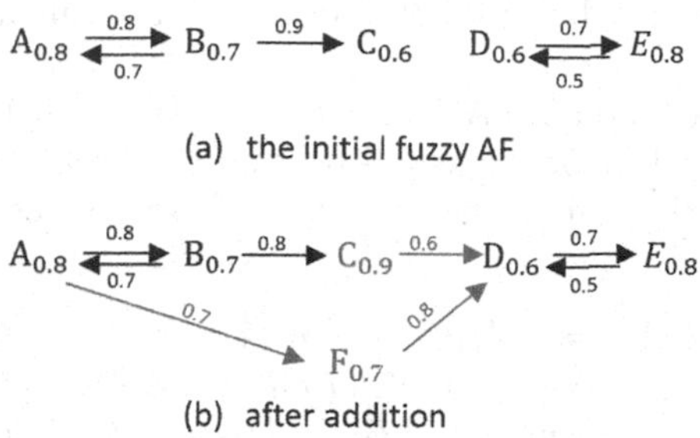

$$A_{0.8} \underset{0.7}{\overset{0.8}{\rightleftarrows}} B_{0.7} \xrightarrow{0.9} C_{0.6} \quad D_{0.6} \underset{0.5}{\overset{0.7}{\rightleftarrows}} E_{0.8}$$

(a) the initial fuzzy AF

$$A_{0.8} \underset{0.7}{\overset{0.8}{\rightleftarrows}} B_{0.7} \xrightarrow{0.8} C_{0.9} \xrightarrow{0.6} D_{0.6} \underset{0.5}{\overset{0.7}{\rightleftarrows}} E_{0.8}$$

$$F_{0.7}$$

(b) after addition

Fig. 3. The computation of semantics of an updated fuzzy argumentation framework (Example 4)

Example 4. *Let* $FAF = \langle \mathcal{A}, \rho \rangle$, *in which* $\mathcal{A} = \{(A, 0.8), (B, 0.7), (C, 0.6),$ $(D, 0.6), (E, 0.8)\}$ *and* $\rho = \{((A, B), 0.8), ((B, A), 0.7), ((B, C), 0.9), ((D, E),$ $0.7), ((E, D), 0.5)\}$. *Let* $(\mathcal{B}, \mathcal{I}_{Ar_1 : Ar_2} \cup \mathcal{I}_{Ar_1})$ *be an addition, in which* $\mathcal{B} = \{(C, 0.9), (F, 0.7)\}$, *and* $\mathcal{I}_{Ar_1 : Ar_2} \cup \mathcal{I}_{Ar_1} = \{((A, F), 0.7), ((C, D), 0.6), ((F, D), 0.8)\}$. *Then, updated FAF is* $\langle \{(A, 0.8), (B, 0.7), (C, 0.9), (D, 0.6), (E, 0.8), (F, 0.7)\},$ $\{((A, B), 0.8), ((B, A), 0.7), ((B, C), 0.8), ((C, D), 0.6), ((D, E), 0.7), ((E, D), 0.5),$ $((A, F), 0.7), ((F, D), 0.8)\} \rangle$, *the division of the updated FAF is showed as follows:*

- $\langle \mathcal{A}_a^{\oplus}, \rho_a^{\oplus} \rangle = \langle \{(C, 0.9), (D, 0.6), (E, 0.8), (F, 0.7)\}, \{((F, D), 0.8), ((C, D), 0.6),$ $((D, E), 0.7), ((E, D), 0.5)\} \rangle$;
- $\langle \mathcal{A}_u^{\oplus}, \rho_u^{\oplus} \rangle = \langle \{(A, 0.8), (B, 0.7)\}, \{((A, B), 0.8), ((B, A), 0.7)\} \rangle$;
- $(\mathcal{A}_c^{\oplus}, \rho_c^{\oplus}) = (\{(A, 0.8), (B, 0.7)\}, \{((A, F), 0.7), ((B, C), 0.8)\})$.

We can obtain CFAF $= (\langle \mathcal{A}_a^{\oplus}, \rho_a^{\oplus} \rangle, (\mathcal{A}_c^{\oplus}, \rho_c^{\oplus}))$. *For simplicity, we only discuss the case under the preferred semantics. And we only consider the limit cases.*

Under preferred semantics, $\mathcal{E}_{PR}(\langle \mathcal{A}_u^{\oplus}, \rho_u^{\oplus} \rangle) = \{E \cap \mathcal{A}_u^{\oplus} \mid E \in \mathcal{E}_{PR}(\langle \mathcal{A}^{\oplus}, \rho^{\oplus} \rangle)\}$. *Two limit cases are* $E_1 = \{(A, 0.8), (B, 0.2)\}, E_2 = \{(A, 0.3), (B, 0.7)\}$. *Then we get two assigned CFAFs:* CFAF$[E_1]$, CFAF$[E_2]$. *Next, we compute the preferred extensions of* CFAF$[E_1]$ *and* CFAF$[E_2]$ *according to Definitions 12 and 13. For simplicity, we only show a preferred extension* $\hat{E}_1$ *of* CFAF$[E_1]$ *and a preferred extension* $\hat{E}_2$ *of* CFAF$[E_2]$, *where* $\hat{E}_1 = \{(C, 0.8), (D, 0.4), (E, 0.6), (F, 0.3)\}$ *and* $\hat{E}_2 = \{(C, 0.3), (D, 0.3), (E, 0.7), (F, 0.7)\}$. *Finally, we combine the semantics extensions of* $\langle \mathcal{A}_u^{\oplus}, \rho_u^{\oplus} \rangle$ *and* CFAF. *From Theorem 1,* $E_1 \cup \hat{E}_1, E_2 \cup \hat{E}_2$ *are two preferred extensions of the updated FAF.*

5.6 The Conclusion About the Dynamics of FAF w.r.t. a Deletion of FAF

The dynamics of FAF have been explored when attached with an addition of FAF. In addition, from Definition 6, there exists the case of the deletion of

FAF. Indeed, we only need to explore the case of the removing of the arguments and attack relation. This is because the decrease of initial degree of arguments or attack relation can be regarded as we first remove the arguments or attack relation, and then we add the new belief degree of arguments or attack relation to the FAF.

Since the case of deletion of FAFs is similar to the addition of FAFs, we only list some definitions and theorems as follows and the proof procedure is omitted. And we only provide the case of the removing of arguments and attack relation.

Definition 18. *Let* $FAF = \langle \mathcal{A}, \rho \rangle$, *where* $\mathcal{A} : Ar_1 \to (0,1]$ *and* $\rho : Ar_1 \times Ar_1 \to (0,1]$ *are total functions. A deletion of FAF is represented as a tuple* $(\mathcal{B}, \mathcal{I}_{Ar_1 \backslash Ar_2} \cup \mathcal{I}_{Ar_1 \backslash Ar_2 : Ar_2})$, *in which,* $\mathcal{B} \subseteq \mathcal{A}$ *is a set of fuzzy arguments to be removed and* $Supp(\mathcal{B}) = Ar_2$, $\forall A \in Ar_2$, $\mathcal{B}(A) = \mathcal{A}(A)$, $\mathcal{I}_{Ar_1 \backslash Ar_2} \cup \mathcal{I}_{Ar_1 \backslash Ar_2 : Ar_2}$ *is a set of fuzzy attacks to be removed and* $\forall (A,B) \in Supp(\mathcal{I}_{Ar_1 \backslash Ar_2} \cup \mathcal{I}_{Ar_1 \backslash Ar_2 : Ar_2})$, $\mathcal{I}_{Ar_1 \backslash Ar_2} \cup \mathcal{I}_{Ar_1 \backslash Ar_2 : Ar_2}(A,B) = \rho(A,B)$.

Definition 19. *Let* $FAF = \langle \mathcal{A}, \rho \rangle$, *in which* $\mathcal{A} : Ar_1 \to (0,1]$ *and* $\rho : Ar_1 \times Ar_1 \to (0,1]$ *are total functions. Let* $(\mathcal{B}, \mathcal{I}_{Ar_1 \backslash Ar_2} \cup \mathcal{I}_{Ar_1 \backslash Ar_2 : Ar_2})$ *be a deletion. The updated FAF w.r.t.* $(\mathcal{B}, \mathcal{I}_{Ar_1 \backslash Ar_2} \cup \mathcal{I}_{Ar_1 \backslash Ar_2 : Ar_2})$ *is represented as follows:*

$$\langle \mathcal{A}, \rho \rangle \ominus (\mathcal{B}, \mathcal{I}_{Ar_1 \backslash Ar_2} \cup \mathcal{I}_{Ar_1 \backslash Ar_2 : Ar_2}) = \langle \mathcal{A} - \mathcal{B}, \rho - \mathcal{I}_{Ar_1 \backslash Ar_2} \cup \mathcal{I}_{Ar_1 \backslash Ar_2 : Ar_2} \rangle$$

From the above definition, given an updated FAF $\langle \mathcal{A} - \mathcal{B}, \rho - \mathcal{I}_{Ar_1 \backslash Ar_2} \cup \mathcal{I}_{Ar_1 \backslash Ar_2 : Ar_2} \rangle$ with a deletion of FAF $(\mathcal{B}, \mathcal{I}_{Ar_1 \backslash Ar_2} \cup \mathcal{I}_{Ar_1 \backslash Ar_2 : Ar_2})$, we can identify the subset of $\mathcal{A}$ which is affected by $\mathcal{B}$ or $\mathcal{I}_{Ar_1 \backslash Ar_2} \cup \mathcal{I}_{Ar_1 \backslash Ar_2 : Ar_2}$. Therefore, we are ready to define the concept of the division of an updated FAF. When a deletion $(\mathcal{B}, \mathcal{I}_{Ar_1 \backslash Ar_2} \cup \mathcal{I}_{Ar_1 \backslash Ar_2 : Ar_2})$ is deleted from an $FAF = \langle \mathcal{A}, \rho \rangle$, the updated FAF will be divided into three parts:

- a component of $\mathcal{A}$ that is affected by $(\mathcal{B}, \mathcal{I}_{Ar_1 \backslash Ar_2} \cup \mathcal{I}_{Ar_1 \backslash Ar_2 : Ar_2})$;
- a component of $\mathcal{A}$ that is unaffected by $(\mathcal{B}, \mathcal{I}_{Ar_1 \backslash Ar_2} \cup \mathcal{I}_{Ar_1 \backslash Ar_2 : Ar_2})$;
- a subset of the unaffected component that conditions the affected components.

Formally, we can provide the definition of the division of an FAF w.r.t. an addition $(\mathcal{B}, \mathcal{I}_{Ar_1 \backslash Ar_2} \cup \mathcal{I}_{Ar_1 \backslash Ar_2 : Ar_2})$.

Definition 20. *Let* $FAF = \langle \mathcal{A}, \rho \rangle$, *and* $Supp(\mathcal{A}) = Ar_1$. *Suppose* $(\mathcal{B}, \mathcal{I}_{Ar_1 \backslash Ar_2 : Ar_2} \cup \mathcal{I}_{Ar_1 \backslash Ar_2})$ *be a deletion to the FAF. The updated FAF* $\langle \mathcal{A}^{\ominus}, \rho^{\ominus} \rangle$ *is divided into three parts:* $\langle \mathcal{A}_a^{\ominus}, \rho_a^{\ominus} \rangle$, $\langle \mathcal{A}_u^{\ominus}, \rho_u^{\ominus} \rangle$, $(\mathcal{A}_c^{\ominus}, \rho_c^{\ominus})$ *where* a, u *and* c *stand for, respectively, affected, unaffected and conditioning.*
$\mathcal{A}_a^{\ominus} = \{(A, \mathcal{A}^{\ominus}(A)) \mid A$ *is affected by* $\mathcal{B}$ *w.r.t.* $\mathcal{I}_{Ar_1 \backslash Ar_2 : Ar_2}$ *or* A *is affected by* $\mathcal{I}_{Ar_1 \backslash Ar_2}$ *or* A *is affected by an argument in* $Supp(\mathcal{A}_a^{\ominus})$ *w.r.t.* $\rho^{\ominus}\}$
$\mathcal{A}_u^{\ominus} = \mathcal{A}^{\ominus} - \mathcal{A}_a^{\ominus}$
$\mathcal{A}_c^{\ominus} = \{(A, \mathcal{A}^{\ominus}(A)) \in \mathcal{A}_u^{\ominus} \mid \exists B \in Supp(\mathcal{A}_a) \text{ s.t. } (B, A) \in Supp(\rho^{\ominus}) \text{ w.r.t. } \rho^{\ominus}\}$
$\rho_a^{\ominus} = \rho^{\ominus} \cap \rho_{Supp(\mathcal{A}_a^{\ominus})}$
$\rho_u^{\ominus} = \rho^{\ominus} \cap \rho_{Supp(\mathcal{A}_u^{\ominus})}$
$\rho_c^{\ominus} = \rho^{\ominus} \cap \rho_{(Supp(\mathcal{A}_c^{\ominus}), Supp(\mathcal{A}_a^{\ominus}))}$

In this definition, for a given updated FAF $\langle \mathcal{A}^\ominus, \rho^\ominus \rangle$, $\mathcal{A}_u^\ominus$ coincides with the arguments that are unaffected by $(\mathcal{B}, \mathcal{I}_{Ar_1 \backslash Ar_2} \cup \mathcal{I}_{Ar_1 \backslash Ar_2 : Ar_2})$, $\mathcal{A}_a^\ominus$ coincides with the arguments that are affected by $(\mathcal{B}, \mathcal{I}_{Ar_1 \backslash Ar_2} \cup \mathcal{I}_{Ar_1 \backslash Ar_2 : Ar_2})$ $\mathcal{A}_c^\ominus$ coincides with the arguments in $\mathcal{A}_u^\ominus$ that attack $\mathcal{A}_a^\ominus$.

After we have the division of the updated FAF, the next step is to construct two sub-frameworks of the updated FAF $\langle \mathcal{A}^\ominus, \rho^\ominus \rangle$: the unaffected FAF and the affected FAF under the condition. The unaffected FAF is $\langle \mathcal{A}_u^\ominus, \rho_u^\ominus \rangle$. And the conditioned FAF w.r.t. $\langle \mathcal{A}_u^\ominus, \rho_a^\ominus \rangle$ is constructed as:

$$CFAF = (\langle \mathcal{A}_a^\ominus, \rho_a^\ominus \rangle, (\mathcal{A}_c^\ominus, \rho_c^\ominus))$$

From Definition 20, we have $\mathcal{A}_c^\ominus \cap \mathcal{A}_a^\ominus = \emptyset$, $\mathcal{A}_c^\ominus \subseteq \mathcal{A}_u^\ominus$ and $\rho_c^\ominus \subseteq \rho_{(\mathcal{A}_c^\ominus, \mathcal{A}_a^\ominus)}$. Namely, it satisfies the definition of condition.

Based on the extensions of the two kinds of sub-frameworks, we will compute the extensions of $\langle \mathcal{A}^\ominus, \rho^\ominus \rangle$ by combining $\mathcal{E}_\mathcal{S}(\langle \mathcal{A}_u^\ominus, \rho_u^\ominus \rangle)$ and $\mathcal{E}_\mathcal{S}(CFAF[E])$, in which $E \in \mathcal{E}_\mathcal{S}(\langle \mathcal{A}_u^\ominus, \rho_u^\ominus \rangle)$.

Definition 21. *Let $\langle \mathcal{A}_u^\ominus, \rho_u^\ominus \rangle$ be the unaffected sub-framework of $FAF = \langle \mathcal{A}, \rho \rangle$ w.r.t. a deletion $(\mathcal{B}, \mathcal{I}_{Ar_1 \backslash Ar_2} \cup \mathcal{I}_{Ar_1 \backslash Ar_2 : Ar_2})$, $\mathcal{E}_\mathcal{S}\langle \mathcal{A}_u^\ominus, \rho_u^\ominus \rangle$ be the set of extensions of $\langle \mathcal{A}_u^\ominus, \rho_u^\ominus \rangle$, and $CFAF[E_1] = (\langle \mathcal{A}_a^\ominus, \rho_a^\ominus \rangle, (\mathcal{A}_c^\ominus[E_1], \rho_c^\ominus))$ be an assigned conditioned FAF w.r.t. $E_1 \in \mathcal{E}_\mathcal{S}\langle \mathcal{A}_u^\ominus, \rho_u^\ominus \rangle$. The result of combining $\mathcal{E}_\mathcal{S}\langle \mathcal{A}_u^\ominus, \rho_u^\ominus \rangle$ and $\mathcal{E}_\mathcal{S}(CFAF[E_1])$, $\forall E_1 \in \mathcal{E}_\mathcal{S}\langle \mathcal{A}_u^\ominus, \rho_u^\ominus \rangle$, to form the set of combined extensions of $\langle \mathcal{A}^\ominus, \rho^\ominus \rangle$, denoted as $CombExt_\mathcal{S}(\langle \mathcal{A}^\ominus, \rho^\ominus \rangle)$, is defined as follows:*

$$CombExt_\mathcal{S}(\langle \mathcal{A}^\ominus, \rho^\ominus \rangle) = \{E_1 \cup E_2 \mid E_1 \in \mathcal{E}_\mathcal{S}(\langle \mathcal{A}_u^\ominus, \rho_u^\ominus \rangle) \wedge E_2 \in \mathcal{E}_\mathcal{S}(CFAF[E_1])\}$$

Next, we prove that under each semantic $\mathcal{S} \in \{\mathcal{CO}, \mathcal{PR}, \mathcal{GR}\}$, the extension of an updated framework $\langle \mathcal{A}^\ominus, \rho^\ominus \rangle)$ coincides with the $CombExt_\mathcal{S}(\langle \mathcal{A}^\ominus, R^\ominus \rangle)$. We have the following important conclusion.

Lemma 3. *Under each semantics $\mathcal{S} \in \{\mathcal{CO}, \mathcal{PR}, \mathcal{GR}\}$, $\forall E \in \mathcal{E}_\mathcal{S}(\langle \mathcal{A}^\ominus, \rho^\ominus \rangle)$, it holds that $E \cap \mathcal{A}_a^\ominus \in \mathcal{E}_\mathcal{S}(CFAF[E_1])$, in which $E_1 = E \cap \mathcal{A}_u^\ominus$.*

Based on Lemmas 3, the coincidence of the semantics extensions and the combined extensions can be showed as follows:

Theorem 3. *Under each argumentation semantics $\mathcal{S} \in \{\mathcal{CO}, \mathcal{PR}, \mathcal{GR}\}$, $\forall E \in CombExt_\mathcal{S}(\langle \mathcal{A}^\ominus, \rho^\ominus \rangle)$, it holds that $E \in \mathcal{E}_\mathcal{S}(\langle \mathcal{A}^\ominus, \rho^\ominus \rangle)$, in which $E = E_1 \cup E_2$, an extension by combining $E_1 \in \mathcal{E}_\mathcal{S}(\langle \mathcal{A}_u^\ominus, \rho_u^\ominus \rangle)$ and $E_2 \in \mathcal{E}_\mathcal{S}(CFAF[E_1])$.*

Theorem 4. *Under each semantics $\mathcal{S} \in \{\mathcal{CO}, \mathcal{PR}, \mathcal{GR}\}$, $\forall E \in \mathcal{E}_\mathcal{S}(\langle \mathcal{A}^\ominus, \rho^\ominus \rangle)$, it holds that $E \in CombExt_\mathcal{S}(\langle \mathcal{A}^\ominus, \rho^\ominus \rangle)$.*

6   Conclusion

In this paper, we explore the dynamics of FAFs. The changing of the argument and attack relation as well as the initial belief degree of the arguments and attack relation is an intrinsic property of FAFs with the changes of observations, basic knowledge, and information.

First, we list the whole changes in the dynamics of FAFs. The dynamics of FAFs include not only the changes of arguments and attack relation but also the changes of initial belief degree of arguments and attack relation. Furthermore, the arbitrary combination of these cases is also a dynamic FAF. Additionally, our main task is to compute the semantics of the dynamics FAFs. We focus on the complete, preferred and grounded semantics by extending Liao's division-based approach. First, we divide the updated FAF into three parts: affected FAF, unaffected FAF, conditioned FAF. Then we compute the semantics of the affected FAFs under the conditioned FAF. Due to the directionality principle, the semantics of the unaffected AF are directly obtained from the previous FAF. Thus, this algorithm conserves part of the semantics in the previous FAF.

In the future, we will continue exploring the residual semantics of the dynamics of FAFs, such as stable semantics, ideal semantics. We also want to prove that a variety of principles are satisfied in FAFs, such as reinstatement principle and SCC-recursiveness principle. Then we can provide an incremental computation in FAFs which can efficiently compute the semantics by the topology-related properties.

References

1. Baroni, P., Giacomin, M., Guida, G.: SCC-recursiveness: a general schema for argumentation semantics. Artif. Intell. **168**(1–2), 162–210 (2005)
2. Bench-Capon, T., Dunne, P.: Argumentation in artificial intelligence. Artif. Intell. **171**(10–15), 619–641 (2007)
3. Capobianco, M., Chesñevar, C., Simari, G.: Argumentation and the dynamics of warranted beliefs in changing environments. Auton. Agents Multi-Agent Syst. **11**(2), 127–151 (2005). https://doi.org/10.1007/s10458-005-1354-8
4. Cayrol, C., de Saint-Cyr, F., Lagasquie-Schiex, M.: Change in abstract argumentation frameworks: adding an argument. J. Artif. Intell. Res. **38**, 49–84 (2010)
5. da Costa Pereira, C., Tettamanzi, A., Villata, S.: Changing one's mind: erase or rewind? Possibilistic belief revision with fuzzy argumentation based on trust. In: Twenty-Second International Joint Conference on Artificial Intelligence (2011)
6. Coste-Marquis, S., Devred, C., Konieczny, S., Lagasquie-Schiex, M., Marquis, P.: On the merging of dung's argumentation systems. Artif. Intell. **171**(10–15), 730–753 (2007)
7. Dung, P.: On the acceptability of arguments and its fundamental role in non-monotonic reasoning, logic programming and n-person games. Artif. Intell. **77**(2), 321–357 (1995)
8. Dunne, P., Hunter, A., McBurney, P., Parsons, S., Wooldridge, M.: Weighted argument systems: basic definitions, algorithms, and complexity results. Artif. Intell. **175**(2), 457–486 (2011)
9. Hunter, A.: A probabilistic approach to modelling uncertain logical arguments. Int. J. Approximate Reasoning **54**(1), 47–81 (2013)
10. Janssen, J., De Cock, M., Vermeir, D.: Fuzzy argumentation frameworks. In: Information Processing and Management of Uncertainty in Knowledge-Based Systems, pp. 513–520 (2008)

11. Kakas, A., Miller, R., Toni, F.: An argumentation framework for reasoning about actions and change. In: Gelfond, M., Leone, N., Pfeifer, G. (eds.) LPNMR 1999. LNCS (LNAI), vol. 1730, pp. 78–91. Springer, Heidelberg (1999). https://doi.org/10.1007/3-540-46767-X_6
12. Li, H., Oren, N., Norman, T.J.: Probabilistic argumentation frameworks. In: Modgil, S., Oren, N., Toni, F. (eds.) TAFA 2011. LNCS (LNAI), vol. 7132, pp. 1–16. Springer, Heidelberg (2012). https://doi.org/10.1007/978-3-642-29184-5_1
13. Liao, B., Jin, L., Koons, R.: Dynamics of argumentation systems: a division-based method. Artif. Intell. **175**(11), 1790–1814 (2011)
14. Rotstein, N., Moguillansky, M., Garcia, A., Simari, G.: An abstract argumentation framework for handling dynamics. In: Proceedings of the Argument, Dialogue and Decision Workshop in NMR, pp. 131–139 (2008)
15. Wu, J., Li, H., Oren, N., Norman, T.: Gödel fuzzy argumentation frameworks. In: COMMA, pp. 447–458 (2016)
16. Zadeh, L.: Fuzzy sets. Inf. Control **8**(3), 338–353 (1965)

Probabilistic Three-Valued Argumentation Frameworks

Jiachao Wu[1] and Hengfei Li[2(✉)]

[1] Department of Mathematics and Statistics, Shandong Normal University,
Jinan 250014, China
wujiachao1981@hotmail.com
[2] School of Computer Science and Technology, Shandong Jianzhu University,
Jinan 250101, China
hengfei2014@outlook.com

Abstract. Dung' AF has been extended in many different directions. One particular direction is to allow uncertainty in AFs. Among others, probability and fuzzy theory are typical approaches used in this direction. In this paper, we argue that arguments can be both fuzzy and random. We thus introduce probabilistic-fuzzy argumentation frameworks in which probabilities and fuzzy values are combined to describe fuzzy and random arguments. We introduce an algorithm for revising probabilities. Based on this algorithm, we study semantics of probabilistic-fuzzy argumentation frameworks.

1 Introduction

An abstract argumentation framework (AF) [5] contains a set of arguments and an attack relation between the arguments. Dung's AF theory [1,5] selects various kinds of accepted arguments. This theory has been applied in many fields in artificial intelligence, such as decision making, multi-agent systems, the law and so on.

Dung's theory has been extended in many different directions. One particular direction is to allow uncertainty in AFs. Among others, probability and fuzzy theory are typical techniques used in this direction. For example, probabilities are assigned to arguments and/or attacks to capture uncertainty in AFs in [4,8–10, 13]. Fuzzy theory is adopted to extend AFs in [2,3,11,12,14]. However, there are relatively sparse works on combining these two techniques in AFs. Probabilities and fuzzy values are joint together in [3], but arguments are evaluated in separate layers in each of which either probability-based or fuzzy-based analysis is carried out.

As discussed in [3], probabilistic and vague (fuzzy) arguments can co-exist in a dialectical process. In certain cases, information expressed by an argument can be both fuzzy and random. To illustrate, consider the following argument:

Ar: The weather forecast says it will rain tomorrow. The football match should be cancelled.

© Springer Nature Switzerland AG 2020
M. Dastani et al. (Eds.): CLAR 2020, LNAI 12061, pp. 308–323, 2020.
https://doi.org/10.1007/978-3-030-44638-3_19

This argument is both fuzzy and random. On the one hand, it is fuzzy because different people have different cognition that the rain prevents the match. For example, most football matches continue in light rain; some matches are played in moderate rain; and few important matches may be took place in heavy rain. Thus for different states of the rain, the argument can have different fuzzy statuses. On the other hand, the forecasted rain has randomness. There will be chances of light rain, moderate rain and heavy rain. Hence, the argument **Ar** is random.

In this paper, we present a novel argumentation framework, called *probabilistic-fuzzy argumentation framework (PFAF)*, in which arguments can be both fuzzy and random. The fuzzyness and randomness of arguments are described by a model called PF-matrices. We study semantics of PFAFs based on revising the probabilities of fuzzy statuses.

The contents are arranged as follows: In the next section, we introduce PF-matrices for describing fuzzy and random arguments. We then present our probabilistic-fuzzy argumentation frameworks. In Sect. 3, we introduce an algorithm to revising the probabilities. In Sect. 4, we study semantics of PFAFs. We discuss how our work is related to other works in Sect. 5 and we conclude in Sect. 6.

2   Definition of PFAFs

We introduce PFAFs in this section. We begin with how we describe fuzzyness and randomness of arguments. In this paper, we simplify the fuzzyness, i.e., for each argument, we only consider three fuzzy statuses. We denote them by values 0, 0.5 and 1. We then assign a probability value to each fuzzy status to capture the randomness. For an argument A, its fuzzy and probability values form a matrix as shown in the following:

$$\mathbb{M}_A = \begin{bmatrix} 1 & P_{1,A} \\ 0.5 & P_{0.5,A} \\ 0 & P_{0,A} \end{bmatrix},$$

In the above matrix, the first column shows the three statuses of argument A and the second column shows the probabilities of the three statuses.

For every argument, there are three fuzzy statuses of it and the probabilities assigned to the three statuses should sum up to 1. Thus we have the following the definition of probabilistic-fuzzy matrices. These matrices describe fuzzyness and randomness of arguments.

Definition 1. *Given an argument A, the probabilistic-fuzzy matrix (PF-matrix) is a matrix*

$$\mathbb{M}_A = \begin{bmatrix} 1 & P_{1,A} \\ 0.5 & P_{0.5,A} \\ 0 & P_{0,A} \end{bmatrix}, \tag{1}$$

where $P_{1,A} + P_{0.5,A} + P_{0,A} = 1$.

In order to characterize the semantics of PFAFs, we introduce an order between the PF-matrices.

Take the argument **Ar** for an example. If it has two PF-matrices $\mathbb{M}$ and $\mathbb{M}'$. then each of them represents a forecast of the rain. Which forecast indicates heavier rain?

Intuitively, if the probability of heavy rain is higher and the probability of light rain is lower, then we can recognize that the forecast shows heavier rain. In other words, if $P_1 \leq P_1'$ and $P_0 \geq P_0'$, then the rain forecasted by PF-matrix $\mathbb{M}$ will be no heavier than the one forecasted by PF-matrix $\mathbb{M}'$. Similarly, the order between the PF-matrices is introduced as follow:

Definition 2. *Given two PF-matrices* $\mathbb{M}_A$ *and* $\mathbb{M}_B$, $\mathbb{M}_A \leq \mathbb{M}_B$ *if and only if* $P_{1,A} \leq P_{1,B}$ *and* $P_{0,A} \geq P_{0,B}$.

Particularly, $\mathbb{M}_A < \mathbb{M}_B$ if and only if $\mathbb{M}_A \leq \mathbb{M}_B$ and $\mathbb{M}_A \neq \mathbb{M}_B$[1].

Given a PFAF, let $Args$ be the set of all the arguments and $\mathcal{M}$ be the set of all the PF-matrices. In order to show the probabilities of the fuzzy statuses of the arguments, each argument is associated with a PF-matrix. It can be represented by a function $S: Args \rightarrow \mathcal{M}$, where $\forall A \in Args$, $S(A) = \mathbb{M}_A$ is the PF-matrix of A. Similar to the fuzzy sets, the function S is called a PF-set on $Args$ here. Particularly, if the set

$$ Ar = \{A \in Args \colon S(A) \neq \begin{bmatrix} 1 & 0 \\ 0.5 & 0 \\ 0 & 1 \end{bmatrix}\} \subseteq Args $$

is finite, the set S can be represented in the form $S = \{(A, \mathbb{M}_A) \colon A \in Ar\}$.

Given two PF-sets S_1 and S_2 on $Args$, we say that S_1 is included in S_2, denoted by $S_1 \subseteq S_2$, iff $S_1(A) \leq S_2(A)$, for all $A \in Args$.

The empty set $\emptyset$ stands for the PF-set S, s.t. for all $A \in Args$, in the PF-matrix $S(A)$, $P_{0,A} = 1$. Obviously, $\emptyset$ is the least element of all the PF-sets on $Args$ w.r.t. the set inclusion $\subseteq$.

With the notion of PF-sets, PFAFs can now be formally introduced.

Definition 3. *Let* $(Args, Atts)$ *be a Dung's AF. A PFAF is a tuple* $(\mathbb{A}, Atts)$, *where* $\mathbb{A}: Args \rightarrow \mathcal{M}$ *is a PF-set on* $Args$.

Example 1. A conference is beginning in 45 min. The organizers are discussing whether or not to wait for Jim.

A: Hi, all. Jim is driving here. But he is still 60 miles away. He may arrive very late. I don't think we should wait for him.

B: The speed limit of the highway is 80 mph. He can drive fast and arrive nearly on time. I think we'd better wait for him.

---

[1] If $\mathbb{M}_A \leq \mathbb{M}_B$ and $\mathbb{M}_B \leq \mathbb{M}_A$, $\mathbb{M}_A = \mathbb{M}_B$. It is the same as the common "=" between matrices in algebra.

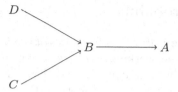

Fig. 1. AF of Example 1

C: In general, the speed limit is 80 mph. But it rains now. And the forecast says the rain is going heavier soon. Jim can't drive so fast. His speed may decrease to 60 mph or 40 mph.

B: How heavy the rain will be?

C: By the forecast, there is a 20% chance of a heavy rain, a 30% chance of a moderate rain, and a 50% chance of a light rain.

D: By the way, I heard that some lanes of the highway are closed for road working. It may also decrease Jim's speed.

B: Are you sure? How serious?

D: I don't think it is serious. I think there is a roughly 40% chance that the work is already finished, a 30% chance that one lane is still closed and a 30% chance that two lanes are still closed.

The discussion in the above scenario can be represented by a Dung's AF depicted as follows:

In Fig. 1, the arrows stand for the relation *attack* and the arguments are as follows:

A: Jim will arrive very late. We should not wait for him.

B: On the highway, Jim drives very fast.

C: The rain goes heavier. Jim cannot drive so fast in the rain.

D: The road working drops Jim's speed down.

The PF-matrices of C and D are obvious. For argument B, its probabilities are determined by the driving habit of Jim. But there is no information about his driving habit. In this case, we suppose that Jim will drive as quickly as possible. In other words, the initial probability of "driving fast and late for not long" is 1, i.e., in the PF-matrix of B, $P_{1,B} = 1$. It follows that $P_{0.5,B} = P_{0,B} = 0$. Similarly, we suppose $P_{1,A} = 1$ and $P_{0.5,A} = P_{0,A} = 0$ initially. Then the function $\mathbb{A} \colon Args \to \mathcal{M}$ in the PFAF $(\mathbb{A}, Atts)$ can be shown as follows:

$$\mathbb{A}(D) = \mathbb{M}_D = \begin{bmatrix} 1 & 0.3 \\ 0.5 & 0.3 \\ 0 & 0.4 \end{bmatrix}, \quad \mathbb{A}(C) = \mathbb{M}_C = \begin{bmatrix} 1 & 0.2 \\ 0.5 & 0.3 \\ 0 & 0.5 \end{bmatrix},$$

$$\mathbb{A}(B) = \mathbb{M}_B = \begin{bmatrix} 1 & 1 \\ 0.5 & 0 \\ 0 & 0 \end{bmatrix}, \quad \mathbb{A}(A) = \mathbb{M}_A = \begin{bmatrix} 1 & 1 \\ 0.5 & 0 \\ 0 & 0 \end{bmatrix}.$$

3   Revising the Probabilities

In the scenario of Example 1, if the probabilities of the fuzzy statuses of the arguments C (rain) and D (road working) are already known, then the probabilities of the fuzzy statuses of the arguments B and A are determined. Decisions can be made according to the probabilities (of A). In this paper, we will concentrate on the algorithm to calculate the probabilities. The process of making decisions will not be discussed here.

In a PFAF, the initial matrices (or the initial probabilities) of the arguments may not be consistent, for instance, the arguments B and C in the scenario. In this section, we will introduce a method to revise the probabilities of the arguments, so that they become consistent in some sense.

Firstly, let's only consider the effect of C on B. The probabilities of Jim's speed and arrival time are determined by the probabilities of the rain. Then the probabilities in the PF-matrix of B should be revised according to the PF-matrix of C. More specifically, if the rain is heavy, his speed is around 40 mph; if the rain is moderate, his speed is around 60 mph; and if the rain is light, his speed is around 80 mph. As a result, the probability that Jim drives very fast is 50%, which is the probability of light rain; the probability that Jim drives at moderate speed is 30%, which is the probability of moderate rain; and the probability that Jim drives very slowly is 20%, which is the probability of heavy rain. Then the PF-matrix of B should be revised to the following:

$$M'_B = \begin{bmatrix} 1 & 0.5 \\ 0.5 & 0.3 \\ 0 & 0.2 \end{bmatrix}$$

Now, consider the arguments D in the scenario together. Because B is attacked by C and D, the probabilities of the statuses of B should be influenced by the probabilities of C and D. Let's check the probabilities of the status of B. Suppose C and D are independent.

Case 1: The fuzzy degree of argument B is 1, i.e., Jim drives very fast. This requires that the rain is light and the road working has been finished. In other words, the fuzzy degrees of both C and D are 0. The probability $P_{1,B}$ should be revised to the product of $P_{0,C}$ and $P_{0,D}$. Denote the revised probability by $P'_{1,B}$. We then have:

$$P'_{1,B} = P_{0,C} \times P_{0,D}.$$

Case 2: The fuzzy degree of B is 0, i.e., Jim drives very slowly. In general, Jim drives so slowly, either because the rain is heavy or because the road working limits the speed seriously. In other words, either C or D is of degree 1. And the probability is the probabilistic sum of $P_{1,C}$ and $P_{1,D}$. Denote the revised probability of $P_{0,B}$ by $P'_{0,B}$. We have:

$$P'_{0,B} = P_{1,C} + P_{1,D} - P_{1,C} \times P_{1,D} = 1 - (P_{0,C} + P_{0.5,C}) \times (P_{0,D} + P_{0.5,D}).$$

Case 3: Otherwise, the argument B is of fuzzy degree 0.5, i.e., Jim drives at moderate speed. Its revised probability can be obtained by the following equation:

$$P'_{0.5,B} = 1 - P'_{0,B} - P'_{1,B}.$$

Putting the three values $P'_{1,B}$, $P'_{0.5,B}$ and $P'_{0,B}$ into a PF-matrix, we obtain the revised probabilities of the fuzzy degrees of B. This illustrates the idea of revising probabilities. It should be noted that in the above calculations of $P_{1,B}$, $P_{0.5,B}$ and $P_{0,B}$, we assumed the following:

- **Independence** All arguments are independent. With this assumption, the probabilities can be calculated easily.
- **Maximum** The attack relation cannot increase the probability of an argument. In other words, the revised PF-matrix of an argument is no more than its initial PF-matrix w.r.t. the order between PF-matrices.

An algorithm for revising the PF-matrix of an argument is then introduced in the next definition.

Definition 4. *Suppose an argument B with a PF-matrix $\mathbb{M}_B$ is attacked by a finite set of arguments $\{A_i : i = 1, 2, ..., n\}$, and for each argument A_i, $i = 1, 2, ..., n$, its PF-matrix is*

$$\mathbb{M}_{A_i} = \begin{bmatrix} 1 & P_{1,A_i} \\ 0.5 & P_{0.5,A_i} \\ 0 & P_{0,A_i} \end{bmatrix}.$$

We say that the PF-set $\{(A_i, \mathbb{M}_{A_i}) : i = 1, 2, ..., n\}$ revises B's PF-matrix

$$\mathbb{M}_B = \begin{bmatrix} 1 & P_{1,B} \\ 0.5 & P_{0.5,B} \\ 0 & P_{0,B} \end{bmatrix} \text{ to } \mathbb{M}'_B = \begin{bmatrix} 1 & P'_{1,B} \\ 0.5 & P'_{0.5,B} \\ 0 & P'_{0,B} \end{bmatrix}$$

where

$$P'_{1,B} = \min\{P_{1,B}, \ \prod_{i=1}^{n} P_{0,A_i}\},$$

$$P'_{0,B} = \max\{P_{0,B}, \ 1 - \prod_{i=1}^{n}(P_{0,A_i} + P_{0.5,A_i})\}$$

and

$$P'_{0.5,B} = 1 - P'_{1,B} - P'_{0,B}.$$

Obviously, the revised PF-matrix $\mathbb{M}'_B$ is no more than the original PF-matrix $\mathbb{M}_B$, i.e. $\mathbb{M}'_B \leq \mathbb{M}_B$.

Example 2. Consider the PFAF in Example 1. The initial matrices of the three arguments B, C and D are:

$$\mathbb{M}_B = \begin{bmatrix} 1 & 1 \\ 0.5 & 0 \\ 0 & 0 \end{bmatrix}, \quad \mathbb{M}_C = \begin{bmatrix} 1 & 0.2 \\ 0.5 & 0.3 \\ 0 & 0.5 \end{bmatrix} \text{ and } \mathbb{M}_D = \begin{bmatrix} 1 & 0.3 \\ 0.5 & 0.3 \\ 0 & 0.4 \end{bmatrix}.$$

We can obtain:
$$P'_{1,B} = P_{0,C} \times P_{0,D} = 0.5 \times 0.4 = 0.2,$$

$$P'_{0,B} = 1 - (P_{0,C} + P_{0.5,C}) \times (P_{0,D} + P_{0.5,D}) = 1 - (0.3 + 0.5) \times (0.3 + 0.4) = 0.44,$$

and
$$P'_{0.5,B} = 1 - P'_{0,B} - P'_{1,B} = 1 - 0.2 - 0.44 = 0.36.$$

In other words, the PF-matrix of B is revised to:

$$\mathbb{M}'_B = \begin{bmatrix} 1 & 0.2 \\ 0.5 & 0.36 \\ 0 & 0.44 \end{bmatrix}.$$

Similarly, the PF-matrix of A is revised by $(B, \mathbb{M}'_B)$ to

$$\mathbb{M}'_A = \begin{bmatrix} 1 & 0.44 \\ 0.5 & 0.36 \\ 0 & 0.2 \end{bmatrix}.$$

From this PF-matrix, there is a 44% chance that Jim will be late for a long time, a 36% chance that he will be late for a moderate time, and a 20% chance that he will arrive nearly on time. Then the decision can be made according to the probabilities.

Suppose $S \subseteq \mathbb{A}$ is a PF-set in a PFAF $(\mathbb{A}, Atts)$. Let's consider that it revises the PF-matrix of an argument $A \in Args$. Obviously, A is only influenced by the arguments B with $(B, A) \in Atts$. Then we have the following definition.

Definition 5. *In a PFAF $(\mathbb{A}, Atts)$, suppose $S \subseteq \mathbb{A}$ is a PF-set on Args. S revises the PF-matrix $\mathbb{M}_A$ of an argument A to $\mathbb{M}'_A$, if and only if the PF-set $\{(B, S(B)): (B, A) \in Atts\}$ revises $\mathbb{M}_A$ to $\mathbb{M}'_A$.*

In Definition 4, the PF-set $\{(A_i, \mathbb{M}_{A_i}): i = 1, 2, ..., n\}$ is on $\{A_i: i = 1, 2, ..., n\}$, which is not *Args* in general. This is the distinction between Definitions 4 and 5.

Note that in general, $P'_{0.5,B} \leq P_{0.5,B}$ is not valid. But we have the following proposition.

Proposition 1. *In a PFAF, if the PF-matrix of B is revised to $\mathbb{M}'_B$, then $P'_{0.5,B} + P'_{1,B} \leq P_{0.5,B} + P_{1,B}$.*

Proof. Because $P'_{0,B} \geq P_{0,B}$, we have $1 - P'_{0,B} \leq 1 - P_{0,B}$. It is $P'_{0.5,B} + P'_{1,B} \leq P_{0.5,B} + P_{1,B}$.

Next proposition shows the monotonicity of the revision, which follows obviously from Definition 4.

Proposition 2. *Let $S \subseteq S'$ be two PF-sets and $\mathbb{M}_A \leq \mathbb{M}'_A$ be two PF-matrices of an argument A.*

1. *If S revises $\mathbb{M}_A$ to $\mathbb{M}_{A,1}$ and S' revises $\mathbb{M}_A$ to $\mathbb{M}_{A,2}$, then $\mathbb{M}_{A,1} \geq \mathbb{M}_{A,2}$.*
2. *If S revises $\mathbb{M}_A$ to $\mathbb{M}_{A,1}$ and S revises $\mathbb{M}'_A$ to $\mathbb{M}_{A,2}$, then $\mathbb{M}_{A,1} \leq \mathbb{M}_{A,2}$.*

Next definition introduces the revision between PF-sets.

Definition 6. *Let S_1 and S_2 be two PF-sets in a PFAF. S_1 revises S_2 to S'_2, iff for each $A \in Args$, S_1 revises the PF-matrix $S_2(A)$ to the PF-matrix $S'_2(A)$.*
Particularly, if S_2 is a single point set $\{(A, \mathbb{M}_A)\}$, we simply say that S_1 revises $(A, \mathbb{M}_A)$ to $(A, \mathbb{M}'_A)$.

The following proposition follow from Proposition 1.

Proposition 3. *If S is revised to S', then $\forall A \in Args$, $S'(A) \leq S(A)$, i.e., $S' \subseteq S$.*

4   PFAF Semantics

In this section, we will explore the consistency of the probabilities of the arguments in a PFAF. We then establish a semantics system that parallels Dung's theory [5].

4.1   Conflict-Free Semantics

Consider arguments B and C in the PFAF of the scenario, and their associated PF-matrices $\mathbb{M}_B$ and $\mathbb{M}_C$. Since $P_{1,C} = 0.2$, there is a 20% chance that it will rain heavily; and since $P_{1,B} = 1$ it is certain (a 100% chance) that Jim will drive around 80 mph. They are obviously in contradiction. Thus we can reach the conclusion that the two arguments with such PF-matrices are conflict with each other.

On the other hand, suppose $\mathbb{M}_B$ is revised to

$$\mathbb{M}'_B = \begin{bmatrix} 1 & 0.2 \\ 0.5 & 0.36 \\ 0 & 0.44 \end{bmatrix}.$$

This matrix means that there are 20%, 36% and 44% chances that Jim drives around 80 mph, 60 mph and 40 mph respectively. From this matrix and argument C, we obtain that there is:

- 20% chance that it rains heavily and Jim drives around 40 mph;
- 30% chance that it rains moderately and Jim drives at 40 mph (24% chance) or 60 mph (6% chance);[2]
- 50% chance that it rains lightly, and Jim drives at 60 mph (30% chance) or 80 mph (20% chance).

Now we can conclude that $(B, \mathbb{M}'_B)$ is no longer conflict with $(C, \mathbb{M}_C)$.

Similarly, in PFAFs if a PF-set S revises $(A, \mathbb{M}_A)$ to $(A, \mathbb{M}'_A)$, S is consistent with $(A, \mathbb{M}'_A)$. This is similar to the conflict-free semantics in AFs.

Definition 7. *In a PFAF* $(\mathbb{A}, Atts)$*, a PF-set* $S \colon Args \to \mathcal{M}$ *is conflict-free, iff for any* $A \in Args$*,* S *revises* $S(A)$ *to itself, i.e.* S *revises* S *to itself.*

Example 3. Consider the PFAF in the scenario. The PF-set S is conflict-free, where S is defined as follows:

$$S(D) = \mathbb{M}_D = \begin{bmatrix} 1 & 0.3 \\ 0.5 & 0.3 \\ 0 & 0.4 \end{bmatrix}, \ S(C) = \mathbb{M}_C = \begin{bmatrix} 1 & 0.2 \\ 0.5 & 0.3 \\ 0 & 0.5 \end{bmatrix},$$

$$S(B) = \mathbb{M}_B = \begin{bmatrix} 1 & 0.2 \\ 0.5 & 0.36 \\ 0 & 0.44 \end{bmatrix}, \ S(A) = \mathbb{M}_A = \begin{bmatrix} 1 & 0.44 \\ 0.5 & 0.36 \\ 0 & 0.2 \end{bmatrix}.$$

Note that from Definition 7, the empty PF-set $\emptyset$ is conflict-free. It seems un-intuitive. For example, in the scenario, the empty PF-set means that $P_{0,B} = 1$ and $P_{0,A} = 1$ hold at the same time. In other words, Jim drives at no more than 40 mph and Jim is late for no more than 10 min. How can these two events happen at the same time? In our opinion, it can be illustrated as follows. If the speed is 80 mph, then Jim is certainly not late very much. But if the speed is not so high, Jim may also not be late very much. For instance, there may be some shortcuts such that Jim can arrive not very late in the speed 40 mph. Therefore, we permit the conflict-free between the two cases, though they are not perfect.

On the other hand, according to the definition of conflict-free sets, the attacks between PF-sets can be classified into two kinds. Here, we introduce the sufficient attacks from a PF-set to an argument with a PF-matrix.

Definition 8. *In a PFAF, let* S *be a PF-set and* A *be an argument with a PF-matrix* $\mathbb{M}$*. Suppose* S *revises* $(A, \mathbb{M})$ *to* $(A, \mathbb{M}')$*. If* $\mathbb{M} > \mathbb{M}'$*, then we say* S *sufficiently attacks* $(A, \mathbb{M})$*.*

Then the conflict-free sets can be represented by the sufficient attacks.

Proposition 4. *Let* S *be a PF-set in a PFAF.* S *is conflict-free, iff* $\forall A \in Args$*,* S *does not sufficiently attack* $(A, S(A))$*.*

Proof. ($\Rightarrow$) Suppose S is conflict-free. Then S revises $S(A)$ to itself, i.e., S does not sufficiently attack $(A, S(A))$.

($\Leftarrow$) Because for all $A \in Args$, S does not sufficiently attack $(A, S(A))$, we have S revises $S(A)$ to $\mathbb{M}'$ such that $\mathbb{M}' \leq S(A)$. Hence, S revises $S(A)$ to itself, i.e., S is conflict-free.

---

[2] The two percentages 24% and 6% show the influence of the road working.

4.2 Acceptability

The acceptability is a core concept in Dung's theory [5]. All the extension-based semantics are built on it. In this paper, our semantics are also established on the acceptability. We first introduce the acceptability in PFAFs.

Consider the PFAF in the scenario. Since the rain and the road working drop Jim's speed down, Jim arrives late. When only the fuzzy degrees or the probabilities are considered, we have:

Fuzziness If the rain is heavier and the road working occupies more lanes, then Jim's speed will be lower. It follows that Jim arrives later.

Probability If the probabilities of the rain and the road working are higher, the probability that Jim drives fast is lower. Then the probabilities that Jim arrive late will be higher.

When both the fuzziness and the randomness are considered together, we will discuss the consistency between the probabilities of the fuzzy statuses of the arguments. For example, if the probability of heavy rain is 20%, the probability of closing two or more lanes is 30%, then the probability that Jim's speed is less than 40 mph is 44%. Consequently, we can get the probability that Jim is late for a long time is 44%. It can be read as that the two probabilities (20% of heavy rain and 30% of closing two or more lanes) defend the probability 44% of Jim's late arrival in some sense. Similarly, because the probability of the light rain is 50% and the probability that the road working has been finished is 40%, there is a 20% chance that Jim will drive around 80 mph and will arrive nearly on time. From the probabilities of statuses of C and D, the probability that Jim drives around 60 mph and arrives late for around 20 min is $1 - 44\% - 20\% = 36\%$. These three can be represented by the PF-matrices:

The arguments C, D with the PF-matrices $\mathbb{M}_C$ and $\mathbb{M}_D$ defend the argument A with a PF-matrix

$$\mathbb{M}_A = \begin{bmatrix} 1 & 0.44 \\ 0.5 & 0.36 \\ 0 & 0.2 \end{bmatrix}$$

by revising the PF-matrix $\mathbb{M}_B$ of B.

Following the above idea, the defence relation in PFAFs can be defined.

Definition 9. *In a PFAF* $(\mathbb{A}, Atts)$, *an argument* A *with a PF-matrix* $\mathbb{M}_A \leq \mathbb{A}(A)$ *is acceptable to a PF-set* $S \subseteq \mathbb{A}$, *iff* $\forall B$ *with* $(B, A) \in Atts$ *and* $\mathbb{M}_B \leq \mathbb{A}(B)$, S *revises* $\mathbb{M}_B$ *to* $\mathbb{M}'_B$, *such that the PF-set* $\{(B, \mathbb{M}'_B) : (B, A) \in Atts\}$ *revises* $\mathbb{M}_A$ *to itself.*

Simply, we say $(A, \mathbb{M}_A)$ *is acceptable to (or defended by)* S.

Note that the function $\mathbb{A}$ shows the initial probabilities of the arguments, which are also the highest probabilities of the arguments. In a semantics, for any argument, the probabilities should not be higher than it. Therefore, in Definition 9, we require that $\mathbb{M}_A \leq \mathbb{A}(A)$, $\mathbb{M}_B \leq \mathbb{A}(B)$ and $S \subseteq \mathbb{A}$.

Because of $\mathbb{M}_B \leq \mathbb{A}(B)$ from the second part of Proposition 2, we have the following proposition.

Proposition 5. *In a PFAF, $(A, \mathbb{M}_A)$ is acceptable to (or defended by) S, iff $\forall B$ with $(B, A) \in Atts$, S revises $\mathbb{A}(B)$ to $\mathbb{M}'_B$, such that the PF-set $\{(B, \mathbb{M}'_B) : (B, A) \in Atts\}$ revises $\mathbb{M}_A$ to itself.*

This proposition help us to calculate the acceptability easily.

Example 4. Consider the conflict-free PF-set S in Example 3. It revises $\mathbb{A}(B)$ to

$$\mathbb{M}'_B = \begin{bmatrix} 1 & 0.2 \\ 0.5 & 0.36 \\ 0 & 0.44 \end{bmatrix}.$$

Because $\mathbb{M}'_B$ revises

$$\mathbb{M}'_A = \begin{bmatrix} 1 & 0.44 \\ 0.5 & 0.36 \\ 0 & 0.2 \end{bmatrix}$$

to itself, S defends $(A, \mathbb{M}'_A)$.

On the other hand, $\mathbb{M}'_B$ revises

$$\mathbb{M}_A = \begin{bmatrix} 1 & 1 \\ 0.5 & 0 \\ 0 & 0 \end{bmatrix} \text{ to } \mathbb{M}'_A = \begin{bmatrix} 1 & 0.44 \\ 0.5 & 0.36 \\ 0 & 0.2 \end{bmatrix}.$$

Hence, S does not defend $(A, \mathbb{M}_A)$.

Example 5. Consider the empty set $\emptyset$ in the PFAF in Example 1. It revises $\mathbb{A}(C)$ and $\mathbb{A}(D)$ to themselves. Because $\{(C, \mathbb{A}(C)), (D, \mathbb{A}(D))\}$ revises

$$\mathbb{M}'_B = \begin{bmatrix} 1 & 0.2 \\ 0.5 & 0.36 \\ 0 & 0.44 \end{bmatrix}$$

to itself, we get that $\emptyset$ defends $(B, \mathbb{M}'_B)$.

But $\emptyset$ does not defend $(A, \mathbb{M}'_A)$, where

$$\mathbb{M}'_A = \begin{bmatrix} 1 & 0.44 \\ 0.5 & 0.36 \\ 0 & 0.2 \end{bmatrix}.$$

Because $\emptyset$ revises $\mathbb{A}(B)$ to itself, which revises $\mathbb{M}'_A$ to $\begin{bmatrix} 1 & 0 \\ 0.5 & 0 \\ 0 & 1 \end{bmatrix}$.

The monotonicity of the acceptability follows obviously from the first part of Proposition 2.

Proposition 6. *Let $S_1 \subseteq S_2$ be two PF-sets in a PFAF. If S_1 defends $(A, \mathbb{M}_A)$, then S_2 defends it.*

Proof. For any B with $(B, A) \in Atts$, suppose S_1 revises $\mathbb{M}_B$ to $\mathbb{M}_{B,1}$ and S_2 revises $\mathbb{M}_{\mathbb{B}}$ to $\mathbb{M}_{B,2}$. Because $S_1 \subseteq S_2$, we have $\mathbb{M}_{B,2} \leq \mathbb{M}_{B,1}$.

Suppose the PF-set $\{(B, \mathbb{M}_{B,2}\colon (B, A) \in Atts\}$ revises $\mathbb{M}_A$ to $\mathbb{M}'_A$. Because the PF-set $\{(B, \mathbb{M}_{B,1}\colon (B, A) \in Atts\}$ revises $\mathbb{M}_A$ to itself, from Proposition 2 we have the $\mathbb{M}_A \leq \mathbb{M}'_A$. Together with $\mathbb{M}'_A \leq \mathbb{M}_A$, we have $\mathbb{M}_A = \mathbb{M}'_A$. It ends the proof.

Given a PFAF $(\mathbb{A}, Atts)$, let $\mathcal{S}$ be the set of all the PF-sets in it, i.e., $\mathcal{S} = \{S \subseteq \mathbb{A} \mid S\colon Args \to \mathcal{M}\}$.

Definition 10. *Let $(\mathbb{A}, Atts)$ be a PFAF. Suppose the function $F\colon \mathcal{S} \to \mathcal{S}$ is defined as follows:*

$$F(S) = \{(A, \mathbb{M}_A) \in \mathbb{A}\colon (A, \mathbb{M}_A) \text{ is defended by } S\}, \ \forall S \in \mathcal{S}.$$

Then F is called the characteristic function of the PFAF.

It follows from proposition 2 that F is monotone.

Proposition 7. *Let F be the characteristic function of a PFAF. Suppose $S_1 \subseteq S_2 \subseteq \mathbb{A}$. Then $F(S_1) \subseteq F(S_2)$.*

4.3   Extension-Based Semantics

In this part, we establish the semantics of PFAFs similar to Dung's extensions.

Definition 11. *In a PFAF $(\mathbb{A}, Atts)$, $S \subseteq \mathbb{A}$ is a conflict-free PF-set. A PF-set S is*

admissible *if it defends itself, i.e., $S \subseteq F(S)$.*
complete *if it defends itself and does not defend any $(A, \mathbb{M}_A)$ with $\mathbb{M}_A > S(A)$, i.e., $F(S) = S$.*
preferred *if it is a maximal admissible PF-set w.r.t. set inclusion.*
grounded *if it is the least complete PF-set.*
stable *if for any $(A, \mathbb{M}_A)$ with $\mathbb{M}_A > S(A)$, S revises $\mathbb{M}_A$ to $S(A)$.*

Example 6. Consider the PFAF in Example 1. The PF-set S is admissible, complete, preferred, grounded and stable.

The empty set $\emptyset$ is admissible. From Example 5, it is not complete. Thus it is not preferred or grounded.

Example 7. Consider the PFAF $(\mathbb{A}, Atts)$, where

$$\mathbb{A}(A) = \begin{bmatrix} 1 & 1 \\ 0.5 & 0 \\ 0 & 0 \end{bmatrix}, \mathbb{A}(B) = \begin{bmatrix} 1 & 1 \\ 0.5 & 0 \\ 0 & 0 \end{bmatrix}$$

and $Atts = \{(A, B), (B, A)\}$. It is the graph $A \rightleftarrows B$.

The grounded extension is the empty PF-set $\emptyset$. It is also complete, but not preferred.

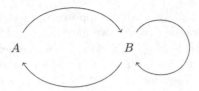

Fig. 2. A simple PFAF

The following four PF-sets are preferred, which are also complete and stable.

$$S_1: S_1(A) = \begin{bmatrix} 1 & 1 \\ 0.5 & 0 \\ 0 & 0 \end{bmatrix} \text{ and } S_1(B) = \begin{bmatrix} 1 & 0 \\ 0.5 & 0 \\ 0 & 1 \end{bmatrix}.$$

$$S_2: S_2(A) = \begin{bmatrix} 1 & 0 \\ 0.5 & 1 \\ 0 & 0 \end{bmatrix} \text{ and } S_2(B) = \begin{bmatrix} 1 & 0 \\ 0.5 & 1 \\ 0 & 0 \end{bmatrix}.$$

$$S_3: S_3(A) = \begin{bmatrix} 1 & 0.7 \\ 0.5 & 0 \\ 0 & 0.3 \end{bmatrix} \text{ and } S_3(B) = \begin{bmatrix} 1 & 0.3 \\ 0.5 & 0 \\ 0 & 0.7 \end{bmatrix}.$$

$$S_4: S_4(A) = \begin{bmatrix} 1 & x \\ 0.5 & 1-x-y \\ 0 & y \end{bmatrix} \text{ and } S_4(B) = \begin{bmatrix} 1 & y \\ 0.5 & 1-x-y \\ 0 & x \end{bmatrix}, \text{ where } x, y \in$$

$[0, 0.5]$.

For these four PF-sets, S_1 is a preferred extension in Dung's theory; S_2 is a preferred extension in PFAFs; S_3 is a special semantics of crisp probabilistic AFs; and S_4 shows the general case of preferred PF-sets in our theory.

Example 8. Consider the PFAF in Fig. 2, where the initial PF-matrix of each argument is

$$\begin{bmatrix} 1 & 1 \\ 0.5 & 0 \\ 0 & 0 \end{bmatrix}.$$

The PF-set S is preferred but not stable, where

$$S(A) = \begin{bmatrix} 1 & 0.75 \\ 0.5 & 0 \\ 0 & 0.25 \end{bmatrix} \text{ and } S(B) = \begin{bmatrix} 1 & 0.2 \\ 0.5 & 0 \\ 0 & 0.8 \end{bmatrix}.$$

Obviously, S is admissible and maximal w.r.t. set inclusion. But S revises

$$\mathbb{M}_A = \begin{bmatrix} 1 & 0.8 \\ 0.5 & 0 \\ 0 & 0.2 \end{bmatrix}$$

to itself, which does not equal to $S(A)$.

5   Related Works

In this section, we compare PFAFs with related works. Dondio [3] introduces multi-valued and probabilistic argumentation frameworks. Our work is motivated by a similar intention to this work, i.e., modelling probabilistic and fuzzy (vague) arguments. But the two works differs significantly. A key difference lies in the use of probabilities. In [3], probabilities are assigned to arguments to represent whether or not (e.g., $P(A)$ and $1 - P(A)$) arguments hold. In our work, probabilities are assigned to the fuzzy statuses of arguments to represent the likelihood of fuzzy statuses, e.g., $P_{1,A}$, $P_{0.5,A}$ and $P_{0,A}$. This leads to different approaches for analysing arguments. In [3], probabilities and fuzzy values (referred to as "multi-valued" in [3]) are used separately. More specifically, arguments are evaluated in a two-layer model. At the first layer, probabilistic analysis is carried out based on the approach in [13] and at the second layer fuzzy analysis is done based on multi-valued argumentation frameworks [3]. In PFAFs, fuzzy values are fixed and we revise probabilities in order to make them coherent with the fuzzy statuses and the AF structure. Based revising probabilities, semantics of PFAFs is defined in an analogue way to Dung's theory.

Probability theory has been used to extend AFs in various forms. Dung and Thang [4] introduce a probabilistic argumentation model designed for jury-based dispute resolution. In this model, a probability distribution over subsets of arguments is used to represent how an individual juror weight the arguments. The model then computes the probability of arguments being in grounded extension as the juror's degree of acceptance of the arguments. The jury's decision is then obtained by certain criteria aggregating all jurors' opinions. The work by Li et al. [13] generalize the idea of [4] and introduce probabilistic argumentation frameworks. In this proposal, probabilities are assigned to arguments and attacks to describe the likelihood that arguments and attacks exist in the AF. The semantics of PrAFs is captured by the notion of probabilistic justification that indicates the likelihood of a set of arguments being accepted under certain AF semantics.

The approach of [13] and [4] uses probabilities to capture uncertain in argumentation. The semantics is based on theories of probability and possible worlds. In PFAFs, probabilities are associated with fuzzy statuses to describe the likelihood of fuzzy statuses. The semantics of PFAFs is based on revising probabilities.

Hunter [8] introduces the epistemic approach to probabilistic argumentation. In this approach, a probability distribution is associated with the set of subgraphs. The probability of an individual argument is obtained by computing the marginal probability. This probability represents the degree of belief one puts in the argument. Hunter then studies a set of postulates that a probability distribution over subgraphs should satisfy in order to be coherent with respect to the structure of the argument graph. For example, a probability distribution is called rational iff for all argument A attacks argument B, if $P(A) > 0.5$, then $P(B) < 0.5$.

It seems that the probabilities associated with arguments in the epistemic approach play a similar role to the fuzzy values in PFAFs, because it is reasonable to read fuzzy values as belief degrees. Probabilities in PFAFs describe the likelihood of different belief degrees. A coherent probability distribution over fuzzy statuses is achieved by revising probabilities.

Regarding fuzzy argumentation, there are two main ways to discuss the fuzzy degrees of the arguments in fuzzy AFs. One is to find algorithms to revise the fuzzy degrees. The works [2,6,7] introduce an equation to revise the fuzzy degrees of the arguments according to the attackers' fuzzy degrees. In order to deal with the degrees of the arguments in cycles, the values are revised step by step, and the limit values are the semantics of the fuzzy AFs. The other is to built extension systems by fuzzy sets. [11] introduces equations such that if a fuzzy set satisfies some equations, it is a corresponding extension. [14] defines conflict-free sets and acceptability by developing the methods in [2,7]. A variety of extension-based semantics are then introduced in Dung's way. The main idea of this paper is similar to [14]. We introduce an algorithm to revise the PF-matrices of the arguments. Based on it, the conflict-free sets and the acceptability are then defined and the extension-based semantics are established in Dung's way. In a PFAF, if for every argument, the probability of one of its three fuzzy status is 1, then the PFAF can be seen as a fuzzy AF in [14] where the fuzzy status are restricted to three cases of all the arguments. In this case, our semantics will coincide with the semantics in [14].

6 Conclusion

In this paper, we discussed the need for the presence of both fuzzyness and randomness in AFs. We introduced PF-matrices and probabilistic-fuzzy argumentation frameworks. We designed an algorithm for revising PF-matrices of arguments in a PFAF. Based on this algorithm, we studied semantics of PFAFs. We showed by examples that PF-matrices and PFAFs are a feasible approach to the goal of allowing for fuzzyness and randomness in AFs. We discussed how PFAFs are related with other works.

This paper contributes on the following aspects: First, a formal definition of PFAFs is introduced based on PF-matrices with finite (three) fuzzy statuses. This forms a basis for the future study of fuzzy and random AFs. Second, the PF-matrices are applied to characterize the semantics of PFAFs. We have shown that PF-matrices are an effective tool for investigating PFAFs. Finally, the semantics of PFAFs is introduced, which provides a theory for analysing fuzzy and random arguments.

Regarding future work, the current work presented in this paper has limitations and weakness. For example, the arguments' fuzzy statuses are discrete and finite; the arguments are assumed to be independent; and when revising an argument's PF-matrix, the PF-matrix of itself is neglected. These all give directions for future work.

Acknowledgements. This work is supported by the National Natural Science Foundation of China (11601288), the Natural Science Foundation of Shandong (ZR2016AQ21). The authors thank the anonymous reviewers for their helpful comments.

References

1. Baroni, P., Caminada, M., Giacomin, M.: An introduction to argumentation semantics. Knowl. Eng. Rev. **26**(04), 365–410 (2011)
2. Da Costa Pereira, C., Tettamanzi, A.G.B., Villata, S.: Changing one's mind: erase or rewind? Possibilistic belief revision with fuzzy argumentation based on trust. In: Proceedings of the Twenty-Second International Joint Conference on Artificial Intelligence, IJCAI 2011, pp. 164–171. AAAI Press (2011)
3. Dondio, P.: Multi-valued and probabilistic argumentation frameworks. In: Proceedings of the 5th International Conference on Computational Models of Argument, pp. 253–260 (2014)
4. Dung, P.M., Thang, P.M.: Towards (probabilistic) argumentation for jury-based dispute resolution. In: Computational Models of Argument, Proceedings of COMMA 2010, pp. 171–182. IOS Press, Amsterdam (2010)
5. Dung, P.: On the acceptability of arguments and its fundamental role in non-monotonic reasoning, logic programming and n-person games. Artif. Intell. **77**(2), 321–357 (1995)
6. Gabbay, D.: Equational approach to argumentation networks. Argum. Comput. **3**(2–3), 87–142 (2012)
7. Gabbay, D.M., Rodrigues, O.: Equilibrium states in numerical argumentation networks. Log. Univers. **9**(4), 411–473 (2015). https://doi.org/10.1007/s11787-015-0119-7
8. Hunter, A.: A probabilistic approach to modelling uncertain logical arguments. Int. J. Approximate Reasoning **54**(1), 47–81 (2013)
9. Hunter, A.: Probabilistic qualification of attack in abstract argumentation. Int. J. Approximate Reasoning **55**(2), 607–638 (2014)
10. Hunter, A., Thimm, M.: Probabilistic reasoning with abstract argumentation frameworks. J. Artif. Intell. Res. **59**, 565–611 (2017)
11. Janssen, J., Cock, M.D., Vermeir, D.: Fuzzy argumentation frameworks. In: Information Processing and Management of Uncertainty in Knowledge-Based Systems, pp. 513–520 (2008)
12. Kaci, S., Labreuche, C.: Argumentation framework with fuzzy preference relations. In: Hüllermeier, E., Kruse, R., Hoffmann, F. (eds.) IPMU 2010. LNCS (LNAI), vol. 6178, pp. 554–563. Springer, Heidelberg (2010). https://doi.org/10.1007/978-3-642-14049-5_57
13. Li, H., Oren, N., Norman, T.J.: Probabilistic argumentation frameworks. In: Modgil, S., Oren, N., Toni, F. (eds.) TAFA 2011. LNCS (LNAI), vol. 7132, pp. 1–16. Springer, Heidelberg (2012). https://doi.org/10.1007/978-3-642-29184-5_1
14. Wu, J., Li, H., Oren, N., Norman, T.: Gödel fuzzy argumentation frameworks. In: Computational Models of Argument: Proceedings of COMMA 2016, vol. 287, p. 447 (2016)

Further Steps Towards a Logic of Polarization in Social Networks

Mina Young Pedersen[3(✉)], Sonja Smets[1,3], and Thomas Ågotnes[2,3]

[1] ILLC, University of Amsterdam, Amsterdam, The Netherlands
S.J.L.Smets@uva.nl
[2] ILI, Southwest University, Chongqing, China
[3] Department of Information Science and Media Studies, University of Bergen,
Bergen, Norway
{mina.pedersen,thomas.agotnes}@uib.no

Abstract. In this paper we look at different ways of modally defining properties related to the concept of balance in signed social networks where relations can be either positive or negative. The motivation is to be able to formally reason about the social phenomenon of group polarization, for which balance theory forms a network-theoretical underpinning. The starting point is a recently developed basic modal logic that axiomatizes the class of social networks that are balanced up to a certain degree. This property is not modally definable but can be captured using a deduction rule. In this paper we examine different possibilities for extending this basic language, in order to, first, be able to define frame properties such as balance and related properties such as non-overlapping positive and negative relations and collective connectedness as axioms, and, second, be able to define the property of *full* balance rather than balanced-up-to-a-degree. We consider extensions with both static modalities such as the universal and the difference modality, the intersection modality, and nominals known from hybrid logic, as well as dynamic global bridge modalities known from sabotage logic. Along the way we provide axioms for weak balance. Finally, to explore measures of how far a network is from polarization, we consider and compare variations of distance measures between models in relation to balance.

Keywords: Polarization · Balance · Social network logic · Modal logic · Network theory

1 Introduction

The way in which we receive and exchange information changes rapidly with the advances of new technology in our current world. Simultaneously we are facing local and global issues that are driving our opinions to the extremes of the political landscape. A social phenomenon related to these trends considered to be increasingly dangerous is *group polarization.*

© Springer Nature Switzerland AG 2020
M. Dastani et al. (Eds.): CLAR 2020, LNAI 12061, pp. 324–345, 2020.
https://doi.org/10.1007/978-3-030-44638-3_20

Group polarization, or polarization for short, is not a new concept but has gained increasing relevance in the age of social media [20]. The phenomenon has been extensively researched by, among others, Cass Sunstein [28,29]. Polarization describes the tendency for people to develop more extreme views after deliberation within a group. Although issues up for debate often are complex and dependent on a number of factors, an effect of polarization is that fine lines are blurred and that answers to complicated questions are driven into opposing parties of either 'for' or 'against'. This applies to juries in court rooms and participants in political discussions, but can also find its way into mundane everyday social settings.

Reasons behind polarization include a combination of peer pressure and the way information exchange is carried out within group settings [29]. One important aspect of this process is that individuals with a weak inclination towards one opinion are likely to be confronted with louder voices expressing a radicalized version of the same opinion. As a result of exposure to new arguments and desire to be part of a community, uncertain agents might leave their insecurities behind and adopt a stronger position.

One purely network-theoretical factor related to polarization phenomena is *balance theory*. Balance theory goes back to the foundation of the field of social network analysis [17], and asserts that certain configurations of connections between friends and enemies in a signed network with positive and negative links, such as a triangle of two positive and one negative relation, are unstable and therefore comparatively rarely observed. Key results in balance theory originating in the works of Harary [17] link this local property of unstable configurations to the global property of a formation of groups of friends who are enemies with everyone else. Group polarization is captured precisely in this global balance property of networks divided into opposing parties.

In this paper we are interested in formal reasoning about polarization and therefore about balance. First steps in this direction have been made: positive and negative relations logic (**PNL**) [31,32] is a basic modal logic that uses two-sorted Kripke frames to model networks where agents can be related positively or negatively, but not both, and is used to axiomatize the class of networks that are balanced (to a certain degree). While **PNL** can be seen as a logical foundation for reasoning about balance, it has two particular downsides. First, balance properties, and related properties such as non-overlapping positive and negative relations and collective connectedness, are not modally definable in the logical language, but can only be captured using a deduction rule. Second, the logic only axiomatises the class of "almost" balanced networks, networks that are balanced up to a degree set by a fixed parameter, and not the class of all fully balanced networks. In this paper we study possible extensions of the basic language of **PNL** in order to increase the expressive power in general and in particular to be able to define the mentioned properties, including full balance, as axioms. Towards this end, we systematically look at several expressive modalities known from the literature, both static modalities such as the universal and the difference modalities, the intersection modality, and nominals known from hybrid logic, and dynamic global bridge modalities known from sabotage modal logic [4]. We focus on the possibility of modal definability of the mentioned properties, as first steps towards possible axiomatisations. In particular, we provide a logical-dynamic characterisation of (full) balance. Along the way we also characterize *weak* balance, which has not been logically characterized before.

We also introduce and evaluate several distance metrics on the class of models, and develop a tool to measure the distance between models which enables us for any network to determine how far it is from being polarized.

The structure of the remainder of the paper is as follows. The following Sect. 2 consists of preliminaries; we present the social concept of balance and polarization as well as the basic **PNL**. In the next Sect. 3 we propose additions to **PNL** in order to define a balance axiom, and show that the logic with these extensions is not compact. Then in Sect. 4 we look at the in **PNL** modally undefinable frame properties: collective connectedness and non-overlapping positive/negative relations. We discuss and compare the inclusion of various known modalities with respect to definability. Section 5 is devoted to measures of distance in terms of balance to analyze how close a network is to polarization. We present three metrics and discuss strengths and weaknesses before using an example for comparison. In the final Sect. 6 we conclude the paper and discuss future directions of the work.

2   Preliminaries: Balance and PNL

We begin by presenting **PNL** which we extend and use in later sections. We also look at structural balance theory and its relation to polarization while studying how this particular logic expresses essential properties of the theory. The section concludes with a discussion of motivations to expand on this framework.

As a well-known concept from the field of social network analysis, balance is defined on *signed* social networks. A signed network is an undirected graph consisting of agents and relations between them, represented as strictly either positive or negative, but not both. For simplification we think of agents as friends if they share a positive edge and as enemies if they are connected by a negative edge.

Positive and negative relations logic (**PNL**) [31,32] models signed networks as two-sorted Kripke frames[1] with a set of possible worlds representing agents and positive '+' and negative '−' binary relations representing friendships and enmities, respectively. See Fig. 1 for an example.

2.1   Syntax and Semantics of PNL

Definition 1 (Syntax of PNL [31]). *Let* At *be a countable set of propositional letters. We define the well-formed formulas of the language* $\mathcal{L}_{PNL}$ *to be generated by the following grammar:*

$$\phi ::= p \mid \neg\phi \mid (\phi \wedge \phi) \mid \oplus\phi \mid \ominus\phi$$

---

[1] We will assume some familiarity with Kripke semantics for modal logic; see, e.g., [5].

where $p \in$ At. We define propositional connectives like $\lor, \rightarrow$ and the formulas $\top, \bot$ as usual. Further, we define the duals as standard $\boxplus := \neg \diamondsuit \neg$ and $\boxminus := \neg \diamondsuit \neg$.

To rightfully depict relations R^+ and R^- as edges in a signed graph, both relations are symmetric as signed graphs are undirected. R^+ is reflexive, demanding agents to have a positive relation to themselves. Moreover, relations are *non-overlapping* [31,32]: no two agents can be related by both a positive and negative relation. Some networks, but not all, are *collectively connected*: all agents in the graph or subgraph that constitutes the network under consideration, are related, either positively or negatively. Formal definitions of non-overlapping and collective connectedness follow.

Definition 2 (Non-overlapping and Collective Connectedness). *Let A be a non-empty set of agents and R^+ and R^- be two binary relations on A. We define the following properties of R^+ and R^-:*

- *R^+ and R^- are **non-overlapping** iff $\forall a, b \in A : (a,b) \notin R^+$ or $(a,b) \notin R^-$.*
- *R^+ and R^- are **collectively connected** iff $\forall a, b \in A : aR^+b$ or aR^-b.*

We can now define signed frames and models, and the semantics of **PNL**.

Definition 3 (Signed Frame and Model [31]). *Let A be a non-empty set of agents and R^+ and R^- be two symmetric and non-overlapping binary relations on A where R^+ is reflexive. Further, let $V :$ At $\rightarrow \wp(A)$ be a valuation function. A **signed model** is a tuple $\mathbb{M} = \langle A, R^+, R^-, V \rangle$. We define a **pointed signed model** $(\mathbb{M}, a)$ where $\mathbb{M}$ is a signed model and $a \in A$ its distinguished point, at which evaluation takes place.*

*We call a signed model without valuation $\mathbb{F} = \langle A, R^+, R^- \rangle$ a **signed frame**.*

Definition 4 (Semantics of PNL [31]). *Let $\mathbb{M}$ be a signed model and a an agent in A. We define the truth conditions for **PNL** as follows:*

$$\mathbb{M}, a \Vdash p \ \textit{iff} \ a \in V(p)$$
$$\mathbb{M}, a \Vdash \neg \phi \ \textit{iff} \ \mathbb{M}, a \nVdash \phi$$
$$\mathbb{M}, a \Vdash \phi \land \psi \ \textit{iff} \ \mathbb{M}, a \Vdash \phi \ \textit{and} \ \mathbb{M}, a \Vdash \psi$$
$$\mathbb{M}, a \Vdash \diamondsuit\phi \ \textit{iff} \ \exists b \in A \ \textit{such that} \ aR^+b \ \textit{and} \ \mathbb{M}, b \Vdash \phi$$
$$\mathbb{M}, a \Vdash \diamondsuit\phi \ \textit{iff} \ \exists b \in A \ \textit{such that} \ aR^-b \ \textit{and} \ \mathbb{M}, b \Vdash \phi$$

For a signed frame $\mathbb{F}$ and a formula $\phi \in \mathcal{L}_{PNL}$, we write $\mathbb{F} \Vdash \phi$ when ϕ is valid in $\mathbb{F}$: if ϕ is valid at every agent in $\mathbb{F}$.

Intuitively, we read $\diamondsuit\phi$ to hold at an agent if and only if the current agent is positively related to an agent where ϕ is true. Similarly, we read $\diamondsuit\phi$ to hold at an agent if and only if the current agent is related negatively to an agent where ϕ holds.

2.2   The Balance Theorem: Polarized Networks

Structural balance, referred to as balance for short, originates from theories in social psychology [19], and also carries empirical support (in e.g. [22]). We first define balance on a collectively connected network. A collectively connected network with the balance property consists of triangles with either all positive edges, or two negative edges and one positive edge. These triangles correspond to the sociology-psychological motivation that "the enemy of my enemy is my friend" and similarly "the friend of my enemy is my enemy" and "the friend of my friend is my friend". The last tendency has also been characterized as triadic closure in social networks [16] and has been formalized in a logical framework in [25]. We formally define balance on collectively connected signed frames as *local balance*.

Definition 5 (Local Balance [32]). *A signed frame* $\mathbb{F} = \langle A, R^+, R^- \rangle$ *has the* **local balance** *property iff* $\forall a, b, c \in A$:

- *if* aR^+b *and* bR^+c, *or* aR^-b *and* bR^-c, *then* aR^+c, *and*
- *if* aR^+b *and* bR^-c, *or* aR^-b *and* bR^+c, *then* aR^-c.

We note that a network can have the local balance property without being collectively connected: it can have single disconnected agents or consist of disconnected subgraphs each of which are collectively connected.

The Balance Theorem, proved by Harary in 1953 [17] shows an equivalence on collectively connected networks between the local property of sets of three agents and a global property of the network in its entirety: that all agents can be divided into two groups where agents within groups are friends and agents across groups are enemies.

The general version of the Balance Theorem defined on general signed networks as discussed in [13] states the following equivalence: a signed network can be divided into two opposing groups if and only if it is possible to "fill in the missing edges" to construct a collectively connected signed frame with the local balance property. See the signed frame $\mathbb{F}$ in Fig. 1 for an example. For simplicity, we have omitted positive reflexive arrows. Here we can divide agents into the two sets $X = \{a, c\}$ and $Y = \{b, d\}$ where within the sets, agents are friends, and, if related, enemies towards members of the other set. Note that we can "fill in" a negative relation between c and d such that the signed frame has the local balance property.

The characterization of balance does not end here: a signed frame is balanced if and only if there are no *simple cycles* with an odd number of negative edges [8]. We refer to these cycles as *negative cycles*. A simple cycle, often just called a *cycle*, is defined in graph theory as a path of nodes and at least three edges, in which the first and last nodes are the same and visited exactly twice [13]. Otherwise all nodes are distinct. Examples of cycles in Fig. 1 are $aR^-bR^-cR^+a$ and $aR^-bR^+dR^-a$. We note in agreement with the Balance Theorem that the cycles are not negative. The general Balance Theorem is summarized below.

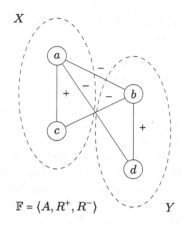

Fig. 1. Division of agents in A into sets X and Y.

Theorem 1 (The Balance Theorem). *Let* $\mathbb{F} = \langle A, R^+, R^- \rangle$ *be a signed frame.* $\mathbb{F}$ *has the **balance** property iff it satisfies the following equivalent properties:*

1. *There exists a collectively connected signed frame* $\mathbb{F}' = \langle A', R^{+'}, R^{-'} \rangle$ *such that* $A = A'$, $R^+ \subseteq R^{+'}$ *and* $R^- \subseteq R^{-'}$ *that has the local balance property;*
2. *There exists a set of agents* $S \subseteq A$ *such that* $\forall a, b \in A$:
    - *if* aR^+b, *then* $a, b \in S$ *or* $a, b \in A \setminus S$, *and*
    - *if* aR^-b, *then* $a \in S$ *and* $b \in A \setminus S$, *or* $a \in A \setminus S$ *and* $b \in A$;
3. *There are no negative cycles in* $\mathbb{F}$.

The resemblance between balance and polarization is captured in the global definition of balance. A balanced signed frame can be divided into two opposing groups, just as in a polarized social setting. A balanced network is a polarized one. However, it is important that we specify that this interpretation of polarization is not a general definition; we are looking specifically at signed networks of positive and negative relations constructed on certain properties like symmetry and non-overlapping. Still, we also note that to speak of polarization one must assume some positive and negative attitudes. Signed networks turn out to provide a useful foundation for analyzing a simplification of personal and collective opinion, and of polarization in particular. Analogies between balance and polarization is not novel in this paper, and can be found in literature such as [6,10,30]. We will therefore use the terms balance and polarization interchangeably in what follows.

2.3   Weak Balance: More than Two Extremes

Before we turn to examine the axiomatization of **PNL**, we briefly introduce the notion of *weak balance*, first proposed by Davis in 1967 [10]. Weakly locally balanced frames are supersets of locally balanced frames that disallow only one type of triangle: with two positive edges and one negative edge.

Definition 6 (Weak Local Balance). *A signed frame* $\mathbb{F} = \langle A, R^+, R^- \rangle$ *has the **weak local balance** property iff* $\forall a, b, c \in A$:

- *if* aR^+b *and* bR^+c, *then* aR^+c, *and*
- *if* aR^+b *and* bR^-c, *or* aR^-b *and* bR^+c, *then* aR^-c.

Davis [10] proved a similar Balance Theorem for weak balance, although in this case the global property of weak balance characterizes the possibility of dividing agents into not just two, but any number of sets of 'friends'. Weakly balanced signed frames are polarized with respect to a collection of groups, where relations within each group are positive and all relations between agents in different groups are negative. Analogous to (strong) balance, a weakly balanced signed frame also has a cycle property: it cannot contain a simple cycle with only *one* negative edge. We state the Weak Balance Theorem as follows.

Theorem 2 (Weak Balance Theorem). *Let* $\mathbb{F} = \langle A, R^+, R^- \rangle$ *be a signed frame.* $\mathbb{F}$ *has the **weak balance** property iff it satisfies the following equivalent properties:*

1. *There exists a collectively connected signed frame* $\mathbb{F}' = \langle A', R^{+'}, R^{-'} \rangle$ *such that* $A = A'$, $R^+ \subseteq R^{+'}$ *and* $R^- \subseteq R^{-'}$ *that has the weak local balance property;*
2. $\exists S_1, \ldots, S_n \subseteq A$ *for* $n \in \mathbb{N}$ *such that* $\forall a, b \in A$:
   - *if* aR^+b, *then* $a, b \in S_m$ *for some* m, *and*
   - *if* aR^-b, *then* $a \in S_s$ *and* $b \in S_t$ *for some* $s \neq t$;
3. *There are no cycles with exactly one negative edge in* $\mathbb{F}$.

Studies, such as [21], have found strong balance to be too restrictive as a common property of real-world social networks and propose weak balance as a more likely alternative. In the literature on **PNL**, weak balance is only mentioned in passing and not included in the formalization. We keep both definitions as they serve different purposes. A network of football fans might converge to a weakly balanced graph structure where supporters of the same team agree and disagree with supporters from other teams in plural. In the context of particular political issues, like Brexit or anti-vaccination, the same network could converge to a strongly polarized network in camps of 'yes' and 'no'. Depending on the social context and research goal, both balance definitions are valuable in their own respect.

2.4   Axiomatization

It is important to first note that balance, non-overlapping and collective connectedness are all undefinable in the language of **PNL**. Balance (up to a degree n) and non-overlapping are defined in the axiomatization given in [32] with a rule, not an axiom, and there is no axiomatization for full balance. In later sections we discuss possible extensions to the language of **PNL** to define these properties with axioms.

As shown in [32], local balance is definable by the following axiom **4B**.

$$((\blacklozenge\blacklozenge p \vee \lozenge\lozenge p) \to \blacklozenge p) \wedge ((\blacklozenge\lozenge p \vee \lozenge\blacklozenge p) \to \lozenge p) \qquad (4B)$$

Lemma 1 ([32]). *For any signed frame* $\mathbb{F}$, $\mathbb{F} \Vdash$ *4B iff* $\mathbb{F}$ *has the local balance property.*

Recall that local balance is the balance property relevant for collectively connected signed frames, where we assume that all agents are related to one another. For this reason, the **4B**-axiom is not included in the axiomatic system for **PNL**.

By modifying the **4B**-axiom to adapt to the local weak balance conditions, we get the **4W**-axiom with the corresponding lemma, novel in this paper.

$$(\blacklozenge\blacklozenge p \to \blacklozenge p) \wedge ((\blacklozenge\lozenge p \vee \lozenge\blacklozenge p) \to \lozenge p) \qquad (4W)$$

Lemma 2. *For any signed frame* $\mathbb{F}$, $\mathbb{F} \Vdash$ *4W iff* $\mathbb{F}$ *has the weak local balance property.*

Proof. ($\Rightarrow$) Proof by contraposition. Let $\mathbb{F} = \langle A, R^+, R^-\rangle$ be a signed frame without the weak local balance property. Then, without loss of generality $\exists a, b, c \in A$ such that aR^+b, bR^+c and aR^-c. Now, let V be a valuation on $\mathbb{F}$ such that $V(p) = \{c\}$. It follows that $\langle\mathbb{F}, V\rangle, a \Vdash \blacklozenge\blacklozenge p$. However, by the non-overlapping property, we have that $(a, c) \notin R^+$. Thus $\langle\mathbb{F}, V\rangle, a \nVdash \blacklozenge p$. We have that $\langle\mathbb{F}, V\rangle, a \nVdash \blacklozenge\blacklozenge p \to \blacklozenge p$ and hence $\mathbb{F} \nVdash$ **4W**.

($\Leftarrow$) Let $\mathbb{F} = \langle A, R^+, R^-\rangle$ be a signed frame with the weak local balance property and fix an arbitrary valuation V and $a \in A$. Assume that $\langle\mathbb{F}, V\rangle, a \Vdash \blacklozenge\blacklozenge p$. Then $\exists b \in A$ such that aR^+b and $\langle\mathbb{F}, V\rangle, b \Vdash \blacklozenge p$. Thus it follows that $\exists c \in A$ such that bR^+c and $\langle\mathbb{F}, V\rangle, c \Vdash p$. By the weak local balance property aR^+c and hence $\langle\mathbb{F}, V\rangle, a \Vdash \blacklozenge\blacklozenge p \to \blacklozenge p$. Now assume that $\langle\mathbb{F}, V\rangle, a \Vdash \blacklozenge\lozenge p$. Then $\exists b, c \in A$ such that aR^+b and bR^-c where $\langle\mathbb{F}, V\rangle, c \Vdash p$. The weak local balance property of $\mathbb{F}$ demand aR^-c and therefore $\langle\mathbb{F}, V\rangle, a \Vdash \lozenge p$. By similar reasoning $\langle\mathbb{F}, V\rangle, a \Vdash \lozenge p$ if we assume $\langle\mathbb{F}, V\rangle, a \Vdash \lozenge\blacklozenge p$. Hence it follows that $\langle\mathbb{F}, V\rangle, a \Vdash (\blacklozenge\blacklozenge p \to \blacklozenge p) \wedge ((\blacklozenge\lozenge p \vee \lozenge\blacklozenge p) \to \lozenge p)$ and as we fixed an arbitrary V and $a \in A$ we conclude that $\mathbb{F} \Vdash$ **4W**. $\square$

In [32], the axiomatic system called $\mathbf{pnl}_n$ over the language $\mathcal{L}_{PNL}$ is introduced for each $n \in \mathbb{N}^+$.[2] The number represents balance up to the *degree* n: that there are no negative cycles of length less than or equal to n. [32] proves that $\mathbf{pnl}_n$ is sound and weakly complete with respect to the class of n-balanced models. This gives us an axiomatization of n-balance, not of balance in the general sense. Included in the axiomatization as the only component dependent on n is an inference rule called $\mathbf{Nb}_n$. As this rule requires an extensive presentation of concepts with details outside the scope of this paper, we refer to the original literature in [32] or to the presentation of **PNL** in [24].

---

[2] We denote $\mathbb{N} \setminus \{0\}$ as $\mathbb{N}^+$.

We conclude this preliminary section with a short recap of the essential properties of **PNL** and the motivations leading us to expand on this framework. **PNL** is a two-sorted modal logic developed to analyze the concept of balance in social networks. A full axiomatic system is given, but there is no formula in $\mathcal{L}_{PNL}$ that defines the frame property of being balanced for all signed frames; balance is captured by a rule, not an axiom. Additionally, this rule only defines n-balance, not general balance. Furthermore, the non-overlapping property, i.e., that no two agents can be both positively and negatively related, is similarly not modally definable in **PNL** and also captured by the $\mathbf{Nb}_n$-rule. Local balance is the balance property on signed frames that are collectively connected: where all agents have a relation to each other. Signed frames with single disconnected points or a set of collectively connected frames disconnected to one another can also have the local balance property. Local balance is characterized with the **4B**-axiom, whereas collective connectedness is modally undefinable. We extend the formal landscape by taking weak balance into account and define the **4W**-axiom. Motivated by the undefinability of the properties mentioned above, in the next sections we explore additions to the language of **PNL** such that they become definable.

3   Speaking of Balance

In this section we introduce a universal operator and dynamic modalities for global link addition to define a dynamic characterization of balance. We also show that this extended fragment of **PNL** is non-compact.

3.1   A Balance Axiom

Recall that the only formula we have in **PNL** to define balance on a signed frame is axiom **4B** defining the local balance property. To begin to resolve the issue of defining balance, we introduce the standard global modality $[A]$ and global link-adding modalities $\langle \mathcal{M}+ \rangle$ and $\langle \mathcal{M}- \rangle$. The global link-adding modalities take inspiration from sabotage modal logic [4] and bridge operators found in literature such as [3]. The semantics of these modalities is presented below.

Definition 7 (Semantics of Global Addition Modalities). *Let* $\mathbb{M} = \langle A, R^+, R^-, V \rangle$ *be a signed model and* $a \in A$. *We define truth conditions for the new modalities as follows:*

$$\mathbb{M}, a \Vdash [A]\phi \text{ iff } \forall b \in A : \mathbb{M}, b \Vdash \phi$$

$$\mathbb{M}, a \Vdash \langle \mathcal{M}+ \rangle \phi \text{ iff } \exists b, c \in A \text{ such that } b, c \notin R^- \text{ and}$$
$$\langle A, R^+ \cup \{(b,c),(c,b)\}, R^-, V \rangle, a \Vdash \phi$$

$$\mathbb{M}, a \Vdash \langle \mathcal{M}- \rangle \phi \text{ iff } \exists b, c \in A \text{ such that } b, c \notin R^+ \text{ and}$$
$$\langle A, R^+, R^- \cup \{(b,c),(c,b)\}, V \rangle, a \Vdash \phi$$

Intuitively, the formula $[A]\phi$ states that ϕ is true at all agents in the network. $\langle \mathbb{M}+\rangle \phi$ is forced at an agent if and only if ϕ is true at the current agent after adding a positive link somewhere in the network. Similarly in the negative sense for $\langle \mathbb{M}-\rangle \phi$.

We also include *choice* and *iteration* modalities inspired by known dynamic logics such as propositional dynamic logic (PDL) [5]. We accommodate them to the global link-adding modalities of our language and define them accordingly.

Definition 8 (Semantics of Choice and Iteration Modalities). *Let* $\mathbb{M} = \langle A, R^+, R^-, V \rangle$ *be a signed model and* $a \in A$. *We define truth conditions for the global addition choice and iteration modalities as follows:*

$$\mathbb{M}, a \Vdash \langle \mathbb{M}+\cup \mathbb{M}-\rangle \phi \text{ iff } \langle \mathbb{M}+\rangle \phi \text{ or } \langle \mathbb{M}-\rangle \phi$$

$$\mathbb{M}, a \Vdash \langle (\mathbb{M}+\cup \mathbb{M}-)*\rangle \phi \text{ iff } \exists n \geq 0 \text{ such that}$$

$$\mathbb{M}, a \Vdash \underbrace{\langle \mathbb{M}+\cup \mathbb{M}-\rangle \cdots \langle \mathbb{M}+\cup \mathbb{M}-\rangle}_{n} \phi$$

$\langle \mathbb{M}+\cup \mathbb{M}-\rangle \phi$ is true at an agent if and only if ϕ is true at the current agent after adding a positive or negative link somewhere in the network. We read the iterated modality as $\langle (\mathbb{M}+\cup \mathbb{M}-)*\rangle \phi$ true at an agent if and only if ϕ holds at the current agent after adding a finite number of positive or negative edges to the signed frame. With the newly defined modalities we present the axiom $\mathbf{B}_G$.

$$\langle (\mathbb{M}+\cup \mathbb{M}-)*\rangle [A]\mathbf{4B} \tag{$\mathbf{B}_G$}$$

To show that $\mathbf{B}_G$ defines balance, we need Corollary 1 of the Balance Theorem.

Corollary 1. *A locally balanced signed frame* $\mathbb{F} = \langle A, R^+, R^- \rangle$ *is balanced.*

When a signed frame $\mathbb{F}$ is locally balanced *and* collectively connected, Corollary 1 is one direction of the Balance Theorem. As mentioned, a frame can however have the local balance property while not being collectively connected. It might consist of groups (subgraphs) each of which are collectively connected, but not related to each other. Yet, this locally balanced signed frame will still be generally balanced. By the Balance Theorem, every disconnected component of the frame will have the cyclic balance property. Having them together in the same frame will not affect this cyclicness. Hence, the corollary follows directly from the Balance Theorem. We now present the subsequent lemma.

Lemma 3. *For any finite signed frame* $\mathbb{F}$, $\mathbb{F} \Vdash \mathbf{B}_G$ *iff* $\mathbb{F}$ *has the balance property.*

Proof. ($\Rightarrow$) Let $\mathbb{F} = \langle A, R^+, R^- \rangle$ be a finite signed frame such that $\mathbb{F} \Vdash \mathbf{B}_G$. Let V be an arbitrary valuation on $\mathbb{F}$ and let $\mathbb{M} = \langle \mathbb{F}, V \rangle$. Let $a \in A$. We have that $\mathbb{M}, a \Vdash \mathbf{B}_G$. Then there exists $b_1, \ldots, b_j \in A$ such that $\langle A, R^+ \cup \{(b_m, b_n), \ldots\}, R^- \cup \{(b_s, b_t), \ldots\}, V \rangle \Vdash [A]\mathbf{4B}$. For simplicity, call

$\langle A, R^+ \cup \{(b_m, b_n), \dots\}, R^- \cup \{(b_s, b_t), \dots\}\rangle = \mathbb{F}'$ and $\langle \mathbb{F}', V\rangle = \mathbb{M}'$. We now have that $\forall b \in A$, $\mathbb{M}', b \Vdash \mathbf{4B}$. Since we fixed an arbitrary valuation V, it follows that $\mathbb{F}' \Vdash \mathbf{4B}$. By Lemma 1 we have that $\mathbb{F}'$ has the local balance property. By Corollary 1, $\mathbb{F}'$ is balanced and thus by the Balance Theorem 1 there exists a collectively connected frame $\mathbb{F}'' = \langle A'', R^{+''}, R^{-''}\rangle$ with the local balance property such that $A'' = A'$, $R^{+'} \subseteq R^{+''}$ and $R^{-'} \subseteq R^{-''}$. Since $\mathbb{F} \subseteq \mathbb{F}' \subseteq \mathbb{F}''$ it follows that $\mathbb{F} \subseteq \mathbb{F}''$ and hence again by the Balance Theorem, $\mathbb{F}$ has the balance property.

($\Leftarrow$) Let $\mathbb{F} = \langle A, R^+, R^-\rangle$ be a finite signed frame with the balance property. Then by the Balance Theorem 1 there exists a collectively connected frame $\mathbb{F}' = \langle A', R^{+'}, R^{-'}\rangle$ such that $A = A'$, $R^+ \subseteq R^{+'}$ and $R^- \subseteq R^{-'}$ that has the local balance property. It follows from Lemma 1 that $\mathbb{F}' \Vdash \mathbf{4B}$. Fix an arbitrary valuation V and an arbitrary $a \in A$. It follows that $\langle \mathbb{F}', V\rangle, a \Vdash [A]\mathbf{4B}$. Since $A = A'$, $R^+ \subseteq R^{+'}$ and $R^- \subseteq R^{-'}$, it follows directly that $\langle \mathbb{F}, V\rangle, a \Vdash \langle (\mathbb{M}+ \cup \mathbb{M}-)*\rangle[A]\mathbf{4B}$. As we chose an arbitrary V and $a \in A$, we conclude that $\mathbb{F} \Vdash \mathbf{B}_G$.   □

The $\mathbf{B}_G$ formula holds at any agent in the network if and only if axiom $\mathbf{4B}$ will be forced at all agents after adding a finite number of positive and negative edges anywhere in the signed frame. This is essentially characterizing the Balance Theorem: the formula holds at an agent in a signed frame $\mathbb{F}$ if and only if there exists a superframe of $\mathbb{F}$ where the local balance property holds.

It follows directly that we have the analogous $\mathbf{B}_W$-axiom relative to weak balance with a lemma proved similarly as in the case of Lemma 3.

$$\langle (\mathbb{M}+ \cup \mathbb{M}-)*\rangle[A]\mathbf{4W} \tag{$\mathbf{B}_W$}$$

Lemma 4. *For any signed frame $\mathbb{F}$, $\mathbb{F} \Vdash \mathbf{B}_W$ iff $\mathbb{F}$ has the weak balance property.*

3.2 Non-compactness

Logics with iteration modalities such as common knowledge [15] or iteration in PDL [5], are often not *compact*. Non-compactness is a consequence of the interaction of the iteration modalities and the other modalities, and it is not completely obvious that the extended logic with the iteration modality introduced above is not compact. However, we show that it is not. As a counter example to compactness, consider the following theory, where $\mathcal{S}^*$ denotes the set of finite strings of symbols from the set $\mathcal{S}$ (so $\{\langle \mathbb{M}+\rangle, \langle \mathbb{M}-\rangle\}^*$ below denotes the set of all sequences of the $\langle \mathbb{M}+\rangle$ and $\langle \mathbb{M}-\rangle$ modalities; e.g, $\langle \mathbb{M}+\rangle\langle \mathbb{M}-\rangle\langle \mathbb{M}-\rangle$):

$$\Gamma = \{\langle (\mathbb{M}+ \cup \mathbb{M}-)*\rangle \boxminus \Diamond p, \neg X \boxminus \Diamond p : X \in \{\langle \mathbb{M}+\rangle, \langle \mathbb{M}-\rangle\}^*\}$$

Γ is not satisfiable (there is no pointed signed model that satisfies all formulas in Γ): if $\mathbb{M}, a \Vdash \langle (\mathbb{M}+ \cup \mathbb{M}-)*\rangle \boxminus \Diamond p$ then there is some n such that $\mathbb{M}, a \Vdash \langle \mathbb{M}+ \cup \mathbb{M}-\rangle^n \boxminus \Diamond p$, which by the semantics means that $\mathbb{M}, a \Vdash X \boxminus \Diamond p$ for some $X \in \{\langle \mathbb{M}+\rangle, \langle \mathbb{M}-\rangle\}$ with $|X| = n$, which is a contradiction.

However, every finite subset Γ' of Γ is satisfiable. First, observe that if Γ' does not contain $\langle(\mathbb{M}+\cup\mathbb{M}-)*\rangle\boxminus\diamondsuit p$ it is trivially satisfiable (say, by two connected points where p is false in both). Second, assume that $\langle(\mathbb{M}+\cup\mathbb{M}-)*\rangle\boxminus\diamondsuit p \in \Gamma'$ and let $m \geq 0$ be the largest m such that there is a $X \in \{\langle\mathbb{M}+\rangle, \langle\mathbb{M}-\rangle\}^*$ with $|X| = m$ and $\neg X\boxminus\diamondsuit p \in \Gamma'$. Let $\mathbb{M}$ be the model in Fig. 2. We see that $\mathbb{M}, a \Vdash \neg Y\boxminus\diamondsuit p$ for any $Y \in \{\langle\mathbb{M}+\rangle, \langle\mathbb{M}-\rangle\}^*$ with $|Y| \leq m$; all $m+1$ dotted edges need to be added for $\boxminus\diamondsuit p$ to be true in a – which is exactly why $\mathbb{M}, a \Vdash \langle(\mathbb{M}+\cup\mathbb{M}-)*\rangle\boxminus\diamondsuit p$ as well.

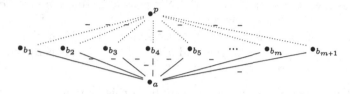

Fig. 2. Model $\mathbb{M}$, consisting of all points and the solid edges. The dotted edges are the potential edges that if added make $\boxminus\diamondsuit p$ true in a. All edges are symmetric. Positive reflexive loops omitted.

Consequently, the logic with the iteration modality is not strongly axiomatizable.

4   Collective Connectedness and Non-overlapping

We proceed with a discussion of additions to $\mathcal{L}_{PNL}$ to define collective connectedness and non-overlapping. We show that collective connectedness can be defined by the inclusion of the universal modality introduced in the previous section. We present nominals, an intersection modality and a difference operator as possible candidates for extensions guaranteeing an axiom for non-overlapping, where the latter also gives us a collective connectedness axiom without the universal modality.

4.1   Universal Modality

Recall that the collective connectedness property is modally undefinable in **PNL**. By adding the global modality $[A]$ we get the axiom **C** for collective connectedness.

$$(\boxplus p \to [A]p) \vee (\boxminus p \to [A]p) \tag{C}$$

Lemma 5. *For any signed frame* $\mathbb{F}$, $\mathbb{F} \Vdash C$ *iff* $\mathbb{F}$ *satisfies collective connectedness.*

Proof. ($\Rightarrow$) Let $\mathbb{F} = \langle A, R^+, R^- \rangle$ be a signed frame and $\mathbb{F} \Vdash (\boxplus p \to [A]p) \vee (\boxminus p \to [A]p)$. Fix $a \in A$ arbitrarily. For any $V : \langle \mathbb{F}, V \rangle, a \Vdash (\boxplus p \to [A]p) \vee (\boxminus p \to [A]p)$. Then $\langle \mathbb{F}, V \rangle, a \Vdash \boxplus p \to [A]p$ or $\langle \mathbb{F}, V \rangle, a \Vdash \boxminus p \to [A]p$. Let $V(p) = \{b \mid aR^+b \text{ or } aR^-b\}$. Fix $c \in A$ arbitrarily. We want to prove that $\langle \mathbb{F}, V \rangle, c \Vdash p$. Assume that $\langle \mathbb{F}, V \rangle, a \Vdash \boxplus p \to [A]p$. By V, we have $\langle \mathbb{F}, V \rangle, a \Vdash \boxplus p$ and thus $\langle \mathbb{F}, V \rangle, a \Vdash [A]p$. Therefore $\langle \mathbb{F}, V \rangle, c \Vdash p$. Similarly for the case where $\langle \mathbb{F}, V \rangle, a \Vdash \boxminus p \to [A]p$. Since we fixed $a, c \in A$ arbitrarily, we conclude that $\mathbb{F}$ is collectively connected.

($\Leftarrow$) Let $\mathbb{F} = \langle A, R^+, R^- \rangle$ be a signed frame with the collective connectedness property. Then $\forall a, b \in A : aR^+b$ or aR^-b. Suppose for reduction that $\exists a \in A$ and V such that $\langle \mathbb{F}, V \rangle, a \nVdash (\boxplus p \to [A]p) \vee (\boxminus p \to [A]p)$. Then $\langle \mathbb{F}, V \rangle, a \Vdash \neg(\boxplus p \to [A]p) \wedge \neg(\boxminus p \to [A]p)$. Thus $\langle \mathbb{F}, V \rangle, a \Vdash (\boxplus p \wedge \boxminus p) \wedge \neg[A]p$. Then $\exists b \in A$ such that $\langle \mathbb{F}, V \rangle, b \nVdash p$. As $\langle \mathbb{F}, V \rangle, a \Vdash \boxplus p \wedge \boxminus p$ and aR^+b or aR^-b, this is a contradiction. Hence $\mathbb{F} \Vdash (\boxplus p \to [A]p) \vee (\boxminus p \to [A]p)$. $\square$

The following corollaries follow directly from this lemma.

Corollary 2. *For any signed frame $\mathbb{F}$, $\mathbb{F} \Vdash 4B + C$ iff $\mathbb{F}$ is locally balanced and has the collective connectedness property.*

Corollary 3. *For any signed frame $\mathbb{F} = \langle A, R^+, R^- \rangle$, $\mathbb{F} \Vdash B_G$ iff $\exists \mathbb{F}' = \langle A', R^{+'}, R^{-'} \rangle$ such that $A = A'$, $R^+ \subseteq R^{+'}$, $R^- \subseteq R^{-'}$ and $\mathbb{F}' \Vdash 4B + C$.*

4.2 Nominals

One possibility is to add nominals in the hybrid tradition. We keep the formal discussion of nominals rather brief and suggest that the reader turns to [2] for further details. Nominals are a set of propositional variables where output of the valuation function is a singleton: any nominal can only be true at exactly one world. In practice, this lets us assign a *name* to individual agents in the network.

We extend the set of propositional variables to be the union of two sets At and Nom with an empty intersection. At is the set of propositional atoms, whereas Nom is the set of nominals. We also modify our valuation function and call it V_H such that $V_H : \text{At} \cup \text{Nom} \to \wp(A)$ satisfies the property: for all $i \in \text{Nom}$, $|V_H(i)| = 1$. We denote members of $\text{At} = \{p, q, r, \dots\}$ and $\text{Nom} = \{i, j, k, \dots\}$. Satisfaction of nominals in a signed model with nominals $\mathbb{M} = \langle A, R^+, R^-, V_H \rangle$ and $a \in A$ is defined as with propositional variables:

$$\mathbb{M}, a \Vdash i \text{ iff } a \in V_H(i)$$

We call the language of **PNL** including nominals $\mathcal{L}_{PNL_i}$ and present the nominal axiom for non-overlapping $\mathbf{N}_H$ with a matching lemma.

$$i \to \boxminus(\diamondsuit i \to i) \tag{$\mathbf{N}_H$}$$

Since we defined signed frames as already having the non-overlapping property, we define *general frames* and *general models* to be signed frames and models without any restrictions on the binary relations R^+ and R^-.

Definition 9 (General Frame and Model). *Let A be a non-empty set of agents and R^+ and R^- be two binary relations on A. Further, let $V : \mathsf{At} \to \wp(A)$ be a valuation function. A **general model** is a tuple $\mathbb{M} = \langle A, R^+, R^-, V \rangle$.*

*We call a general model without valuation $\mathbb{F} = \langle A, R^+, R^- \rangle$ a **general frame**.*

Lemma 6. *For any symmetric general frame $\mathbb{F} = \langle A, R^+, R^- \rangle$ of $\mathcal{L}_{PNL_i}$, $\mathbb{F} \Vdash N_H$ iff $\mathbb{F}$ has the non-overlapping property.*

Proof. ($\Rightarrow$) Proof by contraposition. Let $\mathbb{F} = \langle A, R^+, R^- \rangle$ be a symmetric general frame without the non-overlapping property. Then $\exists a, b \in A$ such that aR^+b and aR^-b. Let $V_H(i) = \{a\}$ be a valuation on $\mathbb{F}$. It follows that $\langle \mathbb{F}, V_H \rangle, b \nVdash i$. By symmetry bR^+a and thus $\langle \mathbb{F}, V_H \rangle, b \Vdash \diamondsuit i$. Therefore we have $\langle \mathbb{F}, V_H \rangle, b \Vdash \neg(\diamondsuit i \to i)$ and as aR^-b it follows that $\langle \mathbb{F}, V_H \rangle, a \nVdash \boxminus(\diamondsuit i \to i)$. Hence $\mathbb{F} \nVdash i \to \boxminus(\diamondsuit i \to i)$.

($\Leftarrow$) Let $\mathbb{F} = \langle A, R^+, R^- \rangle$ be a symmetric general frame with the non-overlapping property. Suppose for reduction that there exists $a \in A$ and a valuation V_H on $\mathbb{F}$ such that $\langle \mathbb{F}, V_H \rangle, a \nVdash i \to \boxminus(\diamondsuit i \to i)$. Then $\langle \mathbb{F}, V_H \rangle, a \Vdash i$ and $\langle \mathbb{F}, V_H \rangle, a \Vdash \diamondsuit(\diamondsuit i \wedge \neg i)$. It follows that $\exists b \in A$ such that aR^-b and $\langle \mathbb{F}, V_H \rangle, b \Vdash \diamondsuit i \wedge \neg i$. Since $|V_H(i)| = 1$, it must be the case that bR^+a. By symmetry bR^-a and thus we have reached a contradiction by non-overlapping. We conclude that $\mathbb{F} \Vdash i \to \boxminus(\diamondsuit i \to i)$. $\quad\square$

Nominals greatly extends the expressivity of a logic. It is not always evident what the motivation is beyond simply being allowed to express otherwise undefinable properties like irreflexivity, asymmetry, antisymmetry and intransitivity, to mention some. However, when modeling agent based networks with a logic like **PNL**, we already have an incentive to add nominals to make it clear *who* we are modeling. Of course, this is not a novel approach to social network logics, see, e.g., [9,25,27].

4.3 Intersection

Another possible option is to introduce an intersection modality, perhaps most commonly used as a distributed knowledge operator known in the literature of dynamic epistemic logic, such as [11,26]. We modify it to our purpose.

Definition 10 (Semantics of Intersection Modality). *Let $\mathbb{M} = \langle A, R^+, R^-, V \rangle$ be a general model and let $a \in A$. We define the semantics of the intersection modality $\langle + \cap - \rangle$ as follows:*

$$\mathbb{M}, a \Vdash \langle + \cap - \rangle \phi \text{ iff } \exists b \in A \text{ such that } aR^+b, aR^-b \text{ and } \mathbb{M}, b \Vdash \phi$$

By including this operator, the axiom for non-overlapping N_I would simply be:

$$\langle + \cap - \rangle \perp \tag{N_I}$$

Lemma 7. *For any general frame* $\mathbb{F} = \langle A, R^+, R^- \rangle$, $\mathbb{F} \Vdash \boldsymbol{N_I}$ *iff* $\mathbb{F}$ *has the non-overlapping property.*

We read $\langle + \cap - \rangle \phi$ to hold at an agent if and only if there exists another agent that is both a friend and an enemy of the current agent where ϕ is true. That two agents *cannot* be both friends and enemies is a property assumed in the original work on signed graphs, and it is therefore difficult to see how the intersection operator would have any application outside axiomatizing the non-overlapping property.

4.4 Difference

A third possible solution is to introduce the difference operator $\langle D \rangle$.

Definition 11 (Semantics of Difference Operator [5]). *Let* $\mathbb{M} = \langle A, R^+, R^-, V \rangle$ *be a general model and let* $a \in A$. *The semantics of* $\langle D \rangle$ *is defined as follows:*

$$\mathbb{M}, a \Vdash \langle D \rangle \phi \text{ iff } \exists b \in A \text{ such that } b \neq a \text{ and } \mathbb{M}, b \Vdash \phi.$$

With this definition, we introduce the axiom $\boldsymbol{N_D}$ for the non-overlapping property:

$$(p \wedge \neg \langle D \rangle p) \rightarrow (\boxplus(\diamondsuit p \rightarrow p) \wedge \boxminus(\diamondsuit p \rightarrow p)) \tag{$\boldsymbol{N_D}$}$$

Inclusion of the $\langle D \rangle$ modality is not hard to motivate. $\langle D \rangle \phi$ holds at an agent if and only if there is another agent in the network where ϕ is true. We show the following lemma.

Lemma 8. *For any symmetric general frame* $\mathbb{F} = \langle A, R^+, R^- \rangle$, $\mathbb{F} \Vdash \boldsymbol{N_D}$ *iff* $\mathbb{F}$ *has the non-overlapping property.*

Proof. ($\Rightarrow$) Let $\mathbb{F} = \langle A, R^+, R^- \rangle$ be a symmetric general frame of $\mathcal{L}_{PNL_{\langle D \rangle}}$ such that $\mathbb{F} \Vdash \boldsymbol{N_D}$. Let $a, b \in A$ and without loss of generality assume that aR^+b. We want to prove that $(a, b) \notin R^-$. Let V be a valuation on $\mathbb{F}$ such that $V(p) = \{a\}$. It follows that $\langle \mathbb{F}, V \rangle, a \Vdash p \wedge \neg \langle D \rangle p$. Since $\mathbb{F} \Vdash (p \wedge \neg \langle D \rangle p) \rightarrow (\boxplus(\diamondsuit p \rightarrow p) \wedge \boxminus(\diamondsuit p \rightarrow p))$, we have that $\langle \mathbb{F}, V \rangle, a \Vdash \boxplus(\diamondsuit p \rightarrow p) \wedge \boxminus(\diamondsuit p \rightarrow p)$. As aR^+b, then $\langle \mathbb{F}, V \rangle, b \Vdash \diamondsuit p \rightarrow p$. We know that $\langle \mathbb{F}, V \rangle, b \not\Vdash p$, thus $\langle \mathbb{F}, V \rangle, b \not\Vdash \diamondsuit p$. Hence, $(b, a) \notin R^-$ and by symmetry $(a, b) \notin R^-$.

($\Leftarrow$) Let $\mathbb{F} = \langle A, R^+, R^- \rangle$ be a symmetric general frame of $\mathcal{L}_{PNL_{\langle D \rangle}}$ with the non-overlapping property. Fix an arbitrary valuation V on $\mathbb{F}$ and $a \in A$. Assume that $\langle \mathbb{F}, V \rangle, a \Vdash p \wedge \neg \langle D \rangle p$. Then $\neg \exists b \in A$ such that $b \neq a$ and $\langle \mathbb{F}, V \rangle, b \Vdash p$. It follows that $V(p) = \{a\}$. Let $c \in A$ such that aR^+c. By symmetry and non-overlapping $(c, a) \notin R^-$. Thus $\langle \mathbb{F}, V \rangle, c \not\Vdash \diamondsuit p$ and hence $\langle \mathbb{F}, V \rangle, c \Vdash \diamondsuit p \rightarrow p$. Then $\langle \mathbb{F}, V \rangle, a \Vdash \boxplus(\diamondsuit p \rightarrow p)$. Now, let $d \in A$ such that aR^-d. By similar reasoning $\langle \mathbb{F}, V \rangle, d \Vdash \diamondsuit p \rightarrow p$ and thus $\langle \mathbb{F}, V \rangle, a \Vdash \boxminus(\diamondsuit p \rightarrow p)$. It follows that $\langle \mathbb{F}, V \rangle, a \Vdash (p \wedge \neg \langle D \rangle p) \rightarrow (\boxplus(\diamondsuit p \rightarrow p) \wedge \boxminus(\diamondsuit p \rightarrow p))$ and as we chose an arbitrary V and $a \in A$, we conclude that $\mathbb{F} \Vdash \boldsymbol{N_D}$. $\square$

We show that we can also define collective connectedness with this operator:

$$(p \vee \langle D \rangle p) \rightarrow (\oplus p \vee \ominus p) \qquad \qquad (\mathbf{C}_D)$$

Lemma 9. *For any signed frame* $\mathbb{F} = \langle A, R^+, R^- \rangle$, $\mathbb{F} \Vdash \mathbf{C}_D$ *iff* $\mathbb{F}$ *has the collective connectedness property.*

Proof. ($\Rightarrow$) Proof by contraposition. Let $\mathbb{F} = \langle A, R^+, R^- \rangle$ be a signed frame without the collective connectedness property. Then $\exists a, b \in A$ such that $(a, b) \notin R^+$ and $(a, b) \notin R^-$. Now let $V(p) = \{b\}$ be a valuation on $\mathbb{F}$. Thus, $\langle \mathbb{F}, V \rangle, a \Vdash \langle D \rangle p$. Yet we have that $\langle \mathbb{F}, V \rangle, a \Vdash \neg \oplus p \wedge \neg \ominus p$ as a and b are neither positively nor negatively related. It follows that $\langle \mathbb{F}, V \rangle, a \nVdash (p \vee \langle D \rangle p) \rightarrow (\oplus p \vee \ominus p)$ and hence $\mathbb{F} \nVdash (p \vee \langle D \rangle p) \rightarrow (\oplus p \vee \ominus p)$.

($\Leftarrow$) Let $\mathbb{F} = \langle A, R^+, R^- \rangle$ be a signed frame with the collective connectedness property. Let $a \in A$ be an arbitrary agent and V an arbitrary valuation on $\mathbb{F}$. Now assume that $\langle \mathbb{F}, V \rangle, a \Vdash p \vee \langle D \rangle p$. Then $\exists b \in A$ such that $\langle \mathbb{F}, V \rangle, b \Vdash p$. By the collective connectedness property aR^+b or aR^-b and thus $\langle \mathbb{F}, V \rangle, a \Vdash \oplus p \vee \ominus p$. Since we chose a and V arbitrarily we conclude that $\mathbb{F} \Vdash (p \vee \langle D \rangle p) \rightarrow (\oplus p \vee \ominus p)$. □

5 Measuring Polarization

The aim of this section is to investigate networks that can change from imbalanced to balanced, and in particular to analyze how far a network is to being polarized. We begin by assessing different properties that a measure of distance might have. Then we introduce several measures of distance from a balanced model found in the literature, but accommodated to a logical framework. We contrast advantages and disadvantages of each metric and compare them using an example.

5.1 Distance Properties

In literature such as [1,7], the distance between two standard Kripke models is defined as a mapping from an ordered pair of two models to a real number. This mapping usually has to satisfy certain properties. The core feature of what we will call *balanced distance* is to measure how far a signed model is from being balanced. Therefore, we define balanced distance as a mapping from *one* signed model to a real number.

Definition 12 (Balanced Distance Measure). *Let* $\mathcal{M}$ *be the class of signed models. A **balanced distance measure** is a mapping* $d : \mathcal{M} \rightarrow \mathbb{R}$ *which satisfies the following properties:*

[nonnegativity] $d(\mathbb{M}) \geq 0$,
[balance indistinguishability] $d(\mathbb{M}) = 0$ *iff* $\mathbb{M}$ *is balanced.*

There are other restrictions we can impose on balanced distance depending on motivation and purpose. One candidate is *long cycle discrimination*. Studies show that longer cycles have less effect on people's tension than shorter cycles [14]. Moreover, the number of cycles in a network of a given length generally increases with length [21]. A count of cycles would therefore be dominated by long cycles. This might motivate the need for a metric that downplays the role of longer cycles in the calculation.

By simply counting the number of negative cycles, we do not distinguish between cases where the cycles overlap and cases where they do not. Imagine a network containing only two overlapping negative cycles on one edge. There is only need of a single link change for the network to become balanced. In a network of the same two negative cycles, however in this case not overlapped, we require two link changes for the purpose of a balanced network. Counting the number of negative cycles determines the same balanced distance between these two networks. This problem might provoke the need for an *overlapping cycle discrimination*.

Lastly, note that for all measures of balanced distance there is a corresponding weakly balanced version. As balance always entails weak balance, balanced and weakly balanced measures might, but not necessarily, be identical. With all properties listed here in mind, we turn to examine some options for a concrete notion of balanced distance.

5.2   Counting Cycles

By the Balance Theorem, imbalance is directly related to negative cycles. This observation was applied to balanced distance already in a paper by Cartwright and Harary in 1956 [8] and realized as *degree of balance*. Degree of balance in its original form is the number of non-negative cycles, divided by the total number of cycles. To ensure output 0 when the model is balanced, we appropriately rename our variation *degree of imbalance* and divide the number of negative cycles by the number of cycles. We also consider the weak version in the following definition.

Definition 13 (Degree of Imbalance). *Let $c^-(\mathbb{M})$ be the number of negative cycles in $\mathbb{M}$, and $c(\mathbb{M})$ be the total number of cycles in $\mathbb{M}$. Let $c^{-W}(\mathbb{M})$ be the number of cycles in $\mathbb{M}$ that have exactly one single negative edge. Note that $c^{-W}(\mathbb{M}) \subseteq c^-(\mathbb{M}) \subseteq c(\mathbb{M})$. Let $\mathcal{M}$ be the class of signed models. The **degree of imbalance** is the map $d_{DB} : \mathcal{M} \to \mathbb{R}$ such that $d_{DB}(\mathbb{M}) = \frac{c^-(\mathbb{M})}{c(\mathbb{M})}$. The **degree of weak imbalance** is the map $d_{DBW} : \mathcal{M} \to \mathbb{R}$ such that $d_{DBW}(\mathbb{M}) = \frac{c^{-W}(\mathbb{M})}{c(\mathbb{M})}$.*

We observe that although this simple measure of distance is a balanced distance metric by Definition 12, it does not satisfy neither the long cycle nor the overlapping cycle discrimination property. [21] defines another cycle counting measure of balance motivated by long cycle discrimination, called *level of imbalance*.

Definition 14 (Level of Imbalance [21]). *Let $\mathcal{M}$ be the class of signed models. The **level of imbalance** is the map $d_{Bz} : \mathcal{M} \to \mathbb{R}$ such that $d_{Bz}(\mathbb{M}) =$*

$\sum_{k=1}^{\infty} \frac{I_k}{z^k}$ where I_k is the number of negative cycles of length k and $z > 1$ is a free parameter. The **weak level of imbalance** is the map $d_{BzW} : \mathcal{M} \to \mathbb{R}$ such that $d_{BzW}(\mathbb{M}) = \sum_{k=1}^{\infty} \frac{I_{Wk}}{z^k}$ where I_{Wk} is the number of cycles with a single negative edge of length k.

The level of imbalance satisfies the long cycle discrimination property in addition to being a measure of balanced distance. The measure divides the number of negative cycles by a free parameter that increases by the negative cycle's length. Like the degree of imbalance, this metric does not satisfy the overlapping cycle discrimination property.

5.3   Line Index of Imbalance

Line index of imbalance was proposed by Harary in 1959 [18] and follows a simple idea: it measures the minimal number of edges to be deleted for the network to be balanced. The measure has also been implemented in terms of weak balance in [12].

Transition from a signed model to a submodel of fewer edges can seem unintuitive when we imagine links between agents to represent positive and negative relations. Where it is easy to imagine relations in a network to be created, it might be slightly harder to think of situations where agents completely lose touch. We can still of course regard line index of imbalance as a fruitful measurement, although we also remark that the minimal number of edges deleted is the same number as the smallest number of edges changing signs in order to make the network balanced. The reasoning is as follows. By the Balance Theorem, a network is balanced if and only if it has the potential to have the local structural balance property for each set of three agents. That is, as long as it is possible to fill in missing edges such as to create a collectively connected model where all triangles have either three positive signs or one positive and two negative, the signed model is balanced. Thus, changing signs in an imbalanced network have the same purpose as deleting edges in terms of balance: each edge needed to change signs could be deleted and now have the potential of the desired sign.

We present a novel definition of line index of imbalance for signed models.

Definition 15 (Line Index of Imbalance). *Let $\mathcal{M}$ be the class of signed models. The **line index of imbalance** is the map $d_{LI} : \mathcal{M} \to \mathbb{R}$ such that $d_{LI}(\mathbb{M}) = min\{\sum_{i \in \{+,-\}} |\frac{|R^i| - |R^{i'}|}{2(|R^+ \cup R^-| - |A|)}| \mid \mathbb{M}' = \langle A', R^{+'}, R^{-'}, V' \rangle$ where $A' = A$ and $\mathbb{M}'$ is balanced\} where $\mathbb{M} = \langle A, R^+, R^-, V \rangle$. The **line index of weak imbalance** is the map $d_{LIW} : \mathcal{M} \to \mathbb{R}$ such that $d_{LIW}(\mathbb{M}) = min\{\sum_{i \in \{+,-\}} |\frac{|R^i| - |R^{i'}|}{2(|R^+ \cup R^-| - |A|)}| \mid \mathbb{M}' = \langle A', R^{+'}, R^{-'}, V' \rangle$ where $A' = A$ and $\mathbb{M}'$ is weakly balanced\} where $\mathbb{M} = \langle A, R^+, R^-, V \rangle$.*

Line index of imbalance satisfies the properties of a balanced distance. It does not discriminate long cycles; in a network with both shorter and longer negative cycles, line index of imbalance will output a number independent on the ratio between short and long negative cycles. As mentioned, line index of imbalance satisfies the overlapping cycle property: in networks where cycles overlap, this metric will not count twice any edges needed to be changed for the purpose of balance.

5.4   Comparing Measures: How Far from Polarization?

We now look at an example to compare the different measures we have considered in this section. How far the network is from being polarized or weakly polarized is decided with respect to the measure one chooses to adopt. Consider the network in Fig. 3 and call it $\mathbb{M}$. Positive reflexive arrows are omitted for simplicity. We calculate and compare the distance towards polarization in Table 1.

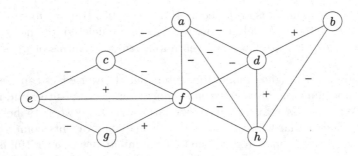

Fig. 3. A network that is not yet polarized.

We make some observations on Table 1. For the level of imbalance, z is a free parameter with the choice $z = 3$ made deliberately for comparison. The degree of imbalance is higher than the level of imbalance and line index of imbalance for strong polarization. We also note that line index of imbalance has a slightly higher measure than the other metrics with respect to weak polarization. As a general analysis over all three measurements, we see that the network is relatively far from being strongly polarized. Nevertheless, this is a social setting quite close

Table 1. How far is $\mathbb{M}$ in Fig. 3 from being polarized?

Strong polarization	Weak polarization
Degree of Imbalance	
$d_{DB}(\mathbb{M}) = \dfrac{c^-(\mathbb{M})}{c(\mathbb{M})} = \frac{15}{27} \approx 0.556$	$d_{DBW}(\mathbb{M}) = \dfrac{c^{-W}(\mathbb{M})}{c(\mathbb{M})} = \frac{2}{27} \approx 0.074$
Level of Imbalance	
$d_{Bz}(\mathbb{M}) = \sum_{k=1}^{\infty} \dfrac{I_k}{z^k} = \frac{183}{729} \approx 0.251$ for $z = 3$	$d_{BzW}(\mathbb{M}) = \sum_{k=1}^{\infty} \dfrac{I_{Wk}}{z^k} = \frac{2}{27} \approx 0.074$ for $z = 3$
Line Index of Imbalance	
$d_{LI}(\mathbb{M}) = \frac{1}{4} = 0.25$	$d_{LIW}(\mathbb{M}) = \frac{1}{6} \approx 0.167$

to being weakly polarized. Recall that this would indicate a situation where the agents are divided into a number of groups where there would be friendships within, but hostility towards all other groups.

6   Conclusions and Future Work

After introducing structural balance and group polarization through positive and negative relations logic known from the literature, we set out to expand this logical framework with several intentions in mind. We presented a number of additions to **PNL** to be able to define previously undefinable frame properties. By extending the language with the universal modality and dynamic modalities we introduced a dynamic characterization of the balance property. We also showed that an axiom for collective connectedness is secured by the universal modality or the difference operator, while non-overlapping can be defined with an axiom by inclusion of nominals, an intersection modality or the difference operator. Finally, we considered and compared a variation of distances in relation to balance to explore measures of how far a network is from polarization.

One obvious direction for future work is to prove completeness for the different logics with the axioms we have identified. This is not trivial. First, as far as we know there is no complete axiomatization of sabotage modal logic with the bridge modality. Second, as we already pointed out, if we include the global iteration modality together with the global addition modalities, the logic becomes non-compact. As a consequence, the standard canonical model method cannot be used (the standard truth lemma does not hold), but finitary methods, such as using an appropriate notion of closure like in completeness proofs for PDL, can possibly be used.

Another exciting prospect for future directions is to analyze network change in signed models, by extensions to the language of **PNL** with further dynamic modalities. Possible candidates are the following local link change and addition modalities inspired by sabotage modal logic, most notably [4,23].

Definition 16 (Semantics of Local Dynamic Modalities). *Let* $\mathbb{M} = \langle A, R^+, R^-, V \rangle$ *be a signed model and* $a \in A$. *We define truth conditions for the local link change modalities as follows:*

$$\mathbb{M}, a \Vdash \langle \oplus \rangle_L \phi \text{ iff } \exists b \in A \text{ such that } aR^- b \text{ and}$$
$$\langle A, R^+ \cup \{(a,b),(b,a)\}, R^- \smallsetminus \{(a,b),(b,a)\}, V \rangle, a \Vdash \phi$$

$$\mathbb{M}, a \Vdash \langle \ominus \rangle_L \phi \text{ iff } \exists b \in A \text{ such that } aR^+ b, a \neq b \text{ and}$$
$$\langle A, R^+ \smallsetminus \{(a,b),(b,a)\}, R^- \cup \{(a,b),(b,a)\}, V \rangle, a \Vdash \phi$$

$$\mathbb{M}, a \Vdash \langle \mathbb{M} + \rangle_L \phi \text{ iff } \exists b \in A \text{ such that } (a,b) \notin R^+, (a,b) \notin R^- \text{ and}$$
$$\langle A, R^+ \cup \{(a,b),(b,a)\}, R^-, V \rangle, a \Vdash \phi$$

$$\mathbb{M}, a \Vdash \langle \mathbb{M} - \rangle_L \phi \text{ iff } \exists b \in A \text{ such that } (a,b) \notin R^+, (a,b) \notin R^- \text{ and}$$
$$\langle A, R^+, R^- \cup \{(a,b),(b,a)\}, V \rangle, a \Vdash \phi$$

We read $\langle\oplus\rangle_L\phi$ to be true at an agent if and only if ϕ holds at the current agent after changing one edge connected to this agent from *negative to positive*. Similarly, we read $\langle\ominus\rangle_L\phi$ to be true at an agent if and only if ϕ holds at the current agent after changing one edge connected to this agent from *positive to negative*. The modalities $\langle\mathbb{M}+\rangle_L$ and $\langle\mathbb{M}-\rangle_L$ operate in a close similarity to $\langle\mathbb{M}+\rangle$ and $\langle\mathbb{M}-\rangle$. Although where $\langle\mathbb{M}+\rangle\phi$ holds at an agent if and only if ϕ is true at the current agent after *any* link addition to the signed model, $\langle\mathbb{M}+\rangle_L\phi$ holds if and only if ϕ is true at the current agent after a link addition to the signed model at that specific agent. Note that $\langle\mathbb{M}+\rangle_L\phi$ implies $\langle\mathbb{M}+\rangle\phi$, but the converse does not hold. The analogous implication holds for $\langle\mathbb{M}-\rangle$ and $\langle\mathbb{M}-\rangle_L$. These modalities enable stepwise analyses of the network dynamics from the perspective of single agents. In a network $\mathbb{M}$ and agent $a \in \mathbb{M}$, we could have formulas like $\mathbb{M}, a \Vdash \langle\mathbb{M}+\rangle_L\langle\ominus\rangle_L\langle D\rangle\phi$ stating that ϕ holds at another agent than a after adding a positive link to a and changing a negative link to positive from a.

On a final note, in light of logical analyses of social concepts it could be interesting to give certain attributes to agents in the network. One alternative is knowledge, as in epistemic frameworks such as [27]: could a polarized setting change depending on what agents know about their social situations? Another is communication: by implementing an information flow in the network we could analyze which agents are likely to become friends based on information and information access, e.g., by adopting a dynamic epistemic logic approach including public and private announcements [11].

References

1. Ågotnes, T., van der Hoek, W., Wooldridge, M.: Conservative social laws. In: Proceedings of the 20th European Conference on Artificial Intelligence, pp. 49–54. IOS Press (2012)
2. Areces, C., ten Cate, B.: Hybrid logics. In: van Benthem, J., Blackburn, P., Wolter, F. (eds.) Handbook of Modal Logic, pp. 821–868. Elsevier, Amsterdam (2006)
3. Areces, C., Fervari, R., Hoffmann, G.: Relation-changing modal operators. Log. J. IGPL **23**(4), 601–627 (2015)
4. Aucher, G., van Benthem, J., Grossi, D.: Modal logics of sabotage revisited. J. Logic Comput. **28**(2), 269–303 (2017)
5. Blackburn, P., de Rijke, M., Venema, Y.: Modal Logic. Cambridge University Press, New York (2001)
6. Bramson, A., et al.: Understanding polarization: meanings, measures, and model evaluation. Philos. Sci. **84**(1), 115–159 (2017)
7. Caridroit, T., Konieczny, S., de Lima, T., Marquis, P.: On distances between KD45n Kripke models and their use for belief revision. In: Proceedings of the ECAI, pp. 1053–1061. IOS Press (2016)
8. Cartwright, D., Harary, F.: Structural balance: a generalization of Heider's theory. Psychol. Rev. **63**(5), 277–293 (1956)
9. Christoff, Z., Hansen, J.U.: A logic for diffusion in social networks. J. Appl. Logic **13**(1), 48–77 (2015)

10. Davis, J.A.: Clustering and structural balance in graphs. Hum. Relat. **20**(2), 181–187 (1967)
11. van Ditmarsch, H., van der Hoek, W., Kooi, B.: Dynamic Epistemic Logic. SYLI, vol. 337. Springer, Dordrecht (2007). https://doi.org/10.1007/978-1-4020-5839-4
12. Doreian, P., Mrvar, A.: A partitioning approach to structural balance. Soc. Netw. **18**(2), 149–168 (1996)
13. Easley, D., Kleinberg, J.: Networks, Crowds and Markets. Cambridge University Press, New York (2010)
14. Estrada, E., Benzi, M.: Walk-based measure of balance in signed networks: detecting lack of balance in social networks. Phys. Rev. E **90**(4), 042802 (2014)
15. Fagin, R., Halpern, J.Y., Moses, Y., Vardi, M.Y.: Reasoning About Knowledge. The MIT Press, Cambridge (1995)
16. Granovetter, M.S.: The strength of weak ties. In: Social Networks, pp. 347–367. Academic Press (1977)
17. Harary, F.: On the notion of balance of a signed graph. Mich. Math. J. **2**(2), 143–146 (1953)
18. Harary, F.: On the measurement of structural balance. Behav. Sci. **4**(4), 316–323 (1959)
19. Heider, F.: Attitudes and cognitive organization. J. Psychol. **21**, 107–112 (1946)
20. Hendricks, V.F., Hansen, P.G.: Infostorms. Springer, Cham (2016). https://doi.org/10.1007/978-3-319-32765-5
21. Kirkley, A., Cantwell, G.T., Newman, M.E.J.: Balance in signed networks. Phys. Rev. E **99**(1), 012320 (2019)
22. Leskovec, J., Huttenlocker, D., Kleinberg, J.: Signed networks in social media. In: Proceedings of the SIGCHI Conference on Human Factors in Computing Systems, pp. 1361–1370 (2010)
23. Li, D.: Losing Connection: the Modal Logic of Definable Link Deletion. ILLC Technical Notes Series, X-2019-01 (2019)
24. Pedersen, M.Y.: Polarization and echo chambers: a logical analysis of balance and triadic closure in social networks. Master of Logic Thesis Series, MoL-2019-10 (2019)
25. Pedersen, M.Y., Smets, S., Ågotnes, T.: Analyzing echo chambers: a logic of strong and weak ties. In: Blackburn, P., Lorini, E., Guo, M. (eds.) LORI 2019. LNCS, vol. 11813, pp. 183–198. Springer, Heidelberg (2019). https://doi.org/10.1007/978-3-662-60292-8_14
26. Roelofsen, F.: Distributed knowledge. J. Appl. Non-Class. Logics **17**(2), 255–273 (2007)
27. Seligman, J., Liu, F., Girard, P.: Facebook and the epistemic logic of friendship. In Proceedings of the Conference on Theoretical Aspects of Rationality and Knowledge, pp. 229–238 (2013)
28. Sunstein, C.R.: The law of group polarization. J. Political Philos. **10**(2), 175–195 (2002)
29. Sunstein, C.R.: Group polarization and 12 angry men. Negot. J. **23**(4), 443–447 (2007)
30. Xia, W., Cao, M., Johansson, K.H.: Structural balance and opinion separation in trust-mistrust social networks. IEEE Trans. Control Netw. Syst. **3**(1), 46–56 (2015)
31. Xiong, Z.: On the logic of multicast messaging and balance in social networks. Doctoral dissertation, University of Bergen (2017)
32. Xiong, Z., Ågotnes, T.: On the logic of balance in social networks. J. Logic Lang. Inf. **29**, 53–75 (2020). https://doi.org/10.1007/s10849-019-09297-0

A Formalization of the Slippery Slope Argument

Zhe Yu[✉]

Institute of Logic and Cognition, Department of Philosophy,
Sun Yat-sen University, Guangzhou 510275, China
yuzh28@mail.sysu.edu.cn

Abstract. To bridge the gap between human reasoning and machine reasoning, one of the key problems in argumentation research is how to model natural language arguments by formal argumentation. The slippery slope argument (SSA) is a commonly used type of argument in the context of deliberation, with the intent of persuading people not to take a particular action. In this paper, an argumentation theory for the basic form of SSA is given based on the formal argumentation framework $ASPIC^+$ and argumentation schemes of SSA. Then, an SSA occurrence in a popular blog post about gene editing is taken as an example. By analyzing the case, this paper tries to model these arguments based on our argumentation theory and evaluates the arguments using abstract argumentation frameworks. The paper then points out that since whether an SSA is persuasive rests on whether its ultimate consequence is really unacceptable to the audience, value judgement should play an important role in the deliberation.

Keywords: Formal argumentation · Argumentation schemes · Slippery slope argument · Structured argumentation

1 Introduction

Argumentation is a cross-disciplinary topic involving multiple subjects such as philosophy, cognitive science, logic, linguistics and computer science. There are several research directions in the field of artificial intelligence, such as natural language processing and argumentation mining, that can be combined with argumentation and benefits from it [5]. As an approach for non-monotonic reasoning, formal argumentation is promising to bridge the gap between human reasoning and machine reasoning. To achieve this goal, a key problem is how to model natural language arguments by formal argumentation.

I would like to thank the anonymous reviewers for their valuable comments. This work is supported by the China Postdoctoral Science Foundation [No. 2019M663353] and the MOE Project of Key Research Institute of Humanities and Social Sciences in Universities [No. 18JJD720005].

M. Dastani et al. (Eds.): CLAR 2020, LNAI 12061, pp. 346–361, 2020.
https://doi.org/10.1007/978-3-030-44638-3_21

Based on this concern, argumentation schemes can be seen as a "semi-formal" generalization of arguments [18]. Many researchers have shown their interests in the formalization of argumentation schemes, such as the concerns for the argumentation scheme of argument from expert opinion [1,9,16].

In [20], Walton mentioned that the slippery slope argument (SSA), as a subclass of argument from negative consequences, is commonly used in the context of deliberation, with the intent of persuading people not to take an action that is under consideration. Here is an interpretation of the possible applications of SSA, taken from a book on informal logic [19].

Example 1. "You may hear such arguments in court. For example, the prosecuting attorney may encourage you (the jury) to be stern, severe, and courageous and not to shrink from your duty of demanding severe punishment for this guilty defendant; otherwise, this crime will be unpunished, criminals will run amok, and the social fabric of society will be threatened."

Though has been introduced in many logic textbooks as a sort of fallacy, there is also a lot of researchers hold the opinion that slippery slope arguments can be legitimate if good reasons are given for deeming that the first action will lead to catastrophic consequences [10,11,19,20]. Typically, SSA can be found in the discussions about legal, biomedical, and ethical issues. For instance, the topics of abortion, gay marriage, euthanasia, human gene therapy, etc.

This paper aims to formalise slippery slope arguments based on formal argumentation theory, and discuss if we can evaluate a slippery slope argument using formal methods. Firstly, by consulting the argumentation schemes for slippery slope argument presented by Walton [21,22], we give a formal model of slippery slope argument based on the structured argumentation framework $ASPIC^+$ [14,15]. Afterwards, we attempt to give a formal definition of the Critical Questions for slippery slope argument schemes, thus bring the informal way for evaluating a slippery slope argument into our theory. Meanwhile, we point out that the value judgement is an important factor in the evaluation of a slippery slope argument. For illustration, this paper models an application of the slippery slope argument found in a popular blog post using our argumentation theory.

The rest of this paper is structured as follows. In Sect. 2, we first summarize the basic features of SSA according to Walton's basic argumentation scheme for SSA. Then an argumentation theory for SSA (called SSAT) based on a formal argumentation system is constructed. After that, we try to define the Critical Questions for evaluation of SSA. In Sect. 3, we analyze an SSA from nature language text, and model it by SSAT. In Sect. 4, we briefly discuss some key ideas of this paper and list several related works, while in Sect. 5 we summarize this paper.

2   Argumentation Theory for SSA

In this section, we model the slippery slope argument based on Walton's basic scheme for this kind of argument and the structured argumentation framework $ASPIC^+$.

2.1 Basic Components of SSA

Several kinds of SSA as well as their schemes have been mentioned in [10,20, 23], such as the Causal Slippery Slope Argument, the Sorites Slippery Slope Argument, etc. In [21], Walton gives a basic scheme for SSA, intending to capture the basic features of SSA. He also emphasized that "there are factors that help to propel the argument and series of consequences along the sequence, making it progressively harder for the agent to resist continuing to move ahead". These factors have been called "Drivers" [21].

Based on Walton's interpretation, in this paper we use 'a_0' to denote an action under consideration, 'a_n' to denote a catastrophic outcome; '$a_1, a_2, \ldots, a_x, \ldots, a_y$' denotes a sequence of action or events between 'a_0' and 'a_n', each causes the next one, and 'd_i' ($i = 1, 2, 3, \ldots$) denotes the drivers. Then we can set out that an SSA has the following 8 basic components:

1. An initial event/action a_0.
2. A sequence of events/actions: $a_0, a_1, a_2, \ldots, a_x, \ldots, a_y, \ldots, a_n$. As the sequence proceeds, the consequences tend to become more serious.
3. Drivers: d_i. Catalyst that helps to propel the argument along the sequence in the argument. Drivers could be factors like precedent, public acceptance, vagueness, climate of social opinion, public acceptance, etc. [21]
4. Gray area: the area that starts at an undetermined point x (denoted by a_x), and end at another undetermined point y (denoted by a_y). In this area a slippery slope argument is turning form controllable to uncontrollable.
5. Controllable area: the area between the initial event/action and the gray area.
6. Uncontrollable area: the area between the gray area and the catastrophic consequence.
7. Catastrophic consequence: a_n, which should be avoided if possible.
8. Conclusion: not to take the initial step a_0.

According to this summarization, the developing process of an SSA can be illustrated by Fig. 1.[1]

2.2 SSAT

Our current work is mainly based on the structured argumentation framework $ASPIC^+$, which is proposed by Prakken et al. in [14]. $ASPIC^+$ is not a system but a framework, so that people can specify or extend it as an instantiation, as long as meeting some specific requirements.

Based on the above analysis of SSA, we can define an argumentation theory for SSA. First of all, an argumentation theory starts with a logical language $\mathcal{L}$. Since an SSA always leads to a negative consequence, we add a symbol "$\bot$" into the language of the argumentation theory, which denotes "bad/unwanted (consequence)".

---

[1] In a proper SSA, Drivers should always exist within every step. Here we write d_1, d_2 and d_3 as an example.

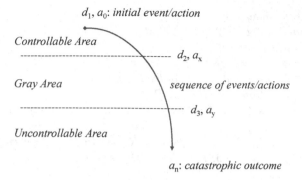

Fig. 1. Process of an SSA

What's more, we divide the rules used in the SSA into two kinds: slippery slope rules and consequence judgements rules, denote as $\mathcal{R}_{sl}$ and $\mathcal{R}_j$ respectively. The slippery slope rules are always defeasible, and that's the reason an SSA is "sloping"; on the contrary, since an SSA must include a bad/unwanted consequence, the consequence judgements rules are always strict.

Then a knowledge base $\mathcal{K}$ is needed, which contains the premise sets of an argumentation theory, and from which we can proceed to build arguments. We put "$\neg\bot$" into the premise set, because if something is bad/unwanted, people are supposed to resist it instinctively. As for the premises of the SSA, the initial step is more like a presumption, or something that is still under consideration, so that we use $\mathcal{K}_0 = \{a_0, b_0, c_0, \ldots\}$ to denote the set of initial actions/events.[2] Since an argument $A = a_0$ represents a pending event or action, if A attacks other arguments without any supporter, it seems counterintuitive. Conversely, if A is not attacked by any other argument, it should be acceptable. Meanwhile, there is no reason not to accept any argument that depend on A, otherwise the entire SSA and its sub-arguments would be unacceptable.

Last but not least, we use C to denote the set of actions/events, and D to denote the set of drivers.

An argumentation theory for SSA can be defined as follows.

Definition 1 (SSAT). *A slippery slope argumentation theory (SSAT) is a tuple $SSAT = (\mathcal{L}, ^-, \mathcal{R}, n, \mathcal{K}, C, D)$, where:*

---

[2] The idea of $\mathcal{K}_0$ was inspired by Prakken [15], where the knowledge base $\mathcal{K}$ consists of 4 disjoint subsets: $\mathcal{K}_n, \mathcal{K}_p, \mathcal{K}_a, \mathcal{K}_i$, which are respectively the sets of axioms, ordinary premises, assumptions, and issues. The definitions of the axioms and the ordinary premises are the same as in this paper, while attacks on the assumptions are always succeed, and an issue must always be backed with a further argument. However, since the initial premise in the SSA is not only an event/action under consideration, but also the premise of the SSA and its sub-arguments, none of the above premise sets is particularly suitable as the set of initial premises of the SSA.

- $\mathcal{L}$ is a logical language; $\perp \in \mathcal{L}$.
- $^-$ is a function from $\mathcal{L}$ to $2^{\mathcal{L}}$, such that
  1. φ is a contrary of ψ if $\varphi \in \overline{\psi}$, $\psi \notin \overline{\varphi}$;
  2. φ is a contradictory of ψ, if $\varphi \in \overline{\psi}$, $\psi \in \overline{\varphi}$ (denoted by '$\varphi = -\psi$'); [3]
  3. each $\varphi \in \mathcal{L}$ has at least one contradictory.
- n is a partial function such that $n: \mathcal{R}_d \to \mathcal{L}$.
- $\mathcal{R} = \mathcal{R}_s \cup \mathcal{R}_d$ is a set of strict ($\mathcal{R}_s$) and defeasible ($\mathcal{R}_d$) inference rules of the form $\varphi_1, \ldots, \varphi_n \to \varphi$ and $\varphi_1, \ldots, \varphi_n \Rightarrow \varphi$ respectively (φ_i, φ are elements in $\mathcal{L}$), and $\mathcal{R}_s \cap \mathcal{R}_d = \emptyset$. $r_{sl} \in \mathcal{R}_{sl} \subseteq \mathcal{R}_d$ is slippery slope rule of the form $\varphi_1, \ldots, \varphi_n \Rightarrow_{sl} \varphi$, $\mathcal{R}_{sl} \neq \emptyset$; $r_j \in \mathcal{R}_j \subseteq \mathcal{R}_s$ is consequence judging rule of the form $r_j = \varphi_1, \ldots, \varphi_n \to_j \perp$, $\mathcal{R}_j \neq \emptyset$.
- $\mathcal{K} \subseteq \mathcal{L}$ is a knowledge base in an argumentation system, consisting of three disjoint subsets $\mathcal{K}_n$, $\mathcal{K}_p$ and $\mathcal{K}_0$ (i.e. $\mathcal{K} = \mathcal{K}_n \cup \mathcal{K}_p \cup \mathcal{K}_0$), where:
  1. $\mathcal{K}_n$ is a set of axioms;
  2. $\mathcal{K}_p$ is a set of the ordinary premises, such that $\neg \perp \in \mathcal{K}_n \cup \mathcal{K}_p$;
  3. $\mathcal{K}_0$ is a set of initial steps in a slippery slope argument of the form $\mathcal{K}_0 = \{a_0, b_0, c_0, \ldots\}$, where a_0, b_0, c_0 are initial actions or events.
- C is a set of actions or events in a slippery slope argument of the form $C = \{a_0, \ldots, a_n, b_0, \ldots, b_m, c_0, \ldots, c_q, \ldots\} \subseteq \mathcal{L}$, where a_i, b_j, c_k are actions or events; $\mathcal{K}_0 \subseteq C$.
- D is a set of drivers, $D = \{d_1, \ldots, d_n\} \subseteq \mathcal{K}_p$, where d_i is a driver.

We use $Prem(A)$ to denote all the formulas of $\mathcal{K}$ that used to build an argument A, $Conc(A)$ to denote the conclusion of A, $Sub(A)$ to denote all the sub-arguments of A, $DefRule(A)$ to denote all the defeasible rules of A, and $TopRule(A)$ to denote the last rule of A. Depending on $ASPIC^+$, an argument in $SSAT$ can be defined as follows.

Definition 2 (Arguments). *An argument A on the basis of an $SSAT = (\mathcal{L}, ^-, \mathcal{R}, n, \mathcal{K}, C, D)$ is defined as:*

1. φ *if* $\varphi \in \mathcal{K}$ *with:* $Prem(A) = \{\varphi\}$, $Conc(A) = \varphi$, $Sub(A) = \{\varphi\}$, $DefRules(A) = \emptyset$, $TopRule(A) = undefined$.
2. $A_1, \ldots, A_n \to \psi$ *if* $A_1, \ldots, A_n$ $(n \geq 1)$ *are arguments such that there exists a strict rule* $Conc(A_1), \ldots, Conc(A_n) \to \psi$ *in* $\mathcal{R}_s$ *with:* $Prem(A) = Prem(A_1) \cup \ldots \cup Prem(A_n)$; $Conc(A) = \psi$; $Sub(A) = Sub(A_1) \cup \ldots \cup Sub(A_n) \cup \{A\}$; $DefRules(A) = DefRules(A_1) \cup \ldots \cup DefRules(A_n)$; $TopRule(A) = Conc(A_1) \ldots Conc(A_n) \to \psi$.
3. $A_1, \ldots, A_n \Rightarrow \psi$ *if* $A_1, \ldots, A_n$ $(n \geq 1)$ *are arguments such that there exists a defeasible rule* $Conc(A_1), \ldots, Conc(A_n) \Rightarrow \psi$ *in* $\mathcal{R}_d$ *with:* $Prem(A) = Prem(A_1) \cup \ldots \cup Prem(A_n)$; $Conc(A) = \psi$; $Sub(A) = Sub(A_1) \cup \ldots \cup Sub(A_n) \cup \{A\}$; $DefRules(A) = DefRules(A_1) \cup \ldots \cup DefRules(\alpha_n) \cup \{Conc(A_1), \ldots, Conc(A_n) \Rightarrow \psi\}$; $TopRule(A) = Conc(A_1) \ldots Conc(A_n) \Rightarrow \psi$.

---

[3] For all $\varphi \in \mathcal{L}$, we have $\neg - \varphi \in \overline{\varphi}$ and for all $\neg\varphi \in \mathcal{L}$, we have $\varphi \in \overline{\neg\varphi}$.

According to Walton [20–22], an integrated SSA should consists of two main lines, one from the initial action a_0 to a catastrophic consequence, and the other from the undesirability of the catastrophic consequence to the final conclusion ($\neg a_0$). However, from Example 1 we can see that in practical applications, the proponent of an SSA may only state the first line explicitly. If the SSA is used properly, the audiences will automatically infer the second line through rational intuition, and draw a conclusion $\neg a_0$. Since the main focus of this paper is on SSAs expressed in natural language, we consider an arguments containing the components in the first line as an SSA. Therefore, we define an SSA in the SSAT as follows.

Definition 3 (SSA). *If an argument A in $SSAT = (\mathcal{L},^-, \mathcal{R}, n, \mathcal{K}, C, D)$, such that: $Prem(A) \cap \mathcal{K}_0 \neq \emptyset$, $Prem(A) \cap D \neq \emptyset$, $SlRule(A) \neq \emptyset$, $JRule(A) \neq \emptyset$, $Conc(A) = \bot$, for every $A' \in Sub(A)$ and $A' \neq A$, $Conc(A') \in C \cup D$, then A is a slippery slope argument (SSA).*

Note that Definition 3 is not strictly corresponding to Walton's basic scheme of SSA, for it does not include the final conclusion. We have two reasons for this. On the one hand, with this definition, we can better identify an SSA, for the conclusion of an SSA is omitted in many cases. On the other hand, based on the current argumentation theory, an argument with the conclusion $\neg a_0$ would otherwise attack its sub-argument with the conclusion a_0 (see Definition 5). As a result, the SSA will cause inconsistency and cannot be accepted.

By claiming that the bad outcome is unacceptable, the slippery slope argument always attempt to draw a conclusion that the initial step should not be taken. To capture this feature, in addition to transposition under strict rules required by $ASPIC^+$, we define a "weak transposition" for the slippery slope rule used in the SSA.

Definition 4 (Transposition and Weak Transposition). *Let $SSAT = (\mathcal{L},^-, \mathcal{R}, n, \mathcal{K}, C, D)$ be an $SSAT$, $SSAT$ is closed under transposition and weak transposition, iff the following two conditions hold:*

1. *if $\varphi_1, \ldots, \varphi_n \rightarrow \psi \in \mathcal{R}_s$, then for each $i = 1 \ldots n$, there is $\varphi_1, \ldots, \varphi_{i-1}, -\psi, \varphi_{i+1}, \ldots \varphi_n \rightarrow -\varphi_i \in \mathcal{R}_s$;*
2. *if $\varphi_1, \ldots, \varphi_n \Rightarrow_{sl} \psi \in \mathcal{R}_{sl}$, then for each $i = 1, \ldots, n$, such that $\varphi_i \in C$, there is $\varphi_1, \ldots, \varphi_{i-1}, -\psi, \varphi_{i+1}, \ldots \varphi_n \Rightarrow_{slt} -\varphi_i \in \mathcal{R}_d$. The set of transposed rules is denoted as $\mathcal{R}_{slt} \subseteq \mathcal{R}_d$; the transposed rule of a slippery slope rule $r_i \in \mathcal{R}_{sl}$ ($i = 1 \ldots n$) is denoted as $r_{it} \in \mathcal{R}_{slt}$.*

Weak transposition enables us to achieve the second main line of reasoning of the SSA. According to this definition, the weak transposition can only apply on the sequence of action/events that are linked by slippery slope rules. It is possible that one of the drivers is in fact refutable. However, on the one hand, the attack on drivers can be achieved by means other than weak transposition; on the other hand, we realize that applying transposition to all defeasible rules is dangerous because it can lead to counter-intuitive results. The transposition of slippery slope rules may still cause some disagreement, we will discuss this in Sect. 4.

In $ASPIC^+$, arguments could be attacked in three ways: (1) undermining attack on the ordinary premises; (2) rebutting attack on the conclusions (only when the last rule is defeasible); (3) undercutting attack on the defeasible rules. In this paper we add a special set of premises $\mathcal{K}_0$, whose elements are more like presumptions. So that we define the undermining attack slightly different from in $ASPIC^+$. Besides, since we have defined the weak transposition, the undercutting attack should also become different. Thus the attack relation in SSAT is defined as follows.

Definition 5 (Attack).   *Let A, B and X be arguments in $SSAT =$ $(\mathcal{L}, {}^{-}, \mathcal{R}, n, \mathcal{K}, C, D)$, $\varphi, \psi \in \mathcal{L}$. A attacks B (and X), iff A undercuts, rebuts or undermines B, where:*

- *A undercuts B on B' iff:*
  1. *$B' \in Sub(B)$ such that $TopRule(B') = r$ and $r \in \mathcal{R}_d$, $Conc(A) \in \overline{n(r)}$[4];*
  2. *$\exists X$, $X' \in Sub(X)$, $\underline{TopRule(X')} = r_i (i = 1, \ldots, n)$, $r_i \in \mathcal{R}_{sl}$, and $\exists r_{it} \in \mathcal{R}_{slt}$[5], $Conc(A) \in \overline{n(r_i)}$ (i.e. A undercuts X on X'), while $B' \in Sub(B)$, such that $TopRule(B') = r_{it}$.*
- *A rebuts B on B', iff $Conc(A) \in \overline{\varphi}$ for some $B' \in Sub(B)$ of the form $B''_1, \ldots, B''_n \Rightarrow \varphi$, and if $A = \psi$, then $\psi \notin \mathcal{K}_0$; A contrary-rebuts B iff $Conc(A)$ is a contrary of φ.*
- *A undermines B on B', iff:*
  1. *$B' = \varphi$ and $\varphi \in Prem(B) \cap \mathcal{K}_p$, such that $Conc(A) \in \overline{\varphi}$ and if $A = \psi$, then $\psi \notin \mathcal{K}_0$;*
  2. *$B' = \varphi$ and $\varphi \in Prem(B) \cap \mathcal{K}_0$, such that $Conc(A) \in \overline{\varphi}$.*
  A contrary-undermines B iff $Conc(A)$ is a contrary of φ.

Based on this definition, if an argument undercuts an SSA on one of its slippery slope rules r_i, it will also undercut another argument that contains the defeasible rule r_{it}, which is obtained by applying weak transposition on r_i. Besides, a presumption can only attack another presumption, which means that an argument consisting only of element in $\mathcal{K}_0$ can merely undermine another argument that is also consisted only of element in $\mathcal{K}_0$.

In $ASPIC^+$, whether an attack from A to B (on its sub-argument B') succeeds as a defeat depends on the relative strength of A and B'. In [14], this is determined by a binary ordering $\preceq$ on the set of all arguments. With arguments and the defeat relations, we can evaluate the status of arguments using Dung style abstract argumentation frameworks [8] and decide the set of arguments that jointly acceptable (called an extension) under particular argumentation semantics. Due to limitation of space, we omit the formal introduction of defeat relation in $ASPIC^+$ and the abstract argumentation framework here, the readers are referred to paper [8] and [14] to find more details.

---

[4] '$n(r)$' means that rule r is applicable.
[5] r_{it} is the transposed rule of r_i.

2.3   Evaluation of SSA

According to the set-up of argumentation schemes, each scheme is corresponded with a specific sequence of critical questions. Basically, there are two ways to evaluate a given argument: (1) use relevant schemes to check the form of the argument; (2) ask the corresponding critical questions, to see if the questions can be answered satisfactorily.

In this section, we try to give some way to evaluate a slippery slope argument based on formal argumentation. The main idea is to formalize the critical questions of the argumentation scheme for SSA, thus we can involve the critical questions into an argumentation framework and evaluate all the arguments together.

Critical Questions. In [22], the author gives 5 critical questions for the basic scheme of SSA, as described below.

CQ1 What intervening links in the sequence of events $a_1, a_2, \ldots, a_i$ needed to drive the slope forward from a_0 to a_n are explicitly stated?

CQ2 What missing steps are required as links to fill in the sequence of events from a_0 to a_n, to make the transition forward from a_0 to a_n plausible?

CQ3 What are the weakest links in the sequence, where additional evidence needs to be given on whether one event will really lead to another?

CQ4 Is the sequence of argumentation meant to be deductive, so that if the first step is taken, it is claimed that the final outcome a_n must necessarily come about?

CQ5 Is the final outcome a_n shown to be catastrophic by the value-based reasoning needed to support this claim?

Suppose that a proposed SSA fails to answer CQ1, CQ2 or CQ4 properly, it means that (at least one of) the links from the initial step a_0 to the bad outcome a_n is too weak. In other words, the slippery slope rules between premises to the conclusion is too weak to apply (then we have $\overline{n(r_{sl})}$). And if a proposed SSA fails to answer CQ3 properly, it perhaps that there lacks a driver to back up the 'sloping', or the given driver is not good enough. For the first situation, it could also be seen as that the related link is too weak; for the second situation, it means at least one of the given drivers has been attacked (then we have $\overline{d_i}$). At last, if a proposed slippery slope argument cannot answer CQ5, it means that the final outcome of this argument is not really unacceptable or cause resistance as it has been claimed to (then we have $\overline{\neg\perp}$).

Thus we define the critical questions for slippery slope argument as following.

Definition 6 (Critical Question).   *Let argument A, B be arguments in $SSAT = (\mathcal{L}, {}^-, \mathcal{R}, n, \mathcal{K}, C, D)$, $\varphi, \psi \in \mathcal{L}$. Let A be an SSA, such that $d_i \in Prem(A)$, $r_{sli} \in SlRule(A)$, $Conc(A) = \perp$. B is an argument of critical question for A (denoted by CQA) iff $TopRule(B) = \varphi_1, \ldots, \varphi_n \rightarrow / \Rightarrow \psi$, while $\psi = \overline{n(r_{sli})}$, $\psi = \overline{d_i}$ or $\psi = \overline{\neg\perp}$.*

Here the CQ5 make us aware that the persuasive powers of an SSA should be rested on the fact that the ultimate consequence is catastrophic and really unacceptable to its audiences. Which indicates that the value judgement of the audience may need to be taken into account. Through the case analysis in Sect. 3, the readers should be able to see this point clearer, then we could look back upon this issue and further discuss about it.

3   A Case Analysis

In this section, we apply our argumentation theory for SSA on a slippery slope argument observed in natural language text. The argument came from a Chinese biologist's comments on the Chinese gene editing baby experiment exposed in November 2018.

3.1   The Gene Editing Baby Case: A Practical Application of SSA

On November 26, 2018, Chinese researcher Jiankui He claims that his lab had been editing embryos' genetic codes for seven couples undergoing in-vitro fertilization. Twin girls had been born with DNA altered to make them resistant to HIV, which is the virus that causes AIDS.[6] He used a tool known as CRISPR-cas9 to disable a gene called CCR5, which could form a protein doorway that allows HIV to enter a cell. By doing this, as He claimed, the twin babies are immune to HIV.

Editing the genes of embryos intended for pregnancy is banned in many countries, while in some other countries, editing of embryos may be permitted for research purposes with strict regulatory approval. Jiankui He's experiment is the world's first case of germline gene therapy that performed on humans, which is likely to spark significant ethical questions around gene editing and so-called designer babies. This action shocked and outraged scientists around the world.

Liming Wang, a professor of Zhejiang University who is familiar with genetic technology, released a blog post online to announce his attitude to this event immediately after the news was announced. In which he clearly explained his opinion from several perspectives. In short, there are already many ways to control the genetics of AIDS and reduce the impact of it on patients' lives, therefore the benefit of this action to the newborn children is actually negligible. In turn, the risk of gene editing, including CRISPR-cas9 technique, is still unpredictable and uncontrollable. Furthermore, Wang says, "In addition to the scientific considerations, I have deeper concerns: concerns about the future fate of human beings." In the following text, we can clearly find an application of slippery slope argument. From the following excerpts, we can see more distinctly (translate from Chinese):

---

[6] The news can be find at the following websites: https://edition.cnn.com/2018/11/26/health/china-crispr-gene-editing-twin-babies-first-intl/index.html, https://www.theguardian.com/science/2018/nov/26/worlds-first-gene-edited-babies-created-in-china-claims-scientist, etc.

Example 2. "... from "treatment" to "prevention" greatly extends the application of gene editing technology. An apparent question is: **where is the boundary** of this technology? You will find it's very difficult to **draw a line.**"

"Since editing CCR5 for treating AIDS is reasonable, then isn't it nature to modify CCR5 gene in advance for protection? In this case, is it wrong that an ordinary person also want to protect his children from AIDS? **Take one more step**, if a person has 1% higher risk of getting a genetic disease, isn't it reasonable that he asks for gene editing to reduce the risk? If it is reasonable, can one in ten thousand of the risks be genetically edited? How about one in a million? If it is unreasonable, how much risk can make us allow the gene editing?"

"What more terrible is that once the boundaries of 'treatment' and 'prevention' are broken, it will be much easier to **break the line** between 'prevention' and 'improvement'! What if people want their children to get more muscle, get taller, have blonde hair, double eyelids, or high nose bridges? Even further, what if they want their children to be smarter, have greater abilities on language, analysis and leadership? "

"Though so far, our knowledge about human genes may not achieve these goals, I believe that one day in the future we can figure out all of these things. At that time, will the development of gene technology **bring human beings into the abyss**? Will gene editing destroy the diversity of human gene pool? Will it make human beings monotonous and uncharacteristic? Most seriously, will it cause eternal inequalities? ...... If some people's children get genetically improved, they may have competitive advantages not only in appearance but also in intelligence. What even worse is that these advantages are written into the genome and can be inherited. Thus the other children may never catch up with them!"

The words like "draw a line", "boundary", "one more step", "even further", "break the line", "bring ... to the abyss" appearing in these statements indicate that the SSA is applied.

3.2   Modeling of SSA

The SSA in Example 2 contains arguments from precedent and causal arguments. Apart from some analogies and metaphors in the detail, the author's main idea is as follows:

Firstly, because the boundary of gene editing application is difficult to delimit, if using gene editing to prevent AIDS is approved, then we can hardly stop people to use gene editing on the prevention of other genetic diseases, even if the possibility of getting these diseases are very small but the risks are unpredictable;

Next, since it's much easier to break the line between 'prevention' and 'improvement', then from appearance, physique to intelligence, gradually people will use gene editing techniques to achieve human enhancement.

Then the author gives several negative consequences that may occur. Apparently, he believes that the public will think the most unwanted consequence is "causing eternal inequalities", which is because those people who cannot get genetic improvement, including their offspring, will never be able to catch up with those who have adopted genetic improvement.

In this process, the substantial changing is from *approving the gene-edited HIV-immune babies* (a presumption, the initial step), to *the abuse of gene editing techniques on genetic diseases prevention* (the first step), then to *use gene editing techniques for human enhancement* (the second step), and ultimately lead to *eternal inequalities of human society* (disastrous consequence) and other bad consequences.

The first and second steps can be seen as indications for the beginning and ending of the "gray area" in this SSA respectively. The author gives three reasons to support his statements: (1) *it's very difficult to draw a line*; (2) *it will be much easier to break the line between 'prevention' and 'improvement'*; and (3) *the other children may never catch up with them*.

We use a_0 to denote "approving the gene-edited HIV-immune babies", a_x to denote "abuse of gene editing techniques on genetic diseases prevention", a_y to denote "use gene editing techniques for human enhancement", a_n to denote "eternal inequalities of human society"; [7] d_1, d_2, and d_3 denote the three reasons (drivers) respectively. According to the definition of SSAT in Sect. 2.2, we can get the following argumentation theory.

Example 3 (Example 2 continued). $\mathcal{L} = \{a_0, a_x, a_y, a_n, d_1, d_2, d_3, \bot, \neg\bot\}$;
$\mathcal{K} = \{a_0, d_1, d_2, d_3, \neg\bot\}$; $\mathcal{K}_0 = \{t_0\}$;
$\mathcal{K}_n = \{\}$; $\mathcal{K}_p = \{d_1, d_2, d_3, \neg\bot\}$;
$\mathcal{R}_d = \mathcal{R}_{sl} \cup \mathcal{R}_{slt} = \{a_0, d_1 \Rightarrow_{sl} a_x; a_x, d_2 \Rightarrow_{sl} a_y; a_y, d_3 \Rightarrow_{sl} a_n\}$
$\cup\{\neg a_x, d_1 \Rightarrow_{slt} \neg a_0; \neg a_y, d_2 \Rightarrow_{slt} \neg a_x; \neg a_n, d_3 \Rightarrow_{slt} \neg a_y\}$;
$\mathcal{R}_s = \{a_n \rightarrow_j \bot\} \cup \{\neg\bot \rightarrow \neg a_n\}$.

Arguments are:

$A_1 : a_0$	$A_2 : d_1$	$A_3 : d_2$
$A_4 : d_3$	$A_5 : A_1, A_2 \Rightarrow_{sl} a_x$	$A_6 : A_3, A_5 \Rightarrow a_y$
$A_7 : A_4, A_6 \Rightarrow a_n$	$A_8 : A_7 \rightarrow_j \bot$	$A_9 : \neg\bot$
$A_{10} : A_9 \rightarrow \neg a_n$	$A_{11} : A_4, A_{10} \Rightarrow_{slt} \neg a_y$	$A_{12} : A_3, A_{11} \Rightarrow_{slt} \neg a_x$
$A_{13} : A_2, A_{12} \Rightarrow_{slt} \neg a_0$		

According to Definition 5, assuming that all the attack relations we get are success as defeats, we have the following set $\mathcal{D}$ of defeat relations:

$\mathcal{D} = \{(A_5, A_{12}), (A_5, A_{13}), (A_6, A_{11}), (A_6, A_{12}), (A_6, A_{13}), (A_8, A_9), (A_8, A_{10}),$
$(A_8, A_{11}), (A_8, A_{12}), (A_8, A_{13}), (A_{10}, A_7), (A_{10}, A_8), (A_{11}, A_6), (A_{11}, A_7), (A_{11}, A_8),$
$(A_{12}, A_5), (A_{12}, A_6), (A_{12}, A_7), (A_{12}, A_8), (A_{13}, A_1), (A_{13}, A_5), (A_{13}, A_6), (A_{13}, A_7),$
$(A_{13}, A_8)\}$.[8]

---

[7] We use x, y and n instead of $1, 2$ and 3 because actually between these steps, many intervening small steps are omitted.

[8] Due to the restricted rebutting applied in $ASPIC^+$, A_9 does not directly attack A_8 because the last rule of A_8 is strict. Instead, A_{10} obtained by the transposition of rule '$a_n \rightarrow_j \bot$' rebuts A_8's sub-argument A_7, and thus also attacks A_8.

Now we can get an abstract argumentation framework based on [8] as shown in Fig. 2.

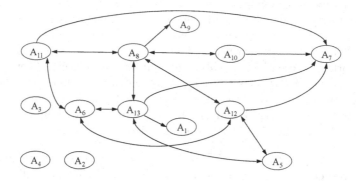

Fig. 2. An abstract argumentation framework

Applying the argumentation semantics [8], we can get four extensions under preferred semantics: $E_{\mathcal{P}1} = \{A_2, A_3, A_4, A_9, A_{10}, A_{11}, A_{12}, A_{13}\}$, $E_{\mathcal{P}2} = \{A_1, A_2, A_3, A_4, A_5, A_9, A_{10}, A_{11}\}$, $E_{\mathcal{P}3} = \{A_1, A_2, A_3, A_4, A_5, A_6, A_7, A_8\}$, $E_{\mathcal{P}4} = \{A_1, A_2, A_3, A_4, A_5, A_6, A_9, A_{10}\}$. Compared with extensions under other semantics, preferred extensions can reflect a more credulous attitude. If the arguments has equal priorities and there is no additional information, a credulous agent may accept one of the above extensions.[9] Besides, we can get one extension under grounded semantics: $E_{\mathcal{G}1} = \{A_2, A_3, A_4\}$. The grounded extension reflects the most skeptical attitude of agents. In the argumentation framework of Fig. 2, only argument A_2, A_3 and A_4 (whose conclusions are d_1, d_2 and d_3 respectively) are not attacked, thus a very skeptical agent will only accept these three arguments. There are other argumentation semantics introduced in [8], [2], etc. Here we only take two of them for instance.

In Example 2, the blogger mentions that the key reason he disagree with the CCR5 gene-edited babies experiment is that the benefit it will bring is far less than the risk. Apparently, in addition to the unpredictable accidents such as "off-target effects" during operations, the catastrophic consequence (i.e. *cause eternal inequalities in human society*) mentioned in his SSA is also one of the risks - perhaps the worst one. This kind of statements reflects his value judgement:

---

[9] The proponent of an SSA will expect the audience to accept $E_{\mathcal{P}1}$. However, the persuasiveness of an SSA depends on audiences, and many factors will affect their final decision. For example, whether the audience is worried enough about the catastrophic consequence. Since we has assumed that all the attacks are successful (while the proponent won't consider that a_8 will defeats a_9), from the perspective of the audience, we believe that the current result is in line with human intuition, i.e. some audiences are successfully persuaded by the SSA (thus accepting $\neg a_0$), whereas some audiences are not.

The value of avoiding the catastrophic consequence is much higher than the value of enjoying the benefit of CCR5 gene editing. And he believes that the public will agree with this opinion.

In fact, many other experts also expressed their opposition to this experiment in the mass media.[10] In popular social media platforms in China, such as Weibo, people almost unanimously criticized the experiment of He's team. Liming Wang's blog post has also been widely reposted by users of various social media platforms. These phenomena reveal that Wang's point of view and value judgment are generally approved, and his arguments are convincing to the public.

In argumentation theory, the statement "the babies are immune to HIV, which is good; good thing should not be resisted and we should approve the gene-edited HIV-immune babies" can be modeled as:

Example 4 (Example 3 continued). ('*imH*' and '*G*' denote 'immune to HIV' and 'good' respectively, $\neg\bot$ denotes 'not be resisted'[11], here we add them into $\mathcal{L}$. Three more rules are obtained: $a_0 \Rightarrow imH$, $imH \Rightarrow G$ and $G \to \neg\bot$. We add them into $\mathcal{R}_d$ and $\mathcal{R}_s$ respectively.)

$$A_{14} : A_1 \Rightarrow imH \qquad A_{15} : A_{14} \Rightarrow G \qquad A_{16} : A_{15} \Rightarrow \overline{\neg\bot}$$
$$A_{17} : A_{15} \Rightarrow a_0$$

According to Definition 5, A_{16} conflicts with argument A_9 and arguments $A_{10}, A_{11}, A_{12}, A_{13}$ (because A_9 is their sub-argument), A_{17} conflicts with argument A_{13}. Suppose that based on argument $A_1 - A_{17}$, there is an audience who prefer a_0 than $\neg a_0$, $\overline{\neg\bot}$ than $\neg\bot$, then the only preferred extension and grounded extension of the updated argumentation framework will be $\{A_1, A_2, A_3, A_4, A_5, A_6, A_7, A_8, A_{14}, A_{15}, A_{16}, A_{17}\}$. So that the initial action a_0 is acceptable to this particular audience. On the contrary, if we obtain an ordering on arguments according to the value judgement of most people in this case, it's more likely that A_{13} will has higher priority than A_{17}, A_9 will has higher priority than A_{16}, thus both the attack from A_{16} to A_{13} and from A_{17} to A_{9-13} will not be successful.

4   Discussion and Related Work

In this section we discuss some basic ideas and important issues in this paper, and introduce some related works.

4.1   Discussion About the Weak Transposition

Firstly, in addition to defining the transposition of strict rules, we also give a definition of 'weak transposition' of defeasible rules in Sect. 2.2. The reason lies in the operating mechanism of the slippery slope argument: unacceptable outcomes

---

[10] Refer to the news https://edition.cnn.com/2018/11/26/health/china-crispr-gene-editing-twin-babies-first-intl/index.html and [24, 25].

[11] Remember that $\neg\bot$ in $\mathcal{K}$ represents "resistance to something bad/unwanted".

indicate that its premise is unacceptable. Though going through a long chain, it still implies a backward reasoning. What's more, without the weak transposition, in order to come up with a final conclusion (which is "not to take the first step"), the slippery slope argument is self-attacking based on the formal argumentation theory.

However, although the application of this transposition may raise criticism and controversy, the current paper is neither the unique nor the first to propose the contraposition/transposition of defeasible rules. In [7], Caminada examined Socrates's elenchus, which always leads the audience to make an inference that discredits his own reasoning (thus called "hang yourself argument"), and put forward the issue of contraposition and defeasible reasoning. Then in [6], he distinguished between epistemical reasoning and constitutive reasoning, and concluded that whether there should be contraposition of defeasible rules depends on which type of reasoning one is considering. In many aspects, the slippery slope argument is comparable to the "hang yourself argument", thus analysis in [6,7] are considerable references.

4.2 Discussion About Value Judgement

Through the case analysis in Sect. 3, it is not difficult to find that: if there is a counter-argument which asserts that the benefits may outweigh the harm claimed by an SSA, whether the attacks will succeed depends on the value judgement of the audience.

As Walton mentioned in [22], SSA is a subspecies of argument from negative consequence, and could also be seen as an approach to achieve practical reasoning. A slippery slope argument works by claiming that take the first step will lead to a highly undesirable consequence, which means that the consequence strongly contravenes values held by the audience [22].

In the current work, we model the negative value by adding a symbol "$\perp$" into the language $\mathcal{L}$ of an argumentation system. Correspondingly, we add a symbol "$\neg\perp$" into the knowledge base $\mathcal{K}$ to represent the intrinsic unacceptability of something bad. Then a slippery slope argument can be attacked by statements like "the final outcome is not as bad as it has been claimed", i.e., based on Definition 6, a CQA with the conclusion $\overline{\neg\perp}$. In $ASPIC^+$, conflicts can be resolved by comparing arguments based on preference, thus when we consider the preference in an SSAT, value judgement deserved to be taken into account.

Several systems that consider values based on formal argumentation have already been proposed. In [12], Liao and Oren et al. introduced a hierarchical abstract theory of normative system (called HANS) to resolve conflicts amongst norms. In simpler terms, this system associated numbers that indicating priorities of norms to an abstract theory of normative system defined by Tosatto et al. [17]. When conflicts arise between norms, HANS resolve it by the priorities assigned to them, and derive extensions according to different detachment procedure. In [13], Liao and Slavkovik et al. consider moral values and present an approach based on formal argumentation and normative systems to reach moral agreements. In [3], Bench-Capon clarified the role of persuasion in practical argumentation, and extends the abstract argumentation frameworks to a value-based argumentation framework (VAFs). In [4], Bench-Capon and Atkinson et al. focus on legal reasoning and discusses how to instantiate a VAF.

5   Summary

On the basis of the basic scheme of an SSA given in [21] and the formal argumentation framework $ASPIC^+$ [14,15], the present paper gives an argumentation theory for SSA (called SSAT). In addition, we give a definition of critical questions. Accordingly, based on the SSAT, we can model the basic form of SSA and evaluate it by formal argumentation system.

We apply this argumentation theory to model an SSA found in a popular blog post, which criticized the gene-edited babies experiment. The blog post has got a lot of attention since the news released in last November. The blogger, a Chinese biologist, used an SSA to back up the opinion that the benefits of adopting such an experiment are far less than the risk. By argumentation evaluation based on an abstract argumentation framework, we get extensions of arguments (and thus we can get the corresponding extensions of conclusions). It shows that our SSAT is able to model SSAs found in natural language text, and get reasonable results.

Furthermore, we point out that value judgement plays an important role in the evaluation of effectiveness of an SSA. How to lift preference on arguments through the value assignment or ranking in SSA, is a topic for future studies.

References

1. Atkinson, K., Bench-Capon, T.: Abstract argumentation scheme frameworks. In: Dochev, D., Pistore, M., Traverso, P. (eds.) AIMSA 2008. LNCS (LNAI), vol. 5253, pp. 220–234. Springer, Heidelberg (2008). https://doi.org/10.1007/978-3-540-85776-1_19
2. Baroni, P., Caminada, M., Giacomin, M.: An introduction to argumentation semantics. Knowl. Eng. Rev. **26**(4), 365–410 (2011)
3. Bench-Capon, T.: Persuasion in practical argument using value-based argumentation frameworks. J. Logic Comput. **13**(3), 429–448 (2003)
4. Bench-Capon, T., Atkinson, K., Chorley, A.: Persuasion and value in legal argument. J. Logic Comput. **15**(6), 1075–1097 (2005)
5. Cabrio, E., Hirst, G., Villata, S., Wyner, A.: Natural language argumentation: mining, processing, and reasoning over textual arguments (Dagstuhl seminar 16161). Technical report, Schloss Dagstuhl-Leibniz-Zentrum fuer Informatik, Dagstuhl, Germany (2016)
6. Caminada, M.: On the issue of contraposition of defeasible rules. In: Computational Models of Argument: Proceedings of COMMA 2008, Toulouse, France, 28–30 May 2008, vol. 172, pp. 109–115, January 2008
7. Caminada., M.: For the sake of the argument; explorations into argument-based reasoning. Ph.D. thesis, Vrije University Amsterdam, Amsterdam (2004)

8. Dung, P.M.: On the acceptability of arguments and its fundamental role in non-monotonic reasoning, logic programming and n-person games. Artif. Intell. **77**(2), 321–357 (1995)
9. Gabbay, D.M., Thiruvasagam, P.K.: Reasoning schemes, expert opinion and critical questions. Sex offenders case study. In: FLAP, vol. 4 (2017)
10. Govier, T.: What's wrong with slippery slope arguments? Can. J. Philos. **12**(2), 303–316 (1982)
11. Johnson, R.H., Blair, J.A.: Logical Self-defense, 2nd edn. McGraw-Hill Ryerson, Toronto (1983)
12. Liao, B., Oren, N., van der Torre, L., Villata, S.: Prioritized norms and defaults in formal argumentation. In: Proceedings of the 13th International Conference on Deontic Logic and Normative Systems (DEON 2016), pp. 139–154 (2016)
13. Liao, B., Slavkovik, M., van der Torre, L.W.N.: Building Jiminy cricket: an architecture for moral agreements among stakeholders. In: Proceedings of the 2019 AAAI/ACM Conference on AI, Ethics, and Society, AIES 2019, Honolulu, HI, USA, 27–28 January 2019, pp. 147–153 (2019)
14. Modgil, S., Prakken, H.: A general account of argumentation with preferences. Artif. Intell. **195**, 361–397 (2013)
15. Prakken, H.: An abstract framework for argumentation with structured arguments. Argum. Comput. **1**(2), 93–124 (2010)
16. Prakken, H., Wyner, A., Bench-Capon, T., Atkinson, K.: A formalization of argumentation schemes for legal case-based reasoning in ASPIC+. J. Logic Comput. **25**(5), 1141–1166 (2015)
17. Tosatto, S.C., Boella, G., van der Torre, L., Villata, S.: Abstract normative systems: semantics and proof theory. In: Brewka, G., Eiter, T., McIlraith, S.A. (eds.) Proceedings of the Thirteenth International Conference on Principles of Knowledge Representation and Reasoning, KR 2012, Rome, Italy, pp. 358–368 (2012)
18. Verheij, B.: The toulmin argument model in artificial intelligence. In: Simari, G., Rahwan, I. (eds.) Argumentation in Artificial Intelligence, pp. 219–238. Springer, Boston (2009). https://doi.org/10.1007/978-0-387-98197-0_11
19. Waller, B.N.: Critical Thinking: Consider the Verdict, 6th edn. Prentice Hall, Upper Saddle River (1998)
20. Walton, D.: Slippery Slope Arguments. Oxford UniversityPress, Oxford (1992)
21. Walton, D.: The basic slippery slope argument. Informal Logic **35**(3), 273–311 (2015)
22. Walton, D.: The slippery slope argument in the ethical debate on genetic engineering of humans. Sci. Eng. Ethics **23**(6), 1507–1528 (2017)
23. Walton, D., Reed, C., Macagno, F.: Argumentation Schemes. Cambridge University Press, Cambridge (2008)
24. Wang, C., Zhai, X., Zhang, X., Li, L., Wang, J., Liu, D.P.: Gene-edited babies: Chinese academy of medical sciences' response and action. Lancet **393**(10166), 25–26 (2019)
25. Zhang, L., Zhong, P., Zhai, X., Shao, Y., Lu, S.: Open letter from Chinese HIV professionals on human genome editing. Lancet **393**(10166), 26–27 (2019)

Author Index

Printed in the United States
By Bookmasters